The
LUTHERAN TRAIL

The LUTHERAN TRAIL

A History of the Synodical Conference
Lutheran Churches in Northern Illinois

By Louis J. Schwartzkopf

CONCORDIA PUBLISHING HOUSE
SAINT LOUIS, MISSOURI

CONCORDIA PUBLISHING HOUSE
Saint Louis, Missouri

Printed in the United States of America

This work, The Lutheran Trail, *we dedicate to the blessed memory of the sainted Fathers of The Lutheran Church-Missouri Synod, who, under God, have blazed a trail through the prairies of northern Illinois, leaving to their children a sacred heritage, a Church with the Word of God and His Holy Ordinances pure and undefiled.*

We further dedicate this record of the accomplishments of God's grace within the Lutheran Church to all fellow Lutherans of this region, particularly to our children and to future generations, praying that they ever may be mindful of the rich blessings which the Lord our God has wrought so abundantly in our midst during the past century, and that they may prove to be worthy administrators of their inheritance.

Preface

IT was with wavering courage that the undersigned yielded to the request submitted to him in 1944 by the Centennial Historical Committee appointed by the Rev. Ernest T. Lams, then President of the Northern Illinois District, to prepare a history of "True Lutheranism, Its Part in the Development of Greater Chicago." The committee, consisting of Pastors Ferdinand L. Gehrs, Paul Sauer, and William Gahl, subsequently forwarded to all pastors in charge of Missouri Synod congregations in the area of immediate concern a friendly appeal for support in this venture, with the specific request that "every pastor compile a history of his congregation." All data were to be in the hands of the committee by February 1, 1945. Approximately one year later, a comparatively large number received another, but more urgent, appeal for historical data: "Please do not stand back, but send the history of your congregation or a brief sketch of it before *September* 1, 1946, to . . ." (the undersigned).

Meanwhile, at several special meetings with the Centennial Historical Committee in the central office of the Northern Illinois District, 77 West Washington Street, Chicago, the outline and the scope of the proposed history were enthusiastically and thoroughly discussed; these meetings invariably were followed by personal visits to many sources of pertinent information: pastors, teachers, laymen, libraries, historical deposits, etc., which resulted in a tremendous amount of copying, most of which was competently done by a daughter of an 1884 graduate of the old Teachers' Seminary in Addison, Emma, nee Gerlach, my wife. From the more than 6,000 standard-size double-spaced typed sheets, progress toward adequate conciseness was understandably slow. With the unstinted aid of John L. Astley-Cock, associate editor of Religion and Education, *The Chicago Tribune,* and of Dr. John G. Kunstmann, associate professor in the Department of Germanic Languages and Literatures, The University of Chicago, the basic objective was reached during the winter months of 1946-1947. Grateful acknowledgment is herewith directed also to Mr. C. W. Tennant of the Western United Gas and Electric Co., Aurora, for supplying copies of the "Service Bulletins" containing valuable data concerning various points of local historical interest; likewise, to the Rev. Walter G. Stallmann, through whose voluntary efforts access was prepared to F. O. Peterson & Sons, printers in Aurora, from whom a well-preserved copy of *The Centennial Record of Aurora* was secured; also to Miss Clara Schweppe for her cheerful co-operation while searching for salient facts regarding pastors and day school teachers in the files of the Statistical Bureau, Concordia Publishing House; to Miss Lillian Brune for her patience in trying to convince us of her choice of design and general make-up; to Prof. L. Blankenbuehler and his associates for their meticulous proofreading; to Dr. Martin Piehler and his staff for supplying needed copies of synodical *Proceedings*; and to all others who in any way participated in bringing the task to a successful finish.

Difficulties which arose in the printing trade prevented the publishing of this historical volume, the title of which was altered to "The Lutheran Trail," in 1947—the Missouri Synod's centennial year. After a long lapse of time this writer was informed that Synod's Centennial Committee was desirous of having the history published, with the understanding, however, that it would be brought up to date. Additional data were forthwith gathered, and several months afterward the publishers began the actual printing job.

The feasibility of presenting an, albeit somewhat sketchy, account of Lutheran activities in America which preceded the inception of Lutheranism in this part of our country probably will not be seriously questioned. The purpose seems obvious. Neither will the chronological arrangement of the 250 congregations constitute a grievous problem; moreover, it is hoped that the reader's imagination will not be stretched too taut as he approaches the end of an article in "1949" and at the beginning of the next one suddenly is whisked back, in spirit, to "1860" or "1900."

An attempt to supply vital information concerning the Missouri Synod's founding and gradual development and the various educational institutions and charitable organizations in the Northern Illinois area is exemplified in Part Three.

If the "Trail" has not been properly blazed, we shall soon find out. May all who follow in its wake charitably consider the manifold obstacles that had to be overcome on this its first peregrination.

Vista of the Midway Plaisance
1443 East Sixtieth Street
Chicago 37, Illinois

LOUIS J. SCHWARTZKOPF

Contents

Part Six. From Homewood to Arlington Heights 540

Plates

The
LUTHERAN TRAIL

Part One

The Trail Starts

"Martyrum Sanguis Semen Ecclesiae"—"The blood of the martyrs is the seed of the Church"—and martyrdom marks the genesis of the Lutheran Trail!

Admiral de Coligny, the eminent Huguenot leader, in the year 1564 had established a settlement near St. Augustine, Fla., a territory over which Spain claimed dominion. Whereupon Pedro Menendez was dispatched under commission "to destroy the Lutheran French who had dared to settle there." Accordingly, on September 20, 1565, occurred the Massacre of Fort Caroline. Two hundred and thirty-three members of the settlement were beheaded, and a placard was placed over their graves bearing the inscription: "We slew them not as Frenchmen, but as Lutherans."*

But with this sanguinary execution of his mission Menendez signed his death warrant. There were seven survivors of the massacre. They, together with the Levantine sailors of the expedition, mutinied against Menendez, killed him, and betook themselves in his ship to Denmark, and it was from Denmark that history, fifty-four years later, erected another

*Some historians refer to these French settlers as "heretics."

marker on the Lutheran Trail, again associated with death.

Captain Jens Munck with crews of two Danish vessels set out to discover the northwest passage to India. In 1619 he anchored in Hudson Bay and set up winter quarters on the western shore, now part of the Province of Manitoba. That winter forty of his crew died. Chaplain to the expedition was the Rev. Rasmus Jensen. He read the funeral service over these sailors who were buried in a plot he had previously staked out, and thus was dedicated the first Lutheran cemetery on the North American continent. The chaplain's last recorded pastoral act was celebration of the Lord's Supper on Christmas Day of that year. On February 20, 1620, he died and was interred alongside the flock to which he had so faithfully ministered.

Overshadowed as the Lutheran Trail was by mass murder in the sixteenth century and the tragedy of death in the seventeenth, it was further darkened by massacre in the first half of the eighteenth century.

In 1710 a migration of Lutherans from Switzerland settled at New Berne in North Carolina. Indians almost wiped out the colony the following year, and the survivors fled to Virginia. In 1739 some German Lutherans had founded a colony on the "wild and forbidding" coast of Maine where today the town of Waldoboro is situated. Seven years later the settlement was raided by Indians, who murdered the majority, carried the remainder into captivity, and by burning their primitive homes "turned the whole region into a dreary waste." But the Salzburgers, harassed for three years in their homeland, who emigrated to Georgia, found a goodly heritage.

The Salzburgers were a persecuted group from the Alpine district of Austria, so called because they formed a confederacy named the Salzbund. They existed on a diet of salt and bread, and vowed never to prove untrue to their Lutheran convictions. On October 31, 1731, an order was issued that they change their faith or emigrate, leaving behind all children not of age. A considerable number so did, and they were welcomed at Charleston in March, 1734, by General Oglethorpe. A few days later, accompanied by the Rev. J. M. Belzius and the Rev. I. C. Gronau, they were allotted territory near Savannah. They named their settlement Ebenezer—"Rock of Salvation."

Let none think, however, that at this early period the Lutheran Trail was nought but sporadically stained with blood; along its way are many historic markers recording heroes and deeds of first instance.

There was the first Lutheran pastor to work among settlers in America, the Rev. Reorus Torkillus. He arrived on April 17, 1640, a passenger of the second expedition from Sweden. He became pastor of the Swedes who had settled on Christina Creek, where they had erected a fort, named in honor of their Queen, Christina.

Then there was the first missioner who erected the first church, the Rev. Johan Campanius of Sweden. In 1645 he brought the evangel to the northeastern coast of America and forthwith busied himself translating the Small Catechism of Dr. Martin Luther into the Iroquois dialect. On September 4, 1646, he dedicated the first Lutheran church, "a handsome wooden building," on the Isle of Tinicum, about fifteen miles from the mouth of the Delaware River, known now as Tenacon Island.

Also there was the first pastor to the Dutch, who had settled in 1623 at Fort Orange on Manhattan Island, the Rev. Johannes Ernestus Goetwater (Gutwasser). He was commissioned by the Lutheran ministry of Amsterdam "to minister to the Lutherans in the Hudson Valley," and arrived at his post early in 1657.[1]

Next was the first pastor of the German Evangelical Lutheran Church in America, the Rev. Justus Falckner, who holds the distinction of being the first Lutheran minister to be ordained in this country. His ordination took place in the Swedish church at Wicaco on November 24, 1703. The site is now included in the "City of Brotherly Love"—Philadelphia, Pa. After a ministry of about twenty years, mostly in the States of New York and New Jersey, he died in 1723.[2]

Finally, there was the Rev. Henry Melchior Muhlenberg, founder of the Ministerium of Pennsylvania in 1748, the mother synod of the Lutheran Church, originally called "United Pastors and United Congregations."[3]

The Lutheran Trail now enters on an era of continuous achievement. Those unrelated, indistinct by-paths, started variously from Hudson Bay to the Atlantic Ocean, at last converge to form the objective of this chronicle. All preceding was prophetic of what Lutherans had to surmount as the Trail began to traverse the State of Illinois before it ended in the Centennial accomplishment of the Missouri Synod in northern Illinois.

Before blazing this trail, however, attendant circumstances and society must be briefly sketched better to apprehend the arduous labors of those pioneers in the past century.

By the Peace of Paris in 1763 Illinois was ceded by France to Great Britain. Seven years after the adoption of the Declaration of Independence (1776), Illinois was ceded to the United States of America and was then known as "Illinois County of Virginia." "The two extremes of the early civilization of America were immensely influenced by two very opposite forms of the religious idea, namely, that which the Puritans represented in the East and that which the Jesuits represented in the West."[4]

In 1787, one year before the organization of the second Lutheran synod in this country, the New York Ministerium, Illinois became a part of the Great Northern Territory.

When Thomas Jefferson was elected the third President of the United States, in 1800, Illinois was made a part of Indiana Territory, with General William Henry Harrison as governor and the seat of government at Vincennes, Ind. By this time "the New York Ministerium had completely fallen away from Lutheranism." Rationalism was the monster that had pounced upon a large section of Lutheranism.[5]

In 1803 the North Carolina Synod, the mother synod of all the Southern synods, was organized by four Lutheran clergymen, including the Rev. Paul Henkel, and fourteen laymen at Salisbury, N.C.[6]

For the first time in the history of the Lutheran Church in America—now about 166 years old—the "language question" became an issue in 1806. Henry Melchior Muhlenberg, William C. Berkenmeyer, and other German as well as Swedish clergymen had been preaching in the English language without serious disapproval or drastic interference. But now, in 1806, under the leadership of John Peter Gabriel Muhlenberg, an illustrious son of the "patriarch of the Lutheran Church in America" and colonel in the Continental Army, some of the members of Saint Michael's Congregation in the "City of Brotherly Love," Philadelphia, Pa., insisted upon calling an English-speaking minister to replace their own two German ministers. Most of the votes cast were in favor of abiding by the existing arrangement. The minority left and established a church of its own—Saint John's.

Near Saint Michael's stood Zion Church. Under the auspices of the United States Government a memorial service for "the Father of his Country"—George Washington—who died December 14, 1799, was held in the latter Lutheran church on December 26, 1799. Members of the Senate and the Supreme Court as well as many generals and other officers who had served under General Washington's brilliant leadership attended that service. General "Light Horse Harry" Henry Lee gave the principal address on this occasion, and it was here that the now familiar words were heard for the first time: "First in war, first in peace, and first in the hearts of his countrymen."

In 1815 Saint Michael's Congregation was again disquieted by the "language question"; and in September of the following year another separation occurred, resulting in the founding of Saint Matthew's Congregation.[7]

In 1809 Illinois was made a separate territory, with Ninian Edwards as governor and the seat of government in the old French village of Kaskaskia,[8] in what now is Randolph County in the southwestern part of the State.*

During the "era of good feeling," which began in 1816, or slightly less than four years after the United States Government had signed the treaty of peace with England, the fifth President of the nation, James Monroe, in his second annual message to the Congress of the United States, declared: "I communicate with great satisfaction the accession of another State [Illinois] to our Union, because I perceive from the proof afforded by the additions already made the regular progress and sure consummation of a policy of which history affords no example, and of which the good effect cannot be too highly estimated. By extending our Government on the principles of our Constitution over the vast territory within our limits, on the Lakes and the Mississippi and its numerous streams, new life and vigor are fused into every part of our system."[9] Thus Illinois, in 1818, became the eighth State to be admitted to the Union.

What constitutes a State?
Not high-rais'd battlements, nor labored mound,
Thick wall, nor moated gate;
Nor cities proud, with spires and turrets crown'd,
Nor starr'd and spangled courts,
Where low-born baseness wafts perfume to pride:

*In 1820 the seat of government was moved to Vandalia, where it remained until moved to Springfield in 1837.

But *men!* high-minded men,
Who their *duties* know, but know their *rights*,
And knowing, *dare* maintain them.[10]

In the same year, 1818, the Evangelical Lutheran Synod of Ohio and Adjoining States, constituting the western part of the Pennsylvania Ministerium, was founded at Somerset, Perry County, Ohio.[11]

It was during the decade 1820-1830 that the great westward trek was in progress. The gradual opening of new territories beyond the Appalachian Mountains, combined with the widely publicized offer of low-priced land and relief from the hard times which had been brought on by the recent War of 1812, lured many people away from the Atlantic seaboard. "Overland in great Conestoga wagons, and driving their herds before them, came settlers from Ohio, Pennsylvania, New York, and Virginia, entering the eastern borders of Indiana, establishing their homes and subduing the wilderness. From the sunny Southland came hardy pioneers, desiring to improve their temporal conditions, and to escape the baneful influence of slavery. Everywhere the woodman's ax was heard, and the smoke ascended from hundreds of clearings, where the finest poplar, oak, and walnut were consigned to the flames to make room for the corn and wheat of the thrifty farmer."[12] Among the participants in that great early "Cavalcade of America" were numerous Lutherans. "Lutherans of Pennsylvania and New York moved into Ohio, Indiana, and Illinois, and many from Maryland and Virginia and the Carolinas went to southern Ohio, Kentucky, Tennessee, and even Missouri."[13]

First settled in the southern section, Illinois as a United States territory and State, derived its earliest population largely from southern and southeastern States. The first known Lutheran clergyman in the young State was the Rev. John L. Markert from Ohio.[14] According to Wagner, however, the Rev. Daniel Scherer "may justly be regarded as the patriarch of the

Lutheran Church in Illinois"; in fact, Wagner goes so far as to say that Scherer was for a number of years the only Lutheran pastor in the State.[15]

Illinois, the "most level" of the forty-eight States, has an area of approximately 56,650 square miles. The northern section, which is our immediate concern, comprises approximately eleven thousand square miles. Hence, only about one fifth of the State's total area is the theater in which the events between 1840 and 1949, chronicled in these pages, took place.

Inasmuch as Chicago will be referred to more frequently than any other city, town, or village in Illinois, no apologies are offered for presenting at least a brief outline of this great metropolitan center's history and development.

The wars which had ravaged the northwestern frontiers were terminated on August 3, 1795, by General "Mad Anthony" Wayne when a treaty of peace with the hostile Indian tribes was successfully negotiated at Greenville, Ohio. By that treaty, signed for the United States by General Wayne and for the Indians by Chief Little Turtle, the Indians ceded, along with other items, "one piece of land six miles square, at the mouth of the Chikagou River, emptying into the southwest end of Lake Michigan, where a fort formerly stood."

The fort alluded to probably had been built by the French during the latter part of the seventeenth century. In 1804 another fort was erected on or near the same site and named "Dearborn," in honor of General Henry Dearborn, an officer in the American Revolution and later Secretary of War. It was located on the south bank of the Chicago River, directly east of what was the Rush Street Bridge.* At that time the "Chikagou" River took a sharp turn to the south, just east of the fort, and made its way into the lake over a heavy sandbar near the now eastern end of Madison Street. "Far in the wilderness," the fort was reached from Detroit by a woodland trail.

*Rush Street no longer extends as far south as the river; also, the bridge has long since been non-existent.

When, in 1812, this nation became involved in war with Great Britain, the Indians independently went on the warpath and in this part of the country attacked Fort Dearborn. Obedient to an order from General William Hull, at Detroit, Mich., Captain Nathan Heald and his party abandoned Fort Dearborn in the middle of August, 1812. On the fifteenth day of that month the company was attacked by Indians among the sand hills along the lake shore. Most of the Americans, "including twelve children, were massacred and their scalps sold to Colonel Proctor, who had offered a premium for American scalps."

For four years after this tragic event the place was deserted by all save the Indians. . . . Chicago seemed to have been recommitted to aboriginal obscurity. At the end of that dark period, however, the pendulum started a powerful swing backward, and a great change took place in the dramatic presentations, particularly in the "Northern Illinois Theater."

In 1816 the fort was rebuilt under the direction of Captain Hezekiah Bradley, and thereafter it was continuously occupied by United States troops for twenty-one years, except for a short time in 1831. In 1827 the town of Chicago was composed of six or seven families, a number of half-breeds, and a lot of idle, vagabond Indians loitering about. For several years mail was brought once or twice a month from the nearest post office—Fort Wayne, Ind.

At that time, Cook County, named after Daniel P. Cook, one of Illinois' first Congressmen and perhaps better known as the "father of the Illinois-Michigan Canal," embraced all the territory now included in the counties of Lake, McHenry, Du Page, Will, and Iroquois. For a short time prior to that, the entire northern portion of the State of Illinois was included in Peoria County.

According to George S. Phillips the period between the second building of the fort until 1830 was, geologically speaking, the Saurian period of Chicago's history. The first white settler was John Kinzie, and the first white child born in Chicago was Ellen Marion Kinzie. Reputedly, however, a Negro, Jean Baptiste Pointe du Sable, has the distinction of having been the first "Chicagoan."

In the spring of 1831 the United States Government Postal Department in Washington, D.C., established a post office in the village of Chicago, which during the previous year had been laid out to cover an area of only three eighths of a square mile and "had streets marked off, although these were indistinguishable in the mud." The time required for mail to come from New York, via Cleveland, Ohio, and Detroit, Mich., was about twenty days.

The Government troops which had been dispatched to expel the Indians from the "Great Northwest" returned to their respective homes in 1832 and there sang the praises of the fertile valleys which they had discovered along the banks of the Illinois, the Fox, and the Rock Rivers. This resulted in the beginning of a great influx of immigrants into this area; many of them preferred to settle in the little town of Chicago at Lake Michigan, "the great water."

When Andrew Jackson in 1833 started upon his second term in the White House, the Congress made an appropriation for a harbor at Chicago. Piers were built out into the lake, a channel was cut through the old sandbar, and the heavy spring rains, together with the melting snow, gave it a thorough and much needed cleansing.

On August 10, 1833, the incorporation record of the "village" Chicago, numbering 250 inhabitants, was registered in the now thirteen-year-old capital, Vandalia. A few weeks later, September 26, the treaty of peace with the Potawatomis, Ottawas, and Chippewas was definitely completed, and soon afterward the Indians, accompanied by Chief Sauganash, were on their trek toward their new reservation on the western side of the Mississippi River, "the Father of Waters." Two years after its incorporation the village's population had increased to 3,297.

In 1836 the digging of the Illinois-Michigan Canal, linking Lake Michigan and the Chicago River with the Illinois River and the apparently boundless riches of the vast Mississippi Valley, was begun. In the following year, 1837, when Martin Van Buren became the eighth President of the United States and had to cope with an acute financial panic, the first candidates for the mayoralty of Chicago were nominated: the Democrat William Butler Ogden and the Whig John H. Kinzie. Ogden was elected with a majority of 282 votes—809 being the total number of votes cast.

At that time Chicago's population was 4,180. There were 398 dwellings, 29 dry goods stores, 5 drugstores, 5 hardware stores, 4 warehouses, 45 grocery stores, 10 taverns, 17 law offices, and 5 churches when the struggling village was reincorporated as a city in 1837.

The financial panic referred to affected the Chicagoans to such an extent that for a time it appeared as though it would have been better for most of them to have remained at the Eastern seaboard, if not in the "old country." More and more they were being fettered by poverty and practically profitless toil. The real estate boom burst like a bubble; the value of landed property declined with almost incredible speed; cash money was virtually out of circulation; and trade and commerce lay wholly prostrate.

A factor which very materially helped to prevent Chicago from sinking back into oblivion was the construction of the Illinois-Michigan Canal, which provided an income for many Chicago laborers. Other early settlers moved into the country districts round about and engaged in farming and truck gardening on a greater or lesser scale. This fact may account for the familiar reference to Chicago as the "Garden City."

According to Lewis and Smith, Chicago's incorporation as a city included the selected motto "Urbs in Horto" (City in a Garden). The depression lasted for seven long years, and during this time some of the inhabitants supplied food for their tables by hunting and fishing. The Madison Street Bridge was a popular place for duck hunting. "As late as 1838 wolves could be heard at night howling in the woods around this little town."

The first census of Chicago was taken July 1, 1839. It showed a grand total of 4,170 persons, of whom 3,989 were white, 77 Negroes, and 104 sailors.

As the 1840's dawned, 4,470 inhabitants sat along "Garlic Creek"—more politely called the Chicago River—wondering if they were justified in referring to their community as the Garden City, or if the slurs of certain other people after all had more basis in fact, namely, that Chicago was only a "mudhole in the prairie," or a huge dismal swamp. Perhaps some of them opined that they had jumped out of the frying pan into the fire.

The climax of the depression came in 1843, when, due to the complete exhaustion of essential materials, work on the canal was halted. A loan from the United States Government, in 1844 or 1845, made possible the resumption of work on this project. Despite the hard times the city's population had increased to twice its pre-depression size—about 8,000. The reason for this sharp increase was probably the restoration of economic stability in the country at large, and many people, hoping to improve their lot, were streaming from the Eastern States and from the southern to the northern part of Illinois to the Chicago area. The rising generation sought its own place. So soon as they felt that they could properly handle an ax and a rifle, the young men set out for the "Far West." And older people who could not live peaceably with their relatives or neighbors went along with the young folks.

In those days there was no Lutheran church in Chicago. The first Christian Sunday school was opened on August 19, 1832, in a log house at the Point, on the west side of the river's south branch. The first pupils, fifteen in number, were mostly children of the French and half-breed residents.

A Methodist minister conducted services in a portion of his own double log house near the river bank, where the north and south branches meet, in 1832. It was here also that the first services of the Presbyterian denomination were held in 1833. According to Charles Cleaver, however, the building which constituted the locale for various denominational beginnings in Chicago "had five or six windows on the side fronting on Franklin Street . . . owned, so we afterward found, by the Baptists, but then used, being the only one in the village, by the Presbyterians and Methodists as well." The first Baptist church was organized on October 19, 1833. The first Roman Catholic resident priest in Chicago was the Rev. Saint Cyr, who come from Saint Louis, Mo., in 1833. The first church of this denomination was built "somewhere on State Street" and called Saint Mary's. The first Episcopal parish, Saint James, was organized in 1834 in a wooden building which stood on the corner of Wolcott (now North State Street) and Kinzie Streets. The first church building was erected on land donated by the Kinzie family. In the month of July, 1837, the Rev. Jacob Boas, who at that time had charge of the Miami Circuit (Ohio) of the Evangelical Association, came on horseback through the wilds of Indiana on a missionary visit to Chicago—the first German Protestant minister that penetrated these parts—and in August preached the first sermon in the German language in Chicago in the old Methodist frame church, near the corner of Washington and Clark Streets. An organization was not deemed practicable at this time, and Mr. Boas, after having confirmed the organization of several societies in the country and visited and preached in other settlements, as for instance at Dunklees Grove, returned to his charge in Ohio.[16]

"In 1846 the Illinois Methodist Conference sent the Rev. Philip Barth from St. Louis to serve the German emigrants settling here. Finding no parsonage, no church, and no congregation, compelled to sell his furniture in order to feed himself and his family, the Rev. Mr. Barth nevertheless organized a congregation, and a year later built a church on Indiana, now Grand Avenue, between Wells and Franklin."[17]

Between 1840 and 1850 Pittsburgh, Louisville, Detroit, and Cincinnati all doubled their population, while the increase in the case of St. Louis was nearly fivefold and in the case of Chicago sixfold.[18]

The Lutheran Trail is now passing through the "roaring forties."

Part Two

From Duncklees Grove to Cummings Corner

1. Duncklees Grove

The dawn of Lutheranism in this part of the country was dimly foreshadowed, not at the center—Chicago—but at the periphery, slightly less than twenty miles northwest of Chicago, on an island, not a body of land surrounded by water, but an island of trees surrounded by prairies (*Waldinsel*—grove). There were many such "islands," or groves, in the vicinity of the "Garden City," or, as Chicago was also known, the "Prairie City by the Lake," as will be seen in subsequent chapters.

The first of these groves to be considered was named Duncklees Grove.* Presumably this island of trees was named in honor of the first settler in that region. History, it would seem, has thus far failed to ascertain the nationality of this settler. T. John Grosse merely points out that at the time the first German settlers arrived there, in June, 1834, only "two Americans, M. Smith and H. Duncklee, sojourned here"

*Other spellings: Dunkel and Dunckley.

("hielten sich damals hier auf") and that the other inhabitants of the wild prairie were Indians.

Vague and fragmentary records of the territory and of its earliest white inhabitants lead one to the belief that among them was a Jan Hinrich Rothenfeld, who, while residing in "Amt Stolpe" in the province of Hanover, Germany, developed the desire to emigrate to "fabulous America" and to seek out Duncklees Grove, about which he had heard numerous and, perhaps, only glowing accounts, for the establishing of a homestead. Eventually he came to Chicago and thence walked along Indian trails to the place of his not altogether wild dreams—Duncklees Grove. Without undue delay he purchased from certain "Yankees" a suitable tract of land; and before long he realized that the soil, which he forthwith began to cultivate, by far surpassed that of "Amt Stolpe." Yearning for good, amiable, and industrious neighbors of his own kind, with whom he might associate and leisurely converse ("en baeten wat snakken"), he soon corresponded with his relatives in the "Old Country," wishing to lure them across the Atlantic. Surely he did not fail to tell them about the source of good meat: deer, grouse, rabbits, etc. Grosse relates that one day a number of prairie chickens gathered on top of the chimney of Fred Stuenkel's log house. Mr. Stuenkel shot one of them; it fell down through the chimney and directly into a pot of boiling soup.

Numerous relatives of Jan Hinrich Rothenfeld, pleased with the prospect of better living conditions, at more or less frequent intervals, appeared on the scene, and each group, according to its means, then purchased real estate, the price of which was raised in proportion to the increase in the number of purchasers. A flourishing and prospering German settlement was the result of this influx. There were difficulties, to be sure, including altercations with interloping "Yankees" who from time to time appeared in the vicinity of Duncklees

Grove to stake claims of land already bought and paid for by the German settlers. The names of some of the earliest German settlers, 1834–1844, appear below*

The social life of these pioneers can, perhaps, be more readily imagined than described. That the conversations were carried on in their native language or dialects may be regarded as a foregone conclusion. But, of course, religious life nowhere in the world originates in the fertile soil or in agricultural enterprises. Having been reared in a religious atmosphere, those German settlers surrounded themselves with a similar atmosphere in their new home at or near the "island of trees," Duncklees Grove. However, for quite some time, so it would seem, no serious attempt at erecting a church building was made by them. Moreover, unlike the Saxon settlers in Missouri (1839), there were no ordained clergymen among the Duncklees Grovers.

Discussions of church matters culminated in the decision, in 1838, to organize a Christian congregation. Viewed in the light of subsequent history, this congregation actually proved to be a very strange compound of conflicting, contradictory, and incongruous religious elements.

The first preacher to serve the newly organized congregation was a Prussian, Ludwig Cachand-Ervendberg. After only about two years of "spiritual activity" (1837-1839) at Duncklees Grove he departed for the State of Texas (then the independent republic of Texas),† where for a time he served a congregation as pastor. In 1863 he was killed by Mexican Indians.

*Mr. and Mrs. Ludwig Blecke
Mrs. G. Buchholz
Mr. and Mrs. Ludwig Leeseberg
Mr. and Mrs. Friedrich Leeseberg
Mrs. Sophia Mesenbrink
Mrs. Dorothea Preuszner
Friedrich Graue
Heinrich Buchholz
Friedrich Knigge
Wilhelm Rabe
Mr. and Mrs. Wilhelm Boeske
Mr. and Mrs. Friedrich Stuenkel
Mrs. Sophia Tonne
Mrs. Dorothea Plagge
Wilhelm Buchholz
Friedrich Krage
Heinrich Stuenkel
Mr. and Mrs. Dietrich Hahn
Mr. and Mrs. Friedrich Eickhoff
August Graue
Heinrich Hackmeister

†Texas was admitted to the Union in 1845; shortly afterward the United States was at war with Mexico, 1845-1848.

Ervendberg's successor as preacher among the Germans of Duncklees Grove (1840) was eighteen-year-old Francis Arnold Hoffmann, a printer by trade and a youth whose heart was filled with enterprise. Being obliged to earn his living during the week, he was unable to prepare sermons for Sunday delivery and at first read sermons "out of a book." Later he prepared and delivered lectures on various religious subjects, and before the close of the second year of his adopted profession as a preacher, young Hoffmann was officially recognized as the congregation's spiritual leader and pastor, "without further examination and ordination." After three years he left the congregation, and during his absence a Jew who had joined the Methodist Church preached several times. According to Grosse, Pastor Hoffmann returned to Duncklees Grove in August, 1844, and pleaded for forgiveness. Not only was he forgiven, but reinstated in the pastorate. Karl Kretzmann disagrees with Grosse's version; he says: "The truth is that Hoffmann, apparently early in 1841, traveled to Southeastern Michigan, where he received whatever theological training could be obtained in those days, probably from the Rev. Friedrich Schmid of Ann Arbor, president of the Michigan Synod. 'By diligent study he soon became so proficient that the superintendent of the circuit, a Hannoverian by the name of Wyneken, could ordain him, after he had passed his examination' (*Hannoversche Tagespost,* April 16, 1861). Nor is there any room for the claim of Grosse that Hoffmann 'looked for a better congregation.' His temporary absence from Addison is accounted for by his trip to Michigan and by his missionary activities in the territory assigned to him by the Michigan Synod in Northeastern Illinois, covering the counties of Du Page, Cook, and Will, in Illinois, and Lake County, Indiana, an area of about 4,000 square miles. . . . In 1844, on February 22, in Crown Point, Ind., Hoffmann married a young lady of English antecedents, Miss Cynthia Gilbert, who had been born

May 18, 1825, in Columbiana Co., Ohio, where C. A. T. Selle held a pastorate in 1844-45."*

In 1842 a tract of land comprising forty-eight acres was purchased for $200, and upon it was erected the first church. No official records having been kept prior to 1844, the exact date of the formal dedication cannot be definitely established, but it is believed to have taken place on a Sunday in November, 1842. Its official name was "Die deutsche vereinigt reformirt lutherische Gemeinde zu Addison, Du Page County, Illinois" ("The German United Reformed Lutheran Congregation at Addison, etc."). A paragraph of its constitution contained this broad and liberal statement: "The faith and the confession of the teacher and the hearer shall never be taken into consideration in this congregation." The author of this document was a surveyor, Dunlop by name. In later years Dr. Martin Luther's Small Catechism, introduced by Pastor Hoffmann, was used for instruction in Christian doctrine.

In the fall of 1842 a German man, well reputed and generally known in Chicago, suddenly died. His family at once dispatched some of its members to Duncklees Grove in an endeavor to secure Pastor Hoffmann to conduct the service of interment. The road through the woods proved impassable, and plans to bring Pastor Hoffmann to Chicago for the funeral had to be abandoned. Meanwhile a colporteur, found in the city, was engaged to speak at the service. Many of the Germans of Chicago attended the rites. Most of these were sorely disappointed with the appearance and message of the man who had been pressed into service. This situation tended to heighten the desire for an organized church and a full-time pastor who would uphold the faith and language of the Prussian State Church.

Pastor Hoffmann remained with the United Reformed Lutheran Church of Duncklees Grove until 1847, when he ac-

Concordia Historical Institute Quarterly

cepted a call to the near-by German settlement of Sarah's Grove (Schaumburg). Thereupon three candidates presented themselves for the vacant place, and each preached a trial sermon. One, F. W. Poeschke, a converted Jew, selected for his theme "The Jewish Laws Regarding the Ten Commandments." When he had come to "fourteenthly," only three people remained in the church. When neighbors inquired as to what had kept them so long at church, they replied: "Why, we are getting home early. The preacher has more than a hundred commandments to explain; we left at the fourteenth; the last will come at about four o'clock tomorrow morning." Of course, this candidate completely annihilated his chance of being called as Hoffmann's successor. Candidate Ernst August Brauer, who had the assurance of the Consistory in Hanover, Germany, that upon his return from America he could enter the State Church at Hanover, was ordained and installed at Duncklees Grove December 15, 1847. He accepted the pastorate on the condition that the congregation should become thoroughly Lutheran. It was determined upon; but then came bitter opposition from the rationalistic party, which in February, 1848, separated from the "mother" congregation and built a church of their own a short distance from the first one.

The way having been prepared for a sounder type of Lutheranism, Pastor Brauer experienced on the one hand the joy of seeing a change in the congregation's name to that of "Evangelical Lutheran" and, on the other hand, the sorrow of witnessing a defection. Within the next two years, however, it became increasingly apparent that the defection did not have the expected damaging effect upon the "mother" church; in fact, the increase in membership necessitated enlargement of the church building, in 1850, and on October 8, 1851, the parish was divided into four parts: North, South, East, and West.

During the following thirty-five years special school districts were established in various centers of the large parish. The eastern district was organized on May 2, 1852; the southern, at "Franzosenbusch"—approximately nine miles south of Duncklees Grove—now known as Proviso, October, 1852; the northern, November 4, 1855; another portion of the southern, about one mile southeast of Lombard—at a place called York Center, 1860; the Elmhurst district, March 8, 1879; the Town Bloomingdale district, July 25, 1880; and the Itasca district, July 29, 1885. The "home district" had been established on January 14, 1849. In the latter, the following served as teachers: H. Bartling, G. Seitz, Miss Regina Rotermund, A. Albers, J. Brackmann, Adolph Gruhl, Karl Koebel, W. Kammann, Christian Greve, Miss Liesette Leeseberg, Miss Bertha Heidemann, Miss Amalia Brauer, Edmund Brust, and G. Ritzmann.

The following served in the eastern district:* F. Griese, H. Riebling, W. Kohlmann, G. Seitz, W. Fuerstenau, Frederick Polzin, A. Daake, H. D. Cluever, C. A. Louis Wuellner, and C. Theo. Diesner.

School activities in the northern district were begun in a private home. A certain Mr. Gehring, who "happened to be staying with Pastor Brauer," was engaged to teach; he left in May, 1857, and joined a "sectarian church." Other teachers were Fred Gehrke, Henry Gehrke, R. Vogel (he died of the cholera in 1866), A. Albers, A. Ehmann, E. F. Rosen, Adolph Kastner, Eugene Schulz, Martin Eggerding, and Walter G. Gerth.

In March, 1856, the congregation, now known as Zion Evangelical Lutheran Congregation, was received into membership with the Missouri Synod, which had been organized in 1847, in Chicago.

In March, 1857, Pastor Brauer accepted a call to Pittsburgh, Pa. His place at Duncklees Grove was taken by the Rev. A. G.

* This district was closed from September, 1860, to April, 1861.

G. Francke, called from Cook's Store, Lafayette County, Mo. He was installed as pastor of Zion Congregation on August 28, 1857. That year also marked the beginning of extensive mission activities in the surrounding territory, including the following communities: Proviso, York Center, Elmhurst, Itasca, Bloomingdale, Bensenville, and Elk Grove. In January, 1878, the Rev. Traugott John Grosse, professor at the Teachers' Seminary at Addison, a short distance west of Duncklees Grove, was called as assistant pastor of Zion Congregation, and, upon the death of Pastor Francke at the age of 58 years, January 3, 1879, Pastor Grosse was installed as permanent pastor on May 11, 1879. The Rev. Prof. J. C. W. Lindemann, first director of the Teachers' Seminary, died at the age of 52 on January 15, 1879. Addressing himself to the students, the Rev. Henry Wunder of Chicago, in the course of a memorial address on January 20 in the institution, said: "Here below you can no longer thank your instructor for what he has done for you; so, then, follow his footprints: become humble students of the Word, fervent in the faith, zealous in godliness, faithful in your profession."

During the winter of 1888-1889 services were conducted every other week in near-by Bensenville; but pecause of poor attendance they were soon discontinued.

In 1892 the members residing in the Elmhurst school district were granted permission to withdraw from Zion and to organize their own congregation; it was named Immanuel.

Beginning in June, 1892, afternoon worship services were held on alternate Sundays in the chapel of the Teachers' Seminary for the students and for other Lutherans living in the vicinity of that institution. Beginning the first Sunday in November of the same year, forenoon services were held there, with Professors C. August T. Selle, E. A. William Krauss, John Theodore Brohm, and Frederick Koenig serving according to a prearranged schedule. On September 8, 1893, Prof.

Frederick Lindemann was called by Zion Congregation to serve as assistant pastor.

In January, 1895, the Duncklees Grove congregation was reincorporated under the name "German Evangelical Lutheran Zion Congregation of Addison, Du Page Co., Ill." By that time the "claim wars" of the early pioneer days probably had been completely forgotten; but another kind of problem had arisen: horse thieves—how to handle them? These disturbers of the peace took advantage of the opportunity to ply a profitable "trade"—particularly, it seems, while the Duncklees Grovers were attending worship services or meetings and their patient horses were tied to the hitching posts outside. So, the congregation hired a special watchman and paid him for his services—fifty cents for daytime watching and one dollar for nighttime.

In April, 1907, the western and Bloomingdale Township school districts were released to Saint Paul's Evangelical Lutheran Congregation in Addison. At the same time a pastor was called to conduct services and teach school in the Itasca school district. With eleven members released from Zion, Saint Luke's Congregation was organized in the village of Itasca in 1907. Prof. Frederick Lindemann died Dec. 13, 1907.

Pastor Grosse died February 14, 1919. His successor, the Rev. Oscar H. Weinrich of Janesville, Calif., was installed June 15, 1919.

A severe hailstorm in 1927 destroyed all the windows of the church building. In January, 1929, the congregation decided to content itself with only eight acres of the original property purchased in 1842. Forty acres were sold to Harvey Branigar of Chicago. Three of the retained acres on the east end comprise the cemetery, while on the other five acres are the church, the parsonage, and the janitor's dwelling.

During the ten-year period 1927-1937 English and German services were repeatedly shuffled; a regular schedule of three

English and four German services was maintained after that time, with an additional English service combined with Communion on the fifth Sunday of certain months.

On August 19, 1937, the church was struck by lightning, and after burning for three hours the fire was extinguished, but in its wake was a mass of wreck and ruin.

On April 20, 1945, Pastor Weinrich died. His successor in the Zion pastorate, the Rev. Erwin H. Heidorn of Hoxie, Kans., was installed September 2, 1945.

Many of the congregation's children now attend the central school in Itasca, maintained by Zion of Duncklees Grove (now called Churchville) and Saint Luke's of Itasca. The teachers: Gerhard Elbert, Mrs. W. Danker, Miss Edna Bonitz. Recently a new school was established by Zion—the first one on the original church property—taught by Alfred C. Abel.

A large number of Lutheran pastors and teachers could point to Duncklees Grove and say: "That's where I was born." The names of some of them are listed below.*

Among those who died while studying at the Teachers' Seminary at Addison were August Mesenbrink (March 7, 1869), Ernest Bartling (May 9, 1881), and Edward Hoppenstaedt (October 11, 1887).[19]

2. Chicago, First Saint Paul's

Returning from Duncklees Grove by way of the Indian Trail (Lake Street), the Lutheran Trail at once proceeds to what is now known as Chicago's near North Side. Prior to the year 1846, seemingly, there was no evidence of Lutheranism anywhere in the "Garden City."

*Pastors: William Bartling, Augustus Reinke, F. Wesemann, Henry Norden, Fred Lindemann, George Rosenwinkel, W. Burmeister, H. L. Pflug, J. Johl, Adolph Bartling, William Koepchen, and W. Baeder. Karl Selle, a student at Concordia Seminary in St. Louis, Mo., died on March 12, 1885.
Teachers: George Bartling, Ernest Selle, Louis Selle, Henry Brauer, Carl Appel, William Leeseberg, Louis Rittmueller, William Pflug, Herman Weiss, Clem. Kambeiss, Alfred Johnson, Hermann Maudanz, Albert Rossmann, and Henry Grosse.

Standing at the portal of that eventful and memorable year, outstanding events in Chicago's history during the previous record must be reviewed.

In 1836 several members of the German Evangelical Association had emigrated from Warren, Pa., to this then remote and insignificant village at the Lake. In the spring of 1837 a number of families from the same place had followed, settling in what is now the village of Northfield, others in Naperville, and a few of them in McHenry County. In the summer of 1840 the first society of that Association had been organized in Chicago by the Rev. Isaac Huffert. Three years later Chicago had been selected as a center of mission activity under the direction of the Rev. Frederick Wahl. A lot on the northeast corner of Wabash Avenue and Monroe Street had been donated by the old Canal Company, and upon it a church, 32x38 feet, had been erected. This, then, was the first German Evangelical church in Chicago.

In the year 1840 the Rev. Frederick C. D. Wyneken of Fort Wayne, Ind., started out on horseback to investigate mission possibilities in the Chicago area. Because of inclement weather he could not go beyond Elkhart, Ind., where he then spent some time doing mission work.

One Sunday afternoon, late in 1843, during a heavy blizzard, nine men and several women met by arrangement in a grocery store at the corner of Franklin and Lake Streets definitely to attempt the organization of a congregation. As was the custom in Germany, these men organized themselves into a church council and appointed a "ways and means committee" of five men to select and obtain a building lot; and they decided upon the name Saint Paul for the new congregation. The names of the founders are on record: George Schaiver, Karl Teschner, John Pfund, Charles Stein, B. A. Beyer, H. H. Rantze, Arnold Kroeger, William Frank, and Jacob Letz. Pfund was a baker, and Letz a shoemaker.

In that year the "city fathers" decreed that the farming citizens ("Ackerbuerger") must not permit their pigs to roam about in the streets and lanes of the city.

Before the end of the year 1843 the little German congregation received as a gift from William Butler Ogden—"the city's richest man"—and Walter L. Newberry a spacious piece of property on the southwest corner of Ohio Street and La Salle Avenue, in an area which at the time was largely swampland, dotted here and there with small groves of trees; the nearest building, a small frame house, stood at the corner of Ohio and Clark Streets. The small and unpretentious church building, 20x60 feet, was completed in February, 1844. The men of the congregation had carried the lumber on their shoulders to the building site all the way from the Jackson Street Bridge, about a mile south.

During the first year of its existence the congregation did not have its own pastor. Various unpleasant experiences with self-styled "clergymen" induced the leaders of Saint Paul's Congregation to appoint a special committee for the purpose of carefully selecting and calling a competent and dependable preacher and pastor. "In those primitive times," says Solon Justus Buck, "it was not thought to be necessary that a teacher of religion should be a scholar. . . . However ignorant these first preachers may have been, they could be at no loss to find congregations still more ignorant, so that they were still capable of instructing someone." Obviously, such was not the case here. The little group had had enough of Catilinarian practices and "ravening wolves in sheep's clothing." Through the mediation of the Rev. J. Fred Winkler, a Lutheran pastor in Detroit, Mich., to whom the first call had been extended, but by whom it was declined, presumably for cogent reasons, the committee extended a call to the Rev. Christian August Thomas Selle of New Lisbon, Ohio. He accepted the call on the condition that he "could serve the congregation as a Lutheran congregation and in a building suited for Lutheran worship services" (" . . . dass er die Gemeinde als eine lutherische, in einem fuer lutherische Gottesdienste geeigneten Gebaeude bedienen koenne").

After a long trip, partly by wagon and partly by boat, from New Lisbon, Columbiana County, Ohio, by way of Detroit, the Strait of Mackinac, and Milwaukee, Wis., the new pastor arrived in Chicago on Easter Day, April 18, 1846, and on the following day, also a church holiday, he preached his first sermon here (in German) on the topic: "Christ is Risen Indeed." Within the next few days the first Lutheran parochial or day school in Chicago was opened with twenty-six pupils, a Lutheran constitution was unanimously adopted, and Pastor Selle was, upon his request, recognized as a *Lutheran* pastor and preacher. About two years later, April 9, 1848, this constitution was repudiated and rejected by an overwhelming majority of the members, and one with "Reformed" tendencies was substituted. Pastor Selle and only four of his members, R. Ohm, C. Michel, C. Bluess, and W. Brockschmidt, although in a veritable sea of troubles, declared their adherence to the Lutheran constitution. After the meeting these four men appeared in Pastor Selle's home to assure him of their determination to assist in the continuation of the Lutheran congregation, even though its membership might never be increased.

At that time, the city limits extended from the Lake to Wood Street, and from North Avenue to 22nd Street, now Cermak Road. "The years from 1833 to 1848 had been, in every sense, elemental." During the latter part of that period the war with Mexico was in progress, and between seven and eight hundred men of Chicago had volunteered to help terminate that conflict. Chicago was at the dawn of a new commercial and political and industrial era. The great new region west of the Appalachian Mountains was on the march, and Chicago was becoming its dynamic expression. In another respect the 1840's may be regarded as an age "characteristic for its 'dollar magazines, shilling theaters, shilling concerts, penny papers, beggarly office seekers, rascally politicians, unprincipled bankers, cut-throat financiers, doubtful saints, miserable Wall Street editors, and fine women.'" But what about that remnant of Saint Paul's Congregation, which on April 9, 1848, was like a ship tossed to and fro on the sea of life? Cognizant of the fact that the majority group by withdrawing had established a new and non-Lutheran congregation, the minority group, abiding by the Lutheran constitution and considering itself the true continuation of Saint Paul's Evangelical Lutheran Congregation, henceforth called itself "First Saint Paul's." On the next day, Sunday, April 10 (Judica Sunday), the entire confirmation class, composed of sixteen members, appeared for instruction at Pastor Selle's home. All declared their intention of vowing loyalty to the Lord as Lutherans on the following Sunday, even though it would be necessary to be confirmed in a nook ("Winkel"). Contrary to all expectation, in the course of the first week after the separation had taken place, eight of the former voting members returned to join the minority group. The confirmation took place, not in a "nook," but in the County Court House, at the southeast corner of Clark and Randolph Streets, and 250 persons attended.

In connection with the "Chicago Charter Jubilee," a bronze plaque, authenticated by the Chicago Historical Society, was placed on the wall of the building now standing on the site of the original Lutheran church.

Desirous of erecting a church of its own, First Saint Paul's Congregation purchased a piece of property on Indiana Avenue (now Grand), between Wells and Franklin Streets, at a cost of $600. On February 8, 1849, the following resolution was passed: "Dass der Kirchenrath beauftragt sei, mit dem Baumeister einen Kontrakt abzuschliessen ueber den Bau einer Kirche (34x55 Fuss) mit einem Turm, der Arbeitslohn die Summe von $260 nicht uebersteigend." ("That the church council be instructed to make a contract with the architect for the erection of a church building, 34x55 feet, with a steeple, the cost of labor not to exceed the sum of $260."

In March, 1849, the Chicago River was the scene of a disastrous flood.

At the third annual convention* of the German Evangelical Lutheran Synod of Missouri, Ohio, and Other States, popularly known as the Missouri Synod, which had been organized in Saint Paul's Church at Ohio Street and La Salle Avenue (now forfeited to the aforementioned majority group), First Saint Paul's Congregation was accepted into membership. One month later, July 15, 1849, its church was dedicated. By 1851 the congregation had a membership of fifty voters, and the enrollment in the day school, conducted from the beginning by the pastor, was 49. The time, therefore, had come to give serious consideration to the calling of a teacher in order somewhat to alleviate the pastor's growing burden. A young man, who had expressed the desire to enter the teaching profession, was at first engaged as an assistant instructor. Should he prove his teaching ability, he was to be called permanently. In the preliminary dealings, however, it became apparent that the young man under observation was an obstinate and arrogant individual ("ein eigensinniger und hoffaertiger Mensch"). Among other things, he declared that an annual salary of $100 would be insufficient; he wanted $104; also he refused to "fire up" for the school, because he insisted that he was no "Feuerjunge" (fire boy). Later he dropped these "ridiculous" demands; but the congregation did not call him, not even as assistant.

This happened at the time when the streets of Chicago

*June 6-16, 1849, in Fort Wayne, Ind.

were being planked and, for the first time, the city was lighted by gas.

In February, 1851, Pastor Selle received a call to Crete, Ill. Among the reasons advanced for accepting the call, Pastor Selle gave the following as "probably the principal one: "Dass ich meine Hausmiete nicht mehr erschwingen konnte, ohne Schulden zu machen, zu deren Abtragung ich keine Aussicht hatte, waehrend ich freilich zugleich hoffte, des Herrn Werk in Chicago werde um so herrlicher voranschreiten unter einem andern treuen Pastor, auf dessen Namen nicht in den Augen des allgemeinen Publikums das Odium bestandener heftiger Kaempfe lastete. Vor der Trennung war, meine ich, mein Jahresgehalt $300 gewesen; die drei Jahre nach derselben nie ueber $130. Davon forderte die Miete $50, die Feuerung $50, und der Rest ging auf Milch, und Wasser, das beim Fass gekauft werden musste." ("I could no longer raise enough money for my house rent without going into debt, for the settlement of which there was no prospect; while, at the same time, of course, I hoped that the Lord's work in Chicago would progress more gloriously under the guidance of another faithful pastor, upon whose name, in the eyes of the general public, did not rest the odium of furious battles of the kind to which I had been subjected. Prior to the separation, I think, my annual salary had been $300; during the three years following the separation it was never above $130; of this amount, rent required $50, fuel $50, and the rest was used for milk, and water, which had to be purchased by the keg.") Bessie Louise Pierce says that in those days water was transported to consumers by carts, from which householders could buy a barrel for ten cents.

Of more than passing interest is the following quotation which concerns Pastor Selle, who was not, as below intimated, "the founder of the Missouri Synod": "Persoenlich war an diesem wuerdigen und gewissenhaften Manne nicht das Mindeste auszusetzen. Aber er war ein orthodoxer Lutheraner und *gruendete* gegen Wunsch und Willen der Gemeinde, deren Mitglieder zumeist aus der sogenannten unierten Kirche hervorgegangen waren, *im Jahre* 1847 *auf einer von* 16 *Gemeinden beschickten Konferenz die lutherische Missouri Synode.*" ("So far as his person was concerned, there was not the least reason for censuring this worthy and conscientious man. But he was an orthodox Lutheran, and *founded,* contrary to the wish and will of the congregation, most of whose members had come from the so-called 'united' church, *in the year* 1847, *at a conference to which sixteen congregations had sent delegates, the Lutheran Missouri Synod.*" (Italics our own.)

In his biography Pastor Selle states that his congregation approved of the invitation, but decided not to join the Synod immediately.

Pastor Selle did not at once follow the call to Crete, Ill.; he accepted it in April, 1851, and went there in September of that year.

On January 19, 1851, George Henry Fischer was installed as First Saint Paul's first day school teacher. Eight months later, September 21, 1851, the congregation's second pastor, the Rev. Henry Wunder of Centerville, near Millstadt, Ill., was installed.

During the decade 1850-1860 the membership grew to such an extent that the church on Indiana Avenue, erected in 1849, became too small. A site on the corner of Franklin and Superior Streets was purchased for $5,400, and upon it a church building was erected. It was dedicated in December, 1864.

Late April, 1859, four cars of the Chicago City Railway, laden with Chicagoans enthusiastic over the new method of transportation, made the initial trip from Lake to Twelfth Street.

During the period 1857-1863 a great missionary effort was made by the "Missouri" Lutherans of Chicago, which resulted in the organization of many new congregations throughout the Middle West—in the States of Indiana, Iowa, Michigan, and Wisconsin. The vast and comprehensive mission program was sponsored jointly by First Saint Paul's and its first "daughter" congregation, First Immanuel (founded 1854). In the course of time the following three young clergymen were called to serve as assistant pastors for both congregations: William Heinemann, Gotthilf Simon Loeber, and H. F. Fruechtenicht. Later, First Saint Paul's independently called, consecutively, as assistant pastors: Traugott John Grosse, who was ordained and installed before the close of the seminary term because of the prevailing pressing circumstances ("unter den obwaltenden noetigenden Umstaenden"); Grosse served as assistant until First Saint John's Congregation, another daughter of First Saint Paul's, was organized in 1867; then, in 1869, Candidate Herman W. Querl, who served as assistant until Saint James (Sankt Jakobi) was organized in 1869; next came Herman Brauns, and then Herman Sauer. And then occurred a tragic interruption.

> Men said at vespers: "All is well."
> In one wild night the city fell;
> Fell shrines of prayer and marts of gain
> Before the fiery hurricane.
>
> On threescore spires had sunset shone,
> Where ghastly sunrise looked on none.
> Men clasped each other's hands and said:
> "The City of the West is dead!"*

At ten o'clock in the forenoon of October 9, 1871, the church, which had been solemnly dedicated less than seven years before, fell a victim of the flames of the Great Chicago Fire. The only article saved was the wooden figure of an angel which used to hang on the wall above the pulpit and which

*First two stanzas of "Chicago," by John Greenleaf Whittier.

PLATE I

(PLATE II *following page*)

The Weekly Chicago Democrat

IS PUBLISHED EVERY TUESDAY MORNING AT

NO. 107 LAKE-ST., CHICAGO, ILLS.

AT THREE DOLLARS A YEAR,

From which one dollar will be deducted when payment is made in advance.

ADVERTISEMENTS

Will be inserted on reasonable terms and a larger and better circulation given to them than by any other paper in the State.

There is also issued from this office the

Daily Democrat,

☞ Five Dollars a year, or Fifty Cents for one month.

Weekly Chi

NEW SERIES, VOL. XI, NO. 24. CHICAGO, ILLS.,

TUESDAY, APRIL 27, 1847.

HARBOR AND RIVER CONVENTION.

ADDRESS OF THE CHICAGO COMMITTEE.

The high prices of freight, taken in connection with the loss of life and property upon the western waters, last season, caused several public meetings to be held in various sections of the country, for the purpose of devising the best means of remedying these and other evils of which the great mass of the people interested in commerce, were complaining. At all these meetings, the propriety of holding a convention at some convenient point, was discussed and universally concurred in.

In consequence of Chicago having been generally named as the proper point, its citizens called a meeting, named the fifth of July as the appropriate time, and chose the undersigned a committee to draft an address, setting forth the objects of the convention.

The movers in this matter, have been, from the first, like the undersigned, of entirely different politics, and, so far from there being even in the remotest degree, any political design in the contemplated convention, one of the chief objects of it, is to call together for a common object, the men of all parties, and to convince the people every where that the improvements designed are not now, never have been, and never should be connected with "*Party Politics*" in the ordinary use of that term. Such a connection would, in the minds of all interested, have a very deleterious tendency. It cannot be denied that there is a predisposition among all politicians to support the measures of a chief magistrate of their own party; and hence we have seen western representatives, originally supporting harbor and river improvements, and elected upon express pledges to do so, finally vote to support a *veto* of bills providing for that purpose and assigning as a reason therefor that it was their duty to sustain an executive of their own selection, even though it be in express opposition to the wishes and interests of their constituents. Repeated instances of this kind must eventually give this question somewhat of a political cast, which the undersigned and all who co-operate with them, would seriously regret.

The construction of *harbors* upon our northern lakes, as well as upon the Atlantic, with the improvement of our great rivers, whose commerce is of a national character, necessarily involves no questions of party difference. They are matters that must interest all parties, as they do all *classes*, alike, and Harbor and River bills have been supported by the ablest men of both the great political parties which divide this country. This subject has never entered into any presidential canvass, since each party has always taken it for granted that the candidate of the other was above suspicion upon a matter of such pre-eminent importance. The first Congress that ever assembled under the present constitution, many of whose members helped to frame it, passed a law defraying all expenses which should accrue after the fifteenth of August 1789, in the necessary support, maintenance, and repairs of all light-houses, beacons, buoys, and public piers erected, placed or sunk before the passage of this act, at the entrance of or within any bay, inlet, *harbor*, or ports of the United States, *for rendering the navigation thereof easy and safe*. Gen. Washington signed this bill; and bills for the continuance of such works were also successively signed by Presidents the elder Adams, Jefferson and Madison. The first *Lake Harbor* bill was signed by Mr. *Monroe*. He never raised the constitutional question; nor do the Congressional debates of those days show that any members of either branch of Congress made any distinction between *salt* and *fresh* water improvements, or between foreign and domestic commerce. All at that time were acknowledged alike deserving the fostering care of the General Government, as they also were during the administrations of the younger Adams, Gen Jackson and Mr. Van Buren. Though remarkably scrupulous as to the extent to which the power to construct works of internal improvement should be exercised, General Jackson and Mr. Van Buren signed bills for the improvement of rivers and construction of harbors, to the amount of $7,000,000, and the two bills signed by Gen Jackson in 1836 contained no less than

ILLINOIS TROOPS.

To the two Illinois Reiments is due the credit of winning the battle of Buena Vista. Nearly all the others have had their conduct impeached in one way or an other. But not a voice has ever been raised against our own Illinois sons. On that occasion they honored themselves and their State.

JOLIET SIGNAL.—In far more prosperous times than the present, efforts to keep up a paper at Joliet have proved unsuccessful. Indeed, the idea of being able to support a paper at that town was about being abandoned when the present proprietors, Messrs ZARLEYS, took hold of it.—They were sons of an old democratic farmer, Reazon Zarley, Esq., who imparted to his boys the real fire of the flint. He learnt them in early life that they were no better than other people, and yet were just as good if they only conducted themselves as well. This made them democrats. He worked hard himself and made his boys work, too. This made them both steady and industrious. Fresh from a farm, these two young men took the press almost completely ruined and they have placed it on a permanent foundation. They do their own work, mental and physical, writing and printing. They eschew no sectional or local quarrels, but confine their labors to the advocacy of democratic principals and support of regular nominees. We are glad to see the young men of our State coming forward in this way, gaining popular esteem by their industry, punctuality, economy and virtue. This is practical democracy. The rise of these men will not be meteoric like some of our limbs of the law, nor will their fall be so. But, like the stately oak, their roots will extend so far and so deep, that they will have a strength commensurate with their growth and no storm can overturn them.

ROCK ISLAND.

ROCK ISLAND, Ill., April 21, 1847.

Editor Chicago Democrat:

DEAR SIR: Our returns, for Delegates, are mostly in and the following is the result, so far as ascertained:

	WHIG J. W. Spencer	DEMOCRAT Joseph Knox
Illinois City	9 majority	
Edgington's	30	33
Camden	45	53
Rock Island	113	106
Moline	93	17
Hampton	64	29
Port Byron	35	23
Cordova reported	majority	6
Drury's at noon	5	reported 7
Totals	304	274
	274	
Majority	130	

There were about 750 votes polled out of about 1100. There is not, on a fair trial, more than 30 or 40 whig majority in this county. The majority, last fall on a full vote, was 39 for Killpatrick for Governor and 28 for James Knox for Congress. We are gratified with the course of Wentworth the past winter: and we shall, so far as able, endeavor to sustain his views.

LUTHERAN SYNOD.

The German Evangelical Lutheran Synod of Indiana, Missouri and adjoining States is in session at St. Paul's Church, (Ohio street, north side of the river,) in this city. We learn that there is quite a number of clergymen and lay-delegates of their respective churches.

☞ The elephants, Virginius and Pizaro, attached to Raymond & Waring's menagerie, were drowned on the 14th instant, in attempting to swim the river near Philadelphia.

They had exhibited in that city during the winter and were proceeding on the tour to N. York and the eastward by way of Camden.

VOICE OF THE PEOPLE.

SLAVERY IN ILLINOIS.

We are in favor of putting the words of the Wilmot proviso into our constitution with such an addition as will not only prohibit slavery itself but will prohibit any legislation which acknowledges its existence in any other State. Every human being treading the Illinois soil should be free except in cases provided for by the United States laws. On our own statutes the word slave, or fugitive from labor, or bound to service should not appear. If other States will have slaves, it is a quasi endorsement for us to make laws to facilitate the capture of fugitives.

MINESOTAH is the Sioux name of the St. Peters River, and is composed of two words; *mine*, water, and *sotah*, turbid, or whitish turbid, in contradistinction from the reddish tinge which muddy streams generally have. At the junction of the St. Peters with the Mississippi, especially in the high waters of the spring, the difference in the color of the stream is quite perceptible at a distance of four or five hundred yards. As it appears to be a settled principle to give the new States and Territories the name of the principal stream running through them, as is the case with Illinois, Wisconsin, Iowa and Missouri, the word Minesota, (should be Minesotah,) is quite appropriate, as the St. Peters is undoubtedly the longest, if not the largest river in the New Territory.

GEN. TAYLOR writes, under date of March 4th, after the battle of Buena Vista to General Butler as follows:

"I may observe that I have been also named as a candidate for that high office by a few newspaper editors and others, which has been done without my knowledge, wishes or consent.

This I have assured all who have written me on the subject, assuring them I had no aspirations for that or any other civil office; that my whole energies, mental and physical, were and had been absorbed in such a way as I thought best calculated to bring this war to a speedy and honorable close, believing it was for the interest of both countries the sooner it was done the better—at any rate so far as ours was concerned; and that President-making should be lost sight of until this was accomplished"

It is said that other letters had been received from Gen. Taylor expressing it as his opinion that the North is entitled to the next Presidency and giving a preference to Judge McLean.

DE KALB COUNTY.

De Kalb, April 22, 1847.

We had our county convention at so late a day that we could not get our proceedings to you before election. We passed resolutions in favor of the Wilmot Proviso and against a tea and coffee tax: and also one approving the course of Mr. Wentworth the past winter.

LEE COUNTY.

Dixon, April 24th, 1847.

Dear Sir: I send you the result of the election in Lee county, Ill. The votes canvassed as follows: Col. J. Dement, democrat, 308; W. W. Heaton, whig, 249. Gaston, abolitionist, 63; J. V. Eustice, bolter of democratic nomination, 12; leaving Col. J. Dement a plurality of 59.

DU PAGE CIRCTIT COURT.

On the criminal docket there were 23 cases, of which 17 were disposed of, and 6 convicted.

On the common law docket there were 47 cases, of which 37 were disposed of, and 10 convicted.

In Chancery, there were 21 cases, 13 were disposed of, and 8 convicted.

In all, 91 cases, disposed of, 67, convicted, 24.

☞ We would direct public attention to the concert of vocal and instrumental music at the City Saloon, to-morrow, (Wednesday,) evening for the benefit of the Permanent Temperance Union, of this city Marsten's (Rechabite,) Band, the Harmon Choir, and Mr. Kieth have volunteered their services for the occasion.

DISTANCES FROM VERA CRUZ TO MEXICO.—

WEDNESDAY, APRI

☞ W. G. Fargo, of Buffalo, has route from here to Milwaukee; and from here to St. Charles; and E. to Springfield.

We hope these contractors will come with, as there is now one universal mail disarrangements throughout Illin

The Department, some time ago, o St Charles mail to leave here on Tue Fridays. It now leaves on Wedne and breaks its whole western connecti

DR. TURNER, of the U. S. A., who battle of Buena Vista, is now at the House, in this city, with his lady.

SCHOOL TAXATION.—An article on t in to-day's paper should be read.

Mr. Clay, has been *set up* for nearly Mr. Calhoun for nearly 25, Gen. Cass 15, Gen. Scott for about the same per Van Buren *ever since* he *was* paid in Webster ever since Gen. Jackson's se tion, and Judge McLean ever since I could mention several others who have [illegible] but *not up* for *stereotype*.

The *Union* says the President will c diately about 6000 more volunteer troo service. They are principally intended the places of volunteers whose time o about to expire.

These troops are intended to strengt divisions of our army, viz —at Santa F my in the direction of the Rio Grande, umn of Vera Cruz.

JOHN QUINCY ADAMS.—For more than Mr. ADAMS is understood to have kept which every thing connected with his life is presented with careful minute has been stated, also, that he has writt moir of his father, but he has found tim plete only a single volume, of four or f the plan embraced.

Mr Calhoun has been in Congress, Executive, from time immemorial, a Carolina has learned to think that the e any other man to the Presidency would constitutional Kentucky thinks the Mr. Clay, Massachusetts of Mr. Webst York of Mr. Van Buren, and other other veterans.

QUICK TIME.—The Eastern mail last brought Buffalo papers of Saturday the This makes us feel some nearer that ci

ICE AT MACINAC.

The steamer St. Louis, Capt. Fred has returned to Detroit after an unsucc to Macinac. She reports *twenty miles* the straits.

The Capt. also reports propellers C Oneida, Princeton, Manhattan, and th Windham and Alvin Clark, and one b not known, at Macinac.

LATEST FROM THE GUL

Com. Perry was about leaving with to capture every Mexican port on which had not been taken south of Al A fine one, called Kacotalpel, possesses sheltered harbor.

☞ Alvarado surrendered to Com his sending a flag of truce, before Ge man and his troops came up.

☞ The Cambria [illegible] £400,000, of [illegible] at Halifax.

OPENING OF THE CANA

The New York Canal boards have o open their canals on the first day of Ma

THE GREAT BATTLE.

...go Democrat.

, MAY 4, 1847. OLD SERIES VOL. XV, NO 15.

SCHOOL TAXATION.

Chicago, April 26, 1847.

School Directors of Cook Co., Ill.

...ACH is upon you that the School Law ...and The principal duty in carrying out its ..., relative to taxation for the support of ... Schools, it seems to me that this com... on is appropriately addressed to you.— ...ortance of the subject leads me to hope ... will at once fulfill the duty of your po... ...d having called a meeting of the inhab... your districts respectively as required by ... them the necessity of taxation ...pport of common schools, and its j s-

...egislature at its last session passed a ...w to take effect from and after the first ...ay, 1847, which repeals all former acts ...ubject. This act contains the follow... ...ns relative to the assessment and col... of taxes for the support of common ... to wit:

TAXES.

11. On the first Saturday of May next, ...on the first Saturday of May annually, ..., the inhabitants, legal voters, (2) of ...ool district in this State, may meet to... ...t some convenient place in the district, ...rpose of voting for, or against levying ... the support of common schools, for ... repairing school houses, or for other ..., or to pay existing debts contract... ...ool purposes before that time, in the ... the school directors (3) shall give ten ... of such meeting, by posting up no... at least three public places in the dis... ...ing forth the time, place and object of ...ing: *Provided*, that if five of said in... request it, school directors shall call ...ing to be holden upon any Saturday, ... given as aforesaid.

...1. The inhabitants, legal voters, when ... as above provided, shall organize by ... one of their number chairman, and ...ecretary. They shall then determine ... such manner as they may choose, (4) ...her they will tax themselves for the ..., or either, or any of them, (5) in sec... specified. If two-thirds of the voters shall be for a tax, they shall determine ... rate to be levied for the current year, ...ding fifteen cents on the one hundred ...nd to what purpose or purposes (6) au... ...in sections 109 and 110 hereof, the ...ised by tax shall be applied. The sec... ...ll keep a true record of the proceedings ... meeting, which shall be certified and ... the chairman and secretary, and pre... ...y said secretary, together with the ... all resident tax payers of the district, ...e district treasurer: *provided*, that for ... of lot, or building and furnishing school ...e rate of taxation may be any amount, ...ed by vote as aforesaid, not exceeding ...on the one hundred dollars.

...th section of the act creates a district ..., who is to be appointed by the school ... in the several districts of the township. ...s officer that the proceedings of the ... above spoken of are to be certified.— ...ese proceedings are received by him, ... section of the act makes it his duty "to ...d certify to the clerk of the County ...ioners' Court, BEFORE THE FIRST DAY ... a correct abstract of the votes, (8) and ...nt of money voted to be raised at any ... of the inhabitants, under the provisions ...s 110 and 111." The agency of the ... this matter ceases here, as no other ...g is required of them. The issuing the ...or the collection of the tax and its col... ...re duties imposed upon the County ...d the collector. After the tax is col... ...e district treasurer is authorized to de... ...d receive the amount of the collect...

... be necessary to give a few practical ...s on the subject of sections 110 and ...ifficulties sometimes occur in regard to ...ruction of legislative acts. These sug... ...for clearness I shall make as they oc... ...ding these sections, and number them ...ment reference.

This meeting may be held upon any ... if requested in the manner pointed out ... to this section: but it must be ... for the treasurer to make his re... ...e county clerk, which is before the ... of July.

It is not necessary that all the inhabi... ...he district, legal voters, should be pres... ... meeting. If it is called according to ...ns of the 111th section, any number ...uals attending it, great or small, will, ...ion, constitute a legal meeting.

THURSDAY, APRIL 29.

NOTICE.

A general meeting of the citizens of Chicago, will be held at the Court House, on Saturday evening, May 1st, for the purpose of nominating delegates to the River and Harbor Convention, to be held in this city on July 5th.

A general attendance is particularly requested.

We see no necessity of this meeting at all. Every citizen of Illinois ought to be considered a member of the convention, and every citizen of the United States an invited guest.

Supposing a select few get together on Saturday night and appoint none but members of their own circle or own party as delegates, do they suppose the mass of the people of Chicago will submit to it? No, never!

It has been with great difficulty that jealousy has thus far been kept down. But the matter is well enough now, and will be if a few men do not undertake, on their own responsibility, to resolve their own particular selves into a mass meeting.

Is it intended to have this convention in a school house, a law office, or some other small room that it becomes necessary to exclude any portion of our fellow citizens? We hope this project will be abandoned, and that every body will be allowed to attend the convention.

For the democratic party, we say, once for all, that they have acted thus far in good faith and intend to do so. They, however, know when they are well used; and, unless every body is allowed to take part in the Convention, they will *hand it over, with all its responsibilities*, to that party which is eternally proving itself more nice than wise.

APPOINTMENTS BY THE PRESIDENT.

Brigadier General GIDEON J. PILLOW, to be Major General in the army of the United States, in the place of Thomas H. Benton, who declined to accept.

Brigadier General JOHN A. QUITMAN, to be Major General in the army of the United States, in the place of William Cumming, who declined to accept.

Colonel CALEB CUSHING, to be Brigadier General in the army of the United States, in the place of John A. Quitman, promoted.

☞ Mr. Baptiste Irwin, of Louisville, Ky., was so severely wounded by the premature discharge of a cannon, with which he, with other citizens, was firing a salute in honor of the glorious victory of Buena Vista, as to cause his death on the evening of the next day.

ALVARADO, as every one anticipated, was taken without firing a gun, and the squadron has returned to Vera Cruz. Capt. Mayo has been left as Governor of the town with a small force, while Capt. Tatnall, in the Spitfire, has gone farther up the river to look in at the different towns.

A great number of cannon and other military stores were captured at Alvarado, for there were no less than seven forts and batteries on the water side. It is said that Com. Perry brought off every thing of value.

The two ports reported to have been taken by our forces are Tlacotalpan and Cosamoloapan, above Alvarado. They have fallen without resistance. They are important points, situated upon fine inland waters which have their outlet to the Gulf of Alvarado.

The very latest report at Vera Cruz was that Santa Anna would dispute the passage of our troops to Mexico with an army of 20,000 men.

COL. BENTON.—The last Commercial Bulletin, published in Boonsville, contains the following important letter from Col. Benton:

WASHINGTON CITY, March 21, 1847.

Mr. QUESENBURY—Sir: I see that you have put up my name for the Presidency, at the head of your editorial column: and while I thank you

CANAL TRUSTEES.

The Trustees of the Canal, in behalf of the Foreign Bond holders, Capt. Swift and Mr. Leavitt, arrived, last night, and will proceed to *Lockport*, to-day. They express a determination to complete the work within the year 1847; and with this our people will be satisfied, and this much they expect.

DELEGATES.

We notice in town, the present week, Wm. McClure Esq., of *Will*, and D. H. Whitney Esq., of Boone.

We find both of these gentlemen opposed to all incorporations and exclusive privileges whatever, and for inserting in the constitution a positive prohibition against making any difference between a man as a banker, a merchant, a doctor, or any thing else. They would have a banker brought before a magistrate, for his bills, in the same way as for his notes of hand. And, if one banks, they want all to have the privilege who can so secure the public that the Governor, with the security in the Treasury of the State, will put his name on the bills. Thus all the stockholders can be sued individually at any time, the same as on their notes of hand, and then the Governor has the security in par stocks, dollar for dollar, besides.

We believe every bank-man in this State will oppose any such just restrictions.

VIRGINIA ELECTION.

6th District—Returns from Richmond city, Powhatan and Chesterfield counties, and part of Hanover county, gives Botts, (whig) 620 majority.—He is undoubtedly elected.

8th District—Newton, (whig) supposed to be elected over Willoughby.

9th District—John J. Pendleton, (whig) was re-elected

BATTLE OF BUENA VISTA.

The numbers of killed, wounded and missing, according to Gen. Taylor's tables, are as follows:

Killed.—Commissioned officers, 28; non-commissioned officers, musicians, artificers and privates, 239;—total 267.

Wounded.—Commissioned officers, 41; non-commissioned, &c., 415;—total 456.

Missing.—Non-commissioned officers, musicians, artificers and privates, 23.

Grand total of killed, wounded and missing, 746.

The number of troops engaged in the action was: Commissioned officers, 334; non-commissioned officers, musicians, artificers and privates, 1,425—total, 4,759.

MOVEMENTS OF THE PEOPLE.

A copy of the poll books of Caledonia precinct, Boone Co., has been forwarded us with sixty-three names attached. The questions were put and decided viva voce at the polls, as follows:

For the Wilmot Proviso, ayes 63, noes 00.—For a tea and coffee tax, ayes 0, noes 63. Improvement of harbors, ayes 63, noes 00.

Keep the ball in motion! There will be a chance for other precincts to speak in August.

VERMILLION AND CHAMPAIGNE COUNTIES.—We are gratified to learn that T. R. Webber, Esq., has succeeded in Champaigne Co.; and regret very much that Mr. Davis was beaten in Vermillion, as will all the democrats who know him. He had all the wealth, talents and popularity of the two strongest men in the county, with their host of friends to oppose him, and yet he gave them a hard run.

LAKE CO. OFFICIAL.

Dear Sir,—The following is an abstract of the votes cast in Lake County for delegates to the Convention to amend the Constitution of this State. Yours Respectfully,

A. PATTERSON, Co. Cl'k.

[illegible]

BY AUTHORITY.

LAWS OF THE UNITED STATES passed at the second session of the Twenty-ninth Congress.

JAMES K. POLK, President. GEORGE M. DALLAS, Vice President. JOHN W. DAVIS, Speaker of the House of Representatives.

CHAP. 30.—AN ACT to establish a land office in the northern part of Michigan, and to provide for the sale of mineral lands in the State of Michigan.

[SEC. 1.] Be it enacted by the Senate and House of Representatives of the United States of America in Congress assembled, That all that portion of the public lands in the State of Michigan lying north of the boundaries of the Saginaw and Grand river land districts in said State, commonly called the northern peninsula of the State of Michigan, with the islands in Lakes Superior, Huron and Michigan, and in Green Bay, the straits of Michilimackinac, and the river St. Mary's, within the jurisdiction of said State, be, and the same are hereby, included in a land district. There shall be a land office established at such point therein as the President of the United States may select.

SEC. 2. And be it further enacted, That the Secretary of the Treasury shall cause a geological examination and survey of the lands embraced in said district to be made and reported to the Commissioner of the General Land Office. And the President is hereby authorized to cause such of said lands as may contain copper, lead, or other valuable ores to be exposed to sale, giving six months' notice of the times and places of sales in such newspapers of general circulation in the several States as he may deem expedient, with a brief description of the lands to be offered; showing the number and localities of the mines known, the probability of discovering others, the quality of the ores, the facilities of working the mines, and the means and expense of transporting their products to the principal markets in the United States. And all the lands contained in said district, not reported as aforesaid, shall be sold in the same manner as other lands under the laws now in force for the sale of the public lands, excepting and reserving from such sales section sixteen in each township for the use of schools, and such reservations as the President shall deem necessary for public uses.

SEC. 3. And be it further enacted, That all those persons who are in possession, by actual occupancy, of any portion of the district described in the first section of this act, under authority of a lease from the Secretary of War, for the purpose of mining thereon, and who have fully complied with all the conditions and stipulations of said lease, may enter and purchase the same at any time during the continuance of such lease, and not less, by paying to the United States therefor at the rate of two dollars and fifty cents per acre: *Provided*, That said entry and purchase shall be made to include the original survey of such lease, as near as may be conforming to the lines of the public surveys of sections and subdivisions thereof. And all those persons who are in possession, by actual occupancy, of any of said lands, for mining purposes, under authority of a written permit from the Secretary of War, and who have visible landmarks and monuments as boundaries thereon, and who have, in all other respects, complied with the conditions and stipulations contained in such permit, may enter and purchase the same, to the extent of the tract selected by them and reported to the Secretary of War, [illegible] said permit, and no less, in the same manner [illegible] under leases, and at the same price: *Provided*, such entry and purchase be made before the day said [illegible] shall be offered for sale by order of the President.— And all those persons who shall be in possession, by actual occupancy, of a mine or mines actually discovered [illegible] the passage of this act, and who shall pay the same per cent [illegible] as those who [illegible] under leases, as aforesaid, shall be permitted to enter a [illegible] one section of land, and not less, to include such mine or mines discovered and occupied as aforesaid, by them, by paying to the United States the same price, and at the same time, as required of those who hold under permits [illegible], and all rents accruing from such lessees [illegible] rents shall be paid and delivered to such officers of the Government as the Secretary of the Treasury shall direct: *Provided*, That prior to any such purchase being made under the provisions of this section, proof of possession and occupancy, as aforesaid, in the name of those claimed, shall be made to the register and receiver of the land district, together with the evidence of the payment of all rents due the United States, agreeably to such rules as may be prescribed by the Secretary of the Treasury for that purpose, which register and receiver shall be entitled to receive one dollar for his services therein: *Provided*, That an appeal from the decision of the register and receiver to the Secretary of the Treasury may be [illegible] such regulations as the said Secretary may prescribe. And if two or more persons are in possession of the same section, the first occupant shall be entitled to a [illegible], unless the same can be so divided by legal subdivisions as to give each the discovery claimed by them.

SEC. 4. And be it further enacted, That the said mineral lands shall be offered for sale in quarter sections, [illegible] shall be received at a less rate than five dollars per acre; and if such lands shall not be sold at public sale at such price, they shall thereafter be entered at private sale at that price: *Provided*, That no [illegible] of any of said lands upon which there may be an outstanding lease or [illegible] from the Secretary of War, unexpired or undetermined, and which is [illegible] for mining purposes, and the occupants [illegible] which have complied with all the requisitions of such lease or leases, [illegible] the same, shall [illegible] the determination of such lease or leases by efflux of time, voluntary surrender, or other legal [illegible] thereof, except in such cases as are provided for in the third section of this act, and the lessees respectively shall be entitled to the privileges [illegible] voluntary surrender of the lease or leases held by them.

SEC. 5. And be it further enacted, That the management and control of the mineral lands shall be transferred from the War Department, and placed under the jurisdiction and control of the Treasury Department; and all [illegible], maps, papers, instruments, and other property, [illegible] to be used in [illegible] the mineral agency, [illegible] by the War Department, shall be delivered over and made subject to the disposition of the Secretary of the Treasury.

SEC. 6. And be it further enacted, That the President, by and with the advice and consent of the Senate, [illegible] a sufficient number of townships are surveyed, and [illegible] made to the General Land Office, to allow the commencement of the sales in said district, shall appoint one register and one receiver for the land office in said district, who shall reside at the place designated by the President for the land office, receive such compensation, give security, and discharge all duties pertaining to such office as are prescribed by law.

Approved, March 1, 1847.

CHAP. 31.—AN ACT to amend an act entitled "An act to regulate the carriage of passengers in merchant vessels," and to determine the time when [illegible] take effect.

[SEC. 1.] Be it enacted by the Senate and House of Representatives of the United States of America in Congress assembled, That the act to regulate the carriage of passengers in merchant vessels, approved the twenty-second day of February, eighteen hundred and forty-seven, shall, in regard to all vessels arriving from ports on this side of the capes of Good Hope and Horn, take effect [illegible] in force from and after the thirty-first day of May [illegible], and in regard to all vessels arriving from

PLATE III

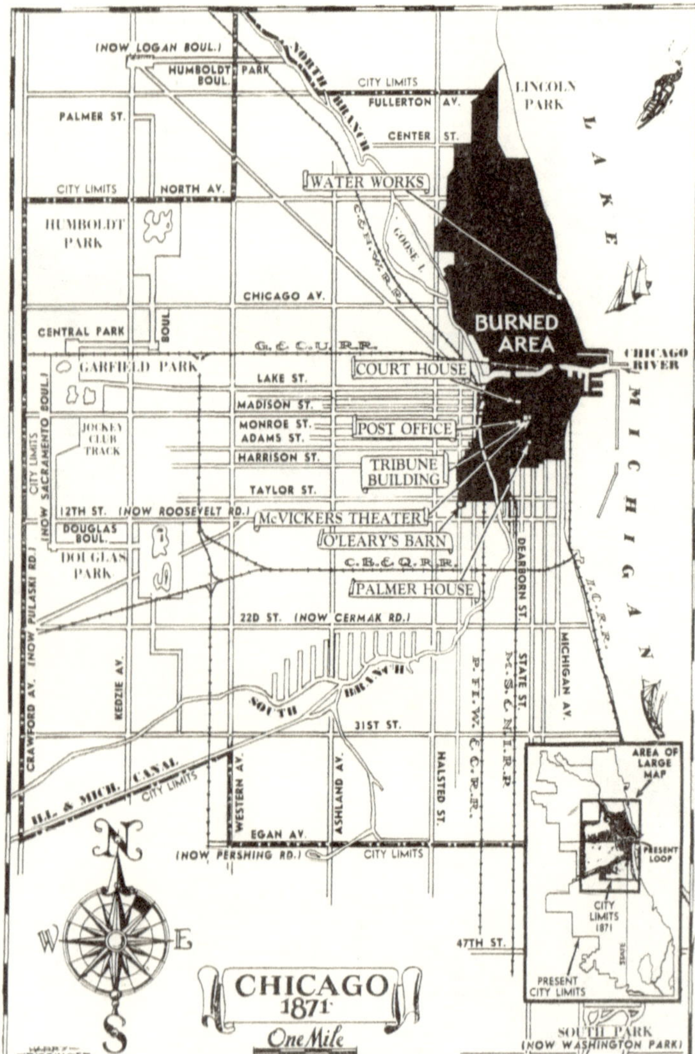
(NOW LOGAN BOUL.)
HUMBOLDT PARK BOUL.
NORTH BRANCH
CITY LIMITS
FULLERTON AV.
LINCOLN PARK
PALMER ST.
CENTER ST.
LAKE
WATER WORKS
CITY LIMITS
NORTH AV.
HUMBOLDT PARK
C. & N. W. R. R.
GOOSE I.
CHICAGO AV.
BURNED AREA
CENTRAL PARK
BOUL.
G. & C. U. R.R.
CHICAGO RIVER
GARFIELD PARK
COURT HOUSE
LAKE ST.
MADISON ST.
MICHIGAN
MONROE ST.
ADAMS ST.
POST OFFICE
JOCKEY CLUB TRACK
HARRISON ST.
TRIBUNE BUILDING
TAYLOR ST.
12TH ST. (NOW ROOSEVELT RD.)
McVICKERS THEATER
DOUGLAS BOUL.
O'LEARY'S BARN
DOUGLAS PARK
C. B. & Q. R. R.
PALMER HOUSE
DEARBORN ST.
I. C. R. R.
CITY LIMITS
(NOW SACRAMENTO BOUL.)
CRAWFORD AV. (NOW PULASKI RD.)
22D ST. (NOW CERMAK RD.)
KEDZIE AV.
SOUTH BRANCH
P. FT. W. & C. R. R.
M. S. & N. I. R. R.
STATE ST.
MICHIGAN AV.
31ST ST.
ILL. & MICH. CANAL
CITY LIMITS
WESTERN AV.
ASHLAND AV.
HALSTED ST.
EGAN AV.
(NOW PERSHING RD.)
CITY LIMITS
AREA OF LARGE MAP
PRESENT LOOP
CITY LIMITS 1871
PRESENT CITY LIMITS
N
W
E
S
47TH ST.
CHICAGO 1871
One Mile
SOUTH PARK (NOW WASHINGTON PARK)

bore the inscription, in German: "Fuerchtet Gott und gebet ihm die Ehre!" ("Fear God, and give glory to Him.")

No attempt will be made here to give a detailed description of this appalling catastrophe. However, a few paragraphs will not lead to boredom.

"The burning of Moscow, in 1812, caused a loss amounting to £30,000,000; but the loss at Chicago was in excess of this amount. The Great Fire of London, in 1666, devastated a tract of 436 acres and destroyed 13,000 buildings; but that of Chicago swept over 1,900 acres and burned more than 17,000 buildings." A. T. Andreas writes: "The following is the statement of the area burned over and of property destroyed, made by the Chicago Relief and Aid Society, and which is probably authoritative: 'The total area burned over the city, including streets, was 2,124 acres, or nearly three and one-third square miles. This area contained about 73 miles of streets, 18,000 buildings, and the homes of 100,000 people.'" Some of us remember the story as it was printed in the *Lesebuch fuer Oberklassen evangelisch-lutherischer Schulen,* in which the author refers to the Great Fire of Chicago as an "unprecedented picture of the transitoriness of earthly things." By others it was called "a grand but awful spectacle"; by still others, an "appalling calamity." "A fellow standing on a piano declared that the fire was the friend of the poor man. He wanted everybody to help himself to the best liquor he could get and continued to yell until someone as drunk as himself flung a bottle at him and knocked him off." J. Pat Maloney, writing in "The Voice of the People" of the *Chicago Tribune,* made the following statement concerning the cause of the great conflagration: "The fire was started by four hobos who were rushing the 'beer can' and sleeping in the hay over the cow barn. One of the four dropped a lighted match in the hay." Mr. Maloney says he got that information from Frank T. Scanlan, who lived two blocks from Saint Patrick's Church on Des Plaines Street. He was sixteen years old at the time and knew the O'Leary family well. On State Street was the fine row of five-story marble-front buildings known as "Booksellers' Row." These magnificent buildings were . . . filled with books and stationery. . . . An exploration of the ruins failed to discover a single book—or a sheet or a quire of paper. "The only legible thing found was a single leaf, badly scorched, of a Bible, and this is said to have contained that part of the first chapter of Jeremiah, which opens: 'How doth the city set solitary that was full of people, how she became as a widow. She weepeth sore in the night, and her tears are on her cheeks.'" Robert Collyer tells this story: "I well remember in our great fire in Chicago a slender young man who undertook to carry a lady and her little child in a light buggy out of the burning city. He was going down Michigan Avenue, the street was crowded to a jam, and he had to stop and wait for the jam to get loose. All at once there came along behind him a great fellow driving a furniture-wagon, who yelled to him, with an oath, to get out of the way or he would run into him. 'I cannot stir,' the man said quietly, "and this lady is sick and has a little babe with her not a week old. Now, you must be quiet and stay where you are, and we will all come out together very soon.' Then the brute swore a great oath that he would come down and pull him out of that and twist the thing out of his way. He jumped out of his wagon to do it. The young man jumped too. They were both on the ground at the same instant, but before the giant had time to strike him or clutch him, the young man had sent his fist about where the brute's dinner would go if he could get any that day, and that brought him down. But as he was coming down, he caught him with the other fist right under the chin, and that brought him up. 'Now,' he said, 'you get onto that wagon and do just as I tell you, or I will give you the greatest licking you ever had since you were born.' The fellow swore horribly, mounted the wagon, and drove down the avenue at the back of the buggy when the jam gave way. But the best of the story is this, and I vouch for its truth, that this young man was a minister in our city, in good standing, a mighty man in preaching and prayer, as I know, a man who wouldn't hurt a mouse and in every way a gentlemen." Unfortunately, the identity of that minister is hidden from us.

One year after the conflagration, James T. Fields, in the course of a lecture, said: "Instead of ruin I found such a grandeur of restoration and strength of enterprise, such an overwhelming result of indomitable will, unfailing industry and courage, that I almost doubted the evidence of my senses and could scarcely believe that any such conflagration as we had heard of, read of, had occurred at all."

Possibly very few people, as they travel by auto on the present beautiful Lake Shore Drive, realize that the greatest portion of the "foundation" for the area between the Illinois Central Railroad tracks and the Lake, which now constitutes a part of Chicago's "front yard," is composed of rocks and debris hauled out there soon after the Great Fire.

As that exciting decade closed, it was reported that Thomas Alva Edison had solved the problem of the electric light.

On August 26, 1896, the Rev. John Baumgaertner, Pastor Wunder's son-in-law, was called as assistant at First Saint Paul's. Following the death of Dr. Wunder* at the age of eighty-three on December 22, 1913, the assistant was installed as full-time pastor.

Toward the close of the first decade of the twentieth century, the congregation became increasingly aware of the fact that it could not much longer remain in the neighborhood, because the entire region was rapidly becoming dotted with factories of various kinds; also, the elevated raidroad (Rapid

* Pastor Wunder received the degree of Doctor of Divinity from Concordia Seminary, St. Louis, Mo., on the occasion of the sixtieth anniversary of his ordination to the ministry, in 1909.

Transit—"L"), erected on the east side of the church edifice, created intolerable disturbances during the services and meetings. These considerations led to the purchase of the present building at the northeast corner of Goethe and North La Salle Streets for $45,000 from a Hebrew congregation. This church was dedicated on August 28, 1910. Less than eight years later, on January 19, 1918, Pastor Baumgaertner, First Saint Paul's third "regular" pastor, died at the age of forty-four. His successor was the Rev. Henry G. W. Kowert, a native of New Zealand, who, before coming to Chicago, had served congregations in Cordelia, Calif., and in Chicago Heights, Ill. Pastor Kowert came to Saint Paul's in 1916. He was installed on September 16, 1917, and served the congregation during Pastor Baumgaertner's last illness.

In 1931 the day school, established in 1846, was closed because there were "too few children to continue." A Sunday school had been started in the fall of 1910. In 1937 the Rev. Louis W. Grother was called as Pastor Kowert's assistant for one year and in 1938 as associate pastor. Pastor Kowert died on August 18, 1944, at the Lutheran Sanatorium, Wheat Ridge, Colo., and shortly afterward the associate pastor became full-time pastor. Pastor Grother accepted a call to Kalamazoo, Mich., and left Chicago soon after Easter, 1949. His successor, the Rev. James G. Manz, assistant pastor of Grace Congregation, River Forest, Ill., since January, 1946, was installed at First Saint Paul's on October 9, 1949.

The following teachers served First Saint Paul's day school: George Henry Fischer, Christian Luecke, Charles Laufer, Christian Schumm, John Nickolaus Haase, G. Koebel, John Doerfler, Louis C. E. Doering, Arthur H. Eggers, Miss M. Koplien, and Gustav A. Niethammer.[20] Eduard Bartling, formerly at Bethlehem in Colehour, served for about four months, 1876-1877. He died February 8, 1877, at the age of 22.

3. Sarah's Grove

The Lutheran Trail now returns to the region of Illinois Lutheranism's inception, by-passes Duncklees Grove and Zion Church, and proceeds about eight miles beyond in a northwesterly direction, until it reaches a community known in the 1840's as Sarah's Grove. In this community the first Lutheran services were conducted in the log huts of various interested German settlers, the majority of whom had very recently immigrated from Hessen-Schaumburg, Germany. The first service was conducted on December 26, 1840 (Second Christmas Day), by the Rev. Francis A. Hoffmann of Duncklees Grove.

Whether or not Pastor Hoffmann was an expert equestrian has not been established; and, for that matter, he never professed to be a good pedestrian; and yet, he must have been just that, according to an account of his journeys from Duncklees Grove to Sarah's Grove, which continued for a period of about six years. "Usually the distance of approximately eight miles was covered on foot." Occasionally some good soul would place at his disposal an old nag ("Klepper"), which today one would scarcely classify as a horse. "Between the point where Salt Creek Station is located," Hoffmann continues, "and a small wooded area known as Sarah's Grove (later known also as Schween's Grove), near which the present Saint Peter's Church stands, and many miles beyond, the region was entirely uninhabited. . . . Immediately after crossing the bridge over Salt Creek, I headed directly for the hickory trees of Sarah's Grove, five or six miles away. At that time there were neither roads nor paths." Near the southern edge of Sarah's Grove the Indians had blazed a trail from Chicago through Bloomingdale to Galena, which the settlers preferred not to use ("den man aber lieber nicht betrat"). One wonders why not.

Additional families having in the course of time settled in

the region, these settlers in co-operation with the Lutherans at Long Grove (some twelve miles north by northeast of Sarah's Grove) in 1846 called the Rev. Simon Duncan,* who had served as missionary of the Michigan Synod (dissolved in that year) to the Chippewa Indians. He began his ministerial activities in these two communities in July, 1846. It was during that same month that a number of Lutheran pastors of Fort Wayne, Ind., and vicinity met in that town mainly for the purpose of discussing and formulating a constitution for a strictly confessional Lutheran synod in America.

In the same year, 1846, the Sarah's Grove Lutherans invested $50 in forty acres of land. Upon it were erected a church and a school, and a section was reserved as a "Gottesacker" (cemetery).

By the end of 1847 the number of Lutheran families had increased beyond the twenty mark, and so the Sarah's Grovers felt confident in their ability to support a pastor of their own, and that was to be none other than the man who had conducted the first service there—the Rev. Francis A. Hoffmann of Duncklees Grove.

In the summer of the same year forty-five members† had adopted and signed the congregation's constitution, which contained a paragraph stipulating "adherence to all confessional writings of the Lutheran Church." Although the congregation had formally organized as Saint Peter's and made provision

*The same as Johann Simon Dumser?

†Conrad Salge	Fried. Hartmann	Fried. Bartels
Ludwig Vette	F Helberg	Conrad Wille
Christian Vette	F. Gieseke	F. Lichhart
Christian Waldemar	F. Redker	H. Thies
J. H. Becker	F. C. Hausing	H. Reckeweg
Heinrich Schierding	H. Kreft	F. Nerge
J. Honeberg	F. Koelling	J. Boeger
J. Engelking	Ch. Rohlwing	Wilkening
Ernst Kinkelhake	Ch. Teigeler	Ch. Koelling
H. Steege	Heinrich Pfingsten	J. C. Biesterfeld
C. Redeker	Ch. Winkelhake	Wente
H. Redeker	Hattendorf	August Claus
Heinrich Schrage	Conrad Kruse	Fried. Trost
Johann Fasse	Ch. Geseke	W. Teyler
Ch. Withaeger	H. Homeier	F. Rascher

for their spiritual needs, the members found themselves in temporal straits. With the exception of a few members, the immigrants, after a long and tedious voyage across the Atlantic, followed by a strenuous journey from the seaboard, had arrived without sufficient funds for the acquisition of food and shelter on the seemingly boundless and very sparsely populated prairie. With the aid of those in somewhat easier circumstances, land was eventually acquired, and everyone began in one way or another to construct log and clay houses. That accomplished, they proceeded with primitive tools to the difficult task of clearing the land and making it arable. "If one had a pair of oxen," writes Hoffmann, "a miserable plow and perhaps also a worn-out wagon, he counted himself a full-fledged farmer" ("ein gemachter Farmer"). Thus the prairie was eventually cultivated and seeded, the wife driving the oxen and the husband wielding the plow handles—probably not always with sublime patience. But, why not?—with the fragrance of a bountiful earth round about and the prospects becoming brighter!

A post office was established at Sarah's Grove in 1848. That was evidence of the intimate relations that even then existed between Pastor Hoffmann and prominent politicians, such as Senator Stephen A. Douglas and Representative "Long John" Wentworth. "Of course," remarked Hoffmann, who had been appointed postmaster, "the mailman appeared but once a week, at times even with an empty bag," which, in such condition, was referred to as "Uncle Sam's tubercular, poorly fed mailbag" (" . . . schwindsuechtiger, kaerglich gefuetterter Postsack"). In 1868 Henry Rohlwing, heretofore mail carrier, was appointed postmaster, and mail was received twice a week.

On a carefully selected portion of the congregation's premises a church building, 24x30 feet, including a fifty-foot steeple, was erected according to a plan agreed upon by fifteen members, each of whom consented to cut down a tree, square it, and haul it to the building site. While the construction work was in progress, the services were conducted in the near-by barn of Mr. Schween, "where not seldom a rooster and a hen boldly held forth with their cackling" ("tapfer drein redeten"). Early in autumn, 1848, services were transferred to the partially completed church, which was dedicated on the Seventeenth Sunday after Trinity, 1848. This church later, for twenty-five years, served as a school.

Impaired health forced the resignation of Pastor Hoffmann in 1851. His successor, the Rev. J. Nick Volkert, hitherto pastor of the Lutheran congregation at Highlands Grove (now Plum Grove), was installed by Pastor Hoffmann on April 9, 1851.

At a town meeting held some time during the period between 1851 and 1854, while E. F. Colby served as supervisor for and within the township, the name of the community was discussed. The Anglo-Americans present insisted upon naming it Lutherville or Lutherburg. But Fred Nerge, a member of Saint Peter's Congregation, suddenly "with the firmness of an old German champion" pounded upon the table and exclaimed: "Schaumburg it shall be called!" ("Schaumburg schall et heiten!") And thenceforth it was Schaumburg!

Concerning the first period of his ministry at Saint Peter's in Schaumburg (not Sarah's Grove or Schween's Grove!), Pastor Volkert writes: "At that time the Ark of God dwelt in board huts, and the flock with its shepherd did not dwell in paneled houses. However, if one then had a small church ("Kirchlein"), 24x30 feet, with a steeple on it, not exactly like a 'peep show' ("Guckkasten"), and, besides, a bell in the same, even though not much larger than a locomotive bell, one could exult and shout for joy. And no matter how breezy ("luftig") and exposed to the heat of summer and the cold of winter, one nonetheless felt happy and content when one finally saw how the wood, which, with the help of a German immigrant and a student, had been cut from obese ("dickleibiger") tree trunks and split, trickling and sighing in the stove, produced heat. When the pastor then with his 'better half' rode in a buggy—respected by him but worn out—then the much-beloved and highly honored President (of the Missouri Synod) could comment thus: 'The Northern Illinois pastors ride in carriages like the prelates.' "

At the first congregational meeting in his new pastorate, Pastor Volkert began to testify against the rationalistic doctrines contained in the hymnbook and in the "Kurhessisch" catechism, which the members insisted upon retaining, despite the fact that at the time they submitted the call to Pastor Volkert at Highlands Grove they agreed to receive instruction in doctrinal matters. The resultant dissension was not "too serious"—only a few members withdrew from Saint Peter's. On September 15, 1853, the congregation resolved to introduce the "Missouri" Synod's hymnal and the Lutheran "Ludwig Catechism," the best to be had at that time.

In 1856 Saint Peter's former pastor, Francis A. Hoffmann, was nominated Lieutenant Governor of Illinois.

In the spring of 1858 Pastor Volkert accepted a call to the congregation at Cook's Store, Lafayette County, Mo., which the Rev. A. G. G. Francke had left less than about one year previously to assume the pastorate at Duncklees Grove (Zion). Two years later, in 1860, he resigned.

Because Saint John's Congregation at Rodenberg (Rothenberg), four miles southwest of Schaumburg, had become vacant by the dismissal of Pastor Seitz, Saint Peter's Congregation joined the former in calling the Rev. Frederick William Richmann from Grand Rapids, Mich., to serve both parishes. He was installed on the Tenth Sunday after Trinity, 1858. In the same year F. W. A. Fuerstenau was called to serve as teacher in both schools. Alternately the pastor preached, and alternately the teacher taught at both places. On October 10, 1860,

Saint Peter's Congregation at Schaumburg was accepted into membership with the Missouri Synod.

In March, 1862, Pastor Richmann unexpectedly received a call to serve as chaplain with the Fifty-eighth Regiment of the Ohio Volunteers. He requested the congregation to give him a leave of absence. The request was granted with the provision that he secure a student of theology to serve as supply pastor during his absence; in the event he failed to heed the congregation's request to return by a specified time, his ministry would automatically terminate. Student John Walther was secured as substitute, and the Rev. A. G. G. Francke of Duncklees Grove performed the official acts. It was at that time that "the halls of the theological seminaries sent forth their young men, whose lips were touched with eloquence, whose hearts kindled with devotion, to serve in the ranks, and make their way to command only as they learned the art of war. Striplings in the colleges, as well as the most gentle and the most studious, those of sweetest temper and loveliest character and brightest genius passed from their classes to the camp. The lumbermen from the forests, the mechanics from their benches, where they had been trained by the exercise of political right to share the life and hope of the Republic, to feel their responsibility to their forefathers, their posterity, and mankind, went to the front, resolved that their dignity as a constituent part of this Republic should not be impaired. Farmers and sons of farmers left the land but half plowed, the grain but half planted, and, taking up the musket, learned to face without fear the presence of peril and the coming of death in the shocks of war, while their hearts were still attracted to their herds and fields and all the tender affections of home." The *Chicago Tribune* reported in 1861 that a new German regiment was raised in Chicago, with recruiting offices in various saloons. On April 21, 1861, 595 men, the first to leave Chicago, boarded an Illinois Central train for Cairo, Ill.

In the middle of May, 1862, Pastor Richmann went to the battle front; but an illness which he had meanwhile contracted forced him to leave the military service, and before the end of that summer he had returned to Schaumburg. "His first report to the *Lutheraner* was written on May 30, 1862, from a camp in the neighborhood of Corinth in northern Mississippi, where he had arrived on May 26 and was received with great joy. General Halleck had just issued a command that all Army chaplains should be held to take command on the battlefield of the men who were ordered to bring the wounded out of the battle lines. . . . Many of the chaplains, on account of impending battle, had 'gone over the hill.' "—"Later the *Lutheraner* reported: Our dear brother Richmann has again been heard from under date of June 24 from Memphis: 'On our marches through the wilderness we endured unspeakable hardships, hunger and thirst, dust, heat, exposure, and rain. . . . Soldiers devoured raw dough and gulped water from muddy puddles which horses and mules disdained to drink.' "

The records of Saint Peter's Congregation contain the following: "After three months of service in the Army, Pastor Richmann, exhausted by the hardships of war and sickness, returned to his congregation."

Teacher Fuerstenau, who had served both parishes, in 1862 followed a call to Zion at Duncklees Grove. Thereupon Saint John's at Rodenberg called a theological candidate, J. N. Niethammer, and Saint Peter's at Schaumburg called a teacher, August Engelke. By this action the alternation above referred to was terminated.

An enlarged church building, of brick, 85x40, with a 127-foot steeple, was dedicated "during a lull on all war fronts"—on November 4, 1863. These alterations and improvements cost $10,000, excluding labor, which was donated by members.

In July, 1869, Pastor Richmann accepted a call to Saint

John's Congregation in Elgin, about eleven miles west of Schaumburg, and on the following October 17 the Rev. Henry Schmidt of Dundee, Ill., was installed as his successor. Pastor Schmidt served the congregation for a period of fourteen years, until July, 1883, when he followed a call to Pittsburgh, Pa. The Rev. Gustav Adolph Mueller of Kankakee, Ill., succeeded him in the Schaumburg pastorate, his installation taking place on November 25, 1883.

Invited to participate in the fiftieth anniversary celebration, the Rev. F. A. Hoffmann (Hans Buschbauer) declined for reasons indicated in the letter reproduced between pages 48 and 49. (See Chapter One.)

On July 11, 1904, during a violent electrical storm, lightning struck the steeple of the church and set it on fire at the very top. Slowly it burnt down to its base. Effort by some of the members prevented complete destruction of the building, but the organ was almost a total loss. The steeple was replaced with one of the same height and form as the original one.

At the turn of the century the following was written by a member of that community: "Schaumburg is the only exclusively German town in Illinois, if not in the United States. Every farm in the township is occupied by Germans. Schaumburg, according to an important English newspaper, has its 'reputation of being the model community of Cook County.' " . . . and Schaumburg still has no jail; someday such a building is to be erected, not, however, for local residents, but for foreigners" (". . . nicht aber fuer ansaessige Buerger, sondern fuer auswaertige").

Physical debility caused the resignation of Pastor Mueller in November, 1905,* but he continued to serve the parish as vacancy pastor until April 29, 1906, when he officiated at the installation of his successor, the Rev. Gottlob Theiss of Hampton, Iowa. At about that time the Missouri Synod's new

*Pastor Mueller served the congregation at Elizabeth, Ill., from 1908 till 1912, in 1913 he resigned, and on Feb. 11, 1923, he died.

Catechism—"Schwan's Exposition of Dr. Martin Luther's Small Catechism"—was introduced in Saint Peter's Church and School.

Following the death of Pastor Theiss in 1935, the Rev. Carl Pfotenhauer of Bright View, Alberta, Canada, was installed as pastor of Saint Peter's Congregation on November 3, 1935. He served here until the spring of 1940, when he followed a call to Zion Congregation in Roseland (Chicago). His successor at Saint Peter's was the Rev. Martin H. Behling of North Plato and Pingree Grove, Ill., who was installed on June 2, 1940. In May, 1948, Pastor Behling accepted a call to Decatur, Ind., and the Rev. Frederick A. Hertwig, Jr., of Milwaukee, Wis., succeeded to St. Peter's, January 30, 1949.

In addition to Mr. Engelke, the following have served in Saint Peter's School:

Herman Brandenburg, 1864-1866
John Hoffmann, 1866-1867
Henry George Grothmann, 1867-1872
John Paul Emrich, 1872-1873
Carl Laufer, 1874-1887
William Simon, 1886-1919
Carl W. Sauer, 1887-1902
F. C. Biermann, 1899-1903
W. A. F. Kath, 1903-1906

Since 1919:
W. H. Luthring
Edwin H. Eggersmann
C. Meinke
F. Hamann
Paul Groenke
W. H. Christian
G. W. Schlie
Roy A. Kolzow

4. Glencoe

From Schaumburg the Trail leads in a northeasterly direction, a distance of about eighteen miles, to Glencoe,* formerly called Gross Point, where in the year 1850 the Rev. C August T. Selle again appears. Having been informed of a settlement of German immigrants on the Cook-Lake county line, Pastor Selle of First Saint Paul's Congregation in Chicago investigated the possibility of conducting worship services for those settlers professing the Lutheran faith. Assured of their interest, he agreed to minister to them once a month; no suitable place being available for worship, the homes of the settlers, particularly that of the John Fehd family, for a

*1940 census: 6,825.

time served the purpose. In 1898 Pastor Selle wrote: "I was privileged to establish a small congregation in Gross Point, twenty miles north of Chicago, which I then served once a month. I also tried to do missionary work elsewhere. This was done especially through a "green" German candidate, Poeschke, who afterwards turned out to be a scoundrel, and through our dear August Lehman, now (1898) long since fallen asleep as our orphan father near St. Louis, both of whom I had received into my house."

In September, 1851, Pastor Selle moved to Crete, Ill., in response to a call from Zion (in 1858 changed to Trinity) Congregation, and for a period of about two years no Lutheran services were held at Gross Point (Glencoe). Then, in 1853, the Rev. Henry Wunder, Pastor Selle's successor in the pastorate of First Saint Paul's in Chicago, once more began services at the county line. The date of the formal organization of the congregation (Trinity) at Glencoe is as yet undetermined. However, it is known that in 1866 the group, now in existence for some time, purchased an acre of land on Green Bay Road, near the county line. Upon this property Trinity Congregation in 1867 erected a church which cost $649.89. At the time of its completion a debt of only $35.66 remained to be paid. Near the site of the property is a granite boulder to which is affixed a bronze plate bearing the reproduction of a tree that in earlier days had served to mark the trail.

The thirty-two settlers* who pledged their support for the purchase of land and building of the church may be considered the original members of Trinity Congregation.

Recording reminiscences on his ninetieth birthday in 1929,

*George Hesler
George Rudolph
Frederick Knoll
Karl Schneider
John Hesler
John Fehd
Julius Nafe
Margaret Beinlich
Edward Mueller
Karl Ludwig
Jacob Behrens
Abraham Frank
Martin Huessel
John Wolff
William Ostermann
Christoph Hohlfelder
George Rosenberger
Paulus Hoffmann
William Bartmus
Frederick Kuhl
Henry Tomfo
Frederick Helke
Carl Unbehauen
Katherine Diesch
M. Gesch
John Pavillard
Christoph Lehmann
Frederick Nerich
Gottlieb Hesler
George Schaefer
Frederick Truempler
Frederick Rudolph

George Hesler, a leading member of Trinity when the first church was built, gives an interesting sidelight of conditions prevailing in the 1850's and 1860's, when the congregation was in its infancy. "There were many hardships to endure. However, there was such a friendly spirit of helpfulness among the neighbors that we were happy then, and certainly more content than we are now. Money was not plentiful in those days, an acre of land costing about $5.00. Work was hard to find; father was willing to undertake any job that was offered at fifty cents per day. The principal means of making a living was the burning of charcoal. This was sold in Chicago at the price of five to ten cents a bushel. The only means of transportation was oxcarts. It took a charcoal wagon three days to make the round trip; one day going, the second day selling, and the third day returning. Another source of revenue was that of chopping cordwood, for which a man received from 35 cents to 40 cents a day. Even we children were obliged to work; many a day I labored at digging potatoes from early morning till late at night, and the wages were five cents a day plus meals."

Pastor Wunder or his pastoral assistant continued conducting services once a month, on Mondays, in Glencoe. In addition to local people, others came from as far south as Evanston—seven miles—and as far north as Lake Forest—ten miles. In August, 1874, however, the congregation called its own pastor, the Rev. Edward Doering, who then served until July, 1881, when he accepted a call to Portland, Oregon. Bethlehem Congregation in Evanston had been organized in 1872; and shortly after Pastor Doering's departure from Glencoe, the two congregations, Trinity of Glencoe and Bethlehem of Evanston, jointly called the Rev. J. Adam Detzer. A resident of Evanston, he conducted services on alternate Sundays for the Glencoe flock. After eight years the Rev. John Dietrich Matthius succeeded to the Evanston pastorate and also continued serving Trinity in Glencoe, until 1902, when Trinity called its second resident pastor, the Rev. Bernard Hintz of Stones Prairie, Mo. Meanwhile, the members of Trinity residing in Highland Park—about four miles north of Glencoe—had established their own parish (1891), which they named Zion.

A day school which Pastor Hintz founded in Glencoe was discontinued in 1917. Following his call to Roseland (Chicago), the congregation in the spring of 1913 secured the services of the Rev. F. C. Israel of Lone, S. Dak., who remained there for the next four years, until 1917, when he accepted a call to Trinity Congregation in Hanson Park (Chicago). Thereupon the Rev. William F. Suhr of Highland Park served as vacancy pastor; and it was upon his recommendation that the old church, dedicated in 1866 on the original church property, was razed and a new one erected at Greenwood and Hawthorne Avenues in Glencoe. The first unit of this church was dedicated April 17, 1921.

The next and fourth pastor, the Rev. Louis H. Nauss of Mora, Minn., served from May, 1925, to May, 1933, when he resigned and moved to Minnesota.

The fifth and present (1949) pastor, Candidate Paul A. Mundinger, was ordained and installed on May 7, 1933.[22]

5. Elk Grove

A news item written by Carl Sallmann, pastor of Saint John's Congregation at Elk Grove, Cook County, Ill., July 3, 1856, and published in the *Lutheraner* August 12, 1856, induces another journey to the "old neighborhood," where in 1842 appeared "Hans Buschbauer," as the Rev. Francis A. Hoffmann was familiarly known in later years. Pastor Sallmann writes thus: "About eight years ago the congregation at Elk Grove, the membership of which was very small, had the courage to erect a small frame chapel ("Kirchlein"), in which services

PLATE IV

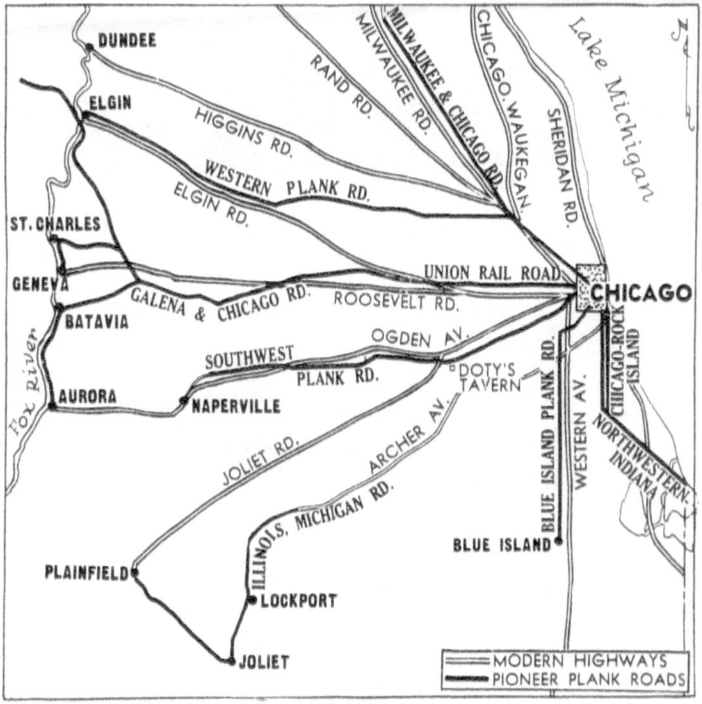
DUNDEE
ELGIN
ST. CHARLES
GENEVA
BATAVIA
AURORA
NAPERVILLE
PLAINFIELD
LOCKPORT
JOLIET
BLUE ISLAND
CHICAGO
Fox River
Lake Michigan
RAND RD.
MILWAUKEE RD.
MILWAUKEE & CHICAGO RD.
CHICAGO-WAUKEGAN.
SHERIDAN RD.
HIGGINS RD.
WESTERN PLANK RD.
ELGIN RD.
UNION RAIL ROAD
GALENA & CHICAGO RD.
ROOSEVELT RD.
OGDEN AV.
SOUTHWEST
PLANK RD.
DOTY'S TAVERN
JOLIET RD.
ARCHER AV.
ILLINOIS, MICHIGAN RD.
BLUE ISLAND PLANK RD.
WESTERN AV.
CHICAGO-ROCK ISLAND
NORTHWESTERN. INDIANA
MODERN HIGHWAYS
PIONEER PLANK ROADS

PLATE V

Hans Buschbauer,
landwirthschaftlicher Redacteur
der Milwaukee Germania,
der Chicago Warte,
des Buffalo Volksblatt,
und Haus- und Bauernfreund.

Buschbauerfarm.

Bei Geo. Brumder in Milwaukee sind folgende Bücher von Hans Buschbauer zu haben:
Praktisches Handbuch des Grasbaus, Futterpflanzenbaus und der Milchwirthschaft. Geb. $1.25.
Amerikanische Bienenzucht. Geb. $1.00.
Der Amerikanische Geflügelzüchter. Geb. $1.50.
Familienschatz. Geb. $1.25.
Amerikanisches Gartenbuch. Geb. $2.00.

Jefferson, Wis., Aug. 23 1897

Grüß Gott!

Ihr freundliches Schreiben empfing ich, als ich eben einen Artikel für die Germania über das Addison Waisenhaus beendet, und darin des Schaumburger Posaunenchors gedacht hatte. Ihnen u. der Schaumburger Gemeinde meinen wärmsten Dank für die Einladung zu der bevorstehenden Jubelfeier. Sie haben keine Ahnung, wie schwer es mir wird, Ihre freundliche Einladung ablehnen zu müssen. Ich kenne kein Ereigniß, dem ich mit meiner alten Grete lieber beiwohnen möchte, als gerade das Jubiläum Ihrer Gemeinde. Es kostet mir viel Ueberwindung und bereitet mir tiefen Schmerz, der Freude, die meiner dort wartet, entsagen zu müssen. Obgleich ich für meine Jahre noch ziemlich stark und rüstig bin, auch arbeitsfreudig und schaffensfähig in meinen Kräften, so darf ich mich kaum den Strapazen einer weiteren Reise, noch weniger aber der Aufregung aussetzen, die das Fest für mich nothwendig im Gefolge haben müßte. Mit schwerem Herzen schreibe ich diese

Zeilen. Meine Gattin, die frühere „Frau Pastörsch" der ihr einst so lieb gewesenen und noch immer unvergeßlichen Schaumburger, dankt ebenfalls für die freundliche Einladung. Sie leidet seit einigen Jahren an einem Fußübel, das ihr das Gehen sehr erschwert und sie an das Haus fesselt.

Gern will ich Ihnen in den nächsten Tagen einige Notizen über die Gründung der Gemeinde zukommen lassen.

Möge der Gott der Gnade über die Schaumburger Gemeinde auch ferner walten. Ich danke aus innersten Herzen allen Gliedern derselben, die sich meiner in Liebe erinnern, und bitte Gott, er möge mir um seiner unendlichen Barmherzigkeit und Christi Blut willen nicht anrechnen, was ich in meiner Amtsführung und sonst verfehlt habe.

Behüt Dich Gott!

Franz A. Hoffmann.

PLATE VI

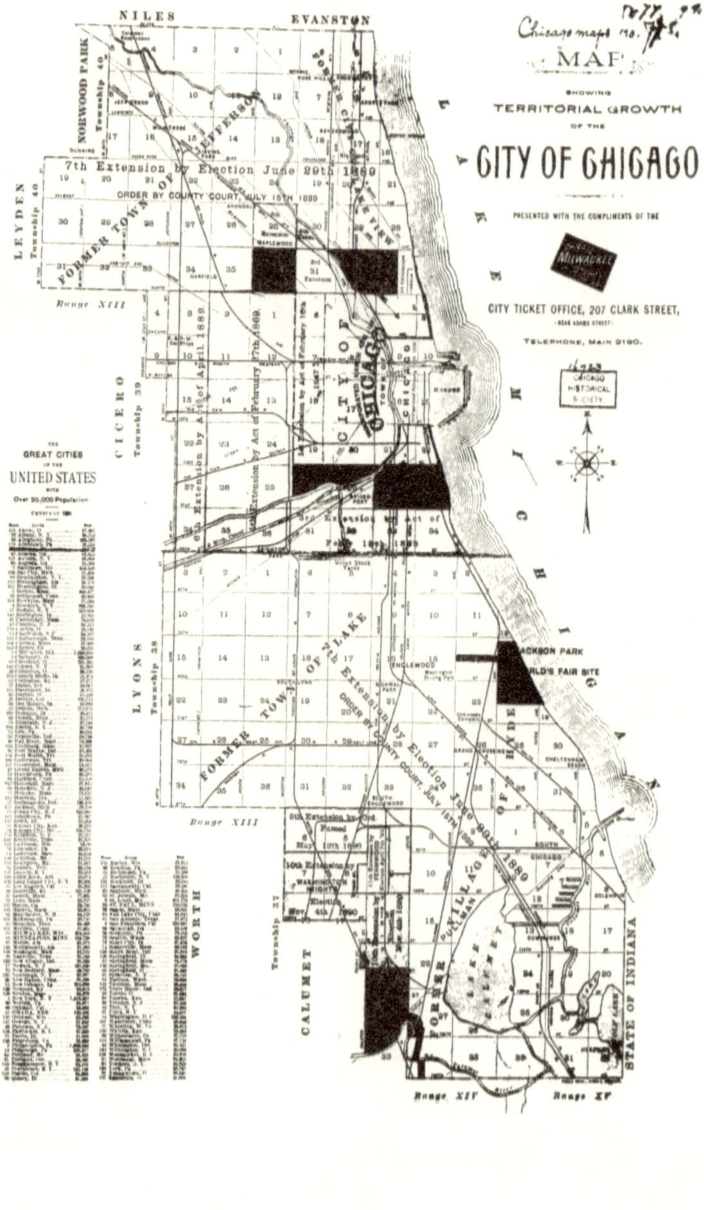

MAP
SHOWING
TERRITORIAL GROWTH
OF THE
CITY OF CHICAGO
PRESENTED WITH THE COMPLIMENTS OF THE
CITY TICKET OFFICE, 207 CLARK STREET,
TELEPHONE, MAIN 2190.
CHICAGO HISTORICAL SOCIETY
NILES
EVANSTON
NORWOOD PARK
Township 40
LEYDEN
7th Extension by Election June 29th 1889
ORDER BY COUNTY COURT, JULY 15TH 1889
FORMER TOWN OF JEFFERSON
LAKE VIEW
CICERO
Township 39
CITY OF CHICAGO
6th Extension by Act of April 1882
5th Extension by Act of February 27th 1869
3rd Extension by Act of Feb. 16th 1863
LYONS
Township 38
FORMER TOWN OF LAKE
7th Extension by Election June 29th 1889
ORDER BY COUNTY COURT, JULY 15TH 1889
JACKSON PARK
WORLD'S FAIR SITE
HYDE PARK
ENGLEWOOD
LAKE MICHIGAN
9th Extension by Ord. Passed May 12th 1890
10th Extension by Election Nov. 4th 1890
FORMER VILLAGE OF PULLMAN
LAKE CALUMET
CALUMET
WORTH
Township 37
STATE OF INDIANA
Range XIII
Range XIV
Range XV
THE GREAT CITIES OF THE UNITED STATES WITH Over 20,000 Population.

were hitherto conducted." Deducting eight from 1856 leaves 1848, the year of the founding of a Lutheran congregation in the community referred to by Pastor Sallmann—Elk Grove, for which no census figure is given.

The arrival of several new families from Hanover, Germany, prompted the Elk Grove Lutherans to organize Saint John's Congregation. A constitution was submitted and discussed and then signed by thirty-two men.*

It was Pastor Hoffmann who in the year prior to the congregation's founding came at more or less regular intervals from Schaumburg (Sarah's Grove) to Elk Grove, a distance of about eight miles, to conduct worship services, at first in the home of Henry Wuestenfeld. In those early days (1848 to about 1855) the Elk Grovers found it difficult to support themselves and their families. There was no market for their farm produce; Chicago was a city of about 32,000 inhabitants, but the roads leading to the "Big City" were well-nigh impassable. For reasons such as these, many would-be settlers, after a brief sojourn at Elk Grove, shook its dust off their feet and went elsewhere.

On January 1, 1849, the Rev. Vincenz Klein became the first resident pastor of Saint John's Congregation. He remained for a very short time, only until the following year, 1850. His successor, the Rev. John George Kunz, served the struggling congregation for less than three years, from September, 1850, until the spring of 1853, when he returned to Indianapolis, Ind., whence he had come.

Poverty compelled the members themselves to undertake

*Conrad Roehler
Christian Linnemann
Christoph Senne
Heinrich Thake
Friedrich Busse
Christian Busse
Heinrich Breuscher
Christoph Mensching
Wilhelm Kleinhans
H. Christoph Senne
Ferdinand Kummer
J. C. Niedert
Christoph Tuernau
Heinrich Busse
Johann Stege
Friedrich Katz
Heinrich Roehler
Heinrich Decke
Phillip Steege
Friedrich Ahrens
Carl Dohme
Heinrich Biesterfeld
Heinrich Thies
Heinrich Behrens
Heinrich Senne
Heinrich Wuestenfeld
Conrad Rehling
Phillip Ostmann
Conrad Moehling
Heinrich Mueller
Carl Kiesel
Conrad Schwake

the construction of a church building in the year 1848. The stately oaks of Elk Grove, as it were, proudly and heroically offered themselves as essential material for the project, and the men promptly responded by cutting some of these "giants" down and, amid showers of flying chips and shavings, reduced them to the desired shapes and proportions. "The knottier the beams and the uprights, the weaker and breezier were the walls and the roof." ("So kernig die Schwellen und Pfeiler waren, um so viel schwaecher und luftiger waren die Waende und das Dach.") Sidings were nailed on the sturdy but rough logs, and homemade shingles were fastened to the rafters. Concerning the dedication of this first crude church in 1848, the Rev. Francis A. Hoffmann some years later wrote: "The first church building, though poor and small, was a temple of the bounteous, omnipotent God. . . . The day of dedication was a festival! On either side of the church door there was a long pole decorated with pumpkins and prairie flowers. The poles were connected at the top with a white cloth bearing the legend: "Gott allein die Ehre" (To God alone the glory). My pony, which had only the one fault that it was not ascertainable as to whether it was lame in one foot or in all four feet, brought me close to the church. There the entire congregation formally welcomed me."

This little church stood on the congregation's property, which at that time comprised forty acres and which had been purchased at $1.25 per acre. Later, fifty per cent of this property was sold, and at the present time (1949) the congregation's real estate possession comprises only the remaining twenty acres.

During Pastor Sallmann's pastorate, 1853-1859, the steady increase in membership led to the construction of a larger church building. It is described in the news item in the *Lutheraner* referred to above. It was dedicated in 1854. In the same year Saint John's Congregation called its first day school teacher, Carl Laufer, and also joined the Missouri Synod. Five years later, near the close of 1859, the congregation suffered a number of terrific blows: both the pastor and the teacher accepted calls to other fields—the pastor, to Independence, Ohio—and fire completely destroyed the parsonage and all its contents, including the church records, minutes of congregational meetings, etc. The pastor and the teacher had occupied the parsonage. They lost all their earthly possessions and barely escaped with their lives. Before construction work on a new residence had begun, both had left Elk Grove. During the ensuing vacancy, which lasted until 1862, the congregation's spiritual needs were supplied by Pastors Christian H. Loeber of Coopers Grove, H. F. Fruechtenicht, assistant pastor at First Saint Paul's and First Immanuel in Chicago, and John George Kuechle of Skunks Grove.

With the promise of an annual salary of two hundred dollars, Candidate William Bartling, a native of Duncklees Grove, accepted the call, which specified preaching and teaching. He served as day school teacher until Samuel Garbisch, in response to a call, arrived at Elk Grove in September, 1862. The teacher's salary was $125 the year, which for the following two years he was obliged to collect himself, a procedure terminated in July, 1864. By calling Mr. Garbisch to the office of teacher, Saint John's Congregation acted in accordance with the practice of the Missouri Synod, which holds that "while, indeed, rooted in the one ministry of the Word, the office of a teacher as a separate and distinct branch of said ministry is not a divine, but an ecclesiastical institution, inasmuch as Christian congregations must not by divine command branch off certain work from the ministry and thus create this office, but they may do so in Christian liberty if circumstances demand it."

Pastor Bartling remained until February 15, 1863, when he followed a call to the State capital, Springfield, Ill. Teacher

Garbisch left Saint John's in 1870. Only one week after Pastor Bartling's departure, February 22, 1863, Candidate Henry Schmidt arrived at Elk Grove to carry on the work; he did so, more extensively than heretofore. He introduced "Christenlehre," a form of religious training which also had its origin in the Reformation, particularly in Germany. "Therefore it was a custom peculiar to the German Lutherans. The 'Christenlehre' was an agency of instruction in a portion of the Catechism or in a certain phase of Bible history, employed by the pastor on Sundays, either after the morning worship or at a special service in the afternoon. The purpose of conducting 'Christenlehre' was 'to further and establish the members of the church in their acquaintance with the doctrines of the church.'" The Rev. Louis Hoelter, pastor of First Immanuel Congregation in Chicago, 1878-1922, is quoted as saying that "the 'Christenlehre' is primarily intended for those past the age of schooling. We ask the children, but have the adults in view."

In 1860 mission projects were inaugurated by Saint John's Congregation and its pastor at Dunton (Arlington Heights), Gilmore, and Russells Grove (now Fairfield), near Lake Zurich. Services at these places were conducted on Sunday afternoons. At the voters' meeting held July 14, 1867, Pastor Schmidt was granted permission to extend his mission activities into the State of Michigan (particularly to Niles and vicinity). At the end of the same year, 1867, Pastor Schmidt received a call from Immanuel Congregation in Dundee, Ill. He accepted it and left Elk Grove on February 9, 1868.

The group at Dunton, in 1860, expressed its willingness to act jointly with Saint John's of Elk Grove in calling a new minister, with the understanding that the pastor would conduct services at Dunton every other Sunday forenoon. Because Saint John's Congregation denied that request, the Dunton group was granted permission to withdraw and to organize its own congregation. It was named Saint Peter's, but the calling of a pastor by the newly organized congregation did not occur until December 29, 1867.

On the Sunday after Easter, 1868, the Rev. William Dorn of Boeuf Creek, Mo., was installed as Saint John's pastor at Elk Grove. Teacher Garbisch, who in March, 1870, had followed a call to Trinity in Springfield, Ill., and there had served for two and a half years, was recalled to Elk Grove in 1872. In the interim, teacher-candidate Gottfried H. C. Burgdorf had charge of the school until the end of 1872, when he, in turn, followed a call to St. Louis, Mo.

In 1873 the members of Saint John's at Elk Grove residing in Des Plaines received their "mother" church's permission to organize a congregation of their own. It was named Immanuel. (See Chapter 60.)

On February 6, 1876, Pastor Dorn accepted a call to Pleasant Ridge, Ill., and in the following August, on the Ninth Sunday after Trinity, the Rev. Herman F. H. Ramelow of Prairietown, Ill., was installed as Saint John's seventh pastor. Following his acceptance of a call to Saint Paul, Ill., in April, 1891, the Rev. J. H. Haake of Chapin (Bethel), Ill., became the eighth pastor here on July 26, 1891. On September 4, 1892, the congregation dedicated its third church. Into its cornerstone the following publications were placed: Luther's Catechism, a German hymnbook, a German and English reader, the *Rundschau,* and a copy of the *Inter-Ocean and Herald.*

On the first Sunday in January, 1898, Christian Busse, who had faithfully served as the congregation's treasurer since 1872, resigned from office on account of advanced age, and his son, H. W. Busse, succeeded him.

Teacher Garbisch was compelled by tuberculosis to resign on August 19, 1900. In addition to a formal written expression of gratitude, the congregation granted him free use of the residence and gardens, plus ten dollars monthly for playing the organ at the church services. He died at the age of fifty-nine on June 5, 1901. In September of the same year a new school of brick construction upon a rock foundation, and considerably closer to the road than the church, was dedicated. The cost, including equipment, was $2,937.09. Prior to the formal ceremonies the entire amount, with the exception of $25.04, had been collected. The remaining small debt was liquidated by means of a "hat collection" at the voters' meeting October, 1901.

In January, 1905, Pastor Haake accepted a call to Holy Cross Congregation in Chicago, and the Rev. Julius Drexler of Millerton, Nebr., became the ninth pastor of Saint John's at Elk Grove on January 29, 1905. Pastor Drexler served here until December 28, 1910, when he resigned.. By special permission of the congregation, however, he continued to occupy the parsonage until March 1, 1911. On March 26, 1911, the tenth pastor, the Rev. Louis J. C. Millies of Hegewisch, Ill., was installed. He served for about one and a half years, when he accepted a call to Redeemer Congregation in Cicero, Ill. On March 31, 1913, the Rev. Ferdinand Louis Gehrs of Marion, N. Dak., was installed as the eleventh pastor of Saint John's.

Of the six young men of Saint John's who served in World War I, one—Ernest Mensching—died on the battlefield shortly before the signing of the Armistice, and another—Theodore Heimsoth—died at sea.

In October, 1918, Luther's Small Catechism in German and English was introduced for confirmation instruction; and in 1923 the pastor was granted permission to conduct English worship services once a month; later, services were held in both languages every Sunday morning.

During the latter part of August, 1922, the chimney of the church was hurled through the roof by a violent storm.

In addition to Carl Laufer, Samuel Garbisch, and Gottfried H. C. Burgdorf, and Pastors Haake and Drexler, the following have served as teachers: Paul Meeske, Miss Helen Meeske, W. H. Heuser, and Delbert V. Stegemann.

One of the daughters of Saint John's, Elk Grove, is Saint Paul's Congregation in Mount Prospect, Ill. (founded 1912), about two miles northeast of Elk Grove. (See Chapter 178, p. 521.)

In a letter dated April 12, 1945, Pastor Gehrs wrote as follows: "Pastor Hoffmann must have been on his toes, ever ready to look up the early Lutheran settlements. . . . Undoubtedly we owe it to him that these congregations became Lutheran instead of Methodist."[23]

6. Coopers Grove

Having covered a distance of about thirty-two miles "as the crow flies," from Elk Grove toward the southeast, the Trail now arrives at another "grove" (Waldinsel) near the southern boundary of Cook County–Coopers Grove, also known, at least in the 1830's, as "Yankee Settlement." It was the center of a little more than a dozen German Lutheran families who settled here in 1846 and 1847, including Henry Werfelmann, F. Diekmann, E. Magnus, F. Stoerckmann, H. Rathe, C. Rathe, Fred vom Berge, Fred Thies, P. Eggers, Henry Bensemann, Henry Stelter, and H. Bodehorst. For some time this group was served spiritually by the Rev. Ernst August Brauer of Duncklees Grove, who, presumably, was the founder of Saint John's Congregation at Coopers Grove. Soon afterward the little flock recognized the necessity of calling its own pastor. On June 28, 1849, the Messrs. J. Nick Volkert and Wolfgang Simon Stubnatzy, who at the synodical convention in Fort Wayne, Ind., had passed their colloquium and been assigned to this region for service in the Church, came to the Rev. C. August T. Selle in Chicago. This pastor immediately informed "a certain man in the settlement of Coopers Grove" that he and Stubnatzy would be in their midst for the purpose of conducting worship service there in the near future. In an elaborate and fascinating account of his experience at that time, Pastor Selle writes: "I also requested Pastor Brauer of Addison to meet us there at the appointed time, but unfortunately he was prevented by illness, and especially by the intrusion of Methodists into his congregation, from accompanying the young brother to his destination. Hence the two of us were compelled to go on our way alone . . . in the afternoon of July 4." T. Johannes Grosse referred to the situation at Addison (Duncklees Grove), saying: "In the year 1853 danger from another direction threatened the congregation. The Methodists continued with ever-increasing determination to attack the congregation. Two members of the congregation who in the earlier days of the congregation's existence had fallen into the hands of the Methodists and poisoned by them, fell away and joined them. . . . One of the apostates presented a tract of land, upon which the Methodists built their own church—only a quarter of a mile from the Lutheran church."

And now, letting Pastor Selle continue his story: "Our first reception in Coopers Grove—twenty-three miles south of Chicago—was not a very encouraging one. Having misunderstood directions which we had received as to which way to follow through the prairie, we drove into a fenced-in field. As we then, realizing our error, deliberated as to how we would get through the fence at the other end of the field, we heard behind us a powerful scream ("starkes Geschrei") combined with fearful cursing ("mit fuerchterlichen Fluechen"). Two men rushed toward us; one of them, cherry-brown with anger ("kirschbraun vor Zorn"), pulled a heavy pole, which had served as part of a scarecrow, out of the ground, with nothing less in mind than to punish us with it. . . . A kind word found a good place; a friendly plea for pardon of our evil deed somewhat appeased the man, especially when he heard that we were Germans. . . . But, what if there were many such people, or even all the people here were of that man's type! Continuing our journey, we arrived at the next farmhouse, where the service was to be held. I was heartily pleased to hear this from several people: 'We have as yet not been well pleased here in America, but we will gladly want to remain here since we can have God's Word. Daily bread we have all the time.' ("Et haett uns hier wohl noch nicht gefallen, aber nu wollt wir gern in Amerika sien, da wi Gottes Word hem koeht. Da dagligt Brod hem wi all lang.")

On July 5, 1849, Candidate Wolfgang Simon Stubnatzy was ordained and installed in the young congregation, known as Saint John's, worshiping temporarily in the E. Magnus home. This building was located about one mile northwest of the forty-acre property purchased in 1850 for $65. About a year later Mr. Magnus left the congregation, and then services were held in the home of Henry Werfelmann, which in more recent years was occupied by the John Koehlers.

Saint John's Congregation at first erected one building, which served as parsonage, church, and school; a portion of the land on a near-by hill was set aside for a cemetery ("Gottesacker"). In 1857 a church was erected, which served the congregation's needs for about seventeen years.

The railroad, in 1857, ran north as far as Lake Forest, then the seat of Lind University; and the *Chicago Tribune* reported the north shore as becoming lined with cottages embowered in elaborate comfort. Conditions at Coopers Grove also were steadily improving; but in the midst of these improved conditions Pastor Stubnatzy accepted a call to Fort Wayne, Ind., in 1862. The second pastor, Christian H. Loeber of Frohna, Mo., was installed on the third day of the Pentecost festival, in 1862. He also taught school for seven years. In 1869 he accepted a call to Milwaukee, Wis. Toward the close of the same year the Rev. Erhard Riedel of Dubuque, Iowa, was called; he began his work at Saint John's at the end of January, 1870.

In the course of the next few years it became increasingly apparent that the church built in 1857 had become too small for the accommodation of the increasing membership. It was decided, therefore, to build a larger church, not of wood, but of stone. The stones were transported by rail from Joliet to Matteson—about five miles south—and thence hauled by wagons to the building site on what is now 183d Street, a short distance east of Cicero Avenue. Not a few of the stones were of such dimensions that a team of horses could pull but one as a load. Other stones were obtained from a quarry near Blue Island, seven or eight miles north of the building site. In the early fifties, Franz Schwartz purchased a piece of land on Crawford Avenue, near what is now West 147th Street (Sibley Boulevard), planning to farm it. As he began to dig a well, he met an obstruction: limestone of superior quality for building purposes. There is a similar quarry near what is now West 135th Street and Claire Boulevard.

The dedication of the stone church, which cost approximately twenty thousand dollars, took place on October 11, 1874.

In the fall of 1876 Pastor Riedel accepted a call to Bloomington, Ill. He was succeeded by the Rev. Ferdinand Doederlein of Marengo, Ill., on Maundy Thursday, March 22, 1877. Pastor Doederlein served here until 1897, when he was called to Venedy, Ill. During the subsequent vacancy of about three months the congregation issued several calls before it succeeded in its quest for a new pastor. The third candidate on the list, the Rev. Matthew Henry Feddersen of New Berlin, Ill., accepted the call and was installed on July 25, 1897. This was at about the same time when the gold rush to the Klondike (Alaska) began. When in the same year the Rev. Carl Moritz Noack left Harvey, the small flock there (Trinity Congregation) became a spiritual orphan. Beginning in the fall of 1898, Pastor Feddersen also served there, until 1902, when he turned that project over to the Rev. Henry Wind, pastor of Saint Paul's Congregation, Dolton-Riverdale. In 1905 Pastor Feddersen started to serve the German-speaking people in the village of Homewood, about three miles due east from Saint John's Church.

In 1929 Pastor Feddersen was forced by illness to resign his pastorate at Coopers Grove. The Rev. Henry F. Meyer of Thornton, Ill., succeeded him on May 12, 1929. Pastor Feddersen died on March 31, 1940.

In June, 1949, the congregation celebrated its 100th anniversary and the 75th anniversary of the church building. One of the festival preachers was the Rev. A. H. A. Loeber of Detroit, Mich., a grandson of St. John's second pastor.

The following teachers have served in Saint John's School:

Otto, 1858-1860
H. Reifert, 1860-1865
J. Wegner, 1865-1866
J. Troeller, 1866-1879
A. E. Eggers, 1879-1906
A. Eggers, 1906-1908
J. G. Hillger, 1909-1914
Richard Hillger, 1914-1929
E. Schuricht, 1930-1948
Elmer Huedepohl, 1948-

Charter Members of Saint John's:
Henry Werfelmann
F. Diekmann
E. Magnus
F. Stoerckmann
H. Rathe
C. Rathe
Friedrich vom Berge
Fr. Thies
P. Eggers
Henry Stelter
Henry Bensenmann
*H. Bodehorst

7. Crete

Proceeding from Coopers Grove in a southeasterly direction, a distance of about ten miles, is a little village named after a well-known island—Crete, in the Mediterranean Sea, and located about two miles south of the Cook-Will county line. The county was named after Dr. Conrad Will, a delegate to the Illinois first constitutional convention.

It is the year 1849. Several members of First Saint Paul's Congregation in Chicago and others who had been frequent visitors in that first Lutheran congregation in the rapidly

*Martin Stelter of Janesville, Wis., had accepted the call and had notified the congregation that he would arrive early in August. In preparation for his trip, Teacher Stelter did some cleaning and tuning up of the engine in his auto. Suddenly the engine burst into flames, and in an attempt to beat down the flames he spilled gasoline over his person and became a flaming torch. A few days later Teacher Stelter died.

growing "Garden City" had moved to this area, and their consultation with Pastor Selle, which obviously included a request for his help in organizing a congregation "'way out there in the country," resulted in securing temporary services of the Rev. Wolfgang Simon Stubnatzy, the newly called pastor of Saint John's at Coopers Grove.

A young man of thirty-seven, with two daughters and his second wife, Elizabeth, nee Laubenheimer,* Anton August Philip Weyel, had arrived in New York City on July 17, 1849. The little group proceeded to Fort Wayne, Ind., where the Rev. Mr. Weyel, who had been pastor of a congregation in Herborn, Hesse-Nassau, and also head teacher at the *Gymnasium* (college) there, was scheduled to submit to a colloquium. "At Fort Wayne the cholera met the immigrants again. It claimed the life of a certain young Pastor Wolter. While performing the last rites at the burial of Pastor Wolter, Pastor Reisener was suddenly stricken with the plague and sank down at the open grave. On the following day Pastor Weyel performed the last rites at the grave of Pastor Reisener. A few weeks later, having satisfactorily passed his colloquium, Pastor Weyel was appointed missionary for 'Will County and surrounding country,' with Crete, Ill.,† as his base."

The Rev. Anton A. P. Weyel was ordained and installed as pastor of this group of Lutherans on October 31, 1849 (Reformation Day). The group was organized as Zion Congregation.

There being no dwelling place for the pastor and his family, the young pastor and his wife furnished the necessary building material at their own expense, and the members subsequently erected a miserable hut ("armselige Huette"), measuring about 12x12 feet, on a plot of ground on the farm of Wilhelm Rinne. "The logs were hauled by ox team from a

*Pastor Weyel's first wife died in Germany. His second wife was a graduate deaconess. The marriage took place on May 17, 1849, at Steeden, Germany.

†Population of Crete, 1940 census, 1,772.

distance, since the surrounding country, sloughs and prairie land, was practically treeless." In this small building, which was divided into two rooms—the one large and the other small—worship services were held for some time. Later, they were held in the upper story of Mr. Rinne's home.

After but a few months' work in Crete, Pastor Weyel in May, 1850, moved to Hickory Creek, near Frankfort and what is now New Lenox, about twelve miles west of Crete. During the vacancy of more than a year and a half, services were again held at regular intervals, with sermons preached by guest clergymen or read by lay members. In September, 1851, the Rev. C. August T. Selle, heretofore pastor of First Saint Paul's Congregation in Chicago, was installed as Zion Congregation's second pastor. At that time there were only twelve members.* There was no railroad connecting Crete with the rest of the world. Seven farm wagons were used to haul Pastor Selle's possessions, including his family. All were brought to the unfinished tiny parsonage ("Pfarrhaeuschen") one and a half miles southeast of Crete. The attic of the parsonage served as a schoolroom. Cheerfully the pastor shared the lot of his parishioners; in fact, their poverty elicited from the pastor the expression of complete satisfaction with rye bread, coffee, and corn bread, even as they seemed satisfied with such provender; but he cherished the hope that later he might be able to eat roasts ("Braten") with them.

In 1852 Zion Congregation joined the Missouri Synod.

Writing of his experiences in Crete, Pastor Selle made these observations: "My relationship with the congregation was a pleasant one, similar to that of a father among his children . . . the seven years of my labors in Crete were the happiest of my life. That is not the same as saying that the devil was

*The 12 voting members in 1851:

Karl Klausing	Konrad Harmening	John F. Koller
John C. Meier	John O. Piepenbrink	Wilhelm Rinne
Konrad Saller	Wilhelm Wehmhoefer	Fritz Wente
Philip Wilharn	John Wilkening	Philip Wille

resting during that time. At first, there occurred occasional instances of very despicable rudeness; particularly did I have to fight against the dance carousals which were customary at dedications of homes and barns. The Low-German is not easily persuaded to give up dancing." (" . . . Der Plattdeutsche laesst sich schwer vom Tanzen abbringen.")

A letter dated December 10, 1945, from a son of Pastor Selle is quoted in the *Lutheran Annual* for 1947: "In Illinois they" (his parents) "lived fourteen years, and they had rather hard times there. Father's salary for the first year was $90 a year, and it took more than half of that to pay his trip to synod.'"

Hardly had the membership of Zion Congregation reached the twenty mark when several members, because of the distance from their homes to the church, expressed the desire to establish a new congregation southeast of Beebe's Grove. The "mother" congregation's approval was given to seven members in 1854, with the result that Saint John's Congregation of Eagle Lake was founded. Another group at Black Walnut, west of Crete, in 1855, built a church and school, but remained a branch of Zion Congregation. Alternately the pastor conducted school in Beebe's Grove and Black Walnut; in winter months, also confirmation classes. Very few of the settlers owned horses, and the journey by oxcart consumed very much time. There were no highways and no bridges, and the roads, if that is the proper name for them, caused much more misery for riders than for walkers. Pastor Selle explained to his people how much better the growth and the progress of the two congregations would be, how many hardships they could spare themselves, their wives, their children, and their pastor, if they would jointly erect a larger church about halfway between the two places, preferably in the vicinity of the village of Crete, and to form one congregation with two school districts. Action upon this proposal was not taken until 1858. At the beginning of that year the two congregations Beebe's

Grove and Black Walnut—with a total of fifty-three members united under the name Trinity ("Evangelisch-lutherische Dreieinigkeits-Gemeinde"). The name Zion now disappears; it reappears in 1911. (See Chapter 162.)

In addition to the thirty-three and a half acres at Beebe's Grove and the ten acres at Black Walnut, which were owned by the two congregations respectively, the new congregation (united) now purchased an acre of land one mile south of Crete as the site of the new church. Before this was accomplished, however, Pastor Selle had accepted a call to Rock Island, Ill. Two of his children lie buried in the Lutheran cemetery just south of Crete. Pastor Selle was successively professor in Fort Wayne, Ind., and at the Teachers Seminary in Addison. His death occurred April 3, 1898, when he was seventy-nine years of age.

Pastor Selle's successor at Trinity Congregation, Crete, was the Rev. William Heinemann, who had been ordained in the fall of 1857 in Chicago, where he had served as assistant for First Saint Paul's and First Immanuel Congregations. He was installed in Crete on the Fourth Sunday after Trinity, 1858, by his predecessor. At the same service, which was held in the shade of the trees surrounding the cemetery, Pastor Selle preached his farewell sermon. The reason for the outdoor service was that both churches were too small to accommodate the crowd.

During Pastor Heinemann's pastorate the present church was built in 1860, at a cost of $2,600, exclusive of furnishings. Pastor Heinemann carried on mission work in the following places: Calumet (West Hammond—now Calumet City), Dolton-Riverdale, Cummings Corner (Oak Glen-Lansing), Bloom (Chicago Heights), and Kankakee. At the beginning of 1866 he followed a call to Neugehlenbeck, Ill. The Rev. Gottlieb Traub of Allen and Adams Counties, Indiana, his successor, was installed on the Fifth Sunday after Trinity. Pastor Traub engaged in mission work in Crown Point, Ind., and in Woodworth, Ash Grove, Watseka, Matteson, and Joliet, Ill. Shortly after his arrival in Crete, Trinity Congregation purchased nine more lots adjoining the plot purchased in 1858.

In August, 1878, Pastor Traub was called to Peoria, Ill., and the Rev. Ernst August Brauer was called from St. Louis, Mo., to Trinity in Crete. Pastor Brauer had served pastorates at Duncklees Grove, Ill., and in Pittsburgh, Pa. In 1863 he had become second professor at the Theological Seminary (Concordia) in St. Louis. Later he became assistant pastor and, still later, pastor of "Old Trinity" in St. Louis, Mo. Having become blind in his left eye, which was surgically removed in order to save the right eye, his physician advised him to take over a small and quiet congregation. Crete was just the place for him. When he arrived there, on Reformation Day, October 31, 1878, the congregation welcomed him with a band and a torchlight procession. He was installed November 3, 1878. In the winter of 1881, when Pastor Brauer was noticeably "aged," his son Karl of Champaign, Ill., was called as assistant and as teacher for the school at Black Walnut. Four years later Pastor Karl Brauer was called to the "daughter" congregation at Eagle Lake—Saint John's. Thereupon Trinity called another son of Pastor Ernst August Brauer, Candidate Friedrich Ernst Brauer, as assistant pastor. In the morning of September 29, 1896, Pastor Ernst August Brauer died at the age of seventy-seven; and on October 11 his son Friedrich was installed as Trinity's pastor.

During the first decade of the twentieth century serious problems confronted Trinity Congregation. Because the church was located at a considerable distance from the village, the members residing in Crete, having no means of transportation and finding it extremely difficult, especially older folks, in winter and in inclement weather of other seasons of the year, to attend the services, gave earnest thought to the advisability of erecting a new church. In order to forestall a separation, it was recommended that the old church be transferred to the village. At a meeting, November 15, 1908, the proposition was put to a vote by ballot, with the result that seventy-six members were for and fifty-six against the proposed change. However, the motion was made unanimous, to which was joined a resolution that the change be made without delay. Evidently, "unanimity" existed only in the minutes or for the time being, for a few weeks later, on January 2, 1909, it was reported that a number of dissenting members had incorporated under the name Zion and were laying claim to the entire property. Synodical officials who had been drawn into the dispute warned against a schism and urged the maintenance of peace. Their effort, however, was futile. The minority, numbering approximately fifty, remained adamant and devoted itself to the idea of building a church on the site of the original church property one and a half miles southeast of the village. This, in turn, induced Trinity Congregation to take legal action and by a writ of injunction from the circuit court (in Joliet) to stay further action by the dissenters. The judge ruled that the property be divided between the contestants. Regarding the judgment as unjust, the constituents of Trinity appealed to the Supreme Court, which rendered a decision in all respects favorable to the appellants. When the dissenters petitioned the Missouri Synod for ministerial service, it was the judgment of this Synod that such a petition should be granted only on the condition that the dissenting group would recognize Trinity as the true and original congregation, implying also an admission of the former's guilt in the schism. Instead of recognizing the validity of Synod's decision and exhortation, the minority group proceeded to call upon the Wisconsin Synod for help in securing a pastor. This action was followed by a formal protest addressed to the latter synod by Trinity. After a prolonged delay, another investigation of the unfortunate case was made, and it was not until June, 1913, that the synodical officials established peaceful relationships between the two congregations. But the final settlement of the case did not come until 1934, at a convention in Mankato, Minn.

Meanwhile Pastor Friedrich Brauer, weary of the continued struggles, petitioned his congregation, Trinity, for a peaceful release to a congregation at Horse Prairie, near Red Bud, Ill., from which he had received a call. The petition was granted. During the eight-month vacancy caused by his departure the Rev. H. William Meyer of Steger, a short distance north of Crete, served Trinity. On April 12, 1912, the Rev. Charles A. Waech, heretofore president of the Texas District of the Missouri Synod, arrived in Crete and immediately occupied the newly erected parsonage. He at once introduced English services, which were held once a month in the evening. The two school districts, Beebe's Grove and Crete, were amalgamated. As a result, Trinity now had about four hundred communicants. In 1913 the entire property of the school and the cemetery association was transferred to Trinity Congregation.

Of the twenty-six men who served in World War I, only one, Martin Biesterfeld, fell in battle. His body was transported from France and interred with military honors in Trinity Cemetery near Crete. During that war the congregation's schools were painted yellow, because the German language was taught there. That action, however, resulted in a yet greater desire on the part of Trinity's members to erect a new and larger school. A much keener interest in Christian education had been aroused.

Briefly summarized are the congregation's school activities. The first teacher in Beebe's Grove school was Peter Nickel, 1850; in the fall of 1858 Ernst Luetge began teaching there, but in the following spring he was called to the Eagle Lake congregation (Saint John's), and Pastor Heinemann again taught school in his own home. In 1862 followed J. Theodore Herrmann; in 1865 he was succeeded by a young man who had been recommended by a Lutheran pastor in Chicago; but, unqualified for the position, he was soon dismissed; and John Riebling was called.

On July 5, 1881, the school which had been erected in 1869 was destroyed by fire, and immediately a new one, but somewhat smaller, with a steeple and a bell, was erected. Later that same bell was installed in the tower of the large brick school building erected in 1923.

John Roecker served as teacher from 1870 until October, 1878, when he was called to Peoria, Ill. His successor was John Brase, who served for a period of thirty-four years, 1878 to January, 1913. When the merger of the Beebe's Grove school district with that of Crete was effected, the congregation pensioned Mr. Brase, "either so long as he would live or until he would receive another call." He desired to serve as substitute teacher in various Lutheran schools in Chicago, but he soon realized that he was unable to bear the strain. Combined with a peaceful release, the privilege was granted him, "in case of need to return to Crete and at any time to knock at our doors." Subsequently he moved to Nebraska, where he made his home with his children.

The first teacher at the school in Black Walnut was Eduard Buehring, 1856; upon his departure, J. Theodore Herrmann of the Beebe's Grove school succeeded him here. In 1866 George Wambsganss was called specifically for the Black Walnut school. He was succeeded by C. Gottlieb Kienzle in 1870; eight years later the latter resigned on account of illness. Then came Hermann Albrecht. He died in July, 1881. For a while then Pastor Karl Brauer served as teacher; upon his acceptance of a call to Saint John's Congregation at Eagle Lake, W. Kluender of Richton (Skunks Grove) was called. He resigned in 1898. A student of theology served as supply teacher until the arrival of Otto Schueler, who served from 1899 until December, 1904. A vacancy existed until 1906, during which time, presumably, the pastor taught. In 1906 Franz C. Stoll took charge and remained until the year 1910, when he accepted a call to Niles (formerly known as Dutchman's Point), Ill. In 1911 the school property was sold.

Up to the year 1871 the children attended school either at Beebe's Grove or Black Walnut, but on April 27, 1873, a school was established in the village of Crete. A room was rented in the public school. The rental of space in the public school had resulted from an agreement reached in 1872, according to which the "city fathers" consented to place one of the rooms at the congregation's disposal for a church school if the congregation would, at the forthcoming election, vote for the construction of a spacious and attractive building. This arrangement continued until June, 1923.

The first teacher in the public school room was Chr. H. Brase, who taught all classes from January 2, 1873, until 1894. In that year the classes were divided, and Miss Christine Schweer was engaged to teach the lower grades. She served until June, 1902. Then Mr. Brase took over the lower grades and John G. Kirsch, formerly of Oak Glen (Cummings Corner), the upper grades. Mr. Brase died in 1909. His successor was Martin Eggerding. After the merging of the Beebe's Grove district with Crete, in 1913, Mr. Eggerding taught the lower grades until the summer of 1918, when Mr. Kirsch left for Fort Wayne, Ind.

While waiting for a new teacher, the work was carried on by Pastor Waech, Edgar Baehrens, and the Rev. Adolph Ernst Beil, (retired pastor*).

In 1919 Albert E. Meyr was called, and in the same year Mr. Eggerding accepted a call to Churchville (Duncklees Grove). Again the pastor, aided by Teacher Jackisch, "substituted"

*Pastor at Thawville, Ill., 1914-1918; retired; died May 21, 1927.

until the following spring, when Edward Stelter was called. He served here until February, 1927, when he followed a call to Gethsemane Congregation in Chicago.

In 1923 a new school and parish house was built directly west of the church building at a cost of $23,524 and dedicated in August, 1923. Construction of a new church building, 56 by 103 feet, on the present site and costing approximately $125,000, will be started in October, 1949. The new church will face west; the old building faced north.

Pastor Waech retired in 1944, and on April 15, 1945, his successor, the Rev. Alfred Theodore Kretzmann of Barrington, Ill., was installed.

The present teachers (1949): Theodore J. Wichmann and Albert E. Meyr.[25]

8. Mokena

Continuing the journey westward from Crete, the Trail crosses another portion of the great prairie and soon comes to a quiet spot near the village of Frankfort*—also in Will County. There are found some of the German settlers who had recently purchased a wooded hill from the United States Government for the purpose of erecting thereon a little frame church building in the following year. Fifteen of these men on November 4, 1850, organized a congregation which they named Immanuel. Their little church was located about three miles southeast of the little village of Mokena.†

The first pastor, whose name on the old church records is "almost undecipherable" and given as "Weiler," doubtless, was the Rev. Anton August Philip Weyel, for, according to the history of Zion (changed to Trinity in 1858) Congregation at Crete, Pastor Weyel in 1849 left that village to carry on mission work in the neighborhood of Frankfort. Moreover, there is reason to believe that the good man had the wander-

*1940 census: 568.
†1940 census: 657.

lust. During his comparatively brief pastorate in Crete he traveled quite extensively; he visited places "as far as fifty miles from Crete—places desolate then, but with flourishing congregations now (1949). He traveled on foot, with his gun and Phylax, a retriever, as company." Among the places which he is said to have visited were Joliet, Dundee, Downers Grove, Homewood, Blue Island, Addison (Duncklees Grove), Schaumburg (Sarah's Grove), and Niles (Dutchman's Point). "At the last three places mentioned he found three who had been his fellow passengers on the sailship. They had settled on prosperous farms and laughed at him for being so foolish as to become a missionary."

All the records covering the first forty years of Immanuel Congregation's history were lost in a fire which destroyed a country home where they had been kept.

The second pastor, the Rev. Elias Hieber of Westville, Ind., served Immanuel Congregation for forty-one years, from 1873 to 1914. His main pastorate was at Sieden Prairie—Saint Paul's Congregation. He died at the latter place on October 19, 1931.

In 1915 the congregation erected a new church in the village of Mokena. The burial plot on the original property in the country was retained for future use. Several Lutheran families who were members of Saint Paul's Congregation (Sieden Prairie) residing in Mokena in 1915 requested the Rev. Raymond R. Reinke, pastor of Salem Congregation in Blue Island, to serve them during the construction and rehabilitation period. Virtually a new congregation had come into existence. Soon afterward (1918) the Rev. Walter J. Kemnitz of Parshall, N. Dak., became Immanuel's pastor; he remained until September, 1924, when he accepted a call as associate pastor of the Rev. Henry Wind at Saint Paul's Church in Dolton-Riverdale, Ill. On September 21, 1924, he was succeeded by the Rev. Daniel C. Hennig of Granfield, Okla.

The school, founded at the beginning of the congregation's

existence, in 1850, and taught by the pastors, was discontinued in 1929. Pastor Hennig served Immanuel Congregation until 1930, when he accepted the position as missionary at large* under the direction of the Northern Illinois District (Missouri Synod).

The Rev. Paul E. Schauer served the parish in Mokena from March 23, 1930, until 1932, during which time Immanuel Congregation became self-sustaining. Pastor Schauer resigned and moved to Joliet, but in the following year, 1933, he accepted a call to Immanuel Congregation in De Kalb, Ill.

The Rev. Walter J. Geffert of Arlington Heights, Ill., where he had been ordained in 1929, succeeded Pastor Schauer and served from 1932 until 1943, when he followed a call to a pastorate at Kingfisher, Okla. In the spring of 1943 the Rev. Albert W. Gode, who had left the active ministry in 1929 and formerly was stationed at Accident, Md., became Immanuel's pastor.[26]

9. Rodenberg

A brief departure must now be made from this section of the great prairie in Will County to return to Du Page County and see how the work is progressing in the vicinity of Schaumburg. Quite a distance to travel; walking is out of the question, so history takes to wagons or oxcarts for the Trail north on Wolf Road, west on the Chicago-Elgin Road as far as Roselle, and again due north on the Roselle Road to Schaumburg (known up to about this time as Sarah's Grove, but for which official census figures are still lacking). Animated discussions are now rife among the young and the old settlers about the great inconveniences suffered attending church services at Saint Peter's in Schaumburg. The children, too, are sorely displeased with the long and wretchedly poor roads. The pastor—Francis A. Hoffmann—and his congregation mani-

*Successor of the Rev. Horace H. Hartmann, who accepted a call to Zoar Congregation in Elmwood Park, Ill.

fest a sympathetic attitude, and they soon approve the establishment of a separate and autonomous parish at Rodenberg (Rothenberg), about two miles west of Roselle.*

It is the year 1851, and the organization of Saint John's Congregation at Rodenberg is effected by only seven former members† of Saint Peter's. During the same year the small group erected a two-story building, 20x30 feet and 16 feet high—the various sections of which were designed to serve as auditorium, school, and parsonage. A ministerial candidate from Frankenhilf, Mich., Ernst Ludwig Hermann Kuehn, became the first pastor of Saint John's Congregation on March 23, 1851. He, however, left a few months afterward to become assistant pastor at Saint Paul's Church in Fort Wayne, Ind. A teacher in the day school of the "mother" church, J. Seitz, was selected as the second pastor. Mr. Seitz submitted to a colloquium as a candidate for the Lutheran ministry and was declared qualified to assume ministerial duties. In 1857 he resigned. During the ensuing vacancy the congregation was served by the Rev. A. G. G. Francke of Duncklees Grove and the Rev. J. Nick Volkert of Saint Peter's, Schaumburg. Shortly afterward, when a vacancy was created in Saint Peter's Congregation by Pastor Volkert's departure, both congregations—Saint John's and Saint Peter's—joined in calling one pastor for both parishes. The pastor was the Rev. Frederick W. Richmann of Grand Rapids, Mich., whose installation took place on August 1, 1858. In 1859 Saint John's Congregation joined the Missouri Synod.

Two years later, 1861, the Hanoverian hymnbook in use heretofore in Saint John's as well as in Saint Peter's was superseded by the hymnbook published by the Missouri Synod.

A short time later Saint John's Congregation sought the

*1940 census: 694.

†Christoph Steffen
Heinrich Hasemann
Friedrich Hinze
Heinrich Mensching
Christopher Ackmann
Conrad Dralle
Conrad Geistfeld

"mother" church's permission to call its own pastor again. Permission was readily granted. Professors C. F. W. Walther and Frederick A. Craemer of Concordia Seminary in Saint Louis, Mo., then advised the congregation to call Candidate J. N. Niethammer, who at the time was engaged as a vicar in Terre Haute, Ind. Candidate Niethammer was installed as Saint John's third resident pastor on October 1, 1862.

A substantial increase in membership at that time resulted in the decision to erect a new and more spacious church. On December 16, 1863, that church was formally dedicated. Less than one year later Pastor Niethammer was released to a pastorate at Lancaster, Ohio. He was succeeded by the Rev. August Heitmueller of Elyria, Ohio. During the latter's pastorate at Rodenberg a controversy concerning "confession and absolution on Sundays" disrupted the congregation. Many members severed their connection with Saint John's. While this controversy was in progress, Pastor Heitmueller was called to Columbus, Ind. (1870), and an old friend, Professor C. August T. Selle of the Teachers Seminary, Addison, served as vacancy pastor until the Rev. L. E. Knief of Millers Landing, Mo., was installed in May, 1870. Only nine months later, in January, 1871, Pastor Knief followed a call to Saint John's Congregation in Neuendettelsau (founded in 1838; one of the twelve congregations which in April, 1847, participated in the founding of the Missouri Synod), a few miles south of Marysville, Ohio. His successor at Rodenberg, the Rev. George William Bruegmann of Canaan, Mo., was installed on February 5, 1871. During the above-mentioned controversy much time, particularly at the voters' meetings, was devoted to the discussion and analysis of the differences between the Lutheran and the Reformed doctrines.

On February 21, 1878, Pastor Bruegmann followed a call to Zion Congregation at Union Hill (Bonfield), Ill. The Rev. Henry Schmidt, pastor of near-by Saint Peter's at Schaumburg, assumed charge of the pastoral duties during the vacancy, which was terminated on June 4, 1878, when the Rev. H. F. C. Grupe of Price City, Mo., was installed. Pastor Grupe served until September 19, 1889, when he was called to Macon City, Mo. From 1889 until 1905 the congregation's pastor was the Rev. Theodore Heine, a native of New Zealand. When he left for Dillon, Iowa, the Rev. Emil F. J. Richter of Garner, Iowa, became the shepherd of the flock at Rodenberg. Pastor Richter had served as a parochial school teacher at Shible, Minn., from 1892 till 1894.

In 1910 a number of members of Saint John's received permission to organize a congregation in the village of Roselle on the condition that the new congregation would agree "with us and our Synod in doctrine and practice." That congregation was named Trinity.

Early in the morning of August 23, 1910, Saint John's Church was completely destroyed by fire, caused by lightning. Already two weeks later the cornerstone for a new church was laid, and the structure was dedicated on February 12, 1911.

On August 31, 1913, Pastor Richter followed a call to Belvidere, Ill. He was succeeded by the Rev. Richard L. Seils of Woodworth, Ill.

In conjunction with the founding of the congregation, Saint John's also established a day school in 1851. In 1878 a building for the exclusive use of its school was erected; in 1908 this school was remodeled and modernized. In the beginning the teachers taught alternately in Schaumburg and Rodenberg. F. W. A. Fuerstenau was the first teacher. Then followed John W. Flach, 1867-1870; C. Meinke, 1888-1900; Louis Detgen, 1900-1906; H. Krentz, 1906-1925; H. E. Albrecht, 1926-1939; and Harry F. Voigt, 1939-1945; Paul W. Schmandt, Jr., 1949—. When the congregation had no "regular" teachers, the respective pastors shouldered also that responsibility. Thus, from 1870 until 1888 Pastors Knief, Bruegmann, and Grupe taught.

In 1929 Pastor Seils resigned because of advanced age. He was succeeded by the Rev. Adolf L. Oetjen of Howard Lake, Minn., on October 14, 1929. Pastor Oetjen served until January 2, 1939, when he accepted a call from Saint Peter's Congregation in Joliet, Ill., as assistant pastor. His successor, the Rev. Martin A. Gassner of Alexander, Ark., was installed at Saint John's on January 22, 1939. He served until September 20, 1942, when he resigned. The Rev. John Rozak, formerly pastor of Zion Congregation in Chicago,* and for some time without a charge, was installed on January 31, 1943. In June, 1948, Pastor Rozak accepted a call to Fairland, Okla. Since November 21, 1948, St. John's Congregation has been served as an affiliate of Immanuel, Ontarioville. (See Chapter 135, p. 439.)

10. Skunks Grove

Instead of heeding Horace Greeley's advice, "Go West, young man, go West!" history wends its way back to the Sauk Trail in the southern region of Cook County and scouts for signs of a Lutheran church. And, lo, there it is, in Skunks Grove—near the northwest corner of what is now Cicero Avenue and the Sauk Trail! "Founded in 1852," the year in which Harriet Beecher Stowe's *Uncle Tom's Cabin* was first published. On February 20 of the same year the first train of the Michigan Southern Railroad, which heretofore had terminated at Elkhart, Ind., steamed into Chicago with the first load of passengers from the East, "while fire bells rang, cannon boomed, and the citizens cheered their heads off." Three months later, on May 21, the first train of the Michigan Central Railroad, using the Illinois Central Railroad's right of way for the last fourteen miles of its route, came into town from the East.

The Rev. John George Kuechle, this congregation's first

*Zion Lithuanian Church, located at the southeast corner of West Cermak Road (Twenty-second Street) and South Bell Avenue.

resident clergyman, relates that in about the year 1850 a number of young unmarried men purchased so-called "soldiers' land" in the fertile prairie bounded on the east by Butterfield's Grove and Thorn Grove and on the west by Skunks Grove (butter-thorn-skunk—what a droll combination!). These bachelors, native Hanoverians, originally settled at Duncklees Grove, some thirty miles to the north, and had belonged to Zion Congregation there. Shortly afterwards they had established themselves in this part of the great prairie and gave serious thought to the matter of having worship services in their own midst. The Rev. Wolfgang S. Stubnatzy of Saint John's Congregation at near-by Coopers Grove ("Yankee Settlement"), about five miles north, partially fulfilled their wish by holding services on Sunday afternoons in the home of Dietrich Dettmering. In the course of a short period of time the Coopers Grovers' dissatisfaction with the makeshift arrangement culminated in the recommendation that the Sauk Trailers, or Skunks Grovers, join the Coopers Grove congregation—Saint John's. Instead, the twenty-two families of the Sauk Trail, in 1852, organized Immanuel Congregation and upon the advice of Pastor Stubnatzy called the Rev. John George Kuechle of Niles (Dutchman's Point), Ill. He preached his introductory sermon at Skunks Grove on June 6, 1852; and two weeks later, on June 20, he was formally installed.

Shortly afterward fifteen acres of land were purchased for "$50.00 in gold" from H. Kruse. Services in private homes were continued, consecutively, in the homes of the following members: Fred Duensing, William Mahler, and Fred Bartling, until 1855, when a two-story building was erected at the northwest corner of the Sauk Trail and Cicero Avenue, the lower story serving as parsonage and the upper as church and school. For some time the schoolwork had been carried on in private homes. The "all-purpose" building was dedicated May 6, 1855. In March, 1853, Henry Fowler, editor of the *Tribune*, wrote:

"On the last Lord's day the cars of the Chicago and Rock Island made a trip to La Salle and back. This is a profanation of the Sabbath on the part of the manager of this road and seems more wanton and inexcusable as there was no real necessity for it."

In 1861, following a period of steady growth in membership, Immanuel Congregation erected a new church. The enrollment in the day school continued apace so that the congregation in the fall of 1862 proceeded to the calling of a teacher, Candidate George Bartling of the Teachers Seminary at Addison and a native of Duncklees Grove. Within the decade 1852-1862 a pastor and a teacher had been called and three buildings, including a parsonage, erected. Pastor Kuechle occupied the new parsonage for only about nine months, for he followed a call to Columbus, Ind., in the summer of 1864.* The Rev. Chr. H. Loeber, successor of Pastor Stubnatzy at Coopers Grove, served during the brief vacancy. On November 20, 1864, Immanuel Congregation installed Candidate Louis Lochner of Milwaukee, Wis. During his pastorate an additional teacher, Candidate D. Koennemann of the Teachers Seminary at Addison, was called for the second classroom. He was unable to accept because of illness. Miss Regina Rotermund, who had been assisting Teacher H. Bartling in Zion School at Duncklees Grove, 1861-1865, was then engaged as temporary teacher. In the following year, 1866, Teacher George Bartling's career as teacher was abruptly ended by the shock of the untimely death of an intimate friend, Frederick Stuenkel, which so affected his mind that he remained in that state of infirmity for the rest of his life, until September 11, 1905, when he died at the age of sixty-three. On November 18, 1866, he was succeeded in Immanuel School by Peter Nickel of Crete, Ill. About one year later Pastor Lochner was called to a

*A son, Herman C. Kuechle, born here in 1858, served as pastor of St. John's Congregation at Marysville (Neuendettelsau), Ohio, 1898-1929. He died at the age of 87 in February, 1947.

pastorate in Richmond, Va. Again Pastor Loeber of Saint John's, Coopers Grove, had charge of the temporarily shepherdless flock, and Miss Maria Helberg was engaged to teach the lower classes.

The next pastor of Immanuel Congregation was the Rev. Theodore Pissel, who had gone there as a ministerial candidate. Shortly after his installation, on December 4, 1877, a branch school was established by Immanuel Congregation in Matteson, a small village about two miles northeast of Immanuel Church, and L. Maurer was placed in charge of it in 1868. In 1870 Mr. Nickel followed a call to Iron Mountain, Mich., and A. Albers of Duncklees Grove, Zion Congregation's northern school district, became the next teacher of Immanuel School at the Sauk Trail. When, in 1876, Mr. Maurer left, Otto Bonneront continued the work in the branch school in Matteson. Changes in Immanuel's day school occurred in rapid succession. In 1876 Mr. Albers followed a call to Saint John's School at Eagle Lake. During the next year and a half J. Jarms taught. Then W. Kluender of Yorkville, Ill., took charge in March, 1877, and taught for about seven years, until 1884.

Shortly before Pastor Pissel's departure for Bath, Ill., in February, 1878, a majority of the members of Immanuel Congregation residing in Matteson organized a congregation of their own, which was called Zion. During the vacancy at Immanuel, which lasted until the following spring, the Rev. Elias Hieber of Saint Paul's Congregation in the Sieden Prairie territory,* had charge of the pastoral work. In 1879 the Rev. Barthold Burfeind of El Paso, Ill., was installed as Immanuel's pastor.

In August, 1884, Mr. Kluender was compelled by illness to discontinue his teaching activities. Accordingly, F. C. Biermann was engaged. After the latter's dismissal in January,

*The Sieden Prairie church, Saint Paul's, is located about three miles north of Immanuel Church on Vollmer Road, between Cicero and Harlem Avenues.

1886, William H. C. Pflug of Benton, Mo., taught for three years and then followed a call to Milwaukee, Wis. In March, 1889, Pastor Burfeind accepted a call to Lemont, Ill. This meant that Immanuel Congregation was without a pastor and a teacher until the arrival of the Rev. John Meyer from Helena, Mont., in August, 1889, and, soon after his installation, of F. A. H. Richert as teacher. The latter remained at Skunks Grove for about one and a half years, and his successor, Gustav E. Brauer of Willow Springs, Ill., served for about four and a half years and then resigned and became a cabinetmaker. In 1894 Pastor Meyer was laid low with sickness. Instead of granting him a release from the pastorate, as he had requested, Immanuel Congregation called an assistant pastor, Candidate A. Holthusen of Concordia Seminary, St. Louis, Mo., with the understanding that he would serve also as schoolteacher. However, shortly after his arrival he, too, became ill and thus was prevented from entering upon any of the assigned duties. In this predicament the congregation engaged a student, Flentje* by name, to assist the pastor in church and school for a term of one year. Before the expiration of this term, his request for a release was granted, in the spring of 1895. At the same time the Rev. Tobias H. Joeckel was called to serve as assistant pastor and as teacher.

On March 1, 1897, Pastor Meyer died at the age of thirty-seven.† In July of the same year Pastor Joeckel became Immanuel's pastor, and M. C. Aherns was installed as teacher on December first. In the spring of 1903 Pastor Joeckel was called to Germantown, Nebr. About three months after his departure the Rev. Christian Merkel of Dieterich, Ill., was

*Mr. Flentje was a member of the Wisconsin Synod.

†Pastor John Meyer was the father of the Rev. Lawrence Bernhard Meyer, D.D., missionary in China, 1917-1925; more recently, Director of Publicity and Missionary Education, Missouri Synod, St. Louis, Mo. He was born at Skunks Grove July 13, 1890. A brother, Henry, is the pastor of Saint Martini Congregation, Chicago, since 1946; and another brother, Theodore, is a teacher at Saint Paul's Congregation in Chicago (Austin), Ill. Dr. L. B. Meyer's wife, Magdalene, is a daughter of the Rev. Friedrich Brauer, who was pastor of Trinity Congregation in Crete, Ill., 1885-1911.

installed in Immanuel Church. On February 28, 1904, Mr. Ahrens sought and received a peaceful dismissal, and a few months later John Richter of Belvidere, Ill., took charge of the school. In the spring of 1920 Pastor Merkel, because of failing memory, which presumably resulted from a serious bodily injury, relinquished the pastorate to the Rev. Emil Hieber of Lone Wolf, Okla., who was installed on June 6, 1920.

In 1929, two weeks after Immanuel Congregation had commemorated Mr. Richter's quarter-century jubilee as teacher in its midst, the auto in which he and his wife were riding was struck by a freight train at a near-by crossing. The injuries sustained by Mrs. Richter proved fatal. Soon after, Mr. Richter resigned. His successor was E. H. Klemp. He, in turn, was succeeded by K. Kraemer. A new school, erected at a cost of $25,000, was dedicated on August 22, 1948.

The following servants of the Church hail from Immanuel Congregation:

Pastors George Bartling, Albert Theodore Merkel, Eduard Paul Merkel, and Lester Hieber; Teachers E. Bartling and Richard Bartels.[27]

11. Chicago, First Immanuel

Having been absent from Chicago for a period of about seven years, history now turns back to 1847 to gather more facts regarding the progress of "Missouri" within the city limits. The first halt is at Cross Point, a spot where a Roman Catholic church now stands—Holy Family Church, Twelfth Street (Roosevelt Road), near Hoosier Avenue (since 1853 known as Blue Island Avenue).* Yes, this is where the first daughter congregation of First Saint Paul's Congregation. organized March 19, 1854, as First Immanuel Congregation, erected its first church—a frame building which provided a

*The name Hoosier was changed to Blue Island because the "avenue" was the most direct road between Chicago's then West Side and Blue Island.

school as well as living quarters for the pastor—at a cost of $1,030.

A brief report on the dedication appeared in the *Lutheraner* a few weeks later: "We have just received the glad tidings that on the Thirteenth Sunday after Trinity, September 10 [1854], the new Immanuel Church in Chicago was dedicated and that on this occasion the Rev. George Schick was solemnly installed by his colleague Pastor Wunder, assisted by Pastor Brauer, upon the direction of the District President, Pastor [George F.] Schieferdecker. Now may the Lord crown the twofold work of the two orthodox preachers of the Gospel with twofold blessings, and may both of them constantly be able to say with the Prophet: 'Here is Immanuel!' Isaiah 8:10." Soon after his arrival, Pastor Schick found a helpmeet: a daughter of one of the leading members. Two years later, in 1856, Pastor Schick accepted the professorship of ancient languages at Concordia College, first in St. Louis, Mo., and then at Fort Wayne, Ind., with the transfer of the college to the latter city in 1861. In Fort Wayne he became senior assistant master of that institution ("Konrektor"), and later senior master ("Rektor"). In 1906 the honorary title of Doctor of Philosophy was conferred upon him by Concordia Seminary, St. Louis, Mo. Dr. Schick retired in 1914 and died in the spring of the following year. He lies buried in Concordia Cemetery, just east of Concordia College in Fort Wayne.

During the dry law wave in the early 1850's Chicago brewers and saloonkeepers, chiefly represented by North Side Germans, organized an opposition to the enforcement of the law. On April 23, 1854, a crowd of them marched across the river, and there were liquor riots on Randolph Street, resulting in the death of at least one man. On June 18, 1855, Joseph Medill joined the *Chicago Tribune* staff. It was to Medill that Horace Greeley gave the advice "Go West, young man, go West!" Medill went West—to Chicago—as did in the same year Dr.

Charles H. Ray, "whose powerful editorials in the *Tribune* were to influence political and economic thoughts in the West for the next decade." The Garden City was destined for two great purposes: to serve as a distributing center for Eastern and foreign manufacturers in the West and Northwest and to serve as a manufacturing center. "Within twenty-four hours in the summer of 1857, 3,400 emigrants were reported as arriving over the Michigan Central alone." Among these there also were many Lutherans.

First Immanual Congregation's second pastor was the Rev. J. A. F. W. Mueller of Manchester, Mo., one of the first graduates of the Lutheran college at Altenburg, Perry County, Mo. He was installed on the Fifth Sunday after Trinity, June 22, 1856. The first teacher in Immanuel's day school was "Kantor" Theodore Ernst Buenger,* formerly of New Orleans, La. Within a comparatively short time the congregation had two schools with a total enrollment of 190 pupils. The second teacher was Theodor Zacharias, who, however, was soon succeeded by G. F. Schachameyer. In 1857 the young congregation was put to a severe test: Although the entire membership recognized the need for a larger church building, it seemed for a while as though everyone had been overcome by a spirit of dejection for the reason that the cost probably would be prohibitive. Nevertheless a new church was erected, a frame building, 40 x 60, and 20 feet high, with a 34-foot steeple, measured from the apex of the roof. And the congregation celebrated—for two days! Two dedicatory services were held on the First Sunday in Advent, 1857, with sermons by Pastor Mueller in the forenoon and by the Rev. Henry Wunder of the "mother" church in the afternoon; and on Monday, the day following, with sermons by the Rev. A. G. G. Francke of Duncklees Grove in the forenoon and the Rev. W. S. Stubnatzy of Coopers Grove in the evening.

*A son of "Kantor" Buenger, Theodore, in 1884, became the second pastor of Trinity Congregation at Bachelors Grove, near Tinley Park.

According to Bessie Louise Pierce, the single nationality which added most to the population of Chicago after 1850 was the German, which helps toward a better understanding of the mushroomlike growth of Lutheran congregations during the following half century. On December 25, 1858, the first through train left Chicago for Pittsburgh, Pa., on what then was known as the Pittsburgh, Fort Wayne and Chicago Railroad. This railroad was taken over by the Pennsylvania Lines in 1869.

It is oral tradition that the regular meetings of the two "Missouri" pastors, Henry Wunder and J. A. F. W. Mueller, marked the beginning of the Lutheran Pastoral Conference of Chicago and environs.

Because of their far-flung mission activities these two pastors were provided with ministerial assistants, including Candidates William Heinemann (1857), Gotthilf Simon Loeber (1858), and Herman F. Fruechtenicht (1860). Beginning in 1865, both congregations independently called such assistant pastors. The following served in that capacity at First Immanuel: W. Richter, 1865-1866; G. A. Barth, 1869; John Merkel, 1881-1883; Jacob Seidel, 1884-1895; and G. C. Bauer, 1933-1934.

In 1863 Pastor Mueller was called to Pittsburgh, Pa. His successor in the First Immanuel parish was the Rev. John Paul Beyer of Altenburg, Perry County, Mo. In September of the same year a mission school was established at Mark Street, between Union and South Halsted Streets, with Christian Weigle as teacher. Another school was begun in a small rented building on Archer Avenue, which not many years later grew into a large congregation, First Trinity, since 1906 at West Thirty-first Street and Lowe Avenue.

It was in July, 1863, that the Battle of Gettysburg was fought in the "Keystone" State, Pennsylvania. In September of the same year it was reported that the population of Chicago had increased to 165,000. However, there was "not a single park or drive in the city, except Dearborn Park with a few shriveled trees, without a flower, overgrown with weeds, the receptacle of tin cans, dead animals, and rubbish. The courthouse is a standing disgrace." On November 3 a hundred head of cattle were driven over the Rush Street Bridge; the bridge collapsed, and a girl was drowned. The horse railway on Blue Island Avenue and on Halsted Street was ready for service.

In order to carry on its work in a more quiet neighborhood, First Immanuel Congregation in 1864 moved its church to Taylor and Brown Streets. According to Sharvy G. Umbeck the congregation was compelled to move to Ashland Avenue and Twelfth Street as early as 1864 by the influx of Catholics. 1864 was the year in which a city-wide fire alarm telegraph system was installed in Chicago; and during that time Chicago streets were full of loafers lounging around. The tunnel under the Chicago River at Washington Street was completed December 31, 1868.

In 1869 First Immanuel established still another mission school, this one in the so-called "Lime Kiln" community (corner of Hinman and Paulina Streets), with William Ganske in charge. This school likewise developed into a large congregation, Holy Cross (1886), whose center now is located at West Thirty-first Place and Racine Avenue. It was during this time that agitation for the establishment of a Lutheran high school was begun at the suggestion of a Mr. Asbrand, a candidate of philology. Meanwhile a second pastor was called as associate, namely, the Rev. Anton Wagner of Collinsville, Ill. (1867). The Rev. John Paul Beyer served as "first" pastor until Easter, 1871, and then followed a call to Pittsburgh, Pa.

It is related that soon after Dr. C. F. W. Walther's *Evangelien-Postille* had been published (1870), Pastor Beyer preached a sermon to which he added the following comment: "Wer von euch heute aufmerksam zugehoert hat, der hat gemerkt, dass ich eine *ausgezeichnete* Predigt gehalten habe! Ich habe mir grosse Muehe gemacht, sie auswendig zu lernen. Sie steht auf Seite soundso in der eben erschienenen *Evangelien-Postille* von Dr. Walther. Alle andern Predigten in diesem Buche sind eben so gut. Kauft es!"

(Those of you who today listened attentively will have noticed that I have preached an *excellent* sermon. I worked hard to memorize it. And it appears on page so-and-so of the *Evangelien-Postille* by Dr. Walther, which has just appeared [on the market]. All the other sermons in this book are equally as good. Buy it!)

In 1848 the first contract was let for construction of a plank road covering the area's worst thoroughfare, the so-called Nine Mile Swamp from Chicago to Doty's tavern in Riverside, a distance of ten miles. The road left Bull's Head tavern on Madison Street, running slightly south of what is now Ogden Avenue, to Doty's tavern. Shortly the Southwest Plank Road had sprouted connections to Brush Hill, sixteen miles farther out, to Naperville, Sycamore, and Oswego, so that by 1851 the mud embargo from Chicago's southwest had been lifted. A year after opening Southwest Plank Road, Northwest Road was begun, connecting the city with the upper Des Plaines Valley. It began near the old Galena depot and left the city on what is now Milwaukee Avenue, with Wheeling its destination. During the next two years it was constructed three miles beyond Dutchman's Point, now Niles. The Western Plank Road was an offspring of the Northwest Road. It branched off the main road at Oak Ridge, seven miles from the city, running west to the boundary of Du Page County, where it connected with the Elgin and Genoa Plank Road, which ran through Elgin to Genoa in Kendall County, fifty miles from Chicago. In 1850 the Southern Plank Road was begun with hopes of leading it down the trail mapped out by that hard-fighting, hard-riding pioneer Gordon Hubbard, from State Street to Middleport in Iroquois County, a distance of seventy-five miles. But the project ran afoul of the Illinois Central Railroad proposal to run a branch into Chicago. The road promoters grew cold and abandoned the project at Kyle's tavern, ten miles out. But the settlers to the south of Chicago were not to be outdone. They laid a plank road from Blue Island running north on the line of Western Avenue, to its junction with Blue Island Avenue, which in 1854, the year of the road's construction, was the southwest corner of the city. Turning northeast, it followed Blue Island Avenue into the city. The road was thirteen miles long, and Governor Bross called it "the avenue across the prairie." Only one other road was constructed before the plank road fever was cured. It ran from the junction of North Avenue, with Clark Street at that time the city limits, parallel with the lake shore to Little River, through Pine Grove to Hood's tavern on Green Bay Road, a distance of about five miles. A few broken planks remained as late as 1861 to plague travelers on Blue Island Avenue.

Pastor Beyer's successor, the Rev. Christian Koerner of Norwich, Conn., served only from 1871 till 1872. On December 8 of the latter year he was succeeded in the First Immanuel pastorate by the Rev. Rudolph Carl Henry Lange of Defiance, Ohio. On June 18, 1876, "Kantor" Buenger died. In 1878 Pastor Lange* was called to a professorship at Concordia Seminary in St. Louis, Mo., a position which he held until his death, which occurred while he was visiting in Chicago, on October 2, 1892.

On February 23, 1868, First Immanuel released a number of its members to organize a congregation of its own, with the center of activities at what now is West Nineteenth and Peoria

*Pastor Lange was the first one of the present generation of the Missourians "to pay special attention to the English language, wrote textbooks on English, which were widely used at the time, and through his work at the Seminary at St. Louis wisely and successfully prepared the way for the present transition period" (1915-1925).

Streets, and known as Zion Church. That "daughter" congregation's first pastor was the Rev. Anton Wagner, associate pastor of First Immanuel, 1867-1868.

Succeeding Pastor Lange at First Immanuel, in 1878, was the Rev. Louis Hoelter of Quincy, Ill. About ten years after his arrival in Chicago, Pastor Hoelter, having observed the population trend in the "sprawling giant at the Lake," came to the conclusion that the congregation's future field of activity lay in an area a little farther west of the present location (Taylor and Brown Streets) and in a more secluded atmosphere. In 1888, therefore, an edifice with a stone front was built on the west side of South Ashland Avenue (formerly Reuben Street), just north of West Twelfth Street (now Roosevelt Road), at a cost of $58,000. Very substantially built, the church originally had a seating capacity of 1,400. "Some of Chicago's best families lived in homes along Ashland and Washington and Jackson Boulevards. After the World's Fair in 1893 the exodus began—to Garfield Park, Oak Park, Hyde Park, and Evanston—and the first signs of decay set in." Mrs. Addie Hibbard Gregory, the 87-year-old author, is quoted as saying (in 1947): "I was quite accustomed, while walking to church with mother, to seeing people standing knee-deep in bogs which were Chicago's early streets. Mother explained that they probably had slipped trying to leap from their high-wheeled buggies to the wooden sidewalks." This was in the early 1860's. At that time also West Madison Street was a "fine shopping district, with specialty shops run by dependable merchants." Now that section, or a part of it, is known as "Skid Row."

Ashland Avenue was a "choice residential boulevard" when First Immanuel Church was built on it in 1888. The house of worship conformed to the architectural features of the neighborhood. "It stands much the same today as at the time of its construction, save that the 185-foot spire, the repairs of which began to become too costly, was removed" in 1919, in the words of Oney Fred Sweet of the *Chicago Tribune* staff (1912-1947). Sweet's account continues: "It was found that the removal of the steeple was timely, for the timbers were found to be rotted, and, with further delay, it might have pitched into the street." Forty feet of vacant land to the north of the church were purchased to preserve light and air.

For many years Pastor Hoelter was assisted by his father-in-law, the Rev. Jacob Seidel.* Later, Pastor Hoelter's son Edward became his ministerial assistant, and, after his father's death, May 30, 1922, Edward was installed as First Immanuel's pastor, which position he held until his death in 1933. His successor was the Rev. Herman M. Bauer of Leola, S. Dak., who served until 1941, when he assumed the duties of a chaplain in the United States Army; at which time, then, the congregation entrusted the pastorate to the Rev. Erwin H. Meinzen, pending Pastor Bauer's return after one year. Because that was not to be, Pastor Meinzen, formerly a missionary at Vadakangulam, in southern India, was formally installed on October 11, 1942. He served First Immanuel until April 11, 1948, when he was re-commissioned as missionary to India. His successor, the Rev. August L. Oltroge of Willow Springs, Ill., was installed on May 16, 1948.

The following have served as day school teachers at First Immanuel: H. H. Hattstaedt, 1881-1914; A. H. J. Abraham, 1883-1909; Charles C. H. Suhr, 1890-1923; Carl Backhaus, 1902-1906; William Bachert, 1903-1911; Martin Rabe, 1911-1922; R. Appelt, 1922-1926; Miss Thea Bittner, 1923-1925; Oscar Bruell, 1925-1928; Christian Seidel, 1926-1930; F. C. Himmler, 1927-1935; Richard F. Held, 1935-1939; Paul A. Lassanske, 1939-1943; Martin F. Wessler, 1942-1946; H. O. Bloch, 1943-1949; Herbert Gade, 1947-1949. Other teachers, whose terms

*Pastor Seidel's first ministerial position was at one of the founding congregations of the Missouri Synod, St. John's in Neuendettelsau (3 miles south of Marysville), Union County, Ohio. (This writer's birthplace.) He was installed there as assistant pastor on Oct. 1, 1847.

of office are not indicated: R. H. Boecher, H. F. L. Roemer, and G. Bartelt.

Miss Clara Heymann has served as Sunday school superintendent since 1933.

Among other historic events that have taken place in First Immanuel Church was the commissioning on March 17, 1946, of the Rev. Alvaro A. Carino, a native of the Philippine Islands, as Lutheran missionary to his people on the "Islands." Born September 19, 1908, in San Juan, on historic Lingayam Gulf, Luzon, P.I., young Carino in the 1920's accompanied a wealthy American tourist to St. Louis, Mo., where, through broadcasts from the Missouri's Synod's radio station, KFUO, he became acquainted with Lutheranism. Soon afterward he entered Saint Paul's College, Concordia, Mo., and, having completed his course there, continued his theological training at Concordia Seminary, St. Louis, Mo., from which he graduated in 1937. For a period of time he served as assistant city missionary in Cook County institutions.[28]

12. Goodfarm

From Ashland and Twelfth in Chicago the Trail heads in a southwesterly direction toward Dwight, Ill., a considerable distance, but after having witnessed so many exciting events in the "Garden City," the sixty-five-mile journey should prove very refreshing.

The year is 1854, and the people down in Grundy County are "keeping the pot boiling" and, although there are cows here, too, there seems to be no danger of any of them coming close enough to kick the pot over and causing a conflagration. Particularly interesting is a settlement known as Goodfarm, four miles northeast of Dwight. Here are discovered some of the originators of another Lutheran congregation. "Die Leit babbern bayrisch!" (These people are conversing in the Bavarian dialect!) Some of them had been parishioners of the

Rev. Johannes Konrad Wilhelm Loehe* in Neuendettelsau, Bavaria, Germany.

Had it not been for the eloquent and impressive salesmanship of the Rev. Henry Wunder, pastor of First Saint Paul's Congregation in Chicago (1851-1913), these settlers probably would have carried out their original intention of joining their kinsfolk in the Saginaw Valley in Michigan. It seems that he persuaded them to remain at Goodfarm by suggesting that it were much better for them to turn the sod of Illinois' prairies than to spend the rest of their lives blowing up or grubbing out stumps for the benefit of their descendants. Manifesting a personal interest in their welfare, Pastor Wunder came, at least part of the long distance, by oxcart, in order to give them spiritual attention and to organize a congregation. In fact, the first Baptisms performed by him at Goodfarm were recorded in the records of First Saint Paul's Congregation in Chicago. Exact data concerning the early history of this congregation, Trinity at Goodfarm, are not available, owing partly to the fact that the first parsonage where the church records were kept was destroyed by fire in 1884, and partly to the fact that the minutes of the voters' meetings, which were kept in the home of the secretary, were likewise destroyed when the home burned down. Information reveals nothing but these simple facts:

Trinity Congregation's first pastor, the Rev. Lorenz Ed. Kaehler, served from 1856 to 1861 and then accepted a call from a Lutheran congregation at Glasgow, Mo. His successor, Franz Schmidt, served from 1861 to 1863. Then came the Rev. Carl Heinrich Gottlieb Schliepsiek from Bloomington,

*Pastor Loehe, in 1842, was visited by the Rev. Friedrich Conrad Dietrich Wyneken, then a member of the Pennsylvania Ministerium. One result of the visit was that Pastor Loehe became intensely interested in Lutheran missionary work in America, and "undertook the task of finding, training, and supporting men for this field." In 1854 the friendly relations were ruptured, and Loehe, unable to agree with the Missouri Synod's doctrine of the Church and the Ministry, founded a separate synod (Iowa), now a member of the American Lutheran Church (organized in 1930 in Toledo, Ohio). Cf. Concordia Cyclopedia (St. Louis, 1927), p. 413 ff.

Ill., who served from 1863 to 1872 and then resigned.* The Rev. Karl Wuensch of Pierceville and Squaw Grove, near Hinckley, Ill., held the pastorate for about four years, from 1872 to 1876, and followed a call to Spring Valley, Mo. Then, it seems, there was a vacancy which lasted about three years. The Rev. Carl W. R. Frederking of Lost Prairie, Ill., took charge in 1879 and resigned in 1896. He died on October 22, 1902. The next man to be installed as Trinity's pastor, A. W. Vogt, came from Des Plaines, Ill., where he had served as a day school teacher from 1893 to 1897 (four miles east of Des Plaines—Saint Matthew's Congregation, affiliated with the Wisconsin Synod). His ordination and installation took place in the Goodfarm church (Trinity) on March 7, 1897. Shortly after he had terminated his pastorate here, in 1902, the Rev. H. Grefe succeeded him. After about four years, in 1906, Pastor Grefe accepted a call to Lemont, Ill. Succeeding him to the Trinity pastorate was the Rev. George Peter Albrecht Schaaf, who served from 1906 to 1911. He died July 28, 1925. In 1911 the Rev. John A. Leimer of Denver, Idaho, became Trinity's pastor. In the latter part of 1916, however, he accepted a call to a mission field in the southwestern part of Chicago, which within the next thirty years developed into one of the largest parishes in the Missouri Synod—Hope Church, at West Sixty-fourth Street and Washtenaw Avenue. In 1917 Trinity received its new pastor, the Rev. Paul J. Danker, hitherto at Jefferson City, Mo. His pastorate at Trinity, like that of Pastor Frederking, covered a period of approximately seventeen years. In 1934 he followed a call to Bonfield (Union Hill), Ill. From the time of his departure from Goodfarm until the installation of his successor, the Rev. David J. Kramer, in 1936, the congregation was served by various students of theology. In 1944 Pastor Kramer accepted a call to Union, Ill., and on December 3, 1944, the Rev. Ernest W. Schwartz

*Later he resumed the ministry at Cayuga and Chenoa, Ill.; resigned in 1889, and died on Aug. 21, 1894.

of Pecatonica, Ill., was installed. On November 14, 1948, the renovated church was dedicated. "Macht's gut, iha lieben Leit von Goodfarm!"

13. Eagle Lake

It is still 1854 as the Trail winds from Goodfarm some forty-five miles toward the northeast in Will County to Eagle Lake, passingly mentioned when on the Crete trail. Here are Lutheran settlers who in company with many other immigrants had come from Germany about four years previously and for some time were affiliated with Zion (in 1858 changed to Trinity) Congregation at Crete. Incidentally, how much did our trip from Goodfarm to Eagle Lake cost? Abraham Lincoln, it is said, recently had covered the distance of 149 miles from Peoria to Chicago in three days and that he spent twelve dollars for the transportation. At that rate, our journey should not have cost more than about four dollars!

In 1854 Saint John's Congregation of Eagle Lake was organized. The constitution was adopted and signed by ten men.* On September 11, 1854, the Rev. W. Gustav Polack of Weisseichen (White Oaks), near Cincinnati, Ohio, was installed as Saint John's first resident pastor by the Rev. C. August T. Selle of Crete. No definite salary was promised the pastor; but he was given the assurance that he would receive all the money paid by the members and earmarked "Pastor's Salary." This method of maintaining the new pastor must not be ascribed to miserliness, but rather to the extreme poverty of the members. At the voters' meeting, January 1, 1855, it was agreed that every family head should pay five dollars for himself, his wife, and his children; children above the age of fourteen were encouraged to pay as much as possible, and young people above twenty-one were expected to pay $2.50 each to-

*Hans H. Tatge	John Scheiwe	F. Rotermund
John Hartmann	Konrad Ohlendorf	Chr. Wassmann
Henry Wassmann	John Windheim	Chr. Scheiwe
		Konrad Tatge

ward the pastor's salary. "An examination of the past," writes a recent President of the United States, "can oftentimes serve a most constructive purpose. By studying the means employed by those who have gone before us, in the solution of their problems, we may obtain light for our guidance in solving the questions which confront us in our own day and time." No doubt Pastor Polack was adequately supported!

The first services were conducted in the home of Hans H. Tatge. In 1856 the first church building was erected upon property donated by Henry Wassmann. Each landowner was asked to pay fifteen dollars toward the erection of the building, while the necessary lumber was donated by the others. Also, in accordance with a formal agreement, every owner of timberland donated two wagonloads of firewood, two fence posts, and six fence rails to the church. The rest of the men had the job of splitting wood.

A parish school had been established in 1855; but there were only three days of school each week, taught by the pastor until 1858, when a student, E. Vogel, was engaged for this work. He left after the first term. It was during this time also that eight members of Saint John's Congregation, having become utterly displeased with the "Scriptural" sermons preached by Pastor Polack, withdrew and organized a congregation of their own several miles to the east (in the State of Indiana) and joined the Reformed Church. Shortly afterward, in 1860, Saint John's Congregation of Eagle Lake joined the Missouri Synod.

Because many immigrants had settled in the area some three or four miles south of the church, a school was built there in 1859. E. Luttje served as teacher until 1861. On October 10, 1861, F. Fathauer began to teach alternately in both schools. By that time the little church at Eagle Lake had outlived its usefulness. A large church was erected at a place approximately halfway between the two schools, or about two miles south of the old church. In 1866 several members, upon their request, were released to organize Saint Paul's Congregation, about two miles northwest of Beecher, Ill. A second teacher, W. Bunge, was called in 1868 for the northern school at Eagle Lake, and in the same year Pastor Polack followed a call to Cape Girardeau, Mo. His successor at Saint John's, the Rev. Jacob Friedrich Nuoffer, heretofore with the Ohio Synod in northern Ohio, began his ministry here in March, 1869. During his pastorate a new school was erected in the southern district at Eagle Lake. By that time the total enrollment in both schools had reached the 185 mark. Mr. Bunge resigned in 1875, and in 1876 A. Albers of Skunks Grove succeeded him. Stricken with illness, Pastor Nuoffer tendered his resignation in April, 1885.* Two months later the Rev. Karl Brauer,† assistant pastor of Trinity (prior to 1858 known as Zion) Congregation at Crete since 1881, was installed in Saint John's pastorate. In 1902 Mr. Fathauer, after forty-one years of teaching at Eagle Lake, retired, and W. Hillger became his immediate successor. Five years later, in 1907, Mr. Albers, having served for thirty-two years at Eagle Lake and, prior to that, about six years at Duncklees Grove and about four at Skunks Grove, likewise terminated his professional activities. He was succeeded by G. Stephani, who resigned after three years. Otto Wegner was the next teacher. In 1911 Pastor Brauer resigned because of ill health. His successor, the Rev. Richard David John Piehler of Sycamore-Genoa, Ill., was installed on November 12, 1911. On March 14, 1917, Christian A. Eickemeyer was placed in charge of the northern school. On May 26 (Pentecost Sunday) of the same year a tornado wrought havoc in this region. Among other property damage in the area, the steeple of Saint John's Church was twisted off. It was replaced with a new one. In

*A son, Herman Gottlieb Nuoffer, born at Eagle Lake on March 21, 1870, was a day school teacher, 1889-1940; he died in Fort Wayne, Ind.

†A son of the Rev. Ernst August Brauer, who began his ministry at Duncklees Grove, December 15, 1847.

1921 Mr. Hillger followed a call to First Trinity, Chicago, and J. D. Bruns took his place at the southern school. In 1925 Walter H. Buethe was installed. He served for about eleven years at the southern school and in 1936 resigned because of illness. Thereupon Candidate W. H. Strum was employed for the school. Then came Richard Hillger. On March 14, 1938, Pastor Piehler died. Saint John's fifth pastor, the Rev. Carl R. Selle* of Milwaukee, Wis., was installed on September 25, 1938, and in the same service Candidate Sturm was formally inducted as teacher. In 1939 the northern school was closed because over a period of years the enrollment was too small to warrant its continuance. Teacher Eickemeyer was offered the use of the house as well as the eight acres adjoining it for as long as he desired to live there.[29] In June, 1947, Pastor Selle accepted a call to Blue Island, Ill., and the Rev. Walter J. Link of Menno, S. Dak., succeeded in this pastorate on August 17, 1947.

14. Aurora, Saint Paul's

While on the Sauk Trail, at Skunks Grove, reports were heard about the first train steaming into Chicago from the south and the east. About two years have elapsed since that time, and newspapers now record "104 trains rumbling in and out of Chicago." This means that soon trips to various Lutheran churches will be by train! What a relief that will be from the muddy wagon and oxcart trail! But what say the local newspapers? "A meeting was called for September 20, 1854, at Aurora [Illinois] of all citizens opposed to the extension of slavery and who are willing to disregard old party distinctions to make common cause to secure free territory for free men." Does this mean the nation is headed for trouble? The answer is but a few years hence. National news of the year 1857 occupies our immediate attention: "Financial panic"

*Not related to the Rev. C. August T. Selle.

—"Mountain Meadow Massacre; 120 immigrants killed by Indians in Utah." From the *Chicago Tribune* is learned something about happenings in the "Big City": "Chicago held its first sailing regatta—the railroad ran north as far as Lake Forest—the north shore is becoming lined with cottages embowered in elaborate comfort—a poor coot, Edward Daly, was fined $1 and ten days at Bridewell for stealing lumber from a vacant lot—Tom Tate, a miserable drunken vagabond, was fined $3 and sentenced to ten days at Bridewell, etc., etc." And here is an item dated September 9, 1857, that must not be overlooked: "Lincoln was often in Chicago during this year and tried one of the most important law cases of his career, 'The Effie Afton or Rock Island Bridge Case.' " Does not the second to the last news item bring to mind the legend about the devil giving a hermit the choice of three great vices, one of which was drunkenness? The hermit chose drunkenness as being the least sinful; he got drunk and committed the other two! "Ancient" vices are not obsolete!

Meanwhile the name "Aurora" looms large on the Trail. According to the 1940 census, Auroa had a population of 47,170. What the population was in the late 1850's, is not known to this narrator, neither does it matter at the moment. As a voting precinct of the newly organized Kane County (in 1836) this place was designated as "Fox River." The entire area was at one time included in an Indian reservation ten miles square. Chief Waubonsie, for some time chief of the Potawatomi tribe, had his headquarters here. For this reason some of the townspeople wanted the whole settlement named Waubonsie; but this name had already been given to another village in Illinois (Wauponsie). Other people liked the name Hartford. Actually, however, most of the people in that area and vicinity simply let it go at "McCarty Mills," at least until about the year 1837, when the Government Postal Department decided that the settlement should have a definite name. It was then that most everybody became vitally interested in the matter of having the village on the Fox River properly named. Many names were suggested, including a large number of Indian titles. At last Elias D. Terry, one of the community's first settlers, suggested the classic and beautiful name "Aurora," after his old home town in the State of New York, Aurora, on the beautiful Cayuga Lake. No doubt, it was explained that Aurora means the same as Waubonsie, "dawn" or "the rising light of the morning." So, the name Aurora was adopted in 1837. Then "things began to happen": a new grist mill was opened; the last of the Indians departed; new settlers came in; business houses were started; small factories opened. The town was on its way! Three Indian trails converged in the heart of the Fox River Valley, with Aurora now in its center; the principal trail was traveled by the Potawotamis, from Chief Waubonsie's village, via Plainfield, to a point a short distance south of Joliet. Early in 1849 the first moves were made toward bringing a railroad to Aurora. Three routes were surveyed, and the one finally adopted started from the eastern bank of the Fox River (in Aurora) and led by way of Batavia (about six miles north), along the river, and then in a northeasterly direction to Turner Junction (now West Chicago). On September 2, 1850, a diminutive "tea kettle" engine, drawing one coach, puffed along the new railroad between Turner Junction and Batavia, and on October 21 the first train on this new railroad reached "the dawn city"—Aurora. This was the day that the nucleus of the Chicago, Burlington and Quincy Railroad ("the Q") was formed. The population of Aurora at this time (in the early 1850's) was estimated at one thousand.

The first German, and nominally Lutheran, service in this "dawning city" was conducted by the Rev. Ernst Buhre in 1854. After futile attempts in near-by Naper (Naperville), about nine miles east, he succeeded in surrounding himself with a small group of Aurorans. Two young men, Fred and Andrew Muschler, who had recently come to Aurora from the Duncklees Grove neighborhood, attended several services as well as a special meeting. When at one of these the clergyman solicited donations and pledges for the support of church work in Aurora, the two young men responded by offering him the contents of their "treasury"—a total of three dollars and fifty cents. Fred said: "Now that the money is gone, we shall fast for at least a day and sleep in some barn until something can be earned." His brother promptly smoothed his (Fred's) ruffled brow with the cheering assurance that "God will never forsake those who live and work for Him!" On the very same day both of them were privileged to see the "dawn of hope"—they were provided with a place where they could eat and sleep until they found employment. In 1855 the first church, a wooden structure, was erected by the small group of Lutherans at the corner of First Avenue (now Benton) and Jackson Street at a cost of about $1,400. The property, which comprised about a quarter of an acre, was donated to the congregation by Benjamin Hackney with the stipulation that it be used for "church purposes." The formal organization of Saint Paul's Congregation was originally scheduled for January 1, 1856; but a serious controversy prevented it from materializing. The lay members had insisted upon the inclusion of certain essential paragraphs in the constitution. The pastor's agreement was conditioned upon the incorporation of his own ideas, some of which, of course, were incorporated. When he, however, submitted the provision that "the pastor shall remain in his holy office with the congregation as long as he lives," the war was on. At the organization meeting on January 1, 1857,* Pastor Buhre swallowed the pill and bit the dust. But, in spite of this yielding to the will of his parishion-

*The record containing the list of the charter members is said to be irretrievably lost.

ers, the next five years were "terrible years for the faithful few." The arguments in the meetings were of such a turbulent and threatening nature that the aid of civil authorities was summoned to forestall a catastrophe. Finally one of the members took up the congregation's cause in a decided manner and on July 11, 1862, brought a lawsuit to a victorious conclusion. The obdurate clergyman and his "confederates" were forcibly expelled from the meeting place. "Even the women helped with their umbrellas; otherwise the men, being outnumbered, would have been defeated." The Lutheran Trail leads through all manner of scenery! Destruction of churches, schools, parsonages, etc., by fire caused by lightning, by cyclones, tornadoes, and arsonists. Sometimes the Trail pauses to "witness" a different kind of "burning" or "storm." Moreover, history dare not overlook all the unpleasant aspects of settlements and their gradual development. And, again, there certainly can be no question about the moral and cultural degeneracy and debasement that went hand in hand with the "great westward movement." Neither was there any question concerning the need of the Church's influence, not only in Aurora, but everywhere!

Several weeks after the first Lutheran congregation had been organized, certain forces of nature went on a rampage in Aurora. A great flood occurred there on February 7, 1857. According to the local newspaper of that week, the ground had been covered with snow a foot deep for sixty days, with the ground frozen hard. On February 5 it began to rain and continued to do so for two days. The railroad bridge blocked the ice, and the water set back all over Stolp's Island (in the heart of the downtown district). Suddenly a gorge two miles up the Fox River gave way, and water and ice came down in irresistible foaming fury, sweeping everything before it. Crash! Crash! Crash! went the three bridges within a few minutes. Shortly after the last echo of another kind of "crash" in Saint

Paul's Church had faded away, the congregation's second pastor arrived from Quincy, Ill., namely, the Rev. H. Baumstark ("tree-strong"). His installation in Aurora took place on April 12, 1863. In the same year, on October 12, the congregation joined the Missouri Synod. At that time, also, a revised constitution was adopted and signed by eighteen men, including the pastor.* Less than two years later, Pastor Baumstark accepted a professorship at Concordia Seminary, St. Louis, Mo.† His successor, the Rev. Johannes Strieter of Stonehill, Wis., was installed as Saint Paul's third pastor on March 19, 1865. About four years later he followed a call to Peru, Ind. Then came the Rev. Johannes Traugott Feiertag, formerly of Watervliet (Bainbridge), Mich., who was installed in Aurora on December 16, 1869.

In 1879 Pastor Feiertag terminated his pastorate in Aurora and began his new pastorate in Wolcottsville, N.Y., where he remained until the spring of 1882, when he returned to northern Illinois to serve as pastor of Bethlehem Congregation in the Colehour area (now South Chicago). The Rev. Walter Krebs of La Rose, Ill., in 1879, became Saint Paul's fifth pastor. His ministry in Aurora was disturbed especially by the "lodge question," which led to the excommunication of a number of members. A new church building, of brick construction and costing about fifteen thousand dollars, was erected in 1884. In the spring of that year the branch line of the North Western Railroad, connecting "the dawning city" with the main line at Geneva, was completed. Seven years

*H. Baumstark, pastor
Friedrich Fickenscher
Johann Adam Brunnemeyer
Johann Friedrich Muschler*
William Fickenscher
Wilhelm Rang
Johann Michael Grometer
Johann Heinrich Rang
Georg Andreas Muschler*
Michael Schoeberlein
Leonhard Schoeberlein
Christoph Baumann
G. Heinrich Brunnemeyer
Louis Kohtz
Johann Georg Grometer
John Hitzler
Friedrich Kehm
Johann Wilhelm Muschler

NOTE: Johann Friedrich (Fred) Muschler and George Andreas (Andrew) Muschler were mentioned as the original promoters of church work in Aurora. The former served for many years as the congregation's treasurer, and the latter as secretary.

†Baumstark followed Dr. Ed Preuss into the Catholic Church, having been misled by the same priest who influenced Preuss.

later, in 1891, Pastor Krebs accepted a call to Trinity Congregation at Bachelors Grove, two miles north of Tinley Park, Ill. His successor, the Rev. Gottlieb Traub, Sr., of Peoria, Ill., arrived in the same year and remained until 1895, when he was forced to resign because of a heart ailment. During his illness the congregation called his son, the Rev. Gottlieb Traub, Jr., to carry on from 1894 until 1896, when he followed a call to Hancock, Mich. On July 1, 1900, Pastor G. Traub, Sr., died. Several weeks previously, on May 21, 1900, Candidate Adolph M. Loth was ordained and installed as the seventh pastor of Saint Paul's Congregation. Two days before the installation twenty-one voters and their families were released to organize a congregation of their own a short distance from the "mother" church, which was named Emmanuel. [See Chapter 143, p. 457.] Thirteen years later the forces of nature again went on a rampage in Aurora. On May 6, 1914, the steeple of Saint Paul's Church was struck by lightning, and the building itself was almost demolished. The edifice was rebuilt and rededicated on May 26, 1918.

Saint Paul's School was founded two years before the congregation was formally organized, in 1854. George Grass taught a few children in a small building at the northwest corner of River and Walnut Streets (1854-1855). "Then selfishness on the part of the leaders and worldly-mindedness on the part of some of the leaders closed the school." In 1865 a school was opened on the city's east side, and Ernst H. Dress was called as the first teacher. On August 27, 1865, the congregation resolved to build a schoolhouse. The attendance soon demanded another teacher, and on April 3, 1870, Fred W. Knaack was called. In 1871 Mr. Dress followed a call to Zanesville, Ohio, and William Henke of Ottawa, Ill., succeeded him at Saint Paul's School. After a brief term he resigned; then H. Mack of Beardstown, Ill., was installed, in December, 1872. In the fall of 1873 he was called to Immanuel School at the "Franzosenbusch"—near Duncklees Grove—Proviso, Ill. For well-nigh two years the congregation then called in vain. On August 15, 1875, John W. Hild of Chester, Ill., was installed. He remained until November, 1880, and then left for Homestead, Iowa. On June 26, 1881, Paul F. W. Otto of Yorkville, Ill., took charge of the school. In 1885 another attempt was made to establish two classes, with the "trained" teacher in charge of the upper grades, while the lower grades were taught by the pastor and, later, by Miss Minnie Rockey. That arrangement prevailed until 1887, when Mr. Otto accepted a call to First Saint John's School in Chicago. He was succeeded by Paul Rupprecht of Brooklyn, N.Y., who worked here until 1891, when he followed a call to Pittsburgh, Pa. Shortly before that Carl Emil Hoffmann had been engaged to teach the primary grades. In 1892 he passed a colloquium at the Teachers' Seminary, Addison, and then assumed charge of the upper grades. In the same year H. Hansen was called to teach the lower grades. The number of pupils had been increasing, and when the total reached 140 in 1897, the congregation faced an acute housing problem. Hence a new school building was erected in 1898 at a cost of about sixteen thousand dollars. In 1899 Miss Emily Traub served as instructor in the third class. In 1902 Mr. Hansen resigned, and H. O. Eirich of Chicago was installed as his successor on March 30, 1902. When Mr. Hoffmann then accepted a call to the near-by "daughter" congregation's school (Emmanuel), Mr. Eirich was placed in charge of the upper grades, while Max Jeske taught the primary grades. On May 18, 1902, H. Maschoff was installed; he taught Grades Two and Three. Mr. Jeske, who left in 1903, was succeeded by Rudolph Bargmann on April 19. In 1907 Teachers Bargmann and Maschoff exchanged classes. When the former in 1911 left for the East, William Bachert of First Immanuel Congregation's day school, Chicago, was called. Mr. Eirich resigned on January 2, 1912. Paul C. Streufert was called, and installed on June 2.* Mr. Maschoff resigned in 1918. His successor, E. G. Starck of Lemont, Ill., was installed on May 5, 1918. Meanwhile, the seventh and eighth grades had been added. Miss Laura Kueffner had been teaching the primary grades from 1912 to 1923. Other women teachers in Saint Paul's School were Miss Clara Fickenscher, Miss Frieda Claus, Miss Dorothy Heerboth, Miss Edna Kluender, and Mrs. Virginia Konrad. John W. Feiertag,† a son of Saint Paul's fourth pastor, of Marengo, Ill., was placed in charge of the primary grades on August 26, 1923. Departmental work was introduced in 1931, at which time a ministerial candidate, Paul Lindenmeyer, was engaged to assist in the school. Because of the economic depression, this additional help had to be discontinued until 1934, when a recent graduate of Concordia Teachers College,‡ River Forest, Ill., E. E. Heimsoth, was engaged to teach Grades Two and Three; he was permanently called and installed on May 17, 1936. C. M. Hutfilz has been on the staff since August, 1948. On February 23, 1936, Candidate Walter G. Stallmann, a native of Aurora, was installed as assistant pastor. Meanwhile Pastor Loth accepted a call to South Gate, Calif.§ On August 23, 1936, the assistant pastor became "first" pastor. The Rev. Belno R. Lange of Plankinton, S. Dak., was installed as assistant pastor on January 25, 1942; less than two years later he followed a call to Stockton, Calif.

Illness brought about the resignation of Teachers J. W. Feiertag§ and E. G. Starck in June, 1946. Thereupon A. E.

*On Sept. 21, 1947, St. Paul's Congregation observed the fiftieth anniversary of this veteran teacher.

†Born Dec. 15, 1872, in the old parsonage of Saint Paul's Church.

‡Prior to 1912 known as the Teachers' Seminary and located at Addison, Ill. (1864-1912.)

§Pastor Loth died on Oct. 23, 1946.

§In March, 1946, Teacher Feiertag was stricken with illness and upon insistence of his doctor retired from active service. Shortly after Easter, 1948, he was hospitalized. Death followed on May 2.—During the 52 years of teaching Mr. Feiertag was absent from the classroom only twenty days. (Cf. *Northern Illinois Messenger*, LXVII, No. 11—June 1, 1948.)

A brother, the Rev. H. H. Feiertag, superintendent of the Evangelical Lutheran Sanatorium, Wheat Ridge, Colo. (1916-1939), died on June 25, 1948, in Los Angeles, Calif.

Wolkenhauer was placed in charge of Grade One and Victor C. Wassermann of Grades Seven to Eight, in 1946. In 1948 Teacher Karl O. Gandt was added to the staff.

The Lutheran Trail will return to Aurora in 1901. It now leaves by way of the old Indian trail, in a southeasterly direction, through Plainfield and Joliet, and then almost due south, crossing the Kankakee River at Wilmington and continuing for about twenty more miles, until it comes to what is known as Townline Road. There must be a Lutheran church in this neighborhood. Behold, there it is—Zion Evangelical Lutheran Church, on the south side of the Townline Road, in Pilot Township! The official address is Bonfield, Ill.[30]

15. Bonfield

During the middle 1850's a number of Lutheran families settled in Pilot and Salina Townships of Kankakee County. Apprised of their presence, the Rev. Wolfgang Simon Stubnatzy, pastor of Saint John's Congregation at Coopers Grove —about thirty-five miles northeast of Bonfield*—volunteered to give them spiritual attention. He conducted worship services in various homes. Early in the year 1859 twenty men† met in the home of A. Betz and organized Zion Congregation (Bonfield). In December of the same year the Lutherans residing in the village of Kankakee (ten miles east of Bonfield) also organized a congregation of their own, which they named Saint Paul's. Jointly the two congregations called Pastor Stubnatzy's assistant, the Rev. George Bernthal. The installation took place on Palm Sunday, April 1, 1860. (See Chapter Twenty-two, page 130.) On June 27, 1861, the cornerstone of the

*1940 census 116..

†Charter members:

C. Brinkmann	F. Brinkmann	A. Betz
C. Meyer	H. Beckmann	J. Burkhart
L. Herscher	H. Dickmann	A. Herscher
F. Kraft	W. Keerbs	F. Kemp
F. Schott	J. Nansen	J. Schwark
T. Wilken	F. Reinhart	J. Reinhart
	J. Winterroth	J. Zuelch

country congregation's first church was laid. Of wooden construction, the building measured 20x34 and cost seven hundred dollars. The building site was donated by the aforementioned Mr. Betz. In March, 1862, Pastor Bernthal accepted a call to Frankenhilf, Mich. His successor as Zion's first resident pastor was the Rev. Franz Schmidt, who then for more than a year served Saint Paul's in Kankakee as an affiliate of Zion, Bonfield. Then, it seems, both congregations once more were served by one pastor, the Rev. Carl A. Meyer of Immanuel Congregation, Proviso ("Franzosenbusch"), Ill., who now resided in Kankakee. His installation took place on August 14, 1864. In 1867 Zion Congregation once more independently called a pastor, the Rev. Franz Lehmann of Jacksonville, Ill., who was installed on December 1 of that year. He served here until the beginning of October, 1871, when he accepted a call to Saint Peter's Congregation in the Town of Lake (Chicago), Ill.* His successor, the Rev. R. Koehler of Sigel, Ill., was installed on October 8, 1871. His pastorate extended into the summer of 1875, when he resigned and moved to Wilmington, Ill.† The Rev. August Schuessler‡ of Ellisville, Mo., was installed on August 22, 1875. His pastorate was a brief one; in February, 1878, he assumed the pastorate at Saint Peter's in Joliet, Ill. On April 11 he was succeeded at Bonfield by the Rev. George William Bruegmann of Rodenberg (two miles west of Roselle), Ill. A new church was erected during the winter and spring months of 1881-1882, the dedication taking place on June 27, 1882. This church, 32x68, also a frame structure but considerably larger than the previous one, was adorned with a seventy-five-foot steeple and cost three thousand dollars. The first school building was erected in the

*Annexed to Chicago in 1889.

†Resignation resulted from advice given to the pastor by the pastors of the Illinois District, "um einer Spaltung . . . vorzubeugen." (*Proceedings, Illinois District*, 1876.)

‡Father of the Rev. Guido Rohe Schuessler, pastor of Our Redeemer Congregation, Chicago, 1901-1946, and president of the English District, 1927-1936; died July 6, 1946.

same year. The pastor served as teacher. In April, 1885, Pastor Bruegmann accepted a call to a dual parish at Vera and Vandalia, Ill. His successor, the Rev. Carl Weber of Mackey's Grove, Boone County, Iowa, was installed on November 15, 1885. He served Zion for about twelve and one-half years, resigning in the spring of 1898 and moving to Chebanse, Ill. Zion's next resident pastor was the Rev. William Henry Meyer of Gillett, Ark. He was installed on July 3, 1898. In June of the following year Zion Congregation joined the Missouri Synod. A new school building was erected in 1902. In August of the same year Pastor Meyer died after a brief illness. The Rev. Frederick Schroeder, pastor of Saint Paul's, Kankakee, assumed the pastoral responsibilities at Bonfield pending the arrival of a new pastor. On November 9, 1902, the Rev. Carl H. Mueller of Mount Carroll, Ill., was installed as Zion's next pastor. In 1909 a number of Zion's members residing in the village of Herscher and vicinity discussed the advisability of organizing their own congregation. Out of these discussions originated a new parish, Trinity. (See Chapter 169, page 507.) Pastor Mueller resigned in 1910. His successor, the Rev. G. Groenow of Mallard, Iowa, was installed on July 31, 1910. He served for about thirteen years, until the summer of 1923.* Then came the Rev. Oswald C. Taege of Anamoose, N. Dak., whose installation took place on September 9, 1923.

English services, twice a month, were introduced in 1924.

The church building was remodeled during the year 1924. The cost, which included raising the building, constructing a basement, decorating the interior, installing a new altar and pulpit as well as a new furnace, was $16,400. Several small buildings which were destroyed by fire in 1925 were replaced at a small cost, covered by the above sum.

*In the *Lutheran Annual* for 1924, the Rev. G. Groenow's address is given as Orange, Calif. He did not, however, have charge of a congregation there. He was 58 years of age at that time.

Pastor Taege resigned in May, 1934, and moved to Arlington Heights, Ill. The Rev. Paul J. Danker of Goodfarm (near Dwight), Ill., formally assumed the pastorate of Zion on January 13, 1935. Soon afterward services were conducted every Sunday in both German and English.

16. Dolton

Ten miles due east of Bonfield the Trail connects with the Illinois Central Railroad, at Kankakee, where as yet (1858) no "Missouri" congregation is to be found. Flitting in a northeasterly direction, about forty miles, the Trail is justified in making a somewhat prolonged pause at Dolton, Ill.,* a village whose name honors the memory of George Dolton. Mr. Dolton, Levi Osterhout, and others, in 1841 were authorized by the State Legislature to build a toll bridge across the Calumet River at Dolton's nearest "sister" village, Riverdale. Two years before the Trail's arrival the toll was discontinued (1856). In Dolton, then, is found an important objective of our journey in the form of a brief report written by the Rev. William Heinemann, which reads: "On Palm Sunday, March 28, 1858, ten children were received into communicant membership with the Evangelical Lutheran Church through the rite of confirmation by the undersigned, Rev. W. Heinemann." This information doubtless implies that the reverend gentleman maintained a more or less definite schedule of activity in the village of Dolton and that, although he was serving as pastor of Zion (the name of which in the same year was changed to Trinity) Congregation at Crete, approximately a dozen miles farther south, he had started giving instructions in Dolton sometime in the preceding autumn. In 1858 he baptized twelve children in Dolton, the first one on March 23. It was during this time that Abraham Lincoln was defeated for the senatorship of Illinois by Stephen A. Douglas. Pastor

*1940 census: 3,068.

Heinemann was assisted, first by the Rev. W. S. Stubnatzy of Saint John's Congregation at Coopers Grove and then by the Rev. Chr. H. Loeber, the latter's successor at the same place, in paving the way for the establishing of a Lutheran congregation in Dolton (formerly known as Hope) (?).

The incorporation of the small congregation, named Saint Paul's, took place on October 19, 1862. About a month prior to this important event in Dolton, "church people of all denominations met in Chicago" to discuss the "Emancipation Question"; a memorial concerning the matter was adopted and a special committee sent to the President of the United States, Abraham Lincoln. On April 1 of that same year it was reported that Chicago was packing more pork than any other city in the United States. On the 9th of the same month the battle of Pittsburgh Landing was fought. By the end of that year Chicago's population had increased to about 135,000. Also in Dolton there were signs of progress. Shortly after its incorporation had been effected, Saint Paul's Congregation erected a church on the property of F. Bachmann. However, its first pastor was not installed until about two years later, in 1864. It was the ministerial candidate Konrad Ludwig Moll. He served for about two years, until the end of 1865, and then accepted a call to Detroit, Mich. He was succeeded in the Dolton parish by the Rev. Johann Jacob Rauschert of Mount Clemens, Mich., on January 7, 1866. The age of baseball had begun, according to a news item in the *Tribune,* July 22, 1866. In the same summer the "Asiatic cholera" appeared in Chicago, and the *Tribune* told how to avoid the disease: "The cleanly person, who drinks water, eats plain and wholesome food, sleeps between clean sheets, bathes regularly, avoids excitement of all kinds, eats the bread of honest labor, owes no man, loves his neighbor and his God, may live above the cholera in the worst cholera season that ever prevailed." Pastor Rauschert served Saint Paul's Congregation until his death, June 18, 1882. Unfortunately, no minutes of congregational (voters') meetings were kept until August 6, 1882. During the year 1882 a new church was built on East 138th Street, where several lots had been donated by F. Rau. Candidate Carl Moritz Noack was ordained and installed as Saint Paul's third resident pastor on July 30, 1882. In 1883 the congregation joined the Missouri Synod. Because the day school enrollment had reached the ninety mark in 1885, the congregation in 1886 made a virtue of necessity by calling a trained teacher, J. C. A. Winterstein, hitherto at Zion School in near-by Roseland, to take charge of the admittedly otherwise unwieldy situation. In the following year a school building, 25x50 feet and costing eleven hundred dollars, was erected. When Mr. Winterstein in 1891 followed a call to Roseville (now Halfway), Mich., he was succeeded in Saint Paul's School by H. Burmeister. In February, 1894, Pastor Noack accepted a call to Sioux City, Iowa, where he held a pastorate until called to Saint Peter's Congregation in Dunton (Arlington Heights), Ill., in September, 1899. His successor in Dolton, the Rev. John Michael Hieber of Sheboygan Falls, Wis., was installed on May 6, 1894. Pastor Hieber ministered to the little flock until his death on August 23, 1901. Two months later, on November 3, 1901, the Rev. Henry H. Wind* of Cheyenne, Wyo., became the next pastor of Saint Paul's. In addition to his ministerial duties in Dolton, Pastor Wind also continued the mission work begun by his predecessors in Riverdale, Oak Glen (Cummings Corner), Hammond (Ind.), Hegewisch, Blue Island, and other places, not overlooking Harvey—about three miles southwest of Dolton—where on February 8, 1903, he assisted in the organization of Trinity

*His first wife, Agnes Amalia (died in 1915), was the youngest daughter of the Rev. John Friedrich Buenger, one of the founders of the Lutheran college at Altenburg, Perry County, Mo. (1839.) *Amalia* was the name of the ship (one of five carrying Saxon immigrants), which was lost.

Congregation, which he served as an affiliate of Saint Paul's, Dolton, until August, 1913.

At the beginning of the 1903-1904 school year, 126 children were enrolled in the new school erected in 1902 on recently purchased property (100x150 feet) on the south side of the street which separates the villages of Dolton and Riverdale (the latter is now within the city limits of Chicago), East 138th Street. Mr. Burmeister resigned on May 24, 1903, and Chr. Seidel became his successor. Assisting him in the flourishing school, in 1903, was William Gaekemeier. On February 26, 1905, Mr. Seidel followed a call to Des Plaines, Ill., where, it seems, he had served for about two years, 1891-1893. (See Chapter 60, p. 263.) About a week after Mr. Seidel's departure, William Maurer stepped into his place in Dolton. Shortly afterward Mr. Gaekemeier went to another school in Chicago, and teacher-candidate A. L. Kaeppel came to Dolton. In May, 1908, Mr. Maurer resigned. In July of the same year F. W. Rademacher became Mr. Kaeppel's new colleague; but about two years later, in the spring of 1912, Mr. Kaeppel went to St. Louis, Mo., and Pastor Wind's son, Henry F., then a student at Concordia Seminary, St. Louis, Mo., served as substitute teacher until the end of that school year. E. W. Grothe became Mr. Rademacher's associate in the same summer, at which time also a Sunday school was brought into being. Upon Mr. Grothe's departure for Belvidere, Ill., in March, 1914, Pastor Wind served in school for about two months, until Alvin Luebker relieved him of those responsibilities in May. In November, 1911, one English service per month was introduced; they were held on Sunday evenings. In 1918 the old church was remodeled and enlarged at a cost of $12,400. In the spring of the following year, 1919, the church was struck by lightning. In August, 1920, Mr. Luebker resigned. His successor was C. F. Keller. When the latter in 1922 accepted a call to Westcliffe, Colo., August C. Bernahl of Hanson Park (Chicago) was called. Two years later, in September, 1924, Saint Paul's Congregation installed the Rev. Walter J. Kemnitz of Mokena, Ill., as its first associate pastor. In the same month regular services in both languages, German and English, were inaugurated. In charge of the English work in the parish, the associate pastor also served as teacher in the primary grades of the day school for about one-half year. In March, 1925, E. Cluever, a student at Concordia Teachers College, River Forest, Ill., was engaged to fill out the school year in these grades.

Having resigned and preached his farewell sermon in Saint Paul's Church on Sunday, July 5, 1925, Pastor Wind "rested for a few months" and then accepted a call to Fillmore, N.Y. A year later he was called to Buffalo, N.Y. He resigned from the active ministry "because of his advanced age" in 1936 and then moved to Creve Coeur, Mo., where he died on October 23, 1943.

At the beginning of the 1925-1926 school year Miss Lillie Homann was engaged as teacher in the primary department; she served in this capacity until the end of 1926, when failing health compelled her to discontinue teaching. Miss Linda Wassmann then took charge of that work in February, 1927. A new school and parish hall, costing $58,000, was dedicated on November 20, 1927. Four bowling alleys in the building cost an additional $5,600. After having served continuously as teacher in Saint Paul's School for twenty-four years, Mr. Rademacher died suddenly on December 5, 1932. Erich O. Haase was his successor; he served here until September, 1943, when he followed a call to Saint Peter's School in Chicago. On January 30, 1944, O. W. Schultz of First Saint John's, Chicago, succeeded him in Dolton-Riverdale. Others who have served as teachers in Saint Paul's day school: William A. Peters, Mrs. Victor Both, W. W. Bloom, Miss Irma Bertram, Miss Norma

Strampe, Mrs. Fern Pfitzer, Mrs. Hazel Koenker, Ernest J. Kemnitz, Pastor Kemnitz's father, a retired school teacher,* B. C. Zimdahl, and Miss Frances Williams.

During the year 1943 the children of Saint Paul's School† made a total contribution of $1,336.75 for home purposes and for projects of the Missouri Synod.[31]

17. Proviso

The Trail now leaves the Dolton-Riverdale territory, crosses the "free" bridge and hastens in a northwesterly direction toward Duncklees Grove, but stops at "Franzosenbusch"—about nine miles south of Duncklees Grove—in a community long since known as Proviso.‡ The census records do not include such a name, at least not for the State of Illinois, to which State present interest is confined. Here in the Proviso community, near the intersection of what now is known as Cermak (West 22d Street) and Wolf Roads, again are found Hanoverian and Pomeranian settlers. Beautiful country, and not a wolf in sight, nor a howl to be heard! At this time (remember, this is the year 1850!), there isn't even a sign of a railroad track or train, much less of railroad yards! And, oh, such country roads! Lacking a church of their own, the Proviso Lutherans on Sunday mornings, for a period of about eight years, attended worship services in Zion Church at Duncklees Grove—not nine city blocks, but nine miles away! However, these Lutherans were willing to let their children suffer the disadvantage of traveling so far to school every day for only about two years. In 1852 the Provisoans obtained permission from their "mother" church, Zion, to establish a school in their own midst; they secured the services of H. Bartling of Duncklees

*Teacher Kemnitz died on June 29, 1942.
†Enrollment in 1943, 154.
‡Named for Wilmot Proviso.

Grove to teach three days a week, in the home of Henry Degener. In 1853 they erected a school building and called a supposedly "trained" teacher, Hahn by name. His teaching career was of very short duration. Nicholas Kirchner succeeded him in 1854. On May 14, 1858, the ambitious settlers sought the "mother" congregation's approval to organize a separate congregation at Proviso. Because there was no indication in the written request for such approval concerning the confessional standard of the proposed new congregation nor a reference to the "type" of pastor to be called, the "mother" congregation, for the present, denied the request. Some of the Provisoans attending the meeting at which the request was submitted and discussed declared that it was their intention to abide by the confessional standards of the Missouri Synod and to call a pastor of this synod. Thereupon Zion Congregation passed this resolution: "If the brethren at Proviso promise us that they want to call only a pastor of our Synod, then we shall not interfere; moreover, as soon as more pastors become available, we shall assist them in securing one." The Provisoans returned to their respective homes. On May 25, 1858, nineteen Provisoans* signed another document, which contained reassurances relative to the matters discussed at the above-mentioned meeting at Duncklees Grove. On July 15, 1858, this document was submitted at a voters' meeting of the "mother" congregation, and the request of the Provisoans was finally approved and granted by unanimous vote. The organization of the new congregation, named Immanuel, was effected on November 27, 1858. Immanuel's first pastor was the Rev. Carl A. Meyer. He was installed on January 12, 1859.

*H. Mesenbrink	August Heidorn	Heinrich Runge
J. Schultz	Heinrich Volberding	Siegfried Kolb
Fried. Hase	Friedrich Weiss	C. Seegers
Wilhelm Mandel	Heinrich Ehrenpfort	Christian Puscheck
Heinrich Evers	Heinrich Degener	C. G. Puscheck
Friedrich Volberding	Friedrich Volberding	F. Meyer
		C. Spannuth

On January 17 twelve more voting members of Zion Congregation were released to the young "daughter" congregation at Proviso.* In the same year, 1859, Immanuel Congregation joined the Missouri Synod.

During the first year of his ministry at Proviso, Pastor Meyer also founded mission stations at Willow Springs and at Harlem (Forest Park). After about five years, in 1864, Pastor Meyer accepted a call to Kankakee. In the fall of that year the Rev. George M. Zucker of Yorkville, Ill., became Immanuel Congregation's second pastor. During the following two years the Proviso Lutherans were diligently formulating and crystallizing plans for the erection of a new church. The edifice was dedicated on July 16, 1868. It cost $10,209.90. Several months later, Gen. Ulysses S. Grant was elected as the eighteenth President of the United States. Meanwhile there had been several changes in the Lutheran school at Proviso: Nicholas Kirchner, in 1861, had been replaced by Carl Herpolsheimer; Herpolsheimer by Fred Rix; and Rix, in turn, by Julius Muenchow; Muenchow, in 1870, was succeeded by C. H. Nagel. In 1870 William Eggers took charge of the newly founded branch school on York Road, north of Hinsdale and west of Immanuel Church. In 1871 F. Polsdoerfer took Mr. Nagel's place in the branch school. At that time also the Sunday school† sessions were begun on Sunday afternoon. By special resolution the voters' meetings were to be conducted through the medium of the High German language (Hochdeutsch). In 1873 Pastor Zucker accepted a call to Defiance, Ohio, and shortly afterward Immanuel had a new—its third—pastor in the person of the Rev. Johannes Strieter‡ of Peru, Ind., as well as a new day school teacher as Mr. Polsdoerfer's succes-

*F. Hoermann	F. Andermann	Ch. Thiele
Ch. Thiele	W. Boeger	H. Mesenbrink, Sr.
Ch. Erich		H. Roehrs
H. Nebel		L. Ridder
L. Wiebe		H. Bergmann

†Probably known as "Christenlehre."

‡Pastor Strieter was pastor of Saint Paul's ongregation in Aurora, Ill., 1865-1869; thence he went to Peru, Ind.

sor, Fred Leutheusser. The latter died in the following year. His successor was A. F. Mack, who served for about four years and then accepted a call to St. Charles, Mo. His successor at Proviso was John Kaeppel. William Wiegrefe of Downers Grove, Ill., was placed in charge of the branch school. He served from 1878 until 1888. In the latter year the school was closed, and some of the children transferred to the main school, while others enrolled in Zion Lutheran School in Hinsdale, which was organized in April, 1888. Mr. Kaeppel had resigned in 1885. Defective hearing caused the resignation of Pastor Strieter in 1902.* His successor in the Proviso pastorate was the Rev. Christoph Droegemueller of Lindenwood, Ill. He served here until 1905, when he accepted a call as superintendent of the Children's Friend Society in Peoria, Ill. Then came the Rev. Henry Roehrs, who served Immanuel Congregation until his death in November, 1928. In February, 1929, the Rev. Otto Heerwagen of Westcliffe, Colo., was installed. His pastorate extended over a period of about sixteen years. He died on January 24, 1945.

On July 2, 1933, a cyclone struck the church steeple. Windows of the parsonage and the teacher's residence were shattered, and many good and beautiful trees on the premises and in the surrounding region were destroyed.

On September 9, 1945, the Rev. Elmer H. Pittelko of Fairmont, Okla., was installed as Immanuel Congregation's seventh pastor.

Teachers, in addition to those already mentioned, who served at Proviso, were the following: William Adolph Herter, Charles Voigt, John H. Daenzer, Edmund C. Brust, Herman Fickenscher, Miss Eunice Hoeger, and Adolph Obermann. The last named, in 1944, followed a call to Saint Peter's in Arlington Heights, Ill. His successor, since March 4, 1945, is Lawrence Pohlmann.[32]

*Pastor Strieter died Aug. 24, 1920.

18. Bachelors Grove

The Trail now picks up another of the many groves in the vast prairie, which is unique so far as its name is concerned—Petzel's Grove, or Berzel's Grove, or Bachelor's Grove. We should, perhaps, go out to the present West 159th Street and Oak Park Avenue for information concerning the correct spelling and pronunciation of that grove's name! This community is located approximately two miles north of Tinley Park* and five miles south of the Calumet Sag Channel; or, perhaps, it is better to say: seven miles southwest of Blue Island.

It may be assumed that the first German settlers at Bachelor's Grove established their church home in the grove instead of in the near-by village because they preferred the former to the latter. However, that was not exactly the case; at any rate, it was not the principal reason. According to reliable sources there were two principal reasons for the choice, and that mentioned is not one of them. First, the group's friendly deference to Saint John's Congregation at Coopers Grove (organized in 1848), with whose expansion program it did not wish to interfere; secondly, the location north of Tinley Park was more central for all those originally concerned with the matter. It was the Rev. W. S. Stubnatzy of the Coopers Grove parish who in 1859 began preaching to this group of Lutherans, thirteen of whom became charter members† of Trinity Congregation at about this time. A short time later the young congregation erected a two-story building, the first floor of which served as living quarters for the pastor (yet to be called) and the second as church and school. Trinity's first pastor, the Rev.

*1940 census: 1,136.

†Friedrich Engelhardt, Philip Huhnstock, Lorenz Burkhardt, Christ. Abbe, Sr., Christian Schilling, Justus Knierim, John Schaller, Lorenz Gaus, Karl Reichert, Friedrich Kimmel, Peter Dehnhardt, John Huhnstock, Sr., George Weber

Herman Wunderlich, was installed on June 19, 1861—about a month before the now memorable Battle of Bull Run was fought, in Virginia.*

Pastor Wunderlich soon came to regard as his mission field Oaklawn to the north, Lemont to the northwest, and Mokena to the southwest. Presumably it was he who served Immanuel Congregation "on the hill" three miles southeast of Mokena for some time before the Rev. Elias Hieber of Sieden Prairie took charge of it as an affiliate of his own congregation, Saint Paul's, which the latter served from 1873 until 1914. (See Chapter 8.) Saint Matthew's Congregation in Lemont was organized in 1874. In Oaklawn, however, there was no Missouri Synod congregation until 1939—Faith. In addition to teaching school for three years, Pastor Wunderlich ministered to Trinity Congregation at Bachelor's Grove and conducted services in those "distant" places, covering the territory on foot or by means of horse and buggy, for about ten years. In 1871 he accepted a call to Tolleston, Ind., now incorporated with Gary, Lake County, Ind., founded in 1906† and named after Elbert H. Gary, a native of Wheaton, Ill. The Rev. John Christian Herman Martin of Dorsey (Bethalto), Ill., became Trinity Congregation's second pastor in 1871. This date recalls the Great Fire in Chicago; and that, in turn, will remind the "children of Trinity" at Bachelor's Grove of the fire which on Christmas Day, 1883, destroyed their first church. A new church was erected and dedicated in 1884; also, Pastor Martin, having followed a call to Brownsdale, Minn., a new pastor came to Trin-

*A second battle took place here during the latter part of August, 1862. By the Confederates these two great battles were called Manassa—after a near-by railroad junction.

†Between the present station of the "South Shore Line" (Chicago, South Shore and South Bend Railroad) and Gary's main thoroughfare, Broadway, there is a metal plaque bearing the legend: "This site once occupied by frame building which housed first Gary post office, 1906. First daily paper published here and headquarters for Gary Land Company." At that time Gary was an "almost impenetrable wilderness of swamps and dunes." Its population (1940) was 111,719. St. John's Congregation (Missouri Synod) was founded in 1870.

ity Church on August 17, 1884—the Rev. Theodore Henry Carl Buenger, from northern Wisconsin, where he had served as missionary for about two years.* This third pastor of Trinity Congregation "really started something"—something unheard of in this territory!—he conducted services in English! In 1888 the members of Trinity residing in and around Orland Park—about five miles northwest of Bachelor's Grove, were released to organize Christ Congregation. Pastor Buenger served this new congregation as an affiliate of Trinity. In 1891 Trinity Congregation joined the Missouri Synod. In the same year Pastor Buenger accepted a call to St. Paul, Minn., where he at first served as pastor of Zion Congregation and later as professor at the Missouri Synod's Concordia College (1893-1896) and as president of the same institution (1893-1927), and for a few more years again as professor. In June, 1891, the Rev. Walter Krebs of Saint Paul's Congregation in Aurora, Ill., was installed as Trinity Congregation's fourth pastor. This pastor and his wife had the sad experience of seeing five of their children die of the "Great White Plague." On March 11, 1917, the pastor died after a long siege of illness. At Easter time in the same year the Rev. William R. Greve came from Lester Prairie, Minn., to become Trinity Congregation's fifth pastor. His father, Christian H. Greve, was a schoolteacher at Duncklees Grove (1874-1887); his mother was Susanna, a daughter of the Rev. A. G. G. Francke at Duncklees Grove (1857-1879). In 1929 a new Lutheran school was erected and dedicated at Bachelor's Grove.

Early in 1935 Pastor Greve entered the Northern Illinois District's service as institutional missionary at the Cook County Infirmary and Sanitarium located at West 159th Street and Cicero Avenue. His successor at Bachelor's Grove, the Rev. Martin Frick of Pontiac, Ill., was installed on March 10, 1935.

*Pastor Buenger was a son of "Kantor" Theodore Ernst Buenger. (See Chapter 11.) Pastor Buenger died on Sept. 9, 1943, in Portland, Oreg.

Shortly afterward a Sunday school was organized, and English services were "introduced." This seems to indicate that such services were discontinued when Pastor Buenger left in 1891. Frank Loeher's observation probably is not entirely irrelevant: "Waere der deutsche Charakter weniger kraftvoll, weniger eigenartig, so waere auch der Uebergang in den englischen leichter und gewinnreicher." ("If the German character [disposition] were less vigorous, less peculiar, then the transition to the English [character] would also be easier and more profitable.")

On September 7, 1940, Pastor Frick assumed the pastorate of Saint Andrew's in Chicago (Brighton Park). The seventh pastor, the Rev. Fred J. Pfotenhauer of Taylor Ridge, Ill., youngest son of the Rev. Frederick Pfotenhauer, D.D.,* was installed on November 24, 1940. He served at Bachelor's Grove for a little more than two years. During the latter part of that period the interior of the church was renovated at a cost of $8,000. However, it became necessary to call an eighth pastor, because the seventh had accepted a call to Concordia Congregation in Chicago before that important work was completed. The eighth pastor was the Rev. Oswald Woelzlein, who had left his congregation at Hillman, Mich., to be installed at Bachelor's Grove on May 9, 1943. He served here until August 8, 1948, when sudden death overtook him.† The Rev. H. David Mensing of Glenshaw, Pa., was installed on November 14, 1948.[33]

The following teachers have served in Trinity's day school:

Herman Reifert, 1875-1880	Walter Schmidt, 1927-1942
Chr. Hassenpflug, 1880-1913	A. E. Doering, 1942-1945
William Schweder, 1913-1914	Harry R. Voigt, 1945-1946
A. T. Christian, 1916-1921	Otto Beccue, 1946
Paul Schaefer, 1921-1926	Mrs. O. G. Beccue

*President of the Missouri Synod, 1911-1935; died Oct. 9, 1939.

†On a recent Saturday, Pastor Woelzlein and wife returned from a two weeks' vacation. On Sunday he preached two sermons (German and English). On Monday morning, Aug. 8, 1948, he mowed the lawn and then moved over into his garden to hoe weeds. He became ill and went into the house to rest. When the noon hour struck, he was dead." (Cf. *Northern Illinois Messenger*, LXVII (No. 18).

19. Dutchman's Point

It is still 1859, and, of course, there are not many villages or communities remaining to be visited unless more immigrants arrive soon to establish new ones. Perhaps some of them will leave Chicago and settle in the surrounding countryside. Even that city is still quite young. It was only last year that the first steam fire engine made its appearance in the "Big City"—nicknamed by the folks, "The Great Skwirt 'Long John' "—after John Wentworth, of whom Abraham Lincoln said: "He knows more than most men." It was in 1859 also that a well-known American preacher, Henry Ward Beecher, said: "Chicago looks like a vast railroad freight depot, and the people have that keen-eyed, restless, penetrating look that belongs to railroad men. One is struck with the magnitude, not only of its stores and business structures, but at the remarkably fine architectural effects which every day are ennobling the streets. . . . It is worth a visit to Chicago to see a new method of digging a city out of the mud." The Lutheran Trail passes right through Chicago, from Bachelor's Grove, and proceeds about twelve miles northwest of the "Big City" to a place then known as Dutchman's Point. The original "point" was a tavern operated by a Dutchman (a Hollander?). Chief distractions were dancing and drinking, so it may be preferable to use the village's more polite name—in fact, its real name: Niles, Ill.*

Records reveal that a Lutheran congregation was founded here on January 12, 1859, and named Saint John's, the first resident pastor of which was the Rev. F. J. Henicke, who served for less than one year. According to a report in the Missouri Synod's *Proceedings* of the year 1851, however, the Rev. John George Kuechle had served the Lutherans at Dutchman's Point as early as 1851. In 1852 he was called from

*1940 census: 2,168.

Dutchman's Point to Skunks Grove. Furthermore, in 1857 the Rev. H. Bauer, "formerly pastor of the congregation at Dutchman's Point, Cook Co., Ill., was called by Saint James (St. Jakobi) Congregation in Wittenberg, Franklin Co., Ohio."

On March 11, 1860, the Rev. Gotthilf Simon Loeber, since 1858 assistant pastor at First Saint Paul's and First Immanuel Congregations (jointly) in Chicago, became Pastor Henicke's successor. In the same year the first church building was erected by Saint John's Congregation. Pastor Loeber taught school until 1870, when August Krueger was called as first teacher. Two years later, in 1872, a school was built. When Mr. Krueger resigned because of illness, in 1874, August Gruhl assumed charge of the school and served until 1883, when H. Jarnecke succeeded. In 1884 Pastor Loeber accepted a call as assistant pastor at First Trinity and First Zion Congregations in Chicago. Candidate Herman Brauer* succeeded Pastor Loeber to the Saint John's pastorate in Niles on July 27, 1884. William Adolph Brauer,* a brother of the new pastor and student at Concordia Seminary, Springfield, Ill., taught school until C. W. Schwanke came to Niles. The latter served until 1893, when he accepted a call to Saint Luke's School in Chicago. Then Rudolph Kranz became teacher. When he followed a call to Saint Peter's School in Dunton (Arlington Heights), Ill., Paul Meeske was called. He served until called to Saint John's School at Elk Grove, in 1906. Then came Edward Schuricht, followed by Franz C. Stoll in 1910. A new church was built in 1902 and dedicated on November 2 in the same year. In 1914 Mr. Stoll moved to Michigan, and Pastor Brauer resigned because of ill health. He was succeeded by the Rev. Louis A. Grotheer, who served Saint John's Congregation until 1942, when he retired. The congregation, however, retained him as "honorary pastor."† The Rev. Daniel

*Pastors Herman and William Brauer were sons of the Rev. Ernest August Brauer, who died at Crete, Ill., on Sept. 29, 1896.

†He died soon afterward, September 4, 1942.

Wenz, for some time institutional missionary for the Northern Illinois District (Missouri Synod), was installed as Pastor Grotheer's successor on May 3, 1942. In the same year a Sunday school was organized.

Miss Esther Piehler taught in the day school from 1921 to 1926. She was then succeeded by Harold Mass, who remained with the school until 1929, when he followed a call to Elkhart, Ind. Edgar Abraham took his place in Saint John's School and remained until 1942, when he accepted a call to Saint Paul's School in Brookfield (Grossdale) Ill. In 1943 Walter L. Papenberg took over the teaching duties. Most, if not all, of Saint John's children now attend the "central school" maintained by Saint Paul's Congregation in Skokie (formerly known as Niles Center), Jerusalem Congregation in Morton Grove (a member of the Wisconsin Synod), and Saint John's of Niles since 1946 in Morton Grove. The teachers of this consolidated school are: Edward M. Lindemann, Walter L. Papenberg, Mrs. Mable Windhorn, and Mrs. Elinor Behrens.

On October 20, 1946, Robert E. Wiltenburg, a recent graduate of Concordia Seminary, St. Louis, Mo., and student at the University of Chicago, was installed as pastor of Saint John's Congregation at what formerly was known as Dutchman's Point. The congregation joined the Missouri Synod in July, 1943.[84]

20. Elgin, Saint John's

The Lutheran Trail now arrives at Elgin* on the Fox River —about twenty-five miles west of Niles—(named after the royal burgh of Scotland, whose ruined cathedral was founded in 1224) an Illinois city, partly in Kane and partly in Cook County, renowned the world over for its timepieces and its observatory famed for "correct time from Arcturus." Hunger compels a halt at a creamery for refreshment with those dairy products

*1940 census: 38,333.

for which this region is famous, and, being interested in Illinois, one may forget Wisconsin to the north momentarily.

One cannot but wonder how this region looked to the Rev. Henry Wunder, pastor of First Saint Paul's Congregation in Chicago, or to the Rev. J. A. F. W. Mueller, pastor of First Immanuel Congregation, also in Chicago, who came out here to gather the scattered Lutherans and to conduct worship services for them. On July 4, 1859, a Lutheran congregation was organized in Elgin and named Saint John's, and on February 23 of the following year a small frame church, located at Spring and Division Streets, was purchased for $550. The future looked bright and promising in Elgin. But the year 1861 saw the outbreak of the Civil War. In addition, in Elgin itself serious trouble was brewing for the budding Saint John's Congregation. A certain young clergyman, von Snell by name, came to serve this congregation. He was imbued with doctrines diametrically opposed to the doctrinal standards subscribed to at the time of Saint John's founding. Thereupon the Rev. Frederick Reinecke, pastor of an Evangelical congregation at Hoosier Grove, took over and served Saint John's until 1865, when he was crowded out of this pastorate by the Rev. R. Dulon, a minister of the Reformed Church. The services of the latter must have proved very unsatisfactory, for on April 29, 1866, the congregation effected a change in the pastorate by calling Professor Carl Israel, a member of the Evangelical Church and, no doubt, of the type the first "Kirchenrath" (church council) of Saint Paul's Congregation in Chicago had in mind when it called the Rev. C. A. T. Selle from New Lisbon, Ohio, about twenty years previously, in 1846. (See Chapter 2, p. 24.) Prior to the coming of Professor Israel the Lutheran constitution had been in force. His influence brought about a decided change in this constitution; its Lutheran character was gone, as was also the word "Lutheran" in the official title. It was then called "Saint John's United Evangelical Church."

The leading spirits in this movement probably felt that everything had been done "decently and in order"; but their attention was soon called to the fact that, even though such may have been the case, it was no proof that the congregation was well and properly founded. Outward order often is but a glittering illusion, an "outer garment." The members who desired Saint John's Congregation to function as a confessional Lutheran congregation strenuously objected to those who obviously wanted a sort of half-and-half religious concoction; also, it was the expressed wish of the minority group that the name "Lutheran" be embodied in the official title. So the struggle for "victory" was off to a good start even before the "foundation" was reasonably well settled.

On January 21, 1867, the "liberal" group appeared before a notary public with a declaration to the effect that the name "Lutheran" in the congregation's property deed had been inserted by mistake and, therefore, demanded that it be officially deleted. Because the desired result was not forthcoming, the same group pursued another course, which was to increase the membership with people whom they could trust as being averse to function as a distinctively Lutheran congregation. The idea was fruitful, at least, for a little while. At a meeting on April 28, 1867, the congregation's name was changed to "United Evangelical Church." Instead of breathing easier, not only the "liberal," but also the "conservative" group suddenly realized that a serious *faux pas* had been made and that the step now taken was leading toward complete disorganization. To extricate all concerned from the muddled situation, someone conceived the idea to authorize the trustees of both groups to sell, *pro forma,* the church to "Saint John's Protestant Congregation" for five hundred dollars. The idea clicked, but the plan failed. According to the wording of the deed and the letter of the law the property remained in the possession of Saint John's Evangelical Lutheran Church. No violence was done to the letter of the law; the law was respected.

On May 20, 1867, another clergyman of the Evangelical Church, the Rev. Prof. W. Buehler, was called. "He was Lutheran in spirit," but remained in Elgin for only about two years; he was succeeded on August 1, 1869, by the Rev. Frederick William Richmann of Schaumburg, Ill. His pastorate in Elgin extended over a period of about six years, until 1875, when he accepted a call to Pittsburgh, Pa.* During his ministry in Elgin, Saint John's Congregation adopted the Missouri Synod's hymnbook (German). The Rev. Henry Schmidt of Saint Peter's Congregation at Schaumburg served as vacancy pastor. On August 15, 1875, Saint John's Congregation, under Pastor Schmidt's direction, adopted a Lutheran constitution. Saint John's next resident pastor, the Rev. Herman F. Fruechtenicht of Ottawa, Ill., was installed on October 10, 1875. This pastor's first major undertaking in Elgin was the building of a new church, of brick, in 1876. The dedication took place on January 14, 1877. Later the seating capacity was increased to accommodate a total of about six hundred persons by the construction of galleries on either side of the nave. In 1904 the congregation called an associate pastor, the Rev. William J. Kowert† of Nokomis, Ill. In 1909 Pastor Fruechtenicht, because of his advanced age, withdrew from the heavy responsibilities of the pastorate, but continued to serve as assistant pastor. Pastor Kowert at that time assumed full responsibility as "first" pastor. English services were established and conducted at first on Sunday evenings and, later, in the mornings. The rapid growth which occurred during his pastorate in Elgin led to the erection of a new church in 1911. This building, "one of the most beautiful churches in Illinois," was dedicated on May 12, 1912. It has a seating capacity of about

*Later he served as chaplain of the Lutheran Hospital and the Wartburg Old Folks' Home in Brooklyn, N.Y. (1883). He died Nov. 7, 1885.

†Brother of the Rev. Henry G. W. Kowert, pastor of First Saint Paul's Congregation, Chicago, 1917-1944.

a thousand and cost $75,185.25. Five years later, in 1917, Saint John's Congregation became a member of the Missouri Synod. Pastor Fruechtenicht died on February 15, 1918, at the age of a little more than eighty-two years. On August 30, 1931, Candidate Elmer T. Grotelueschen of Columbus, Nebr., was ordained and installed as Saint John's associate pastor. On December 30, 1938, an acute attack of appendicitis compelled Pastor Kowert to submit to an emergency operation, which, however, proved to be too late. He died on the following day.

In April, 1939, the congregation purchased six lots on the corner of South Aldine and Van Streets with the view to erecting upon it a bungalow chapel for its "West Side" mission, which shortly afterward, on July 24 of the same year, became Good Shepherd Congregation, whose first pastor, Candidate L. W. Schuth, was ordained and installed on August 13. (See Chapter 234, Elgin, Good Shepherd.) During the same period Saint John's Congregation was making preparations for its own pastoral needs. The Rev. Arthur H. Werfelmann* of Zion Congregation in Hinsdale, Ill., was called to succeed Pastor Kowert in Elgin. He was installed on August 20, 1939. At the same time Rev. E. H. Grotelueschen was officially recognized as Saint John's associate pastor.

When Saint John's School was established is unknown to this writer. From 1866 to 1874 the respective pastors taught the school; it was closed in 1875 and 1876. In the fall of 1876 the school was reopened and taught by Pastor Fruechtenicht. Since 1878 the day school was in charge of trained teachers.

In 1884 a new school building was erected. In 1915 this building was enlarged.

Charles Wolff, Sr., served as trustee for Saint John's Congregation for fifty years and Fred Volstorff as secretary for forty years.[35]

*Pastor Werfelmann is a son of the Rev. Ernst Werfelmann, pastor of Christ Congregation of Logan Square, Chicago, 1885-1933. Mrs. A. H. Werfelmann (Beatrice—daughter of the Rev. and Mrs. Frederick Duever) died on Oct. 31, 1947.

The following have taught in Saint John's School:

Martin Schleier	J. C. Wohlfeil
A. C. Hintze	Paul Stormer
Richard Wismar	L. O. Schafer
Albert Mueller	Theo. Wunderlich
W. L. Laesch	Norman F. Kosche
A. Diesing	Miss Adline Ahrens
John Faisler	Miss Paula Albrecht
Alfred Johnson	Miss Anamae Hoffmann
John Feiertag	Miss Elda Volkening (Kindergarten)
John Rauschert (See note below)	

NOTE: Mr. Rauschert served as teacher in Saint John's School for 47 years.

Three members of the Missouri Synod make up seventy-five per cent of the rural letter carriers out of the post office at Elgin, Ill. Of these, Harold G. Laseman is chairman of Good Shepherd Congregation, Elgin; Fred A. Kamp is trustee of Immanuel Congregation, Dundee, Ill.; and Harold E. Dab is a member of the building committee of St. John's Congregation, Elgin. In giving this information, Mr. Dab remarks: "I might add that we get a good workout every two weeks, when the *Witness* comes out."

21. Lace

About twenty-five miles southeast of Elgin, or five miles southwest of Hinsdale, there is a community known as Lace, for which, however, no census figure is given. The Trail's passage through this little "village" allows time for reflection. There's an eerie silence. A number of old and dilapidated buildings testify to former activities at this spot on Plainfield Road. "There still are indications of what once was a cheese factory, a town hall, a blacksmith shop, and a small trading center along the winding gravel road." According to reliable sources, Lutheran pastors "as far back as 1852 made occasional visits to the neighborhood of Willow Springs and Lace," which would indicate that Lace really was on the map in the 1850's and for some time after that. After 1852 worship services were conducted by the Rev. Ernst August Brauer of Zion Congregation at Duncklees Grove. But where was the church? The services were held in private homes. The Rev. Carl A. Meyer of the "Franzosenbusch" (Proviso) Immanuel Congregation also assisted in laying the groundwork for the upbuilding of a Lutheran congregation in this community. For a time the small group of Lutherans met in a schoolhouse on the

Joliet road for worship services and other functions. In 1859* a congregation was organized under the leadership of the Rev. G. Liesmann by fifteen men† and named Saint John's. In the same year a tract of land, one and one-half miles northeast of Lace, was purchased and the first church erected upon it. A portion of the property was set apart as a "Gottesacker" (cemetery). The promise of the future, indeed, was bright for the little flock—brighter even than the fulfillment of the past. However, already in the following year Saint John's was without a shepherd. On rare occasions were worship services conducted by neighboring pastors. The scarcity of Lutheran clergymen and the infrequent services combined to render the people callous toward religion in general and very indifferent toward specific spiritual values. Spiritual progress was severely impeded and congregational growth stunted. There is evidence, however, of a spiritual revival which began in 1870, noticeable particularly in the congregation's record of Communion attendance of that time.

From 1879 to 1892 Saint John's Congregation was served by the following pastors as an affiliate of the respective congregations: by the Rev. C. A. Trautmann of Trinity Congregation at Willow Springs, 1879-1882; by the Rev. William Uffenbeck of Saint Matthew's Congregation in Lemont, November, 1882—March, 1883; and by the Rev. F. W. Brueggemann‡ of Trinity Congregation at Willow Springs, April, 1883—May, 1892. Up to this time Saint John's Congregation was recognized as a member of the Missouri Synod. During

*"In 1859 Thomas Alva Edison became a train boy selling newspapers and candies on trains of the Grand Trunk Railroad running between Port Huron and Detroit."

†Heinrich Sucher
Johannes Muchel
Friedrich Klein
Valentin Klein
Tobias Hoehn
George Bostetter
Christian Siegfried
Tobias Gailer
Peter Wolf
Jacob Klein
Jacob Hoerbig
George Fix
Philipp Binder
Herman Pilz
George Wolf

‡Pastor Brueggemann died of tetanus, on May 17, 1892.

the following thirteen years the congregation was recognized as an "Evangelical" congregation, for it was served by clergymen affiliated with the Evangelical Church, 1893-1906. In 1899 a new church was erected at Cass Avenue, about a half mile west of the "ancient" village of Lace, and Seventy-fifth Street. During the Lenten season of 1906 Saint John's Congregation resolved to rejoin the Missouri Synod and to call a pastor of this Synod. The Rev. Martin Nickel, a missionary in northern Michigan, where "for about four years he had been ministering to six 'sprawling stations,'" was installed as Saint John's pastor on May 27, 1906. In October of the same year he opened a day school with an enrollment of twenty-five children. In August, 1915, one English service each month, on Sunday mornings, was introduced. On Sunday afternoons Pastor Nickel served the newly organized congregation in Downers Grove, about four miles northwest of Saint John's Church. In December, 1913, Pastor Nickel accepted the call to Zion Congregation in near-by Lyons. His successor, the Rev. Walter Burmeister, was installed in Saint John's Church on December 11, 1913. He continued to serve also the mission congregation (Immanuel) in Downers Grove until Candidate Otto F. Arndt was ordained and installed as Immanuel's first resident pastor in the fall of 1921. It was in November, 1921, also that Pastor Burmeister followed a call to Squaws Grove (Hinckley), Ill., and on December 11, 1921, the Rev. William L. Kupsky of Kensal, N. Dak., was installed as Saint John's new pastor. In July, 1922, the decision was reached to conduct services in the English language on the first and the third Sunday morning of every month. At about this time quite a number of members moved to Downers Grove, Hinsdale, and Lemont; and thus the promise of the future once more became rather dim.

In December, 1926, Pastor Kupsky accepted a call to Bellwood, Ill., continuing, however, with the instruction of the catechumens at Saint John's, Lace, until the end of February,

1927. His successor at Lace, the Rev. Herman August Laufer of Woodstock, Ill., was installed on March 6, 1927. In January, 1932, it was resolved to conduct services in English every Sunday morning, in German on the second and fourth Sundays of each month preceding the English services.[36]

22. Kankakee

In 1858 the Lutheran Trail started out to a complete change of scenery and environment, from the "dawning city on the Fox River," by way of Plainfield, Joliet, and Wilmington. At Wilmington it crossed the Kankakee River and then proceeded to the little village of Bonfield in Pilot Township. This time the Trail, starting at Lace, goes almost due south a distance of about forty miles to the county seat of Kankakee County, Kankakee, Ill.,* on the Kankakee River, which has its rise in English Lake, in northern Indiana, joins the Des Plaines River in Grundy County (Ill.), and with it forms the Illinois River. Kankakee, at the time of the Trail's second arrival, is only about three years old, that is, as an incorporated "village" of northern Illinois. It was laid out in the early 1850's, when the railroad was built. In the late 1850's several Lutheran families in this community were provided with spiritual care by the Rev. W. S. Stubnatzy, pastor of Saint John's Congregation at Coopers Grove, about thirty miles north of Kankakee. On December 9, 1859, these Lutherans organized a congregation and called it Saint Paul's. On the same day the budding congregation also called its first resident pastor, the Rev. George Bernthal, who had been serving as Pastor Stubnatzy's assistant since July 22 of that year. His installation took place on April 1, 1860. For some time worship services were conducted in the county courthouse, in the public school building, and in private homes. Then followed a period of vacancy for about two years, during which the Rev. Franz Schmidt of Zion Con-

*1940 census: 22,241. The name "Kankakee" is the Algonquian word for "raven."

gregation at Bonfield (ten miles west of Kankakee) served. On August 14, 1864, Saint Paul's second pastor, the Rev. Carl A. Meyer of Proviso ("Franzosenbusch") was installed and the first church dedicated. Immediately after his installation, Pastor Meyer opened a day school and taught until H. G. Schuricht took charge. In 1870, when Mr. Schuricht left, Pastor Meyer resigned from the pastorate in Kankakee. His successor was the Rev. Gustav Adolph Mueller of McGregor, Iowa. In 1871 William F. Pott was installed as day school teacher. In the following year, 1872, a new church was built. In 1873 the congregation became a member of the Missouri Synod. In 1876 Mr. Pott followed a call to the State of Alabama, and William G. Schmidt succeeded. He remained about two years and was then succeeded by Chr. Gotsch. In 1883 Mr. Gotsch was called to a school at Columbus, Ind., and Herman F. Reifert came to Kankakee. In the fall of that year, 1883, Pastor Mueller accepted a call to Saint Peter's Congregation at Schaumburg, Ill., and the Rev. Frederick Schroeder of Sadorus, Ill., succeeded him in Saint Paul's pastorate on December 16, 1883. On May 1, 1887, Saint Paul's Church was destroyed by a fire which started from an adjacent conflagration. On December 9, 1888, its new church was dedicated. In 1890 George Seitz of Chicago took charge of the school and served until 1896, when he resigned because of impaired health. Gustav H. W. Kastrup of Cleveland, Ohio, assumed the teaching duties in 1896. Following his acceptance of a call to Sauers, Ind., Martin E. Bittner succeeded him in St. Paul's School.

On September 14, 1916, Pastor Schroeder died.* He was succeeded soon afterward by the Rev. Herman A. Pfotenhauer of Effingham, Ill., who served until his death, December 26, 1921. The Rev. Carl F. Haller of Appleton City, Mo.,

*A son, Werner, is chairman of the Republican Committee of Illinois; he is a member of Bethany Congregation (English District) in the Edgewater community, Chicago.

accepted the formal invitation to fill the vacancy caused by Pastor Pfotenhauer's death and was installed on April 2, 1922.

In August, 1919, Martin Koschmann came to teach; in 1925 he followed a call to Milwaukee, Wis. His successor was Paul Noennig. Mr. Noennig resigned on August 4, 1931, and Paul M. Krotke was engaged to serve until the end of the school year, June, 1932. On the following July 24 R. E. Appelt was installed as teacher. Norman Brinkmann was called to serve as "relief man," beginning to teach with the opening of school in September, 1932. On June 15, 1933, he was installed as a member of the official staff. Miss E. Lange also taught for some time. On March 7, 1943, Candidate Ralph Bartelt was installed as teacher. Oscar Wilde* joined the teaching staff on June 23, 1946, and Frederick Nohl, on September 5, 1948.

In recent years the congregation has been providing its pastor with ministerial assistance. The Rev. Herbert P. Vogel served in this capacity for some time, until he entered the U. S. Army chaplaincy. (Since July, 1947, he has been stationed at El Monte, Calif.) On March 11, 1945, the Rev. Herbert F. Bohlmann of Minneapolis, Minn., was installed as associate pastor. In the spring of 1947 Pastor Haller started a mission in the village of Onarga, about 25 miles south of Kankakee, in Iroquois County. A congregation was organized and named Trinity. Its first resident pastor, the Rev. W. C. A. Martens of Chicago, was installed on August 10, 1947.

23. Mount Carroll

The year 1860 was among the most important in American history, for it saw, among other things, the nomination and the election of Abraham Lincoln as Chief Magistrate of the United States of America. When the news of his election reached Chicago, two hundred guns were fired from the Randolph Street Bridge in celebration of the event. Actually, our

*In 1882 a man by the same name, an Irish poet and dramatist and referred to as "the apostle of the utter," visited in America. Probably no relation

"nation was going down into the Valley of Decision," in the words of a great American statesman, John Hay. "The question which had been debated on thousands of platforms, which had been discussed in countless publications, which, thundered from innumerable pulpits, had caused in their congregations the bitter strife and dissension to which only cases of conscience can give rise, was everywhere." But there were other events which compete for space in the annals of history; such as the completion of the Atlantic Cable* and the banking crisis in Illinois. On June 5, 1860, a great tornado was reported to have occurred in Illinois and Iowa with more than one hundred casualties. Chicago led in giving aid to the sufferers.

A cross-country journey through the great prairie may be somewhat tiresome and monotonous, but it will be well repaid. Straight west from Chicago, 120 miles, is Savanna, Carroll County, on the eastern bank of the Mississippi River. Ten miles east of Savanna is a village with a population of 2,947 less than the former. This village, Mount Carroll, named for Charles Carroll of Maryland, one of the signers of the Declaration of Independence, has 1,845 inhabitants (1940 census), any of whom can point out the Lutheran church. Their direction is: "Take State Route 88 out of town—that way (southeast)—and about four miles out you'll come to what we around here have been calling Black Oak Lutheran Church. In fact, that's where our grandfathers in 1860 helped to organize a congregation. They and most of the other founders were immigrants from Hesse-Darmstadt, Germany." And do you know who this congregation's first past was? Yes; his name was the Rev. Carl Weber, and it was he who—let's see—yes, about seventy-one years ago, in 1878, the same year Professor Walther in St. Louis, Mo., received the D.D. degree from Capital University in Bexley (Columbus), Ohio, caused a split in the congrega-

*The first message transmitted: "Glory to God in the highest, on earth peace, good will toward men."

tion by introducing new hymnbooks printed by the Missouri Synod in St. Louis; some of the members, especially the older ones, preferred the hymnal of the Evangelical Church, and so they withdrew and organized a congregation of their own.

Further inquiry elicits this additional information: "At first worship services were held in a school building; shortly after the small defection had occurred, Pastor Weber followed a call to Carroll, Iowa. From Mount Carroll to Carroll. During the resultant vacancy, which lasted until 1880, the flock was attended by the Rev. Frederick Lussky of Sterling, about twenty miles to the southeast. On July 18, 1880, the church, still in use today (1949), was dedicated."

The second pastor, the Rev. August Haensgen, was installed on the day of church dedication, in the afternoon. After the installation ceremony he preached an English sermon to a strictly German-speaking congregation. In the same year the congregation began to support a full-time day school. During the ten-year period of its existence (1880-1890) the school was in charge of the pastors. Pastor Haensgen remained but a short time; ill health caused his resignation in 1881. John Heinze served as a vicar from the fall of that year until the following July. The third pastor at "Black Oak" was the Rev. Louis J. Schwartz ("black"); he served from July, 1882, until December, 1887, when he accepted a call to Altamont, Ill.

In 1887 a new school was erected. In June, 1888, the congregation's fourth pastor was installed, namely, the Rev. Julius Bernhard Graupner of Broadlands, Ill. He served at "Black Oak" until the fall of 1898, when he accepted a call to Benson, Ill. In October of the same year the Rev. Charles H. Mueller of Champaign, Ill., assumed the pastorate. Presumably it was to him that the Mission Board, at the turn of the century, loaned seventy-five dollars, by way of exception ("ausnahmsweise"), for the purchase of a buggy to enable the pastor to serve the scattered Lutherans in that far-western part of the State. The horse soon kicked and demolished the vehicle. The pastor himself barely escaped with his life. Informed of the hectic experience, the Mission Board related the story at the Illinois District convention (1900). The delegates resolved that the debt be canceled. In the same report, Mount Carroll is referred to as "Daggett." Pastor Mueller served this congregation, known also as Trinity—its official name—until 1902. His successor, the Rev. C. H. Sommer of Leigh, Nebr., served for a similar period of time, about four years, until 1906, when he followed a call to Cayuga, Ill. The pastorate of his successor at "Black Oak," the Rev. Philip Sam. Estel of Nokomis, Ill., extended from October, 1906, until July, 1919, when advancing age compelled him to resign. The Rev. O. Johannes Buenger of Richland, Ill., was installed at "Black Oak" on September 21, 1919. In February, 1933, he resigned. His successor, the Rev. Lawrence C. Hoeppner,* was installed in May of the same year. After about four and one-half years at Trinity, Pastor Hoeppner followed a call to Zion Congregation in Matteson, Ill., near the end of the Illinois Central Railroad's suburban lines. Then came Candidate Erwin Wiedbusch, March 27, 1938. After about four years, he, too, left for another place—Elizabeth, Ill.—about twenty miles northwest of Mount Carroll. The Rev. Lester M. Hiebert† was installed at "Black Oak" on July 12, 1942. He served here until November, 1945, when he accepted a call to Pecatonica, Ill. On November 4, 1945, his successor, the Rev. C. A. Noffke of Wilcox, Nebr., was installed.

Once more the Lutheran Trail stops to allow time for more reflection. It is the year 1860. Less than a century ago, in 1769, when the news of Chief Pontiac's death became known among the Indians, they demanded vengeance upon the Illini Indians. The war was on. Pontiac's three tribes, the Chippe-

*Candidate Hoeppner was ordained in St. John's Church, La Porte, Ind., May 21, 1933.

†Pastor Hieber is a son of the Rev. Emil Hieber, at Immanuel Church, at Cicero Avenue and the Sauk Trail (Skunks Grove).

was, Potawotomis, and Ottawas, arrayed against the Illini tribe. The latter's forces were concentrated at Blue Island and Wildwood. At the latter place (northeast of Blue Island) several important Indian trails converged, and this region was the scene of the first blood bath. Driven from Wildwood, the Illini retreated to Blue Island, where they struggled valiantly against overwhelming odds. However, they were driven from Blue Island to Joliet, and from Joliet to a promontory on the Illinois River, where Fort St. Louis once stood, and since the final defeat of the Illini Indians known as "Starved Rock."

The Trail now proceeds to a city located a few miles northwest of "Starved Rock"—a city named after one of Chief Pontiac's tribes, Ottawa, Ill. It was here that the two well-known characters in Illinois' history, Stephen A. Douglas and Abraham Lincoln, held their now famous debate, on August 21, 1860. Several months before, on May 18, "old rails were carried around in the streets of Chicago"—promoting Lincoln's nomination for the Presidency of the United States.

Prior to that time another man had gone to Ottawa a number of times, not to debate or to listen to a debate, but to preach the Gospel to a group of German immigrants who had settled in that village. The preacher was the Rev. Henry Wunder, pastor of First Saint Paul's in Chicago.[37]

24. Ottawa

In 1860 seventeen German families formed the nucleus of a Lutheran congregation in Ottawa.* They adopted the name Zion and called the Rev. Herman F. Fruechtenicht, assistant pastor at First Saint Paul's, Chicago, as their first pastor.

Although in its early infancy, the congregation had purchased two lots for six hundred dollars at the corner of Jefferson and Sycamore Streets, to which was added, soon afterward, another plot, thus extending the property to a half-

*1940 census: 16,005. The name comes from "adawe," meaning "to trade," "to buy," or "to sell." It was applied to the Indians of the Ottawa tribe because they were traders.

block frontage. No church was built for a considerable period of time. The county courthouse, the Mechanics' Hall, and other places served for worship. Later a modest church was erected for eight hundred dollars.

In 1875 Pastor Fruechtenicht accepted a call to Saint John's Congregation in Elgin, Ill. He was succeeded by the Rev. Herman Sieving of Egypt (Manito), Ill., who, in addition to serving Zion Congregation in Ottawa, also conducted services in Marseilles, Brookfield Township, and Morris. In this work he was assisted by two students of theology, A. Carl T. Ponitz (1876) and August Wilder (1877). On August 11, 1878, Candidate Theodore J. Biltz was ordained as assistant pastor. Soon afterwards, however (May 18, 1879), he was called to Morris, Ill., about thirty-five miles to the east. Shortly before Christmas, 1881, Zion's new church was dedicated. It cost $6,767.37. Pastor Sieving's resignation in 1885* brought the third resident pastor to Zion in Ottawa, the Rev. Ludwig von Schenk of Rockford and Pecatonica, Ill. During his pastorate a few refractory members had the locks on the church doors changed so that no services could be held. Pastor von Schenk left Ottawa early in 1890 for Van Meter, Iowa. In the spring of the same year the Rev. Frederick Lussky of Sterling, Ill., became the fourth pastor of Zion. He was instrumental in organizing congregations at Deer Park and Ransom. He also ministered to the needs of struggling Trinity Congregation in Marseilles, about seven miles east of Ottawa.

In 1895 the congregation "finally had lived down its prejudices against the Synod and joined the Missouri Synod." Zion evidently did not know that "in its relation to the individual congregation Synod is an advisory body" and that Synod "has no right to tell a congregation what to do in its internal affairs, whom to call as pastor or as teacher." It is frequently a question as to the real nature of "prejudice." To

*On Aug. 2, 1885, installed at Trinity, York Center. Chap. 41.)

persuade the congregation to become a member of the Missouri Synod seems to have been a task of unusual proportion —it required just forty-five years to bring about this change of heart. During World War II one of our Lutheran chaplains, Ernest E. Heuer at Fort Belvoir, Va., asked the lone Chinese soldier in a new group: "Are you Protestant, Catholic, Mohammedan, or Confucian?" The Chinese promptly replied: "No; I'm from the Missouri Synod!" The young man, Everett Gum, was a member of the Missouri Synod's "True Light Mission" in New York City's "Chinatown."

The first services in the English language in Zion Church, Ottawa, were held on Reformation Day, October 31, 1914. "Fifty-four years of preaching in German exclusively!" World War I "merely gave added impetus to a process which had been in operation for many years."

Pastor Lussky resigned in 1917, "uncheered, unbewept, and unenvied by the world, but gratefully respected by his faithful followers." His successor was the Rev. John Theodore Mueller from Hubbell, Mich. Although World War I was still raging fiercely at that time and dark clouds were hanging low, interest was aroused in a project that was to cost twenty-eight thousand dollars—Zion Memorial Hall. The building was dedicated in 1919. In 1920 Pastor Mueller accepted a professorship at Concordia Seminary, St. Louis, Mo. In the same year the Rev. Horace H. Hartman became Zion's sixth pastor. He served until 1928, when he accepted the position of missionary at large of the Northern Illinois District. The seventh pastor was the Rev. Hugo Oldsen of Hubbard, Iowa. His installation took place on April 29, 1928. Pastor Oldsen graduated from the Teachers' Seminary, Addison, in 1906, and served as schoolteacher* until 1924, when he passed a colloquium and entered the pastoral profession.

Teachers who have served in Zion School: K. Schmidt, Stu-

*At Wisconsin Rapids, Wis.; St. Paul's, Addison, Ill.; and Zion, Hinsdale, Ill.

dents E. Becker and Joseph Riedel, Paul H. Groenke, and Mrs. P. H. Groenke.[38] The day school was closed in 1947—"because of the prevailing acute teacher shortage" (Cf. *Northern Illinois Messenger*, LXVI, No. 21).

25. Dunton

Following a road which runs diagonally through La Salle and Kendall Counties in the direction of Chicago, the Trail leads to Naperville in Du Page County. Thence the road map: Washington Street, one mile north to Ogden Avenue;* east on Ogden to Naperville Road, to Summit Street, to Roosevelt Road; on Roosevelt Road one mile east; then north on Lombard Road, curving toward the east and north through Glen Ellyn; remaining on Glen Ellyn Road for five miles, it comes to the old Indian trail, Lake Street; east on Lake Street to Swift Road; north to Itasca Road, through the village of Itasca, finally picking up the Arlington Heights Road. How easy is the way through this maze of roads, compared with the experiences of those pioneers less than a century ago!

Particularly interesting, at the moment, is this little village, Dunton—later known as Arlington Heights, Ill.† Musing on a store box over past experiences and the potentialities of the national and religious future in a changing world, one speculates how the evolution of "State and Church" will affect Dunton. The Civil War, of course, was still in the future. Dunton, in 1860, was a straggling community of less than a hundred inhabitants, comprising a few dwellings, two general stores, a hardware store, a blacksmith shop, and a hotel. (Lace, probably, was its counterpart.) Most of the villagers are German immigrants of Lutheran persuasion; but they have no pastor of their own and, of course, no church. Eventually they hear of the Lutheran congregation at Duncklees Grove and its

*Named in honor of Chicago's first mayor, William B. Ogden.
†1940 census: 5,668.

pastor, the Rev. August G. G. Francke. However, ten miles to that church was altogether too far! What about Saint John's Church at Elk Grove? That is seven miles away—still too far, and the roads are terribly bad! Well, if the mountain won't come to Mohammed, Mohammed will be brought to the mountain! The Duntonites asked the Rev. Carl Sallmann of Elk Grove to come and preach for them. But where? In the hotel or in one of the stores? Hardly! Along comes Jacob Sigwalt to offer his home for that purpose. And this was the scene of the first Lutheran worship service in Dunton (1858). In 1859 Pastor Sallmann was called to Independence, Ohio; and when the matter of his successor was considered, the group at Dunton expressed its desire to participate in the calling with the understanding that the new pastor would preach in Dunton every other Sunday in the forenoon. To this proposition, however, the Elk Grovers would not agree; instead, they recommended that the Duntonites organize their own congregation and call their own pastor, which was decided upon at a meeting on March 30, 1860,* but did not take effect till about seven years later. During the summer of 1860 a small frame church with three windows on the north and south sides and a seating capacity of about seventy was erected on South Evergreen Street in Dunton. The "pews" were made of rough boards, with no back rests. Occasionally a visiting clergyman conducted services. When none came, a member of the small parish took charge of the service and read a printed sermon. On November 21, 1860, the Rev. William Bartling began his ministry in the Elk Grove-Dunton parish, but terminated it within less than three years, on February 15, 1863, when he accepted a call to Springfield, Ill.† One week after Pastor Bartling's departure, viz., on February 22, Candidate Henry (Heinrich) Schmidt was installed as pastor of the dual parish.

*The date also of the organization of Saint Peter's Congregation.

†Pastor Bartling returned to northern Illinois in 1870 and became pastor of St. James Congregation in Chicago. In May, 1897, he resigned, and less than a year later he died (March 1, 1898).

Encouraged by him, the congregation at Dunton (Saint Peter's) opened its first day school in the fall of 1864. Henry Knickriem, a carpenter, was engaged to be the teacher. The rear room of a shoemaker's shop served as a classroom for the first year. Sixteen children were enrolled. In the fall of 1865 the school was transferred to the now vacant house of Jacob Sigwalt at the southwest corner of Vail and Sigwalt Streets, and Mr. Knickriem was replaced by Henry Rathe, a church member of advanced years. The first trained teacher, Gottlieb Kienzle, on June 10, 1866, took over the work and carried it on for a few months in the old primitive environments, until the congregation bought the church building formerly used by the Universalists, corner of Vail and St. James Streets, in October, 1866, for seventeen hundred dollars. In April, 1867, Saint Peter's Congregation became a member of the Missouri Synod. In February of the following year, 1868, Pastor Schmidt left the dual parish to accept a call to Immanuel Congregation in Dundee, Ill., fifteen miles to the west.

At a special meeting on December 29, 1867, the voters of Saint Peter's Congregation finally resolved to call a pastor of their own. The call was extended to the Rev. John Edmund Roeder,* a former missionary among the Indians in the Saginaw country in the State of Michigan, and more recently in Ontario, Canada. At the annual meeting, in January, 1868, his message of acceptance was read, and on April 22 he arrived with his family in Dunton.

When Mr. Kienzle was released from his responsibilities as teacher, because the congregation could no longer assume the financial obligation, the pastor at once volunteered to assume charge of the school. He taught until 1870, when the enroll-

*Sent to America in 1847 to study American marketing and business methods, John E. Roeder had come under the influence of the Rev. Theo. J. Brohm in New York City. Induced by him to study for the Gospel ministry, young Roeder attended the Missouri Synod's seminary (then located in Fort Wayne, Ind.) and upon graduating, in 1851, served for four years as missionary among the Chippewa Indians, as Missionary Auch's assistant, in Michigan. In 1855 he was called to serve congregations in Middleton and Rainham, Ontario, Canada.

ment had increased beyond his "capacity and control"—sixty-eight pupils. The congregation then engaged Emil Rudolph. When in April, 1872, Mr. Rudolph relinquished his position, Pastor Roeder again took over the school, until August, 1873, when C. G. Frederick Militzer, a graduate of the Teachers' Seminary, Addison, was installed. Two years later, on May 17, 1875, he married Augusta, daughter of Pastor Roeder.

At first Saint Peter's Congregation was somewhat reluctant to undertake a building program. But the need of providing more space for its growing membership was eventually recognized, and so, in April, 1881, it was resolved to build a brick church measuring 40 by 70 feet. The old plot of land was traded for three acres on the Northwest Highway. Thirty-three men, who at that meeting had agreed to the new venture, subscribed a total of $5,635. Eager to have a part in erecting their church, many members donated their services in the construction and hauled all the necessary building material to the building site. The new church was dedicated October 22, 1882. In spite of defections and unpleasant cases requiring church discipline, together with other sources of irritation, vexation, woes, and griefs, the congregation, both physically and sipritually, was in a healthy state of development.

In 1892 the Evangelical Lutheran Old Folks' Home ("Altenheim")* was established in Arlington Heights (Dunton).

Two years after the dedication of the new church (1884), Pastor Roeder reported a membership of 740 and an enrollment of 116 in the day school. In April, 1898, the pastor's health failed, and the Rev. J. H. Haake of Saint John's at Elk Grove had charge of the pastoral work in Arlington Heights. March, 1899, Rev. Roeder resigned. His successor, the Rev. Carl Moritz Noack, first mentioned when he was struggling with his first mission congregations in Dolton, Oak Glen, Hammond (Ind.), Hegewisch, Blue Island, and Harvey (see

*Recently renamed: Lutheran Home and Service for the Aged.

Chapter 16), was called from Sioux City, Iowa, and installed as Saint Peter's pastor in September, 1899. For some time he was assisted by his predecessor, Pastor Roeder, who also had charge of the spiritual care of the near-by Olk Folks' Home since its inception. Pastor Roeder died on February 21, 1902, and was buried in Saint Peter's Cemetery.

Ten years after Pastor Noack had assumed his pastoral duties in Arlington Heights, the number of individuals on his parish list had increased from 1,048 to 1,380. On September 3, 1899, a new four-room brick school building was dedicated, and by 1925 this building was "taxed" by an enrollment of 239 pupils. By erecting a recreation building in 1925, Saint Peter's felt that it had accommodated itself to the requirements of its youth—"the congregation of tomorrow."

The boom of 1924-1929 added a large number of desirable neighbors to Arlington Heights, including many Lutherans, chiefly from Chicago. These people and their children were accustomed, especially since the First World War, to having regular worship services in the English language. Beginning in January, 1921, one English service a month on a Sunday evening was held, with a sermon either read by Pastor Noack or preached by a visiting minister, frequently by the Rev. Erwin T. Umbach of the Walther League office in Chicago. After five years the arrangement was altered to the extent that on the third Sunday of each month an English service was held in the forenoon in place of the German service. The Rev. Andrew C. Landeck, who had resigned from the active ministry (in Pecatonica) in 1925 because of his health, was then placed in charge of the English preaching and the assisting also at the Communion services. In January, 1927, another change was made: So-called "double header" services (German and English) were arranged for the first and third Sundays of each month. On May 1, 1927, the Rev. Harry C. Fricke of Hinckley, Minn., was called as associate pastor, particularly for the purpose of exploring the missionary possibilities among the unchurched English-speaking residents. On October 16, 1927, was founded a Sunday school with fourteen pupils, and "double-header" services for every Sunday were instituted.

In October, 1943, Pastor Fricke was granted a leave of absence from Saint Peter's Congregation to enter the chaplaincy in the United States Army. The Rev. Luther V. Stephan, for some time "service pastor" employed by the Lutheran (Missouri Synod) Army and Navy Commission and prior to that, beginning 1931, pastor at Stillwater, Okla., was engaged to serve during Pastor Fricke's absence, which was expected to extend over one year. Upon his return from military service, Pastor Fricke was called to Faith Congregation in Clyde (Cicero), and the Rev. L. V. Stephan was installed as Saint Peter's pastor on August 26, 1945.

Pastor Noack died on February 23, 1944, at the age of eighty-six*

During the ten-month period from March through December, 1943, the pupils of Saint Peter's School (enrollment, 226) contributed a total of $748.22 for church purposes.†

A "daughter" congregation, organized on March 10, 1947, as Faith Congregation, has its center in the Scarsdale community south of Arlington Heights. (See Chapter 249.)

The following have taught in Saint Peter's School:

C. G. Frederick Militzer, 1873-1929
Miss Henriette Weinrich (later Mrs. Geffert), 1882-1891
Miss Hedwig Weinrich (later Mrs. Wm. Guenther), 1891-1899
Miss Hulda Noack (later Mrs. E. Meyer), 1901-1906
Carl Jensen, 1907-?
Rudolph Kranz, 1899-1939
William Hildebrandt, 1915
Herman C. Landeck, 1915-1944
William E. Dreyer, 1918-1920
Ottomar Kolb, Jr., 1920-
Theodore Preuss, 1928-1946
Karl Louis Busse, 1929-
Miss L. Glaesel (later Mrs. Pautsch), 1939-1944
Arnold Wm. Bathje, 1939-
Miss G. Dahm, 1942-1943
H. Eugene Burger, 1942-
Miss Ruth Wilkens, 1944
H. W. Adolph Obermann, 1944-

*During the 57 years of his ministry he delivered 2,964 sermons and never failed to preach on a single Sunday.

†Recently St. Peter's School was the beneficiary of a gift of $5,000 from John Henricks, a member of the congregation, which has been designated for the purchase of educational equipment.

NOTE: Mr. and Mrs. Peter Hartmann on Oct. 6, 1947, observed their sixtieth wedding anniversary.

More recently: Mrs. P. Weinrich, Miss Marcella Rubis, Miss Judith Seltz, Miss Elda Halfpap, Elmer Arnst, E. W. Klammer, Luther Schwich, Lester Rush, and the Misses Ruth Going, Claire Highbarger, and Edna Lehenbauer.

26. Forest Park

From Dunton (Arlington Heights) the Trail dawdles back toward Chicago. At 7200 West it turns south on Harlem Avenue, continuing to an attractive sign on the west side of the avenue near Madison Street, reading "Forest Park."* How different this place in 1949 looks from what it did in 1860! Instead of mud roads and open fields, there are now excellent streets, avenues, and boulevards. There is a direct and constant flow of traffic to and from the Loop, especially on Jackson Boulevard, by means of the "L" (Elevated–Rapid Transit), and for the past several years a modern streetcar service. Furthermore, not only transportation, but even the name of the community has been changed from Harlem to Forest Park.

A group of about thirty persons back in 1860 banded together for worship in the afternoon of every other Sunday in a rented hall on what now is Lake Street, near Marion Street, in Kettlestring Grove (now Oak Park). Two Lutheran clergymen for about twelve years shared the work of conducting those services, the Rev. Carl A. Meyer of "Franzosenbusch" (Proviso) and the Rev. George M. Zucker of Yorkville, both coming a distance of about ten miles, on horseback or on foot, to what then was Harlem. In 1867 Saint John's Congregation was organized and within the same year its first church was erected at a total cost of $1,164.67 on the southwest corner of Franklin Street and Marengo Avenue. In 1872 Candidate F. M. Grosse of Macon City, Mo., a recent graduate of Concordia Seminary, St. Louis, Mo., became Saint John's first resident pastor. Two years previously (1870) a day school had been

*1940 census: 14,840.

founded. The first teacher was John Rademacher. In 1873 a new and larger church was erected; the old church was moved to the rear of the lot and used as a school. In 1887 a new school building was erected at Circle and Warren Avenues. In 1904 this building was enlarged. In 1927 more space had to be added, and in 1928 a branch school was opened at 1037 Marengo Avenue.

Pastor Grosse resigned in 1905,* and on July 9, 1905, the Rev. Marcus Edward Wagner of Decatur, Ill., was installed.

On May 3, 1914, the present imposing church building—a large Romanesque edifice, with a seating capacity of more than a thousand and costing sixty thousand dollars—was dedicated. The tower is 150 feet high and is surmounted with a spire ending in a ten-foot cross covered with gold leaf. The bell of the first church was donated to Trinity Congregation in Ardmore (now Villa Park) in 1913. The bell of the second church, erected in 1873, was recast and hung in the tower of the new edifice. In the late 1930's the designer and architect of the new church, Henry J. Schlacke, died. Shortly before his death he visited Saint John's Church with a group of distinguished architects and said: "This, though it was one of the least expensive, is the most beautiful job I ever did." The young people of Saint John's were granted permission to use the old church building as a desirable place for their meetings, parties, entertainments, recreation, and other social functions. In the night of April 26, 1916, this whole building suddenly stood in flames. The spire fell with a great crash. The fire department was powerless, for the conflagration was beyond control. The cause of the fire has not been definitely determined.

On September 1, 1929, the Rev. Alvin Wagner, a son of Pastor Marcus E. Wagner, was installed as assistant pastor of Saint John's.

In 1937 a number of families presented to Saint John's a

*Pastor Grosse died on Oct. 7, 1906.

memorial to their departed loved ones: a set of twenty-four chimes, whose tones are broadcast (periodically) from the tower in melodies of praise.

From the time of the dedication of the new church, in 1914, Saint John's membership has grown from 1,300 to more than 2,700 active communicants, and, including the children, the congregation now numbers nearly 4,000 members.

The chancel with its large mural and white Carrara marble altar, fashioned by craftsmen in northern Italy, where these marble quarries have been worked for about two thousand years and still are regarded as practically inexhaustible, is generally recognized as one of the most inspiring examples of the artist's skill. The mural is an exquisite reproduction of Coletti's *Ascension*. In 1946 new windows, made of imported antique cathedral glass and "fashioned with all the care and beauty of medieval art," were installed. In the same year, 1946, both pastors terminated their services in Forest Park. On May 26 Pastor Marcus E. Wagner* retired from the active ministry, but continued serving as institutional missionary in Chicago until spring, 1949. Pastor Alvin Wagner accepted a call to a newly opened mission field in the Panama Canal Zone.† "Long will we remember Sunday, May 26! Over eleven hundred people crowded the church, and every available space, even the chancel, was occupied. There were tears of sincere sadness in the eyes of the worshipers as they listened with devout attention to the last message of their beloved pastors. It was an unforgettable scene when the whole congregation, one by one, bade them farewell. Many a voice faltered, hands trembled, and tears spoke louder than words," according to Brunhilde Birkigt, secretary in the pastor's office (Saint John's). The Rev. Prof. Paul E. Kretzmann, D.D., formerly a member of the faculty of Concordia Seminary, St. Louis, Mo.,

*Pastor M. E. Wagner received the degree of Doctor of Divinity from Concordia Seminary, Springfield, Ill.

†In North Hollywood, Calif., since February, 1948.

was installed as Saint John's pastor on September 8, 1946. He served until June, 1948, when he resigned. His successor, the Rev. Erwin L. Paul of Milwaukee, Wis., was installed on December 5, 1948.

The following teachers have served in Saint John's School since 1870: John Rademacher, H. Chr. Nehrling, Edwin C. Grube, Henry C. Meier, Andrew F. G. Petersen, Albert G. Guemmer, Henry K. Moeller, A. E. Bruns, Christian W. Linsenmann, A. W. Lindemann, William E. Dreyer, Fred G. Meyer, Paul L. Schaefer, Emil M. Kirsch, Louis Lueker, Robert C. Reuter, Leo. H. Krumme, John Socha, Arvin Hahn, Miss M. Doederlein, Miss N. Steffenhagen, Gerhard Becker, Leo H. Krumme, A. W. Scheiwe, Miss M. Schoeberlein, Owen C. Wood, Mrs. A. Hahn, and Ernest Winter.

27. Dundee

Leaving Forest Park and returning to Harlem Avenue, then north with a left turn at Higgins Road, a mile from the Northwest Highway, and along Higgins Road to the Fox River, the Trail brings us to the eastern part of the village of Dundee, Ill.* Whether the Civil War had anything to do with the division of the village into two parts, nobody knows. But apropos of the Civil War, it should be remembered that 1862 was the year wherein the ironclad naval ships, the Confederate *Merrimac* and the Union *Monitor*, were engaged in a fight which resulted in a draw. Anyway, finding traces of early Lutheranism in this section of the great Prairie State (also known as the "Sucker State") is of immediate concern, and the search seems also to be ending in a draw, so far as determining the date or year is concerned when the first Lutheran congregation in Dundee was organized, more exactly, when the first German congregation became Lutheran in character and practice. Was it 1860, 1861, or 1862? It is advisable, there-

*1940 census: 5,005. Named after a village in New York State.

fore, to seek further into the past for information about the people, for, after all, it is people who are important! Well, here are some of the facts extricated from certain records in Dundee. German immigrants began to drift into this primitive village on the banks of the Fox River late in the 1840's. They knew little about doctrinal distinctions and less about proper church organization. But they felt a longing for the preaching of God's Word, and soon there were preachers offering their services. These were not Lutheran "soul seekers," but, obviously, they were chiefly interested in material compensation. The Dundeeans' experiences with preachers probably were similar to those of the little group which later organized the first Lutheran congregation in Chicago. (See Chapter Two.) The Missouri Synod had been in existence only a few years and did not have a sufficient supply of pastors to provide for the constantly increasing demand. Nevertheless, Lutheran pastors living at what in those days was considered a great distance reached out and tried to establish a church also in Dundee. Because they could not come regularly, it became quite easy for "religious tramps" or "ravening wolves in sheep's clothing" to take possession of the field and to scatter the sheep. Among the Lutheran pastors who began preaching here more or less regularly in 1854 was the Rev. J. Nick Volkert of Saint Peter's Congregation at Schaumburg, about eleven miles southeast of Dundee. (See Chapter Three.) Then, however, a "Mr. Adam" seemingly took over, and the eleventh paragraph of the congregation's constitution, drawn up by this man, reads thus: "The preacher shall be held to instruct the children of the members of the congregation in the usual elementary subjects, reading, writing, and arithmetic, as also the advanced pupils in the Christian religion four days a week." A year later this man was gone. "He was followed by a similar character named Serfling, and another named Bender or Binder. The latter was soon exposed as a drunkard and then also disappeared." A small portion of the flock possessed a "little better knowledge" of church polity and confessions. To these people it was quite evident that the men who had come to them were hirelings and did not preach God's Word. Steadfastly resisting all pressure to join the congregation, they kept themselves aloof, hoping that eventually the unsatisfactory situation would improve and that "Lutheran preaching would again be heard." Theirs was not an idle hope! On March 1, 1859, the Rev. Frederick W. Richmann became Pastor Volkert's successor at Saint Peter's, Schaumburg, and shortly afterward began to conduct services in Dundee. However, dark shadows once more gathered in the little village. Another man (named Schnell - "swift") appeared with pedantry and pretense to serve as the spiritual leader and adviser of these heretofore so often disappointed, misled, and, no doubt, by this time, utterly confused people. This man who "palmed himself off as a preacher" expressed the wish to serve the congregation for the same amount of money they had paid to "outsiders," with the understanding that he would derive an additional income from extraneous services during the week, as a painter. At night and on Sundays he would serve the congregation. Recognizing the advantages of such an arrangement, the congregation hired him for one year. "He," so the account goes on, "not only found time to do those things—he even found time to spend most evenings in the saloon." At his advent the "conservatives" had again stepped aside. He winced at the fact that these people so obstinately resisted his plea to join the congregation. Membership was an extremely simple matter: the applicant pledged a certain sum of money for the year and thus automatically became a member for that period of time; if he failed to pledge for the following year, out he was, just as automatically! At the end of the year the group saw fit to renew the compact. But the preacher could not complete it; after about six months he was exposed as a liar and a fraud." After his departure a committee sought out the Rev. William Bartling, pastor of Saint John's Congregation at Elk Grove—about twelve miles east of Dundee—to secure his services as pastor. He consented to supply the spiritual needs of the Dundeeans. Trouble of still another kind broke out in the "refashioned" congregation—this time from within. The immigrants from various parts of Germany had brought along hymnbooks used in their respective churches in the Old Country. There were eight or more different books, some Lutheran, others Reformed, still others Evangelical. Thus exceeding difficulty was encountered in the selection of hymns. One Sunday when he was prepared to preach on the doctrine of justification by grace through faith in Christ alone, the pastor paged through the books on his desk to find a suitable hymn. His selection was one in the Missouri Synod's hymnbook and included in the Hanoverian hymnbook, but not in the others. When the time had come to sing that particular hymn of "justification" ("Rechtfertigung"), he had regretfully to announce that the other books did not contain it. Consequently many people could not join in the singing. That was not a thing to be passed over lightly. Looking upon it as an open insult to all who happened to have hymnbooks which did not contain that "particular" hymn and who evidently were much displeased with the idea of "just sitting there" and listening to the others sing, men on that afternoon began to congregate near the church—also near the place where the pastor lodged. The more the shadows moved eastward, the larger the crowd grew; with the increasing crowd tempers increased, until what at first had been "sullen disapproval now became violent anger." "No one can say what might have developed had not the Lord sent an angel in the form of a Christian who approached the throng with the utmost calm and poise." Gaining their attention, he made the point that, in order to avoid trouble of a similar nature in the future, they must have identical hymnbooks. Proceeding cautiously, he suggested that, inasmuch as most of the people hailed from two different sections of the Old Country and, as was proper and commendable, had a very high regard for the hymnbook to which they were accustomed, the others, though they had an equally high regard for theirs, might be persuaded, for the sake of peace, to yield to the former, on the condition, however, that these—the majority—would sell enough hymnbooks to eliminate the difficulty facing the whole congregation. Immediately there was a "great calm." The people had heard a sensible argument! Inquiry, however, revealed that there were no hymnbooks to spare; hence, not a book could be sold or bought. Now what? Well, the "angel" had still another sensible suggestion; he would write to the Missouri Synod's publication house* in St. Louis, Mo., and try to get at wholesale price so many books as were required by the Dundeean Lutherans, provided, of course, those present would promise to buy the ordered books from him. This idea seemed good to the attentive listeners, and most of them ordered their hymnbooks then and there. Everybody was well pleased—especially the pastor. And, why not!? Not long after, the congregational singing did not leave much to be desired.

Early in 1863 Immanuel Congregation, now substantially augmented by several more Lutheran families from Germany, sought the advice of the Missouri Synod's officials† in the matter of calling a pastor. The officials recommended a recent graduate of Concordia Seminary, St. Louis, Mo., Candidate August Hermann Burkhardt. The young man was unanimously elected, and the official call ("Beruf") was extended to him. On July 26, 1863, the young candidate was ordained and installed by the Rev. August G. G. Francke, pastor of Zion at

*The St. Louis firm of Wiebusch was termed "synodical" in those years. Concordia Publishing House was founded in 1869.

†The Rev. Frederick C. D. Wyneken, at that time professor at Concordia College, Fort Wayne, Ind., and President of the Missouri Synod (the second—successor to Dr. C. F. W. Walther), 1850-1864.

Duncklees Grove, in the temporary place of worship, an old public school building on Van Buren Street. Construction of a church, 38x60 feet, of brick, was begun in the fall of the same year. The cornerstone was laid October 21, 1863; the building was roofed by 1864 and advanced so far that services could be held. However, it was not completed until spring of the following year, 1865. On June 4, 1865 (Pentecost Sunday), the church was dedicated as Immanuel Church. A schoolroom was provided in the church basement. In November, 1866, the engaging of a temporary teacher was authorized. A man named Baade consented to serve for $175 for the half year. He, however, introduced the "Reformed" catechism for religious instruction. Because Pastor Burkhardt then relieved the teacher of the teaching of religion, another critical situation faced the Dundeeans. The "grievously offended" teacher solicited the members' sympathy by convincingly telling them that the pastor was unbearably domineering and that they ought to see to it that the pastor be ousted. He soon called a special meeting for a test of strength, feeling sure that he would gain the victory. At this meeting he unexpectedly stripped off his cloak of piety and innocence; in fact, he was "exposed as a bigamist." Only half of his term had expired, so he filed suit against the congregation for the rest of the promised salary. Soon after he disappeared from the scene and was never again seen in Dundee. In 1867 Pastor Burkhardt accepted a call to Troy, Ill. His successor as the second pastor of Immanuel, the Rev. Henry Schmidt of Elk Grove, Ill., came in February, 1868. Louis Matterhausen taught school for a short while, and he, too, disappeared. The first "trained" teacher and organist, August Taebel, a graduate of the Teachers' Seminary at Addison, was installed on July 11, 1869. On September 12 it became known throughout Dundee and environs that Pastor Schmidt had received a call from Saint Peter's Congregation at Schaumburg, Ill., which he also accepted early in October.

After several futile attempts at securing a suitable successor, Immanuel Congregation called the Rev. J. H. C. Steege of Ida, Mich. He apparently found it very difficult to decide to accept, but eventually did decide to do so, with the understanding that he would arrive in Dundee shortly after Easter, 1870. During the long wait for the pastor-elect the teacher, Mr. Taebel, taught school, confirmation class, visited the sick and the dying, conducted services, and read sermons. About every three weeks one of the neighboring pastors came to perform official acts in Dundee. On May 1, 1870, Pastor Steege was installed as Immanuel's third pastor. On the following Pentecost Sunday, June 5, 1870, Pastor Steege, with persuasive eloquence, in a sermon on "That and Why an Orthodox Christian Congregation Ought to Affiliate Itself with an Orthodox Lutheran Synod," prevailed upon the members of Immanuel Congregation to pass a resolution to apply for membership with the Missouri Synod. When the chairman of the voters' assembly submitted the question, there was a solitary but very emphatic "No!"—all others voting in favor of the proposal. The man had not even troubled himself to the extent of listening to the sermon, knew nothing about the underlying reasons for the motion, had no arguments against joining the Missouri Synod nor against making application for joining that synod. Of one thing, though, he was absolutely sure; he was against it! And that was that.

Toward the close of the same year, 1870, an addition was built to the church: a vestry, 18x22 feet, to serve also as confirmation instruction room.

In the fall of 1871, when the news of the Great Fire in Chicago reached Dundee, the members of Immanuel Congregation, out of their own poverty, contributed five hundred dollars for the relief of their fellow Lutherans, most of whom were members of First Saint Paul's Congregation. (See Chapter Two.)

By the end of 1872 Immanuel's membership had increased to 1,150, of whom 185 were voting members.

In his researches the Rev. Edward H. H. Gade, Immanuel's sixth pastor, found that prior to 1871 Immanuel Congregation had an initiation fee ranging from six to ten dollars. Upon the plea of Pastor Steege, however, this provision was abolished.

The year 1873 ended with a loss of ninety-three members (including children and women): a number of families moved away; forty-five died during the epidemic, and not a few were removed by the "painful operation" of church discipline.

On September 14, 1873, Candidate Louis Selle was installed as teacher in the day school, and on October 10 the new school building, one block north of the church, was dedicated. About six months later Mr. Selle accepted a call to First Saint John's School in Chicago. Then for about eight months no teacher could be secured for Dundee. Finally, on November 29, 1874, William Kammann was installed as Mr. Selle's successor. In 1881 Immanuel Congregation purchased the Methodist church on Van Buren Street and converted it into a school. The enrollment at that time was 276. Miss Lange of St. Louis, Mo., was engaged as teacher; illness, however, soon forced her to quit teaching and again Pastor Steege had to serve in the schoolroom for about six months. Then Hicko Hicken,* who had recently immigrated from Germany, was engaged "on trial." Approved, he became a member of the teaching staff in Immanuel School. In 1883 Mr. Kammann accepted a call to the Lutheran Orphanage at Des Peres, Saint Louis County, Mo., and H. T. Bollmann succeeded him on August 12, 1883. He served as Immanuel's teacher for about forty years.†

At the close of 1885 the voting membership had increased to 325. In 1886 the repeatedly discussed plan of building a

*Hicko Hicken later studied theology, passed the required colloquium, and entered the ministry; for many years he was pastor of St. Paul's Congregation at Kouts, Ind. (founded in 1882). Retired on March 2, 1947, and moved to Chicago. He died on April 1, 1948; buried at Dundee.

†Teacher Bollmann died May 19, 1921.

larger church loomed larger than ever before. But for a time it seemed as though the congregation would be frightened away from the project. That came about somewhat after this manner. A certain man, pretending strong Lutheran tendencies, came to the members of Immanuel living in Carpentersville, a small community a short distance northwest of Dundee, with the proposal to serve as their pastor. The people reacted with: "Why should we go all the way to Dundee if we can have the same thing right at our door?" Sixteen voting members informed Immanuel that they and their families had severed their connection with Immanuel Congregation by joining the newly founded Evangelical church in Carpentersville. Other members soon followed. Despite this and other serious difficulties, however, a new church, 60 x 100 feet, including bells and an organ and costing about twenty-five thousand dollars, was erected by Immanuel Congregation. The dedication took place on March 20, 1887.

During the years 1884-1900 the following men served as teachers in Immanuel School: Petzold, Schlueter, and Laufer. The enrollment in 1898 was 302. Mr. August Taebel,* who had served as teacher since 1869, resigned in 1904, and in the same year Immanuel Congregation called a "second" pastor to assist Pastor Steege,† the Rev. Paul Doederlein of Marengo, Ill. He was installed in Immanuel Church by his father, the Rev. Ferdinand Doederlein, assistant pastor at Concordia Church, Chicago, on January 22, 1905. Mission work could now be carried on much more extensively and intensively than before. The congregation grew and flourished. In 1908 there were 394 voting members. In 1909 forty-two members, upon their own request, were released to organize a congregation on the west side of the Fox River, in West Dundee. That congregation was organized on December 5, 1909, and named Bethlehem. (See Chapter 170.)

*Teacher Taebel died on Oct. 9, 1911.
†Pastor Steege died in 1917.

In the early 1920's Pastor Doederlein's health became seriously impaired.* During that time the congregation was served by the Rev. Theodore L. Blanken (temporarily without a charge). Immanuel's fifth resident pastor was the Rev. Ernst A. Brauer of Roselle, Ill., who served from 1922 till 1929, when a nervous breakdown induced him to resign. During the ensuing vacancy the Rev. Edward Sylvester of Bethlehem Congregation in West Dundee was in charge also of Immanuel.

On March 2, 1930, the Rev. Edward Herman Henry Gade of Gaylord, Minn., was installed as Immanuel Congregation's sixth pastor. The Rev. Edmund Happel of Natoma, Kans., was installed as assistant pastor on June 8, 1947. The following persons have served as teachers in Immanuel School, Dundee, since 1900: Mr. Chr. Seidel, Miss E. Wendt, the Messrs. F. J. Himmler, J. Wagner, Bahnemen, O. Wachholz, A. E. Diesing, William Bornhoeft, L. C. Pozehl, K. F. Roemer, F. W. Weidman, Theo. Wachholz, and Mrs. F. W. Wiedman.

Sixty-nine years ago, on April 4, 1880, Charles Rahn and Sophie Oehmke were united in holy wedlock in Immanuel Church. . . . Later they moved to Crystal Lake, where Mr. Rahn opened a general merchandise store known as Schueneman & Rahn. Their pastor conducted the devotions on their 67th wedding anniversary; Mr. and Mrs. Rahn are 88 years old (1949), and both enjoy good health.[41]

28. Russells Grove

Cutting across the fields from Dundee in a northeasterly direction a distance of about thirteen miles, there is yet another grove in the great prairie: Russells Grove, Ill.† Switzerland is recalled by the name Zurich, which designates both a village and a lake, near which the Trail "locates" a settlement of German Lutherans mentioned by the folks at Elk Grove. Less than five miles southeast of this spot there is another

*Pastor Doederlein died on Aug. 8, 1922.
†Now known as Fairfield. 1940 census: 4,008.

place much talked about by the early settlers—Long Grove. In those days there was at Long Grove a congregation belonging to the Reformed Church, whose pastors served the German settlers in Russells Grove and vicinity as an affiliate. The place of worship was the public school building. Shortly after President Lincoln's "Emancipation Proclamation" had been issued (January 1, 1863), the pastor of this congregation, the Rev. Mr. Alberti, informed the people over there that, if they desired spiritual ministration, they would have to attend services in Long Grove. A different course, however, was decided upon. The group went to Elk Grove and petitioned the Rev. Henry Schmidt to assist them in solving a difficult problem. He complied with their request and conducted services for them until their own pastor, the Rev. Julius Friedrich of Huntington, Ind., was installed, June 22, 1864. Immediately after the congregation's organization as Saint Matthew's in 1863, a piece of property was purchased and the erection of a church building begun. Supporting the project financially were the Lutheran congregations: Saint Peter's at Schaumburg, Saint John's at Elk Grove, Saint Peter's in Dunton (Arlington Heights), Trinity (prior to 1858 known as Zion) at Crete, the congregation at Badenburg (?), and another in Indiana (Whitley County). The purchase of the property, church, and parsonage cost slightly more than twenty-eight hundred dollars. The church was dedicated on December 10, 1864. Saint Matthew's had joined the Missouri Synod on the day of its organization, which "took place during the time between June and October of the year 1863." In the summer of 1866 Pastor Friedrich accepted a call to Lancaster, Ohio.* His successor in Saint Matthew's pastorate was a ministerial candidate, C. Boese, who served for about a year. "Because of divers dissensions between him and a large portion of the congregation, he found it most advisable ('fuer das ratsamste'), since he be-

*Pastor Friedrich died in 1869 at the age of thirty-eight and was buried in St. Peter's Cemetery, Schaumburg.

lieved it impossible to continue his ministry in a blessed way ('da er doch nicht mehr segensreich wirken zu koennen glaubte'), to request his dismissal; which also was granted." During the ensuing vacancy of nine months the congregation was again served by the Rev. Henry Schmidt of Elk Grove.

During the first years of the congregation's existence, the day school, which had been opened with an enrollment of nineteen children, was conducted by Pastor Friedrich in a near-by dwelling. In 1868 a room for school purposes was added to the rear of the church building.

The third pastor of Saint Matthew's was the Rev. H. W. Wehrs of Dubuque, Iowa. He was installed on March 8, 1868, and served until 1879, when he accepted a call to Saint John's Congregation, six miles southwest of Northbrook, Ill. (See Chapter 93, p. 345.) Then came the Rev. Hermann Lossner of Saint Paul's Congregation, two miles northwest of Beecher, Ill. He was installed in Saint Matthew's Church on December 10, 1879. Frederick Zersen, born on a farm near Lake Zurich, was almost three years old at that time. Later he attended Saint Matthew's School. In 1907 he became pastor of Saint Luke's in Itasca, about fifteen miles south of his birthplace.

In 1887 a new school accommodating a hundred pupils was erected near the church. Two years later, in the spring of 1889, Pastor Lossner followed a call to Fergus Falls, Minn., and on the following 7th of July the Rev. H. W. Castens of Zion Congregation in Wheatland Township, about five miles northeast of Plainfield, Ill., was installed as Saint Matthew's fifth pastor. From Plainfield to Fairfield! Heretofore the pastors had complete charge of the day school. In 1890, however, the congregation, well aware that, efficiently to conduct a school, men especially trained for the profession should be in charge, called a student attending Concordia Seminary in Springfield, Ill., to serve for one year. The young man, Louis A. R. Gresens, did very well; he then returned to complete his theological training at the seminary. From 1891 until 1893 Pastor Castens again assumed the extra burden. In 1893 Fred Herman Bunjes, a graduate of the Teachers' Seminary, Addison, was called. In 1899 he accepted a call to Worden, Ill. Thereupon Pastor Castens again undertook the teaching responsibilities and, assisted by his daughter, conducted school until 1911. At a meeting on January 2, 1911, the congregation called Henry Lotz of Chicago. In the following year Pastor Castens resigned after having served Saint Matthew's for about twenty-three years. His successor, the Rev. Henry Heise of Lohmann, Mo., was installed as the congregation's fifth pastor on July 7, 1912. In 1916 Mr. Lotz resigned and moved to Milwaukee, Wis. In the absence of an organist, Miss Ella Zersen (later, Mrs. Fenner) was engaged for this position. In the same year, 1916, a student attending Concordia Seminary, Springfield, Ill., H. W. Niewald, was engaged to serve for one year. Then, for several years, the following students served as teachers: A. Meyer, Alvin Hitzemann, P. Bretscher, and Kellermann. Albert Bierwagen, as student, served from December, 1923, till June, 1924; Student Reclau, 1924-1925; Albert Bierwagen, graduating from Concordia Teachers' Seminary in Seward, Nebr.,* was installed as permanent teacher on October 6, 1925.

In January, 1928, Pastor Heise, in the sixteenth year of his ministry at Saint Matthew's, accepted a call to a mission congregation in Waukegan, Ill., about sixteen miles northeast of Fairfield. His successor, the Rev. Arthur C. Streufert of White Lake and Plankinton, S. Dak., was installed on May 20, 1928. After fourteen months as Saint Matthew's sixth pastor, Pastor Streufert in September, 1929, accepted a professorship at Concordia College, St. Paul, Minn. He was succeeded by the Rev. Paul G. Gerth of Bertrand, Nebr., who was installed as seventh pastor on November 10, 1929. In the spring of 1910 he and the teacher, Mr. Bierwagen, canvassed the village of Barring-

*The Missouri Synod's second teachers' college, founded in 1894.

ton, about six miles to the southwest, for the purpose of starting a mission. Two years later (1932) a congregation, another Saint Matthew's, was organized there. (See Chapter 217.)

In 1936 the Sunday evening (English) services were discontinued; instead, they were thenceforth held on Sunday morning. At the same time it was decided to conduct services in German on the first and the third Sunday of the month, three quarters of an hour before the English service.

Saint Matthew's Church, erected in 1864, was remodeled and redecorated in 1939. On December 20, 1942, this church was totally destroyed by a fire which was discovered shortly after the morning service (at about 12:45 P. M.). By 4.30 in the afternoon the building had burnt to its very foundation. The fire was attributed to defective wiring.

The cornerstone of the congregation's new church was laid on August 29, 1948. Constructed of Lannon stone with Bedford stone trim, the new church, 80 x 34, with a seating capacity of 222, was dedicated on July 3, 1949. The cost (exclusive of an organ and furniture) was $65,000.

29. Marseilles

Sixty-five miles in 1862 was a great distance "in any language." Eagerly acquitting itself of its whole obligation, the Lutheran Trail proceeds in a southwesterly direction from Lake Zurich and heads for a little village on the Illinois River, Marseilles,* in La Salle County. Lutheran mission work among the German immigrants who settled in and near Marseilles was begun in that year, 1862, by the Rev. Herman F. Fruechtenicht, first resident pastor of Zion Congregation in Ottawa, about eight miles west. Under his direction, Trinity Congregation was organized in Marseilles in the year 1866. From that time until 1883 the catechumens of Marseilles and vicinity were confirmed in Zion Church, Ottawa. The first confir-

*1940 census: 4,455. Named after the city in France.

mation ceremony in Trinity Church, Marseilles, took place on April 20, 1884.

In 1891 Trinity Congregation purchased the Methodist church at the northwest corner of Liberty and Washington Streets for $775. For nearly fifty years the worship services were conducted only in the German language. The first English services were held in 1914, and since the middle 1930's they have been held in this language exclusively. During the pastorate of the Rev. John Theodore Mueller, 1917-1920, most of the services were conducted in English, but in 1919 the congregation resolved to have fifteen-minute services twice a month in German. It was during his pastorate also that the old church was renovated and remodeled at a cost of about ten thousand dollars, and rededicated in September, 1919. In the summer of 1920 Pastor Mueller accepted a professorship at Concordia Seminary, St. Louis, Mo. The next resident pastor of Zion, Ottawa, was the Rev. Horace H. Hartman. After he had served Trinity, Marseilles, for about one year, the latter decided to call its own resident pastor. This was to be the Rev. Emil J. F. Richter of Elizabeth, Ill. He was installed in August, 1921, and served until January, 1923. The Rev. Frank A. P. Wittmer, formerly missionary on the Isle of Pines, Cuba, came in February, 1923, and served as Trinity's second resident pastor until January, 1926, when he accepted a call to the Rogers Park community on Chicago's North Side. During Pastor Wittmer's pastorate, German services were held once a month. The Rev. Louis H. J. Steinbach of Chicago began his pastorate in Marseilles in April, 1926, and remained for about nine years, resigning on account of ill health in April, 1935. During the ensuing vacancy the congregation was served by the Rev. Hugo Oldsen, pastor of Zion in Ottawa. In September, 1936, the Rev. Leonard E. Thalacker was called to serve the congregation on a temporary basis, but on June 7 of the following year he was formally inducted into this pastorate, which he held until May, 1939, when he accepted a call to Hinckley (Squaw Grove), Ill. The next pastor of Trinity was the Rev. Ernest Wenz, who served until the end of 1944, when he was placed in charge of a new mission in Clyde (South Cicero), Ill. Candidate Robert L. Rock, graduate of Concordia Seminary, St. Louis, Mo., was installed on September 2, 1945. In March, 1947, he accepted a call to Kaukauna, Wis. His successor, the Rev. E. L. Burgdorf of St. Charles, Ill., was installed on September 28, 1947.

Leaving the vicinity of "Starved Rock" and its atmosphere of Indian lore, the Trail now leads eastward along the Illinois-Michigan Canal and the Illinois River; at the confluence of the Kankakee and Des Plaines Rivers it winds its way to Joliet; and from Joliet makes a "bee-line" for Cummings Corner, a few miles west of the Illinois-Indiana State line.[42]

30. Cummings Corner

Marked on an old map of the Lutheran Trail is a spot called Cummings Corner. The spot is still there on modern maps, but the name is beyond the ken of the proverbial Oldest Inhabitant, for Cummings Corner has since become Oak Glen. However, this name is not on the map either, for this community, as the road signs on Torrence Avenue clearly indicate, is now included within the village of Lansing, Ill.* All that is left of "Oak Glen" is the name over the Grand Trunk Western Railroad station, on the United States post office, and on the 1949 ecclesiastical map—*The Lutheran Trail.*.

A Lutheran congregation was founded in Oak Glen (Cummings Corner) in 1864, and the first Lutheran services were conducted by the Rev. William Heinemann, pastor of Trinity (prior to 1858, Zion) Congregation at Crete, Ill., in an old frame building which stood on the corner of what now is Torrence and Indiana Avenues. Pastor Heinemann's immediate

*1940 census: Oak Glen, 298; Lansing, 4,462. Total: 4,760.

successor as the little flock's spiritual leader was the Rev. Konrad L. Moll, pastor of Saint Paul's Congregation in Dolton (1864-1866). After he had left Dolton (February, 1866), Saint Paul's Congregation in Dolton called the Rev. John Jacob Rauschert of Mount Clemens, Mich., who served Trinity at Cummings Corner (Oak Glen) as an affiliate until 1882, frequently walking through miles of mud and snow to serve his flock out there near the State line of Illinois and Indiana. Pastor Rauschert died in 1882 and is buried in the cemetery just west of Oak Glen on what now is known as Ridge Road.*

On July 30, 1882, Candidate Carl Moritz Noack became Saint Paul's pastor (Dolton) and simultaneously the shepherd of the Cummings Corner flock. He encountered a serious problem in connection with a proposed building program. The congregation was divided into two parts, even as the villages of Oak Glen and Lansing, a mile east, for many years were separate places. Trinity of Oak Glen and Saint John's of Lansing were the two separate entities. However, strange as it may seem, both congregations continued to be served by the same pastor until 1884, when they agreed that the time had come for both to call their own pastor, instead of being served as an affiliate of Saint Paul's (Dolton). Candidate Carl F. Dietz was installed as the first resident pastor of the dual parish (Oak Glen-Lansing). Five years later, 1889, Trinity Congregation (Oak Glen) dedicated its own new church buiding, on the south side of Indiana Avenue. Soon after its founding, Trinity Congregation made provision for a day school, with the pastor serving part-time as teacher. Bernhard Mohr served for one year, 1879-1880, and was succeeded by Miss Friedericka Rauschert.† In 1892 a ministerial student, E. Schmiege, assisted the pastor in the school. In the following year Paul Schaefer, a student at the Teachers' Seminary, Addison, served in that capacity. The first

*The western end of the Ridge Road is at the Illinois Central Railroad tracks—opposite Homewood Station (formerly known as Thornton Station).

†A daughter of Pastor Rauschert.

full-time teacher, John G. Kirsch, was installed in September, 1893. In July, 1895, Pastor Dietz accepted a call to Concordia Congregation, Chicago (Avondale community), and the Rev. Frederick Brunn, Sr.,* of Strasburg, Ill., soon afterward succeeded him as pastor of the dual parish, Trinity and Saint John's. He served in this capacity for the next thirty-one years. In 1896 a new school was erected in Oak Glen (Cummings Corner). In 1902 Mr. Kirsch followed a call to Trinity (prior to 1858 known as Zion) School at Crete, Ill., and Gustav Faster took his place in Oak Glen. Ill health forced the latter's resignation in 1911. Martin Hesemann, a student at the Teachers' Seminary, Addison, completed the school term. George P. A. Schmandt, who arrived in the summer of 1912, remained until the spring of 1914. In the summer of 1914 William Kraegel of Rochester, N.Y., was installed; he has been with that school for about thirty-three years.

The greatly increased need for religious work in the English language induced Trinity and Saint John's Congregations in 1924 to call an assistant pastor. The Rev. Herbert H. A. Harthun of Midland, Mich., was called. His installation took place in May, 1924. After the death of Pastor Brunn on May 27, 1927, at the age of seventy-one years, sweeping changes were made in the dual parish. Agreeing to become independent of each other, they proceeded to call pastors separately; Saint John's, Lansing, chose Pastor Harthun, while Trinity, Oak Glen, issued a call to the Rev. Alex W. C. Guebert of Bourbon, Mo. Pastor Guebert was installed on September 11, 1927. A Sunday school was founded in 1928. In April, 1941, Pastor Guebert followed a call to Saint Mark's Congregation, at West Twenty-third Street and California Avenue, Chicago. His successor in Oak Glen, Candidate Walter Theo. Rossnagel, was ordained and installed as Trinity's fourth pastor on June 29, 1941. In 1943 the day school with an enrollment of fifty-

*Pastor Brunn's first charge was St. John's Congregation in Town Jefferson—Mayfair—Chicago, November, 1876—November, 1881.

six pupils was becoming too large for one man; the building was remodeled into two rooms, and the classes were divided between Mr. Kraegel and Miss Alice Haar. After one year Miss Haar left, and Miss Florence Lorenz succeeded her.

From Duncklees Grove to Cummings Corner! From the early 1840's to the middle 1860's—from oxcart and spring wagons to buggies and carriages—from caravans and covered wagons to railroad trains and "palace cars"*—from horse thieves to the release of slaves! And "Father Dearborn's" family had increased to 169,353! The whole civilized world had learnt to know of Chicago as a city which had caught hold of its bootstraps and yanked recklessly—with frequent grunts and groans—to raise itself above the swamp and eventually to scrape the sky. Staggering contrasts in numerous respects! Probably most significant of all: the iron "trails"—"stretching over the continent in endless ramifications, like the skeleton of some mighty intelligence, as if the whole system were alive—a new creation of power and beneficence heralding and hailing a new strange and unheard-of civilization in the swift-coming future. . . . " Near the close of the period in which thirty Lutheran congregations affiliated with the Missouri Synod were visited, the movement of immigrants from Europe and the Eastern seaboard of the United States to the Western prairies was intermingled with the movement of uniformed men to save the Union. The signal for war was given by means of guns at Fort Sumter, at the entrance of Charleston Harbor, S.C., on April 13, 1861. On October 8, 1863, the following item appeared in the *Chicago Tribune*: "There is hardly a block in the city or a mercantile house that has not a representative in the Army. The taxes are the heaviest of all times. Yet there was never a year when as many buildings were erected, except perhaps 1856. Many blocks are built to last a century. Marble palaces and new residences everywhere. Rents

*George M. Pullman's model "palace car," named "The Pioneer," was finished in 1864, in the Pullman community, now part of Chicago—near the southern limits.

are still enormous. A frame building on Wabash Avenue which cost $1,500 rents for $600 a year. Dwellings two miles from the Courthouse are $25 and $30 a month. Mechanical labor is at a premium. The sidewalks of Chicago are still in awful condition."—But the Union was saved. The Civil War ended officially on April 10, 1865. The Missouri Synod had been in existence for almost eighteen years, and it, too, was making rapid strides forward. Its membership had grown from about four thousand to about seventy thousand.

"From Duncklees Grove to Cummings Corner." At this juncture history digresses momentarily from the Lutheran Trail in northern Illinois to pick up a pertinent item in the Saxon settlement in Perry County, Missouri, where the Rev. Gotthold Henry Loeber,* as pastor of Trinity Congregation (founded in 1839) at Altenburg, wrote the following thought-provoking greeting and declaration into his congregation's official chronicles: "Grace and peace in Christ Jesus, our eternal, merciful, and almighty Lord and Savior. Amen. With this greeting we greet you, beloved descendants, who probably at a later date, if the Day of Judgment should not intervene, will still be living in this region and will find the present record in the walls of our house of God. Naturally we know not who you will be, and we do but wish that you, together with us, the first settlers in this locality and the founders of this house of God, may avow the same faith and confession unto your salvation. But that you may know who we, your fathers and ancestors, were, whence we came, and upon what faith and confession we here in this land, by the grace of God, were bound together and built up, receive the following brief and trustworthy account.

"1. Both as a body and singly, without exception, we em-

*Pastor Loeber preached the first sermon at the convention in St. Paul's Church, Ohio Street and La Salle Street, Chicago, at the 10 A.M. service, Sunday, April 25, 1847. His text was John 16:16-23. He and the Rev. Wilhelm Sihler, Ph.D., constituted the first committee of the Missouri Synod which officially examined the theological candidates who applied for admission in Synod. Pastor Loeber died on Aug. 19, 1849; Dr. Sihler died on Oct. 27, 1885.

brace the faith of the Evangelical Lutheran Church, which Church in its source and profession is as old as the pure Gospel itself, but which in its name has been named after Dr. Martin Luther, the memorable, highly enlightened, and faithful servant of God, through whom the merciful God more than three hundred years ago, in the blessed work of the Reformation, again brought the pure Gospel to light out of the darkness of the terrible Papacy.

"We firmly believe and are sure that, just as God's Word will not perish, so also Luther's teaching will perish neither now nor ever in the future.

"But we live in most terrible times, times of ingratitude and unbelief, in which people no longer care to endure wholesome doctrine and have gone astray in almost all places. . . ."*

*The preceding document, written in German, was translated for the *Concordia Historical Institute Quarterly* by the Rev. V. C. Frank of Kansas City, Mo. In a prefatory note the Editor of the *Quarterly* "wishes to emphasize that this is merely a reproduction of an important original document."43

Part Three

From Cummings Corner to Sycamore

31. Chicago, First Trinity

At the beginning of the year 1864 it was reported that Chicago covered an area of twenty-four square miles, that it boasted 722 streets, and that it had a population of approximately two hundred thousand. A new skirt was advertised on the first page of the *Chicago Tribune* on November 17, 1864—"a great invention in hoop skirts—a duplex elliptic or double steel spring." And the closing weeks of that memorable year brought the news of Sherman's successful march across the South, from Atlanta to Savannah on the sea . . . hastening the end of the Civil War. President Lincoln's second inaugural, the converging of General Grant's forces on Richmond, and the swift surrender of General Lee . . . and the end of the war at last . . . these were the exciting events recorded in the spring of 1865. Said the great "Honest Abe" on that important occasion, March 4, 1865 (quoting in part): "On the occasion corresponding to this four years ago all thoughts were anxiously directed to an impending civil war. All dreaded it, all sought to avert it. . . . Neither party expected for the war the magnitude or the duration which it has already attained. . . . Fondly do we hope, fervently do we pray, that this mighty scourge of war may speedily pass away. . . . With malice toward none, with charity for all, with firmness in the right as God gives us to see the right, let us strive on to finish this work we are in, to bind up the nation's wounds, to care for him who shall have borne the battle and for his widow and his orphan, to do all which may achieve and cherish a just and lasting peace among ourselves and with all nations." The Civil War ended when General Lee surrendered to General Grant at Appomattox Courthouse, Va., on April 9—officially, on April 10, 1865. Four days later, in the evening of the fourteenth, Good Friday, the Chief Magistrate, Abraham Lincoln, was shot by an assassin in Ford's Theater, Washington, D.C., and at 7:22 A.M., April 15, President Lincoln died—"struck down by those whom he was lifting up."

On May 1, 1865, the funeral train bearing the body of Abraham Lincoln arrived in Chicago. "The casket was opened in the Court House and from 5 o'clock until midnight the people looked on the face of Lincoln." — " 'His countenance was somewhat discolored from the gunshot wound,' said the reporter, 'but exhibited a natural and lifelike appearance more as if slumbering than in the cold embrace of death.' "

Up to this time only two Missouri Synod congregations have been organized in Chicago: First Saint Paul's and First Immanuel.

It was in that year, 1865, which ended another very important period in American history, that the third Missouri Synod congregation in Chicago had its inception. In the fall of 1863 First Immanuel Congregation, supported by its new pastor, the Rev. John Paul Beyer, established a day school (branch) in a small rented building on Archer Avenue. And now, in May, 1865, eleven members of First Immanuel, convinced that the time had come to have regular church services in the Archer Avenue area, southeast of the "mother" congregation's center (since 1864 at Brown and Taylor Streets),* requested their release to organize their own congregation. The release having been granted, Pastor Beyer assisted these men in organizing Trinity Congregation. The first services were conducted in a private home; in the fall of the same year, 1865, the congregation purchased property, 100x125 feet, at Twenty-fifth Place and South Canal Streets, for one thousand dollars. The area then was referred to as "South Chicago"—the southern limits of the "Prairie City." Upon this property Trinity Congregation shortly afterward erected a one-story frame building, 24x50 feet, which was to serve as church and school. At a meeting on November 24, 1865, Trinity called its first pastor, the Rev. Ferdinand Doederlein of Jackson, Mo. The dedication of the new church and the installation of Pastor Doederlein took place on the same day, August 2, 1866.

During the first year of its existence, Trinity's membership rose from twelve to sixty. During the second year the building was reconstructed and a second story added. The lower floor then served as a schoolroom and the upper as a church auditorium. In June, 1867, a teacher-candidate, William Daniel Treide, was called to take charge of the day school. In the meantime a large portion of the membership had become centered in the Bridgeport community, about a mile southwest of Trinity's center and near the confluence of the South Branch and the South Fork of the South Branch of the Chicago River. Accordingly Trinity Congregation in the early part of 1868 purchased two lots on Farrell Street, near Archer Road, and erected a one-story frame school building on the site. Mr. Treide was transferred to this branch school, while a Mr. Baisch took charge of the "home" school. In April, 1869, he was succeeded in the latter school by a Mr. Diersen,

*Formerly located at Blue Island Avenue and Twelfth Street (now Roosevelt Road).

who, in turn, was assisted by a woman teacher for the lower grades.

On July 31, 1870, the congregation dedicated its new church on the original site. It had a 150-foot steeple in the front center.

In 1864 the Stock Yards were laid out "on paper," and "out beyond the southwestern limits of the city, four miles from the downtown section, the Yards were begun on a square mile of land whose level was two feet below the river." The formal opening took place on December 25, 1865. The residential area adjoining the Yards was known as the Hamburger district, which, having rapidly become the center of another large portion of Trinity's members, prompted the congregation, in the fall of 1871, to purchase two lots on Emerald Avenue, between Thirty-sixth and Thirty-seventh Streets. Shortly afterward a one-story frame school building was erected upon this property. On the day of dedication Caspar H. Nagel of Proviso ("Franzosenbusch") was installed as teacher of this branch school. In March, 1872, the woman teacher in the "home" school was replaced by a male teacher. In the same year the one-story school building on Farrell Street in Bridgeport was converted into a two-story building, and a Mr. Schmidt was placed in charge of the lower grades. At the end of 1873 Mr. Treide was called to Lancaster, Ohio, and A. Kaeppel succeeded him in the Bridgeport school. When Mr. Diersen left in 1876, Richard H. Treiber,* of Quincy, Ill., took charge of the "home" school. On May 3, 1876 (a Saturday), in the afternoon, the church steeple was blown down by a cyclone. In March, 1877, Pastor Doederlein accepted a call to Saint John's Congregation at Coopers Grove, Ill. His successor, the Rev. Louis Lochner of Richmond, Va.,† was installed

*Richard H. Treiber died on June 12, 1930. His wife, Caroline Sophie Tatge, daughter of Conrad Tatge—charter member of Saint John's, Eagle Lake, Ill., died March 15, 1947—ten days before her ninety-fourth birthday anniversary.

†Pastor Lochner's first charge was at Skunks Grove, Ill., 1864-1867.

as Trinity's pastor on August 26, 1877. In February, 1879, Mr. Kaeppel followed a call to Immanuel Congregation at Proviso ("Franzosenbusch"). Thereupon John Richter took charge of the Bridgeport branch school. In the fall of the same year teacher-candidate C. W. Schlueter was called to the same school as teacher in the lower grades.

In 1880 the establishing of still another branch school became necessary in a settlement in the vicinity of Forty-ninth Street and Loomis Avenue, a short distance southwest of the Hamburger community, where many of Trinity's members lived. Hence also there several lots were purchased, a school was built on the site, and the building dedicated on August 15, 1880. Mr. Schlueter was placed in charge of this branch school. From then on worship services were conducted in this building on alternate Sundays, together with "Christenlehre."

In 1882 Trinity Congregation called an assistant for its pastor, Candidate Fred C. Leeb, a recent graduate of Concordia Seminary, Springfield, Ill. In the summer of the same year, Trinity Congregation dedicated a new four-story brick school building at Arch and Lyman Streets and enlarged the Hamburger branch school to a two-story building, adding a woman teacher to the staff. Having outlived its usefulness, the old branch school on Farrell Street in Bridgeport was sold. Assistant Pastor Fred C. Leeb then began to teach in the branch school at Forty-ninth Street and Loomis Avenue, while Mr. Schlueter was transferred back to the Bridgeport branch school, where teacher-candidate August Breuer had served since August, 1880.

In the summer of 1881 the woman teacher in the "home" school was replaced by teacher-candidate J. G. J. Hillger. In 1886 Mr. Hillger followed a call to Milwaukee, Wis., and his successor was Herman Burmeister. In the following year, 1887, the condition of the branch school on Emerald Avenue (Hamburger) had become "steadily worse." Accordingly it was razed, and, instead, a two-story brick building was erected on Thirty-fifth Court, near Halsted Street. Mr. Breuer was transferred to the upper grades of this school and Mr. Nagel to the lower.

In the fall of 1882 the one-story school building in the Hamburger community was enlarged into a two-story building, and a woman teacher engaged for the second classroom.

In the summer of 1883 Trinity bought two more lots, this time on Wood Street, near Thirty-sixth, upon which was erected a one-story brick school building; the dedication took place in October, 1883. The first teacher here was William F. Diener. Here also services were conducted on alternate Sunday afternoons, combined with "Christenlehre."

In the fall of 1884 the congregation called teacher-candidate J. H. William Helmkamp for the third class in the Bridgeport school, and in March, 1884, William Kammann of Des Peres, Mo., for the fourth class in the same school.

First Trinity had as assistant pastors, jointly with First Zion: Gotthilf Simon Loeber (1884-1890) and August Lange (1890-1893).

In 1906 Trinity moved from West Twenty-fifth Place and Canal Street to West Thirty-first Street and Lowe Avenue. In March, 1910, the Rev. Arthur H. C. Both of Crown Point, Ind., succeeded Pastor Lochner, who died on November 9, 1909. During the depression in the early 1930's Trinity's day school was discontinued. The last teacher to serve here was George Duensing.

Trinity's branch schools developed into a number of flourishing congregations: the one at Forty-ninth and Loomis became Saint Martini Congregation (1884); the one in Bridgeport became Holy Cross (1886); the one in the Hamburger district became Saint Andrew's (1888). To which should be added the fact that a number of Lutheran families residing in the vicinity of Fortieth and State (Vincennes Trail) Streets, who for some time attended church services at Trinity as "guests" in September, 1871, organized Saint Peter's Congregation. Also, in the early 1930's many of Trinity's members were moving farther south in the city, into the neighborhood of West Seventy-ninth Street and Ashland Avenue, and Trinity Congregation took an active part in the establishing of a church there. Timothy Congregation was organized in 1935. (See Chapter 222, p. 588.) Trinity, the third* Missouri Synod congregation to be organized within the city limits between 1847 and 1865 and which thirty years after its founding had a communicant membership of almost twelve hundred, despite the substantial "releases" for separately functioning congregations, now (1949) has a little less than three hundred communicants.[44]

32. Plainfield

There is an almost straight road leading from Chicago toward the southwest, today (1949) well known as Route No. 66, or, locally, as Joliet Road. On this road at a spot about five miles this site of Plainfield,† in Will County, out there in the country where since 1887 some of the greatest plowing matches have been held (Wheatland Township), is a Lutheran church named Zion, whose beginning dates back to 1854. In 1854 the Rev. G. Liesmann of Naperville, eight miles north of Zion Church, began to conduct services for the "Wheatland" Lutherans in a public school building. His successors as workers in this mission field were Pastors Herman W. Querl and Ernst Buhre. In 1864 Robert Clow, a friend and neighbor, donated one acre of land for church-building purposes. On this site a Colonial-style church was erected. Jacob Fry donated the necessary stone from his own quarry, and his son, David, then twelve years old, assisted in the construction work. A devoted

*Inasmuch as subsequently other Lutheran congregations in Chicago were also named Trinity, this "third" Missouri Synod congregation henceforth will be referred to as First Trinity.

†1940 census: 1,485.

member of Zion all his life, David died on July 22, 1934. The church was dedicated on Christmas Day, 1864. Thereupon, Zion Congregation secured the services of the Rev. William Uffenbeck, pastor of Saint Matthew's Congregation in Lemont, about seven miles to the east and directly on the other side of the Des Plaines River. At the same time Zion Congregation joined the Missouri Synod.

On August 17, 1879, Candidate Frederick Henry Siebrandt was ordained and installed as Zion's first resident pastor. A school was established. In 1884 Pastor Siebrandt accepted a call to Spencer, Wis., and his successor, the Rev. H. W. Castens of Burton, Mo, was installed on July 20, 1884. A school building was erected in 1889, and in the same year Pastor Castens accepted a call to Saint Matthew's Congregation at Russells Grove (Fairfield), Ill. (From *Plain*field to *Fair*field!) On July 28, 1889, the Rev. Frederick Zagel of Van Wert, Ohio, became Zion's third pastor. He remained for five years and in 1894 followed a call to Effingham, Ill. The fourth pastor was the Rev. John Christian Kueffner of Coal City, Ill. He served until his death, October 20, 1911. From November 17, 1912, until October, 1921, the Rev. August Christlieb Carl Meyer, formerly pastor of Zion Congregation in Summit, Ill., served as Zion (Wheatland) Congregation's fifth pastor. He then followed a call to Elizabeth, Ill. On November 21, 1921, the Rev. Gustav H. Voss of Bingham, Mich., was installed as the sixth pastor of Zion. On January 9, 1927, he resigned and moved to North Aurora, Ill. In July of the same year the Rev. William Bramscher of Genoa, Ill., became the seventh pastor in Wheatland Township. It is to the "seventh pastor" that we are indebted for satisfying our curiosity concerning the name of a place in that vicinity which for some time was known as Tokio. He relates the story as he heard it: "About fifty years ago, before rural free delivery was instituted, the U.S. mail was sent to Plainfield; in the countryside there were little post offices. The farmer would get the mail for his neighborhood and bring it all out to his home; then the neighbors would come and get their mail from him. And so about a quarter of a mile north of my church there was such a little post office in a farm house, and the people called the place 'Tokio.' A certain farmer, William Clow, had a Japanese farmhand who was always talking about Tokio; so the people called the post office Tokio. Within a radius of about five miles there were five such little post offices: East Wheatland, Tokio, Hoddam, Copenhagen, and Tamarack. The two last-mentioned are still known by these names." The good preacher volunteered this additional information: "Plainfield is older than Chicago," and then submits this question: "Do you know that the lumber for the first house in Chicago was milled at a sawmill in Plainfield?" Was it for John Kinzie or for Jean Baptiste Point du Sable [the Negro]?

33. Beecher

Cutting diagonally across the prairie toward the southeast, a distance of thirty-five miles as the crow flies, the Trail approaches within a few miles the centers visited considerably aforetime: Crete, Black Walnut, Skunks Grove, etc. This place is known as Beecher, Ill.* Two miles northwest of the village is Saint Paul's Church, organized jointly with a day school in 1865. The edifice was dedicated, and the first pastor, the Rev. Hermann Lossner from the State of Missouri, was installed in the same year. For about fourteen years this first pastor served Saint Paul's Congregation. He also taught school until 1869, when J. Brackmann took charge, teaching until 1872; again the pastor served as teacher, until 1875, when Albert Dorn relieved him of these responsibilities. In November, 1879, Pastor Lossner accepted a call to Russells Grove (Fairfield), Ill., and on February 1, 1880, the second pastor, the Rev. Albert H. Brauer of Worden, Ill., was in-

*1940 census: 742.

stalled. His pastorate extended over a period of about thirty-five years.*

Schoolteachers in addition to those mentioned before were: Miss Katie Nuoffer, 1881-1888; Miss Marie Roecker, 1892-1894; Miss Emma Kruse, for a short time in 1894; William Joeckel, 1894-1904; Gustav L. Maschoff, 1904-1910; William George Bewie, 1910-1926.

Pastor Brauer died very suddenly on August 29, 1915. His successor in Saint Paul's pastorate was the Rev. Ernst George Herman Zucker of Lockport, Ill. After about seven years, in September, 1922, he resigned and moved to Fort Wayne, Ind. The fourth pastor was the Rev. E. A. Klaus,† who a short time before had resigned the superintendency of the orphanage at Addison. He served for only about three years and in the summer of 1926 moved to Wauwatosa, Wis., to become assistant superintendent of the Lutheran Children's Home. Candidate Paul J. Eickstaedt, the fifth shepherd of this flock, was ordained and installed on October 24, 1926, and remained with it for fifteen years. In 1943 he accepted a call to Gethsemane Congregation in Chicago. In 1927 George Leimer took charge of the day school and remained until 1936, when, probably owing to the economic depression, the school was closed. On March 14, 1943, the Rev. Henry F. Hoffmeyer of Sigel, Ill., became the sixth pastor of Saint Paul's—the congregation two miles northwest of Beecher.

34. Willow Springs

In 1839, when the Saxon Lutheran pilgrims arrived in the State of Missouri, a small group of Lutherans established homes in the vicinity of Willow Springs, Cook County, Ill.‡

*The oldest son of the Rev. Albert H. Brauer, Ernest A. Brauer, has been pastor at Roselle from 1917 to 1922, at Dundee from 1922 to 1929, and institutional missionary since 1930; at present he is prison chaplain at Joliet. Another son of the Rev. Albert H. Brauer, Arthur August Brauer, has been pastor of St. Paul's Congregation in Chicago Heights since June 27, 1926

†A daughter is the wife of the Rev. A. G. Merkens, Ph.D., Director of Christian Education, Northern Illinois District, since May, 1945.

‡1940 census: 948.

In 1851 an ex-teacher of the Reformed Church offered to take care of the spiritual needs of these people as well as of those residing in Downers Grove, about eight miles northwest of Willow Springs, and in Naperville, fifteen miles west. His offer was accepted. After one year, however, he was released. In 1852 the Rev. Ernst August Brauer, pastor of Zion Congregation at Duncklees Grove (Addison) visited the Lutherans in these parts and submitted plans whereby he thought he might be able to serve them as an affiliate congregation of Zion. The demands of his own parish, however, made it impossible to carry this plan into effect; so after but two services he counseled the Willow Springers to conduct services themselves and to have orthodox sermons read. This was done in the homes of members until 1853, when the Lutherans of Willow Springs and those of Downers Grove jointly called a pastor of the Missouri Synod, the Rev. Frederick Ottmann, formerly assistant pastor of a congregation in Cincinnati, Ohio. He was installed on September 4, 1853. In the spring of 1855 he followed a call to New Melle, Mo. During the next three years, 1855-1858, the dual parish was served by the Rev. Richard Riedel of Long Grove (Kendall County) and, beginning in the summer of 1856, by the Rev. J. A. F. W. Mueller, pastor of First Immanuel Congregation (1856-1863), and the Rev. Gotthilf Simon Loeber, assistant pastor for both First Saint Paul's and First Immanuel Congregations in Chicago.

When in November, 1858, Immanuel Congregation was organized at Proviso ("Franzosenbusch"), new hope was kindled in the hearts of the Lutherans in the Willow Springs community. Now they felt that, if and when the roads were passable, they could attend church services with the Provisoans—a little more than eight miles north of Willow Springs. After some time they petitioned the Provisoans to permit their pastor to serve the Willow Springs group as an affiliate of Immanuel. Accordingly the Rev. Carl A. Meyer conducted services and administered the Sacraments in private homes near Willow Springs. Two men of the latter community, Charles Mihm and Henry Boedecker, joined Immanuel Congregation in 1861, but continued their effort to organize a Lutheran congregation in or near Willow Springs. In 1865 the Rev. George M. Zucker, Pastor Meyer's successor in the Immanuel pastorate (Proviso), assisted the Willow Springers in organizing Trinity Congregation. In the same year the first church was built. The dedication took place on December 17, 1865.

George Bancroft, historian and American ambassador to England at the time of the Missouri Synod's founding (1847), made his famous oration before the Congress of the United States in Washington, D.C., on February 12, 1866. The oration began thus: "Senators, Representatives of America: That God rules in the affairs of men is as certain as any truth of physical science. On the great moving Power which is from the beginning hangs the world of the senses and the world of thought and action . . ."

Trinity Congregation's first resident pastor, the Rev. Theodore Mertens, a recent ministerial candidate ordained in Champaign, Ill., was installed at Willow Springs on March 18, 1866. Three years later, in January, 1869, he accepted a call to York Center, about a mile southeast of Lombard, Ill. During the ensuing vacancy, which lasted for more than a year, Pastor Zucker of Proviso again served at Willow Springs, preaching once every four weeks. Then, in May, 1870, the Rev. Herman W. Querl, assistant pastor at First Saint Paul's Congregation, Chicago, became Trinity's second resident pastor. In the following year, 1871, Trinity joined the Missouri Synod. In June, 1874, Pastor Querl followed a call to Toledo, Ohio. His successor was Candidate Carl A. Trautmann, graduate of Concordia Seminary, St. Louis, Mo. In 1881 a parsonage was erected. Hitherto the upper floor of the church had served as the pastor's residence. In October, 1882, Pastor Trautmann was called to a pastorate in Columbus, Ind. In January, 1883, the Rev. Frederick W. Brueggemann of Darmstadt, Ind., became the fourth resident pastor of Trinity at Willow Springs. During his pastorate the congregation called Gustav E. Brauer for its day school. He served until 1891, when he followed a call to Immanuel School at Skunks Grove (Sauk Trail and Cicero Avenue), near Richton, Ill. On May 17, 1892, Pastor Brueggemann died of tetanus.* The fifth pastor, the Rev. Hugo Schwarzkopf of Danvers, Ill., was installed at Willow Springs on August 7, 1892. During his pastorate five acres of land south of the original church property were purchased, and upon it was erected a new church costing $6,229.87. On August 5, 1903, Pastor Schwarzkopf was fatally injured in a streetcar accident in Detroit, Mich.

George Wambsganss and W. Schulz served as teachers in Trinity School from 1895 to 1900; W. H. Grosse, 1906-1908; and J. F. Wunderlich, 1910-1913. Pastor Schwarzkopf's successor at Willow Springs, the Rev. Herman Meyer of Ruma, Ill., was installed on November 8, 1903. In August, 1913, he accepted a call to Saint John's Congregation in Bellwood, Ill., about ten miles north of Willow Springs, and the Rev. Albert Henry Teyler,† then pastor in New Zealand in the South Pacific and president of the New Zealand District, Evangelical Lutheran Synod in Australia (organized in 1836),‡ was installed as Trinity's seventh pastor on February 15, 1914. During a violent electrical storm on June 9, 1915, the church was struck by lightning. At about 5:30 in the afternoon Henry Buege, a

*A son of Pastor Brueggemann, William, born at Willow Springs on the day after Christmas, 1885, in 1908 became a Lutheran (Missouri Synod) pastor and served in the State of Nebraska. In 1912 he married Lydia Noack, a daughter of the Rev. Carl Moritz Noack, pastor of St. Peter's Congregation in Arlington Heights, Ill., 1899-1944. A sister of Pastor William Brueggemann was married to the Rev. S. Daniel Poellot, pastor of Immanuel Congregation in Palatine, Ill., 1910-1940.

†A. H. Teyler hailed from St. Matthew's Congregation at Russells Grove (Fairfield), Ill. He began his ministry in 1900 at Anamoose, N. Dak. In 1904 he accepted a call to New Zealand.

‡The Australian Synod consists of five Districts.

member, noticed the flames shooting from the south end of the building. For several hours the fire raged within, and it was utterly impossible to save anything, and by seven o'clock nothing remained but a smoldering heap. The old building, erected in 1865, was then again used for worship services.

In November, 1924, Pastor Teyler accepted a call to Willow City, N. Dak. (From Willow Springs to Willow City!) During the ensuing vacancy of about one-half year's duration the Rev. William L. Kupsky, pastor of the near-by Saint John's Congregation at Lace, served Trinity. On June 7, 1925, the Rev. Herman Charles Schoenbeck of Norwood Township (now within Chicago's limits) became Trinity's eighth pastor. Shortly afterward Trinity's new church, its third one, was erected. The dedication took place on May 16, 1926. In 1935 Pastor Schoenbeck resigned from the ministry. Candidate William L. Bartling, graduate of Concordia Seminary, St. Louis, Mo., became the congregation's ninth pastor on December 1, 1935. In the first meeting, shortly after his installation, Trinity resolved to build a new school, costing $5,500. Dedication took place on December 6, 1936. In August, 1941, Owen C. Wood of Tigerton, Wis., was installed as day school teacher. He remained until 1944 and then accepted a call to Saint John's School in Forest Park (Harlem), Ill. His successor in Willow Springs, Arthur B. Stoeckel, was installed in November of the same year. A change in the pastorate also had occurred: In July, 1944, Pastor Bartling accepted the call to the Church of the Apostles, a short distance north of Melrose Park, Ill., and Trinity's tenth pastor, the Rev. August L. Oltroge of Yuma, Colo., assumed the Willow Springs pastorate on September 3, 1944.[45] In May, 1948, Pastor Oltroge accepted a call to First Immanuel in Chicago, and on October 10, 1948, his successor in Willow Springs, the Rev. John H. Bohlmann of Altamont, Ill., was installed.

35. Squaw Grove

From Willow Springs, by way of Aurora, the Trail proceeds in the direction of Hinckley, Ill.*—a distance of about forty miles, thirteen miles west of the "dawning city." The first white settlers arrived in this region in 1834 and established their homes a short distance from the village of Hinckley. At that time Indians occupied much of that territory. When the white settlers arrived at this particular spot, the "braves" had gone on a hunting expedition, leaving the squaws behind; and 'tis said that it was from this circumstance that the settlement was named Squaw Grove. Just east of this place was a small grove which was called Papoose Grove. Squaw Grove—a delightful place, as most all the "groves" were a century ago. Comparing our mode of transportation with that of the pioneer days, one can visualize the difficulties confronting the Rev. Johannes Strieter when, on Good Friday in the year 1865, he traveled thither to conduct the first Lutheran service in Hartman's public school. Presumably he made that trip quite frequently while he served Saint Paul's Congregation in Aurora. Immanuel Congregation of Squaw Grove and the Lutheran group in Pierce Township (Pierceville) in 1868 jointly called the Rev. Karl Wuensch of State Center, Iowa. This first resident pastor was installed on November 29, 1868. During his pastorate, which lasted until September, 1872, the Pierceville group withdrew from the Lutheran communion and affiliated with the United Evangelical Church. Doubtless, a very logical procedure. "Truthful separation is far better than dishonest union," writes C. P. Krauth, "and two churches are happier and more kindly in their mutual relations when their differences are frankly confessed." And who will deny that "the Lutheran Church has been the ultimate spring of almost all the profound theological thought of mod-

*1940 census: 710.

ern times"? – "Even Calvinism, without it, would not have been. Calvin was saved, we might almost say created, by being first Lutheranized." Dr. William Arndt in 1940 made the solemn declaration that "Luther . . . is still the great Reformer of the Church, and the teachings brought before us in the Lutheran Confessions are still the hope of sinning, suffering, despairing, war-torn humanity." The very name "Lutherans" was not adopted by the free choice of those who were known by that name, but it was formally inflicted upon them in a bull published by Pope Leo X, on January 3, 1521.

In 1872, the year in which the Evangelical Lutheran Synodical Conference of North America* was organized in Milwaukee, Wis., Pastor Wuensch accepted a call to Trinity Congregation at Goodfarm in Grundy County, four miles northeast of Dwight, Ill. From 1872 to 1873 the Squaw Grove (Immanuel) congregation was again served as an affiliate of another Lutheran congregation, this time of Cross Congregation at Long Grove in Kendall County, three miles south of Yorkville, and served by its pastor, the Rev. J. F. William Hallerberg. In 1873 Immanuel's first church was erected and dedicated. After Pastor Hallerberg the Rev. J. Henry Doermann served in a similar "accommodating" manner during the year 1874. On November 8, 1874, the Rev. Henry Herman Norden† of Pebble Creek, Nebr., took over the Squaw Grove (Immanuel) pastorate, serving until September, 1887, when he accepted a call to Jarvis, Mo. His successor, the Rev. Gottlieb Schroeder of Oshkosh, Wis., was installed on January 8, 1888. During the same year Immanuel's first school was built. The pastor was the first teacher. Candidate Frederick Starke, graduate of

*A federation of synods, comprising at this time (1949) the Missouri Synod, the Joint Synod of Wisconsin, the Slovak Ev. Lutheran Synod of America, and the Norwegian Ev. Lutheran Synod.

†A son of Pastor Norden, Theodore Ludwig, was born at Squaw Grove on Sept. 3, 1879. A graduate of Concordia Seminary, Springfield, Ill., in 1907, he served in the Lutheran ministry until 1941, when he retired and moved to Fremont, Nebr. He died Aug. 20, 1946.

Concordia Seminary, Springfield, Ill., served as teacher until January 1, 1898, followed by William J. H. Buck on September 3, 1898. Mr. Buck left in August, 1901, which implies that the pastor again taught school.

A new church at Squaw Grove was dedicated on November 17, 1901. Relief for the pastor came on August 31, 1902, when teacher-candidate Christian F. Heine was installed. A call from Luzerne, Iowa, terminated Pastor Schroeder's pastorate at Immanuel on April 2, 1905. Approximately two months later, on June 18, the Rev. Frederick Kroeger of New Holland, Ill., was installed. On August 25, 1907, Mr. Heine was called to a school in Milwaukee, Wis., and shortly afterward was succeeded by Emil L. Marquardt. Two years later, in 1909, he also followed a call to Milwaukee.

In 1910 the congregation felt that the time had come to conduct services in the English language—that is, in addition to what they already had; so, once a month the pastor conducted an English service. Possibly on certain special occasions services were held in both German and English—only a conjecture, since specific information is lacking. On September 18, 1910, Mr. Heine resumed his work in the Lutheran school at Squaw Grove. He not only liked the place, but preferred it even to Milwaukee! He remained here till the fall of 1923 and then, nevertheless, went back to Milwaukee. In September, 1921, Pastor Kroeger* accepted a call to Richland, Ill. His successor at Squaw Grove (Immanuel), the Rev. Walter Burmeister of Saint John's Congregation near Lace, Ill., was installed on November 27, 1921. In 1922 two services were held on Sundays, the one in German and the other in English. On April 26, 1924, Henry Burmeister, a teacher formerly in Chicago, assumed charge of Immanuel School at Squaw Grove. Illness caused his resignation in December, 1927; Walter A. Meier of Palatine, Ill., became his successor on June 17, 1928.

*Pastor Kroeger died Jan. 20, 1943.

Less than two years later, on April 2, 1932, he likewise resigned. Herman E. Ellermann taught from August 21, 1932, until June 7, 1933.

Fire destroyed Immanuel's parsonage on February 22, 1929 (Washington's birthday). Ten years later, on March 17, 1939, Pastor Burmeister resigned from the active ministry because of ill health. The Rev. Herman Hagist,* who in the previous year had retired from the ministry at Elberfeld, Ind., and now as "pastor emeritus" was living in Aurora, took charge of the shepherdless flock at Squaw Grove until June 11, 1939, when the Rev. Leonard E. Thalacker of Marseilles, Ill., was installed as Immanuel's sixth resident pastor. In the same month the congregation joined the Missouri Synod. After Mr. Ellermann's resignation, caused by ill health, teacher-candidate F. E. Lietz was engaged to serve temporarily. Two other teachers served here for several years: Richard O. Krause and D. V. Stegemann.[46]

Teacher Walter F. Stahlke, formerly teacher in our Lutheran Mission in Nigeria, West Africa, was installed Aug. 14, 1949.

In May, 1947, Pastor Thalacker accepted a call to Deer Lodge, Mont., and on August 17, 1947, his successor, the Rev. Herbert Stelter of Sheboygan, Wis., was installed.

36. Long Grove

About thirteen miles southeast of Hinckley there is a delightful village named Yorkville,† in Kendall County. It is the year 1866, and it has just been reported that 'way down South ("in the land o' cotton") there is a movement against congressional reconstruction, referred to as the Ku Klux Klan, a secret society whose principal objective was to prevent the Negro from voting or holding political positions; it was likewise anti-Semitic and anti-Catholic. Furthermore, in Mexico

*Pastor H. Hagist died at Magnolia, Iowa, July 23, 1948.
†1940 census: 562.

Emperor Maximilian has relinquished his throne. But up here in Kendall County German settlers were quietly and peacefully going about their daily business and on Sundays gathered for Lutheran worship services, as they had been doing since they had come here in the course of the previous decade, except that during the four Civil War years they probably also patriotically participated in the great effort to save the Union. About one year after that war had officially ended, these Kendall County Lutherans, in 1866, organized as "Kreuz-Gemeinde" (Cross Congregation), under the leadership of the Rev. Johannes Strieter, pastor of Saint Paul's Congregation in Aurora. On a piece of "good earth," comprising two acres* and located about three miles south of Yorkville, a church building, 24x36x16 feet, was erected soon afterward. For fifteen years Cross Congregation, the first in Kendall County affiliated with the Missouri Synod, was served by pastors of the Missouri Synod.†

In lieu of specific information it may be assumed that this congregation originally went by a different name, perhaps until 1881, when a division was caused by the "Election and Predestination Controversy." It is known, however, that in December of that year, 1881, the group‡ which subscribed to the principles and doctrines of the Missouri Synod called a pastor of this synod, the Rev. John Rabe of Kansas City, Mo., and that this congregation, now known as Cross, in 1882 joined the Missouri Synod.

*This real estate was donated by William Kollmann.

†According to a report submitted at the ninth general convention of the Missouri Synod, October 14-24, 1857. "Pastor C. R. Riedel, formerly pastor of the Lutheran congregation at Long Grove, Kendall Co., Ill., was called as assistant pastor and schoolteacher to St. John's Congregation at Minden, Washington Co., Ill." He was installed in the latter place on the 22d Sunday after Trinity, 1856.

‡Charter members:

William Kollmann
Fred Hage
Ernest Ahrens
Fred Behrens
William Thanepohn
Henry Ahrens
William Freise
Charles Siebert
Henry Hotop
August Wilkening
Henry Wilkening
Christ. Kollmann
Fred Duhse
William Wollenweber
August Hage

In May, 1895, it was resolved to erect a new church building to accommodate approximately two hundred worshipers. The formal dedication followed on August 30, 1896. Pastor Rabe served as schoolteacher during his entire pastorate at Long Grove (Yorkville), thirty-eight and one-half years. After a brief illness of two days Pastor Rabe (for many years pronounced "Rah-beh") died on March 1, 1920. His successor, the Rev. Clamor Fuelling of Chicago,* was installed as Cross Congregation's second resident pastor on June 13, 1920. He also taught school until 1925, when E. J. Dreyer, a student at Concordia Seminary, Springfield, Ill., took charge and taught for one year. At that time the grade system was introduced in Cross School. During the following three years the school was in charge of these students of theology: Theodore Schroeder, 1926-1927; W. E. Heddrich, 1927-1928; and J. Schlichting, 1928-1929.

On Palm Sunday, March 24, 1929, while addressing the confirmation class and, no doubt, encouraging his hearers to be "faithful unto death" (Rev. 2:10), Pastor Fuelling suddenly collapsed; however, he was able, though with great difficulty, to conclude the service. Escorted to his home near by, he lay down in bed. Three weeks later, on April 13, 1929, he died at the age of thirty-two. Two weeks after Pastor Fuelling's death Cross Congregation extended a call to the Rev. Reinhold H. Bekemeier of Berkley, Mich. He was installed on July 7, 1929. In April, 1929, teacher-candidate James Strayer, graduate of Concordia Teachers College, River Forest, was called to serve in Cross School. In 1941 he was succeeded by Floyd H. Rogner; and he, in turn, by Otto C. Tinner, in 1943, who remained here until 1945. Then came G. F. Klammer. In 1931 a new two-room school was erected. "The remodeled and enlarged Cross Church . . . was rededicated on April 18 (1948). . . . The tower was moved up, adding nine feet to the length

*Pastor Clamor Fuelling was a son of the Rev. Martin Fuelling, pastor of Emmaus Congregation, Chicago, 1888-1940.

of the nave and increasing the seating capacity. This, in addition to the enlarged balcony, provides seating accommodations for 275. The chancel was rebuilt, ceilings and walls were covered with nuwood. New chancel furniture, tile floor coverings, lighting fixtures, and organ chimes were installed. The cost of the project was $40,000 plus the many hours of labor donated by members of the congregation. . . . One charter member, Mr. August Hage, Sr., aged 94, was privileged to attend the rededication services."—(*Northern Illinois Messenger*, *Lutheran Witness* LXVII, 11.) "The Parent-Teachers Association of Cross Congregation . . . has solved* the problem of transporting its children to school by purchasing a used panel truck and converting it into a school bus"—accommodating forty passengers. "Fifty-two shares of $25 each, sold to members . . . paid the initial cost. Fares which are being collected pay the running expenses, and the surplus will be returned to the investors. . . . The pastor . . . and the teacher . . . share the responsibilities as drivers of the bus." But now to return to the "overgrown country town" on Lake Michigan.[47]

37. Chicago, First Saint John's

Western Avenue—three miles from the lake, whose name is derived from "Mit-chaw-sa-gie-gan," meaning "great water"—was the western city limits of Chicago, which then had a population of over 160,000. The northern limits were Fullerton Avenue, and the southern, Thirty-ninth Street. Behold the many improvements made since First Saint Paul's Congregation in 1863 established a branch school at 842 Noble Street, near Chicago Avenue, two blocks east of Ashland Avenue! The water tower, a crib in the lake, and a water tunnel to provide better drinking water for the rapidly developing "infant prodigy of the West." Christian Luecke, the teacher whom

*In 1945.

Saint Paul's Congregation in 1863 placed in charge of the branch school "away out there" in the northwestern section of Chicago, writes: "We were surrounded by 'Welschkorn' (maize), and I reluctantly unpacked my trunks at the thought of living in this wilderness." ("Es wuchs noch Welschkorn rings um uns, und zoegernd packte ich meinen Koffer aus, denn ich sollte in dieser Wildnis wohnen.") Every Thursday evening, until the fall of 1864, the Rev. Henry Wunder, pastor of First Saint Paul's, preached in this branch school. Gradually the little schoolhouse became surrounded by residences, many of which were occupied by German Lutherans. In the 1860 census of Chicago the number of "German-born represented more than twenty per cent of the total population. In the next ten years the German-born group more than doubled, but their percentage of the total population decreased." Beginning in November, 1864, Saint Paul's assistant pastor, the Rev. Traugott Johannes Grosse, conducted the weekday services there; but already in the following year the responsibilities had increased to such an extent that the "mother" congregation provided a residence for him in the very productive mission field—no longer merely a cornfield! From January until August, 1865, services were held on Sunday mornings in addition to those on Thursday evenings.* In the same year the school was divided into two classes, and Karl Koebel became Mr. Luecke's colleague in this school.

In December, 1866, the matter of organizing a congregation in the "cornfield" was broached; but nothing came of it. Instead, the decision was reached to conduct a voters' meeting in the Noble Street school every third Sunday in the month for the purpose of discussing doctrinal matters only. However, at the very first of the proposed meetings it became very evident that the desire to organize a separate congregation was stronger

*Discontinued in August, 1865.

than at first seemed. On March 3, 1867, several members decided to request their release from First Saint Paul's Congregation and forthwith prepared a list of additional names. But reluctance on the part of many to sever their connection with the "mother" congregation augured disappointment and positive failure for the project. The original promoters, unwilling to recognize the possibility of failing in their endeavor, became yet more persistent and, fully confident of their ability to succeed, again submitted their request for a peaceful release. The release was granted to sixteen men and their families. Four days later, on March 28, 1867, the new congregation was organized and named Saint John's.* One week later twenty-five more names were added to the record of organization. And four weeks after that the young congregation resolved to purchase real estate. Four lots at the corner of Bickerdike and West Superior Streets were purchased, and soon afterward a church was erected thereon. This first church of Saint John's was dedicated on October 13, 1867. During the month of August the old school building, which the new congregation purchased from First Saint Paul's for seven hundred dollars,† was moved from Noble Street to the congregation's "center" and placed beside the new church.

By the end of that year, 1867, Saint John's voting membership had increased to seventy-two. A complete constitution comprising eighteen paragraphs was adopted by Saint John's Congregation. A somewhat striking provision in that original constitution was that "the language in school and church is and shall remain for all future times only and exclusively Ger-

*Because other Lutheran congregations in the course of time adopted the same name, this first St. John's Congregation subsequently was called First St John's Ev. Lutheran. It is No. 4 of the Missouri Synod congregations organized in Chicago.

†First St. Paul's reduced the price from $800 (the amount first asked) to $700, "under the promise of always remaining true to God's Word and the Lutheran symbols, and charging St. Paul's children no higher tuition than their own." (First St. John's *Diamond Jubilee Booklet*—1867-1942).

man," which, however, was invalidated in 1925. (See Part One, page 5.)* The minutes of Saint John's voters' meetings are "replete with interesting and amusing discussion of details. Voters' meetings seemed to be about the only diversion, and our members made the most of them. The minutes offer no clue why the location south of Chicago Avenue was better, but Mr. Luecke's son, Paul,† remembered that the pupils of our St. John's School and those of St. Boniface, across the street, did not always live up to the principle of mild and loving St. John nor to the meaning of Boniface, i.e., 'well-doer.' They carried the idea of the Church Militant too far in their street brawls. In a particular melee when brickbats flew freely, Teacher Luecke, at the danger of bodily harm, grabbed a noisy ringleader from the other camp, locked him up in a closet, and after school handed him over to the priest."

In 1868 a branch school was opened by Saint John's Congregation at North Paulina Street, near Milwaukee Avenue, in the Holstein area, and Louis Appelt was called to teach there. In the following year the seating capacity in the church was doubled by means of a "Kreuzbau." A brick basement for school purposes was constructed under the church and a steeple above it, at a total cost of ten thousand dollars. The enlarged church was dedicated on October 2, 1869. Prior to that time, in August of the same year, a branch school‡ was established on leased property, a short distance toward the southwest, at the corner of Paulina and Fulton Streets. Albert F. W. Rose was called to teach in this school. In the same

*At about the time the State of Illinois was admitted to the Union, 1818, statements such as the following were put on record in congregational meetings: "As long as the grass grows green, and as long as water will not run uphill, this is to remain a German-speaking congregation." And again: "Even in Paradise the Lord spoke to Adam in German, for do we not read in the third chapter of Genesis: The Lord God called unto Adam and said unto him, 'Wo bist du?' " (Neve-Allbeck, *History of the Lutheran Church in America* (The Lutheran Literary Board, Burlington, Iowa, 1934), Third Revised Edition, p. 67f.

†Pastor of St. John's Congregation (Mayfair), Chicago, 1886-1944.

‡In 1875 this school building was moved to St. John's recently acquired property on Oakley Avenue, near Fulton Street. In 1888 the land and the building were donated to the newly organized Emmaus Congregation, whose first pastor was the Rev. Martin Fuelling.

year the "home" school (at Superior and Bickerdike Streets) had been increased to four classes, taught by four teachers: Christian Luecke, John P. Johnson, and Louis Steinbach; shortly afterward Miss Kluever was added to the staff, but resigned in October, 1870. A student, Abraham, then taught for eight months and then resumed his studies at the Teachers' Seminary, Addison.

In 1873 a third branch school was established at the corner of Wood and Cornelia Streets. In this two-story structure the first teachers were Christian Luecke and John P. Johnson. Increase in enrollment resulted in the erection of a two-story brick building next to the old frame building in 1884.

On October 3, 1875, Pastor Grosse accepted a professorship at the Teachers' Seminary at Addison, Ill., and on November 21 of the same year he was succeeded in First Saint John's pastorate by the Rev. Henry Succop of Sebringville, Ontario, Canada. On August 7, 1881, Professor J. Theodore Brohm of the Teachers' Seminary faculty (Addison) became Pastor Succop's assistant pastor. In 1883 a parsonage was erected at a cost of $4,390. This building was sold some years later to the Roman Catholics, who converted it into a nunnery. In the course of time, Pastor Succop became afflicted with a throat ailment, and when the report thereof reached the State of Iowa, "the Fort Dodge congregation called him, saying that if his throat were sore, he would not last long in Chicago, whereas in the pure air of Iowa he could recuperate and serve the Church much longer." He remained in Chicago, kept up a daily gargling with salt water, and lived another thirty-three years.

In 1890 a three-story school building was erected next to the church. It was here that for some time the first Lutherans of Slovak antecedents had their worship services, conducted by their pastor, the Rev. Ladislaus Boor. (See Chapter 127, page 425.)

"In 1901 Pastor Succop's health began to decline due to a

chronic stomach ailment, which he suspected was cancer. He was constantly under the care of a physician, who did not commit himself; but early in 1902 he promised the writer* he would recommend a long vacation to the patient upon his next visit. The congregation concurring, Pastor Succop, a near skeleton, in May left for Hamburg, Germany, to enter the famous Eppendorfer Sanatorium, where in Pavilion 42 he underwent a two months' 'solitary confinement.' He was not allowed to read or write, nor, he said jokingly, to think. He was completely cured of nothing more than a nervous stomach trouble. His characteristic humor never left him, and upon his return he had many comical stories to tell, e.g., of the streetcar conductor who at the end of the line made a remark in Low German about the two 'Amerikaner,' Pastor Succop and Deacon Wm. Streger, who went along. The conductor did not know that Pastor Succop always spoke to his mother in the language of Fritz Reuter. . . . In October, after six months, he returned to Chicago, hale and hearty, and lived another seventeen years."

In 1905 the church on Bickerdike and Superior Streets was sold, and First Saint John's Congregation moved its "center" to the southwest corner of Walton Street and North Hoyne Avenue, where its new church was dedicated on February 11, 1906, "an ideal winter day, bright and mild." The cost of the church, including the organ and equipment, was $45,641. Directly south of it a large new school was erected at a cost of $24,223, and opposite the church, a parsonage costing $6,765. The lots cost $10,000. The total investment amounted to $86,-630. The confidence of those original sixteen members was not misplaced! – "The church and the main school were now near the western end of the parish. All members lived to the east, many even east of Ashland Avenue." The branch school on Wood Street was retained for some time, with J. A. Kast-

*Pastor Succop's nephew and successor, the Rev. Paul Sauer, later spent seven weeks in the Black Forest of Switzerland and was also cured of a lingering cold.

ner, Nicholaus Lampe, and A. Rose in charge. The other four teachers, E. Mueller, P. Otto, Gustav Guettler, and Louis Selle, were in charge of the new school on Hoyne Avenue.

Soon after his graduation from Concordia Seminary, St. Louis, Mo., Candidate Paul Sauer was ordained and installed as assistant pastor of First Saint John's Congregation.* This took place on July 26, 1896. Upon Pastor Succop's resignation in 1919 the assistant became "first" pastor. Until this time, for a period of fifty-two years, the services of First Saint John's Congregation had been conducted exclusively in the German language. But now, in 1919, regular English preaching was begun, and a Sunday school was organized. For the next six years there were two English services each month; since 1925, services in both languages every Sunday morning.

In September, 1939, Candidate Raymond Fechner† was engaged to assist Pastor Sauer. He remained until November 15, 1942, when he accepted a call to Faith Congregation in Oaklawn, Ill. In the summer of 1946 Pastor Sauer retired after celebrating his fiftieth anniversary as pastor of First Saint John's. On September 8, 1946, his successor in this pastorate, the Rev. Carl E. Krog of Reinbeck, Iowa, was installed.

The largest day school enrollment in First Saint John's history was 935. From 1870‡ until 1906 there were always seven or more teachers, with a peak of ten in 1887. In 1940 the enrollment dropped to sixty-three. Owing to an influx of war workers from the country, the enrollment during the Second World War increased to more than one hundred.

On August 10, 1935, the church steeple was struck by lightning, and the tapering portion was destroyed by the ensuing fire; this was not replaced by a new one.

*The following clergymen have served as assistant pastors: John Heyer, G. Johannes, J. Th. Brohm, B. H. Succop, G. H. Loeber, Ed. Pardieck, Emil Zapf, Herman Sauer, Paul Sauer, and Raymond Fechner.

†A son of the Rev. W. G. Fechner, pastor of St. John's Congregation, six miles southwest of Northbrook, Ill.

‡After the critical years in the 1870's there was a tremendous influx of immigrants, particularly from Germany, which included large numbers of Lutherans.

A large percentage of the present membership resides west and northwest of the church's "center"—Hoyne and Walton. Fifty graduates of First Saint John's School thus far have entered the professional service of the Lutheran Church: thirty-three as pastors and seventeen as day school teachers. "Daughter" congregations are: First Bethlehem (originally a branch school on North Paulina Street, near Milwaukee Avenue; now at the southeast corner of North Paulina Street and Le Moyne Avenue); Emmaus (developed from the branch school on Oakley Avenue, near Fulton Street).

In addition to the teachers already mentioned, the following also served at First Saint John's School: August Schoeverling, L. Drews, William Schmidt, J. Lipps, H. Plesse, J. Doerr, Herman Schumacher, O. Vieweg, Walter Schriefer, Theodore Appelt, H. Boester, Herman Fickenscher, Clarence A. Kurth, O. W. Schultz, Delbert V. Stegmann, H. O. Bloch, Miss Thusnelda Ferber, Mrs. Bertha Janusch, Mrs. Margaret Ross, Mrs. Carl Weber.

38. Wheaton

During the year in which First Saint John's Congregation was organized in Chicago, 1867, there was considerable Lutheran activity about twenty-two miles west of Chicago's western limits (Western Avenue), in Du Page County, in and about a little village called Wheaton.* For some time prior to the year 1867 Lutheran services were conducted in a private home. Then, however, came the Rev. Prof. C. August T. Selle of the Teachers' Seminary, Addison, and gathered the Lutheran immigrants into a congregation and served them regularly until 1871. On Easter Sunday of that year (April 9) twenty-eight persons attended the Lord's Supper celebration. From 1871 to 1874 the Rev. George Bruegmann, pastor of Saint John's Congregation at Rodenberg, two miles west

*1940 census: 7,389. Named for Warren L. and Jesse Wheaton, first settlers.

of Roselle, served what now is known as Saint John's English Evangelical Lutheran Church at Wheaton, Ill. During the following six years this congregation was served by the pastors of neighboring congregations: the Rev. J. H. C. Steege of Dundee; the Rev. Herman F. Fruechtenicht of Elgin; the Rev. H. F. C. Grupe* of Chicago; the Rev. Henry Freese of Algonquin; the Rev. C. L. W. Wagner, assistant pastor at First Zion Congregation in Chicago; and Professors J. Theodore Brohm and Traugott Johannes Grosse of the Teachers' Seminary at Addison.

In the thirteenth year of its existence, Saint John's Congregation in Wheaton received its first resident pastor. On October 31, 1880 (Reformation Day), the Rev. Karl William Gerhard Koch (a native of Chicago) was installed. During his pastorate the congregation purchased a school building and converted it into a place of worship. A school and a parsonage were erected next to the church. In the fall of 1886 Pastor Koch accepted a call to Saint Matthew's Congregation in Lemont, Ill., and his successor in Wheaton, the Rev. John Heyer of Saint John's Congregation at Mayfair in Town Jefferson† (Chicago), was installed on October 24, 1886. He, however, remained only until 1888, when he followed a call to Winterrowd (Effingham County), Ill. Then L. August Heerboth, a recent graduate of Concordia Seminary, Springfield, Ill., came to Wheaton in the summer of 1888. On August 12, 1888, he was ordained and installed as Saint John's third resident pastor.

In its early years this parish included the communities of Winfield, Turner Junction (West Chicago), Glen Ellyn, and Lombard. Trinity Congregation in West Chicago was organized in 1884; Saint John's, Lombard, was organized in

*Grupe was born April 6, 1840, in Germany; he emigrated to America and settled in Chicago. He was confirmed by Pastor Henry Wunder in First Saint Paul's Church.

†In 1889 Town Jefferson, Lake View, Hyde Park, part of Cicero, and Town Lake were annexed to Chicago.

1893; Grace, in Glen Ellyn, was organized in 1909 as one of the first congregations in the Northern Illinois District territory affiliated with the English Synod, which, in 1911, joined the Missouri Synod as a non-territorial District. In recent years services have been conducted in a meetinghouse in Winfield, but as yet there is no organized congregation belonging to the Missouri Synod. In those "early years" handcars carried the pastors over the North Western Railroad to the various preaching places.

Pastor Heerboth retired from the active ministry in July, 1940.* His successor as Saint John's fourth resident pastor was Candidate Franz A. T. Frese,† a 1936 graduate of Concordia Seminary, St. Louis, Mo. He served until the Lutheran Army and Navy Commission (Missouri Synod) in 1943 called him into its far-flung activity as service pastor. On January 27, 1944, the Rev. Harold H. Tessmann of Raleigh, N.C., was installed as Saint John's fifth resident pastor. In the same year the congregation, anticipating a building need, purchased additional property adjoining the church. The congregation had become self-sustaining in October, 1942.

39. Dwight

It will be recalled that in 1859 the Lutheran Trail, while crossing Grundy County, met up with some "deitsche Leit" who, except for the astute salesmanship of the Rev. Henry Wunder, pastor of First Saint Paul's Congregation, Chicago, would have found their way to the Franconian (Bavarian) settlements in the Saginaw Valley of Michigan. It so happened, however, that these good "deutsche Leute" (German folk) settled at Goodfarm, about four miles north of Dwight.

*Pastor Heerboth received the honorary degree of Doctor of Divinity from Concordia Seminary, Springfield, Ill., on Sept. 7, 1944. A son, Martin L. Heerboth, graduate of Concordia Seminary, St. Louis, Mo., is a Lutheran pastor in St. Louis, Mo., serving in the correspondence department of the Lutheran Hour headquarters; a grandson, Paul H., is missionary in Japan.

†Pastor Franz A. T. Frese is a son of the Rev. F. J. T. Frese, pastor of Peace Congregation, Chicago, who died on Feb. 29, 1948.

Unfortunately the Lutherans in Dwight inform us that the records of their congregation, known as Emmanuel, were destroyed in the same fire in which Trinity Congregation "out there in the country" at Goodfarm lost its records and minutes of congregational meetings in August, 1884. However, a remnant of the Dwight congregation's early history has been gleaned from notes jotted down by the Rev. G. Frederick W. Westerkamp, Emmanuel's first resident pastor, 1893-1898. Emmanuel Congregation was organized in 1867 and at first was served by the Rev. Franz Schmidt, pastor of Trinity at Goodfarm. Worship services were conducted in private homes and, later, in public halls. A few months later the Rev. C. H. G. Schliepsiek, Pastor Schmidt's successor at Goodfarm, took charge of young Emmanuel Congregation in 1863; and in the same year a church, rather small, was erected in Dwight. In 1872 Pastor Schliepsiek resigned; shortly afterward, however, he resumed ministerial work at Cayuga and Chenoa, Ill. He continued to serve Emmanuel in Dwight as an affiliate of his two small congregations in the afore-mentioned villages, conducting services in Dwight once a month, until 1883. During the next nine years, 1884-1893, Emmanuel was again served as an affiliate of Trinity at Goodfarm by its pastor, the Rev. Carl W. R. Frederking. In the early part of 1893 the Sunday services were placed in charge of Prof. Reinhold Pieper of Concordia Seminary, Springfield, Ill., more than one hundred miles southwest of Dwight. He was assisted by a colleague, Prof. John Frederick Streckfuss. Occasionally the professors sent a seminary student to preach in Dwight. On March 19, 1893, Professor Pieper presided at the meeting at which a graduate of the class of 1893, G. Frederick William Westerkamp, was called as Emmanuel's first resident pastor. The ordination and installation took place on September 3, 1893, the Rev. Prof. Streckfuss officiating. When the problem of financing a church building faced Emmanuel Congregation, one of its members, G. M. Hahn, contributed one thousand dollars as a gift. In the fall of 1895 the new church was dedicated. It had a seating capacity of 250—far too large for the original flock. Alterations and renovations have been made since then; but the original church still stands. In January, 1898, Pastor Westerkamp accepted a call to Cleveland, Ohio. His successor, the Rev. Gustav Ernst Wockenfuss, served from January, 1898, until June, 1907. He, in turn, was succeeded in June, 1907, by the Rev. W. O. J. Kistemann of Pingree Grove, Ill. Seven years later, in June, 1914, Pastor Kistemann accepted a call to Hamler, Ohio. Emmanuel's fourth resident pastor, the Rev. Martin H. Mueller of Marena, Okla., was installed on August 23, 1914. The day school which was conducted in the early years of the congregation's existence was closed "for lack of interest."[49]

40. Sieden Prairie

Leaving Dwight and, by choice, passing through the Goodfarm community, the Trail now is headed in the direction of Chicago. A goodly portion of the great prairie is crossed, and, after covering approximately forty-five miles, the Trail arrives in a community or territory known as Sieden Prairie. And, speaking of prairies, it seems somewhat strange that so few communities in this great "Prairie State" have been named after their natural or accidental characteristics. There is a Prairie Du Rocher (with a population of 576—1940 census) in Illinois, but that's about thirty-five miles south of St. Louis, Mo. Another place northwest of Chicago, not far from Saint Matthew's Church of Lake Zurich fame, is known as Prairie View; also, there is a Prairie du Chien in Wisconsin, just north of the Illinois-Wisconsin line. Now, reckoning from Prairie View, Ill., forty-five miles directly south, via Cicero Avenue, there is another spot with "Prairie" as part of its title. Its approximate location is north of Butterfield Creek, on Vollmer Road, between Cicero and Harlem Avenues. The name? Sieden Prairie. How or where it got this name is not yet definitely determined. "Sieden" is a German word, meaning "to boil, to seethe, to stew, to make soap." A "Siedenhaus" may be a "salthouse" or a "boilinghouse." Do the local philologists know the real meaning of their "community"?

The early settlers in that part of the prairie—beginning probably in the 1840's—were ministered to by a succession of clergymen, including the following, whose Christian names could not be ascertained: Kies, Flott, Mayer, and Richter. The first Missouri Synod pastor serving this congregation, known as Saint Paul's of Sieden Prairie, was the Rev. Hans Christian Harmening. He was installed on November 24, 1867, and served Saint Paul's until October, 1869, when he followed a call to Dissen, Mo. His successor, the Rev. John Christian Friedrich Hartmann, was installed on February 6, 1870. In the fall of 1873 Pastor Hartmann accepted a call to Saint Paul's Congregation at Woodworth, Ill. On December 3, 1873, the Rev. Elias Hieber of Westville (and Otis), Ind., was installed in Sieden Prairie. He also served Immanuel Congregation "on the hill" about three miles southeast of Mokena, Ill.

All of the official records of Saint Paul's Congregation, together with the pastor's library, were destroyed during a violent storm in 1917. Hence historically interesting and valuable items are very scant.

Pastor Hieber retired from the ministry in 1926.* Saint Paul's fourth resident pastor was the Rev. Frank L. Treskow of Beemer, Nebr. In 1927 the congregation became a member of the Missouri Synod.

Pastor Treskow resigned in 1948. His successor, the Rev. John W. Peterson of Creighton, Nebr., was installed on August 29, 1948.

*Pastor Hieber died on Oct. 19, 1931. A son, Emil, has served as pastor of Immanuel Congregation, Sauk Trail and Cicero Avenue, near Richton, Ill. (Skunks Grove), since June 6, 1920.

41. Chicago, First Zion

Forsaking the unbroken monotony of the prairie, the Trail returns to inquire into the progress of the four Missouri Lutheran congregations in Chicago. To find answer to the query: "Has the tremendous growth of the city opened up further mission possibilities?" the Trail skirts the prairie on Johnson (now Peoria) Street, about a mile west of the business district, and on the southwest side, to Nineteenth Street. There it arrives at a spot previously visited in connection with the organization of First Immanuel Congregation at Twelfth Street, near Hoosier (now Blue Island) Avenue. In September, 1863, that congregation established a branch school in this community, actually on Mark Street, between Union and Halsted Streets, with Christian Weigle as teacher. Midweek services were conducted in the same building by the Rev. John Paul Beyer, "first" pastor of First Immanuel. In 1865 a four-room school was dedicated, and Frederick J. Schachameyer was assigned to that school. On September 23, 1865, it was reported that "a man attempting to cross Clark Street at Randolph was knocked down by the careless driver of a swill wagon." And it was pointed out that "such accidents were becoming frequent."

On December 20, 1867, the Rev. Anton Wagner of Collinsville, Ill., was installed as assistant to Pastor Beyer at First Immanuel, with the special assignment to serve this Mark Street mission, so that Mr. Schachameyer would resume his work at the main school.

On February 23, 1868, Zion Congregation was organized in this mission station. But how restricted! How can this (second) "granddaughter" of the First Saint Paul's grow and prosper—in the midst of such unfavorable conditions?! The growth —vertically (north and south)—was noteworthy; that of east and west—horizontally—comparatively insignificant, well-nigh pathetic—because of the industrialization of that area. In some years more members were released to sister congregations than were gained from them or other sources.

On the day after Zion's organization, February 24, 1868, something strange occurred in the nation's capital: "The House of Representatives by vote of 126 to 47 accepted a resolution 'That Andrew Johnson, President of the United States, be impeached of high crimes and misdemeanors.'" Ignoring the heat of summer, the Trail hurries to the month of September. What's this we read, on the very first day of the month which signifies "seventh" but actually is the ninth month? "Annihilation of time and space. . . . hailed with the dispatch of a letter from San Francisco to Chicago in ten days!"

On October 18, 1868, First Zion's first church was dedicated. Prior to this time the members worshiped jointly with First Immanuel Congregation as "guests." The pastors alternated preaching in mission places: Crown Point (Lake County Court House), Ind., Belvidere, Ill., and other places, with the result that each Sunday one of them was gone. In the same year the Rev. Anton Wagner, heretofore assistant pastor at First Immanuel, was installed as First Zion's "first" pastor. In 1886 the church was placed upon a stone foundation; its roof was slated, and the walls were brick-veneered. The entire front, together with the steeple, had been removed, and a new structure—including a steeple—built to provide more room for the growing congregation. Assisting the teachers in the flourishing day school was the Rev. C. L. W. Wagner, who served temporarily as assistant pastor at First Zion (summer, 1879-Easter, 1880). Every other Sunday he conducted services in Wheaton and Turner Junction (West Chicago), Ill. In 1880 this assistant pastor accepted a call to San Francisco, Calif. The Rev. Gotthilf Simon Loeber served as assistant pastor of Trinity and Zion simultaneously from 1884 until August 17, 1890, when he accepted a call to Wayside, Wis., where he died on March 31, 1891. Succeeding him in the same dual position was the Rev. A. Lange, from the fall of 1890 until September, 1893. Later, Professors J. Theo. Brohm and Frederick Lindemann of the Teachers' Seminary, Addison, served as assistants, until Candidate Frederick Knief was ordained and installed as assistant pastor in the summer of 1895.

In 1878 First Zion recognized the feasibility of dividing the parish into two school districts. Property was purchased at the corner of Loomis Street and Zion Place, and the two-story school building moved to the new site. In 1882 another two-story brick building was erected on the same site, and the frame building was converted into a teachers' residence.* Pastor Wagner retired in the spring of 1909.† His successor, the Rev. Adolph Kuring of Laurium, Mich., was installed on July 8, 1909.

The names of the following teachers are recorded without the corresponding years of service: Frederick A. Schachameyer, H. Timmermann, H. Riebling, George Wambsganss, J. Brackmann, Miss Bertha Lossau, Carl Backhaus, William Burhenn, Andreas Mueller, Herman Ruhland, Ernest Strieter, John F. Reuter, Henry Maschhoff, W. Kammrath, George Seitz, Ludwig H. Ilse, Fred F. Asmussen, A. F. Hintze, S. John Richter, Chr. Eckhardt, J. Meyer, Richard G. A. Bendick, W. T. Diener, Elmer Jackisch, Ernest Mueller, W. Rickmeyer, Albert Scheer, Chr. F. Scheer, and C. H. M. Wagner.

The names of some of the "sons of First Zion Congregation" appear at the bottom of this and the next page.‡

*In 1888 there were 915 children in Zion School; nine teachers taught school at that time.

†Pastor Anton Wagner died on Jan. 10, 1914.

‡Sons of First Zion, Chicago:

Paul Budach
Otto Burhenn
William Burhenn
William Broecker
C. H. Burmeister
William Dallmann
Paul Eickstaedt, Sr.
Karl J. Fricke
F. Forster
A. Grambauer
J. P. Graupner
Carl Huth
Frederick Israel
William Israel
Mr. Landeck
Frederick W. Mahnke

Pastor Kuring retired on July 27, 1942.* His successor, Candidate Carl G. Kruse, graduate of Concordia Seminary, St. Louis, Mo., was installed as First Zion's third resident pastor on September 20, 1942.

The prairie was converted into a busy section of Chicago! And First Zion's influence was felt far beyond all the prairies of the great Midwest. It would take us too far afield if we would include but a brief description of the work done by some of Zion's sons and daughters!—Broecker, Dallmann, Huth, Eickstaedt, Miessler, etc. One of these, the Rev. William Dallmann, D.D., saw Zion Church, 19th and Peoria, "go up; was confirmed in it; preached at the fiftieth anniversary (1918); preached at the seventy-fifth anniversay, October 17" (1943).[50]

42. York Center

Sometime during the decade 1840-1850 a young Lutheran, Henry Goltermann, came to the region about five miles south of Duncklees Grove. Soon after that other German immigrants settled in the same neighborhood and attended the services in Zion Church (Duncklees Grove—now Churchville), to the north. In 1860 the Duncklees Grove congregation recognized the desirability of establishing a school district at this place, which is located at what now is known as the intersection of Roosevelt and Meyers Roads, about one mile southeast of the "City of Lilacia" (lilacs), Lombard. The leaders in the undertaking were Friedrich Ahrens, Jobst Goltermann, Henry Goltermann, Ehler Ahrens, and Friedrich Meier. After the school building had been erected, Christian Weigle was placed

*Pastor Kuring died on July 1, 1948.

‡Sons of First Zion, Chicago:

Henry Kuring
Frederick Miessler
Louis Millies
Albert Menkens
Ed. Pautsch
Henry Prekel
Victor Richter
Frederick Schwandt
C. L. W. Wagner

in charge of the institution. A few years later he was succeeded by G. Grothmann. On June 15, 1868, twelve members of Zion (Duncklees Grove)* submitted four reasons for withdrawing from the "mother" congregation and organizing a congregation in their own community, York Center.† The voters of Zion, however, were not convinced by the reasons stated that the necessity of organizing a congregation at York Center was so apparent and urged the applicants for releases to call another teacher and to continue their membership with Zion. The request was repeated on October 13, 1868, by three representatives of Zion's members living in that part of the "mother's" school district. Although still unconvinced, Zion's voters, for the sake of maintaining peace ("um des Friedens willen") finally yielded and granted the releases. Before the end of that year Trinity Congregation was organized at York Center. The exact date is not known. On January 26, 1869, the Rev. Theodore Mertens of Trinity Congregation at Willow Springs, Ill., was installed as the first pastor. He remained but a short time; in July, 1871, he followed a call to Fort Dodge, Iowa. During those early years of Trinity's existence a defection occurred in its own midst; a group left and organized an "opposition" congregation. The "mother's" apprehensions had actually materialized ("die Befuerchtungen waren wirklich eingetroffen"). In 1871 another teacher, Mr. Kleinsteuber, was placed in charge of the day school. Pastor Mertens' successor in the Trinity pastorate, the Rev. George Theo. Gotsch of Akron, Ohio, was installed on August 2, 1872. In 1882 Mr. Steinkraus succeeded Mr. Kleinsteuber as teacher in

*Jobst Goltermann — Heinrich Goltermann
F. Goltermann — W. Goltermann
Ehler Ahrens — Friedrich Ahrens
Friedrich Meier — D. Schallau
H. Hogrefe — F. Schumacher
J. Ulhorn — H. Niemann

†1. The great distance to church; 2. the unwillingness on the part of the teachers to remain at York Center, for reasons included in "1"; 3. the granting of the opportunity to other German settlers in the York Center area to hear God's Word; and 4, guarding against the possibility of having a "united" ("unierte") church established at York Center.

Trinity School. After about two years he left, and J. G. Roecker took charge of the school in 1884. Pastor Gotsch served for twelve years; in 1884 he followed a call to a congregation in Indiana. Trinity's third pastor, the Rev. Herman Sieving of Ottawa, Ill., was installed on August 2, 1885. In 1891 two young men from the Teachers' Seminary, Addison, successively had charge of the school: Frederick W. Polinske and Henry Scheiderer.* On July 21, 1901, Pastor Sieving died of a heart attack, and his successor in the Trinity pastorate, the Rev. Henry Dannenfeldt of Woodstock, Ill., was installed on October 6, 1901.

In 1911 Albert Ortlip assumed his duties in Trinity School and served until 1914, when he was succeeded by Ed. Bunge. Religious instructions in the English language were begun in the school during 1918; in 1931 worship services in English once a month were introduced. Candidate Herbert A. Mueller was called in 1939 to assist Pastor Dannenfeldt and, particularly, to assume the steadily increasing "English work" in the parish. On January 29, 1940, Pastor Dannenfeldt retired from the ministry, and the assistant pastor was given full charge of the pastorate. In 1942 Elmer Becker was called as teacher of the day school. In August, 1943, Pastor Mueller accepted a call to Bethlehem Congregation in West Dundee, and on October 24, 1943, the Rev. A. H. Constien of Charleston, Ill., was installed as Trinity's sixth pastor. In September, 1949, Pastor Constien accepted a call to Holy Cross Congregation in (Bridgeport) Chicago.

Pastor Dannenfeldt died on June 13, 1945.[51]

The congregation's new school and parish hall was dedicated on August 24, 1947.

*Mr. Scheiderer discontinued his studies at the Addison Seminary, returned to his birthplace in Neuendettelsau (near Maryville, Ohio), and became a very successful farmer and dairyman. He was the youngest of twelve children of Casper Scheiderer, a charter member of St. John's Congregation (org. 1838). Three sisters and one brother, all in their 80's, still live there (1949)—one of them, Dorothea, this writer's mother. During the night of March 11, 1912, Henry was mysteriously killed in Columbus, Ohio.

43. Crown Point, Indiana

Several references have been made to the "Hoosier State," and since the Lutheran Trail is not confined solely to northern Illinois, there is ample justification slightly to deviate and proceed in a southeasterly direction, by way of "Franzosenbusch" (Proviso), "the Blue Island," Riverdale-Dolton, and Cummings Corner (Oak Glen), to the first town in Lake County, Indiana, to be surveyed and platted (in 1840), and originally called Lake County Court House—now well known as Crown Point, Ind.* It was there that several afore-mentioned Lutheran clergymen, who, besides serving congregations in northern Illinois, carried on mission activities "across the border." Among these was the Rev. W. Gustav Polack, pastor of Saint John's Congregation at Eagle Lake,† seven miles northeast of Beecher, Ill. In 1861 Pastor Polack, in response to Nicolaus Sauermann's urgent request, conducted the first Lutheran services in the latter's home in Crown Point, every two weeks, sometimes on Sunday afternoons and sometimes on Monday afternoons. Later on they were held in the Lake County courthouse. When in the spring of 1868 the aged pastor's health failed, the Rev. John Paul Beyer, pastor of First Immanuel Congregation in Chicago, was prevailed upon to assume charge of this mission in Crown Point. Soon afterward the organization of a congregation was effected. The precise date is August 8, 1868. About a year later, on August 28, 1869, Trinity Congregation dedicated its first church and on the same day witnessed the ordination and installation of its first resident pastor, Candidate C. F. W. Huge. His successor, in 1871, was the Rev. George Heintz of Mercer, Ohio. For almost twenty years Pastor Heintz served Trinity Congregation and, besides, carried on an extensive missionary campaign in northwestern Indiana. On July 4, 1911, he died at

*1940 census: 4,643.
†Pastor Polack served St. John's, Eagle Lake, from 1854 to 1868.

the age of seventy-seven. His successor in Crown Point was the Rev. August Schuelke of Berlin (since 1914 known as Kitchener),* Ontario, Canada. He held this Crown Point pastorate from July 20, 1890, until August, 1906, when he accepted a professorship at the Missouri Synod's second teachers' seminary at Seward, Nebr.† The Rev. Arthur Henry Claudius Both of Kouts, Ind., succeeded Pastor Schuelke as Trinity's pastor. In January, 1910, Pastor Both accepted a call to become the third pastor of the third Missouri Synod congregation in Chicago, First Trinity, which in 1906 had moved its "center" from Twenty-fifth Place and Canal Street to West Thirty-first Street and Lowe Avenue. On February 6, 1910, the Rev. August Biester of North Judson, Ind., came to Trinity in Crown Point. In 1939 Trinity Congregation placed at Pastor Biester's side a young assistant, Candidate William J. Schepman, graduate of Concordia Seminary, St. Louis, Mo. About a year later Pastor Biester resigned the pastorate, and the assistant pastor was ordained and installed as Trinity's fifth pastor on November 3, 1940. At the same time the retired pastor was honored with the title "Pastor Emeritus" and a life pension granted him by Trinity Congregation. On February 3, 1947, Pastor Biester died.

During its early beginnings, Trinity Congregation established a day school. Pastor Heintz taught for fifteen years, and his successor, Pastor Schuelke, continued serving in the same capacity until the number of pupils had increased to the point where assistance became imperative. Following is a list of the teachers who since then have had charge of the day school in Crown Point: August Fathauer, W. F. Willert, Carl Strieter, William H. Heidbreder, Lillian Bauer, Violet Krueger, Martha Vornemann, Walter Muehl, Miss A. Lovekamp, and Rebecca Duesing. In recent years the Rev. Frederick L. Miller

*Berlin (Kitchener) was originally settled by Pennsylvania Dutch and later by Germans from Europe. (*The Encyclopedia Americana*, 1941, Vol. XVI, p. 465.)

†Pastor August Schuelke died on March 21, 1932.

of Valparaiso University,* Valparaiso, Ind., has served as assistant pastor of Trinity in Crown Point.[52]

Pastor Schepman accepted a call to Manhattan Beach, Calif., at the beginning of May, 1949. The Rev. Herbert J. Meyer of Alliance, Nebr., was installed as Pastor Schepman's successor on August 28, 1949.

44. Palatine

With the Lutheran Trail's brief divergence into northern Indiana completed, it now wends back to Chicago. The city by this time, 1869, has acquired two nicknames. "Queen of the Lakes," which doubtless inspired Will Careton's description: "The golden-crowned, glorious Chicago, the Queen of the North and West," and "The Windy City." The former epithet is now conversationally defunct; the latter exists to this day. Vital statistics, too, have made a mighty leap upward. The population is 306,605, half of them foreign-born, some twenty-five thousand of them German, and almost as many Irish; Chicago's churchgoing population is estimated at one hundred and fifty thousand a Sunday. Of the 156 churches, 25 are Catholic, 21 Methodist, 20 Baptist, 19 Presbyterian, five Jewish, five Missouri Synod Lutheran,† and the remainder of other denominations or sects.

Were a trail vocal, it might pause to reflect on another derogatory epithet Chicago had at this time—"the wickedest city on earth"—but the demands of history are too insistent, so it proceeds northwest for three and one-half miles beyond Dunton (Arlington Heights), to halt at Palatine, Ill.‡

Here is a group of men on the Chicago & North Western Railroad station platform discussing plans to organize a Lutheran congregation in this community. The meeting took

*Purchased by the Lutheran University Association in 1925. (See Sec. III, page 640.

†First St. Paul, First Immanuel, First Trinity, First St. John, and First Zion. The sixth, St. James (Sankt Jakobi), was not organized until Aug. 29, 1869.

‡1940 census: 2,222. Named from the Rhenish Palatinate, Germany.

place on February 20, 1869. Less than ten days later, on March 1, Immanuel Congregation was organized*—at the same place, because there was no other public meeting place available. For approximately two years, then, services were held in the basement of a bakery shop† located at the southwest corner of Wood and Bothwell Streets. During these two years the struggling congregation in Palatine was served by the Rev. John E. Roeder, pastor of Saint Peter's Congregation in Dunton (Arlington Heights), about four miles to the southeast. Immanuel Congregation's first pastor, Candidate Hinrich Rathjen, recent graduate of Concordia Seminary, St. Louis, Mo., was ordained and installed on July 24, 1870. A day school was founded, and Pastor Rathjen served as teacher until June, 1872. Meanwhile, in 1870, Immanuel Congregation purchased "four acres of land bordering on Chicago Avenue and running south to and including the present cemetery." Soon afterward plans for the erection of a church were formulated. Lumber and other building materials were delivered to the building site. Then occurred a serious intervention. "Which of you, intending to build a tower, sitteth not down first and counteth the cost, whether he have sufficient to finish it? Lest haply, after he hath laid the foundation and is not able to finish it, all that behold it begin to mock him, saying: This man began to build and was not able to finish." (Luke 14:28-30.) Immanuel intended to build a church, but, somewhat belatedly, realized that "considerably more money was needed than the congregation was able to raise in order to finish building the church." Fortunately a satisfactory alternative appeared in the nature of a report to the effect that a church building formerly used by another church denomination (Camp-

*Charter members:

H. C. Batterman
Conrad Engelking
Otto Engelking
F. Grebe
H. Schroeder
H. Knickrehm
E. Prellberg
F. S. Senne
H. Schirding

†Rappold Bakery.

bellites?) could be purchased at "a very reasonable price." Fortunately, also, one of the "founding fathers," Henry Battermann, "came to the rescue and took the building material and a considerable part of the land off their hands." The lumber was utilized in the construction of a flax mill. After Pastor Rathjen's acceptance of a call, in June, 1872, to Mayville, Wis., a vacancy of approximately four and one-half years' duration existed in Immanuel's pastorate, during which time the Rev. Henry Schmidt, pastor of Saint Peter's at Schaumburg, ministered to the somewhat hard-pressed flock in Palatine. In May, 1873, Immanuel Congregation became a member of the Missouri Synod. In the spring of the same year the first day school teacher, E. Zachow, was installed. But a few months later he accepted a call to Danville, Ill. His successor was August Koch of Des Plaines, Ill. He served in Immanuel School until April, 1876. On November 19, 1876, the Rev. A. Pohl formally terminated the congregation's long search for a pastor to succeed Pastor Rathjen by being installed in Palatine. He served in this pastorate until 1880, when the Rev. William Graef succeeded him as Immanuel's third resident pastor. In 1881 Mr. Zachow resumed work in the school. The story is told that he was in the habit of wearing a silk top hat to church, where he regularly took his place among the school children. "One fine spring morning, after several services had been held without building a fire in the stove, which stood near the altar, Teacher Zachow entered the church and, as usual, placed his hat on the stove before sitting down. But that Sunday morning a fire had been started. During the sermon the hat burst into flame, and all the efforts of Teacher Zachow to extinguish it were of no avail. When he finally did put out the flame, he had nothing but the brim left in his hand." In October, 1886, Pastor Graef accepted a call to Concord, Wis., and again the Rev. John E. Roeder of Dunton (Arlington Heights) consented to perform services and official acts for the shepherdless flock for a period of about eight months. The vacancy was ended with the installation of Immanuel's fourth resident pastor, the Rev. Adolph Pfotenhauer,* on Feb. 6, 1887. Meanwhile, changes in the teaching personnel had occurred: In 1884 H. Dauel became Mr. Zachow's successor. He resigned in 1886.† Then came Charles G. Decker, who served in the day school from 1887 until July, 1892. He, in turn, was succeeded in the same year by Paul Cutkowsky. Then, in July, 1895, another change took place in the pastorate. Pastor Pfotenhauer followed a call to Saint Matthew's Congregation in Lemont, Ill. His successor in Palatine was the Rev. John Henry Christoph Droegemueller of Arenzville, Ill. In April, 1900, Mr. Cutkowsky followed a call to a school at Rochester, Minn., and Ernest Schreiner took his place in Palatine. He served until December, 1908, and followed a call to Troy, Ill. In September, 1910, Pastor Droegemueller accepted a call to Denham, Ind., and the Rev. Siegfried Daniel Poellot of Huntley, Ill., was installed as his successor on October 2, 1910. From the time of Mr. Schreiner's departure from Palatine until the arrival of Ernest Harks in the fall of 1911 the school was in charge, consecutively, of Teachers W. Grosse and H. Bertram. Mr. Harks served until 1913 and was succeeded by Chr. F. Scheer of Chicago. In the spring of 1914 construction of a new church at Plum Grove and Wood Streets was begun. The old church was sold to Charles Plate for $250, who shortly afterward moved it to a farm on Algonquin Road. The proceeds of the sale were used to purchase the vacant building located at the site occupied by the present school. The new church was dedicated on November 22, 1914. In 1924 Mr. Scheer resigned because of ill health, and W. A. Meier suc-

*Pastor Pfotenhauer was a brother of the Rev. Frederick Pfotenhauer, D.D., President of the Missouri Synod, 1911-1935.

†William Adolph Brauer, a student at Concordia Seminary, Springfield, Ill., taught school in Palatine, 1886-1887. He was pastor of St. John's Congregation, Hammond, Ind., 1889-1941; he died Jan. 15, 1941.

ceeded him in July of the same year, serving until 1928, when, upon his request, he was released from service in the school. Then came H. L. Schroeder, who served until May 4, 1934, when he suddenly died. His temporary assistant for some time, beginning in April, 1931, was J. Breitenfeld. Mr. Schroeder's successor was Bernhard C. Zimdahl. At that time Pastor Poellot's son, Daniel,* a student at Concordia Seminary, St. Louis, Mo., taught the lower grades; during a part of the next school year W. O. Heinemeier served in that capacity. In January, 1936, George Beyer took charge of this department. Teachers who have served in Immanuel School since that time include the following: Miss Iona Stradtman, Miss Jean Swain, Miss Erica Runge, Miss Julia Runge, Miss Marilyn Glade, and Paul Leimer. In 1940 Pastor Poellot resigned.† His successor, the Rev. Wilbur C. Koester, who had served as assistant pastor in Saint Stephen's Congregation, St. Louis, Mo., was installed as Immanuel's seventh resident pastor on September 1, 1940.

45. Chicago, Saint James

Conversations in Palatine on the reported expansion of the Missouri Synod in Chicago beyond North Avenue bend the Trail cityward to Willow and Burling Streets. Here, in 1857, a "Schulverein" (school society), composed of members of First Saint Paul's Congregation and other Lutherans in the vicinity, had been established, with Wednesday evening services in the school conducted by the Rev. Henry Wunder and his assistant pastor. (See Chapter Two, p. 24.) In 1866 his congregation acquired the property and placed A. F. H. Gebhard in charge of the school.

In 1869 the old one-horse cars disappeared from Chicago's

*In July, 1936, Candidate Daniel E. Poellot was installed as assistant pastor of St. Paul's Congregation in Addison, Ill. Upon Pastor Adolph Pfotenhauer's death, in 1939, the assistant pastor was installed as "first" pastor (Sept. 24, 1939).

†The Rev. S. Daniel Poellot died on Jan. 12, 1942.

streets. On May 10 of the same year the Union and Central Pacific Railroad to the Pacific Coast was completed. In the summer of this year thirty members of First Saint Paul's Congregation in Chicago were released to organize, in conjunction with other Lutherans, the "deutsche evangelisch-lutherische Sankt Jakobi-Gemeinde" (German Evangelical Lutheran Saint James Congregation). This was accomplished on August 29, 1869. The "mother" congregation donated the school building at Willow and Burling Streets to this new congregation—the sixth of the Missouri Synod in Chicago. On May 1, 1870, the Rev. William Bartling* of Springfield, Ill., was installed as Saint James' first pastor. At that time the population of Chicago was 298,927, of whom 154,420 were American-born. "Every language was spoken here, and every religion had its believers." During the middle of March, 1870, the city was snowbound. On September 5, 1870, a block of stores on Wabash Avenue was destroyed by fire, and the *Chicago Tribune* posed the query after the statement: "This is the third time that Chicago has been visited with such a calamity.—Shall it be the last?"

In the fall of 1870 Saint James Congregation dedicated its first church building at Fremont and Sophia Streets (now Dickens Avenue).† This building was so constructed that the auditorium was high above the ground, thus providing space below for classrooms (three). The large influx of German immigrants resulted in a fast-growing congregation and overtaxing the schools also in this section of Chicago, and Saint James Congregation purchased a piece of land at Fullerton Avenue and High Street and erected a school upon it. The Great Fire of October 9, 1871, threatened to engulf the school

*Pastor Bartling was pastor of St. John's Congregation at Elk Grove, Ill., from September, 1862, until February, 1863. From Elk Grove he went to Springfield, Ill.

†Prior to the calling of Pastor Bartling, the congregation purchased a church-building site on Burling Street for $3,700. In the first meeting attended by Pastor Bartling it was resolved to build the church at Fremont and Sophia (changed to Garfield; then to Dickens—its present name).

building at Willow and Burling Streets, but then "God graciously called a halt to the holocaust." A second branch school was established in 1881 on property purchased at the corner of Hoyne Avenue and Wellington Street. Instead of placing a trained teacher there, however, the congregation called an assistant pastor to teach school and to alternate with Pastor Bartling in conducting preaching services in that school on Sundays and weekdays for members of Saint James and other interested persons living in that community. Candidate John Ernst August Mueller, graduate of Concordia Seminary, Springfield, Ill., was ordained and installed on January 8, 1882. At his own expense Pastor Bartling built a branch school at Racine and Oakdale Avenues. His only request was that the congregation call and support a teacher. Fred J. Rieck was placed in charge of this school in 1886. In 1884 the branch school at Hoyne Avenue and Wellington Street developed into a new congregation, Saint Luke's. (See Chapter 86, p. 323.) A short time before that development First Saint Paul's branch school located on Larrabee Street was moved to and combined with the branch school erected and maintained by Saint James Congregation at Fullerton Avenue and High Street. Assistant Pastor Mueller was released by Saint James to become the first pastor of the "daughter" congregation, Saint Luke, in 1884. In 1887 another ministerial candidate was called as assistant pastor at Saint James, William C. Kohn. He served in this capacity until June, 1888, when he became the first pastor of Saint Andrew's Congregation in Chicago. In 1893 Pastor Bartling's son, Albert, was called as assistant pastor. He served for only about two years, until 1895, when he accepted a call to Waterford, Wis.* Pastor William Bartling retired from the ministry in May, 1897, and his successor in the Saint James pastorate, the Rev. Karl Schmidt of Crystal Lake, Ill., was in-

*He died on Feb. 23, 1918, at Laurium, Mich. A son, Victor, is a member of the Concordia Seminary faculty at St. Louis, Mo. The latter's wife is a daughter of Dr. Frederick Pfotenhauer.

stalled on August 17, 1897. In the evening of the same day the new pastor's five-year-old son, Herman, died.

In the early part of the 1890's enrollment in the schools of Saint James "was not faring so well, and the decline continued steadily down to the close of the century." In 1895 the first school, at Willow and Burling, was abandoned. In 1897 the congregation's teaching staff had dwindled from nine to only four. In 1902 the congregation acquired the northwest corner of Montana Street and Greenview Avenue (formerly Perry Street) and erected a two-story building, the first floor of which served as a classroom and the second as a teacher's residence. Two years later, in 1904, the congregation purchased land and three buildings at the northeast corner of Fremont Street and Garfield Avenue (now Dickens), razed the buildings, and in place of them erected a three-story school building with four classrooms, "in the hope of an increased enrollment, which did not materialize." The "home" school beneath the church building, at the southwest corner of the same intersection, was closed at that time.* Beside the church stood a building, erected in 1889 and known as the "Aula,"† which served as a gymnasium, library, and for entertainments. The cost was four thousand dollars.

In February, 1916, the plan for a new church was placed before Saint James Congregation by a committee headed by Charles Zuttermeister. Soon afterward the old church and the "Aula" were torn down, and the new church was erected on the same site at a cost of eighty-five thousand dollars. The dedication took place on February 11, 1917. At about that time also the congregation recognized the need for services in the English language. In October, 1917, Candidate Herman C. Engelbrecht was called to serve particularly in this "new field." In the spring of the following year he accepted a call

*The schools, with the exception of the one at Montana and Perry (now Greenview), were consolidated at Fremont and Sophia (later Garfield, now Dickens).

†"Aula"—a Greek word, meaning "a hall or court."

to Grace Congregation in Oak Park.* Then came the Rev. Reinhold Freche, a former missionary in India; he died in 1923. Meanwhile this assistant pastor's son, Martin, a ministerial candidate, was called to assist in the school and in other parish activities. In 1926 he accepted a call to Tuscola, Ill. In that year Pastor Schmidt's health broke down completely. During the following winter months and until July, 1927, the Rev. Herman C. Guebert† was in charge of the pastorate. Pastor Schmidt's successor, the Rev. Louis Seidel of Freeport, Ill., was installed on July 10, 1927. In 1929 the congregation's last branch school, at Montana and Greenview (formerly Perry), ceased to enroll pupils. On October 18, 1929, Pastor Schmidt died at the age of seventy.‡ In 1931 Pastor Seidel confirmed the last class of children in the German language, seventeen boys and fifteen girls. The other eighteen children were confirmed in English; since 1932 all children have been confirmed in the English language. After an illness of eight months' duration, Pastor Seidel died on January 5, 1937, at the age of fifty-eight years. In November, 1936, the congregation called the Rev. Arthur C. Dahms, since 1918 pastor of Our Savior Congregation of the Deaf in Chicago, as associate pastor. He succeeded Pastor Seidel as "first" pastor of Saint James. Serving as assistants in recent years were the Rev. Alex Ullrich, formerly pastor of Saint John's Congregation in La Grange, Ill. (1893-1944), the Rev. Charles A. Waech, formerly pastor of Trinity Congregation in Crete, Ill. (1912-1944), and more recently the Rev. William H. Schuetz, formerly pastor of Zion Congregation in Beecher, Ill. (1923-1943).

*Later Grace Congregation's "center" was moved to the campus of Concordia Teachers College, River Forest, Ill. (See Note below.)

†Resigned at Zion Church, Hinsdale, Ill., March 12, 1922.

‡A son, Otto H. Schmidt, for some time served Immanuel Congregation in Valparaiso, Ind. Since 1940 he has served as executive secretary for the Missouri Synod's Board of Foreign Missions, St. Louis, Mo.

NOTE: In 1921 the English language was permitted for the Sunday school Christmas celebration in the afternoon of Christmas Day.

Teachers who have served in the Saint James' day schools:

Carl Laufer, 1869-1874;
C. W. Laesch, 1869-1871;
William Hoppe, 1870-1882;
August Ross, 1870-1872;
Gottfried Dreyer, 1871-1876;
Bernard Tessmann, 1872-1876;
J. Grothmann, 1872-1873;
Fred Kringel, 1873-1929;
Christian Schwartz, 1873-1902;
Louis Doering, 1876-1893;
Carl H. Schliebe, 1876-1881;
Miss Dreyer, 1879-1880;*
Louis Heitbrink, 1880-1935;†
Paul Appelt, 1881-1893;
William Ernst, 1882-1887;
Miss Johanna Bartling, 1883-1885;*
Miss Sophie Bartling, 1883-1885;*
Fred E. Zimmermann, 1887-1889;
Gustav A. Niethammer, 1887-1897;‡
Mrs. Eggold, 1893-1894;*
Miss Schliebe, 1895-1896;*
H. Schroeder, 1902-1910;
Miss Fischer, 1905-1908;*
John G. Schmid, 1910-
Theodore Gerhard Naeser, 1918-
Miss D. Schmidt, 1920-1921;*
Walter J. Kallies, 1923-1947;
Miss M. Hilger, 1927-1931;*
Norman J. Rogers, 1931-
W. H. Tetting, 1948-

*"Employed teachers."

†Teacher Heitbrink died on March 10, 1946, at the age of eighty-five.

‡Mr. Niethammer was among the last teachers to serve in First Saint Paul's Congregation's day school prior to its discontinuance in 1931.

46. Belvidere

According to the dictionary, the word "belvedere" is derived from the Italian "bel" (beautiful) and "vedere" (a view). "In Italian architecture, the belvedere is the uppermost story of a building, open to the air, at least on one side, and frequently on all, for the purpose of giving a view of the country, and to admit the evening breeze." About sixty miles northwest of Chicago there is a city by that name, although the middle letter of it is not an "e" but an "i"—Belvidere.§ Whether Daniel Boone had anything to do with the founding of Belvidere is not known, but, anyway, the city is the county seat of Boone County, important at the moment as, in 1867, it was the first city in this county with a Lutheran congregation. The Rev. Anton Wagner, assistant pastor of First Immanuel Congregation in Chicago, conducted the first services in Belvidere in 1867. During the years 1867 to 1869 three other Lutheran clergymen conducted the services, the Rev. George M. Zucker of Proviso ("Franzosenbusch"), Prof. C. August T. Selle of the

§1940 census: 8,094.

"It is claimed by some that this city was named by one of the founders for his birthplace in Canada. Another authority has it that it was named "by Samuel P. Doty, the first white settler, who claimed that he named it at the suggestion of Mark Beaubien, an early French settler of Chicago, who fancied the country around it resembled Belvidere near Weimar in Saxe-Gotha, Germany."
(Stennen, p. 43—quoted in *Journal of the Illinois State Historical Society*. 199, Vol. XXIX, No. 3.)

Teachers' Seminary, Addison, and the Rev. Theodore Mertens of Willow Springs. On November 21, 1869, Immanuel Congregation was organized* and its first pastor, the Rev. Philip Estel of Grand Rapids, Wis., installed. The services were held at first in the Boone County Courthouse and, later, in the home of John Suhr. In October, 1870, Pastor Estel accepted a call to Baden (now part of St. Louis), Mo. Then followed a long period of vacancy, during which the congregation was served by these neighboring pastors: the Rev. Henry Schmidt of Schaumburg, the Rev. Theodore Mertens, now of York Center, the Rev. J. H. C. Steege of East Dundee, the Rev. H. W. Wehrs of Russells Grove (now Fairfield), the Rev. John T. Feiertag of Saint Paul's Congregation, Aurora, the Rev. John E. Roeder of Dunton (Arlington Heights), and the Rev. F. M. Grosse of Harlem (Forest Park). On July 13, 1873, the Rev. Louis Steinrauf of Huntley, Ill., was installed as Immanuel's second resident pastor. Two years later, in 1875, the congregation purchased the property of the Congregationalists, Main and Church Streets, and on July 18, 1875, dedicated the building as a Lutheran church. In 1877 Pastor Steinrauf followed a call to Stringtown, Mo., and his successor in Belvidere, Candidate Carl F. Eissfeldt, graduate of Concordia Seminary, St. Louis, Mo., was installed on August 12, 1877. Less than two years later, on April 6, 1879, Pastor Eissfeldt accepted a call to Immanuel Congregation in Colehour (now South Chicago), Ill. During the next seven years the Rev. John Ernst Baumgaertner of Huntley preached here every other Sunday, until June 27, 1886, when the Rev. Theodore Kohn of Dallas, Tex., was installed. For four years Pastor Kohn also served Saint

*Immanuel's charter members:

John Suhr, Sr.	C. Gehlbeck	J. Sturm
J. H. Buhlmeyer	John Riedel	C. Marske
Friedrich Sturm	Christian Grawe	C. Johannes II
J. Gierhahn	John Suhr, Jr.	J. Weber
John Waterman	J. Wascher	A. Lettow, Sr.
John Berg, Jr.	C. Johannes	
Joe Suhr	A. Sandor	

John's Congregation* in Pecatonica every other Sunday. A new school was erected in 1886. August Hoffmann was the first trained teacher. In subsequent years the school was in charge, consecutively, of the following men: Martin J. Schreiner, John Richter, Ludwig Abraham, Henry F. Buls, A. Glammeyer, Edward W. Grothe, Paul Ernst, Alfred Schwausch, and Otto Wm. Schaefer.

When Pastor Kohn in the summer of 1892 accepted a call to Saint Mark's Congregation in Chicago, the Rev. Ernst Heinemann of Geneseo, Ill., succeeded him at Immanuel in Belvidere, being installed on October 30, 1892. The new church was dedicated on October 15, 1893. In 1896 the church steeple was struck by lightning and damaged to the extent that a new one had to be constructed. Pastor Heinemann resigned on August 2, 1913, and was succeeded by the Rev. Emil J. F. Richter of Saint John's at Rodenberg, two miles west of Roselle, Ill. Three years later, in 1916, Pastor Richter accepted a call to Elizabeth, Ill. His successor, the Rev. J. H. Rupprecht of Lemont, Ill., served from February, 1917, until September 4, 1919, when he resigned because of ill health. Then the congregation called its former pastor, the Rev. Ernst Heinemann, who was installed for the second time, on November 16, 1919. He continued in the pastorate here in Belvidere until July, 1926, when ill health again compelled him to resign.† He was succeeded on October 24, 1926, by the Rev. Frederick Ewald Gohlke of Merrill, Wis. After serving in Belvidere for about seventeen years, he also was compelled by ill health to resign, August 8, 1943.‡ During his retirement he lived in Des Plaines, Ill. Pastor Gohlke's successor in the Immanuel pastorate was the Rev. Wilbert Frederick Theiss of Sharon, Wis.,§ who served until November, 1945, when he accepted a call to

*Founded in 1875.

†Pastor Heinemann died on March 3, 1927.

‡Pastor Gohlke died Jan. 4, 1947.

§Pastor Theiss's father, the Rev. Gottlob Theiss, served as pastor of Saint Peter's Congregation, Schaumburg, Ill., 1906-1935.

Port Washington, Wis. He was succeeded in Belvidere by the Rev. Herman W. Bauer, pastor of First Immanuel Congregation in Chicago (1933-1941) and more recently a chaplain in the United States Army. He was installed on December 16, 1945, and served until June, 1948, when he accepted a call to Peace Congregation in Chicago. His successor in Belvidere, the Rev. Walter H. Rengstorf of Devils Lake, N. Dak., was installed on August 29, 1948.

47. Yellowhead

It is the year 1869, and the Lutheran Trail goes from "the beautiful view" (Belvidere) to Yellowhead—a distance of about ninety miles toward the southeastern part of the Northern Illinois District—in Kankakee County. History of the formative years of this region relates of a company of soldiers rushing from Danville, Ill., to the rescue of Chicago (Fort Dearborn) from an Indian massacre. They followed an Indian trail (later known as Vincennes Trail and, a portion of it, as Hubbard's Trace), swimming over Beaver Creek and crossing the Kankakee River at the island near Momenza (Momence); then they passed Yellowhead's village. The old Chief Yellowhead of the Potawotami tribe,* and the squaws and papooses, besides a few old Indian men, were at home. The young men were on a hunting expedition. Tarrying here a little while, the soldiers again set out, proceeding a distance of about five miles, and then encamped at the point of the timber on Yellowhead's creek. The next morning they continued on their way, crossing a branch of the Calumet to the west of "the Blue Island." "Hubbard knew the way!"

It was in the decade 1860-1870 that this section of the country was extensively settled for the most part by immigrants from Germany, including Hanoverians, Mecklenburgers, Pomeranians, Schleswig-Holsteiners, Hessians, Swabians, and

*His Indian name was Minnemaung, or Winnemung, meaning "catfish."

Franconians (Bavarians—"deitsche Leit"!). But these settlers, unlike German settlers in other parts of the United States, were inexplicably dilatory in organizing a congregation. Possibly the mixture was too "strong." Not until 1868, so far as can be determined, was there any kind of "church" activity in the Yellowhead region. A clergyman, Reinecke by name, occasionally conducted services in this community for about one year. Presumably it was he who laid the foundation for the organization of a Lutheran congregation. His plan was followed in 1869 by the Rev. Kilian Barth. On July 11, 1869, the congregation was organized and named Saint Paul's. Seemingly, however, the congregation at first was not strictly Lutheran, if one may make such a deduction from the official name: "The Evangelical Saint Paul's Congregation of Yellowhead." The names of twenty-seven men appear in the records dated July 11, 1869, as the original contributors.* Saint Paul's first church was dedicated on December 19, 1869. Through the accession of five members, who recently arrived at Yellowhead from Duncklees Grove, Saint Paul's Congregation was strengthened in its confidence to support a pastor. Candidate Heinrich Hunziger was installed as Saint Paul's first resident pastor. His pastorate was very short; about one year after his arrival he was succeeded by a minister affiliated with the Evangelical Church, the Rev. Friedrich Woelfele, who likewise remained for only one year. On December 14, 1873, a "Missouri" pastor, the Rev. Lorenz Traub, ordained in Bleeker, N.Y., in 1870, and for a short time pastor of a congregation at Monticello, Iowa, and, more recently, 1872-1873, pastor of Zion Congrega-

*George Hoevet	Henrich Blanke	George Johe
Wilhelm Mussmann	Friedrich Poppe	William Hoevet
Jacob Theede	Dietrich Meyer	Christian Deerson
William Backhaus	Juergen Greve	Johann Mitsch
Jacob Frahm	Matthias Hoevet	Friedrich Meyer
Jeronimus Hansen	Friedrich Hobzmann	Heinrich Pfingsten
Jonathan Oster	Christian Hecht	Carl Hoevet
Claus Stoevet	Claus Frahm	Friedrich Kuecker
Cord Rosenbrock	Hans Casper	S. F. Meyer

NOTE: The names Friedrich Meyer and Friedrich Kuecker appear in the record of vital statistics of Zion Congregation—Duncklees Grove.

tion at Sollitt, Ill., was installed as Saint Paul's next pastor. He resigned in the following year, 1874.* His successor at Yellowhead, the Rev. Peter Graef of Augusta, Mo., was installed on June 27, 1875.

During the night of January 24, 1880, the church and the parsonage were completely destroyed by fire. The first church records were lost in the flames. The minutes of the year 1880 indicate that the congregation immediately applied itself to the task of building a new church as well as a parsonage. The church was dedicated on November 7, 1880. The same minutes also point to the fact that Pastor Graef devoted considerable time to the presentation at voters' meetings of a series of twenty-four theses on the topic: "The Evangelical Lutheran Church, the True Visible Church of God."†

On June 13, 1886, Saint Paul's Congregation, having adopted the Lutheran confessional standards, was received into membership with the Missouri Synod. In the same year "Christenlehre" was introduced. In that same month Pastor Graef followed a call to Immanuel Congregation in Des Plaines, Ill. On the following September 5 his successor at Yellowhead, the Rev. Joachim Henry Gose, was installed. He served here until his death, November 9, 1905, and was buried in the church cemetery. On May 6, 1906, the Rev. H. William Meyer succeeded Pastor Gose. During his pastorate Saint Paul's Congregation increased its pastor's salary from five hundred to eight hundred dollars a year. Pastor Meyer's pastorate at Yellowhead was interrupted by a call from Immanuel Congregation in Columbia Heights (Steger), Ill. His successor, the Rev. J. C. G. Horsch of Wapakoneta, Ohio, was installed on April 23, 1911. During his pastorate the church was completely rebuilt and enlarged. The rededication service was held on November 26, 1916. English services were introduced in 1918.

*Two years later he re-entered the active ministry at New London, N.Y.

†In 1867 a book, written by the Rev. C. F. W. Walther (St. Louis, Mo.), was published, titled: "*The Evangelical Lutheran Church, the True Visible Church on Earth*"—("*Die evangelisch-lutherische Kirche, die wahre sichtbare Kirche auf Erden.*")

In October, 1921, Pastor Horsch followed a call to Trinity Congregation in Hanson Park (Chicago). His successor at Yellowhead—located about six miles northeast of the little village of Grant Park—was a man who was born on the S.S. *Marseilles* in New York harbor on April 5, 1892, the Rev. Karl A. Guenther, until recently a missionary in Argentina, South America. Pastor Guenther was on furlough in the United States when he received and accepted the call to Saint Paul's. He was installed on December 4, 1921. Pastor Guenther preached his last sermon on February 4, 1944. Ill for about a year, he died on February 6, 1945. The Rev. Chr. Adam of Kankakee, institutional missionary for the Northern Illinois District (Missouri Synod), took charge of the pastorate during Pastor Guenther's illness and until the next pastor arrived. The Rev. Reimar A. Frick of Waterloo, Ill., was installed as Saint Paul's pastor on July 1, 1945. On April 7, 1948, a tornado struck this territory. In its path were the homes and possessions of six members of Saint Paul's Congregation: Mrs. Minnie Junker, Otto Braatz, Albert Haase, Erwin Trubach, Frank Wille, and Harold Mussman.[54]

48. Washington Heights, Zion

From Yellowhead to Washington Heights. Still following Hubbard's Trace northward out of Yellowhead, the Lutheran Trail tracks to "the Blue Island," passes Horse Thief Hollow, and comes to a halt at Washington Heights. Prior to 1869 the entire "island" or "ridge" was known by the general name "Blue Island." It is about six miles long, and Washington Heights is located at the northern end of it. Here is a Lutheran mission, Zion, which differs from the majority of Lutheran congregations in that it was not founded by missionary pioneers of Lutheran heritage. Prior to 1870 Zion Congregation, which owned a church building at what now is known as the corner of West Ninety-ninth Street and Winston Avenue, held membership with the Evangelical Church. In 1870 internal dissension in that denomination resulted in the desire on the part of Zion Congregation to become Lutheran in name as well as in character. Moreover, its most recent pastor had been exposed as a swindler and defrocked. Zion Congregation thereupon referred its problem to the Rev. Augustus Reinke, pastor of the first and, at the time, only Lutheran congregation in near-by Blue Island. Soon afterward Zion Congregation* adopted a Lutheran constitution and joined the Missouri Synod. On October 1, 1871, Pastor Reinke accepted a call to First Bethlehem Congregation in the Holstein community of Chicago. His successor in Blue Island was the Rev. H. Ernst, under whose direction a day school was established on November 10, 1878, with an initial enrollment of thirty pupils. The first teacher, Henry F. Mertens, came here as a candidate from the Teachers' Seminary, Addison, and was installed on August 4, 1879. His annual salary was $350. Meanwhile Pastor Ernst had followed a call to Michigan City, Ind., and in the same year, 1879, the Rev. H. P. Duborg succeeded him in the Zion pastorate. In 1881 the congregation became involved in the Election and Predestination Controversy within the Evangelical Lutheran Synodical Conference of North America. Pastor Duborg held and taught the doctrine of the Ohio Synod. A majority of the members shared his views, and when the dissension reached a climax, this group established a church a few blocks from Zion and joined the Ohio Synod. During the controversy Mr. Mertens followed a call to Manistee, Mich. The Rev. Carl F. Eissfeldt, pastor of Immanuel Congregation in Colehour (South Chicago), for some time served the "rem-

*Charter members of Zion Congregation:

Joachim Zander
John Hansen
David Mell
C. Degenhardt
Peter Jacob
John Haas
J. Borndell
William Zander
William Beyer
Albert Jansen
Julius Bohm
Jacob Landeck
Henry Fink
Michael Hemmrich
Julius Boelter

nant" of Zion, as did also the Rev. Louis Hoelter, pastor of First Immanuel Congregation in Chicago. The "Missouri" congregation in Blue Island, served by Pastor Duborg as an affiliate of Zion, also joined the Ohio Synod at that time, and "only a few of its members broke relations" and came to Zion Congregation (Missouri Synod) in Washington Heights.

On July 9, 1882, Zion again secured a pastor of its own in the person of Candidate Henry Theo. L. Felten, who also served as schoolteacher until 1890, when, because of impaired health, he followed a call to Sheboygan, Wis.* [On Nov. 4, 1890, the Village of Washington Heights was annexed to Chicago.] His successor as pastor of Zion, the Rev. Richard Paul Budach of Luverne, Iowa, was installed on May 11, 1890. Now new life began to manifest itself, and the constant growth in membership soon necessitated the erection of a more spacious church building. The old church was converted into a school. The new frame church was dedicated on November 8, 1891. In the evening of that day the first English sermon was preached before Zion Congregation by the Rev. A. Sloan Bartholomew, pastor of Christ English Congregation, Chicago.† Pastor Budach taught school for two years. In 1892 August Seefurth, recently graduated from the Teachers' Seminary, Addison, took charge of the school. Two years later he was succeeded by Paul L. Schaefer, likewise a recent graduate of the same institution. In the same year, 1894, a bell was purchased for the new church. It had been cast for another church and was to be used as part of a three-bell ensemble, but was slightly off pitch. Zion obtained the bell, which was priced at $1,750, for three hundred dollars. The old bell was presented to the Missouri Synod's Concordia College in St. Paul, Minn. In 1901 Mr. Schaefer accepted a call elsewhere, and B. J. Seitz succeeded him in Zion School. In the summer of 1903 Pastor

*He died in Sheboygan Oct. 20, 1899.

†The first congregation in northern Illinois to join the English Synod, which in 1911 joined the "German" Missouri Synod as a non-territorial District.

Budach accepted a call to Bay City, Mich., and on July 6, 1903, the Rev. Leonhardt Brenner of Pecatonica, Ill., took charge of the Zion pastorate in Washington Heights. He served only until 1906, when he followed a call to Concord, Wis.* Then came the Rev. Edward Tappenbeck of Olmstead, Ill.

After Teacher Seitz's resignation in 1911, due to failing health, Zion Congregation extended calls to nine men in succession until finally R. G. A. Bendick of Chicago responded favorably in 1913. Already a year later, in 1914, Mr. Bendick followed a call to Indiana. Again there was a long vacancy in the day school, and for three years the work was done by temporarily employed teachers. Alwin R. Roschke, graduate of Concordia Teachers College River Forest, Ill., was installed as teacher on September 6, 1914. In the course of the next few years the school was divided into two classes, and Miss Paula Roschke taught from 1921 to 1924. In 1923 a new brick school building was erected. The dedication took place on November 10, 1923. In 1924 Miss Ruth Piehler taught the primary grades, and in 1926 her sister, Esther, succeeded to that position. In 1928 Miss Martha Brauer of Sydney, Nebr., took charge of the four lower grades.

On Easter Sunday, April 20, 1930, Pastor Tappenbeck preached his last sermon, and after an illness of several weeks' duration he died on May 8. Thus ended a twenty-four-year ministry in Washington Heights. His successor, the Rev. Carl L. Abel of Sollitt, Ill.,† was installed on August 17, 1930.

Late in 1937 a Lehigh-stone church was erected at a cost of sixty thousand dollars and dedicated on January 30, 1938.‡

*Pastor Brenner died Dec. 18, 1941, at the age of seventy-four.

†Pastor Abel is a son of the Rev. Carl Abel, pastor of Immanuel Congregation, Elmhurst, Ill., 1911-1943. The father died suddenly in Elmhurst on March 13, 1947.

‡"That we now have a flourishing congregation here is due, under God, mainly to the almost singlehanded fight put up by a sturdy pioneer named Landeck (Andreas Christian), a simple layman, during the controversy on Election and Predestination, when this man was indefatigable in visiting and admonishing, in distributing tracts and other reading material, working day and night to hold a congregation together." (Cf. *Concordia Historical Institute Quarterly*, St. Louis, Mo., Vol. XI, No. 1, p. 4.)

In September, 1938, Candidate Victor H. Mattfeld, graduate of Concordia Teachers College, River Forest, Ill., was engaged as teacher for the lower grades; later, on March 19, 1939, he was formally inducted into office. He resigned from the teaching profession in 1948. In 1945 Mrs. Lora Boehm was engaged to assist in school; in 1946 Mrs. Theodore Gose took her place;[55] . . . she, in turn, was replaced by Miss Lenore Menze. Candidate Theodore Knauft was installed as teacher on August 29, 1948.

49. Crystal Lake

From Washington Heights the Lutheran Trail takes a long swing northwestward to a village located approximately forty-five miles beyond Chicago, past Dunton (Arlington Heights) and Palatine, to Crystal Lake.* The Rev. Henry Schmidt of Dundee, Ill., conducted the first Lutheran services in Crystal Lake on October 17, 1869. He continued his work here for about one year, conducting services every two weeks in a rented hall. Following his departure from Dundee, the little group in Crystal Lake was served with worship services every fourth Sunday and on weekdays by the Rev. Frederick W. Richmann, pastor of Saint John's, Elgin. On December 26, 1870, Immanuel Congregation in Crystal Lake was organized by thirty-six members, some of whom resided at Woodstock and McHenry, about eight miles northwest of Crystal Lake. A day school also was established under the direction of Pastor Richmann. In 1873 the latter left the pastorate in Elgin and followed a call to Pittsburgh, Pa. Then the Rev. Adam Detzer of Des Plaines—about twenty-seven miles southeast—took over the pastoral responsibilities in Crystal Lake, in addition to attending to his own parish in Des Plaines. He was assisted in the work at Crystal Lake by the Rev. George Reinsch of Janesville, Wis., and by the Rev. John E. Roeder of Dunton (Ar-

*1940 census: 3,917.

lington Heights), Ill. Candidate Henry G. Schmidt became Immanuel's first resident pastor on July 25, 1875. Three weeks later the congregation decided to build a school and to continue worshiping in rented quarters, pending the coming of a more auspicious time for the erection of a church. The school building, 20 x 37 feet, cost $575. It was erected midway between two "Lutheran settlements"–one of which was near the railroad and the other near the lake. In 1877 a church building was purchased and moved to the congregation's property, next to the school building. A steeple and a sacristy were added to this structure. In 1880 Pastor Schmidt accepted a call to Rochester, Minn., and the Rev. Max Heyer of Winfield Junction, N.Y., succeeded him at Immanuel in Crystal Lake on September 19, 1880. When in 1883 he followed a call to Minnesota Lake, Minn., the Rev. Karl Schmidt* of Rochester, Minn., became Immanuel's pastor in December of the same year.

In the summer of 1884 the congregation called Hicko Hicken† from Dundee, Ill., to become its first trained teacher. By this time the school building had outlived its usefulness, and a new building was erected at a cost of $850. Two years later the problem of increased enrollment recurred, but it was not until 1893 that a second class was organized and Pastor Schmidt became its instructor. By 1895 the congregation's membership had increased to about seven hundred, which meant that more adequate provision had become necessary for the worship services. Four lots south of the school were purchased for $450, and a new church was erected on this site. The contract called for five thousand dollars and the interior appointments an additional fourteen hundred dollars.

In July, 1897, Pastor Schmidt accepted a call to Saint James

*The two pastors were brothers.

†After eighteen years of teaching here Hicko Hicken went to Altamont, Ill. Soon afterward, in 1907, he passed a colloquium and entered the ministry. He served a pastorate at Kouts, Ind. He preached the sermons when Immanuel Ev. Lutheran Congregation at Crystal Lake, Ill., celebrated its fiftieth and seventy-fifth anniversary. He retired March 2, 1947, and moved to Chicago; he died on April 1, 1948, and was buried at Dundee.

(Sankt Jakobi) Congregation in Chicago, and on September 19, 1897, the Rev. Gardus Bertram of Pecatonica, Ill., succeeded him at Immanuel in Crystal Lake. Mr. Hicken, in 1903, was succeeded as teacher by A. D. Abraham. On October 9, 1904, Pastor Bertram accepted a call to Reinbeck, Iowa. His place in Crystal Lake was taken on December 18, 1904, by the Rev. Friedrich Gerhard Kuehnert of Omaha, Nebr. At that time the school enrollment was 130, and the new pastor taught the lower grades for the remainder of that school year. When the enrollment had risen to 150 in 1905, John Hue,* recent graduate of the Teachers' Seminary, Addison, took charge of that part of the school. A new school building costing $9,400 was erected and dedicated in 1906. In 1927 Mr. Abraham was succeeded by Alvin Hitzemann. In the spring of 1934 Pastor Kuehnert resigned. On June 10, 1934, the Rev. Gerhard A. Gehrs† of Fox Valley, Saskatchewan, Canada, was installed as Immanuel's pastor. In 1939 Mr. Hitzemann followed a call to Bay City, Mich. Then came Walter T. Voigt from Ottawa, Ill. In March, 1946, Mr. Voigt followed a call to Wyandotte, Mich. He, in turn, was succeeded by Walter G. Gerth, on June 20, 1946. The most recent change took place in February, 1947, when Leo H. Krumme took over the responsibilities in Immanuel School.[56] In October, 1949, Pastor Gehrs accepted a call to Crystal, N. Dak. (From Crystal Lake to Crystal!). His successor, the Rev. Arnold A. Wessler, was installed on January 22, 1950.

Mr. and Mrs. Charles Rahn on Sunday, April 14, 1948, observed their 68th wedding anniversary. (See Chapter 27.)

50. Sterling

The Lutheran Trail now continues westward as far as Rockford, and from there in a southwesterly direction, along the

*Teacher Hue died on Dec. 31, 1945, in Crystal Lake.

†A son of the Rev. F. L. Gehrs, pastor of St. John's Congregation at Elk Grove, Ill., since March 31, 1913.

banks of the beautiful Rock River, to Sterling,* in Whiteside County, Ill. Here are many "German Lutherans," the majority of whom live near the river. Also ten miles north, in Hopkins Township, and in the prairie west of the village are other German groups. Some of these early settlers at first attended services conducted by an itinerant German preacher "of the revivalistic type"—a type which did not appeal to these German Lutherans. But what could they do? Turning eastward, in search of Lutheran services, which probably would appeal to them, they found nothing within fifty miles.† Informed of the presence of a Lutheran pastor at Lyons (now Clinton), Iowa, where a congregation had been organized about fifteen years previously—in 1855—they forwarded, in 1870, a request to that pastor for spiritual care. The pastor in Lyons, the Rev. Claus Seuel, began occasional ministration, at first once-a-month excursions across the Mississippi River into Illinois, and by horse and buggy, on horseback, or by sled over rugged and sometimes well-nigh impassable roads to Sterling, thirty miles to the east. Also to be taken into account was the fact that Pastor Seuel was serving as schoolteacher in Lyons. It should be noted, *en passant*, that on rare occasions could he come by train on the Chicago and North Western Railroad, that is, when the "local" was running at the opportune time.

On October 4, 1874, Pastor Seuel was succeeded in the Lyons (Iowa) pastorate by the Rev. Frederick Lussky. Continuing the ministrations among the Lutherans in Whiteside County, Ill., Pastor Lussky conducted forenoon services about once each month in the Hopewell School of Hopkins Township and in the Swedish Lutheran church at Sterling. On April 25, 1875, the two groups adopted their new constitutions, the first group in the forenoon and the second in the afternoon. There-

*Named for Col. Samuel Sterling of Pennsylvania. The town was formed by consolidating the villages of Harrisburg and Chatham.—1940 census: 11,363.

†Even today, in 1949, Rochelle, Ill.—41 miles east of Sterling—is the nearest Lutheran (Missouri Synod) parish center, which at that time was non-existent.

upon the two congregations jointly called the Rev. H. Laven of San Francisco, Calif. When he declined the call, the formal "diploma" was addressed to the Rev. Frederick Lussky, who had taken a leading part in organizing the two parishes. Seventy years later (in 1945) Pastor Lussky gave the following account of what transpired after the California clergyman had returned the "diploma":

"Then they wanted me to come. I explained that it would be impossible, since I had been only a short time in Lyons and had my school. It remained as heretofore, and I continued to serve them from Lyons. Then, quite unexpectedly, without a word having been said to me about it beforehand, the call was sent to me. It was dated August 8, 1875, and was sent 'in the name of both congregations, Albert J. Alberts, chairman.' What should I do? Iowa at the time belonged to the Western District [Missouri Synod]. Pastor Buenger of St. Louis happened to come to Lyons on a trip and called on me. He advised me to accept the call since the people had gained such confidence in me, and persuaded the Lyons congregation, which had been served for a few years by our Synod, to grant me a dismissal. So I became pastor of both congregations. Some time elapsed, however, before I could make my home in Sterling." Pastor Lussky was installed on October 24, 1875, and received into the Illinois District in June, 1876. The congregations, however, did not join Synod at that time.

In those days it was not at all an uncommon thing for Lutheran families and individuals to emigrate from "the Old Country," accept the hospitality of friends and relatives in this area over winter or for a year or more, and then to strike out elsewhere on their own in Iowa or other points West.

On October 14, 1877, Pastor Lussky conducted the first Communion service in a near-by mission station, Nelson, Ill. This missionary activity, carried on in a schoolhouse, was discontinued in 1884. Many years ago the first two volumes of minutes of the voters' meetings were 'wantonly destroyed" by some malcontent, whose evil deed, doubtless, has long since been forgiven. Because of that deed, however, there are unfillable gaps in the long early history of these old congregations. For the same reason it cannot be definitely determined when the two lots on Second Avenue at East Tenth Street in Sterling were purchased.

Soon after his arrival in Sterling, Pastor Lussky founded a Sunday school, the sessions being conducted in Mrs. Grossmann's residence—directly behind the Swedish church on Kilgour Road. The first church, or "Kirchlein" (tiny church) as the Rev. J. Fackler of Lyons (Clinton), Iowa, in the course of his dedicatory sermon called it, was lighted by kerosene lamps.

Soon after the congregation in Sterling had been organized, the distillery where "some of the members made kegs" and others "tended to the Texas steers which were brought to Sterling for fattening on the mash," was destroyed by fire. Though partially rebuilt, it was never restored to its former status; finally it disappeared, and some of the members who had been employed there shook Sterling's dust off their feet and went elsewhere for employment.

Between the years 1870 and 1875 local children of confirmation age boarded in Lyons for two winters to attend the day school maintained by Saint John's Congregation in that city. After the organization of the congregation in Sterling, such a school was conducted during the winter months—from the autumn harvest until the beginning of farm work in the following spring. The first school building was erected in the summer of 1883. Pastor Lussky officiated at the dedication ceremonies; but before the new school year opened, he had become the first "full time" pastor of the congregation in Hopkins Township, eight miles northwest of Sterling. (See Chapter 69, page 286). He left Sterling on September 23, 1883, and his successor, the Rev. John Merkel of Chicago, was installed in Sterling on December 9, 1883. Apparently during Pastor Merkel's pastorate another attempt was made to establish another congregation in this part of northwestern Illinois, for the church records indicate that a Communion service was conducted by him in Jordan Township on September 25, 1885. A second entry of a similar service on April 25, 1886, concludes all references to this mission. In August, 1886, Pastor Merkel followed a call to Mascoutah, Ill. Then Pastor Lussky was called. At first he served as "vacancy pastor," and from the early part of 1887 until May, 1890, when he followed a call to Zion Congregation in Ottawa, Ill., he again had charge of both parishes. On June 8, 1890, the Rev. A. Carl Theo. Ponitz of Hahlen, Ill., was installed as pastor of the country parish, Hopkins Township. He served until April, 1892, and then followed a call to Genoa and Sycamore, Ill. His successor, Candidate Otto E. Richter, a recent graduate of Concordia Seminary, Springfield, Ill., was installed a short time later. On June 11, 1893, a new pastor was installed also in the Sterling parish, the Rev. F. Uplegger of Gresham, Wis. In September of the same year the latter was granted permission to preach an English sermon "now and then." He remained only until January 21, 1894, when he accepted a call to Gillett, Wis. Apparently the privilege of preaching in English was not exercised for the next twenty-three years. During the vacancy caused by Pastor Uplegger's departure the congregation in Sterling was served by a student of theology, William Meyer.* While the latter taught school, the Rev. Louis A. R. Gresens† of Germantown, Nebr., was called. His installation took place on May 21, 1894. The first "real" day school was organized under the direction of Pastor Gresens, who remained in Sterling until September, 1915, when he accepted a call to Coal City, near Wilmington, Ill.

*In 1902 a pastor, William H. Meyer, died in St. Louis, Mo., at the age of thirty-two—apparently the same man who taught school in Sterling, Ill., 1894.

†Louis A. R. Gresens, as a seminary student, taught school at Fairfield (St. Matthew's), Ill., in the early 1890's.

On October 24 in the same year the Rev. William John Voeltz* of Rochelle, Ill., was installed in Sterling. Services in German and English were conducted every Sunday, beginning in 1923. On January 7, 1929, the old name, "The First German Evangelical Lutheran Church," was changed to "Second Avenue Evangelical Lutheran Church." On April 20, 1938, Second Avenue Congregation joined the Missouri Synod. When Pastor Voeltz in the latter part of 1939 suffered a serious heart attack, the congregation engaged Candidate Eldor Mueller as assistant to the pastor. Pastor Voeltz died on February 21, 1940, and on the following June 23 Candidate Mueller was ordained and installed as pastor of Second Avenue Congregation in Sterling. In January, 1940, the number of German services per month was reduced to two, and in October, 1942, further reduced to four each year with Communion. Worthy of note is the fact that this congregation's spiritual activity derived support from the West—beyond the Mississippi River, in that Pastors Seuel and Lussky both came from the State of Iowa. In March, 1946, Mr. Schultz, custodian of Second Avenue Congregation, "began to deposit in a mite box the coins which he swept off the floor. After ten months the mite box was richer by 88 cents. Please do not write to the congregation suggesting possibilities of investment."[57]

51. Huntley

When the Lutheran Trail was at Belvidere, it might have anticipated history by fording the Kishwaukee River, a tributary of the Rock River, to explore Huntley,† situated on the opposite bank. But Huntley's first Lutheran (Missouri Synod) congregation was organized two years later than Immanuel in

*William J. Voeltz was born and reared in McHenry, Ill., not far from Sterling.

†1940 census: 674. Named for T. S. Huntley, an early settler and owner of the site.

Belvidere. German families from Pomerania, Germany, settled there shortly after the Civil War. Meanwhile, also, a Lutheran congregation had been organized in Dundee, about ten miles to the southeast. The pastor of that congregation, the Rev. Henry Schmidt, came over to serve the Lutherans in the Huntley community for a short time, 1868-1869. He was succeeded in this work by the Rev. Frederick W. Richmann, pastor of Saint John's Congregation in Elgin. It was under his leadership that Trinity Congregation was organized on March 5, 1871. The constitution was signed by more than the twenty-four men whose names appear at the bottom of this page.* On July 6, 1873, Trinity's first resident pastor, the Rev. Louis Steinrauf, was installed. Soon after the new church had been erected and dedicated, many members defected and joined the Reformed Church. In June, 1875, Pastor Steinrauf accepted a call to Immanuel Congregation in Belvidere, Ill. On September 24, 1876, the Rev. John Ernst Baumgaertner, in response to a call from the "remnant" of Trinity in Huntley came from Appleton, Mo., to Huntley and restored peace, and soon regained many of those who had caused the dissension. A sturdy missionary and organizer, he also ministered to the spiritual needs of Lutheran families living around Hampshire, Burlington, North Plato, Union, Marengo, Belvidere, Cherry Valley—preaching in private homes, schoolhouses, town halls, and even in a blacksmith shop, on Sundays and during the week. In 1886 he resigned and moved to western

*Charter members of Trinity, Huntley:

J. Schroeder
J. Cuetschow
F. Mueller
F. Peters
C. Vollman
Christ. Berner
H. Heuer
C. Gruetzmacher
F. Zimmermann
F. Sahs
J. Peters
C. Petschow
H. Schrader
H. Heinemann, Sr.
C. Fuhrmann
C. Weltzien
L. Schroeder
J. Weltzien
J. Trost
Wm. Henning
F. Felgenhauer
L. Engel
C. Lorenz
J. Awe

Nebraska, where, however, in the following year, he again assumed a pastorate. Thereupon Trinity of Huntley, together with the Lutheran congregations in Marengo and Hampshire, called the Rev. J. Lorenz Craemer of Fort Dodge, Iowa. He was installed on November 14, 1886. Less than two years later, in April, 1888, he accepted a call to Decatur, Ill. The next pastor, the Rev. Gottlieb C. Guelker of Aurelia, Iowa, was installed on November 11, 1888. He also taught school and remained for fifteen years, until 1903. In the same year the Rev. Siegfried Daniel Poellot became Trinity's pastor. Trinity had become "lodge-infested." Many of its members objected to the congregation's acceptance of Lutheran principles concerning membership in secret societies. Those who persisted in objecting were excommunicated. In failing health, Pastor Poellot in September, 1910, accepted a call to Immanuel Congregation in Palatine, about twenty miles east of Huntley. Trinity's next pastor was the Rev. Louis Baumgaertner of Hampshire, Ill. He was installed in December of the same year. Both he and his wife taught school, the attendance of which increased from twelve to fifty-six. Soon afterward a new school was erected, and in 1916 B. J. Seitz was placed in charge of the school. A short time later he accepted a call to Kendallville, Ind. Pastor Baumgaertner then again took over and taught until 1947, when he resigned from the active ministry. His successor, the Rev. Arthur F. Schroeder of Milwaukee, Wis., was installed on July 3, 1949.

52. Lockport

The Trail proceeds a few miles east of Huntley and then follows the Fox River from Elgin to Aurora; and thence it continues in a southeasterly direction, crossing the Du Page-Will county line in the prairie; and, after crossing the Des

Plaines River and the Sanitary and Ship Canal, it takes us, without further delay, to Lockport, Ill.* Unfortunately, "the records are very incomplete and give nothing but the barest facts." Saint Paul's Congregation in Lockport was organized on June 11, 1871. Soon after that the congregation purchased an old frame church building from the Episcopalians and moved it across the street, on Eleventh and Jefferson Streets. This building, now one hundred and thirteen years old, served as a church and school until 1912, when the new church was erected. The old church is still being used as a parish hall.

From 1871 until 1910 Saint Paul's of Lockport was served by the following neighboring pastors: the Rev. C. H. Rohde of Joliet, 1871-1874; the Rev. William Uffenbeck of Lemont, 1874-1886; the Rev. Karl A. Koch of Lemont, 1886-1888; the Rev. Barthold Burfeind of Lemont, 1888-1895; the Rev. August Schuessler of Joliet, 1895-1901; the Rev. Adolph Pfotenhauer of Lemont, 1901-1906; the Rev. H. Grefe of Lemont, 1906-1910. Saint Paul's first resident pastor, the Rev. Ernest George Zucker of Fargo, N. Dak., was installed on September 10, 1910. He served until November, 1915, when he accepted a call to Zion Congregation in Beecher, Ill. His successor was the Rev. Charles W. Tedrahn of Olmsted, Ill. He held this pastorate from January 9, 1916, until May, 1917, when he unexpectedly resigned. After the congregation had for some time called in vain, Pastor Tedrahn submitted a satisfactory reason for his "hasty resignation," whereupon Saint Paul's Congregation reinstated him in this pastorate, which he retained until January, 1923, when he accepted a call to Saint Peter's Congregation in Chicago. Saint Paul's third resident pastor, the Rev. Walter Bezold of Ferndale, Calif., was installed on December 12, 1923, and he is the present pastor (1949).

The day school was closed in 1917.[58]

*Lockport is named for its location at the locks of the old Illinois-Michigan Canal. Its population—1940 census: 3,475.

53. Summit

The Trail now follows the Des Plaines River and the Sanitary and Ship Canal* toward Chicago, but halts at Summit† —about twenty miles from Lockport. In this community Lutheran mission work was carried on from 1869 to 1871 by the Rev. G. A. Barth, assistant pastor at First Immanuel Church in Chicago. It was during the year 1871 that Zion Congregation was organized in Summit. In the following year F. Petersdorf donated a piece of ground to the new congregation, on which in the same year a church was erected. After Pastor Barth's discontinuance of service in Summit the Rev. Herman W. Querl, pastor of Trinity Congregation at near-by Willow Springs, served as "vacancy pastor" in Summit until 1873. Then came the Rev. M. Sandhaus, whose pastorate extended until 1875. In October of 1875 he was persuaded to leave his post in Summit. He resigned and moved to St. Louis, Mo. He was succeeded by the Rev. Wessel Bohlen of Macon, Nebr.; he remained for thirty-one years, 1876-1907. The Rev. G. Hintze, who came from the Danish Free Church, served from November 17, 1907, to the fall of 1908, and then resigned. The Rev. August Christlieb Carl Meyer of Coal City, Ill., served from November 1, 1908, until November, 1912, when he accepted a call to Zion Congregation in Wheatland Township (Plainfield), Ill. A new church was erected in 1913 under the pastorate of the Rev. Richard C. Neitzel of Kansas City, Kans., who served Zion Congregation from January, 1913, until August, 1918, when he accepted a professorship at Concordia Seminary, Springfield, Ill. Following him to Zion in Summit was the Rev. John Henry Mueller of Lone Elm,

*"Construction of two pipe line projects between Joliet and the Pulaski Road facility of the Chicago Pipe Line Company, People's Gas, Light and Coke Company subsidiary . . . is expected to be completed by next fall (1947) . . . most of the pumping equipment will not be installed until 1948." (Cf. The *Chicago Tribune*, Jan. 31, 1947.) The pipe lines run parallel to the Des Plaines River and the Drainage Canal.

†1940 census: 7,043. Named from its location on high land.

Mo., who held this pastorate from August, 1918, until May, 1925, and then accepted a call to Bellwood, about seven miles north by northwest of Summit. His successor in Summit was the Rev. August H. Lange of Madison, Nebr. After twenty-one years of pastoral service in Summit, begun in September, 1925, Pastor Lange retired from the active ministry in the spring of 1946, but continued to live in Summit. On June 30, 1946, the Rev. Herman E. Brauer, pastor of Saint Martini Congregation in Chicago since 1929, was installed as Zion's eighth resident pastor.

Zion Congregation has maintained a day school since the time of its organization in 1871. For about thirty-eight years this school was conducted by the respective pastors. In 1909 the first trained teacher, J. Schultz, was installed. Other teachers successively in charge of Zion School were: Herman Hilbig, Robert C. Runge, F. Martin, Paul Bachmann, Martin Hesemann, W. J. Rudow, Miss Mildred Schroeder, H. Bauer, P. Vetter, Rudolph T. Stahlecker, H. Timmermann, Eric W. Christian, the Rev. A. C. Staats (retired pastor, 1905-1924 in Marengo–Zion Congregation), Hugo E. Becker, E. A. Meyer, Karl Helmkamp, M. H. Eggerding, Richard Popp, Miss Miriam Kuehn, E. A. Muchow, Ernest R. Ebert,* Miss Wilma Schmidt, and Mrs. C. Anderson. A Sunday school was established in 1926. On September 21, 1947, the cornerstone for a school and parish building (90x110) was laid.

Erected at a cost of "more than $200,000," the new building was dedicated on Sunday, September 18, 1949. "Out of the congregation came the architect, mason, carpenter, electrician, and plumber."

In 1925 several members of Zion were released to organize Messiah Congregation in the Clearing industrial area, a few miles east of Summit. In 1929 members residing in the village of Spring Forest were released to organize Grace Congrega-

*Installed as teacher on Sept. 29, 1945; in June, 1948, he was transferred to Cuyahoga Falls, Ohio.

tion. In 1939 and 1940 about fifty members were transferred to the recently organized Gloria Dei Congregation, whose "center" is located at West Fifty-third Street and South Major Avenue, Chicago. And again in 1940 a few members were transferred to Holy Trinity Congregation* in the Bridgeview community, about two miles south of Summit.[59]

54. Chicago, First Bethlehem

From Summit the Trail follows arching Archer Road to the old western limits of Chicago, Western Avenue, a distance of about seven miles; thence north to North Avenue and into a community known as Holstein. It is the year 1871—a year which looms large both in the history of Chicago and that of the Missouri Synod in northern Illinois. First Saint John's Congregation, second "daughter" of First Saint Paul's, cradled in a branch school at Noble and Cornell Streets, began to function autonomously on March 28, 1867. The following year, 1868, a mission school was established by First Saint John's on North Paulina Street, near Milwaukee Avenue, and taught by Louis Appelt. (See Chapter 37, page 189.) In 1871 the members of First Saint John's, whose children attended this branch school, obtained permission to organize their own congregation. On June 26 of the same year the organization of Bethlehem Congregation was effected by thirty-one men.† The "mother" congregation combined the formal release not only with kind words, but also with the presentation of the school property on Paulina Street. Con-

*Organized in 1940.

†Charter members of First Bethlehem:

Fritz Rachow	Wilhelm Balwanz	Friedrich Spierling
Karl Richter	August Stricke	Herman Ebert
Christoph Blum	Franz Behnke	Carl Kemming
Christian Juers	F. Wilhelm Kopplin	Friedrich Schultz
Wilhelm Tuegel	Wilhelm Fraedrich	Louis Appelt
Wilhelm Hormann	Johann Borgiwald	Martin Gromell
Heinrich Hoeppe	Wilhelm Schiefelbein	Carl Maina
Carl Marten	Johann Lange	Dietrich von Horn
Friedrich Rohde	Wilhelm Doss	Wilhelm Kopplin
Ferdinand Fraedrich	Ferdinand Abraham	Johann Blankschen
Johann Dittmann		

struction of a church at the southeast corner of Paulina and McReynolds (now Le Moyne Avenue) Streets was begun in September. Meanwhile a call had been extended to the Rev. Augustus Reinke in Blue Island, Ill. After twice declining it, he accepted it when it was returned for the third time. He was installed as Bethlehem's first pastor on October 1, 1871. While the church was under construction, a large section of Chicago was destroyed by fire. The contractors engaged by Bethlehem's building committee voided their contracts, because the cost of labor and material had risen to unprecedented heights. On the basis of revised figures the church cost several thousand dollars more than had been anticipated. The church, a frame structure on a brick substructure, was dedicated on March 17, 1872, and for some time served as a place of worship, a basement-school, and a parsonage. Although Bethlehem Congregation had been spared any loss in the Great Fire, many of the homeless moved into the community and affiliated with this congregation. Whether or not this circumstance justifies the assertion that the fire was beneficial is difficult to determine. However, in certain respects the fire left in its wake definite benefits, alluded to in expressions such as: "The city came up from its ruins far more palatial, splendid, strong, and imperishable than before . . . a class of structure far better, in every essential respect, than before the conflagration." In an editorial in *The Lutheran and Missionary,* ten days after the fire, the Rev. W. A. Passavant, D.D.,* wrote (we quote in part): "But this wonderful city, which arose as if by magic above the marshes of the Chicago River and Lake and in little more than a generation became a mighty mart of trade and a teeming center of population from many lands, cannot remain in ashes. It will be rebuilt more substantially than ever, and even in a material sense, this appalling destruction

*The Passavant Memorial Hospital in Chicago was founded by Dr. Passavant.

of property and capital will 'work together for good,' though tens of thousands who have lost their all will be scattered as the chaff before the wind. 'The Lord reigneth,' and the devouring fire as well as the stormy wind fulfill His Word. It is a noble spectacle to witness the general and widespread sympathy with the sufferers . . . ."

The population of Chicago grew rapidly, particularly through a heavy wave of immigration from Germany; and the membership of Bethlehem Congregation, like that of the other Lutheran congregations in the city, was correspondingly increased. The financial "crash" of 1873, which affected virtually the entire civilized world, was not immediately felt by Chicago, which experienced its "hard times" during the years 1874-1877. In Chicago's business center another fire occurred on July 14, 1874. About 800 houses, for the most part cheap emergency dwellings hastily put up soon after the Great Fire, were destroyed.

In 1882 Bethlehem Congregation called an assistant pastor, Candidate Ernst Werfelmann of Concordia Seminary, Springfield, Ill., placing him in charge of its branch school,* a newly constructed frame building on Stave Street in the Humboldt community. Four years later, in 1886, this school developed into Christ Congregation. Bethlehem maintained two other branch schools, one on Girard Street, near Clybourn Place, and another at North Leavitt and Franklin Streets. Candidate John Dietrich Matthius served as assistant pastor at First Bethlehem from 1888 until 1890.†

In 1889, at a cost of $35,000, the church was enlarged to a seating capacity of fifteen hundred, and a 186-foot steeple was added. The auditorium has seven exits, so that an entirely filled church can be vacated within two minutes. The pews are circular, so that one immediately realizes how deeply those people were concerned with the matter of utilizing

*The Stave Street school was dedicated in July, 1882.

†In 1890 the Rev. J. D. Matthius accepted a call to Evanston, Ill.

every available inch, in order to provide room for one more hearer (". . . so dass man sofort erkennt, wie aengstlich man darauf bedacht gewesen ist, womoeglich jeden Zoll so auszunutzen, dass noch ein Sitz mehr fuer einen Zuhoerer gewonnen wuerde"). In 1896 Bethlehem Congregation* was recognized as the largest in the Missouri Synod.

On November 18, 1899, Pastor Reinke died. His eldest son, Edwin, who had been installed as assistant pastor on July 2, 1893, succeeded to the full pastorate in December, 1899. On June 17, 1900, Edwin's brother, Arthur L., was installed as assistant pastor.

In 1905 a large brick school building was erected directly east of the church; and in 1906 the eighth grade was added. On December 3, 1911, the branch school on Leavitt Street was closed, and the pupils were transferred to the "home" school at North Paulina and McReynolds (now Le Moyne Avenue) Streets.

Pastor Edwin Reinke died on March 12, 1919. His brother, Arthur L., then assumed full charge of the pastorate. In the same year, 1919, monthly services in the English language were begun. This schedule was adhered to for about ten years. In 1929 services in both German and English were conducted every Sunday morning.

Pastor Arthur L. Reinke died in 1934. His successor in the Bethlehem pastorate, which for about sixty-three years had been held by Reinkes, was the Rev. Clemens Thies of Edmonton,† Alberta, Canada. In February, 1945, Pastor Thies joined the faculty of Luther Institute and on June 8, 1947, was installed as assistant pastor of Saint Paul's (Austin), Chicago. In May, 1945, the Rev. Norman W. Heimsoth of Woodworth, Ill., became First Bethlehem's pastor. In April, 1949,

*Because other Lutheran congregations in Chicago adopted the name "Bethlehem," this eighth congregation of the Missouri Synod in Chicago has added the word "First" to its name.

†The Missouri Synod's first Concordia College in Canada was officially opened in Edmonton on Oct. 31, 1921.

he accepted a call to Grand Junction, Colo. His successor, the Rev. Arthur E. Krause of West Bend, Iowa, was installed in the old Holstein pastorate on Sunday, July 17, 1949.

According to the Missouri Synod's *Statistical Yearbook* for 1949 First Bethlehem's communicant membership currently is 808 as compared with 3,000 in 1896; 50 voting members as compared with 680 at that time; its day school enrollment, 149, compared with 975 fifty-three years earlier.

The long list of teachers* is an indication of Bethlehem Congregation's attention to the Christian education and training of its youth. A certain Lutheran pastor who in 1877 addressed the delegates of the Evangelical Lutheran Synodical Conference surely did not have in mind congregations like Bethlehem in Chicago when he said that it is "the sacred duty of pastors in congregations which are too poor to en-

*Teachers:

Louis Appelt, 1871-1913
Bernard Tessmann, 1872
F. Haertel, 1872-1876
F. Krumsieg, 1872-1893
R. Abel, 1874-1906
L. Karan, 1876-1898
C. Appelt, 1879
E. Steinkrauss, 1879-1906
E. Carsten, 1882-1931
Rev. Ernst Werfelmann, 1882-1885
C. Brandt, 1882-1931
R. Wismar, 1886-1914
Rev. J. D. Matthius, 1888-1890
Paul Bonnorant, 1890-1893
H. Lehwaldt, 1893-1927
E. Wagner, 1897-1903
C. Scheer, 1898-1905
O. Wagner, 1902-1910
A. Johnson, 1903-1911
Herman Maudanz, 1905-1908
A. Eggers, 1906
Paul T. Buszin, 1906-1918
F. Reuter, 1907-1908
B. Stellwagen, 1911-1916
F. J. Priehs, 1914-1923
K. J. Helmkamp, 1916-1945
W. C. Hoeltje, 1918-1922
A. Nottke, 1922-1937
W. F. Kolzow, 1923-1944
R. C. Marten, 1936
A. W. Grauer, 1937-1943
A. C. Abel, 1945
Paul T. Luebke, 1945-1947
Miss Brauns, 1882
Miss Massari, 1891-1894
Miss B. Paehler, 1893
Miss H. Karau, 1893-1897
F. Krumsieg, Jr., 1901-1902
W. Kammrath, 1902-1903
Miss E. Classen, 1903-1911
D. Meyn, 1903
Paul Engelmann, 1906
J. Fred Briel, 1906
R. A. Wismar, 1906
Miss A. Classen, 1906-1907
Miss A. List, 1906-1907
T. Bernett, 1908-1909
Miss Sippel, 1910-1911
Miss Volkmann, 1911-1917
Miss Gremel, 1911-1912
Miss Pfotenhauer, 1912
Samuel Goehringer, 1913
J. Bruns, 1923
Rev. Enno Gahl, 1936
G. Spruth, 1937
A. Abel, 1937-1938
Miss N. Bussmann, 1937-1939
Mrs. E. Gose, 1940-1943
Mrs. T. Leitz, 1944-1945
Miss Ruth Abel, 1944-1945
G. Becker, 1944-1945
Lester Beyer, 1945
Miss E. Leimer, 1945-1946
Miss Esther Abel, 1945
Mrs. A. Barman
M. E. Lorenz
Miss Ethel Piotkowski
Miss Lorraine Novak
Miss Luella Hetzke

gage a trained teacher for the instruction of their children to take over this work themselves at least three days each week. Unless this is done, such congregations have no future." Moreover, the large number of women teachers in First Bethlehem's schools seems to indicate that the congregation recognized the value of the "weaker sex" in the classroom. Or as A. H. Kramer puts it: "It is fortunate for our schools that many women teach in them. The touch of woman's hand is pleasantly felt. Woman is ideally fitted for the work of teaching children."

In June, 1928, a report embodying the following paragraph was adopted by the Northern Illinois District's delegates assembled in convention in River Forest: "1. The Sunday school cannot supplant the day school; 2. It does, however, enlarge and complete the educational program of the church by supplementing the work of the day school down to the cradle roll and up to the adult Bible classes, and by training and developing the devotional life in church surroundings; 3. It should be a very effective missionary agency for the extension of the Lord's kingdom in the local church and its day school." At the same convention the following resolution was adopted: "Das Bedauern des Distrikts darueber auszusprechen, dass in demselben noch 42 Gemeinden ohne regelrechte Gemeindeschule sind." ("That the District's regret be expressed at the fact that forty-two of its congregations still have no regular parochial school.")

Representing the Missouri Synod's Board of Directors, the Rev. G. Christian Barth appeared before the delegates of the same District and said: "Let us not despise the Christian day school and make every effort to establish one, neither let us look down upon the pastor who has no school, since despite his best efforts he may not succeed in establishing one." Long before this, in 1913, this statement was made and recorded at the convention of the Northern Illinois District:

"We must emphasize the day school more, and use the Sunday school only as a substitute through which we must gain children for the day school."

55. Chicago, Saint Peter's

The Lutheran Trail now veers toward the near South Side of Chicago, to the Town of Lake, just beyond Thirty-ninth Street, then the city limits. The majority of the Lutherans residing in this area—"in the woods and on the prairie"—in the 1860's and early part of the 1870's attended worship services in First Trinity Church, then located at Twenty-fifth and Canal Streets. They were regarded as "guests" of this third Missouri Synod congregation in the "Big City." The Rev. Ferdinand Doederlein, pastor of First Trinity at the time, writes: "I spent many a half night walking about, trying to win the people on Forest Avenue and vicinity, and finally succeeded in interesting them in establishing a day school."*

At Fortieth and State Streets an attic was rented, and on January 9, 1871, G. H. F. Pieritz began teaching there with seven pupils under his care. Pastor Doederlein preached in that schoolroom on Wednesday evenings; occasionally it was necessary for the teacher to conduct services and to read "prepared" sermons. Soon afterward three lots on Dearborn Street, between Thirty-ninth and Fortieth Streets, were purchased for $2,100. On September 5, 1871, seven men† organized a congregation and named it Saint Peter's.

On October 8, 1871—the day before the Great Fire—Saint Peter's first pastor, the Rev. Frank Lehmann of Bonfield, Ill., was installed. Upon the property which the new congrega-

*"Manche halbe Nacht bin ich in jenen Waeldern an Forest Avenue und Nachbarschaft herumgelaufen, um die Leute zu gewinnen; brachte sie auch endlich so weit, dass sie sich vereinigten, eine Schule zu errichten." *Geschichte der Ev. Luth. Gemeinden, U.A.C., zu Chicago, Ill.*, p. 81.)

†Charter members of St. Peter's:

Ludwig Bunde	Gottfried Rackow	John Wilk
Frederick Hardt	Carl Polzin	William Polzin
	Carl Hohn	

tion had taken over at the time of the organization a two-story frame building was erected, the upper story designed as a parsonage and the lower as a church and school. This building was dedicated on April 9, 1872 (Easter Day). Induced by the rapidly increasing church attendance, Saint Peter's Congregation erected a larger church edifice, costing seven thousand dollars, at the corner of Dearborn and Thirty-ninth Streets.* The dedication took place on the Sunday before Christmas in 1874. A more adequate school building was erected next to this church. In the same year, 1874, G. A. Albers was placed in charge of this school. He served until 1878, the year in which Thomas A. Edison's inventions were coming to world attention, among them the gramophone, or phonograph. Mr. Albers' successor at Saint Peter's School was H. G. Reifert. During this time the enrollment increased from 75 to 245. In 1879 the school building was enlarged and another teacher called, C. A. Riess.

Failing health of the pastor induced the congregation in 1878 to call a student of theology to assist him. John A. Streckfuss was ordained as "Pastor Vikarius" on June 30, 1878. Not long afterward, however, the "Pastor Vikarius" accepted a call to Davenport, Iowa. Pastor Lehmann died on May 19, 1883. His successor was the erstwhile assistant, now the Rev. John A. Streckfuss of Davenport, Iowa. During his pastorate a branch school was established at Forty-sixth and School Streets (now Princeton Avenue), and the church building was enlarged at a cost of five thousand dollars. On July 15, 1889, the Town of Lake was annexed to Chicago.† In the same year a number of members left Saint Peter's to found a separate congregation, which they named Gethsemane. A short interruption in Saint Peter's membership with the

*A year after the Great Fire there were more houses in Chicago than on the day before the fire.

†It was in 1889 that Dwight L. Moody, the noted evangelist, is reported to have said that "if Gabriel himself came to Chicago, he would lose his character before he had been here six weeks." (Philip Kinsley, *The Chicago Tribune—Its First Hundred Years*, Vol. III, p. 142.)

Missouri Synod occurred in 1891, resulting from the fact that the congregation regarded the suspension of its pastor from Synod as unjust and therefore also withdrew.* In 1892, however, the congregation rejoined Synod. For some years afterward the former pastor served as proofreader at Concordia Publishing House in St. Louis, Mo. On June 7, 1891, the Rev. F. Paul Merbitz† of Beardstown, Ill., was installed as the congregation's third pastor.

The shifting of the population, which included many members of Saint Peter's, resulted in the purchase of property on the southwest corner of West Seventy-fourth Street and Michigan Avenue. On this site a "basement" church was constructed in 1920. The bell of the old church was donated to Saint Paul's Congregation (Grand Crossing), Chicago, and is still in use.‡ Pastor Merbitz conducted services for the last time on January 1, 1923; on the first Sunday of the new year a stroke of apoplexy seriously affected his speech. In the hope that the disorder would be corrected, the congregation in that same month called an assistant pastor, the Rev. Charles W. Tedrahn of Lockport, Ill., but on May 1, 1924, Pastor Merbitz resigned, and Pastor Tedrahn assumed full charge of the pastorate. During his ministry a Sunday school was organized (1923), a parish school was built (1926), and the superstructure of the "basement" church was completed and dedicated, March 13, 1927. In August, 1936, Pastor Tedrahn resigned.§ His successor, the Rev. Arthur Preisinger

*Synodical officials sometimes also blunder. One of the first presidents of the Western District (Missouri Synod) was divested of the pastorate because he taught false doctrine. Later he renounced his error and rejoined the Missouri Synod as a pastor. (See *Concordia Cyclopedia*, 1927, p. 683.)

†His wife was a daughter of the Rev. Frederick Lochner, a Lutheran pioneer (1822-1902). As a youth, Lochner was a copper-plate engraver ("Kupferstecher").

‡This bell was formally dedicated in 1892.

§Re-entered the ministry Oct. 22, 1940, serving as first pastor of Markham Congregation, Markham, Ill.; since November, 1946, in charge of a pastorate at El Cajon, Calif.

of Hamilton, Ontario, Canada, but a native Chicagoan, was installed as Saint Peter's pastor on January 3, 1937.*

Saint Peter's School, which had its inception in the attic of a rented building on the old Vincennes Trail (State Street) in January, 1871, has had an uninterrupted existence down to the present time. The following have served as teachers:†

G. H. F. Pieritz
G. A. Albers
H. F. Reifert
Miss Reifert
C. A. Riess
Paul Bonneront
C. H. Wagner
Miss Streckfuss
Miss Conrad
Mrs. H. Schwanke
B. Bruening
J. A. Theiss
Miss Stubnatzy
Gustav A. Niethammer
O. Wegner
E. Meier
Albert L. Daenzer
Bernhard Hoppe
Miss Elaine Blau
Walter H. Wilke
B. Wambsganss
W. Schweder
Louis Doering
W. A. Meier
Samuel Goehringer
Miss Martha Schneider
J. Vornsand
A. H. Schulz
Reinhold Arkebauer
Miss L. Homann
W. H. Cholcher
Miss Esther Rewoldt
Miss Esther Arndt
Miss Emma Wendler
W. C. Marten
R. P. Ruehs
J. Beck
Erich O. Haase
Miss Lois Haase
Theo. P. Klammer
Aaron Valleskey[61]

56. Chicago, Saint Matthew's

Reversing its track northward, the Trail next reaches the "Lime Kiln" territory, at the intersection of 2100 South and 2100 West. Here, in 1869, First Immanuel Congregation had set up a one-room branch school on a corner lot, now South Paulina Street and West Twenty-first Place. The first teacher was William H. Ganske, who was among the many Germans that immigrated to America in 1867. There was no adequate place for public meetings in this community, so the Rev. J. Paul Beyer, pastor of First Immanuel, and the newly called schoolteacher simply ascended a "brick wagon" which had been drawn upon the school premises for the important occasion; and there, before a large crowd of people, the solemn

*The pastor's son, Daniel C. Preisinger, was ordained in St. Peter's Church on Sunday, Oct. 5, 1948; he is now stationed in Edmonton, Alberta, Canada.

†Includes teachers in branch school at 46th and School Streets (now Princeton Avenue).

installation of Mr. Ganske was performed. On the following day, school was opened with forty-five pupils. In the course of the next few years many more people established their homes in this community. Soon the school building was made to serve also as a place of public worship. The services on weekday evenings were conducted alternately by Pastor Beyer and the Rev. Anton Wagner, pastor of First Zion Congregation, located at Nineteenth and Johnson (now Peoria) Streets.

In 1871 about thirty members of First Immanuel obtained their release to organize their own congregation in the new residential area, north of the old docks on the South Branch of the Chicago River ("Garlic Creek"), or about a mile and a half north of "Bridgeport." On September 13, 1871, the organization of Saint Matthew's Congregation was effected. Without delay the congregation purchased a large plot of ground comprising fifty lots, forty-two of which were offered for sale at $350 each, preferably to members of Saint Matthew's. The remaining eight lots located at the northwest corner of Twenty-first Street and Hoyne Avenue were reserved for the congregation's own use. Upon this site a large church building with an 180-foot steeple was erected.* The dedication took place on December 1, 1872. Less than a month prior to this event, Saint Matthew's resolved to call its own pastor, the Rev. Martin Guenther of Saginaw, Mich. The pastor-elect, however, could not come to Chicago until the following June; the installation was performed by the Rev. Henry Wunder, pastor of the "grandmother" congregation—First Saint Paul's—on June 16, 1872. In the same year Saint Matthew's became a member of the Missouri Synod; the first parsonage was erected at a cost of $1,424; and school picnics were inaugurated.

While still in the embryonic stage, Saint Matthew's lost

*This church was a frame building, 55 x 106 feet, erected at a cost of $20,825. The high basement was used for schoolroom purposes until 1875; a portion of it was used for similar purposes until 1882.

its first pastor. On July 28, 1873, Pastor Guenther accepted a professorship at Concordia Seminary, St. Louis, Mo. He was also given the position as managing editor of the *Lutheraner*, and in 1877 became the first editor of a magazine designed especially for Lutheran pastors, *Homiletisches Magazin*, which later was combined with two other periodicals, *Lehre und Wehre* and *Theological Monthly*. Pastor Guenther died in St. Louis on May 22, 1893.

The Rev. Herman H. Engelbrecht of Lowden, Iowa, succeeded to Saint Matthew's on Oct. 12, 1873. In the years following, the membership rapidly increased, as happened in other congregations in Chicago—First Saint John's, First Bethlehem, First Zion, First Trinity—since many German immigrants settled in the neighborhood. Professor C. August T. Selle of the Teachers' Seminary, Addison, was called to preach in Saint Matthew's Church every second Sunday of each month, but this extra help for the pastor soon proved insufficient; the congregation, therefore, called an assistant pastor, Candidate Paul Brauns, who was installed on February 1, 1885. He served until July, 1891, when he accepted a call to Concordia Congregation* in the Avondale community, at Belmont and Washtenaw Avenues, Chicago.

In 1875 a new school was erected behind the church and in 1882 another opposite the church, on Hoyne Avenue.

On July 23, 1887, the church building was completely destroyed by fire, which originated in the tower, where repairs were being made. Swept by a strong wind, the flames soon enveloped the entire building. Everything was destroyed, including the four basement schoolrooms, with the exception of the Communion vessels, pulpit robes, the book of rituals and liturgy ("Agende"), the pulpit Bible, and the crucifix. A new church with a seating capacity of two thousand and cost-

*Concordia Congregation was organized on June 29, 1891. Four years later Pastor Brauns and a large part of this congregation defected and organized a congregation which then joined the Evangelical Church. (See Chapter 121.)

ing sixty thousand dollars was dedicated on September 30, 1888. At that time Saint Matthew's Congregation had a membership of 5,500, which included 3,480 communicants and 475 voting members. The school enrollment was 1,060. 1888 was the year in which electric lights were beginning to take the place of gas in Chicago's street-lighting system.

In the previous year, 1887, a number of members residing farther west, in the neighborhood of Twenty-second Street (now known also as Cermak Road) and California Avenue, were released to organize their own congregation, which was named Saint Mark's. This congregation grew out of a branch school which Saint Matthew's had established in that community in 1884.(See Chapter 103.)

On February 23, 1896, the Rev. Herman Engelbrecht, Jr., of Woodstock, Ill., was installed as assistant pastor of Saint Matthew's. He served in this capacity until 1907, when he resigned. In the same year Candidate Theodore F. Siemon,* graduate of Concordia Seminary, St. Louis, Mo., was installed as assistant pastor. He served in this capacity until September 15, 1915, when he succeeded Pastor Herman H. Engelbrecht to the full pastorate.†

In 1925 the church steeple was dismantled because of its weakened condition, which constituted a serious hazard, and. incidentally, also because of the high maintenance cost. In the same year a Sunday school was established.

On May 1, 1946, Pastor Siemon retired from the ministry. His successor, the Rev. Ewald F. Lorenz of Vernon Center, Minn., was installed as Saint Matthew's pastor on September 22, 1946.

The history of Saint Matthew's Congregation, like unto that of many other Missouri Synod congregations throughout the country, begins with a day school. During the ninety-year

*A son of the Rev. Otto Siemon, D.D., professor at Concordia College, Fort Wayne, Ind., 1881-1902. Dr. Siemon died Nov. 23, 1902.

†Pastor Engelbrecht died June 3, 1915.

period, from 1869 to 1949, the following have served as teachers at Saint Matthew's:

William H. Ganske	F. Wiedmann
F. Rusch	M. Frieser
J. Backhaus	J. Meyer
R. Nimmer	Mildred Frese
A. Paul	M. Dobberfuhl
W. Schneider	Emil A. Zutz
M. Eggerding	J. L. Bachaus
E. Lietke	J. Faitz
Edward Kopittke	F. Vieweg
W. Freide	F. Polinske
J. Rademacher	H. Christopher
H. Borchers	F. Klenner
H. Heyne	E. Warnke
J. Lettermann	Armin Grams
P. Czamanske	Mrs. Marie Nestle
Mrs. E. Warnke	Leroy A. Bendien
Herman Grote	Miss Ruth Abel
C. Appelt	Roy Kolzow62

57. Sollitt

Forty miles straight south from Chicago's Loop is the hamlet known as Sollitt, in Will County.* Here is Zion Church, the "center" of a "daughter" congregation of Saint Paul's near Beecher. Zion was organized on March 13, 1872, by thirteen men† under the direction of the Rev. Herman Lossner, pastor of Saint Paul's. Two acres of land were bought, and a building, which served as church, school, and parsonage, was erected at a cost of $1,925. Zion's first resident pastor was the Rev. Lorenz Traub of Monticello, Iowa, who served from November 28, 1872, until December 1, 1873, when he accepted a call to Saint Paul's Congregation at Yellowhead, six miles northeast of Grant Park, Ill. He was succeeded by the Rev. Carl W. R. Frederking, who remained

*1940 census: 55.

†Charter members:

Chr. Schroeder	O. Matthias
F. Heidemann	D. Scharnhorst
P. Buhr	H. Wehling
L. Stade	C. Molthan (a)
A. Luhmann	H. Roetter
F. Luhmann	F. Trebesch
C. Nottorf	

(a) Father of the Rev. John F. C. Molthan, pastor of Immanuel Congregation in Batavia, Ill., 1921-1934.

from May 14, 1874, until October 19, 1876, and then accepted a call to Lost Prairie, Ill. It was during his pastorate that Zion joined the Missouri Synod. After a ten-month vacancy, Candidate Albert Wangerin* was ordained and installed as Zion's third pastor, on August 5, 1877. He served this parish for about forty-eight and a half years, until January 3, 1926, when he died. During his pastorate, in 1899, the church was enlarged and a parsonage erected. Pastor Wangerin was succeeded by the Rev. Carl L. Abel, recently ordained by his father in Elmhurst, Ill.† He was installed as Zion's fourth pastor on July 18, 1926. In 1927 English services were introduced in addition to the German services. Pastor Abel preached his farewell sermon in Sollitt's Zion Church on July 27, 1930, and followed a call to Zion Congregation in Washington Heights (Chicago). Throughout the years of its existence Zion School was in charge of the respective pastors. Pastor Abel's successor in the Zion pastorate, the Rev. Daniel A. Gimbel of Fort Frances, Ontario, Canada, was installed in the early part of the following fall. In January, 1938, he accepted a pastorate in Norfolk, Nebr. On May 1, 1938, the Rev. Walter F. Feddersen of Tracy, Ind., was installed as Zion's sixth pastor.‡ In the following year, 1939, a Sunday school was established; in 1943 a basement under the church was constructed, and several other improvements were made, costing altogether eight thousand dollars.

A vivid description of a tornado which struck this territory on April 7, 1948, appears in the *Northern Illinois Messenger* of May 18, 1948 (LXVII, 10). (See Chapter 47.)

*A son, Albert D. Wangerin, was pastor of Tabor Congregation, Chicago, from 1908 until 1940. He died on May 17, 1940. Another son, Walter C. Wangerin, was pastor of St. John's Congregation in Lombard, Ill. ("City of Lilacia"), from March, 1919, until 1930, when he accepted a call to Grand Rapids, Mich. He died on September 19, 1948.

†The Rev. Carl Abel, Sr., was pastor of Immanuel Congregation, Elmhurst, Ill., from 1911 until 1943. He died on March 13, 1947.

‡His father, the Rev. Matthew H. Feddersen, was pastor of St. John's at Coopers Grove, Ill., 1897-1929. He died on March 31, 1940.

58. Evanston

Returning by way of the Dixie Highway, northward, the Trail goes through Chicago, coming out at the other end in Evanston, Ill.* Evanston was not the high-toned "Chicago's dormitory" that it is today, and there were but few Lutherans in this community in the early 1870's, for it is recorded that, "being too small in number to support a minister in their midst, the Lutherans turned to the Rev. Augustus Reinke," pastor of First Bethlehem Congregation in Chicago, "to take the new congregation under his spiritual care and to serve the people as well as could be reasonably expected," all of which Pastor Reinke faithfully did despite the exacting conditions of time and distance. However, before the close of the first year of such service, 1872, which also was the founding year of Bethlehem in Evanston, Pastor Reinke found it impossible, because of his manifold duties and responsibilities in his large Chicago parish, to continue serving this little flock. Thereupon the congregation turned for aid to the Rev. Gotthilf S. Loeber, pastor of Saint John's Congregation at Dutchman's Point (now Niles). He served the Evanstonians until some time in 1873. It was during the previous year that the first Japanese vessel ever to come to the United States arrived in San Francisco, Calif., with a cargo of tea, on August 13, 1872. In the same year the Japanese embassy visited Chicago and donated five thousand dollars to the sufferers of losses in the Great Fire of October 9, 1871. Later a quarter million dollars' worth of livestock and farm implements were purchased by them in Chicago.

After Pastor Loeber had terminated his service in Evanston, it would seem, the Evanstonians were left more or less isolated

*Evanston was named after John Evans, who in 1861 submitted a petition for a railroad linking Evanston with Chicago. The lake shore from Lake View (north of Fullerton Avenue) to Evanston, according to Mr. Evans' petition, was a waste. John Evans, in the 1890's, served as territorial governor of Colorado. Evanston—1940 census: 65,389.

or orphaned, for it was not until 1875 that arrangements were made with the Rev. Edward Doering, pastor of Trinity Congregation at Gross Point (Glencoe), Ill., to serve the Evanston Lutherans in conjunction with his pastorate some seven miles to the north. This arrangement functioned satisfactorily until July, 1881, when Pastor Doering accepted a call to Portland, Oreg. In the same year the Rev. Adam Detzer, Jr.,* succeeded him to the dual pastorate; however, he established his home, not in Glencoe, but in Evanston, and thereby brought about a reversal of the eight-year system. Trinity of Glencoe was now served as an affiliate of Bethlehem in Evanston.†

The first church erected by Bethlehem Congregation in 1876 served its purpose for about ten years. A new one was erected in 1886. The *Evanston Index* under date of November 27, 1886, carried this news item: "A small society, mostly poor Lutheran Christians, who lived in the midst of a wealthy village, concluded to build a better and more commodious house of worship. Scarcely had the frame of the building been erected when a fierce hurricane swept over the village, and when you awoke in the morning, your eyes looked upon the ruins of what had been your joy." The original building, a frame structure, was sold to the Swedish Lutheran congregation and later resold to the Norwegian Lutheran congregation, where it still is being used for worship in a remodeled and enlarged state.

Pastor Detzer's pastorate in the Evanston-Glencoe parish ended in May, 1890, when he accepted a call to Highland Park, Ill.

Pastor Detzer's successor in the dual parish was the Rev. John Dietrich Matthius, hitherto assistant pastor at First

*He was orlained and installed by his father, the Rev. John Adam Detzer, Sr., who in 1845 was sent by Pastor J. K. Wilhelm Loehe of Neuendettelsau, Bavaria, Germany, to America to serve as missionary in northern Ohio. He was pastor of Immanuel, Des Plaines, Ill., 1873-1881, was in office for 58 years, and died in Niles Center (now Skokie) in 1903.

†Bethlehem Congregation joined the Missouri Synod in 1884.

Bethlehem Congregation in Chicago. In 1902 he relinquished the Glencoe pastorate,* but continued serving the congregation in Evanston until the fall of 1910, when he accepted a call to Indianapolis, Ind. The Rev. C. F. W. Meyer of Baltimore, Md., served Bethlehem Congregation from October, 1910, until October, 1916, when he followed a call to East Rutherford, N.J. Then came the Rev. Paul W. Luecke, Jr.,† of Roselle, Ill. He was Bethlehem's pastor from December, 1916, until the spring of 1932, when he resigned from the ministry. His successor, the Rev. Karl Kurth of Saint Peter's in Joliet, Ill., held this pastorate for about four years, from July, 1932, until June, 1936, when he accepted a call to St. Louis, Mo. Next came the Rev. Theodore F. Andres from Valparaiso University, Valparaiso, Ind., who remained for about three years and then, in 1939, accepted a call to Madison, Wis. The successor, the Rev. Walter E. Gehrs‡ of Anamoose, N. Dak., served for about six years; in December, 1946, he returned to North Dakota to assume charge of a dual parish in that State, Langdon and Dresden. He was succeeded in Evanston on June 8, 1947, by the Rev. Samuel E. Rathke of Santa Ana, Calif.

Although residing in Gross Point (Glencoe), Pastor Doering, in 1880, began teaching school in the newly organized day school of Bethlehem Congregation in Evanston. The first school building was erected in 1882; a new school building was erected in 1889 and dedicated in 1890. That building served its purpose until 1921, when a new school was erected. In 1884 Pastor Detzer was relieved of the teaching duties when a layman, Herman Feuchter, consented to assume that responsibility—there being no teacher-graduate available at the time. In 1886 a trained teacher, Martin E. Bittner, was called.

*In 1902 Trinity in Glencoe called its own (second) pastor, the Rev. Bernhard Hintz of Stones Prairie, Mo.

†A son of the Rev. Paul Luecke, pastor of St. John's (Mayfair), Chicago, 1886-1937. The father died on Feb. 15, 1944, the son on July 19, 1943.

‡A son of the Rev. F. L. Gehrs, pastor of St. John's, Elk Grove, Ill., since March 31, 1913. He came to Elk Grove from Marion, N. Dak.

He served until 1905 and then accepted a call to Saint Paul's School in Kankakee, Ill. The following have taught in Bethlehem School since that time:

R. Mangelsdorf
Ernst Mossner
John A. Jaeger
Fred Toenies
William Luebkert
Miss Norma Stolte
Otto Schaefer
Fred W. Toenies
Miss Mathilde Doederlein
Carl E. Kasten
Walter M. Mirow
Mrs. John A. Jaeger
Mrs. Richard Schlake63

59. Woodworth

Eighty miles south of Chicago's Loop is another German community, too small to be numbered in the census; its name is Woodworth. Prior to 1870 this whole area was very sparsely populated. "It was a paradise for the birds of the air, but not for human beings." ("Es war ein Paradies fuer die Voegel des Himmels, aber nicht fuer Menschen.") German settlers purchased land at very low prices and cultivated it. Being Lutherans, they seriously considered having regular worship services in their own midst; but their number was so small that they realized their inability of supporting a pastor. They, too, had heard about a Lutheran congregation "not far away" —at Crete, whose pastor was the Rev. Gottlieb Traub. To him a plea for spiritual attention was submitted. He readily consented to serve the Woodworth group as an affiliate of Trinity (prior to 1858 known as Zion). On some Sundays, however, it was utterly impossible for him to appear at Woodworth; in such instances, then, a reading service ("Lesegottesdienst") was conducted by laymen, at first in the homes of Henry Rehborg and August Luecke and later in the school building. The organization of the congregation was effected in July. 1872.* The first minutes of voters' meetings containing

*Charter members:
August Wm. Schwer
August Luecke
Philip Redeker
August Pfingsten
Heinrich Schrage
Wilhelm Hue
Christoph Munstermann
Dietrich Langelett
Carl Raddatz
Heinrich Rippe
Heinrich Rehborg
Heinrich Schumacher

references to the young congregation's activities are dated April 20, 1873. At that meeting it was resolved to build a church. The farmers had relatively little leisure time, but not one of them indicated unwillingness to participate in the venture and to bring it to a successful conclusion. The project involved more than ordinary building problems and brawn. Stone had to be hauled by wagon all the way from Momenza (Momence)—about thirty-five miles north of the building site. In the fall of that year, 1873, Saint Paul's first pastor, the Rev. John Christian Friedrich Hartmann of Sieden Prairie, four miles southeast of Tinley Park, Ill., was installed. On October 26 of the same year the first church was dedicated. Twice the congregation was disturbed by defections within the next few years. In 1887 a new church was erected. An assistant pastor, Candidate Heinrich Christian Friedrich Neben, was installed on September 13, 1896. Less than a year later, on April 4, 1897, the assistant pastor accepted a call to Zion Congregation in Matteson, Ill. Saint Paul's School, established in 1872, was completely in charge of the respective pastors until 1878, when H. R. U. Richert assumed this responsibility. His successor in 1882 was Theodore Benecke. Meanwhile the congregation was rapidly expanding, although roads from every direction leading to church and school were often impassable. Therefore a branch school was erected in the northern section of the large parish and Wilhelm von Dissen placed in charge. After Mr. Benecke's departure, L. Zeile took over the work in the main or "home" school, until 1887. He was followed by Chr. Merkenschlager,* who served until 1890. Miss Christiana Hartmann took over the branch school, and Mr. von Dissen was transferred to the "home" school. Student Gans rendered temporary assistance until 1893, when teacher-candidate Albert C. Scheer was inducted as teacher at the branch school.

*A son, the Rev. Albert G. Merkens, of Pittsburgh, Pa., was installed in Chicago as Director of Religious Education, May 20, 1945.

Pastor Hartmann resigned in 1898. His successor, the Rev. Richard L. Seils of Swiss Alp, Tex., was installed in 1899.

In 1907 Theodore Trautmann took Mr. von Dissen's place at the "home" school. In 1909 Mr. Scheer accepted a call to Peace School in Chicago, and J. D. Bruns came to the branch school. Henry Waldschmidt followed Mr. Trautmann in the "home" school in 1911. By the end of 1913 the congregation was without a pastor; Saint John's at Rodenberg, two miles west of Roselle, Ill., convinced Pastor Seils that his services were more necessary in that field. On April 26, 1914, his successor at Woodworth, the Rev. Friedrich Adolf Carl Meyer of Cole Camp, Mo., was installed as Saint Paul's third pastor. In 1915 a new school was erected. In 1916 Mr. Scheer was called back from Peace School in Chicago, and Mr. Waldschmidt left. Karl F. Roemer came in 1920 to take the place of Mr. Bruns in the branch school. In 1922 a new branch school was built.

In 1925 Pastor Meyer resigned.* He was succeeded on August 16, 1926, by the Rev. Rudolph F. W. Jeschke of Amarillo, Tex.

In 1934 C. H. Kraemer took Mr. Roemer's place in the branch school.† Not long afterward Pastor Jeschke resigned, and the Rev. Norman W. Heimsoth of Arriba, Colo., became Saint Paul's fifth pastor. In 1940 Mr. Scheer was compelled by failing health to resign.‡ Melvin Bernhard was installed in August, 1940; and in 1942 Leonard Laubenstein was added to the teaching staff. In May, 1945, Pastor Heimsoth accepted a call to First Bethlehem Congregation in Chicago, and the Rev. Carl H. Fruendt of Renault, Ill., became Saint Paul's sixth pastor.

*In 1926, however, his name appears as pastor in Centralia, Ill.

†Karl F. Roemer accepted a call to Immanuel in Dundee, Ill.

‡Mr. Scheer, after his resignation, did supply work at St. John's School at near-by Ash Grove. "During his 48 years of service Mr. Scheer was absent from his classroom but four days." He died on Dec. 6, 1946, at the age of 73 years and six months and lies buried in St. Paul's Cemetery at Woodworth.

NOTE: St. John's at Ash Grove is a "daughter" congregation—organized in 1887.

60. Des Plaines

History is now in the memorable year of the financial panic—1873— and turning back a few of its pages, one reads about the Rev. Henry Wunder's missionary calls in the village of Des Plaines, Ill.,* about fifteen miles northwest from his Chicago parish. He found people who called themselves Evangelical Lutheran, but nevertheless "inclined unionistically." Did W. Kolb have Des Plaines in mind when he made the pithy statement: "The [church] union . . . is lifeless, dead, and already smells . . ."?† Probably he did not even know that a place like Des Plaines existed. Three years after Pastor Wunder started his visits in this community, in 1876, the Rev. F. J. Biltz, president of the Western District (Missouri Synod), in the course of his presidential address at the convention of Synod, said: "Of course, we would gladly lay the sword aside and build the walls of Zion only with the trowel; but so long as the truth is spoken against, the mouth of faithful witnesses dare not become silent." ("Gerne moechten wir freilich das Schwert niederlegen und nur mit der Kelle an den Mauern Zions bauen, aber so lange der Wahrheit widersprochen wird, darf der Mund treuer Zeugen nicht verstummen.")‡ Perhaps yet more appropriate is the observation of the Rev. Franz Pieper: "We American Lutherans of a strictly confessional position have not the slightest reason for exalting ourselves above others. Without doubt we should be swimming in the same misdirected current if divine grace had not placed us amidst an entirely different church environment. We—the second and third generations—have received our theological training under the most favorable conditions conceivable."

*1940 census: 9,518. So named from the presence of a species of maple, "plaine" in French.

†"Die Union ist . . . stark verblichen, entschlafen und riechet, st. . . . schon. Das merkt man allgemein." (Cf. *Der Lutheraner*, XIII, 26, p. 203.)

‡*Proceedings of the Western District*, convention held in Trinity Ev. Lutheran Church, St. Louis, Mo., 1876. Page 12.

The Lutherans in Des Plaines originally were organized as the Evangelical Lutheran Saint Stephanus Congregation. Quoting a portion of its constitution (translated from the German): "The congregation acknowledges the Holy Bible as the revealed Word of God and accepts it as the sole source and standard of faith and life; but it is guided in its exposition of it by the general confessions of the Christian Church. The distinctive doctrines of the German Evangelical Church, however, we do not deem necessary to salvation, but adhere in regard to these to the expressed words of Holy Scripture, and therefore we do not deny any Christian, may he call himself Lutheran, Reformed, or United, participation in the Lord's Supper and other church privileges. Anyone paying the fee determined upon by the congregation is eligible for membership." A similar principle was adopted more recently by the Confessional Synod ("Bekenntnissynode") in Halle, Germany, twelve years ago, in 1937: "Affiliation with the Reformed Church is no reason for being excluded from the (Lord's) Supper celebrated by a congregation of the Lutheran Confession, nor is affiliation with the Lutheran Church a reason for being excluded from the Supper celebrated by a Reformed congregation; therefore, members of the Lutheran, Reformed, and Union churches can celebrate the Lord's Supper together without coming in conflict with the Scriptural administration of the Holy Supper."

Some of the Lutherans in Des Plaines refused to subscribe or adhere to such un-Lutheran and unscriptural principles, so they consulted with the Rev. Henry Wunder in the matter of securing a Lutheran pastor, with the result that the Rev. John Ed. Roeder of Dunton (Arlington Heights), assisted by the Rev. William Dorn of Elk Grove and Professor C. August T. Selle of the Teachers' Seminary, Addison, conducted the services and shared in the pastoral activities in Des Plaines. Meanwhile, on May 18, 1873, the congregation was reorganized as Immanuel, and the Rev. John Adam Detzer, Sr., of Defiance, Ohio, was installed as its first pastor. In 1881 Pastor Detzer accepted a call to Colon, Nebr., and was succeeded in Des Plaines by the Rev. George Johannes of Rockford, Ill., in 1882.

In 1874 the first trained teacher, H. Rademacher, assumed charge of Immanuel School. He served until March, 1891, and was succeeded by Chris. Seidel.

Pastor Johannes' successor in January, 1886, was the Rev. Peter Graef of Yellowhead, six miles northeast of Grant Park, Ill. In 1891 Pastor Graef accepted a call to Fremont, Nebr. On July 12 in that year the Rev. William Lewerenz of Effingham, Ill., was installed as his successor.

On January 10, 1892, Immanuel Congregation voted to join the Missouri Synod. In the following year, 1893, Mr. Seidel followed a call to Seymour, Ind., and A. W. Vogt succeeded him at Immanuel. When he left Des Plaines in 1897, the congregation called two teachers: H. Schroeder of Effingham, Ill., and Ernst Lewerenz. On May 4, 1902, Mr. Schroeder accepted a call to Saint James' School in Chicago, and Ernst Schmidt of Chicago came to Immanuel in Des Plaines. Miss Bertha Lewerenz then took charge of the primary grades. In 1905 Mr. Schmidt went to Red Wing, Minn.

On September 14, 1911, Pastor Lewerenz died and was buried in Concordia Cemetery in Forest Park, Ill. Immanuel's next pastor, the Rev. Walter Frederick Pieper of Farmersville, Ill., was installed on November 19, 1911.

On March 30, 1913, August Koch was inducted into the office of day school teacher in Immanuel School, which he occupied until August, 1917. In the fall of the same year two teachers were installed: Erich H. Schalk of Bristol, Conn., and Theodore Markworth of South Chicago. In the fall of 1918 Herman Ninnemann became a teacher in this school, and Walter Lauing in 1922. Others were Armin Meyermann.

Herbert Gatzke, Mrs. Ruth Gatzke (his wife), Miss Ruth Knopp, Mrs. Loretta Zielke, Miss Margaret Kaste, Henry Becker, and Theodore Appold, the last mentioned resigning in October, 1942.

In July, 1929, Pastor Pieper accepted a call to Saint Matthew's in Lemont, Ill. His successor was the Rev. Otto Carl August Boecler, a member of the Concordia Seminary faculty, St. Louis, Mo., since February, 1925.* On December 17, 1942, the Rev. Allen Feddert† of Tipton, Ind., was installed as Immanuel's assistant pastor. Upon the death of Pastor Boecler, in 1942, the assistant pastor was given full charge of the pastorate, officially by the rite of installation, on January 24, 1943.

The Rev. Robert Stade, missionary in West Africa, hails from Immanuel Congregation.

Immanuel Church is located at the northeast corner of Lee and Thacker Streets. "As motorists drive into Des Plaines from any direction, signs erected by the Chamber of Commerce greet their eyes setting forth the declaration that Des Plaines is the 'City of Roses.' . . . and we might add carnations and orchids as well. Many who attended the National Flower Show at Chicago's International Amphitheater recently and admired the great beauty displayed there were unaware of the fact that many of the finest roses and carnations exhibited were grown right here in Des Plaines. And it is a little-known fact, too, that these prize-winning blooms find their way into flower shops in three fifths of the United States, moving by air and fast express daily from area distributors." With such pleasant odors in its nostrils the Lutheran Trail returns to the "Garden City" with its "Garlic

*The Rev. O. C. A. Boecler served as assistant pastor of Immanuel Congregation in Grand Rapids, Mich. (1906-1909); held a professorship at Concordia Seminary, Springfield, Ill., from 1909 to 1917; was pastor of St. Luke's Congregation in Chicago, 1917-1925; and from there went to Concordia Seminary, St. Louis, Mo., the institution from which he graduated in 1898, but now in entirely new buildings in a different part of the big city on the big river—in Clayton.

†A son of the Rev. Oscar Fedder, pastor of St. Stephen's Congregation, Chicago, since Feb. 8, 1925.

Creek." Although offensive smells still arise here and there in the "Big City," it is fortunate that the Trail is by this time far removed from "the middle 1840's"—for, according to the *Chicago Daily Journal* under date of April 24, 1845, a certain traveler was convinced that Chicago should be called "the City of Pestiferous Odour." About two weeks before the Missouri Synod was organized in Chicago (April, 1847), the *Weekly Chicago Democrat* under date of April 13, 1847, made references to "dogs and hogs and cattle running at large in streets." In its June 8 issue the same newspaper had something to say about dumping manure in public places. But it now is the year 1873. In that year occurred a somewhat unusual development in Chicago: Two Norwegian Lutheran groups were organized by the Rev. J. Krohn and the Rev. I. L. P. Dietrichsen, respectively, as Saint Paul's and Saint Peter's.

61. Chicago, Saint Paul's (Norwegian)

The introduction is borrowed from *Grace for Grace**—"Up to the year 1843 there were no organized Lutheran congregations among the Norwegian immigrants, and no services had been conducted in the manner to which they had been accustomed in the homeland. Elling Eielsen arranged to be ordained privately by a Lutheran pastor, F. A. Hoffmann, whose standing in any Lutheran body no one up to this time has been able to determine. This ordination was said to have been performed in Chicago." The first church building of Saint Paul's Norwegian Lutheran Congregation was erected on the corner of Park and Lincoln Streets in Chicago. Saint Peter's Congregation had its meeting place at Campbell Avenue and Frederick (now Hirsch) Street. In 1887 these two congregations were consolidated under the ministry of the Rev. O. C. O. Hjorth. Soon afterward lots were purchased

*"Brief History of the Norwegian Synod," Lutheran Synod Book Company, Mankato, Minn., 1943.

on West North Avenue, in the block now known as "2200 West," and a "basement" church was constructed. Several years later the superstructure was added, and the entire building was dedicated on November 13, 1892, by the Rev. H. A. Preus, then president of the Norwegian Lutheran Synod.

In addition to the pastors mentioned, the following have served this parish since 1876, when Pastor Dietrichsen left:

H. Johnson, 1876-1878	I. B. Torrison, 1891-1899
A. Mikkelsen, 1879-1881	O. E. Heimdahl, 1899-1902
O. H. Lee, 1879-1881*	G. A. Gullixson, 1902-1933
Student Arvesen, 1881-1882	G. A. R. Gullixson, 1933-1940
J. I. Walo, 1882-1887	B. W. Teigen, 1941-1945
O. C. O. Hjorth, 1887-1890	Eivind G. Unseth, 1945-

62. Colehour, Immanuel

Had it not been for the fact that the United States Government in the 1860's made the Calumet River navigable and built a harbor at its mouth near the foot of what now is East Ninety-fifth Street, this part of the story probably could not be written. As it is, many Germans and Danes moved into that region and found employment. Near the northern end of the Illinois-Indiana State line, between Sheffield, Ill., and Whiting, Ind., there was a place called Robertsdale. At that time (in the 1860's) it was extremely difficult to get to that place; and, actually, there were only two modes of "transportation"—either on foot or by train. Unfortunately, however, there was no railroad station in Robertsdale; and so it happened that the missionaries from Chicago† came out here on a Lake Shore and Michigan Southern train and, as they approached Robertsdale, made careful preparations to jump from the train, and then proceeded to the preaching station.

One day the Rev. Ferdinand Doederlein was informed that Colonel Borrens, president of the Canal and Dock Company, desired to have a meeting with him regarding the donation of lots for a church in Colehour (now South Chicago). The

*Assistant.

†The Rev. J. Paul Beyer, pastor of First Immanuel, and the Rev. Ferdinand Doederlein, pastor of First Trinity.

pastor subsequently appeared at the company's main office, where the generous offer was formally submitted to him. On a section of the donated property, comprising three lots, a small school building, also to serve as a church, was erected. Briefly, that was the beginning of Lutheranism in this section of the northern Illinois area. In 1890 Colehour, together with a number of other communities, was annexed to the city of Chicago.

Three congregations evolved from the Robertsdale mission: Immanuel and Bethlehem in what now is South Chicago and Saint John's in Whiting, Ind.

Immanuel in South Chicago, today at 9035 Houston Avenue, will be the first discussed. On June 20, 1873, nine Lutheran men, under the direction of the Rev. H. P. Duborg, who was conversant with the Danish language, organized Immanuel Congregation. In the same year a day school was established in the home of Mr. and Mrs. Carl Leverenz. In 1874 two other groups were organized as Immanuel's "daughter" congregations, both of them, however, remaining connected with Immanuel for a few more years: Bethlehem until 1879 and Saint John's (Whiting) until 1881. Pastor Duborg also taught school until 1875, when trained teachers were placed in charge of the schools at Immanuel and at Bethlehem, Louis Doering and Edward O. Bartling. The three congregations joined the Missouri Synod at the same time. In the following year Pastor Duborg also conducted monthly worship services in Porter, Ind.

A news "flash" from New York City interrupts the Trail for a few moments: "A company was formed here to introduce Edison's electric light, but there was considerable doubt expressed that he had solved the problem."* In the early part of 1879 Pastor Duborg left Colehour to assume

*"As the year 1879 closed, it was reported that Edison had at last solved the problem of electric light." (*The Chicago Tribune— Its First Hundred Years*, 1945, Vol. II, p. 319.) "In 1880 a Chicago company was incorporated to use the Edison light patent whenever it was in working condition." *Ut supra*, p. 324.

the pastorate of the first Lutheran congregation in Blue Island, Ill. In the spring of the same year the Rev. Carl F. Eissfeldt of Belvidere, Ill., became the pastor of the triple parish in this rather large community. In 1880 a school building was erected on the lot next to Immanuel Church. In 1881, when Saint John's in Whiting, Ind., became autonomous, Immanuel Congregation was severely disturbed and disrupted by the Election and Predestination Controversy in the Ev. Lutheran Synodical Conference of North America. On April 4 of that year J. H. Welp was installed as teacher; he served for about two years, until the spring of 1883, and was succeeded by W. A. Herter, who likewise served for about two years, until July, 1885. Then came Frederick Gose, who remained until April, 1905. Mr. Gose was assisted by Rudolph G. Kranz,* 1891-1893, and by O. Damkoehler, 1893-1894. In 1886 a second classroom was added to the school, and Theodore Ruhland, a student, was placed in charge of the lower grades. In the following year, 1887, missionary work was begun in the Grand Crossing area, resulting in the organization of a third "daughter" congregation—Saint Paul's, whose center now is at East Seventy-sixth Street and Dorchester Avenue, Chicago (1888). This congregation, however, also remained a part of the South Chicago (Immanuel) parish, until 1890.

In 1889 Immanuel Church was remodeled and enlarged to twice its former capacity. In 1896 Pastor Eissfeldt was forced by illness to resign. His successor, the Rev. Ferdinand Sievers of Monitor, Mich., was installed on June 14, 1896. On November 1 of the same year the beginning of English services was made. In 1907 three additional lots were pur-

*Teacher Rudolph G. Kranz, graduate of the Teachers' Seminary, Addison, in 1889, began his teaching career at the Lutheran Orphanage in Wittenberg, Wis. His second charge was in Colehour; from 1893-1899 he served St. John's School at Dutchman's Point (Niles), Ill. From May, 1899, until May, 1944, he was on the staff of St. Peter's School in Arlington Heights (formerly Dunton), Ill. He died May 16, 1944.

chased and a new church erected; the dedication took place on January 26, 1908.

In the following year, 1909, Pastor Sievers organized Salem Congregation in Blue Island. The Rev. Raymond R. Reinke, a son of the founder of the first Lutheran congregation at Blue Island, which later joined the Ohio Synod—Pastor Augustus Reinke—served Salem Congregation from 1909 until January 30, 1947, when he died.

In 1913 some eighty members of Immanuel were released to organize a congregation in the Windsor Park community, due north.

On November 3, 1918—eight days prior to the Armistice of World War I—the Rev. William C. A. Martens of Quincy, Ill., was installed as Immanuel's fourth pastor. He served Immanuel until midsummer, 1947, when he accepted a call to the mission congregation (Trinity) in Onarga, Ill. His successor, the Rev. Walter C. Greve of Hegewisch, Ill., was installed on November 9, 1947.

On March 16, 1919, a Sunday school was organized. Beginning March 13, 1921, separate services in German and English on Sundays and all festival days were conducted. In November, 1923, the day school enrollment reached the "high mark"—223. On December 25, 1937, the church was damaged by fire. On July 6, 1941, the girls' chorus of Immanuel sang before an audience of over two thousand people in an open-air concert in the county forest preserve, directed by Theodore F. Gose. At the conclusion of the program the announcement was made over the public address amplifiers: "This is the fourth time the Immanuel Lutheran Girls' Chorus has here presented the Sunday afternoon program, and they rank among the best of the many choruses."

In addition to those already mentioned, the following have taught or are teaching in Immanuel School:

L. Schieferdecker, 1887-1888
Miss Dreyer, 1888-1891
S. Koestering, 1893-1894
Elfrieda Steinkraus, 1915-1917
Martha Gose, 1920-1923
Paula Wuerffel, 1924-1930

M. Kopplin, 1895-1899
Gertrude Steinkraus, 1912-1915
Editha Kitzke, 1917-1920
Cordelia Ferber, 1923-1927
Ruth Martens, 1927-1928
John Klitzke, 1904-1921
Theodore F. Gose, 1909-1942
Paul A. Wendler, 1922-1931
R. C. Marten, 1930-1936
Robert C. Oestreich, 1936-
Fred W. Haack, 1941-
Lydia Gose, 1906-1912
Anna Pause, 1928-1933
A. H. Fischer, 1905-1909
A. H. Schulz, 1921-1922
Samuel Goehringer, 1922-1924
E. C. Sieving, 1931-1937
E. F. Kolb, 1937-1939
Arthur H. Busch
Mrs. Anna Patzer
W. F. Schmidt
Student R. Greising
Mrs. A. H. Busch

63. Lemont

Twenty miles straight west from Colehour (South Chicago) is Archer Road (now Avenue). Turning south on that road, the Trail passes over the Sag Bridge and, following the Chicago-Joliet Road for a distance of only about four miles, arrives at Lemont, Ill.,* noted for its fields of limestone (Lemont "marble")—used largely in rebuilding Chicago after the Great Fire of October 9, 1871. Prior to that time it had furnished the stones for the upper stories of the present capitol building in Springfield, Ill.

Development of Lutheranism in this community began early in the 1870's. The Rev. G. A. Barth, assistant pastor at First Immanuel, Chicago, and the Rev. Herman W. Querl, pastor of Trinity, near Willow Springs, gathered Lutherans in and around Lemont and conducted worship services in the homes of various Lutherans. In the spring of 1874 a congregation was organized and named Saint Matthew's and a modest building acquired to serve as a church.

On April 8, 1874, Candidate William Uffenbeck was assigned to Saint Matthew's Congregation in Lemont by the Missouri Synod's "College of Presidents." On July 2, 1882, E. Petzold was called to teach in the day school. Four years later, in August, 1886, Pastor Uffenbeck accepted a call to Holy Cross Congregation in the Bridgeport community, Chicago. His successor in Lemont was the Rev. Karl W. G. Koch of Wheaton, Ill. A new church building was erected in 1887. On March 20, 1889, Pastor Koch died; and on the 26th of

*1940 census: 2,557. Named from its elevated location, "the mountain."

March the Rev. Barthold Burfeind of Immanuel Congregation on the Sauk Trail (at Cicero—"Skunks Grove") became Saint Matthew's third resident pastor. In May, 1890, Saint Matthew's joined the Missouri Synod. Pastor Burfeind resigned in the summer of 1895.* In August of the same year the Rev. Adolph Pfotenhauer of Palatine, Ill., became Saint Matthew's fourth pastor. In 1906 he accepted a call to Saint Paul's in Addison,† Ill. In 1907 the Rev. H. Grefe of Goodfarm, near Dwight, Ill., became the fifth pastor in the Lemont parish. Upon his acceptance of a call in the fall of 1910 to Germantown, Iowa,‡ he was succeeded on December 10 by the Rev. J. H. Rupprecht, who remained until the end of 1916, when he accepted a call to Belvidere, Ill. The Rev. Karl F. Lohrmann of Boonville, Mo., was installed as the seventh pastor of Saint Matthew's on January 21, 1917. One year later, on January 18, 1918, the church was destroyed by fire; and six days after the signing of the Armistice of World War I, the rebuilt church was dedicated, November 17, 1918. In May, 1929, Pastor Lohrmann accepted a call to Good Shepherd Congregation in Berwyn, Ill., and the Rev. Walter Pieper of Immanuel, Des Plaines, Ill., was installed on July 7, 1929, as Saint Matthew's eighth pastor.

Teachers who have served in St. Matthew's School since 1933: Miss Tilly Jan, Miss Cordelia Ferber, Miss O. Banke, Miss Gertrude Drews, Miss Mildred Eichelberger, Donald Becker, Student G. Streufert, Miss Elaine Gundermann, Miss Ruth Nauss, and Norman Vonderheid.

64. Colehour, Bethlehem

From Lemont the Trail goes right back to Colehour (South Chicago), where on June 20, 1873, Immanuel Congregation

*Pastor Burfeind carried on missionary work in Wilmette and Winnetka, Ill., 1898-1902. (See Chapter 151.)

†St. Paul's in Addison was organized in 1906.

‡Pastor H. Grefe died at Germantown, Iowa, Sept. 6, 1912.

was organized and where the first church-and-school building was erected on land donated by Colonel Borrens. Across the Calumet River, a short distance south of Immanuel's "center," is the old Colehour area, where Bethlehem Congregation developed almost simultaneously. A romantic spot it was in the 1860's, with its lake shore covered with tall and stately oak trees; where Indians set up their tents and wigwams to spend the summer months in fishing and raising cattle.

In 1874 Charles Colehour and a Mr. Taylor donated three lots at the corner of 103d Street and Avenue G as a church building site. On December 27, 1874, ten Lutheran men* organized Bethlehem Congregation. Shortly afterward construction of a combination church and school building was begun. This building was dedicated on May 13, 1875. In the same month a trained teacher, Edward Bartling, was placed in charge of the school. In 1879 Pastor Duborg, who had served Bethlehem and Saint John's in Whiting, Ind., as affiliates of Immanuel, accepted the pastorate of the first Lutheran church of Blue Island, Ill. In the same year Bethlehem became autonomous and on August 3, 1879, installed Candidate John Heyer as its first resident pastor, who also assumed charge of the day school. At that time Bethlehem was faced with a financial problem. Money was scarce; and when a loan in the amount of four hundred dollars became due, all the members were asked to contribute out of their poverty toward the liquidation of this debt. The fund-raising campaign was well worth while; a total of $368 was at hand to pay the lender. But, of course, the full amount had not been collected to meet the obligation; thirty-two dollars constituted "quite a gap." Pastor Heyer came to the rescue by handing over one month's salary. Perhaps this covered the

*F. Kraetzer	H. Prigge	C. Brandt
F. Eggers	G. Dietrich	G. Kraetzer
J. Meyer	J. Capretz	W. Wuersig
	H. P. Duborg	

principal; but what about the interest amounting to thirty dollars? Well, the story goes something like this: A Mr. Eggers, presumably one of the charter members of Bethlehem, was on his way to the shopping district to purchase supplies for his family. On this little trip he happened to meet the man to whom Bethlehem was obligated. Mr. Eggers dug down into his pockets and drew out all the money he had—thirty-one dollars, and having practically paid the congregation's remaining debt, he returned home without the supplies.

In 1876 Mr. Bartling accepted a call to First Saint Paul's School in Chicago, where he served for only about four months and on February 8, 1877, died at the age of twenty-two.

In December, 1881, Pastor Heyer accepted a call to Saint John's Congregation in Town Jefferson (Mayfair).* His successor, the Rev. Johannes Traugott Feiertag of Wolcottsville, N.Y.,† was installed on April 16, 1882. The establishment of lumber companies in the Colehour area resulted in a great influx of workers, principally from Chicago, which included many members of Lutheran congregations. The growth of the congregation was rapid and sound. At that time the neighborhood comprising 103d Street and Avenues G and H was swampland, with good fishing for pickerels. A two-story parsonage with steps leading over the water was erected. "One often saw rafts with boys floating around, and the rafts were made from boards of the steps. When frozen over in winter time, skates were used by many parishioners to travel back and forth, to and from church and school. Alfred H. Meyer's brief description of "the Calumet prairie" fits into this picture in that Colehour is an important part of the great Calumet area: "Much of the Calumet prairie in the pioneer days was too wet for settlement, and far-flung marshes on the lake

*St. John's Congregation at Mayfair was organized in the spring of 1875. Its first pastor, the Rev. Frederick Brunn, served from November, 1876, till November, 1881. In 1889 Town Jefferson and other large areas were annexed to Chicago.

†The Rev. J. T. Feiertag was pastor of St. Paul's Congregation, Aurora, Ill., from 1869 to 1879; thence he went to Wolcottsville, N.Y.

plain, between the east-west ridges of beach-dune sand, made approach to Lake Michigan from the south extremely difficult. This landscape phenomenon doubtless explains in part the failure of the 'phantom' river and lake-port sites to establish a metropolitan community at the 'head' of Lake Michigan in competition with the Fort Dearborn settlement at Chicago."

In 1883 A. F. Ahner, recent graduate of the Teachers' Seminary, Addison, was placed in charge of the day school. In 1884 the church was enlarged and a 2,500-pound bell purchased; unfortunately, however, the steeple was found inadequate to support the great weight. Therefore, a special "Glockenstuhl" (bell tower) was constructed beside the church. In the same year, 1884, a joint mission festival was held for the first time, in Dolton, with the following congregations participating: Saint Paul's of Hammond, Ind., Trinity of Cummings Corner (Oak Glen), Saint John's of Lansing, Zion of Washington Heights, Saint Paul's of Thornton, Immanuel of South Chicago, Bethlehem of Colehour, and Saint Paul's of Dolton-Riverdale. Tugboats conveyed many Lutherans to Riverdale-Dolton via the Calumet River, a distance of about seven miles, and a rather circuitous route —but how thrilling it must have been!

In 1885 a woman teacher was engaged for a branch school in Hegewisch,* a community about three miles south of Colehour. During the period 1887-1888 Pastor Feiertag provided the Lutherans in this community with spiritual care; other Lutheran pastors, including the Rev. Carl M. Noack of Dolton-Riverdale and the Rev. G. F. Luebker of Saint Paul's Congregation in Hammond, Ind., shared this responsibility. In 1890, the year in which Colehour, together with other communities, was annexed to Chicago, another trained teacher, A. C. Renn, began teaching in Bethlehem School. The local post office dropped the name Colehour, and beginning

*Trinity Congregation in Hegewisch was organized Oct. 1, 1887.

at that time Bethlehem of Colehour called itself "Die evangelisch-lutherische Bethlehems-Gemeinde an der 103. Strasse, Chicago, Illinois." In the following year, 1891, a new church, 50x100 feet, with two steeples—one of which was 160 feet tall—was erected. The dedication took place on November 22. From 1890 to 1891 Pastor Feiertag also served Saint John's Congregation in Whiting, Ind. In the latter year the formal organization of this congregation was effected and its first resident pastor called, the Rev. Herman Philip Wille of Geneseo, Ill.

In the latter part of 1895 Mr. Ahner resigned as teacher, and his successor was John Richter, heretofore on the teaching staff of First Trinity in Chicago.* Others who taught in Bethlehem School were H. G. L. Paul, G. Windisch, C. Homeier, and W. Landeck.

Pastor Feiertag resigned in 1909.† He was the author of *Geschichte der Ev. Lutherischen Gemeinden, U.A.C.,‡ zu Chicago, 1846-1896*, published in 1896 and frequently referred to in this history. His successor in the pastorate of Bethlehem was the Rev. Herman L. Pflug of Hanson Park, Chicago; he was installed on November 28, 1909. Teachers in Bethlehem School at that time were Theodore Markworth, A. H. Falke, Miss Ella Kleist, and August Schumann. In 1909 a Sunday school was organized; also, one English service each month was inaugurated.

In August, 1913, Pastor Pflug accepted a call to Saint Andrew's Congregation in Chicago, and on the 24th of that month the Rev. Traugott Thieme of Shelbyville, Ill., succeeded him to Bethlehem.

In January, 1918, Bethlehem Church was destroyed by fire, the origin of which was never positively determined. A new

*John Richter was called by First Trinity in 1879 to take charge of the branch school in Bridgeport; when in 1886 this school developed into Holy Cross Congregation, Mr. Richter was retained as teacher for several years (until 1891?)

†The Rev. Johannes Traugott Feiertag died on Aug. 18, 1916.

‡"Ungeaenderter Augsburgischer Confession" ("of the Unaltered Augsburg Confession"—the implied designation of all congregations affiliated with the Evangelical Lutheran Synodical Conference of North America.

church as well as a new school was erected, the double dedication taking place on October 12, 1919.

John W. Brodhagen began his teaching duties here in 1918; at that time religious instruction through the medium of English was started. In 1927 the eighth grade was added; in 1928 the enrollment increased to 135. For six years, 1928-1934, young women taught the lower grades. In 1934 Gerhard A. Korntheuer was engaged to teach these grades. He served until 1944, when he accepted a call to Holy Cross in Chicago. His successor was Norman J. Mattfeld of Paullina, Iowa.

Late in 1937 Pastor Thieme was appointed institutional missionary for the Northern Illinois District in Chicago. On February 27, 1938, the Rev. Edgar R. Pflug of Buffalo, N.Y., was installed as his successor.

Bethlehem's day school teachers in recent years were the Messrs. Falke, Brodhagen, Mattfeld, Mrs. Otto Herbener, and the Misses Dorothy Dust and Ethel Ball, Mrs. Eleanore Kressmann, Mrs. Adolph Mueller, and Mrs. Robert Bartz. Louis Cross served on the school board 25 years.

The following members of Bethlehem entered the Lutheran ministry: Richard Seils, George Wolter, H. H. Feiertag, B. Saager, John Feiertag, and Adolph Dietrich.

65. Joliet, Saint Peter's

The county seat of Will County has been crossed several times by the Lutheran Trail, but prior to 1875 there has been no sign of Missouri Lutheran activity in this place, which is located on the Des Plaines River and the old Illinois-Michigan Canal. The name of this important city did not always have the spelling which appears in the caption. It was first named Juliet. "The townspeople," according to Miss Bernadine Skeels, "must have wanted a corner on Shakespearean names, for they became considerably annoyed at a near-by hamlet for romantically calling itself Romeo.* So they looked around and selected Joliet, first, for its similarity in spelling to Juliet,† and second, because as one of the Town Board said: 'This here Jolyette chap what traveled through here with Columbus was a bigger man than Juliet.'" But, so far as the Lutheran Trail is concerned, the origin or derivation of names cannot hinder its progress; moreover, it is interested in people and—will it bear repetition?—it's people that count!

Once more is found a somewhat incongruous agglomeration: "German United Evangelical Lutheran Saint Peter's Congregation." This congregation in Joliet was organized on May 24, 1857, by twenty-six persons, presumably all men. Three days after the organization had been effected, the cornerstone of a church was laid. A frame structure, this church was located at what now is known as 320 North Broadway. "United" Saint Peter's Congregation had for its first pastor the Rev. Christian Bofinger, who served from 1857 until 1860, when he was succeeded by the Rev. Christian Sans, who served until 1870; then came a pastor who after some time persuaded the congregation to adopt a Lutheran constitution: the Rev. Carl H. Rohde. In 1875 the charter and the name of Saint Peter's Congregation were changed from "United" (Reformed) to "Evangelical Lutheran." By the same token its character was also changed; its teachings were to be based upon the "Unaltered Augsburg Confession" ("U.A.C.") of the year 1530. After these alterations had been concluded, Saint Peter's membership increased to such an extent that a larger church building had to be erected. This new church was dedicated on January 20, 1884. Meanwhile, however, there had also been a change in the pastorate. Pastor Rohde in 1878 had accepted

*Romeo, with a population of 170 (1940 census), is located about eight miles north of Joliet, a mile east of the Des Plaines River. Joliet's population, 1940 census: 42,365.

†According to Gannett, "this place was named Juliet for Juliet Campbell, daughter of the founder. By an act of the State Legislature the name was changed in honor of Louis Jolliet, or Joliet, the French explorer."

a call to Detroit, Mich., and the Rev. August Schuessler of Bonfield, Ill.,* had succeeded him to the pastorate in Joliet. In 1891 the congregation became a member of the Missouri Synod. Pastor Schuessler died on January 8, 1913. In February of this year the Rev. Henry G. Sandvoss of Chicago Heights, Ill., assumed the pastorate in Joliet. In 1919 the church was rebuilt at a cost of approximately twenty-two thousand dollars. In the following year, 1920, Pastor Sandvoss accepted a call from the Chicago City Mission Society, which position he held until his death on September 15, 1934. Then came the Rev. Karl Kurth of Beatrice, Nebr. It was during his pastorate that the broadcasting of the second worship service every Sunday morning over a local radio station, WCLS,† was initiated. "This broadcast, more than any other human factor, accounts for the fact that for many years Saint Peter's Church leads all other congregations in the Northern Illinois District in the number of adults confirmed and baptized." In July, 1932, Pastor Kurth accepted a call to Bethlehem Congregation in Evanston, Ill. In October of the same year his successor in Saint Peter's pastorate was installed, the Rev. Erdmann W. Frenk of De Kalb, Ill. In 1936 further structural changes were made in the interior of the church.

A few years after the congregation had been organized, a day school was established and taught by its pastors. The first trained teacher came in 1869. The first school, a frame structure, stood at about the same location where in 1902 a large school building was erected, about a block south of the church. This building, which comprises not only classrooms, but also meeting rooms for the various auxiliary organizations of Saint Peter's, was dedicated on January 4, 1903. Converted into an eight-grade school, Saint Peter's School was fully accredited by the Joliet Township High School, in 1918.

Recent teachers on the day school staff were Martin F.

*His post office address, while pastor of Zion at Bonfield, was Union Hill, Ill.—about six miles southwest of Bonfield.

†Later, Station WJOL.

Dobberfuhl, Otto H. Schumm, Kurt Schmid, Miss Virginia Bachmann, and Miss Jean Burke.

On June 22, 1947, Martin Luther Frenk, a son of Pastor Frenk and recent graduate of Concordia Seminary in St. Louis, Mo., was ordained and installed as assistant pastor.

66. Chicago, Saint John's

The Trail returns to Chicago—this time not to the southeast side, but to the northwest side—to a community a few miles southeast of Dutchman's Point (Niles), known as Town Jefferson.* It is now 1874; and there appears again the Rev. John Adam Detzer, now pastor of Immanuel Congregation in Des Plaines. He is busy gathering Germans for the organization of a Lutheran congregation. Within the year his efforts were successful. In the spring of 1875 eleven men gathered in the home of a certain Mr. Salamann and organized Saint John's Congregation. On October 5 the constitution was adopted and signed by fourteen men.† Worship services were conducted in a Congregational church until the first church was erected. This was a frame structure, 30x50 feet, with a steeple and bells, and arranged for parsonage, church, and school purposes, located on Montrose Boulevard (Avenue), a short distance east of Milwaukee Avenue. The dedication took place on October 14, 1876. From then on Saint John's Congregation was served by the Rev. Augustus Reinke, pastor of First Bethlehem Congregation, Chicago, and by Candidate Frederick Brunn. The latter was ordained and installed as Saint John's first pastor on November 26, 1876. He served this parish until November, 1881, when he accepted a call

*Annexed to Chicago July 15, 1889.

†Charter members:

John Lorenz
Karl Behning
Edward Kuester
Fred Mahler
William Frick
Karl Meyer
Joachim Ganschow
Karl Sass
John Karnatz
Karl Willig
W. Suchow
Reimer Schmook
Fred Jacobs
John Hamann

to Strasburg, Ill.* His successor at Saint John's, the Rev. John Heyer of Bethlehem Congregation in Colehour (South Chicago), was installed on January 8, 1882. About five years—less three months—later, in October, 1886, Pastor Heyer accepted a call to Wheaton, Ill., and on November 14 his successor, the Rev. Paul Luecke of Merrill, Wis., was installed in the "Mayfair" parish. Until Easter, 1887, the respective pastors also had charge of the day school. Then for about two years this work was done by students of the Teachers' Seminary at Addison. In September, 1889, Saint John's first trained teacher, Candidate William Battermann, graduate of the afore-mentioned seminary, was installed. In 1890 the church building was enlarged at a cost of $11,350 and rededicated on September 14, 1890. In October, 1892, the former first teacher of First Saint John's Congregation in Chicago, Christian Luecke, was called to take the place of the woman teacher in the second classroom established during the preceding year. A new school building was erected in 1914; and in 1925 the enrollment was 325. A new church and parish hall were erected during the years 1929 and 1930 at a cost estimated at $150,000, exclusive of the organ, which alone cost fifteen thousand dollars. In 1937 Pastor Luecke retired, but, upon the congregation's request, continued to serve as honorary pastor until February 15, 1944, when he died. His successor, the Rev. Henry H. Blanke of Leavenworth, Kans., was installed in September, 1937. Eight years later, on September 9, 1945, his son, Candidate Henry A. Blanke, graduate of Concordia Seminary, St. Louis, Mo., was installed as assistant pastor. In June, 1947, the son accepted a call to Houston, Tex. Former teachers in Saint John's School: August Besch, E. Setzer, Arthur Schmehling, Miss M. Luecke, and Miss E. Dorre. Teachers in recent years: E. G. Becker, Carl Michel,

*In 1895 the Rev. Frederick Brunn was called from Strasburg, Ill., to Trinity, Cummings Corner—now Oak Glen—and St. John's, Lansing, dual parish. He served there until 1927. He died on May 27, 1927. Pastor Brunn was president of the Northern Illinois District, 1913-1927.

Rudolph E. Hasemann, Miss Marie Ehlers, Miss Lily Nafzger, Miss Lorraine Thiele, Miss Viola Rabey, Mrs. Cordia Becker, Miss D. Reese, Erwin Meyer, Miss Cordelia Ferber, Miss Elvira Preuss, and Miss Gertrude Dahm.

67. Woodstock

When the Lutheran Trail was at Crystal Lake (1875), it was about eight miles from Woodstock, Ill.,* formerly called Centreville. This place was settled by German pioneers whose spiritual needs, were supplied by an occasional ministry beginning early in 1869, performed by the Rev. Henry Schmidt, pastor of Immanuel in Dundee, then by the Rev. F. W. Richmann, pastor of Saint John's in Elgin, and by the Rev. John Adam Detzer, pastor of Immanuel in Des Plaines. From 1869 to 1875 the services were conducted in private homes; thereafter in the lecture room of the old Methodist Episcopal church and in the hall of the Grand Army of the Republic (G.A.R.). In the fall of 1875 a dozen or more men, under the leadership of Pastor Henry Schmidt, then at Schaumburg,† organized Saint John's Congregation and adopted a Lutheran constitution. In 1892 Saint John's, comprising about twenty-five families, purchased a vacant church building for $1,700. The necessary alterations had hardly been completed when the church was destroyed by fire. On October 16, 1898, a new church, costing approximately three thousand dollars, including interior decorations, was dedicated. In 1910 a day school was founded, served for the next seven years by the respective pastors.

Besides the pastors mentioned above, the following have served here: The Rev. Max Heyer, who, coming to Woodstock from Winfield Junction, N.Y., served from 1880 until

*1940 census: 6,123. Woodstock is located about eight miles northwest of Crystal Lake; it was named by Joel H. Johnson, a railroad director, for his native place in Vermont.

†The Rev. Henry Schmidt served Immanuel in Dundee, 1868-1869. Oct. 17, 1869, he was installed as pastor of St. Peter's in Schaumburg and served in this parish until July, 1883; thence he went to Pittsburgh, Pa.

1883, when he accepted a call to Minnesota Lake, Minn.; the Rev. Karl Schmidt of Rochester, Minn., from 1883 to 1894, when he accepted a call to Saint James in Chicago; Candidate Herman Engelbrecht, 1894-1896, who on February 23, 1896, became assistant pastor in his father's congregation, Saint Matthew's in Chicago; the Rev. Henry Dannenfeldt of Lynville (now Lindenwood), Ill., who came to Woodstock in 1896 and in 1902 accepted a call to Trinity Congregation at York Center, about one mile southeast of Lombard, Ill.; Candidate J. Gardus Bertram, who came in 1902 and remained for ten years, accepting a call in 1912 to Osage, Iowa. His successor at Saint John's in Woodstock was the Rev. Herman A. Laufer of Litchfield, Nebr. After about fifteen years in Woodstock he accepted a call to Lace, Ill. The Rev. Paul R. Reetz remained but a short time, from 1927 until 1929; he had come from Alamosa, Colo., and it seems he resigned from the ministry in Woodstock. Then followed the Rev. Herman P. Meyer, formerly missionary in the Belmont Heights and Addison Heights communities on the then northwestern limits of Chicago. He served from 1929 until 1942, when he accepted a call to Zion Congregation in Matteson, Ill. His successor at Saint John's in Woodstock came from Libby, Mont.—the Rev. H. L. Pfotenhauer.* For some time the latter also served the mission at near-by Wonder Lake.

68. Pecatonica

Westward moves the Lutheran Trail, in the early fall of 1875, twenty-five miles from Woodstock to the Rock River, by-passing the city of Rockford along the northern outskirts and, after fording the Rock River, continuing another sixteen or so miles due west, it stops at an interesting village named Pecatonica, Ill.† Whether this place, which, it is said,

*A son of the Rev. Adolph Pfotenhauer, pastor of St. Paul's Congregation in Addison, Ill., from 1906 until April 29, 1939, the day of his death.

†1940 census: 1,302.

means "crooked river," was named after the river or vice versa is not known. But there are quite a number of Lutherans here, and again the Rev. Louis Steinrauf of Huntley appears on the scene. It was under his direction that on October 3, 1875, Saint John's Congregation was organized in Pecatonica. In February of the following year a small chapel on a lot, 132x50 feet, was purchased from the Baptist congregation for one thousand dollars. From 1877 until 1879 the Rev. Carl F. Eissfeldt served Saint John's in Pecatonica as an affiliate of his congregation, Immanuel, in Belvidere—about twenty-seven miles east of Pecatonica. On August 24, 1879, Candidate Karl Schwan* was installed as Saint John's first resident pastor. After a brief period Pastor Schwan resigned, and the congregation became an affiliate of Saint Paul's Congregation in Rockford under the ministry of the Rev. George Johannes, 1880-1882.† It was served under the same arrangement by the Rev. Ludwig von Schenk, 1882-1884, who in the latter year was called to the pastorate in Pecatonica. But he also terminated his ministry at Saint John's after a short time, in 1885, by accepting a call to Zion Congregation in Ottawa, Ill. A prolonged vacancy followed, during which the congregation in Pecatonica was provided with spiritual care by the Rev. Henry G. Schmidt,‡ pastor of Immanuel Congregation in Freeport, until 1886, when the Rev. Theodore F. Kohn, who in the same year assumed the pastorate of Immanuel in Belvidere, included Saint John's of Pecatonica in his field of activity, until 1890. During this period a new church was erected, which was formally dedi-

*The Rev. Karl Schwan was a son of the Rev. Henry Christian Schwan, author of the Missouri Synod's *Exposition of Doctor Martin Luther's Small Catechism* and President of the Missouri Synod, 1878-1899. This book was accepted by the Missouri Synod in 1896. The Rev. H. C. Schwan received the honorary degree of Doctor of Divinity from Luther Seminary of the Norwegian Lutheran Synod in 1893. He was pastor of Zion Congregation, Cleveland, Ohio, 1851-1899.

†In 1882 the Rev. George Johannes became the pastor of Immanuel in Des Plaines, Ill.

‡The Rev. Henry G. Schmidt was pastor in Crystal Lake, Ill., 1875-1880; in Rochester, Minn., 1880-1881; in Freeport, 1881-1899; in Milwaukee, Wis., 1899-1927; his last charge was at Sharon, Wis., 1927-1929. He died on March 21, 1929.

cated on March 12, 1888. Since 1891 Pecatonica had its own resident pastors. The first of these was the Rev. F. Gardus Bertram, from 1891 to 1897. He accepted a call to Crystal Lake, Ill., and shortly afterward his successor, the Rev. Leonhardt Brenner of Golconda, Ill., was installed. He served until 1903, when he accepted a call to Zion in Washington Heights (since 1890 part of Chicago). The next pastor, the Rev. Emil Meyer, came to Pecatonica from Lena, Ill., and remained until 1910. In the same year he was succeeded by the Rev. Andreas (Andrew) C. Landeck of Freeport, Ill.* Pastor Landeck's pastorate in Pecatonica extended over a period of about fifteen years. He resigned in 1925. On February 21, 1938, he died at the age of eighty-four. His successor at Saint John's, the Rev. Ernest W. Schwartz, a "son" of Saint Mark's Congregation in Chicago, held the pastorate in Pecatonica from 1924 until December, 1944, when he accepted a call to Goodfarm, Ill. On August 26, 1945, the Rev. Lester M. Hieber of Mount Carroll, Ill., was installed as Saint John's sixth resident pastor.†

69. Hopkins Township

The Trail now proceeds forty miles in a southwesterly direction, seeking information about the progress of Missouri Lutherans in Whiteside County, at a point about halfway between Sterling and Morrison, in Hopkins Township, where lives a man (remember, this is 1875) mentioned several years ago—a clergyman from Lyons (now Clinton), Iowa—the Rev. Claus Seuel, who is conducting services for the Lutherans out here in the public school building at Round Grove, Ill.‡ In 1874 Pastor Seuel's successor at Lyons, the Rev. John Carl Frederick Lussky, continued this work, and on April 25, 1875,

*See Chapter 48, page 223.

†Pastor Hieber's father, the Rev. Emil Hieber, has been pastor of Immanuel Congregation near Richton (Skunks Grove) since June 6, 1920.

‡1940 census: 153.

thirty-three Lutheran men,* under this pastor's leadership, organized "the first German Evangelical Lutheran Church of Hopkins Township." At the group's second meeting, a month later, it was resolved to build a church, 36x48 feet, at a cost not to exceed twenty-five hundred dollars. On the following August 8, Pastor Lussky was installed as pastor of the dual parish, Sterling and Hopkins Township. In 1883 he moved into the new parsonage in the country and served only that congregation, whose "center" was located approximately eight miles northwest of Sterling.† However, he did missionary work in a community known as Lyndon, resulting in the organization of Saint Peter's Congregation in 1885, which later transferred its "center" to near-by Morrison, Ill. In April, 1890, Pastor Lussky accepted a call to Zion in Ottawa, Ill., and the Rev. A. Carl Theo. Ponitz of Hahlen, Ill., succeeded him on June 1, 1890. Pastor Ponitz remained only until May, 1892, when he accepted a call to the Genoa-Sycamore parish, Ill. In October of the same year he was succeeded by the Rev. Emanuel Meyer of Oakley, Kans., who then served the last-named dual parish for about sixteen years, until 1908, when he went to Coal City, Ill. His successor in Hopkins Township was a son of the "founding father," the Rev. Arthur William Lussky,‡ who served until September, 1913, and then accepted a call to Jehovah Congregation in Chicago. On October 26, 1913, the Rev. Arthur W. Oetting of Perry, Okla., became the pastor of this parish,

*Charter members of "Die erste ev.-luth. Kirche in Hopkins Twp., Whiteside Co., Ill.' Only 22 names are available.

Johann Jaffe
Friedrich Matzwick
Johann Folkers
C. F. Ohms
Wilhelm Hinrichs
Wilhelm Kleihauer
Hillerw. Arians
Johan. Janssen
Eduard Dauen
Rudolph Ohnen
Henry Johnson
Henry Stern
Adam Reithel
Gerd Eden
John Darjus
Wilhelm Koch
George Hinrichs
Enke Hinrichs
Herman Abken
Eibe Heern. Folkers
Harm Onken
H. F. Behrens

†On Jan. 7, 1929, the old name was changed to "Second Avenue Evangelical Lutheran Church." (See Chapter 50.)

‡The Rev. A. W. Lussky was ordained in 1903 at Anaheim, Calif.

which until the year 1915 confined itself to the use of the German language in church activities. What was organized as the First German Evangelical Lutheran Church (1875) is now the entirely "English" congregation, now known as Our Savior's, in Hopkins Township, Whiteside County—eight miles northwest of Sterling, Ill.

70. Glenview

The Trail once more heads eastward in the direction of Chicago. Four miles due north of Dutchman's Point (Niles) there is the next village to be visited, named Glenview, Ill.,* formerly called Oak Glen. Were it not for the commendable custom of placing certain important church documents, books, and other pertinent records, including current literature, into the cornerstones of church buildings, it would have been virtually impossible to recover the early history of Lutheranism in this part of Lake County, Ill. Fortunately the pastor who originally served the Lutheran settlers in and about Glenview had written a document on April 22, 1876, which was preserved in the cornerstone of the first Lutheran church and discovered when this building was razed. Quoting in part, the document reveals that "for many years a number of Lutherans lived in this vicinity. They desired to remain true to the faith of their fathers and to their Church. Their ambition has been realized. For many years ministers of other denominations were called, but the real Lutherans bided their time and fervently hoped that sometime, sooner or later, their wish would be fulfilled and they would get a truly Lutheran pastor. Realizing that their hopes would never materialize so long as they remained with this church, these members left the church and applied to the Rev. Adam Detzer, pastor at Des Plaines, who was affiliated with the Ev. Lutheran Missouri Synod, to come and hold services for them and or-

*1940 census: 2,500.

ganize a Lutheran church in this vicinity. He came, and in January, 1876, a congregation was organized. Already in March of the same year a contract was let for the building of a new church. Although the roads were almost impassable, the members gave their time and teams to haul necessary material . . . . (Signed) Adam Detzer, Luth. Pastor."

At first services were conducted in a public school house on Telegraph Road. When, however, a short time later this building was no longer available, the congregation purchased a two-acre tract of land west of the North Branch of the Chicago River, on Lake Avenue. In 1876 a church was built on this site. The first resident pastor was the Rev. John Zimmermann of Rosehill, Tex. Sickness terminated his pastorate after about two years of service. He then moved to Van Wert, Ohio, where he died two years later. For about one year the congregation was without a pastor. On November 23, 1879, the Rev. Henry W. Wehrs of Saint Matthew's Congregation near Russells Grove (now Fairfield), Ill., was installed as pastor of this congregation, known as Immanuel. He served this parish for about forty years and also taught school. Later Pastor Wehrs wrote: "During the time of my pastorate (at Glenview) many changes were made on the property. When I came, the parsonage consisted of only four small rooms.* There was no cellar under the house nor foundation. The pastor expressed the wish that the parsonage be enlarged and a cellar and foundation be built. This was done. There was a bell in the church, but no lighting fixtures and no musical instrument. The benches were primitive and uncomfortable. Part of the cemetery was low and without proper drainage, and it would happen that a grave was filled with water when the casket was lowered into it. However, things were all taken care of in due time." In 1885 Pastor

*Compare experiences of the Rev. C. August T. Selle and the Rev. Anton Weyel, as related in Chapter Seven.

Wehrs started a mission in West Northfield, about six miles southwest of the present Northbrook.* On July 6, 1913, the pastor's son, Edward W., who had returned from the mission field in South America, was installed as assistant pastor. In 1916 Immanuel joined the Missouri Synod; in the same year one English service a month was introduced. Upon the senior pastor's retirement, in 1918, the Rev. Edward W. Wehrs was installed as "first" pastor. In 1921 Pastor Edward W. Wehrs followed a call to Big Falls, Wis.† His successor at Immanuel was the Rev. Arthur H. Werfelmann of Lindenwood (formerly Lynville), Ill. Pastor Werfelmann served here until November, 1931, when he accepted a call to Zion Congregation in Hinsdale (Fullersburg), Ill. His successor at Glenview was the Rev. Paul E. Meyer of Wahpeton, N. Dak.; he was installed on June 19, 1932, and served until the summer of 1943. In September he was installed as missionary in the Ida B. Wells Government Housing Project for Negroes in Chicago. On July 1, 1945, he became pastor of Calvary Congregation in Milford, Ill. Immanuel's first trained teacher, Frederick C. L. Weber, graduate of Concordia Teachers College, River Forest, Ill., was installed in 1922.‡ In the spring of the same year Immanuel Church was partially wrecked during a violent windstorm.

Other day school teachers were the Misses Marie Reuter, Marie Meyer, and Edna Hellberg, Russell Patzer, Mrs. Louise McLean, Edgar A. Abraham, Miss Doris Gullixson, and Mrs. Theo. Kanitz.

*St. John's, six miles southwest of Northbrook, was organized in 1886. The Rev. Walter G. Fechner has served St. John's since March 2, 1919.

†The Rev. Edward Wehrs died on Aug. 7, 1930. The Rev. Henry W. Wehrs died on April 28, 1940, at the age of about ninety-eight. Another son, the Rev. Herman C. Wehrs, died at Freistadt, Wis., on June 27, 1949, at age 76.

‡He died on Nov. 1, 1947.

NOTE: On February 5, 1948, Mr. and Mrs. Charles Sternberg, both members of Immanuel since its organization in 1876, celebrated their sixtieth wedding anniversary. Mr. Sternberg held the office of elder for forty-five years; since then he has been an honorary elder.

71. Algonquin

Disregarding for the nonce the numerous diagonal roads leading out of Chicago in a northwesterly direction, and taking a beeline across today's fields and gardens for twenty-six miles out of Glenview, the Trail arrives at Algonquin, Ill.* The name of this village signifies "the spearing-place for fish and eels." Inasmuch as no tribe of Indians by this name ever frequented this region, it may be presumed it was so named by an early settler from the valley of the St. Lawrence River, home of the Algonquins, who was familiar with the Algonquin dialect and found good fishing in the Fox River. Because the development of Lutheranism in these parts is particularly interesting, to be first visited is a public school house, about two miles east of Algonquin, where the Rev. J. H. C. Steege, pastor of Immanuel Congregation in Dundee (in the early 1870's) conducted the first Lutheran services. Directed by this pastor, Saint John's Congregation was organized on March 1, 1876, by seventeen men.† In the very first congregational meeting it was resolved to erect a church building with a large "sacristy," which should serve also as a schoolroom. Saint John's first resident pastor, the Rev. Henry Freese, was installed on December 10, 1876. After a brief pastorate he was succeeded by the Rev. Ludwig von Schenk of Rochester, Minn., on November 17, 1878. He remained in Algonquin until February, 1882, when he accepted a call to Saint Paul's Congregation in Rockford, Ill. His successor was his own

*1940 census: 926.

†Charter members:

Fred Richards
Fred Duensing
Christian Patasche
William Wodrich
John Calbow
Christian Dahn
Carl Bueckle
Henry Rogman
Henry Albrecht
Henry Henk
Christian Pinnow
John Zorn
Carl Schoening
John Wienke
Fred Ahrens
Fred Preuss
J. H. C. Steege, pastor

brother, Walter, who for some time had been serving as a day school teacher in Chicago. Candidate Walter von Schenk* was ordained and installed in Saint John's Church on September 17, 1882. During his pastorate in Algonquin, Pastor von Schenk also ministered to the Lutheran groups at Harvard and Hebron, some twenty miles to the northwest and north, respectively. In 1889 Pastor von Schenk was succeeded in Algonquin by the Rev. William Steffen of Genoa, Ill., who, however, shortly after his arrival was stricken with serious illness. While he was ill in bed, the parsonage was destroyed by fire, as also were the church records. He died here on February 8, 1894. His successor, the Rev. Paul von Toerne of Saint John's Congregation, six miles southwest of Northbrook, Ill., was installed on January 17, 1892. He resigned in 1900 and left the Missouri Synod in 1902. On September 16, 1900, the Rev. Henry Moldenhauer of Hanson Park (Chicago) became Saint John's next pastor—the sixth—and as such served for about thirty-seven years, resigning because of ill health in 1939.† During his pastorate a new church and a new school were erected. His successor, the Rev. Theodore Bornemann of Galveston, Tex., was installed on August 6, 1939.

The following trained teachers have served in Saint John's School: Ernest Militzer; John L. Schroeder (1907-1912), B. Seitz (1912-1914), Theodore Wunderlich (1914-1917), Otto Meier (1917-1919), Henry Maschhoff (1919-1921), and Alfred T. Christian (since 1921).

*According to the Rev. Prof. Ludwig E. Fuerbringer, D.D., who died on May 6, 1947, Pastor Ludwig von Schenk married Theresa Lange, daughter of the Rev. C. H. Rudolph Lange, pastor of First Immanuel Congregation in Chicago, 1872-1878; his brother, Pastor Walter von Schenk, married Theresa's sister, Anna. A third sister, Betty, was married to the Rev. August Lange, for many years editor of *Die Abendschule* in St. Louis, Mo. The mother of the three young women was a daughter of the Rev. Carl F. Gruber, one of the pastors of the Saxon group in Perry County, Missouri. (80 *Eventful Years*, Concordia Publishing House, St. Louis, Mo., 1944, page 122.)

†Died Jan. 10, 1941.

72. Sycamore

Oh, for a cottage among the sycamores! Or what did Geoffrey Chaucer, "the father of English poetry" (1340-1400 A.D.), write?—

The hegge also, that yede in compas
And closed in all the green herbere,
With sycamour was set, and eglatere.*

Bernadine Skeels opines that "it may have been that the favorite trysting place for a young brave and his best girl was the paw-paw tree 'essemiauk'—Somonauk—or 'kishwaukee' —Sycamore."

From Algonquin the Trail now proceeds in a southwesterly direction, a distance of about twenty-four miles, to Sycamore, Ill.†—but alas, not to a cottage, but to a jury room in the old courthouse! It was here that the Lutherans of this community at first conducted their services, led by the Rev. Henry H. Norden of Squaw Grove near Hinckley. The first service was held on May 28, 1876. For some time afterward the services were held in the homes of the people. At a meeting on December 10, 1876, a Lutheran constitution was adopted and signed by five men.‡ At that time the Congregational Society of Sycamore owned a piece of property described as "Lot three (3) of Block thirteen (13) in the original Town of Sycamore, on which the old church stood." This property, 60x120 feet, was purchased by the Lutheran group for thirteen hundred dollars. Included were the church, the bell, the altar, etc. The church, 36x70, was "sadly in need of repairs."

After Pastor Norden's acceptance of a call to Horine (Jarvis), Mo., in the summer of 1887, the congregation, known as Saint John's, was served for several years by the Rev. Prof. C. August T. Selle of the Teachers' Seminary at Addison

**Flower and Leaf*—54.
†1940 census: 4,702.
‡Charter members:

H. Lossmann
Claus Loptien
Joachim Wieltzien
J. Hindenburg
Joachim Carnehl

and ex-Professor John Merkel; but precisely how long these men served Saint John's cannot be definitely established. The same is true in the case of some of their successors as "vacancy" pastors. However, it is known that the former Professor Merkel was succeeded by the Rev. A. Carl Th. Ponitz of "the first German Ev. Lutheran Church" in Hopkins Township, eight miles northwest of Sterling, Ill. He was installed in Sycamore in May, 1892, and, like his predecessors, served Genoa—about seven miles north of Sycamore. Pastor Ponitz moved to Iowa, where he soon died. His successor in Sycamore* was the Rev. William Steffen of Algonquin, Ill.† His successor in the dual parish was the Rev. Richard D. J. Piehler of Klinger, Iowa. He served until October, 1911, when he accepted a call to Saint John's Congregation at Eagle Lake, seven miles northeast of Beecher, Ill.

On April 25, 1909, the Rev. August Fred Parge of Bemidji, Minn., was installed as the first resident pastor of Saint John's in Sycamore. In 1918 he was compelled by illness to resign. On August 4, 1918, the Rev. Emil A. Bartusch of Havelock, Nebr., succeeded him. He served until October, 1924, when he accepted a call to Rochelle, Ill. On January 18, 1925, the Rev. Erdmann William Frenk of Bemidji, Minn., succeeded Pastor Bartusch and served here until June 1, 1928. He devoted much time and effort to the congregation in De Kalb—about five miles south of Sycamore; in addition, he performed pastoral work at several State or public institutions.

Instead of attempting to call a resident pastor to succeed Pastor Frenk, who had accepted a call to Saint Peter's Congregation in Joliet, Ill., a delegation was sent to the Rev. Henry E. Tessmann at Genoa with the request that he serve Saint John's in Sycamore to the best of his ability until the congregation could again call its own pastor. Thereupon Pastor Tessmann served Saint John's as an affiliate of Trinity

*Trinity Congregation at Genoa was served as an affiliate.
†The Rev. William Steffen died on Feb. 8, 1894, in Algonquin, Ill.

in Genoa. In 1937 Pastor Tessmann was installed as resident pastor in Sycamore. Without delay, funds were gathered for the construction of a new church building. However, the members well knew that their thousand dollars—collected up to that time—would not be sufficient to cover the cost of the contemplated building program. It was at that time, in 1937, that Paul A. Nehring, a member of Saint John's Congregation, called together the members of the church board, including Pastor Tessmann, and made this announcement: "I have purchased two lots on the northwest corner of South Main and Ottawa Streets and am donating them to Saint John's Congregation for the erection of a house of God." Mrs. Nehring added: "I am donating the residence across the street to be used as a parsonage."* The news spread like wildfire. As soon as possible, a meeting of the congregation was called. Forthwith a building committee was elected, and by November 28 of that year—"a very cold day"—the cornerstone was laid. The beautiful church edifice, costing almost one hundred thousand dollars—most of it donated by Mr. Nehring—was dedicated on June 12, 1938. Pastor Tessmann retired on January 6, 1946. His successor, the Rev. Raymond T. Eissfeldt of Addison, Ill.,† was installed on January 13, 1946.

Having visited forty different Lutheran "centers" since the Trail left Cummings Corner (Oak Glen), where but in the shade of a sycamore could be found a more desirable spot for sweet repose? Sycamore on the map of the Lutheran Trail is "Station Number Seventy-two." Figures are not always uninteresting. Remembering that it is now the year 1877, the fact appears like the aurora borealis that the Missouri Synod was founded thirty years ago. Only three of its pastor-founders have died: The Rev. G. H. Loeber (1849), the Rev. G. K. Schuster (1869), and the Rev. G. H. Jaebker (1877).

*The former Nehring residence.

†Home of the Lutheran Child Welfare Association.

Part Four

From Sycamore to Columbia Heights

73. Freeport

A little more than fifty miles northwest of Sycamore is the city of Freeport, Ill.* "One William Baker, innkeeper, was a bighearted idealist. His wife, who belonged to the workaday world, became so fed up with her husband's non-paying guest policy that she tartly observed their settlement should be named 'Freeport,' and so it was."† For the first time since the Lutheran Trail started from Duncklees Grove, the Lutheran Pastoral Conference of Northern Illinois, recently organized, took an active interest in the development in this area. That body requested Professor T. Johannes Grosse of the Teachers' Seminary at Addison to make a survey of the missionary possibilities in Freeport. He was furnished with the names of several people; but upon finding them, they discouraged him. Then a certain woman, who formerly lived in Oak Park, which at first was known as Kettlestring's Grove, mistook the professor for the Rev. F. M.

*1940 census: 22,366.
†Freeport was once known as Winneshiek.

Grosse, pastor of Saint John's Congregation in Harlem (Forest Park). When he had informed her of his mission in Freeport, she joyfully brought the news to the elders of the Evangelical congregation, who thereupon requested him to preach in their church, because their own pastor had just resigned. On the condition that the retired pastor would agree to the idea and that he (Professor Grosse) would be permitted to conduct a Lutheran service, the professor accepted the invitation. On the following Sunday, February 25, 1877,* two services were conducted—one in the morning and another in the evening. On March 18 the service was held in the public school building. On May 6 a Lutheran congregation was organized and named Immanuel. Soon after that, property was purchased, and on September 2, 1877, a combination school and church was dedicated. In the same autumn a teacher was engaged for the day school. The first resident pastor was a young man who came to Freeport as a ministerial candidate, Fred C. Behrens. He was ordained and installed about the same time and served Immanuel until 1881, when he accepted a call to Manito, Ill.† On May 23, 1881, he was succeeded in Freeport by the Rev. Henry G. Schmidt of Rochester, Minn.‡ As Immanuel Congregation increased in membership, it soon became apparent that a larger church was needed. In 1900 a large brick church was erected at the corner of South Chicago and East Pleasant Streets. The combination church-school building then became the school only. In April, 1899, Pastor Schmidt followed a call to Milwaukee, Wis., and the Rev. Andrew Christian Landeck of St. Paul, Ill., succeeded him in Freeport on April 16, 1899. In 1914 Pastor Landeck accepted a call to Pecatonica, Ill., and his successor, the Rev. Louis Seidel of Joplin, Mo., was

*In 1877 the controversy on Election and Conversion began with Dr. C. F. W. Walther's paper on "Election," read by him at Altenburg, Mo.

†The church was located some distance from Manito, at a place called "Egypt"—probably a postal substation.

‡The Rev. Henry G. Schmidt was pastor of Immanuel Congregation in Crystal Lake, Ill., 1875-1880; thence he went to Rochester, Minn.

installed as Immanuel's fourth pastor on September 13, 1914. In 1923 a new school was erected at a cost of more than sixty thousand dollars. It comprises four large classrooms, a library, a gymnasium, bowling alleys, recreation rooms, and a heating plant. In July, 1927, Pastor Seidel accepted a call to Saint James Congregation in Chicago, and the Rev. Otto Schumacher of Morrison, Ill., succeeded him on October 2, 1927. In 1944 Redeemer Congregation* agreed to pay one fourth of the teachers' salaries with the understanding that its children could attend Immanuel School. The following trained teachers have had charge of this school: R. G. Bendick, H. F. Bode, Miss M. Timmermann, Miss L. Wassmann, Miss Verna Bickel, Miss Ruth Brenner, Arlon Rueter, Miss Doris Polansky, and A. E. Doering.

74. Matteson

Since this history is compiled in chronological order of the various congregations' organization, the Lutheran Trail must now make a trip to the Loop in the "Big City," alight at the Twelfth Street Station of the Illinois Central Railroad, and cross the bridge to catch a southbound electric train labeled "Matteson Special," arriving within an hour at Matteson, Ill.,† a village named for Joel H. Matteson, Governor of Illinois, 1853-1857.

Record is scant about the development of Lutheranism in this area, although it appears that there has been considerable activity at least since 1878, when Zion Congregation was founded in this village. The early Lutherans who desired worship services in their immediate circle were quite willing to share the responsibility of driving to Crete on Sundays and getting the Rev. Gottlieb Traub, pastor of Trinity Congregation (prior to 1858 known as Zion) near that village, to conduct services in Matteson, and then taking

*Redeemer Congregation was organized in 1910; the church is located at 607 South Galena Street. Its present pastor: C. J. Schuth.
†1940 census: 819.

him home again. Later the Rev. Barthold Burfeind of Town Rich (remember Sauk Trail!—"Skunks Grove") served the group in Matteson. On Aug. 10, 1884, Candidate Ernst Kirchner was ordained and installed as Zion's first resident pastor. On April 2, 1890, he accepted a call to Briar Hill, near Youngstown, Ohio, and on June 1 the Rev. John Carl Ludwig Frese of Champaign City, Ill., succeeded him as Zion's second pastor. In March, 1894, Pastor Frese accepted a call to Cowling, Ill. A student at Concordia Seminary, Springfield, Ill., Carl Schroeder, served until August 19, 1894, when Candidate Ferdinand Karl Schmiege, a graduate of the same institution, was ordained and installed. Two years later, in August, 1896, Pastor Schmiege followed a call to Tenhassen, Minn. Student Witschonke, also from Springfield, served as "vicar" until August, 1897, when the Rev. H. C. Friedrich Neben of Woodworth, Ill., succeeded to the Zion pastorate, which he held for only two years, following a call to Campbell, Nebr., in the summer of 1898. In September, 1898, the Rev. Caspar H. Bursick of Lake Ridge, Mich., succeeded Pastor Neben in Matteson. In February, 1905, Pastor Bursick accepted a call to Chandlerville, Ill., where he resigned about a year later.

Zion School was begun at the time of the congregation's organization. The first teacher was a Mr. Maurer; then came a Mr. Bonneront, who served for six years, when Pastor Kirchner, upon assuming charge of the pastorate, also served as teacher in the school. This practice continued until 1931, when Elmer H. Huedepohl was called to teach.

On March 19, 1905, the Rev. Christoph Becker of Sandusky, Wis., was installed as Zion's pastor. He also taught school until the beginning of October, 1937. On the 11th of that month Pastor Becker bumped his head against a hatrack in the lobby of the meeting room. His skull was fractured, and early in the morning of the following day he died. Zion's next pastor was the Rev. Lawrence C. Hoeppner of Mount

Carroll, Ill. Installed on January 23, 1938, Pastor Hoeppner served until April, 1942, when he accepted a call to Elkhart, Ind.* On July 26, 1942, the Rev. Herman P. Meyer of Woodstock, Ill., assumed his new duties in Matteson.† In August, 1945, Mr. Huedepohl left Matteson to take charge of the Lutheran school in Marengo, Ill. At present two men are teaching in Zion School, Werner Wichmann and Ernest Wunderlich.

75. Genoa

Returning to Sycamore, the Trail proceeds directly north a distance of about seven miles to Genoa,‡ where Trinity Congregation was organized in 1878, but whose history for the most part is intimately connected with that of Saint John's in Sycamore. The only additional facts available at the moment concern the pastors who have served Trinity in recent years: the Rev. William Bramscher, who in July, 1927, accepted a call to Zion in Wheatland Township, near Plainfield, Ill.; the Rev. E. M. Telschow of Butternut, Wis., who was installed at Genoa on August 1, 1937; and the Rev. W. C. Vetter of Riceville, Iowa, who was installed as Trinity's pastor on February 18, 1945.

The Trail picks up a few news items as it makes its way southeastward in the direction of Hammond, Ind., a distance of about seventy miles. Strange as it may seem, there is absolutely no information regarding the organization of a Missouri Lutheran congregation in the year 1879, that is, in the Northern Illinois District. A phone call, however, may be expected at any time! In June, 1878, the Bell Telephone

*Trinity, in Elkhart, Ind., was founded in 1872. Pastor Hoeppner's immediate predecessor there was Rev. Paul C. Barth, who in 1942 became Director of Public Relations for the Missouri Synod's Radio Station KFUO on the grounds of Concordia Seminary, St. Louis, Mo. Pastor Barth's brother, Dr. G. Chr. Barth, is president of Concordia Seminary, Springfield, Ill.

†A new school building, costing $25,000, was dedicated on Sept. 3, 1944. The name of the school is imbedded in the concrete walk leading to the building. (Cf. *Northern Illinois District Edition, Lutheran Witness*, LXIII, 20, p. 2.)

‡Named after the town in New York.

Company of Chicago was started. Will the idea click? In the same year the incandescent lamp was invented by Thos. A. Edison. In 1879 the Chicago and Alton Railroad was opened. However, the Trail leads to a station on the Chicago and Eastern Illinois Railroad.

76. Thornton

The village of Thornton, Ill.,* located about three miles west of Cummings Corner (Oak Glen–Lansing), is noted for its extensive stone quarries.

For about five years (1858-1864) German services were conducted here by ministers of the Methodist Church. After an apparent gap of inactivity, the Methodists were superseded in 1866 by ministers of the Evangelical Synod successively stationed at Thornton Station (Homewood), near the western end of Ridge Road, about three miles west of Thornton. In 1880 the Rev. G. Hornborstel, who at the time ministered to the Germans here, reported to the Rev. Henry Wunder, president of the Illinois District (Missouri Synod) and pastor of First St. Paul's Congregation in Chicago, that the Germans in Thornton for the most part were originally ("von Hause aus") Lutherans and therefore should be served by a Lutheran minister. Following his voluntary resignation, Pastor Hornborstel moved to Chicago and there joined a Lutheran congregation. Thereupon, the Thornton Lutherans sent a petition to the faculty of Concordia Seminary, Springfield, Ill., for a student to serve on a temporary basis. Wilhelm Lauer served in this capacity for about two years. In January, 1882, a similar petition, signed by Christ Drews, Johann Lange, Sr., Gustav Lorenz, and Claus Juergensen, in the presence of Pastor Karl Brauer of Crete, was addressed to the same faculty; however, this petition implied "permanency" for the man chosen from the current graduating class. The

*1940 census: 1,101.

official document was submitted by Prof. Friedrich August Craemer, president of the seminary, to Candidate Carl Keller. On August 20, 1882, the young candidate was ordained and installed as the first Lutheran pastor of St. Paul's Congregation by the Rev. Ferdinand Doederlein, pastor of St. John's Congregation, Coopers Grove. Less than four months later, Pastor Keller received from Pastor Brauer in Crete a post card bearing this information: "Pastor Burfeind ist krank, wie Du weisst. Habe gestern fuer ihn gepredigt. Er beauftragte mich, Dir zu schreiben, dass es sein Wunsch sei, die Bloomer-Gemeinde wendete sich ganz an Dich als ihren Prediger. Gehe also getrost hin, trag's den Leuten vor und gewinne die Herzen dieser Leute fuer Dich, resp., fuer Christum. Siehe, so vergroessert sich Deine Parochie!" (Pastor Burfeind is ill, as you know. I preached for him yesterday. He requested me to write you that it is his desire that the congregation at Bloom turn entirely to you as its pastor. Therefore, go there with confidence, submit this matter to the people, and win the hearts of these people for yourself, resp., for Christ. Behold, thus your parish is being enlarged!)

Thus it happened that the two St. Paul congregations constituted one parish from 1882 until 1893, which was served as such by Pastor Keller. Some of the Lutheran farmers volunteered to take him to Bloom (Chicago Heights) "every second Sunday." Occasionally he went there by handcar on the Chicago and Eastern Illinois Railroad. One wonders whether he was assisted with the "pumping" as was the Rev. Johannes T. Feiertag on some of his trips to Batavia from Aurora during the decade 1869-1879. Candidate Karl Henry Schroeder, graduate of Concordia Seminary, Springfield, Ill., was ordained and installed as the first resident pastor of St. Paul's Congregation in Bloom (Chicago Heights) on August 16, 1893, and Pastor Keller continued his pastorate in Thornton until October 7, 1906, when he accepted a call to

Strasburg, Ill. His successor in Thornton, the Rev. Valentine Hornung of Sadorus, Ill., served in Thornton until 1920, when he resigned from the active ministry and moved to Chicago; later, to Des Plaines.

St. Paul's first church building was erected in 1873 on Hunter St., and served its purpose for about thirty years. In 1903 this building was struck by lightning and damaged to such an extent that complete renovation became necessary. Then, on the Friday preceding Palm Sunday, March 25, 1904, the renovated building was completely destroyed by a violent windstorm. "....mit vielen Traenen stand die Gemeinde mit Pastor und Konfirmanden am Truemmerhaufen." ("....with many tears the congregation with its pastor and confirmands stood at the heap of ruins.") Within a few months the amount of approximately $5,000 was gathered in the neighboring congregations, but only $3,000 was needed for the construction of a new church. The surplus was used by St. Paul's Congregation for the support of other small and needy congregations. The new church was dedicated on August 25, 1904.

From 1882 to 1888 the day school was conducted in the Thornton Town Hall. As a direct result of a new law, which became effective on July 1, 1889, and which affected the teaching of religion in Illinois, the school was transferred to the church building. During the next three or four months a school building, 22x28x10, was erected at a cost of $438.57 on property adjoining the parsonage, about a quarter of a mile west of the church. This building was dedicated on October 13, 1889. (Wasn't a whole town laid waste by a great flood on May 31, 1889?—Johnstown, Pa.)

Serving the congregation as vacancy pastors for well-nigh two years after Pastor Hornung's resignation in 1920 were the Rev. Charles A. Waech of Crete and the Rev. Theo. W. Strieter, hitherto a missionary in Brazil, South America. St.

Paul's third resident pastor, the Rev. Henry F. Meyer of Rugby, Ill., was installed on April 30, 1922. He remained here until April, 1929, and then accepted a call to Saint John's Congregation at Coopers Grove, about six miles west of Thornton. His successor was the Rev. A. R. Kasischke, of Neudorf, Saskatchewan, Can. who resigned November 9, 1938.

In November, 1948, Pastor and Mrs. Hornung (the former Bertha Holzman of Grant Park, Ill.,) celebrated their sixty-third wedding anniversary. He died at the age of 89 years on August 12, 1949, in a Palatine (Ill.) hospital.

The Rev. William Schilling was installed as Saint John's next pastor on April 16, 1939. After about four years this pastor accepted a call to Newberry, Mich., and on September 5, 1943, the Rev. Norman M. Streufert of Wooddale, Ill., was installed as his successor. In August, 1948, Pastor Streufert accepted a call to Normandy, Mo., and on May 22, 1949, his successor, the Rev. Henry R. Hardt* of Red Wing, Minn., was installed in Thornton. In 1915 the membership had "melted down" to 94 communicants. In 1948 it was 140.

77. Marengo

The name of the next town to be visited reminds one of Napoleon Bonaparte. In June, 1800, his French soldiers defeated the Austrians at Marengo, Italy. That's the name—Marengo, Ill.,† almost sixty miles northwest of Chicago's Loop.

During the 1870's the first families from Pomerania, Germany, began to settle in the vicinity of this village. Some of these at an early date conferred with the Rev. John E. Baumgaertner, who in 1876 had assumed the pastorate of Trinity in Huntley, ten miles southeast. He came to Marengo and conducted worship services in private homes, in school-

†1940 census: 2,034.

*Son-in-law of the Rev. Chris. Becker of Zion, Matteson, Ill., 1905-1937, who died Oct. 12, 1937.

houses, in town halls, even in blacksmith shops. The first service was held on March 29, 1880 (Easter Monday) in Fay's Public School (Riley Township), located about two and one-half miles south of Marengo. In view of the deep interest manifested by these Pomeranians he promised to continue the services on Sunday afternoons, every other week in summer and once a month in winter. After the second service, on April 25, 1880, the families present on that occasion organized "Zion German Evangelical Lutheran Congregation, U.A.C." Fay's School was used for worship purposes by Zion Congregation until the second Sunday in April, 1881. On April 17, which was Easter Sunday, they met in the basement of the Independent Congregational church, the building which the Lutherans of Marengo shortly afterward purchased for twenty-two hundred dollars, including two lots. The building was dedicated on September 6, 1885. In addition to the forenoon service, an English service was held in the afternoon for the special benefit of non-Lutherans attending the dedicatory services.

In May, 1886, Pastor Baumgaertner resigned and moved to western Nebraska, where, in the following year, he again assumed a pastorate. Jointly with the small "sister" congregations at Huntley (Trinity), Hampshire (Trinity), Union (Saint John's), and other centers, Zion Congregation now called the Rev. J. Lorenz Craemer of Fort Dodge, Iowa. He was installed as pastor of the multiple parish on November 14, 1886. His ministerial service extended over a period of only about eighteen months, until April, 1888, when he accepted a call to Decatur, Ill.

Feeling yet more keenly the need for a pastor of its own, for the growing work in church and school, Zion Congregation now decided to become autonomous and called the Rev. Otto Doederlein of Philo, Ill., to serve as pastor and teacher. He was installed in Marengo on June 3, 1888. In the fall of that same year a day school was opened. "A good barn on the parsonage grounds was moved near the church, remodeled, and converted into a schoolhouse." It served that very purpose for about sixteen years. Pastor Doederlein taught school for about ten years. Then Christian Heine, a student at the Teachers' Seminary, Addison, was engaged for one year.

In May, 1891, Pastor Doederlein declared that because of throat trouble he would soon be obliged to resign. That happened sooner than the members of Zion might have anticipated. Before leaving Marengo, he suggested that the congregation call his brother, Candidate Paul Doederlein, graduate of Concordia Seminary, St. Louis, Mo., as his successor. The congregation recognized the suggestion as "a genuine service." The young candidate was ordained and installed on June 28, 1891.

In the summer of 1901 another classroom was arranged in the second story of the building, and Adolph Fischer, likewise a student, assisted for more than a year. On December 7, 1902, H. E. Kreutz of Lansing, Mich., was installed as Zion School's first resident teacher. In the spring of 1904 a new school building was erected. Pastor Doederlein assisted in hauling and setting up the stones for the foundation. The building was dedicated on August 21, 1904. By 1905 the enrollment had increased to ninety. In January, 1905, Pastor Doederlein accepted a call to Immanuel in Dundee (East), Ill.; his successor in Marengo was the Rev. Adolph C. Staats of Rochelle, Ill. The installation took place on February 26, 1905. On the following August 11 the church was struck by lightning and, together with the old school building near by, burned to the ground. A new church was erected during the following months and dedicated on May 6, 1906.

Meanwhile, progress in the school had been interrupted also by the serious illness of Mr. Kreutz in the fall of 1905. He died in January, 1906, and his successor was J. W. Feiertag; when Mr. Feiertag in 1923 accepted a call to Saint Paul's School in Aurora, Ill., his successor, E. A. Heinitz, took charge of the school in 1924 and remained until 1942.

Soon after the end of the First World War, Pastor Staats' health began to fail, and in June, 1924, he resigned.* He was succeeded in Marengo on August 24, 1924, by the Rev. Herman E. Brauer of Rochelle, Ill. A little more than four years later, in November, 1929, Pastor Brauer accepted a call to Saint Martini Congregation in Chicago, and the Rev. Edward Adam Nauss of Roselle, Ill., succeeded him to the Zion pastorate on January 9, 1930. He served until April 9, 1942—the day of his death—at the age of fifty-two. His successor in Marengo, the Rev. Walter Carl Schaefer of Dale, Wis., was installed on July 12, 1942.

In addition to the teachers already named, the following have also served at Zion School: Miss Ruth Wolter, Miss Dorothy Grundmann, Walter H. Schmidt, Erich O. Haase, Elmer H. Huedepohl, Miss Betty Diesing, Theodore Preuss, Robert Nieting, and Wilbert Frank.

78. Niles Center

Less than three miles northeast of old "Dutchman's Point" —long since changed to Niles—is a village which until a few years ago was well known as Niles Center. Now it is Skokie.† Being in this part of the Chicago area, it is not surprising to meet the Rev. John Adam Detzer once more. As pastor of Immanuel in Des Plaines he was constantly seeking opportunities to establish congregations in various German settlements in the neighborhood of his parish. On December 26, 1880 (Second Christmas Day), he conducted a worship service for the German Lutherans in a hall at Oakton Street

*After resigning, Pastor Staats served various congregations in Chicago and vicinity by occasional teaching and preaching. For nine years he also taught at the "Kinderheim" at Addison.

†1940 census: 7,172. Niles Center, in Niles Township, named from a village in Cayuga County, N.Y.

and Lincoln Avenue. In February of the following year a congregation was organized and named Saint Paul's. Immediately the decision was reached to build a church in Niles Center (Skokie). One of the charter members, Henry Rohr, donated half an acre of land within half a block of the village's business center, and building operations were forthwith begun.

A momentary deviation: On May 21, 1881, the Revised Version of the New Testament Scriptures was published in a special sixteen-page supplement of the *Chicago Tribune*.

In June, 1881, the first church of Saint Paul's Congregation was dedicated.

Another deviation: The twentieth President of the United States, James Abram Garfield, was shot on July 2, 1881, "by a disappointed office seeker named Guiteau in the railroad station at Washington. He lingered eighty days, dying at Long Branch, September 19, 1881."*

On July 31, 1881, Saint Paul's first resident pastor, the Rev. Frederick W. Detzer ("Reiseprediger" in Minnesota, Dakota, Manitoba, and farther West), a son of the founder, was installed in Niles Center (Skokie). Soon afterward a day school was established and taught by the pastor for the next four years. From 1885 on trained teachers were in charge of the school until 1898; consecutively, they were the Messrs. C. Bretall, H. Gosch, J. Wagner, and R. Nimmer. Thereupon the pastor again served as schoolteacher. In 1927, because of lack of adequate support, the day school was discontinued.

During the spring of 1910 Saint Paul's Congregation recognized the need for a larger church building and proceeded with building operations. A new church, built of brick with stone trimmings and seating approximately six hundred, was

*In the course of a memorial address "on the life and character of James A. Garfield," the Hon. James G. Blaine on Feb. 27, 1882, said: "Lincoln fell at the close of a mighty struggle in which the passions of men had been deeply stirred . . . . Garfield was slain in a day of peace, when brother had been reconciled to brother and when anger and hate had been banished from the land." (*Memorial Addresses*, Washington, Government Printing Office, 1903, page 101f.)

dedicated on January 29, 1911. The new church with its excellent facilities for educational and recreational activities infused new life into the membership and attracted many more worshipers.

The years 1921-1928 wrought remarkable changes in the community. Modern concrete roads were built, connecting the village with all the principal streets of Chicago and its northern suburbs. The elevated electric railroad (Rapid Transit—"El" or "L") was extended to Niles Center (Skokie). All of which combined to induce thousands of new residents to settle in this community, including many Lutherans who were eventually adopted by Saint Paul's Congregation.

Having served Saint Paul's as its first pastor for fifty years, Pastor Detzer died on July 10, 1931, and was buried in Saint Paul's Cemetery (established in 1882) on the outskirts of Skokie. The congregation's second pastor, the Rev. Otto F. Arndt of Downers Grove, Ill., was installed on November 15, 1931—fifty years after the congregation's founding. With Pastor Arndt's coming the so-called "double-header" (German-English) arrangement of worship services was made. As a result of the extensive work carried on in the English language, the attendance at the services showed a steady increase from year to year, and in course of time the number of English-speaking worshipers greatly exceeded that of the German-speaking worshipers.

The most recent forward step taken by Saint Paul's of Skokie was the establishment of a consolidated elementary school,* which is being operated jointly with Saint John's of Niles and Jerusalem of Morton Grove.

It is worthy of note that William J. Galitz has served as Saint Paul's second treasurer for almost one-half century; the first treasurer was his father, Ernest Galitz.

Saint Paul's joined the Missouri Synod in 1945. Very re-

*This consolidated school is located a little more than one mile northwest of Skokie in the village of Morton Grove.

cently a Sunday school was started with 28 pupils in the basement of a private home in the northwestern part of Skokie. The Rev. Arthur E. Going is in charge of this project. He lives in Park Ridge.

79. Batavia

In 1881 the Chicago City Railway "ventured to replace the horse-drawn vehicles with cable cars, the motive power being furnished by stationary steam engines in a central plant." That particular kind of noise has completely disappeared from Chicago. It is now the year 1882, and the Trail again returns to the beautiful and quiet valley of the Des Plaines River.

An old Teutonic tribe, known as Batavians, many years ago inhabited a part of the present Holland in Europe, specifically the island of Batavia, formed by that branch of the Rhine River which empties into the sea near Leyden, together with the Waal and the Maas. Tacitus asserts them to have been offsprings of the Catti . . . . At the end of the third century the Salian Franks obtained possession of the island of Batavia. However, history of the Batavia of immediate interest does not date back to the second or third, but only to the first part of the nineteenth century, A.D. It was in the year 1832 that General Scott, during the memorable Black Hawk War, came down this trail to the West and buried many who had died of cholera in an Indian burial place east of Batavia, in Kane County, Ill.* In the following spring, 1833, Christopher Payne used the same trail, taking up a squatter's claim—the first in Kane County—on the east side of the Des Plaines River. In 1835 Payne sold his half section to Isaac Wilson, after whom the principal thoroughfare of Batavia is named. Shortly afterward people of various nationalities settled in this locality, among them Ger-

*1940 census: 5,101. Named for the town in New York, which was named for the Batavian Republic.

man Lutherans. Hence, when the Rev. Ernst Buhre in 1854 came to Aurora ("McCarty Mills") to conduct the first Lutheran service, the Lutherans living in or near Batavia requested him to serve them also. In 1855 Pastor Buhre baptized one child, confirmed a boy, and buried a woman at Batavia. In 1862 he left Aurora and was succeeded by the Rev. H. Baumstark on August 30, 1863. The latter, in turn, was succeeded by the Rev. Johannes Strieter on March 19, 1865. Pastor Strieter baptized seven children in Batavia and officiated at the burial service for a girl. In December, 1869, the Rev. John Traugott Feiertag became pastor of the Aurora parish and continued the work in Batavia. It was in the home of William Wilke that Pastor Feiertag conducted his first service in Batavia. Sometimes he came on a handcar via the Burlington Railroad—members of the Aurora parish pumping the car for him. When the weather was inclement, he came by horse and buggy. In April, 1879, Pastor Feiertag accepted a call to Wolcottsville, N.Y., and on May 11 was succeeded in Aurora by the Rev. Walter Krebs of La Rose, Ill. For twenty-seven years the Batavia Lutherans were served thus intermittently until they formally organized as a congregation, which was effected in 1882 under the direction of Pastor Krebs, and the name Immanuel was adopted.*

In 1887 a lot at Webster and South Van Buren Streets was purchased, and in the following year a church costing $1,289.76 was erected on this site. In 1891, the Rev. Gottlieb Traub, Sr., of Bath, Ill., succeeded Pastor Krebs, who had accepted a call to Trinity Congregation at Bachelors Grove, two miles north of Tinley Park, Ill. Pastor Traub served Batavia for about two years. Beginning in 1893, the Rev. Charles J. Fricke of West Chicago came to preach in Batavia on Sun-

*Charter members:

Walter Krebs, pastor	H. Koepke	W. Schultz
W. Wilke	H. Wilke	A. Schulz
F. Schuldt	H. Bullinger	C. Groener
C. Leipold	C. Miller	F. Pahnke
F. Nurnberg	C. Strobel	

day afternoons. In 1895 Immanuel became a member of the Missouri Synod. In 1900 the recent innovation of permitting men and women to sit together in church was introduced.

On April 13, 1902, the Rev. J. Burkart of Lyonsville (Lyons), Ill., succeeded Pastor Fricke. He was requested also to serve as day school teacher. In the following October he resigned. In November the Rev. Frederick G. Miessler of Ontarioville, Ill., succeeded him. Pastor Miessler began mission work in St. Charles, about four miles north of Batavia, and also on the Des Plaines River, preaching there once every other week. In December, 1909, he followed a call to Trinity Congregation in Hanson Park, Chicago. On April 3, 1910, the Rev. John F. M. Grosse of Watertown, Nebr., and temporarily out of office (since 1909) was installed as Pastor Miessler's successor. On November 10, 1912, the Rev. Herman Christoph Adolf Harms of Standish, Mich., succeeded to the Immanuel parish in Batavia.

Conditions brought about by World War I made it impossible to continue the day school; it was closed. In 1918 a Sunday school was established, and English services were started. In September, 1949, the day school was reopened; Arnold H. Johanns in charge.

In April, 1919, Pastor Harms accepted a call to Davenport, Iowa.* On July 20, 1919, the Rev. Edward C. Krause of Fremont, Nebr., more recently a chaplain in the U.S. Army, was installed as Immanuel's new pastor. In December, 1920, Pastor Krause followed a call to Sheboygan, Wis. His successor at Immanuel, the Rev. John F. C. Molthan of Genoa, Ill., was installed on January 2, 1921. In 1925 a new church was erected at a cost of thirty thousand dollars. Pastor Molthan resigned on July 1, 1934, and on the following August 26 the Rev. W. H. Schlie of Livermore, Iowa, succeeded him in Batavia.

*Presently (1949) First Vice-President of the Missouri Synod.

80. Roseland

In the year 1882 work was begun by the French on the Panama Canal, between North and South America. Near Lake Calumet—about five miles south of Jackson Park on Chicago's lake front—work was begun in the depot of the Illinois Central Railroad at Pullman. This was work of an altogether different nature; but it was hard work. The Rev. Henry Theo. L. Felten of Zion, Washington Heights (Chicago), found several families in this locality and conducted services at different locations: in a hall above a saloon on Front Street—"but straightforward testimony against sin soon resulted in eviction"; so the services were resumed in the home of a Mr. Gieseler on Kensington Avenue; then in Kionka's harness shop on Michigan Avenue and 113th Place. Six men signed the constitution upon which the organization of Zion Congregation was to be based, on August 20, 1882. In that first meeting it was resolved to erect a small church at Michigan Avenue and 113th Place, which was to serve also as a school. The church, 20x30 feet, was erected on Mr. Kionka's empty lot and dedicated on September 24, 1882. Later the congregation purchased the old Methodist church building on East 113th Street and Curtis (now Edbrooke) Avenue and renovated it. A student at the Teachers' Seminary, Addison, S. Roehm, started teaching there in 1882. In 1883 Hugo R. Charle had charge of the school for a very short time; he was succeeded by J. C. A. Winterstein, graduate of the Teachers' Seminary, Addison, who served for about one and one-half years, when he followed a call to nearby Saint Paul's School, Dolton-Riverdale (1886).

Until 1886 Zion Congregation was served as an affiliate of Zion in Washington Heights by the Rev. Mr. Felten. Then for two years as an affiliate of Saint Paul's in Dolton-Riverdale by the Rev. Carl M. Noack. On August 5, 1888, Candidate G. Sievers, graduate of Concordia Seminary, St. Louis, Mo., was ordained and installed as Zion's first resident pastor.

In 1890 a two-room school was built. In the same year, on November 4, West Roseland was annexed to Chicago. In 1894 many of Zion's members were out of work, owing to the strike at the Pullman railroad car shops; during this time "sister" congregations supported the congregation in Roseland.

In 1904 the old church was replaced with a brick structure.

Besides Pastor Sievers, who for several years taught school and later often substituted in emergencies in the day school, the following have served as teachers: W. Hacker, H. Maschhoff, L. Himmler, and P. Juengel; followed in later years by H. Hoppe, E. H. Muenzel, G. M. Meyer, W. Bewie, E. M. Kirsch, R. Appelt; also by several woman teachers, whose names are not now available; furthermore, by R. Schulz, E. Schramm, Candidates Fred Bartling,* John Hubertz,* and A. Schleef,* by Mrs. L. Sander, and by Gerhard Becker.†

In 1890 Pastor Sievers left Zion Congregation in Roseland, and his whereabouts after that time has not been traced. The other pastors of Zion were the Rev. Alfred E. Reinke‡ of Kewanee, Ill., August 5, 1900, to December, 1906, when he accepted a call to Concordia Congregation in the Avondale community, Chicago; his successor, the Rev. Henry Ohldag, from New Fane, Wis., was installed on December 23, 1906, and served until September 14, 1911, when he died. Then came the Rev. Henry C. M. Steger from Arenzville, Ill. His installation took place on September 24, 1911, and he held this pastorate until April, 1913, when he followed a call to Fairbank, Iowa. On the following May 4 the Rev. Bernard Hintz of Glencoe, Ill., began a ministry in Roseland which extended over a period of about fifteen years, until

*Ministerial candidates.

†A son of the Rev. Chr. Becker, pastor of Zion in Matteson, Ill., 1905-1937; since September, 1948, at St. John's, Forest Park, Ill.

‡The Rev. A. E. Reinke, a son of the Rev. Augustus Reinke, served as pastor of Concordia Congregation from Dec. 16, 1906, to Jan. 24, 1943 (date of his death).

April, 1928, when he resigned.* Pastor Hintz was succeeded in Roseland by the Rev. Martin Richard David Piehler of Athens, Wis., who was installed in Zion Church on August 5, 1928. During the convention of the Northern Illinois District (Missouri Synod) in River Forest, Ill., June 24-28, 1940,† Pastor Piehler was installed as stewardship secretary for this District. His successor at Zion in Roseland, the Rev. Carl William Pfotenhauer‡ of Saint Peter's Congregation at Schaumburg, was installed on April 7, 1940.

On the evening of February 19, 1945, a fire broke out in the "vestry" of the church which damaged the building to the extent of about thirty thousand dollars. The cause of the conflagration has not been definitely determined. A new church building at the northwest corner of East 109th Street and South Park Avenue, eight blocks north and five blocks east—or within one mile—of the original site, was erected at a cost of $123,000, including site and all furnishings. Dedication took place on December 4, 1947.

81. Hammond, Indiana

About twelve miles southeast of Roseland another "Missouri" congregation was organized in the year 1882—in Hammond, Ind.§ The name of this place "memorializes the first large industry of the area, the former Geo. H. Hammond Packing Company." The Lutheran Trail comes into this community for the reason that the first German settlers in this northwestern corner of the "Hoosier State" were originally served by pastors from the "Sucker State"—more polite, the "Prairie State." Saint John's Congregation at Tolleston (now part of Gary), Ind., was founded in the year 1870 by the

*Pastor Hintz died on May 19, 1932.

†The office was created at this convention. The installation was performed at the close of the convention sessions, Friday, June 28, 1940, by the president of this District, the Rev. Ernest T. Lams.

‡A son of the Rev. Frederick Pfotenhauer, D.D., President of the Missouri Synod, 1911-1935.

§1940 census: 70,184.

Rev. Henry Wunder, pastor of First Saint Paul's, Chicago. In the following year this congregation received its own pastor, the Rev. Herman Wunderlich of Bachelors Grove (two miles north of Tinley Park), Ill. The first Lutheran service in Hammond, attended by three families, was conducted by Pastor Wunderlich in 1878 in the home of Jacob Rimbach. The organization of Saint Paul's Congregation in Hammond was effected on October 3, 1882, with sixteen founders, and in a subsequent meeting six more were enrolled as charter members. The first church, a frame building, 24x48 feet, was dedicated on July 29, 1883. The first resident pastor, the Rev. Gotthilf F. Luebker of Iuka, Ill., was installed on December 13, 1885. Soon after his arrival he established a day school with an initial enrollment of twenty-three pupils. In October, 1886, the first school building was erected at a cost of $380. As enrollment increased, the pastor was assisted in school by Miss Magdalena Dunsing.* In 1889 the first trained teacher, Henry Maschhoff, graduate of the Teachers' Seminary, Addison, Ill., was placed in charge of Saint Paul's School. In the same year, 1889, several members of Saint Paul's living on the north side of Hammond were released to organize Saint John's Congregation, with its "center" at 4523 Towle Street. Saint John's first pastor was the Rev. William Adolph Brauer† of Appleton City, Mo. His pastorate extended over a period of about fifty-two years. His successor at Saint John's was the Rev. O. W. Linnemeier, twin brother of the Rev. Otto H. Linnemeier, pastor in Rochelle, Ill. The present pastor is the Rev. Henry C. Nickel. During the early years of his ministry in North Hammond Pastor Brauer assisted his father-in-law, the Rev. Johannes T. Feiertag of Colehour, Ill., in missionary activities in Whiting, Ind., and in the organization of Saint John's Congregation there in 1891. (See Chapter 64, page 269).

*Later, Miss Dunsing was known as Mrs. P. W. Meyn.

†He was the ninth and last child of the Rev. E. A. Brauer, second pastor of Zion, Duncklees Grove, Ill. He died on Jan. 15, 1941.

In June, 1889, Pastor Luebker accepted a call to Millerton, Nebr.* His successor at Saint Paul's in Hammond, the Rev. Frederick William Herzberger of Hegewisch, Ill., was installed on July 28, 1889. At this time Hammond experienced a boom; new industries were located here, and new homes were built. In February, 1890, the second church was dedicated. This was a combination church-school building and cost forty-five hundred dollars, including furniture and fixtures. The old church building was moved to the adjacent lot and converted into a parsonage. English preaching in Saint Paul's was begun by Pastor Herzberger. A second teacher for the day school, William Bennhoff, was called in June, 1892. Two years later, June, 1894, Saint Paul's joined the Missouri Synod. In 1895 Mr. Bennhoff followed a call to Fort Wayne, Ind., and was succeeded by John Merkling. In August, 1898, a new school building with four classrooms and a basement was dedicated at Sibley Street and Oakley Avenue in Hammond. It cost about thirteen thousand dollars. In September, 1898, Theodore Militzer of Baltimore, Md., was called to serve in the day school. On June 4, 1899, Pastor Herzberger preached his farewell sermon in Saint Paul's Church and became city missionary of St. Louis, Mo.† He was succeeded in Hammond by the Rev. William Herman Theodore Dau, professor at the English Missouri Synod's‡ college at Conover, N.C., since 1892. Shortly afterward Mr. Militzer resigned as teacher and was replaced by C. G. P. Heintz of Utica, N.Y. A new church, at 215-217 Cilton Street, was dedicated on April 26, 1903. In the same month the Concordia Cemetery Association of Hammond was organized. Two years later, in June, 1905, Pastor Dau accepted a professorship at Concordia Seminary, St. Louis, Mo., and his successor at Saint Paul's, the Rev. Ernst Theo. Claus of Elkhart, Ind.,

*He died in Springfield, Ill., Dec. 17, 1941, and was buried in Oak Hill Cemetery, near Hammond, Ind.

†Author of *The Family Altar* (Brief Daily Devotions).

‡Joined the "German" Missouri Synod as a District in 1911.

was installed on June 18. In 1916 members living in Hessville, Ind., were released to organize Concordia Congregation. The latter's pastor since that time has been the Rev. Paul F. Goltermann. Hessville is now part of Hammond, and Concordia Church is located at 6923 Marshall Street.

Pastor Claus resigned as pastor of Saint Paul's in the spring of 1918, and on June 16 the Rev. Walter F. Lichtsinn of Toronto, Ontario, Canada, was installed as his successor. Several months previously a number of Saint Paul's members, feeling that the congregation was not making sufficient provision for English work, requested their release to organize an entirely English congregation. They organized in the fall of 1918 under the name of Trinity. Trinity's first pastor was the Rev. Henry Mackensen.* His installation in Hammond took place on March 2, 1919. He served until May, 1923, when he accepted a call to Glen Ellyn, Ill. (See Chapter 164, page 496.) He met an untimely death on May 13, 1942. For the next eighteen years Trinity's pastor was the Rev. H. A. Nuoffer.† In 1941 he was succeeded at Trinity by the Rev. Julius William Acker of Evansville, Ind.

Other teachers who followed on Saint Paul's teaching staff were Samuel Goehringer, C. W. Lindemann, A. F. W. Fedder,‡ Miss Clara Peters, H. Werth, H. E. Schroeder, H. C. Meier, J. A. List, A. H. Eggers, Herman Maudanz, H. H. Beiderwieden, and K. W. Mueller; in more recent years: Mrs. E. Jiede, Miss Marie Berg, W. Beckmann, Student T. Schmidt, and E. Unrath.

On September 4, 1927, Pastor Lichtsinn having become president of the Central District (Missouri Synod), and that District having agreed to finance an assistant for him, the Rev.

*Pastor Mackensen's first two charges were at Sophia and Fargo, N. Dak., 1909 and 1912, respectively. From 1918 to 1919 he was a camp pastor.

†Shortly before his acceptance of a call to California, Pastor Nuoffer established a mission at Griffith, Ind., a few miles southeast of Gary, whose first resident pastor was the Rev. Hugo Goetz of La Porte, Ind.

‡A son, the Rev. Oscar Fedder, has served as pastor of St. Stephen's Congregation in Englewood (Chicago) since 1925.

E. W. Sonstroem of Bristol, Conn., was installed. Owing, however, to a shortage of funds in the District, "the arrangement of furnishing the congregation of the president an assistant pastor at the District's expense was discontinued." Accordingly, Pastor Sonstroem was released in May, 1932, when he received a call from New Britain, Conn. On August 7, 1949, Candidate Walter E. Ruehrdanz, Jr., was ordained and installed as assistant pastor.

82. North Plato

About sixty miles northwest of Hammond, Ind., is a little community which is named after an ancient Greek philosopher, Plato Center, Ill.* Saint Peter's Congregation was organized in this hamlet on August 1, 1883.† At first, an old deserted Presbyterian church was used for the worship services, conducted by the Rev. Herman F. Fruechtenicht of Saint John's in Elgin, on Sunday afternoons. The first resident pastor of Saint Peter's, the Rev. Otto Gruner, was installed on August 25, 1888. He served until April, 1895, when he accepted a call to Saint Paul's in Rockford, Ill. He, in turn, was succeeded by the Rev. E. A. Sieving, who held this pastorate until 1900 and then followed a call to Lincoln, Nebr. The Rev. Henry P. Prekel of Hubbell, Mich., served from 1900 until April, 1911, and then accepted a call to Saint John's in West Hammond (Calumet City), Ill. During the ensuing vacancy in the dual parish‡ the Rev. Louis Baumgaertner of Trinity Congregation in Hampshire served Saint Peter's until the Rev. Otto Hitzeroth was installed. He served for about twenty-five years. In 1933 Candidate Paul Hart-

*1940 census: 44.

†Charter members:

Fred Thies	H. Rohrsen	Louis Voltz
Fred H. Thies	Theo. Fischer	J. Kremke
Fred Hartje, Sr.	H. Volkening	J. Lenschow
Chris. Fischer	J. Schroeder	Fred Voltz
Fred Stege	Gus Mueller	W. Luther
C. Kremke	William Schroeder	F. Eineke

‡St. Peter's Congregation at Pingree Grove, four miles northeast of North Plato, was organized in 1890 and has been almost continuously served jointly with St. Peter's of North Plato. (See Chapter 117, page 397.)

mann was called as assistant to the pastor, and when he left, in February, 1936, Candidate William J. Danker, graduate of Concordia Seminary, St. Louis, Mo., continued this dual service for about one year. In the fall of 1936 the Rev. Martin Herman Richard Behling continued in a similar capacity until shortly after the death of Pastor Hitzeroth in May, 1937, when he was installed as Saint Peter's pastor. In May, 1940, Pastor Behling accepted a call to Saint Peter's at Schaumburg, Ill. On the 26th of the same month Candidate Herbert H. Heinemann assumed charge of the dual pastorate, Saint Peter's in North Plato (Plato Center) and Saint Peter's at Pingree Grove. In April, 1945, Pastor Heinemann accepted the pastorate of Saint Matthew's in Barrington, Ill., and the Rev. Kenneth H. Rozak* of David City, Nebr., succeeded him on June 10, 1945.

Saint Peter's in North Plato was self-sustaining from the time of its founding (1883) until 1926 and then received subsidy for its maintenance from the Northern Illinois District.

83. McHenry

About nine miles north of Crystal Lake, where Hanley Creek empties into the Fox River, is a village named McHenry.† Fragmentary information indicates that Lutheranism must have been a factor in this village's history, but the first records of a Lutheran congregation date only from 1875. For many years the congregation, known as Zion, worshiped in the Methodist church, using the German language exclusively. During the first years of its existence it was served as an affiliate of Immanuel Congregation in Crystal Lake by its pastor, the Rev. Henry G. Schmidt. From 1883 down to the present time eight other pastors have served this flock

*His father, the Rev. John Rozak, was pastor of St. John's at Rodenberg, two miles west of Roselle, Ill., from January, 1943, till summer, 1948; now a Fairland, Okla.

†1940 census: 1,354.

in McHenry. Among them was the Rev. Karl Schmidt, brother of the Rev. Henry G. Schmidt. It was during his pastorate (1883-1897) that the present church building was erected and dedicated. In more recent years Zion Congregation has been served as an affiliate of other near-by congregations connected with the Missouri Synod. The Rev. Frederick C. Pudsell, formerly of the Zion Lettish Congregation, Chicago, held this pastorate from May 5, 1946, until early in 1948, when he resigned. His successor, the Rev. Walter C. Johannes of Sweet Springs, Mo., was installed in McHenry on July 4, 1948; however, about eleven months later he accepted a call to the dual parish Concordia in Midlothian and Trinity in Hazel Crest, Ill. His successor, the Rev. Carl Lobitz of Atchison, Kans., was installed on October 9, 1949.

84. Lansing

The Trail now again goes southeast from McHenry, by way of Russells Grove (Fairfield) and Cummings Corner (Oak Glen), to Lansing,* one mile beyond the "Corner." The early history of Saint John's Congregation in Lansing, with its center on Wentworth Avenue about a block south of Ridge Road, is to be found under that of Trinity Congregation at Cummings Corner. Its subsequent history begins with the appointment, on May 11, 1924, of the Rev. Herbert H. A. Harthun of Midland, Mich., as assistant pastor to the Rev. Frederick Brunn, with the specific assignment to perform all necessary English work in both congregations. Upon the death of Pastor Brunn, on May 27, 1927, the two parishes began to function independently. At that time Pastor Harthun was formally given charge of Saint John's in Lansing. In 1931 it became necessary for the young pastor to request help in supporting his congregation. "Practically all the men of the congregation have been unemployed for many months be-

*1940 census: 4,462.

cause of the closing of the brickyards. The local bank, in which a large number of members were interested, has been closed for several months." Later the District granted financial aid for two day school teachers, because the congregation's financial condition had not improved, but rather grown worse.

During the first ten years of Saint John's existence its children attended Trinity School at Cummings Corner (Oak Glen). In 1893, however, the congregation erected its own school building in Lansing. The following have served as teachers in Saint John's School: Miss Liebe, Miss Martha Schulz, H. Kreutz, Eldor G. Handrich, J. H. Hoffmann, Theodore Stelzer, L. B. Abraham, Walter Redeker, Edward Kurth, Lester Baack, Edward M. Streufert, Clarence Zimbrick, and Miss Erna Jochum, Miss Nancy Glass, Miss Caroline Meilahn, and Ralph Boardman.

Plans for the erection of a new church in Lansing are now being formulated.

85. Hampshire

While at North Plato, reference was made to a place called Hampshire,* a village in Kane County, about twelve miles northwest of Elgin, Ill. Lutheranism had its inception here in 1883. Trinity Congregation was organized in that year. The first pastor, the Rev. John Ernst Baumgaertner of Huntley, served from 1883 to 1886; the second pastor, the Rev. J. Lorenz Craemer (also of Huntley), served from 1886 to 1888; then came the Rev. William Steffen of Algonquin and served until 1894.† In 1895 Trinity at Hampshire joined with Saint John's in Burlington—about three miles south—in calling a pastor for both parishes, Candidate Phil. Roesel, who was installed on July 28, 1895. He made his home in Burlington.‡

*1940 census: 757.
†Pastor Wm. Steffen died on Feb. 8, 1894.
‡1940 census: 235.

In 1897 Trinity Congregation erected a new church seating two hundred, which was dedicated on October 24, 1897. The pastor also taught school. In July, 1902, Pastor Roesel accepted a call to Lahoma, Okla. For the interim the Rev. John F. C. Molthan of Genoa's Trinity Congregation served, until August 14, 1904, when Candidate Albert D. Wangerin was ordained and installed as pastor of the dual parish. In February, 1908, Pastor Wangerin accepted a call to Tabor Congregation in Chicago, and the Rev. Louis Baumgaertner of Kampsville, Calhoun County, Ill., became his successor. In the fall of 1910 Pastor Baumgaertner accepted a call to Trinity Congregation in Huntley, about seven miles northeast of Hampshire, and again Pastor Molthan of Genoa took charge of the vacancy, until October 29, 1911, when the dual parish secured the Rev. D. H. Schoof of Gravelton, Mo. After about six years Pastor Schoof was forced by illness to resign,* and during the ensuing vacancy the Rev. Otto Hitzeroth of North Plato served both parishes. In 1921 the Rev. H. J. F. Meier of Ontarioville, Ill., assumed charge of the dual parish. In April, 1929, ill health compelled him also to resign. His successor, the Rev. Werner Schmidtke of Iron Mountain, Mich., was installed on September 1, 1929.† He served until May 1, 1947, when he accepted a call to Fort Wayne, Ind. The Rev. E. F. Kruse of Brazil, South America, was installed as his successor on October 5, 1947.

86. Chicago, Saint Luke's

It is now the year 1884. Grover Cleveland is the twenty-second President of the United States. From Burlington and Hampshire the Lutheran Trail returns to Chicago.

The sixth Missouri Synod congregation in Chicago, Saint

*In 1926 Pastor Schoof resumed ministerial work at Town Center, Rock County, Wis., and again resigned, in 1929. He died on Feb. 7, 1936, at Janesville, Wis.

†A son of the Rev. Leo Schmidtke, who served Bethel Congregation in Chicago from 1914 until 1934 and who died on Nov. 8, 1934.

James (Sankt Jakobi), came under observation in conjunction with the history of First Saint Paul's. Organized in 1869, Saint James in its thirteenth year (1882) had grown to such proportions that an assistant pastor had to be called. Candidate John Ernst August Mueller was ordained and installed on January 8, 1882. On the same day the branch school at Hoyne Avenue and Wellington Street, in what then was the village of Lake View, Ill., was dedicated. Two years later, on January 13, 1884, thirty-four members* of Saint James Congregation were released to organize their own congregation in Lake View, which was named Saint Luke. The new congregation's first day school teacher, Henry D. Cluever, began his activities on April 21, 1884.

In connection with the selection of the site for the proposed church building, at Belmont Avenue and Perry Street (now Greenview Avenue), dissension arose among the members, some of whom strenuously objected to erecting a church building in a "Krautfeld" (cabbage field—truck farm). This resulted in a minor defection.

While the building was under construction, the congregation erected a second or branch school as well as a teacher's residence on Diversey Boulevard, near Southport Avenue. In July, 1884, William Schlake of Belleville, Ill., was called to take charge of this school. In December of the same year, reports concerning the congregation's branch school estab-

*Charter members:

Friedrich Wolff	W. Emskamp	Carl Schroeder
Carl Labahn	Johann Krutz	August Benzin
Fritz Zitzmann	Gottfried Wolski	Carl Benzin
Chas. Mau	Friedrich Scheffler	Wilhelm Witt
Carl Mueller	August Schalk	Herman Krueger
Carl Lietzow	August Schultz	Julius Jordan
W. Jacobs	Johann Lobitz	Joachim Sodemann
C. Wendel	Johannes Koester	John Kuester
John Labahn	Philip Brandel	Wilhelm Kuester
Christian Losehand	Johann Kei	Louis Riemer
F. Jacobs	Heinrich Schalk	Ferdinand Ruebenhagen
	Otto Ristow	

NOTE: In addition to these former members of St. James the following also signed the constitution at the first meeting: Charles Kemnitz, August Jacobs, Joachim Voelker, Friedrich Huxhold, Friedrich Labahn, Julius Ristow, and Carl Deu. ("etc.")

lished in Bowmanville began to appear. This school at the end of December had an enrollment of twenty-two. In September, 1885, Saint Luke's third teacher, H. W. C. Waltke of St. Louis, Mo., was installed. A new school was erected at Belmont and Perry (Greenview) in 1885 and dedicated on the first Sunday of the year 1886. In 1887 the fourth teacher, Konrad A. Leinberger, was added to the staff. In the same year the church building was enlarged to provide a seating capacity of 1,250. The dedication took place on November 11, 1888. On July 15, 1889, Lake View, together with a number of other communities on the North and South Sides, was annexed to Chicago. In 1890 Mr. Schlake resigned as teacher, and Mr. Waltke followed a call back to St. Louis, Mo. A student, J. Zitzmann, served in the classroom vacated by Mr. Schlake until William Burhop of Detroit, Mich., was installed in July, 1890. At the same time William Sagehorn succeeded Mr. Waltke. A third teacher, H. Baumgart, was installed in the same year. In 1890, also, the school at Wellington Street and Hoyne Avenue—a gift from the "mother" congregation—because of its unfavorable location was sold, and a new building of brick and a teacher's residence were erected on Hamilton Avenue, near School Street. In 1892 Charles A. Decker of Palatine, Ill., was placed in charge of the new school. Early in 1893 H. Garbisch was called to take charge of one of the classes of this "constantly growing" school; and shortly thereafter a third teacher, C. Burgdorf of Meriden, Conn., was added to the staff. In 1893 Mr. Cluever resigned from the teaching profession. On October 15, 1893, Conrad J. Schwanke began his work in Saint Luke's day schools—at first in the Diversey Boulevard school and later at the "home" school, Belmont and Greenview. In 1895 H. A. Borchers began teaching at Saint Luke's schools.

On January 29, 1899, during a bitterly cold night, the church was destroyed by fire. Only the side walls and the steeple remained standing. In the interior everything except the altar, the pulpit, and a few pews was completely destroyed. Under the leadership of Pastor Mueller the members organized themselves into a large volunteer group to clear away the debris and to plan for immediate reconstruction; and on July 16 in the same year Saint Luke's third church was dedicated.

In 1900 Mr. Borchers followed a call to Saint Matthew's Congregation in Chicago and was succeeded by H. A. Gehrs. Then, in October, Mr. Baumgart followed a call to Milwaukee, Wis., and on November 15 H. Albrecht succeeded him to Saint Luke's. In 1902 Carl Rupprecht was called from St. Louis, Mo. In the same year, however, Mr. Leinberger followed a call to Saint Martini Congregation in Chicago and was succeeded by Max O. Frieser at Saint Luke's. In 1903 Miss Mathilda Doederlein was added to the teaching staff. In 1905 a modern school building with eight classrooms and an assembly hall was erected on Belmont Avenue, directly west of the church, and two more teachers were called, Herman T. Ellermann of Mount Olive, Ill., and William F. Diener of Saint Andrew's School, Chicago.

At a voters' meeting on September 17, 1905, Pastor Mueller reported that nearly two hundred thousand "bricks" had been donated for the school and hall. While this building was under construction, Mr. Decker followed a call to New Gehlenbeck, Ill.* The dedication of the new building took place on December 10, 1905.

In a special evening service on Easter Day, March 31, 1907, arranged by the young people of Saint Luke's, an English sermon was preached in Saint Luke's Church by a seminary student, William C. Burhop,† son of Teacher Burhop. No doubt, this incident caused not a little commotion in "Lake View," and it probably continued to be "the talk of the town"

*Teacher Decker died on Sept. 3, 1946.

†Now student pastor at the University of Wisconsin in Madison, Wis.

for quite some time. In fact, the voters' assembly in October of the same year reiterated its opposition to English services.

On May 12, 1907, the Rev. Fred W. G. Mueller* of Scott City, Kans., eldest son of Saint Luke's pastor, was installed as assistant pastor. In February, 1910, the young assistant pastor, who also had been serving as teacher in the Hamilton Avenue school, accepted a call to Saint John's Congregation in Wilmette, Ill. Instead of calling another assistant pastor, the congregation now gave its pastor assistance of a different kind—a "Schreiber" (secretary); and the teachers assisted in the "Christenlehre" and in confirmation instruction. Miss Noack was engaged to teach in the branch school on Hamilton Avenue. In 1911 the school property on Diversey Boulevard was sold.

In 1916 Pastor Mueller's health began to fail; during the first part of 1917 he was able to perform most of his pastoral duties, and on Palm Sunday, April 1, although his weakness demanded that he remain seated also through the confirmation blessing, he had the joy of confirming his youngest son, Paul. Pastor and Mrs. Mueller had twelve children.† Pastor Mueller died on August 25, 1917, at the age of fifty-nine and a half years. His successor at Saint Luke's was the Rev. Otto C. A. Boecler, heretofore professor at Concordia Seminary, Springfield, Ill., where for about five years he also served a Negro congregation. He was installed as Saint Luke's second pastor on December 2, 1917. Early in the following year, 1918, English services on Sunday forenoons were introduced. The Sunday school, established in 1918, within its first year had an enrollment of seven hundred. In 1921 Emil

*Fred W. G. Mueller was the first child baptized at St. Luke's (1884).

†Fred W. G. Mueller, pastor, Napoleon, Ohio; Julia (Mrs. Wm. C. Burhop), Madison, Wis.; John E. A. Mueller, pastor in Mount Prospect, Ill.; Lydia (Mrs. Paul T. Diener), Chicago; Hilda (Mrs. Fred Worthmann, Lincoln, Nebr.; Edwin Mueller, Moberly, Mo. (deceased, 1946); Clara (Mrs. Geo. Willer), Moberly, Mo.; Olga (Mrs. Edwin Shoaff), Los Angeles, Calif.; Theodore Mueller, McAllen, Texas; Paul A. J. Mueller, retired rrom the ministry at Edgerton, Ohio, in 1940, and now resides in Fort Wayne, Ind. Two children, Enno and Carl, died in infancy.

Garske of Bethany Congregation was called to serve as teacher. In 1922 Henry Waldschmidt of Kankakee, Ill., was called for the same purpose; and in 1923, Miss Gertrude Doederlein. In September, 1923, the pastor's son, Paul Boecler,* a student at Concordia Seminary, St. Louis, Mo., was engaged to assist in the parish for one year. In 1924 Paul M. Wukasch of Danville, Ill., succeeded Mr. Ellermann, who had resigned. In February, 1925, Pastor Boecler accepted a professorship at Concordia Seminary, St. Louis, Mo. On August 30 of the same year he was succeeded at Saint Luke's by the Rev. Carl J. A. Hoffmann, for some time professor at Concordia Seminary, Springfield, Ill.

In February, 1926, a resolution was adopted to the effect that the minutes of the voters' assembly were to be read in German and English and that all motions were to be made in both languages.

The College of Presidents, in charge of the distribution of calls and meeting in St. Louis, Mo., in 1927, selected Candidate Adalbert R. Kretzmann to fill Saint Luke's petition for an assistant pastor.

Mr. Burhop died on April 3, 1927, and Mr. Gehrs on November 4, 1928. Elmer Pflieger then taught in the branch school, and Charles Plenke assisted during 1928. In 1929 Herbert H. Gross joined Saint Luke's teaching staff. In December, 1930, Pastor Hoffmann accepted a call to Minneapolis, Minn., and in January, 1931, Assistant Pastor Adalbert R. Kretzmann was called as his successor. The Rev. Herman C. Guebert, a retired pastor residing in Oak Park, Ill., was chosen as his assistant and served in this capacity until his death on August 7, 1947. Pastor Paul Sauer thereupon assumed similar responsibilities.

Mr. Cluever died on September 10, 1931. Edgar G. Krenzke of Grace Congregation (Parker and Laramie Avenues, Chi-

*Now pastor in Ladue, St. Louis County, Mo. (1949).

cago) was called as teacher in 1933. Mr. Diener retired in 1936.* In the following year Herbert D. Bruening joined the teaching staff. Mr. Rupprecht died on April 6, 1938, and Mr. Schlake on May 5, 1940. Others on the teaching staff of Saint Luke's: Miss Helen Skaggs, Walter F. Steinberg, Mrs. Linda (nee Wassmann) Wukasch, Edgar R. Spletzer, Miss Lucille Wassmann, Miss Gertrude Doederlein, Henry M. Waldschmidt, Walter H. Hartkopf, Miss Dorothy Kurth, Miss Jeanne Ladewig, and Alfred Mieger. Mr. Wukasch died on April 1, 1942. He was organizer of Saint Luke's children's choir, "which was to become one of the truly well-trained choirs among our Lutheran schools."

Saint Luke's has been served by the following assistant pastors, in addition to those already named: Dr. Otto Paul Kretzmann (since 1941 president of Valparaiso University, Valparaiso, Ind.), brother of Pastor Adalbert R. Kretzmann; the Rev. Otto H. Theiss, executive secretary of the Walther League; Candidate Robert E. Wiltenburg† and Candidate R. C. Proehl.‡

During the course of forty years a total of eight building lots had been acquired on Belmont Avenue. Next to the church there were erected a four-room brick school, a duplex residence for teachers and another building for the fifth class, with an annex to serve as a teacher's residence. As the school continued to expand, an old drugstore on Ashland Avenue, near School Street, was rented to provide for an additional schoolroom. Yet more room was soon needed; however, because no suitable building site was available in the area, the old school next to the church was razed, and one of the teachers' residences was removed, and a large brick building was erected on this site in 1905.

*He celebrated his ninetieth birthday on May 24, 1949, in Chicago.
†Since 1946 pastor of St. John's, Niles (Dutchman's Point), Ill.
‡Since spring, 1947, pastor of a new congregation at Seymour, Ind.

87. Chicago, Saint Martini

It still is the year 1884. The fifth of January was "the coldest day in twenty years—twenty-eight degrees below zero." The old Northwest, with Chicago for its "capital," was beginning to yield to the new Northwest with the inauguration of railroad service on the newly constructed Northern Pacific Railroad. At the beginning of this year the third Missouri Synod congregation in Chicago, Trinity, then at Twenty-fifth and Canal Streets, released a portion of its membership in the Town of Lake, south of the then southern limits of the city, to organize its own congregation. On February 4, 1884, seventeen men* organized and chose the name Saint Martini. Its first pastor was the Rev. Fred C. Leeb, called two years previously as assistant pastor of First Trinity, with the special assignment of schoolteacher in this community. He had also been preaching here once a month and conducting "Christenlehre" on Sunday afternoons. Saint Martini paid its "mother" church thirteen hundred dollars for the property at Forty-ninth Street and Loomis Avenue (in the Town of Lake). In order to be farther removed from the railroad, the original property was sold in April, 1884, and five lots at the corner of Fifty-eighth and Ada Streets—one block north and one block east of original property—were purchased, and the school building was moved to the new site. A new frame church, 46x60 feet, was erected at a cost of $9,500 and dedicated on September 28, 1884. In the preceding August the congregation's first day school teacher, F. Kringel, began his work in the upper classes. For three more years Pastor Leeb also taught, having charge of the lower classes.

In 1886 a mission school was established in Englewood,

*Charter members:

T. Budach	A. Troeder	H. Hansen
J. Abraham	J. Rohwer	E. Dams
H. Fruendt	O. Ciskowski	C. Claussen
C. Kruse	A. Wurst	W. Schmidt
T. Turban	H. Arffe	William Brauer
	H. Claussen	

another community in the Town of Lake. Two lots at the corner of West Fifty-ninth and Green Streets were purchased for $550 and a building, 22x40 feet, erected thereon. On the First Sunday in Advent, 1886, this mission school was dedicated and H. Schulte installed as teacher. From then on Pastor Leeb conducted worship services in this school every other Sunday afternoon, and Mr. Schulte conducted "Christenlehre" every Sunday. As a result of the rapidly growing congregation, Pastor Leeb was relieved of school-teaching duties in 1887, when J. Doepke was placed in charge of this branch school. In 1889 another schoolroom was added, and Miss Gertrude Lange was engaged to teach. After about one year she was succeeded by her sister Jennie.

On January 13, 1889,* Saint Martini released nine of its members to organize a congregation in the mission school. This congregation was named "Sankt Stephanus" (St. Stephen's.) (See Chapter 113, page 389.) Two years later Saint Martini purchased six lots, more centrally located, at Fifty-first Street and Marshfield Avenue, for $3,500. In the fall of 1891 the school was moved from Forty-eighth and Ada Streets to the new site—a distance of slightly less than one mile. A short time later the church building was also moved to the same site and placed upon a nine-foot substructure at the corner. The transfer cost about $7,500. The renovated church was dedicated on February 21, 1892.

Following is a list of teachers installed: J. Grotheer, 1891; G. F. Brill, 1892; Fred Schildmeier, 1893; both Brill and Schildmeier left in 1894 and were succeeded by H. E. Eirich and W. J. Bewie. Miss Jennie Lange taught from 1890 until 1897, when J. George Blumenschein, graduate of Addison, began teaching at Saint Martini. Mr. Grotheer died on March 3, 1901, and his successor was Bernhard Hoppe.

Miss Amalia Haertel of St. Charles, Mo., was engaged to

*On July 15, 1889, the town of Lake, together with several other communities on the North and South Sides, was annexed to Chicago.

teach in the fifth classroom, opened in October, 1900. In February, 1902, Mr. Eirich accepted a call to Saint Paul's School in Aurora, Ill., and Konrad A. Leinberger of Saint Luke's, Chicago, came to Saint Martini. In the same year the congregation established a mission school on Western Avenue for the three lower grades. On June 1, 1902, J. L. List of Pittsburgh, Pa., began teaching activities here. In 1908 Mr. Bewie accepted a call to Zion School in Roseland (Chicago). Decreased enrollment prompted the closing of the fifth classroom of the "home" school at that time. In 1909, when the old kerosene lamps were removed from the schoolrooms and replaced with electric lights, Mr. Leinberger elected to enter the ministry. After his colloquium at Concordia Seminary, Springfield, Ill., he became pastor at Plevna, Kans.* Mr. Leinberger's successor in 1910 was J. P. T. Kirsch. Miss Haertel† was succeeded by Miss Lydia Roehrs in 1913. In July, 1915, Miss Roehrs resigned, and Mr. List came to the "home" school, while Miss Renata Schlechte‡ took charge of the mission school on Western Avenue. In 1915 Miss Lydia Bloedel was placed in charge of the recently reopened fifth classroom in the "home" school. In 1917 the Misses Schlechte and Bloedel resigned and were succeeded by the Misses Helen Kampf and B. Heinemann in the respective places. Each remained for one year. Then came Miss Lillian Claussen for the mission school; after one year she was succeeded by Miss E. Wegmann, and Miss Wegmann, in turn, by Miss Helen Pfotenhauer. Mr. List died in 1922, and Armin G. Zapf§ became his successor. In the same year Mr. Kirsch resigned. The Misses Gertrude Hueschen and Margaret Hartenberger were then engaged to teach in Saint Martini's schools, the former at "home" and the latter in the mission school. In 1923 the

*The Rev. Konrad A. Leinberger died on Sept. 18, 1943, and is buried in Saint Lucas Cemetery in Chicago.

†Miss Amalia Haertel died suddenly on July 13, 1913.

‡Later married to Herbert Leininger, a dental surgeon in Chicago. Dr. Leininger died in 1942.

§A son of the Rev. Emil Zapf, pastor of St. Paul's Congregation, Melrose Park, Ill., 1892-1927; Chicago city missionary, 1927-1937. Pastor Zapf died on July 22, 1937.

erection of a new school on Fifty-first Street, at Marshfield Avenue, was begun. The dedication took place on April 27, 1924. The total cost was $64,000, which included a central heating plant and all necessary facilities. In June, 1924, Miss Hartenberger resigned, and Miss B. Schumann succeeded her in the mission school. In October, 1925, Mr. Zapf accepted a call to Nazareth School at Sixtieth Street and Spaulding Avenue, Chicago, and John Klitzke, formerly at Immanuel School in South Chicago, was installed in November. About two years later the mission school on Western Avenue was discontinued.

In 1929 Pastor Leeb resigned. His successor, the Rev. Herman E. Brauer of Marengo, Ill., was installed on November 24, 1929. In October, 1930, Richard A. Lange, graduate of Concordia Teachers College, River Forest, Ill., was installed as teacher. Soon afterward the school was augmented by a ninth grade, and in June, 1932, the junior high school was fully accredited by the Board of Education of Chicago. Mr. Blumenschein had charge of the ninth grade. The 1933 financial depression forced the city of Chicago to abolish the "junior high school plan," and Saint Martini followed suit.

On September 20, 1942, Candidate Alvaro A. Carino was ordained and installed as assistant to the pastor and commissioned to serve also the Lutheran City Mission. Pastor Brauer's son, Norman E., was ordained and installed as assistant pastor on September 5, 1943. Mr. Blumenschein, having served in Saint Martini School for forty-eight years, retired.* In June, 1946, Pastor Brauer accepted a call to Zion Congregation in Summit, Ill., and in September of the same year his son, Norman E., accepted a call to Bottineau, N. Dak.

In addition to the teachers named, the following have served more recently: Theobald Breihan, Milferd Eggerding, Werner

*Teacher Blumenschein, a native of Marysville, Ohio, after his resignation from the active teaching profession in 1945, continued to assist in other schools of Chicago, including St. Paul's (Grand Crossing) and Peace. Saint Martini observed the fiftieth anniversary of Teacher Blumenschein on Sept. 21, 1947.

M. Wichmann, Ralph Frick, Mrs. V. Brauer, Miss Lucille Peterson, Mrs. Howard Carnitz, H. P. Mroch, Adam E. Scheffler, Mrs. Walter Nadasdy, Roland R. Lassanske, Miss M. Zimmermann, and Miss M. Mahler.

On October 27, 1946, the Rev. Henry Meyer of Cullman, Ala., was installed as Saint Martini's third pastor.

Pastor Leeb died in Chicago on September 30, 1946, at the age of eighty-eight and is buried in Concordia Cemetery in Forest Park, Ill.

88. West Chicago

While in Wheaton, about 1867, it was said that the early clergymen in that territory included West Chicago (Turner Junction) within their parish bounds. Prior to that time, however, work had been done in West Chicago by the Rev. Prof. C. August T. Selle of the Teachers' Seminary, Addison, Ill. He gathered the scattered Lutherans together. From 1880 to 1886 the combined parish was served by the Rev. Karl A. Koch of Wheaton. (See Chapter 38, page 196.) He also conducted the organization meeting in 1884. For about eight years, from 1884 until 1892, the services were conducted on Sunday afternoons in private homes and later in the Methodist church. In 1888 the Rev. L. August Heerboth, pastor of Saint John's Congregation in Wheaton, took charge of this work. In 1893 Trinity called its first pastor, Candidate Charles J. Fricke, who was ordained and installed on August 6, 1893. About eight years later Pastor Fricke accepted a call to Emmanuel Congregation in Aurora, Ill., and his successor at Trinity, the Rev. Fred W. Mahnke of Hanson Park (Chicago), was installed as the second pastor of the congregation on February 9, 1902. In September, 1915, Pastor Mahnke followed a call to Saint Mark's Congregation in Chicago. His successor in West Chicago was the Rev. Louis A. R. Gresens* of Sterling, Ill., whose installation took place on

*Pastor Gresens died on Feb. 27, 1932.

October 3, 1915. During Pastor Gresens' pastorate a new church was built at the corner of George and Sherman Streets. The Rev. Walter Spruth of Foley, Minn., became Trinity's fourth pastor on October 26, 1924; after about eighteen years of service in West Chicago he resigned and secured secular employment. Thereupon the Rev. William J. Danker of Harvard, Ill., assumed the pastorate in West Chicago in 1942. He served here until June 27, 1948, when he was commissioned as the Missouri Synod's first missionary to Japan. On November 4, 1948, the Rev. I. T. Droegemueller of Thorp, Wis., was installed in West Chicago.

A day school, maintained for forty years, was closed for about two decades. In 1944 a modern school was opened and served (more or less consecutively) by Miss Norma Cimaglio, Miss Marie Henriksen, Mrs. Grace Kruse, Student Wilbur Heidorn, Miss Marion Kammeyer, Walter H. Christian, and Miss Rhoda Munderloh.

89. Lyons

Returning eastward from West Chicago by way of the Chicago, Aurora & Elgin Electric Railroad as far as Harlem Avenue, then continuing by bus to the former Southwest Plank Road (now Ogden Avenue) to an intersection about a mile and a quarter in a southwesterly direction, the Lutheran Trail finally arrives at Lyons, Ill.* The earliest records relative to Lutheranism in this community point back to the year 1859, actually the beginning of any religious activities in this village. Old documents refer to a German Lutheran Society, which met biweekly for religious purposes, and the conducting of a Sunday school and preaching services whenever an itinerant clergyman was available. Records of Baptisms and communicants in Lyons (formerly known as Lyonsville) for the period 1859 to 1878 are said to be found

*1940 census: 4,960.

in the files of Immanuel Congregation at "Franzosenbusch" (Proviso). The pastors who served that congregation in the early years of its existence were Karl A. Meyer, George M. Zucker, and Johannes Strieter.

In 1874 the "First Religious Society of Lyons and Riverside," comprising also most of the members of the German Lutheran Society, was organized. The officers were L. Moody, president; Nicolas Meyers, vice-president; Dr. J. Congdon, treasurer. There were three trustees: Dr. George M. Fox, F. C. Dore, and F. Meine. The new organization purchased an old chapel on the "Old Plank Road," and thenceforth services in both German and English were held regularly on Sundays.

In 1878 the Lutherans of Lyons requested the Rev. Wessel Bohlen of Zion Congregation in Summit, about two miles south of Lyons, to serve them every other Sunday afternoon. Shortly afterward the congregation had become distinctly Lutheran in character. On October 4, 1884, this unique organization* founded Zion Evangelical Lutheran Church of Lyons and Riverside, and forthwith transferred all its property to the new congregation.

In 1895 an "English" basement was constructed under the old church, which then served as a temporary schoolroom. On July 28, 1895, Candidate J. Burkart, graduate of Concordia Seminary, St. Louis, Mo., was installed as Zion Congregation's first resident pastor. He also taught in the day school until 1897, when F. A. Schoeneberg took charge of the school. W. C. Meyer took over when Mr. Schoeneberg left. In April, 1902, Pastor Burkart accepted a call to Batavia, Ill., but within the same month a new pastor arrived in Lyons. The Rev. Paul Ladwig was installed on the 27th.

*Charter members of Zion Congregation:

Ferdinand Christian	John Strebing, Sr.	Henry Meine
Fred Kuhlmann, Sr.	Albert Pagels	Louis Lange, Sr.
John Nicolas Meyers	William Graunke	Ferd. Gieseler
Andrew Kirschbaum	John Bermann	Gottlieb Eggert
Charles Lange	William Krueger	Louis Tollner
Ferdinand Schults	Ferd. Buck	Louis Fanter
	Chas. Dehnicke	

In 1907 Mr. Meyer was forced by illness to resign. He was succeeded by William Schweder. In the following year, 1908, Pastor Ladwig* also resigned on account of illness. During the last two years of his pastorate, illness forced his absence for lengthy periods, during which the congregation was served by pastors of neighboring congregations. The next pastor, the Rev. John Schert of River Grove, Ill., was installed on March 22, 1908. In 1909 a new church was erected at what now is known as 7930 Ogden Avenue; it was dedicated on December 19, 1909, and the old church was remodeled to serve as a school. In 1910 John M. Runge succeeded Mr. Schweder in the school, and Miss H. Pfotenhauer was engaged for one year to teach the lower grades. In 1912 Miss Pfotenhauer was succeeded by Miss List. Because of ill health Pastor Schert was obliged to resign in 1913.† His successor in Lyons, the Rev. Martin Nickel of Lace, Ill., about nine miles southwest of Lyons, was installed on December 14, 1913. When Miss List left, Mr. Runge assumed charge of all grades until 1918, when he followed a call to Merrill, Wis. His successor was G. H. Reifschneider. Soon after this it became necessary to reopen the second classroom, in which the following have since taught: Miss L. Homann, Miss Lydia Halboth, Miss Lorraine Behling, Miss Verona Bloedel,‡ and Miss Olga Mueller. In 1913 Mr. Reifschneider followed a call to Cleveland, Ohio. Later, in 1943, he accepted a professorship at Concordia Teachers College, River Forest, Ill. On September 10, 1944, he died. Other more recent teachers at Zion School in Lyons, were A. O. Diersen, B. E. Petrowsky, Miss Maxine Bernhardt, Miss Lora Schumacher, Mrs. W. Liebenow, and Miss Dorothy Steffens. In 1946 Pastor Nickel retired. His

*Pastor Paul Ladwig died on May 25, 1910.

†John Schert was born in Proviso Township, Cook County, Ill., on Jan. 29, 1875. After convalescence in 1914 he re-entered the ministry near Elk River, Minn.; from 1924 to 1940 he was pastor of the congregation at Lester Prairie, Minn. He then retired and moved to Minneapolis, Minn., where he died on March 29, 1943, at the age of sixty-eight.

‡Miss Verona Bloedel is a daughter of the Rev. G. Bloedel, until recently pastor of St. Matthew's Congregation at Hamlet, Ind.

successor, the Rev. Carl F. Spaude of Louisville, Ky., and more recently chaplain in the U.S. Army, was installed as Zion's fourth resident pastor on September 18, 1946.

90. Morrison

After the congregation in Sterling, Whiteside County, had called its own pastor, the Rev. Frederick Lussky, who at this time was serving only the congregation in Hopkins Township, now known as Our Savior's and located about eight miles northwest of Sterling, looked about for another field of labor in which to serve in addition to his comparatively small parish. Having heard that there were some Lutheran families living in the vicinity of Lyndon, he made arrangements to conduct services in that community, too. On the first Sunday in June, 1884, he held the first service in the home of John Helms, on a farm one-half mile north of the village, and the second in the Lyndon public school house. Encouraged by Pastor Lussky, the Lutherans on the first Sunday in January, 1885, organized a congregation and named it Saint Peter's.* For a number of years the congregation continued its worship in the Lyndon public school. Summer and winter, in good weather and bad, Pastor Lussky drove with horse and buggy from "Hopkins" (now Our Savior's Church) to Lyndon on the first Sunday of every month. By January, 1889, Saint Peter's Congregation comprised eighteen families, and it was resolved to build a church. Frank Hayen, a member of Saint Peter's, donated an acre of his farm located about four and one-half miles south of Morrison,† and upon it a small and unpretentious church, 20x30 feet, was

*Charter members of St. Peter's, Morrison:

Carl Kegebein	Albert Brandt	John Helms
Louis Rosenow	John Rosenow	Christ Goesel
Albert Schulz	Albert Stralow	Julius Brandt
Carl Stralow	Fritz Rosenow	Carl Pilgrim

†1940 census: 3,187. Named for Charles Morrison of New York City, by Lyman Johnson, the original owner of the site.

erected at a cost of $576.54. The furniture was made by some of the members.

In April, 1890, Pastor Lussky accepted a call to Ottawa, Ill. His successor, the Rev. A. Carl Theo. Ponitz of Hahlen, Ill., was installed on June 8, 1890. He served here until May, 1892, when he followed a call to the dual parish at Genoa and Sycamore, Ill. In April, 1892, a student, Otto Richter, took charge of the congregation in Sterling* and on the first Sunday of each month conducted services in Lyndon. He also served the congregation in Hopkins Township until the Rev. Emanuel Meyer was installed there on October 23, 1892.

In June, 1905, Saint Peter's Congregation in Lyndon considered building a new church; and on October 7, 1907, a new church was dedicated. A short time later, Pastor Meyer followed a call to Coal City, Ill., and on January 3, 1909, the Rev. Arthur William Lussky, son of the founding pastor of Saint Peter's, was installed. During his pastorate the church "center" was moved into Morrison. The old church building was badly in need of repairs; so the congregation decided to tear it down and to rebuild in Morrison. This was accomplished in 1913. In September, 1913, Pastor Lussky accepted a call to Jehovah Congregation in Chicago, and on October 26 of the same year the Rev. Arthur W. Oetting of Perry, Okla., was installed. The church was dedicated on December 21, 1913. At the same time English services were inaugurated. On March 18, 1917, Saint Peter's Congregation in Morrison called its own pastor. "Thus the ties which had united the mother and the daughter for thirty-two years were severed." Its first pastor was Candidate Paul Weeke; he was ordained and installed on July 8, 1917. Less than two years later, on April 20, 1919, he accepted a call to Superior, Wis. His successor in Morrison, the Rev. Otto Schumacher of Hershey, Nebr., was installed on June 15, 1919. Pastor Schumacher

*Now known as the Second Avenue Ev. Lutheran Church.

served for almost eight years and on September 25, 1927, accepted a call to Immanuel Congregation in Freeport, Ill. Next came the Rev. Theodore Dierks of Waverly, Mo., being installed as Saint Peter's third resident pastor on November 13, 1927. For the special benefit of a few remaining older members German services were held once a month. "The transition from the German to the English was so gradual that it was never accompanied with any serious consequences or any hard feelings." Saint Peter's joined the Missouri Synod in 1928.

91. Elizabeth

The Trail now takes a little jaunt to see what's going on in the little village of Elizabeth, Ill.,* thirty miles from Dubuque, Iowa. "Although services were conducted in Elizabeth prior to 1895, we have no record of who conducted these services . . . . Our official record begins with August 25, 1895." But one cannot return to Chicago without at least a little information about the work done here, even though it be but a meager report. Here it is in a nutshell: The name of the congregation is Saint Paul's. The Rev. Frederick August Scharfenberg, ordained and installed as Saint Paul's pastor in August, 1895, served the Lutherans in and about Elizabeth until about the middle of January, 1904. The Mission Board at one time publicly expressed its sympathy for this pastor because of the insignificant progress. "Die Zahlen sind klein." ("The figures are small.") Pastor Scharfenberg in 1904 accepted a call to Saint John's Congregation at Lena, Ill. His successor, the Rev. Ernest H. F. Baese from Town Sigel, Wood County, Wis., served Saint Paul's from 1904 until 1908 and then accepted a call to West Point, Ill. The next pastor, the Rev. Gustav A. Mueller, came from Mount Pleasant,

*1940 census: 694.

Mich., and served from 1908 till 1913,* when he resigned. Then for about one year Saint Paul's was served by a student, Henry F. Wind, 1913 to 1914. Candidate Edward Paul Merkel was installed in 1914 and remained until 1916, when he followed a call to Waterbury, Conn. From Belvidere ("beautiful view"), Ill., came the Rev. Emil F. J. Richter in 1916. He served this parish until 1921 and then accepted a call to Marseilles, Ill. He was succeeded by the Rev. A. C. C. Meyer of Plainfield (Wheatland Township), Ill., in 1921, who served Saint Paul's until March 29, 1942, when he resigned. The Rev. Erwin A. Wiedbusch has held this pastorate since June 14, 1942.

92. Chicago, Christ of Logan Square

History states that First Bethlehem Congregation in Chicago started a mission school on August 20, 1882, in a new section of Town Jefferson (since 1890 part of Chicago), known as Humboldt—about one and a half miles west of its "center"—on Stave Street, and that its assistant pastor, Candidate Ernst Werfelmann, was ordained and installed here to teach and preach in the mission school. Work began with seventeen children. Soon after this a ladies' aid society ("Frauenverein") was organized. Early in 1885 thirteen members† of First Bethlehem, residents of the Humboldt community, gained permission to organize a congregation of their own in this locality. So on March 8, 1885, Christ Congrega-

*Prior to 1912 the near-by lead mines had attracted many people to Elizabeth; however, these mines became unprofitable and were closed; the banks failed. In 1913 the Mission Board of the Northern Illinois District reported that it had repeatedly reached the decision to merge the small congregation with another near-by parish; but the "sensitive situation" ("zaertliche Lage") is such that such a thing probably is not possible.

†Charter members:

Frederick Buettner	Frederick Lanoch	Andrew Hartmann
Richard Buettner	Henry Bruhns	Carl Britzke
Ingwer Jensen	Albert Adam	Gustav Stolz
Franz Schwahn	Carl Stammer	Gustav Stammer
	Ernst Werfelmann, pastor	

tion was organized, and Pastor Werfelmann was chosen to continue serving the "daughter" congregation. He was installed in August of the same year. At the same time, property was purchased at what now is the southwest corner of Richmond Street and McLean Avenue and a frame church, 26x60 feet, with a fifty-foot steeple, erected. The dedication took place on August 9, 1885. The school building on Stave Street was moved to the new location and enlarged to a two-room building. The cost of the church building was two thousand dollars. On November 29, 1885, the first day school teacher, Louis Steinbach, was installed. Pastor Werfelmann taught the lower grades until April 8, 1888, when Ottomar Kolb of Freeport, Ill., was installed. In 1888 Christ Congregation founded a branch school in the Avondale community —north of Humboldt. This developed into Concordia Congregation, in 1892. A new church was built in 1889, and a four-room school building in 1890. This church, a frame building, measured 50x85 feet and had a seating capacity of about one thousand, costing about eighteen thousand dollars. It had two steeples; one 150 feet, the other 75 feet high. The new school cost four thousand dollars. John Wagner was installed as the third teacher on July 14, 1892. In the same year, 1892, the members of Christ Congregation residing in the Avondale community were released to organize Concordia Congregation, with its "center" at Belmont and Washtenaw Avenues.

During the night of May 29-30, 1896, Christ Church was completely destroyed by fire. It had been the congregation's desire and intention to participate in the fiftieth anniversary of Lutheranism in Chicago on May 31; instead, the members assembled in their school building on that day for a service of mourning and repentance ("Trauer-und Bussgottesdienst"). The opening hymn was Paul Eber's "Wenn wir in hoechsten

Noeten sein" ("When in the Hour of Utmost Need").* It was more weeping than singing ("mehr ein Weinen als ein Singen"). Pastor Werfelmann preached on the text Isaiah 28:29: "This also cometh forth from the Lord of Hosts, which is wonderful in counsel and excellent in working." Sister congregations rushed to Christ Congregation's assistance, and soon a new church of brick occupied the site at Richmond Street and McLean Avenue. In 1899 the congregation called the pastor's father, the Rev. J. H. Werfelmann of Marysville, Ohio, as assistant pastor.†

In 1900 Adam M. Reinhardt was called as teacher in the congregation's branch school in the Pennock community, at 2420 North Lawndale Avenue. This building cost twenty-five hundred dollars. In 1908 a new congregation developed here. It was named Jehovah, and its first pastor was the Rev. Theodore Graebner. (See Chapter 161, page 492.) In 1900 Christ and Saint Luke Congregations jointly purchased seventy-one acres of land on North Crawford Avenue (now Pulaski Road) for a cemetery, known as Saint Lucas.

Illness forced the resignation of Mr. Steinbach in 1900; however, his health being restored, he resumed teaching in 1903 and continued until 1910, when E. L. Marquardt took his place. He served until 1917, when he accepted a call to Tabor School in the Irving Park community. A. Kaeppel served as teacher in Christ School in 1917 and 1918, and in the latter year joined the U.S. Army. Then came Walter L. Sassmannshausen, who served from 1918 to 1929, and then for the rest of his life served as teacher at Pilgrim School,

*This hymn is based on the Latin hymn by Joachim Camerarius, Paul Eber's former teacher, "In tenebris nostrae et densa caligine mentis, etc." The exact time and circumstances of its origin are uncertain. Koch relates that "on Ascension Day, 1547," after the battle of Muehlberg, the Wittenbergers, having received a message from the captive Elector to deliver their city to Emperor Charles V, assembled for prayer in church; and quotes a portion of the prayer by Bugenhagen which greatly resembles Eber's hymn. But that the hymn was written then, we have no proof. . . . the earliest positive date that we have for the text is that it was published in a broadsheet at Nuernberg in 1560. (*The Handbook to the Lutheran Hymnal*, Concordia Publishing House, St. Louis, Mo., 1942, p. 366f.)

†St. John's Church, Neudettelsau, Ohio—organized 1838. Pastor J. H. Werfelmann died in 1905. This writer was baptized by him in 1896.

Chicago.* In 1923 Mr. Wagner, having served in Christ School for about thirty-one years, resigned on account of illness. His successor was E. Brunn, who served from 1923 until 1935. In 1924 the English language was introduced in the worship services, and a Sunday school was organized. In 1929 Pastor Werfelmann submitted his resignation, because ill health hampered his pastoral work; the congregation, however, voted to retain him as honorary pastor, to continue payment of full salary, and to call another pastor. The Rev. Walter George Dippold, assistant pastor at First Trinity,† was installed on June 29, 1929, as Christ Congregation's second pastor. In 1929 Edmund Schroeder was engaged to teach the class relinquished by Mr. Sassmannshausen. In October of the same year the Rev. Frederick H. Schwandt, who in 1927 had resigned from the active ministry on account of ill health at Erie, Pa., was installed as assistant pastor. In 1930 Mr. Schroeder was formally added to the teaching staff by the rite of installation. At that time also another trained teacher was added to the staff, Helmuth A. Stahlecker. In 1932 teacher-candidate Edwin Feddersen was engaged to assist in the school. Pastor Werfelmann died on May 28, 1933. In September, 1934, Mr. Feddersen was installed, and Mr. Kolb, after forty-six years of continuous service at Christ Church, was relieved of his duties as principal of the school. In 1935 Reinhold Arkebauer of Saint Peter's School, Chicago, succeeded Mr. Brunn. In 1938 Mr. Kolb's fiftieth anniversary as a day school teacher was celebrated by the congregation; on that occasion he was given an "honorary release" and a substantial pension.‡ Allan Hart Jahsmann, graduate of Concordia Teachers' College, River Forest, became a member of the teaching staff in September, 1938, but in 1941

*Mr. Sassmannshausen died on Aug. 29, 1945.

†West Thirty-first Street and Lowe Avenue, and a branch congregation at West Eighty-third and Paulina Streets; the latter was later organized as Timothy Congregation.

‡Mr. Kolb's wife, Hulda, died on May 18, 1943; he died on May 1, 1944.

he decided to study for the ministry and shortly afterward entered Concordia Seminary, St. Louis, Mo. Shortly after graduating, in 1945, he received a call to Warren, Ohio. Since 1948 he has been serving as a member of the Missouri Synod's Board for Parish Education in St. Louis, Mo.

Early in the morning of Sunday, February 16, 1941, Pastor Schwandt died at the age of sixty-eight. The Rev. Louis J. Schwartzkopf served as assistant pastor at Christ Church from March, 1941, until December, 1943, when he accepted a call to Hyde Park Congregation on Chicago's near South Side. His son, Luther Edward, a student at Concordia Seminary, St. Louis, Mo., taught in Christ School from January until June, 1941. Presently the principal of this school is Luther Kolander, on the staff since Aug. 15, 1942. Miss Paula Duever has served as the primary teacher since 1909. In the summer of 1949, Mr. Arkebauer accepted a call to Long Beach, Calif., Robert E. Breihan succeeded him here. Other assistant pastors in more recent years were the Rev. Alex Ullrich,* and the Rev. Chas. A. Waech.† In November, 1948, Pastor Dippold resigned from the ministry, and on March 6, 1949, his successor, the Rev. A. H. Fellwock of Wood Lake, Minn., was installed as third resident "first" pastor.

93. Northbrook

Approximately three miles west of Glenview (formerly known as Oak Glen) is Milwaukee Avenue, which the Trail now follows for almost a mile northwest to Lake Avenue, where a left turn brings it to Saint John's Church. Shortly before Christmas in 1885 the Rev. Henry W. Wehrs, pastor of Immanuel Congregation at Glenview, complying with the request of a number of Lutheran men in the western part of Northfield Township, began to conduct services for them in private homes. In March, 1886, Saint John's Congregation

*Pastor Ullrich died on Jan. 24, 1946. He had been pastor of St. John's Congregation, La Grange, Ill., for 48 years, 1893-1942.

†Pastor of Trinity Congregation in Crete, Ill., 1912-1944.

was organized with twelve members.* After worshiping in the English church adjoining Oakwood Cemetery on Milwaukee Avenue, from March until September, Saint John's dedicated its own church in the latter month. During the week this building served as a school. Pastor Wehrs continued to serve Saint John's until August 5, 1890, when Candidate Ernst Scherf, graduate of Concordia Seminary, Springfield, Ill., took charge. He served until September, 1891, when he accepted a call to Sherrill, Iowa. On January 17, 1892, his successor, the Rev. Paul von Toerne of Maple Works, Clark Co., Wis., was installed as Saint John's second pastor. During his pastorate a frame church was erected directly north of Oakwood Cemetery, on the west side of Milwaukee Avenue, and dedicated in September, 1892. In February, 1894, Pastor von Toerne followed a call to Saint John's in Algonquin, Ill., and on August 5 Candidate Gustav William Maede of Concordia Seminary, Springfield, Ill., was ordained and installed. In 1899 an acre of ground east of Milwaukee Avenue, on Lake Avenue, was purchased and set apart as a cemetery. On May 15, 1915, the church was struck by lightning and destroyed by the subsequent fire. A new church of red pressed brick, 34x70 feet, was dedicated on December 19, 1915. In 1918 Pastor Maede was forced by ill health to resign; his successor was the Rev. Alfred Preisinger of Southey, Saskatchewan, Canada.† He was installed as Saint John's fourth pastor. Seven months later, on November 25, this young pastor died of influenza. On March 2, 1919, the Rev. Walter G. Fechner of Vernon, British Columbia, Canada, was installed as Saint John's fifth pastor. In 1930 the congregation joined the Missouri Synod. In the same year a new school building, 32x62 feet, of brick, was erected; the dedication took place

*Charter members:

William Niebuhr	Henry Staak	Herman Knoll
George Sander	Frederick Lemke	John Knoll
John Carnehl	John Wischmann	Herman Mueller
Henry Gaertner	Henry Buhrke	Christ. Justin

†Pastor Preisinger, born in Chicago, was reared in the St. Martini parish.

on August 31, 1930. On the same day teacher-candidate Frank C. Schmiege was installed as teacher. From the time of its founding, in 1890, the school was in charge of the respective pastors, who taught four days a week until 1922 and five days a week from then until 1927, assisted by students from the Teachers' Seminary, Addison, and Concordia Seminary, Springfield, Ill., including Henry Wehrs, F. Thrun, J. H. Becker, and Herman Wehrs. After 1927 the following students served: Raymond Alms, Frank C. Schmiege, Alfred Hoffman, and R. Gotsch, as well as Miss Jeanette Sander. In 1942 Mr. Schmiege accepted a call to Decatur, Ind., and A. E. Christian took his place in Saint John's School in 1943. In November, 1945, Mr. Christian followed a call to Our Savior School, Addison Heights (Chicago), and Wm. C. Marten of Addison, Ill., came to Saint John's School of Northbrook. Actually, Saint John's "center" is located about six miles southwest of Northbrook.*

94. Austin, Saint Paul's

The month of May, 1886, was packed with excitement. "Hysteria rocked Chicago" during the Haymarket Riot, during which a bomb—"so strange and foreign a weapon in an American city"—exploded in a throng which had gathered for a mass meeting on the evening of May 4 on Randolph Street, between Des Plaines Avenue and Halsted Street. Sixty-seven police officers were wounded; seven of them fatally. On May 23, 1886, there was excitement of a different kind in the western suburb of Austin, about six miles to the west. On that day fourteen voting members of Saint John's Congregation in Harlem (now Forest Park) met in the home of Henry Munstermann to organize Saint Paul's Congregation in Austin.† The leader was the Rev. F. M. Grosse of Saint John's (Harlem). Saint Paul's first pastor, the Rev. Theophilus

*1940 census: 1,265.

†Named for Henry W. Austin, the founder.

Stephan, was installed on June 6, 1886. At first, divine services were held in the Austin town hall. When W. H. Austin donated four lots, 100x125 feet, the congregation erected a combination church and school, 30x50 feet, which cost $1,590. The dedication took place on August 15, 1886, four days before seven of the ringleaders in the Haymarket Riot were sentenced to death by Judge Joseph E. Gary. Four of them, Spies, Parsons, Fischer, and Engel, were hanged on November 11, 1887; two had their sentences commuted by Governor Richard Oglesby, and one ended his life in his cell by exploding a dynamite cartridge between his teeth. Digressing yet a little more from Northern Illinois Lutheranism: the Statue of Liberty on Bedloe's Island in New York Harbor was dedicated on October 28, 1886. Back to Austin, Ill. In 1893 Pastor Stephan resigned.* On July 9, 1893, Saint Paul's second pastor, the Rev. Adolf William Bartling, born and reared at Duncklees Grove,† and since 1888 "Reiseprediger" in Montana, was installed. A new church was erected in 1900. Its location officially is 846 North Menard Avenue, Chicago 51, Ill. On February 20, 1938, Candidate Enno Gahl was ordained and installed as assistant pastor. In July, 1943, the fiftieth anniversary of his ordination was commemorated by the congregation. On March 26, 1944, after conducting one of the forenoon services (German) and officiating at a Baptism in the afternoon, Pastor Bartling suddenly died at 7:40 P.M. On May 28 the assistant pastor, Enno Gahl,‡ was installed as Saint Paul's third pastor.

In June, 1946, the steeple of Saint Paul's Church was struck by lightning and destroyed. Soon afterward a new hundred-foot steeple was placed upon the structure. Then, on October 11, the church was destroyed by fire, reputedly started by

*There is uncertainty concerning this pastor's Christian name; also concerning his later activities; according to one account he served for some time as chaplain in the prison at Joliet, Ill. (Compare Chapter 112, page 384. West Hammond, Ill.)

†A. W. Bartling was born on Nov. 10, 1865.

‡A son of the Rev. William Gahl, pastor of Ebenezer Congregation, Chicago, since July 28, 1901.

flames from a blowtorch used by the painters. In December the congregation purchased Saint Luke's Norwegian Lutheran Church at 5916 West Rice Street as a temporary house of worship until such time as a new church would be erected—plans for which had now been formulated. (See Chapter 176, page 516.)

On June 8, 1947, the Rev. Clemens Thies of Luther Institute was installed as assistant pastor.

The following have taught in Saint Paul's School: J. Sagehorn, Theodore Baumgart, Miss Dorothy Heinecke, H. J. Lange, Otto Backhaus, Walter F. Hann, Miss Edna Bartling, Louis E. Schilke, Arthur W. Gross, Theodore Meyer, Miss Margaret Hamann, Miss Peterson, M. Eggers, Mrs. Arvin Hahn, Mrs. Theodore Leitz, Mrs. H. D. Mensing, Miss Jayne Koenig, Miss Elizabeth Humphrey, Miss Carol Schall, Miss Gwendolyn Koss, and Wilbert Krause.

Thirty-one members signed the original constitution of Saint Paul's Congregation in 1886.*

95. Chicago, Holy Cross

In conjunction with the account of flourishing First Trinity Congregation at West Twenty-fifth and Canal Streets†, information was unearthed about one of the parish school districts in the Bridgeport community and the school established in the spring of 1868 at Farrel Street, near Archer Avenue. In 1881 this school was sold and a four-room brick school building erected at the corner of Arch and Lyman

*Charter members:

Henry Munstermann	Herman Voelz	Frederick Buchholz
Henry J. Hankermeyer	Emil Warman	William Voelz
Henry Bergmann	Ludwig Simantzig	Carl Hass
August Stolp	Ad. Schroeder	Leopold Jacobi
Henry Sievers	William Bodenstab	Christ Martens
August F. Voelz	Fredrick Hinrichs, Jr.	Carl Frase
William Hankermeyer	William Schmidt	William Buchholz
William Toedter	Carl Brumm	Carl Hannemann
William Rehr	Frederick Buchholz	Henry Schuette
Peter Munstermann	William Wedekind	Frederick Hass
	Ed. Draheim	

†In 1906 First Trinity's "center" was moved to West Thirty-first Street and Lowe Avenue.

Streets. Incidentally, if the names of some streets seem odd, no Lutheran school or church, so far as has been determined, was ever built on streets known to Chicagoans in the 1860's, such as "Queer Place"—running west from State Street, south of Twenty-second Street (the present Cermak Road), "Moona Way Place"—running south from Twenty-second Street and Archer Road (now Avenue), or "Wrong Place"—running east from Halsted Street, south of Twelfth Street (now also known as Roosevelt Road).

On June 24, 1886, one hundred and sixty-one members of First Trinity residing in the Bridgeport community, south of the South Branch of the Chicago River, were released to organize their own congregation, which was named "Die Evangelisch-Lutherische Gemeinde zum Heiligen Kreuz" (Holy Cross). On August 22, 1886, this new congregation's first pastor, the Rev. William Uffenbeck of Lemont, Ill., was installed. For some time the worship services were conducted in the school building at Arch and Lyman Streets. Four lots at the corner of Ullman Street (now West Thirty-first Place) and James Avenue (now Racine Avenue) were purchased for $2,300, and on the corner lots a church was erected at a cost of thirty thousand dollars. The dedication took place on July 31, 1887. In the same year Holy Cross joined the Missouri Synod. The following teachers continued serving in Bridgeport after First Trinity had formally approved the establishment of the new congregation: John Richter (1879-1891), C. W. Schlueter (1879-1891), J. H. Wm. Helmkamp (1882-1902), and William Kammann (1884-1905).* In 1892 another two-story school building was erected near the church, and two new teachers came to Bridgeport, E. Krumsieg and Miss Lisette Brueggemann; the former serving until 1895 and the latter until 1893. In 1895 Mr. Krumsieg was succeeded by L. H.

*Others who taught during this time: Miss Rose Kranz (1887-1890) and W. Wellensiek (1891-1892); J. H. Rademacher, called in 1891, served until 1917. William Kammann died at Dundee, Ill., Dec. 6, 1929.

Himmler. In the following year H. Schulze was added to the staff. Succeeding Mr. Helmkamp in 1902 was E. Brust; and succeeding Mr. Schulze in 1904 was M. B. Singer. At the end of the same year Pastor Uffenbeck* accepted a call to Portage, Wis., and on February 19, 1905, his successor, the Rev. J. H. Haake of Elk Grove, Ill., was installed. In 1905 Mr. Brust left, and two teachers came to Holy Cross School, Chr. Scheer and J. Merckling. H. Hoppe succeeded Mr. Himmler in 1908; in 1913 A. E. Paul succeeded Mr. Scheer; in 1914 W. F. Preuss succeeded Mr. Merckling; in 1916 Max Zieroth succeeded Mr. Preuss; in 1917 E. Streufert succeeded Mr. Rademacher. On December 5, 1918, Pastor Haake died at the age of sixty-three, and the third pastor of Holy Cross, the Rev. William Roecker of "Gnaden-Gemeinde" (Grace Congregation)† in Oak Park, Ill., was installed on February 2, 1919. In 1921 Mr. Hoppe was succeeded by Elmer Jackisch; in the same year Theodore Meyer was added to the staff, the former serving until 1925 and the latter until 1924. Pastor Roecker died exactly ten years after Pastor Haake, on December 5, 1928. The congregation's fourth pastor, the Rev. Martin A. Pfotenhauer of Springfield, Minn., came in 1929. In 1930 the Rev. Frederick Pfotenhauer, D.D., President of the Missouri Synod (1911-1935), was called as associate pastor.‡

In addition to the teachers mentioned, the following have served in Holy Cross School: Herman Maudanz, E. A. Jahn, J. F. Reuter, J. F. Hergenroeder, John P. Reuter, Gustav Abel, Miss Hartmann, Miss Schwenke, Miss L. Wenz, Miss Elsa Schumann, George Duensing, Gerhard A. Korntheuer, Miss Helen Pfotenhauer, and M. K. Jungkuntz.

Pastor Martin A. Pfotenhauer died unexpectedly on May

*Pastor Uffenbeck died at Portage, Wis., on Nov. 23, 1942. Orphaned at the age of two, he was reared by Mr. and Mrs. Fred Rohlfing in St. Louis, Mo. He was born in St. Louis Oct. 28, 1851. He died at the age of about ninety-one.

†Grace Congregation's center since 1913 is at West Division Street and Bonnie Brae, River Forest—northeast corner of the campus of Concordia Teachers College.

‡Dr. Pfotenhauer died on Oct. 9, 1939, and is buried in Bethania Cemetery, on Archer Avenue, a few miles southwest of Summit, Ill.

16, 1949. His successor, the Rev. Albert H. Constien of York Center, Ill., was installed on September 18, 1949.

96. La Grange

From Racine Avenue and West Thirty-first Place, in "Bridgeport," the Trail next goes west on Thirty-first Street as far as "the heart of Cicero," to the intersection of Fifty-sixth and Ogden (the old Southwest Plank Road) Avenues, and continues in a southwesterly directon on the latter famous thoroughfare about three and a half miles to Lyons; thence west another two miles to La Grange, Ill.* Today one would probably board a suburban train on the "Q Line" (Chicago, Burlington & Quincy) in Cicero for La Grange, but retrospect justifies an historic "Augenblick" in the home of Louis Sieling, on May 30, 1886. Mr. Sieling is seen offering a portion of his farm to twenty Lutheran men for the purpose of erecting a church and a school. The generous offer is gratefully accepted. Shortly afterward a modest church was erected and dedicated, on September 19, 1886. For a period of about seven years Sunday afternoon services were conducted in this church by the Rev. Johannes Strieter, pastor of Immanuel Congregation at "Franzosenbusch" (Proviso), about four miles northwest of La Grange. The first day school teacher was Fred Polsdoerfer, who served for a very short time; his successor, Mr. Lueker, began teaching on Monday, September 27, 1886, the day after the congregation had been formally organized and named Saint John's.† In April, 1892, Mr. Lueker was succeeded by Charles Strieter of Appleton,

*1940 census: 10,479. Named by F. D. Cossitt for Lafayette's homestead of that name in France.

†Charter members:

August Block	Chas. Hoppenrath, Sr.	John Putt
Herman Block	Chas. Hoppenrath, Jr.	Chas. Pankow
William Block	John Hoppenrath	Fred Reinke
Herman Bloedorn	Fred Kenning	Christian Sieling
Henry Bloedorn	Fred Kreienbring	Louis Sieling
William Conrad	Fred Krohn	John Sanborn
Chas. Dallman	Ernst Lueders	Henry Treder
Fred Fehrmann, Sr.	Karl Matz	Asmus Westphal
Fred Fehrmann, Jr.	William Matz	John Westphal
Conrad Grote	Herman Oelker	Herman Wotke
Herman Gieseler	Fred Oelker	

Minn. Candidate Alex Ullrich, graduate of Concordia Seminary, St. Louis, Mo.,* was installed as Saint John's first resident pastor on July 2, 1893. At that time Fred Fehrmann offered a piece of land, 70x135 feet, at what now is the southwest corner of Brainard Avenue and Forty-seventh Street on the south side of La Grange. The offer was gratefully accepted, and the congregation at once proceeded with plans for the erection of a larger church building, 40x60 feet, plus a "vestry," 18x28 feet, at a total cost of $8,500. The building was dedicated on September 30, 1894. In the same year Pastor Ullrich began preaching on Sunday afternoons in Gross Hall, Grossdale (now Brookfield), about two miles east of La Grange. (See Chapter 147, page 466.) In August, 1896, George J. Neumeyer was called as teacher for Saint John's School. He served until 1903, when he accepted a call to Saginaw, Mich. His successor, Theodore Wichmann, served from 1904 until 1906 and then accepted a call to Saint Andrew's School in Chicago. Then came Fred Lustfeldt (1906) and Alfred A. Rumsfeld (1907).

In 1911 the group of Lutherans at Hodgkins, which Pastor Ullrich had served as an affiliate of Saint John's for about nineteen years, organized their own congregation, Immanuel. The old school building was moved to Hodgkins and remodeled to serve as a place of worship. (See Chapter 174, page 512.) During the same year Saint John's Congregation purchased at an auction a public school building on North Kensington Avenue, directly south of Ogden Avenue, for $7,600.

Late in the evening of June 24, 1914, the church was struck by lightning, and a fire broke out in the steeple, but prompt service by the local fire department checked the fire before it reached the main part of the building. In 1916 Mr. Lustfeldt resigned, and William F. Preuss took his place in Saint John's School. In the following year Mr. Rumsfeld was re-

*Alex Ullrich was born Sept. 27, 1872, in Chicago; he received his elementary education at First Saint Paul's School and was confirmed by the Rev. Henry Wunder.

placed by Albert H. Miller. In 1920 Mr. Preuss accepted a call to Seymour, Ind., and Arnold F. Eilers took his place in La Grange. A. H. Eugene Schulz taught from January until April in that year. Miss Helen Fraatz taught the lower grades from 1926 till 1934, when she was succeeded by Miss Edna Eberlein. Other teachers in recent years were Mrs. A. Suter and the Misses N. Hartmann, Bernice Jaster, Esther Thoen, Gertrude Drews, Miss Adelle Gerike, Mrs. Renette Greise, and Miss Dorothy Steffens.

For several years, while Pastor Ullrich served as president of the Northern Illinois District (Missouri Synod), 1927-1936, Saint John's had the following assistant pastors: Arthur C. Piepkorn, August L. Oltroge, and Fred E. Bartling.*

On January 24, 1942, after forty-eight years of service in Saint John's Congregation, Pastor Ullrich retired.† His successor as Saint John's second resident pastor, the Rev. Herold G. Kramer of Van Wert, Ohio, was installed on February 1, 1942. In September, 1949, Teacher Eilers followed a call to Rogers City, Mich.

On the occasion of the congregation's sixtieth anniversary (1946), two members donated two 50-foot lots adjacent to the church to provide parking facilities.

97. Gilberts

It is now the year 1887. On May 7 of this year Dr. C. F. W. Walther, President of the Missouri Synod from the time of its organization in Chicago, April, 1847, until 1850 and from 1864 until 1878, died in St. Louis, Mo. "When the message of his demise reached Fort Wayne, the Monday morn-

*The Rev. A. C. Piepkorn later served a pastorate in Cleveland, Ohio; he is now commandant of the Chaplain School, Carlisle Barracks, Pa. The Rev. A. L. Oltroge became pastor of Trinity Congregation at Willow Springs, Ill., Sept. 3, 1944 and of First Immanuel, Chicago, May 16, 1948. The Rev. Fred E. Bartling, whose brother William L. Bartling served the Willow Springs parish from 1935 until July, 1944, has been pastor of Christ Congregation at North Lake Village, Ill., since 1941.

†After his retirement, Pastor Ullrich served as assistant pastor at St. James and Christ (of Logan Square) Congregations. He died on Jan. 24, 1946.

ing session of Synod was made a mourning service. By request of Synod the funeral was deferred until the 17th of May . . . . The city of St. Louis had never witnessed a larger, grander funeral."*

From La Grange the Trail goes in a northwesterly direction to the now well-known village of Dundee—a distance of about twenty-seven miles, and then about five more miles straight west to Gilberts, Ill.† Here also is a Lutheran congregation, Saint Peter's, which was organized on August 28, 1887.‡ In the same year a church was erected on First Street. Saint John's has been served continuously as an affiliate of Trinity in Huntley, by the following pastors: J. Lorenz Craemer, 1887-1888; Gottlieb C. Guelker, 1888-1903; Siegfried Daniel Poellot, 1903-1910; Louis Baumgaertner, 1910-1947. (See Chapter 50.)

98. Union

Approximately twelve miles northwest of Gilberts, or three miles east of Marengo, is another small village by the sublime name of Union, Ill.,§ where again appears the Rev. J. Lorenz Craemer of Huntley. A congregational meeting is in progress. The date is September 11, 1887. Pastor Craemer takes a very active part in the discussion, particularly in connection with Saint John's first constitution. For the next two years Saint John's was served as an affiliate of Trinity Congregation in Huntley. In 1889 Pastor Guelker, who in the previous year, 1888, succeeded to the Huntley pastorate,

*His first name was not Carl nor Wilhelm, but Ferdinand. In his early years, for instance, in his diary, he signed himself simply as 'F. Walther.' Later his signature was always 'C.F.W.Walther' and as such has gone down in history."—(Fuerbringer, L.E., 80 *Eventful Years*, Concordia Publishing House, St. Louis, Mo., p. 81.)

†1940 census: 170. Named for Amasa Gilbert, an early settler.

‡Charter members (Gilberts):

August Mueller	Albert Mueller	William Puffpaff
Fred Schneidewind	Christian Schultz	Herman Kunke
Frank Ihlenburg	Henry Fritz	Theodore Kunke
	J. L. Craemer, pastor.	

§1940 census: 327.

found it extremely difficult to carry on his pastoral work in four congregations—Saint Peter's, Gilberts; Zion, Marengo; Saint John's, Union—besides teaching school in Huntley. He therefore urged the congregation in Union to unite with Zion of Marengo, to be served by the Rev. Otto Doederlein. In 1892 this congregation (Saint John's) decided to disband, with the understanding, however, that the members would affiliate with one of the nearest Lutheran congregations. But already in the following year the congregation reorganized, with the assurance that the Rev. Paul Doederlein,* pastor of Zion Congregation in Marengo, would also serve Saint John's at Union. This arrangement continued until some time in 1901, when the congregation erected its first church and called its first resident pastor, the Rev. George Lienhardt of Clifton, Tex. He served as Saint John's pastor until the latter part of 1906, when he accepted a call to the State of Nebraska. His successor, the Rev. August Lobitz of Detroit City, Minn., was installed at Union on March 10, 1907. In 1912 Pastor Lobitz followed a call to Ulm, Ark., and was succeeded by the Rev. Henry F. W. Traub of Matangas, near Bath, Ill., on May 21, 1913 (Ascension Day). After about nine years in Union, Pastor Traub at the end of 1922 accepted a call to Darmstadt, Ill., and was succeeded on December 10 of the same year by the Rev. Otto Linnemeier of Hilliards, Ohio.

In 1926 Saint John's Church was struck by lightning and destroyed by the resulting fire. At once the congregation proceeded with plans for a new church. In July, 1928, Pastor Linnemeier accepted a call to Saint Paul's Congregation in Rochelle, Ill. Then came the Rev. William Bartz, who served from October 28, 1928, until September 4, 1938, and then resigned. His successor, the Rev. E. C. Kuehl, was installed on October 30, 1938. In 1943 the interior of the church was de-

*Candidate Paul Doederlein, brother of the Rev. Otto Doederlein, was ordained and installed in Zion Church, Marengo, on June 28, 1891. The latter resigned in May, 1891, on account of a throat ailment.

stroyed by fire. In March, 1944, Pastor Kuehl followed a call to Mancos, Colo.,* and was succeeded at Saint John's, Union, by the Rev. David J. Kramer of Goodfarm, Ill., on April 23, 1944. He served here until December, 1949, when he accepted a call to York Center, Ill.

Saint John's joined the Missouri Synod in October, 1944.

99. Hegewisch

About sixty miles southeast of Union the Trail enters Hegewisch, formerly an independent village, but now a part of the "Queen of the Lakes"—Chicago. There, "where the eastern and the western branches of the Calumet River flow together," about four miles from Lake Michigan, at the "forks," the Rolling Stock Company in 1884 established a railroad coach factory ("Eisenbahn-Fabrik"), according to the Pullman plan. The principal promoter ("Unternehmer") was a German named Adolph Hegewisch. He laid out a village, which in an incredibly short time developed into a rather large community composed largely of factory workers. Among them were also Lutherans, for whom services were conducted by the Rev. Johannes T. Feiertag, pastor of Bethlehem Congregation in Colehour (South Chicago), and by the Rev. Carl M. Noack, pastor of Saint Paul's Congregation in Dolton-Riverdale, and for some time also by the Rev. Gotthilf F. Luebker, pastor of Saint Paul's Congregation in Hammond, Ind., as well as by the Rev. Theodore Buenger of Bachelors Grove (two miles north of Tinley Park, Ill.). A congregation was organized in Hegewisch on October 1, 1887, and named Trinity. Soon a small mission chapel was built on Houston Avenue, the cost being met chiefly by Lutherans of Chicago. The bell was donated by H. Stuckstede, owner of a bell foundry in St. Louis, Mo. Dedication took place on the Sunday before Christmas, 1887. On October 28, 1888, Trinity's first resident pastor, the Rev. F. W. Herzberger, was installed. During his short

*This congregation is located nine miles southeast of Mancos, Colo.

pastorate here he also assisted Pastor Feiertag of Colehour in attending to the spiritual needs of the Lutherans in Whiting, Ind., where Saint John's Congregation was organized in 1891. In July, 1889, Pastor Herzberger assumed the pastorate of Saint Paul's in Hammond, Ind. Then, for about seven years, Trinity in Hegewisch was served as an affiliate of Saint John's in North Hammond, Ind., by the Rev. William Adolph Brauer. The next resident pastor of Trinity was Candidate Martin Kaeppel, who was ordained and installed in Hegewisch on August 2, 1896. A little more than four years later, in November, 1900, he accepted a call to Bunker Hill, Ill.* During the ensuing vacancy this congregation was served by a student of theology, Metzger by name. On August 4, 1901, the Rev. Louis J. C. Millies of Gladstone, Nebr., was installed as Trinity's third resident pastor. He served until March, 1911, when he accepted a call to Elk Grove, Ill. The Rev. A. Wagner of Sydney, Nebr., served Trinity from October 1, 1911, until August, 1914, when he accepted a call to near-by Saint John's Congregation in West Hammond (now Calumet City), Ill., with the understanding, however, that he would be permitted to preach in Hegewisch on the first Sunday of every month in the forenoon and in the afternoon on all other Sundays. This arrangement prevailed until April, 1918, when ill health forced Pastor Wagner to discontinue the work in Hegewisch. Trinity's fifth resident pastor, the Rev. Ernst Kirchner, was installed on April 7, 1918, and served for slightly more than ten years. He died on April 30, 1928. In 1924 a new church was erected at 13200 Burley Avenue. The old church building on Houston Avenue was sold.

Trinity Congregation maintained a day school from 1901 until 1914. Pastor Millies was in charge during his entire pastorate in Hegewisch, as was also his successor while residing in Hegewisch.

*In 1902 Pastor Kaeppel resigned from the ministry.

On August 5, 1928, Pastor Kirchner's successor in Hegewisch, the Rev. Walter C. Greve of Orland Park, Ill., was installed as Trinity's sixth resident pastor. He served here until October, 1947, when he accepted the call to Immanuel Congregation (Colehour), Chicago. His successor, the Rev. Clarence C. Rabe of Pierre, S. Dak., was installed in Hegewisch on May 15, 1949.

100. Ash Grove

The Trail now proceeds southward through the lower portion of Cook County, crosses Will and Kankakee Counties, and takes us into Iroquois County a distance of about twenty-five miles, to a spot known as Ash Grove—the southernmost community on the Lutheran Trail's visiting schedule. Most, if not all, of the Lutherans in this part of the prairie were for some time members of Saint Paul's Congregation at nearby Woodworth.* Less than ten miles southwest of Ash Grove, in the village of Buckley, is Saint John's Church,† which was founded in the year 1870 and whose pastor from 1877 to 1888 was the Rev. G. Blanken.‡ It was he who served the Lutherans of Ash Grove after their separation from Saint Paul's and succeeded in gathering a considerable portion of them together to organize a Missouri Synod congregation, which was also named Saint John's (1887). Its first pastor, Candidate Alfred Grimm (nom de plume: "Alfred Ira"), was ordained and installed on August 19, 1888. He held this pastorate for about three years. In the fall of 1891 he accepted a call to Antigo, Wis.§ His successor at Ash Grove, the Rev. Henry Bode of Wells Creek, Kans., was installed on March 6, 1892. He served Saint John's for a period of almost thirty

*St. Paul's, Woodworth, was organized in July, 1872.

†Since the division of the Illinois District (1907), this congregation has been a member of the Central Illinois District.

‡A son, the Rev. Theodore L. Blanken, was pastor of Messiah Congregation, Chicago, Melvina Street and Patterson Avenue, 1925-1937; now retired and residing in the "City of Lilacs," Lombard, Ill.

§Pastor Grimm died March 12, 1922.

years, resigning in the spring of 1921. The Rev. John Herman Henry Schulz of Orland Park, Ill., succeeded Pastor Bode at Ash Grove on Trinity Sunday, May 22, 1921. He served here for a little more than two years; he died on August 27, 1923. Saint John's fourth resident pastor was the Rev. Gerhard Carl Helmuth Julius Elias Huebener, Lutheran missionary in India 1909-1920, and since then stationed in Shawano County, Wisconsin. He was installed here at Ash Grove on October 28, 1923. His pastorate was the second longest at Saint John's—a little more than twenty years. He resigned on December 1, 1943.* The Rev. John W. Hubertz of Fort Morgan, Colo., became the congregation's fifth pastor on February 6, 1944. Two years later he accepted a call to Hardwick, Minn. On June 29, 1947, his successor, the Rev. Arnold E. Heimsoth of Cole Camp, Mo., who had served as chaplain in the U.S. Army in World War II, was installed as Saint John's sixth pastor.

The day school, established in 1887, was entirely in charge of the respective pastors until 1907, when A. Ortlieb, a trained teacher, took over this part of the congregation's activities. He served in this capacity until 1911, when he was succeeded by F. R. Eberhard. He, in turn, was replaced in 1918 by John Schroeder, a native of Woodworth. In 1922 Mr. Schroeder followed a call to Saint Paul's School in Melrose Park, Ill.† William Schneider took his place at Ash Grove. John D. Bruns, formerly teacher at Immanuel School, Elmhurst, Ill., was called to Saint John's School. D. Schmidt is now in charge.

On July 13, 1948, lightning struck the church building; the resulting fire completely destroyed the building. On June 5, 1949, the cornerstone of a new church was laid.

*He has since been living in retirement in Beecher, Ill.

†Teacher Schroeder died on June 12, 1942—several hours before he was to be officially informed of having been elected as "honorary elder" of Saint Paul's Congregation, Melrose Park, Ill.

101. Coal City

Returning toward Chicago, the Trail proceeds in a northwesterly direction, crossing the northwestern corner of Kankakee County and entering Grundy County, where it soon comes to a village known as Coal City, Ill.* Here a Lutheran congregation was organized in 1887 and named Saint Peter's, concerning which, however, very little can be said at this time.

In 1933 it was reported by the Mission Board of the Northern Illinois District that "most of the communicant members are women; in fact, we have only four men over 21 years of age." Services in the English language are held on alternate Sunday afternoons.

In 1937, or about twelve years ago, it was stated that "the church building and property, once attractive, are now in poor condition."

Reports concerning improvement of the situation at Coal City are being eagerly awaited.

102. Lindenwood

From Coal City the Trail once more heads for Rockford, stopping at a community for some time known as Lynville, but now called Lindenwood, approximately thirteen miles south by southeast of Rockford. The community is not included in the official census records. It is regrettable that "all the early records" of the Lutheran church at Lindenwood "have been lost, with the exception of the official 'Record Book' with its entries of Baptisms, confirmations, marriages, burials, etc." These records provide at least the bare information that Lutheran pastors were active here in the early 1870's, including the following: T. Johannes Grosse, Max Heyer, Johannes T. Feiertag, and W. C. H. Oetting. In the latter part of 1875 the Rev. F. W. Richmann came here

*1940 census: 1,852.

from Elgin to conduct services about every three weeks, at first in private homes and later in the local Union church. From 1878 to 1887 the group was served by the Rev. Henry H. Norden, pastor of Immanuel Congregation at Squaw Grove (five miles northwest of Hinckley). For several months after the departure of Pastor Norden from Hinckley the Lutherans of Lindenwood were spiritually cared for by the Rev. Theodore Kohn of Belvidere and by the Rev. Gotthilf S. Loeber of Niles, until 1888, when the Rev. Louis W. Dorn, new pastor of Saint Paul's in Rockford, began to make regular trips to Lindenwood and, presumably, in the same year directed the organization of Immanuel Congregation in Lindenwood. The constitution drawn up by Pastor Dorn is still in force, although it has since been translated into English.

Soon afterward a tract of land was purchased and a church built upon it, in 1890. Immanuel's first resident pastor, the Rev. Henry Dannenfeldt, who came in 1891, served for about five years,* until 1896, when he accepted a call to Woodstock, Ill. Soon afterward his successor, the Rev. Adolph C. Staats of Clear Creek, Wis., was installed as Immanuel's second resident pastor. He also served the scattered Lutherans at Rochelle; and when these had organized their own (Saint Paul's) congregation, Pastor Staats was called as its first pastor. Thereupon Immanuel of Lindenwood again called a pastor from the State of Wisconsin, the Rev. Christoph Droegemueller of Cecil. He served here for about one year, when illness compelled him to resign. In 1902, however, he resumed the ministry at Immanuel Congregation, Proviso ("Franzosenbusch"), Ill. His successor in Lindenwood was the Rev. Carl Bernhard Schroeder of Bishop, Ill. He served for about ten years, until the fall of 1910, when he accepted a call to Cole Camp, Mo.† Then, on January 8, 1911, followed the Rev. Herman C. Schoenbeck of Rochelle, Ill. Up

*He also served as missionary to the Lutheran settlers at Rochelle, Ill., who in 1900 organized Saint Paul's Congregation.

†The Rev. C. B. Schroeder retired in 1930 and died Oct. 2, 1938.

to this time the work in the congregation had been done exclusively in the German language, but now one English service each month was made the rule. In November, 1915, Pastor Schoenbeck accepted a call to Saint Paul's Congregation in the Norwood Park community in the northwestern section of Chicago, and the Rev. Arthur H. Werfelmann of Culbertson, Mont., was installed as Immanuel's sixth pastor on December 12, 1916. In May, 1921, Pastor Werfelmann accepted a call to Glenview, Ill., and on the following August 21 the Rev. Edwin Henry Schulenburg of Cordova, Nebr., came to Lindenwood. In 1924 a new church was erected, and dedicated in October of the same year. At this time a change was made in the service schedule. Services in English were conducted every Sunday, and in German twice a month. Since January, 1942, no German services have been held in Immanuel Church.

103. Chicago, Saint Mark's

The Trail now returns to 2100 South and 2100 West, where, about one month before the Great Fire, had been founded Saint Matthew's, the second "daughter" congregation of First Immanuel in Chicago—in the "Lime Kiln" area, to become acquainted with a "granddaughter," which evolved from a branch school established by Saint Matthew's Congregation in 1884 on California Avenue, south of West Twenty-second Street (now also known as Cermak Road).* For three years this school was in charge of students and the Rev. Paul Brauns, assistant pastor of Saint Matthew's. In March, 1887, J. C. F. W. Bock was placed in charge of this school, and on the following November 16 thirty-one voting members of Saint Matthew's Congregation organized Saint Mark's Congregation. On March 4, 1888, Saint Mark's first pastor, the Rev. Gustav Rosenwinkel of Berlin, Wis., was

*Named after Anton J. C. Cermak, mayor of Chicago, 1931-1933; died March 6, 1933.

installed, and in the same year Saint Mark's purchased ten lots on the east side of California Avenue, south of West Twenty-third Street, and erected a two-story building, 30x-92 feet, the upper story of which was arranged as a place of worship and the lower for classroom purposes. The cost of the building, which was dedicated on November 11, 1888, was eight thousand dollars. In the summer of 1890 a second teacher, William C. Pipkorn, was installed. Because of failing health, Pastor Rosenwinkel resigned in 1892 and moved to the State of Florida.* His successor, the Rev. Theodore Kohn of Belvidere, Ill., was installed as Saint Mark's second pastor on October 9, 1892. In 1894 a third classroom was arranged, and Frederick Kringel of Milwaukee, Wis., was assigned to the upper class.

A new church was erected and dedicated in 1895. The former church auditorium was converted into classrooms. In January, 1896, a branch school was opened in a store building on Forty-second Avenue (now Keeler), between Twenty-seventh and Twenty-eighth Streets, in the community known as Crawford. Pastor Kohn taught there for about one month; from the beginning of February, 1896, until the middle of July, 1897, the branch school was in charge of two candidates of the teaching profession. In the same summer, teacher-candidates Paul Streufert and Gustav Eberhardt were installed; the congregation now had five teachers and two schools, with an enrollment of 364. On November 26, 1899, a new mission was begun at Twelfth Street and Forty-fourth Avenue (now Kostner). This developed into Ebenezer Congregation, organized in May, 1901, Saint Mark's first "daughter" congregation, served since July 28, 1901, by the Rev. William Gahl. Its present "center" is at West Thirteenth Street and Harding Avenue. In September of the same year the branch school in Crawford had developed into an autonomous

*In 1894 he resumed a pastorate in Milwaukee; later, in Minnesota. He died Sept. 9, 1901.

congregation, named "Gnaden-Gemeinde," Grace Congregation, whose church is located on the northeast corner of West Twenty-eighth Street and South Karlov Avenue.

In April, 1902, the school enrollment had increased to such proportions that another classroom had to be arranged, which was done by building an annex at a cost of seven thousand dollars. F. Metschke was added to the staff on August 17, 1902. Shortly afterward Mr. Pipkorn accepted a call to Wisconsin, and August Haack took his place in Saint Mark's School in February, 1903; after his resignation in May, 1904, H. G. Rabe of Sheboygan, Wis., began teaching here in September, 1904. Mr. Bock died on July 2, 1905. Succeeding him in the classroom was F. G. Krumsieg. In the spring of 1906 Mr. Streufert accepted a call to Zion School in Hinsdale, and teacher-candidate Waldemar Grotheer came to Saint Mark's. In 1908 Mr. Kringel resigned, and J. W. R. List took his place. Mr. Metschke, who resigned in 1910, was succeeded by Herman Krafft.

In 1915 Pastor Kohn accepted a call to St. Paul, Minn., and Saint Mark's third pastor, the Rev. Frederick W. Mahnke of West Chicago (formerly called Turner Junction), Ill., was installed on September 19, 1915.

Mr. List in 1916 was succeeded by M. B. Singer of Holy Cross School, Chicago, who served until 1929, when he followed a call to Saint Mark's first "daughter"—Ebenezer. His successor at Saint Mark's was G. L. Warnke of Staunton, Ill. In the fall of the same year, 1929, Mr. Rabe, who had taught here for about twenty-five years, died.

Pastor Mahnke died on October 24, 1936. During the ensuing vacancy the Rev. William Gahl, circuit visitor, called upon various pastors and students to serve, until February 7, 1937, when Candidate Fred E. Bartling was installed. He served as Saint Mark's fourth pastor until November, 1941, when he accepted a call to a mission congregation in North

Lake Village, Ill. He was succeeded in April, 1941, by the Rev. Alex William C. Guebert of Cummings Corner (Oak Glen), Ill. In August, 1943, Pastor Guebert accepted a professorship at Concordia Seminary, St. Louis, Mo., and on November 7, 1943, Saint Mark's sixth pastor, the Rev. Waldemar Roth of Saginaw, Mich., was installed.

In addition to the teachers mentioned, the following have served in Saint Mark's School: The Misses Olga Schulenberg, Lena Wittrock, Leona Engel, Elsa Schumann, and Doris Rentner, Lyle Stolp, Mrs. Loretta Zielke, Milton Schmidt, Miss Dorothy Schwartzkopf, Miss Arliss Zink, Miss Marie Brenner, and Mrs. Marie Nestel.

104. Chicago, Saint Andrew's

Now to return once more to First Trinity Congregation in Chicago to observe the expansion of this third congregation, whose two "daughters," Holy Cross and Saint Martini, were flourishing and increasing independently, the former since 1886 and the latter since 1884. Approximately two thirds of First Trinity's voting membership constituted the beginning of Holy Cross in "Bridgeport." Saint Martini Congregation did not begin with so large a percentage of the "mother's" voting membership, but it did take along the assistant pastor, the Rev. Fred C. Leeb, making him its own pastor. The "mother" congregation then, together with Zion, at Nineteenth and Peoria Streets, called another assistant pastor, the Rev. Gotthilf Simon Loeber of Niles (Dutchman's Point), Ill. First Trinity in 1883 had purchased two lots on Wood Street, near Thirty-sixth, and within a few months erected thereon a two-story brick school building. So it is not surprising to learn that within a comparatively brief space of time the nucleus of still another congregation was formed in that region, known as Brighton. The practice of conducting preaching services in branch schools was applied also in this case.

On March 4, 1888, First Trinity's members residing in the Brighton community organized the third "daughter" congregation and named it Saint Andrew's. They did not lay claim to the "mother's" assistant pastor, but they did retain the services of "her" teacher in this branch school, William F. Diener. For pastor they called the Rev. William C. Kohn, assistant pastor of the sixth Missouri Synod congregation in Chicago, "Sankt Jakobi" (Saint James), who was installed on July 8, 1888.

The school was enlarged to include two classrooms on the lower floor, with the upper floor set aside for worship. Called to the second classroom was H. Christopher. Within the next few years two more classes were added, to which J. Landeck and H. Proehl were assigned. On July 15, 1889, the Town of Lake was annexed to Chicago.

By 1891 the church had become too small, and it was decided to build. Within one week's time the young congregation of seventy-two members subscribed a total of $8,293 for that purpose, and on January 24, 1892, dedication took place.

Pastor Kohn served until June, 1913, when he accepted the presidency of Concordia Teachers College, River Forest, Ill.* His successor as Saint Andrew's second pastor was the Rev. Herman L. Pflug of South Chicago (Colehour), Ill. His pastorate covered a period of about eight years; he died on March 6, 1921; on May 22, 1921, he was succeeded at Saint Andrew's by the Rev. Ernest Gottlieb Jehn of Howard, S. Dak. The Rev. Frederick Pfotenhauer, D.D., President of the Missouri Synod (1911-1935), served for a number of years as assistant pastor; as did also his successor in that office, the Rev. John W. Behnken, D.D. A Sunday school was established in 1920, and a new school building was erected in 1930.

*Since 1864 located at Addison, Ill., and known as the Teachers' Seminary, the institution was moved to River Forest in 1912. "Director" Kohn died here on March 13, 1943.

In addition to those already mentioned, the following teachers also served in Saint Andrew's School: E. Krause, Carl J. W. Meinke, O. Schaller, T. J. Wichmann, Bernard W. Rubin, K. L. Busse, H. L. Schroeder, T. F. Wunderlich, O. Wegener, A. Schumann, O. Wachholz, E. Haase, Max Zieroth, John Steiner, H. Gersmehl, G. O. Launer, Herman E. Meyer, and Miss Elsa Schumann.

On October 27, 1940, the Rev. Martin Frick of Bachelors Grove (two miles north of Tinley Park), Ill., was installed as associate pastor, and upon Pastor Jehn's resignation the full pastorate was assigned to Pastor Frick.

105. Hinsdale, Zion

The Lutheran Trail now joins the thoroughfare named after Chicago's first mayor, William B. Ogden, Ogden Avenue (once known as the Southwest Plank Road), continuing on it to Cicero's principal intersection and thence southwest through Berwyn, Brookfield (Grossdale), Lyons, and La Grange, to Hinsdale, Ill.,* a distance of about fourteen miles. During the 1880's many Lutheran immigrants from Germany settled in Fullersburg† (now Hinsdale), who, if they desired to attend Lutheran services, would have to journey to Immanuel Church at the "Franzosenbusch" (Proviso), about four miles north. The pastor of that congregation, the Rev. Johannes Strieter, notified them that he was prepared to conduct a service in Fullersburg on November 14, 1886. For some presumably very good reason he could not keep his promise, but he did secure the president of the Teachers' Seminary at Addison, the Rev. Prof. E. A. Wilhelm Krauss, to substitute for him. After January 17, 1887, Pastor Strieter came to Fullersburg (Hinsdale) on alternate Sunday after-

*1940 census: 7,336. Named for W. H. Hinsdale, a prominent railroad man, who formerly lived in Hinsdale, N.Y.

†"The Fullersburg section, north of Hinsdale, is named after an early settler, Jacob Fuller, who came from New England in 1835." (*Chicago Daily News*, Rotogravure Section, June 21, 1947.)

noons and conducted services in an old schoolhouse. On April 15, 1888, these Fullersburg Lutherans got together and organized Zion Congregation. Immediately they considered erecting a church of their own, specifications for which included a steeple with a bell, at a cost of $2,515. On June 1, 1890, Zion Congregation's first pastor, the Rev. John F. C. Molthan of North Judson, Ind., was installed. Soon afterward Pastor Molthan started a day school. In 1891 Zion became a member of the Missouri Synod. In 1894 Nicholas Roemer was called to teach; he remained but a short time and was succeeded by Herman Lemke of Sioux City, Iowa. Then, from 1897 to 1901, Adolph Kastner had charge of the school; after him came Theodore A. Meyer of Mishawaka, Ind.

In August, 1901, Pastor Molthan accepted a call to Genoa, Ill., and on October 27 Zion's second pastor, the Rev. Herman C. Guebert of Baldwin, Ill., was installed. Then followed a period of unpleasantness, occasioned by an increase in the number of members interested in secret societies, which, in turn, led to official disciplinary action, resulting in the withdrawal and dismissal of a number of members.

In 1906 Paul Streufert was called from Saint Mark's Congregation in Chicago to take charge of the day school; at the same time Zion's first woman teacher was engaged, Miss Minnie Kohn. In 1907 Pastor Guebert started mission work in Downers Grove,* and in 1908 English services were introduced. In 1912 Mr. Streufert was succeeded by L. T. Knief. A new church was erected in 1913 at the southwest corner of Grant and Second Streets, Hinsdale. The benches of the old church were donated to the mission congregation in Bellwood (Saint John's), and the bell to Trinity Congregation, two miles northwest of Willow Springs. On March 12, 1922, Pastor Guebert resigned and moved to Oak Park, Ill. His successor at Zion, Hinsdale, on May 21, 1922, was the

*An indication that earlier work in this community proved unsuccessful. (See Chapter 34.)

Rev. Theo. W. Strieter, hitherto a missionary in Brazil, South America.

On March 16, 1922, six voting members were released to organize an all-English congregation, which was named Redeemer. This congregation then joined the English District of the Missouri Synod. Redeemer's first resident pastor, the Rev. Carl F. Dankworth, was installed on September 3, 1922. He still is pastor of Redeemer Congregation.

The minutes of the voters' meeting at Zion on July 14, 1918, reveal that adverse comments were being made regarding the congregation's day school. Articles from official Missouri Synod publications were read indicating that the purpose and objective of a Lutheran school is "not to teach and retain a language, but to give religious instruction and Christian training." Forthwith German grammar and writing were discontinued. In 1923 teaching of religion in the German language was discontinued; and mission work was begun by Pastor Strieter in Westmont, Western Springs, and Naperville.*

Other teachers in Zion School were Miss Clara Ebert, Miss L. Pfotenhauer, R. J. Schultz, Miss Viola Gotsch,† Miss Ethel Fischer, Hugo Oldsen,‡ A. W. Ladwig, H. J. Heyne, Miss Mildred Boger, Miss Paula Schmidt, Mrs. A. W. Ladwig, Luther Mueller, and Miss Elfrieda Timm.

In 1931 Pastor Strieter accepted a position in the Public Relations Department of Valparaiso University, Valparaiso, Ind. On December 15 of the same year the Rev. Arthur H. Werfelmann of Glenview, Ill., was installed as Zion's fourth pastor. In August, 1939, Pastor Werfelmann accepted a call to Saint John's Congregation in Elgin, Ill., and Candidate Paul H. Scheer became Zion's fifth pastor.

*See previous footnote.

†Later married to the Rev. Paul J. Roeder, since Nov. 13, 1938, pastor of Bethany Congregation, Chicago.

‡In 1924 Mr. Oldsen passed a colloquium at Concordia Seminary, Springfield, Ill., and became a candidate for the ministry; pastor of Zion Congregation, Ottawa, Ill., since April 29, 1928.

106. Burlington

About twenty-five miles northwest of Hinsdale (Fullersburg) is the well-known city of Elgin. And thirteen miles straight west of Elgin is a tiny village known as Burlington, Ill.,* which the Trail neared when circling round Sycamore, Hampshire, Gilberts, and Union. Germans who had settled here and in the neighboring prairies in the 1880's for some time went to church either in North Plato or in Hampshire. In 1888 Saint John's Congregation was organized in Burlington by those Lutheran settlers.† They also called their own pastor, the Rev. Otto Gruner, who was installed on August 26, 1888. Their first church building was a small frame structure, at one time a Methodist Episcopal meetinghouse.

The pastor taught school three days a week in Burlington and the same number of days in North Plato (Saint Peter's). In 1893 Saint John's engaged a student of theology, Philip Roesel, to teach five days a week and to preach in Saint John's Church, Burlington, on Sundays. In 1894 this service was rendered by Student Banovsky. From 1893 to 1895 Pastor Gruner performed all the official acts here. After his change of pastorate to Saint Paul's Congregation, Rockford, Ill. (April, 1895), the Rev. Herman F. Fruechtenicht, pastor of Saint John's, Elgin, served in that capacity. On July 28, 1895, Candidate Philip Roesel was ordained and installed as pastor of Trinity in Hampshire and of Saint John's in Burlington, with the pastor's residence in the latter place. Not long afterward a new church, with a seating capacity of about two hundred, was dedicated in Burlington. In the summer of 1902 Pastor Roesel accepted a call to Waukomis, near Lahoma, Okla., and on the following August 24 Candidate Theodore

*1940 census: 235.

†Charter members:

Julius Peplow	Henry Struck	Fred Lenschow
Henry Meyer	August Jahn	William Biesterfeldt
John Kanies	Henry Lenschow	

Samuel Estel succeeded him in the dual parish. Poor health compelled the latter's resignation in 1904.* From 1904 until 1911 Saint John's in Burlington was served as an affiliate of Saint Peter's at North Plato; by its pastor, the Rev. William O. J. Kistemann, until 1907, and then also by his successor at North Plato, the Rev. Henry Prekel, 1907-11.

The following trained teachers served in Saint John's School from 1904 to 1911: Stephanus Mueller, Alfred Kowert, Bernhardt Molthan, Leo Kassemeier, and John Richter.

In 1911 Saint John's of Burlington and Trinity of Hampshire jointly called the Rev. D. H. Schoof of Gravelton, Mo. He was installed on October 29, 1911. Illness forced him to resign in 1918, and during the ensuing vacancy the Rev. John F. C. Molthan of Genoa, Ill., had charge of the work in Burlington. In 1921 the Rev. H. J. F. Meier of Ontarioville, Ill., formally took charge of the dual parish. In the spring of 1929 Pastor Meier was likewise compelled by ill health to relinquish his pastoral office. On October 6, 1929, he was succeeded in the dual parish by the Rev. Werner Schmidtke of Iron Mountain, Mich. He served here until May, 1947, when he accepted a call to Fort Wayne, Ind. On October 26, 1947, the Rev. F. B. Bierwagen of Britton, S. Dak., was installed. (See Chapter 84.)

107. Chicago, Emmaus

On March 28, 1867, was witnessed the founding of the Missouri Synod's fourth congregation in the cornfields of the "overgrown country town"—Chicago. That was First Saint John's, then located at West Noble and Cornell Streets. Four weeks later that congregation bought vacant property at the corner of Bickerdike and West Superior Streets, where on October 13, 1867, its first church was dedicated. In the following year, 1868, First Bethlehem Congregation emerged from

*Later he resumed ministerial work at Shiloh Hill, Ill., and at Platte Center, Nebr. He resigned in 1915.

First Saint John's first school district, the center of which was North Paulina Street, near Milwaukee Avenue. On leased property at Fulton and North Paulina Streets, First Saint John's erected a school building and placed Albert W. Rose in charge of it. In 1875 this building was moved to the congregation's newly acquired property on Oakley Avenue, between Fulton and Kinzie Streets. Meanwhile an old Methodist church on Fulton Street was offered for sale, a fact which aroused in the hearts of First Saint John's members residing in this school district the desire to organize their own congregation. Eleven of them* gained the "mother" congregation's approval, and on April 2, 1888, the organization of Emmaus Congregation was effected by ten men, to which number nine more were added at the same time. The new congregation received from First Saint John's the entire school property as an outright gift. This building served for a brief time as church and school. The first pastor was the Rev. Martin Fuelling, heretofore "Reiseprediger" in North Dakota. He was installed on August 19, 1888. On the same day he officiated at the cornerstone laying of Emmaus Congregation's new church—at first only a basement—at the northwest corner of Walnut Street and North California Avenue. It was arranged for school and church purposes, and the pastor was in charge of both until 1889, when the congregation sold the original property and erected a school building, the upper floor of which was arranged as a parsonage. In August of the same year, 1889, A. B. Johnson, graduate of the Teachers' Seminary, Addison, was installed as teacher. Pastor Fuelling assisted the teacher for a year, and then the congregation engaged Miss Dora Mueller for this work.

In 1891 Pastor Fuelling started a mission at Chicago and Lawndale Avenues, which in June, 1894, developed into Bethel

*Charter members, not including the nine added on April 2, 1888:

F. Katz	Ernst Matz	Heinrich Kropelin
Christ. Ruetz	Christ. Bockelman	Wilhelm Meyer
Franz Schroeder	Christ. Kruse	Louis Lange
Louis Schulz	Christ. Holst	

Congregation. He also assisted the Rev. Theodore Kohn of Saint Andrew's and the Revs. Louis and Edward Hoelter of First Immanuel in the mission field centering at Twelfth Street and Keeler Avenue, which in May, 1901, developed into Ebenezer Congregation.

In December, 1939, Pastor Fuelling retired, and on April 7, 1940, Candidate Walter E. Roschke was ordained and installed as the second pastor of Emmaus.

In January, 1940, Teacher Lassanske accepted a call to First Immanuel School (Chicago), and Teacher Lipske was promoted to the principalship. Candidate Ralph Bartelt, subsidized by the Mission Board, completed the school term in the lower grades. In June, 1941, Mr. Bartelt accepted a call to Kankakee, Ill., and Candidate Delbert Pranschke taught until the end of the school term in June, 1943. In September, 1943, Candidate Norman Vonderheid served as teacher of the lower grades. In the summer of 1944 Principal Lipske accepted a call to Chebanse, Ill. This fact, coupled with the prevailing acute teacher shortage, prompted the congregation to close its day school. During the fifty-six years of its existence, the school was conducted by the following: Pastor Martin Fuelling, Andrew Johnson, E. G. Warman, O. Wegner, H. Seils, Paul Lassanske, L. Helmstetter, Walter E. Buszin, E. H. Koerber, R. Beckemeier, F. J. Schleef, M. Waggazzer, T. H. Hilgendorf, O. Hinrichs, L. A. Buuck, Ralph Stephan, E. F. Jording, L. Klug, Russell Proehl, John Fuelling, H. Kirchmann, Norman Vonderheide, Ralph Bartelt, and Herold Lipske. From 1889 until 1895 the pastor had taught the lower grades; from that time until 1919 these grades were taught by women teachers: Dora Mueller, Mary Gremel, Anna Gallitz, Lena Willner, Anna Listel, Dorothy Heerboth, and Marie Fuelling.

On May 31, 1945, the congregation sold its property on California Avenue to The Church of God in Christ, a Negro congregation. At that time Emmaus Congregation had a monetary deposit on property for a proposed new church building; because of zoning restrictions, however, the congregation was compelled to look for a different site. After considering several lots on the far West Side of Chicago, the congregation purchased a lot on the southeast corner of Austin and Washington Boulevards. On February 24, 1946, the groundbreaking ceremony took place. One week later, Matthew T. Fin and his wife began court proceedings for an injunction against the erection of a church building because of an alleged restriction against any building but a private residence.

From July 1, 1945, until the end of April, 1947, Emmaus Congregation worshiped in the Administration Building of Garfield Park; since that time, from April, 1947, until February 8, 1948, the services were held in a small church building* at Lorel Avenue and West Le Moyne Street. Meanwhile the congregation purchased for $60,000 the Westminster Presbyterian Church, at Gladys and Lotus Streets, where its first worship service was conducted on Ash Wednesday, February 11, 1948. It dedicated this building as a Lutheran church on the Sunday after Easter, April 4, 1948.

108. Rockford

The insatiable wanderlust of the Trail now evokes a journey of seventy-five miles toward the central part of this District to the beautiful city of Rockford on the Rock River.† At this "rocky ford" over the river, 'way back in 1878, the Rev. John Adam Detzer, Sr., conducted mission services in the basement of the Augustana Synod's First Lutheran Church; then in the Grand Army Hall, and still later in Brown's Hall. In the following year this congregation, which was regarded by many as "merely a German club, organized and maintained for the propagation of German culture" and known as Saint Paul's, secured as its first resident pastor the Rev. George

*Property of Christ English Ev. Lutheran Congregation.

†1940 census: 84,637.

Johannes of Chicago, who was installed on November 9, 1879. In October, 1881, he followed a call to Immanuel Congregation in Des Plaines, Ill. On March 5, 1882, the Rev. Ludwig von Schenk of Algonquin, Ill., succeeded Pastor Johannes to this pastorate. Two years later, in 1884, Pastor von Schenk assumed charge of the congregation in Pecatonica, about twenty-eight miles west of Rockford, and, having established residence there, continued serving Saint Paul's in Rockford as an affiliate of Saint John's, Pecatonica. At that time services for the group in Rockford were held in the home of A. Neumeister. It appeared as though Saint Paul's were headed for disintegration; particularly precarious did the situation become when in 1885 Pastor von Schenk left Pecatonica for Ottawa, Ill., where he assumed the pastorate of Zion. However, the dark clouds were soon dispelled by the appearance of Lutheran pastors in Rockford, who, although at infrequent intervals, attended to the spiritual needs of Saint Paul's membership. Among these pastors were Edward Albrecht, Theodore F. Kohn, H. Grupe, Theodore F. Brohm, Anton Wagner, Prof. E. A. Wilhelm Krauss, and others. "The members constituted a large family, knit closely together. On the Sunday when a pastor came to conduct services, all members would gather and spend hours of delightful and instructive conversation and fellowship with their guest. This association fully compensated for the smallness and the scorn of the opponents."

On June 27, 1886, the Rev. Theodore Kohn was placed in charge of three congregations: Immanuel in Belvidere, Saint John's in Pecatonica,* and Saint Paul's in Rockford. In the latter place the number of worshipers soon increased. "The opponents were suffering reverses and now made advances, looking toward reconciliation and amalgamation. However, the efforts failed, and a few years later the former congregation dissolved."

*Pastor Kohn conducted services every other Sunday in Pecatonica.

In 1888 Pastor Kohn, who resided in Belvidere, terminated his services in Rockford, but continued serving Saint John's in Pecatonica until 1890. On March 11, 1888, the Rev. Louis W. Dorn of Collinsville, Ill., was installed as Saint Paul's pastor, who "during his seven years here succeeded in laying a solid foundation for future strength and growth of the congregation." On July 8, 1888, complete reorganization was effected.* In January of the following year Saint Paul's purchased a lot, Number 423, on Chestnut Street, upon which was erected a church, dedicated the following July 22. Pastor Dorn started missions in Lynville (now Lindenwood) and Rochelle, and for a time served Saint John's in Pecatonica. In April, 1895, he accepted a call to Belleville, Ill.† His successor in Rockford, the Rev. Otto Gruner of Pingree Grove, Ill., was installed on April 21, 1895. In 1906 a new church was erected on North Horsman Street, which was dedicated on August 12, 1906. A Sunday school was begun in October, 1917. A day school was fostered shortly after the first building had been erected in 1889, taught by Pastor Dorn, and successively by the following trained teachers: J. F. K. Oberdiek, Theo. Breihan, Miss Augusta Block, Carl Zautner, Alfred Schwausch, W. H. Cholcher, C. F. Wisch, Mrs. C. F. Wisch, Mrs. E. Stolz, and Miss Evelyn Schwanke.

Pastor Gruner died on April 27, 1927. The Rev. F. H. Brunn of Bay City, Mich., succeeded to Saint Paul's pastorate on July 31, 1927.‡ He served here until the summer of 1948 and resigned. On September 19, 1948, the Rev. Erich V. Oelschlaeger of St. Louis, Mo., was installed as Dr. Brunn's successor. The latter was made Doctor of Divinity by Concordia Seminary, Springfield, Ill., on June 7, 1947.

*Charter members:

H. Scharfenberg	G. Schmidt	Mrs. Clara Knott
A. Neumeister	Christian Schmidt	Miss Anna Dietrichsen
F. W. Lueder	Karl Schmidt	August Dietrichsen

†In 1900 Pastor Dorn accepted a professorship at Concordia College, Fort Wayne, Ind., which he held until his death on April 4, 1918.

‡A son of the Rev. Frederick Brunn, pastor of Trinity and Saint John's (Cummings Corner—Oak Glen—and Lansing, Ill.), 1895-1927, and president of the Northern Illinois District, Missouri Synod, 1913-1927.

109. Chicago, Saint Paul's (Grand Crossing)

The Trail next stops at Grand Crossing, nine miles due south of Chicago's Loop. All that can be seen is a little frame building bearing the sign: "Grand Crossing–Nine Miles from Chicago." Thither, nowadays, there is multiple transportaion; but sixty-five years ago the Lutheran Trail found it difficult to traverse, the traditional cowpath being the only approach. Grand Crossing was what the novelists of that era, 1888, termed "a benighted spot," enlivened by a concert of frogs with a buzz-ping obbligato of mosquitoes to the accompaniment of a whistling wind sweeping across the prairie from Lake Michigan. Withal a sorry place to await a train! However, there is no place so sorry or so benighted but that Lutherans there be found, sparse and scattered though they be, whose very existence even was unsuspected when, a while back, the Trail was weaving in the vicinity of Bridgeport and Brighton.

Grand Crossing long ago came into public notice. In 1853 the first train wreck occurred there. "Two stubborn trains smashed . . . and eighteen corpses and forty maimed passengers were brought into the city. Mobs gathered, city dignitaries spoke, and Chicago thereafter made all trains come to a full stop at intersections." Today (1949) it really is a "grand" crossing; the Illinois Central, the Pennsylvania, the Nickel Plate, the Pere Marquette, and the New York Central. The first of these, the "I.C." together with the South Shore Line* and the Michigan Central (now part of the New York Central System), being crossed overhead by the other railroads mentioned; below is South Chicago Avenue.

The German Lutheran settlers who lived in this community in the 1870's attended services in Immanuel Church in South Chicago. In October, 1887, the Rev. Carl F. Eissfeldt of that

NOTE: Until July 15, 1889, Grand Crossing was included in the "Village of Hyde." Together with other communities, it was annexed to Chicago at that time.

*Chicago, South Shore & South Bend Electric Railroad.

congregation began to conduct services in Turner Hall, Grand Crossing. When on July 4, 1888, this building was destroyed by fire, the group was granted permission to have its services in the Ingleside (Avenue) Methodist Church. On July 18, 1888, five Lutheran men* met in the home of H. Nagel to effect an organization; two weeks later they incorporated as "Die Deutsche Evangelisch-Lutherische Gemeinde zu Grand Crossing, Ill." On September 2 the constitution was signed by the five men. Then three lots on Madison Street (now Dorchester Avenue), near Seventy-sixth Street, were purchased for nine hundred dollars, and a small frame church, which was also to serve as a school, was erected, the dedication taking place on December 9, 1888. Pastor Eissfeldt continued serving the little flock, and Student Ruesskamp began his work in the day school in January, 1889, with fourteen pupils.

On December 7, 1890, Saint Paul's first resident pastor, the Rev. August Frederking, former "Reiseprediger" in the State of Arkansas, was installed. In May, 1891, the congregation joined the Missouri Synod. After Student Ruesskamp's departure in December, 1890, Pastor Frederking assumed charge of the school and taught until the fall of 1892, when J. Andrew Sohn of York, Pa., was installed; Mr. Sohn, however, in April, 1893, followed a call to Beardstown, Ill.

On December 23, 1894, a new church was dedicated with three special services—the evening service in the English language with the sermon by the Rev. F. Paul Merbitz, pastor of Saint Peter's Congregation, whose "center" at that time was at the corner of Dearborn and Thirty-ninth Streets, Chicago. The cost of the new church was about six thousand dollars; the bell now (1949) in use came from the old church of Saint Peter's as a donation to Saint Paul's in the early 1920's, when the former transferred its "center" to East Seventy-fourth Street and Michigan Avenue.

†W. Ruehle H. Nagel
H. Troeller L. Mauch
H. Jeske

In December, 1928, Pastor Frederking was compelled by ill health to resign.* His successor, the Rev. Theodore Herman Dorn† of Halfway, Mich., was installed as Saint Paul's second resident pastor on January 13, 1929. A two-story addition to the school, measuring 38x52 feet and costing $50,000, was dedicated on January 25, 1948.

A new school was erected in 1934. In addition to those mentioned, the following have served as teachers in Saint Paul's School:

Henry Heiden, 1896-1899
Adolph Liebe, 1901-1904
A. C. Renn, 1904-1910
Ed. M. Streufert, 1910-1917
A. H. Kuntz, 1917-1922
J. H. Burmeister, 1922-1923‡
E. A. Boseck, 1923-1930
Edward J. Krause, 1930-
Arthur Schaeffer
Walter Beilstein, 1937-1939§
Walter J. Bergmann
Adolph K. Krause
Miss Edna Thies||
Vernon Doering
Vernon L. Wilharm
Mrs. August Mueller
J. George Blumenschein.‡

On May 22, 1938, Pastor Dorn accepted a call to Saint Paul's Congregation in Cleveland, Ohio, and his successor as Saint Paul's third pastor (in Grand Crossing), the Rev. Edwin H. Pflug of St. Charles, Ill., was installed on July 17, 1938.

110. Lombard

A straight line being the shortest distance between two points, the distance between Grand Crossing and Lombard, Ill.,** is exactly twenty-four miles, toward the northwest. The name of this village reminds one of the Low Latin "longobardus,"—"long beard." Lombard is located less than a mile east of the Du Page River and is famous for its extensive cultivation of "Syringa Vulgaris"—lilacs.†† Early in the 1860's

*Pastor Frederking died Nov. 18, 1930.

†Pastor Frederking's son-in-law; son of the Rev. Louis W. Dorn, pastor of Saint Paul's, Rockford, 1888-1895; later, professor at Concordia College, Fort Wayne, Ind.

‡Served as substitutes.

§Died suddenly April 17, 1939, age 22.

||Now the wife of the Rev. Armin H. Breihan, Joliet, Ill.

**1940 census: 7,075. Named for Joshiah L. Lombard, who purchased extensive lands in this vicinity. Formerly called Babcock's Grove, for the original owner.

††Col. William R. Plum, a Chicago lawyer and Civil War veteran, who built his home in Lombard in 1867, gave Lilacia Park to the village. The old Plum home is the town's library today, and the horse barn has been converted into an administration building by the park board. (*Chicago Daily News*, March 28, 1947, p. 7.)

Zion Congregation of Duncklees Grove, about five miles to the northeast, established a school district for its members residing in the neighborhood of Lombard (See Chapter 42, page 205.) In 1868 a congregation was organized in Zion's branch school located about a mile southeast of Lombard, at York Center, at what now is known as the intersection of Roosevelt and Meyers Roads; soon afterward the new congregation, named Trinity, installed its own pastor, the Rev. Theodore Mertens of Willow Springs, Ill., and erected its own church. This development, of course, benefited also the Lutherans living in the village, Lombard, most of whom now attended services at York Center. Less than twenty years later the Lombardians* decided to erect a combination church-school and to call a trained teacher. Neighboring Lutheran pastors conducted the worship services. Then, at a voters' meeting held on May 23, 1893, it was resolved to call a resident pastor. Presiding at this meeting was the Rev. William Uffenbeck, circuit visitor and pastor of Holy Cross Congregation, Chicago. After three unsuccessful "calls"† the Rev. Otto R. Massmann of Three Rivers, Mich., accepted. Installed as pastor of the new congregation on October 15, 1893, Pastor Massmann served for a period of about twenty-five years, the first fourteen of these also as day school teacher. The first school was dedicated in June, 1888. The first teacher was F. Bodenstein, graduate of the Teachers' Seminary, Addison. He remained until December, 1892, when he followed a call to Cleveland, Ohio. From that time until May, 1893, Miss Clara Graue had charge of this work. Mr. Gotsch completed the term. Mr. Schoenbeck taught from the opening of the next school year until the middle of October, when Pastor Massmann took also the school under his care. On September 1, 1907, teacher-candidate H. W. Schreiber was installed. At this time the enrollment was fifty-five. In 1918

*Not Lombardeers—for this word means "pawnbrokers."

†The call had been extended to the Rev. Wm. Koepchen in New York, to the Rev. Carl Abel at Mount Olive, Ill., and to the Rev. Wm. Baeder.

Pastor Massmann accepted a call to Dudleytown, Ind.* His successor as Saint John's second pastor, the Rev. Walter C. Wangerin of Lexington, Ky., was installed on March 30, 1919. A second classroom was opened in 1925 in the church "vestry," with Miss Malinda Volberding in charge of the lower grades. In the following year a new school building was erected; it was dedicated on October 17, 1926. In February, 1930, Pastor Wangerin accepted a call to Immanuel Congregation, Grand Rapids, Mich.,† and his successor, the Rev. Otto August Groth of Clyman, Wis., was installed as Saint John's third resident pastor on March 23, 1930. In September, 1931, R. A. Kolzow was placed in charge of the intermediate grades. Because of illness in her family, Miss Volberding in October, 1935, requested to be released from school teaching. Succeeding her was Miss Phyllis Dosien, who served until April, 1937, and then also resigned. Then came Miss Helen Schaper; and, more recently, H. W. Hann and Mrs. J. Marquardt.

Saint John's Church, erected in 1897, is located at 205 West Maple Street, Lombard. The congregation's first constitution was adopted and signed by thirty members.‡

111. Orland Park

From "Lilacia Park" (Lombard) the Trail now passes through another familiar section of the great prairie, by way of Fullersburg (Hinsdale) and Willow Springs, where it crosses

*Resigned from the ministry in 1932 and moved to Libertyville, Ill.

†Son of the Rev. Albert Wangerin, pastor of Zion Congregation in Sollitt, Ill., 1877-1926 (died Jan. 3, 1926), and brother of the Rev. A. D. Wangerin, pastor of Tabor Congregation, Chicago, Ill., 1908-1940 (died May 17, 1940). Pastor Walter C. Wangerin died Sept. 19, 1948.

‡F. Marguardt, John Bandemer, H. Malwitz, D. Klusmeyer, Carl Birr, J. Speckman, C. Mech, H. Koester, H. Surkamer, F. Luedeke, G. Assmann, Wm. Wehrs, H. Matthews, F. Fleege, H. Rosenwinkel, H. Oetke, F. Kloth, R. Yaeche, F. Knopp, J. Holtz, John Schuetz, Louis Marquardt, W. Albers, A. Rengstorf, J. Greinke, W. Hellmer, H. Kruse, G. Kruse, A. Stock, C. Luedeke

the Des Plaines River, the Sanitary and Ship Canal, and the old Illinois-Michigan Canal, and then directly south to 131st Street, then around McGinnes Lake, to Orland Park, Ill.,* where the Southwest Highway connects with 143d Street. The village adjoins the southeast corner of the Taylor Park Forest Preserve, which, incidentally, includes Lake McGinnes.

During the middle 1880's, while serving Trinity Congregation at Bachelors Grove (two miles north of Tinley Park), the Rev. J. H. C. Martin conducted services in various homes and in the Orland Park public school. On September 16, 1888, ten Lutheran men adopted a constitution for the congregation, organized as Christ Congregation. By that time Pastor Martin had accepted a call to Brownsdale, Minn., and in August, 1884, the Rev. Theodore H. C. Buenger had assumed the pastorate at Bachelors Grove, but continued serving the group in Orland Park and its immediate vicinity. Pastor Buenger's successor in 1891, the Rev. Walter Krebs, did the same until 1898, when Christ Congregation called its own pastor, Candidate John Herman Henry Schulz, graduate of Concordia Seminary, Springfield, Ill. He was installed on September 4, 1898. The congregation's first church was erected at the southeast corner of 143d Street and West Avenue in 1897 and dedicated on February 6, 1898. For some time at the turn of the century Pastor Schulz also served a mission at near-by Chicago Ridge, where a Lutheran manufacturer ("Fabrikant") had provided a building for church and school purposes. On March 13, 1921, Pastor Schulz accepted a call to Ash Grove in Iroquois County, Ill. His successor in Orland Park, the Rev. Walter C. Greve, temporarily without a charge and formerly at Kingsville, Tex., was installed as Christ Congregation's second resident pastor on May 21, 1921. A new school building was erected in 1922. Pastor Greve, like his predecessor, also taught school. In July, 1928, he accepted a

*1940 census: 631.

call to Trinity Congregation in Hegewisch (Chicago).* On September 2, 1928, the Rev. William H. Medler of Westville, Ind., became Christ Congregation's third resident pastor, serving until called as missionary at large for the Northern Illinois District, Missouri Synod, in the spring of 1931. His successor in Orland Park was the Rev. Adolf Lach of Bazine, Kans., who was installed on May 3, 1931.

112. West Hammond

When the white man first came to the Calumet area, the Indians had a name for the river and the same name for one lake of the chain of lakes. The largest lake was called Wolf Lake, and the smallest Bear Lake. Lake Calumet survives. On the earliest maps this lake was designated "Konomick," which in an Indian dialect means "snow beaver," or "white beaver." It was somewhat difficult for the white man to understand the lingo of the aborigines. The word "calumet"—meaning "pipe of peace"†—was the one Indian word well known everywhere, and the early white settlers took the grunted "konomick" to be "calumet"—and so it has been for a hundred years or more. Originally known as West Hammond, Calumet City was only a small village in the 1880's, built in and surrounded by marshes, which after every rainstorm well-nigh isolated the community, most of whose inhabitants were immigrants from Germany. The majority of the men found employment in the packing plant of the Geo. H. Hammond Packing Co. "across the border," in Indiana.‡ In that Indiana community, named after the founder of its major industry, Hammond, a Lutheran congregation was organized on October 3, 1882, and named Saint Paul's. Many

*Trinity in Hegewisch was organized on Oct. 1, 1887—about two weeks after the organization of Christ Congregation in Orland Park.

†According to Alfred H. Meyer, "calumet" is derived from "chalumean," meaning "Hollow Reed River." *Toponomy in Sequent Occupance Geography*, Vol. 54, Calumet Region, Indiana-Illinois—Proceedings of the Academy of Science. (Reprint), p. 145.

‡Established in 1869. In 1901 the plant was destroyed by fire, and the company moved to the Union Stock Yards in Chicago.

of the settlers in West Hammond (Calumet City) joined this congregation, but a larger number remained without any church connections. This was due in part to the difficulties of traveling more than several blocks after every downpour and in part to their brief residence in a new and strange land.

One of the members of the school board of the public school—the only public building at the time—desirous of creating a civic spirit in the villagers, one day complained to one of his fellow workers that there was no organization in the village, and then submitted the query: "Why don't you Germans get together and form a church?" Upon being told that no building was available for worship services, the constructive-minded complainant forthwith offered the use of the school building for such purposes. The idea developed into action, and in August, 1887, a meeting of the settlers in West Hammond was called to discuss the project. But who will conduct the services? Someone suggested that the pastor of the dual parish at Cummings Corner (Oak Glen) and Lansing, Ill., the Rev. Carl Dietz, be asked to serve this group as an affiliate of his parish. This was done; and on August 14, 1887, Pastor Dietz conducted the first Lutheran service in the West Hammond public school, located on the site of the present Douglas School. Arrangements were made to have services once every two weeks. These were conductd alternately by Pastor Dietz and the Rev. Carl M. Noack of Saint Paul's Congregation at Dolton-Riverdale. In November, 1888, the Rev. Frederick W. Herzberger, pastor of Trinity Congregation, Hegewisch—a short distance to the north—began serving the West Hammonders as an affiliate of his own congregation. On December 9, 1888, a congregation was organized in West Hammond and named Saint John's.* The

*Charter members:

Carl Lindner	William Gehrke
H. Leber	Fred Kork
M. Neubert	Fred Rohrbein
August Mayer	H. Schulz
Robert Knott	F. Rickmann

Johann Rohloff (unable to attend the organization meeting "because he had to work")

constitution adopted on February 24, 1889, still serves in a translated and somewhat revised form. In July, 1889, Pastor Herzberger accepted a call to Saint Paul's in Hammond, Ind., but continued serving Saint John's as an affiliate of his new parish. From January 1 to June 1, 1891, Pastor Herzberger received ten dollars from Saint John's, presumably as payment for his services. The organist was paid a dollar per Sunday; the janitor received seventy-five cents per month; and someone else received fifty cents for making a copy of the constitution.

In December, 1890, Saint John's purchased three lots at Harding and Gordon Streets for six hundred dollars and erected a church costing, without furnishings, $839.96, more than a third of which amount was contributed by "its sister congregation." The location was so low that the buildings, including the church, were often surrounded by water; this condition was somewhat improved by filling the premises with many loads of sand.

Candidate Theophilus Stephan was ordained and installed as Saint John's first resident pastor on September 6, 1891. His salary was fifteen dollars a month, for which he also opened and taught school. About thirteen months later, however, in November, 1892, he left West Hammond.* Again Pastor Herzberger was called upon to take charge of Saint John's, and a student, Mr. Frese, was placed in charge of the day school. The emergency was terminated on July 2, 1893, when the Rev. Karl Spannuth of South Pittsburgh, Pa., was installed as Saint John's second resident pastor; he also taught school, replacing Mr. Frese. A little more than three years later, in November, 1896, Pastor Spannuth accepted a call to Defiance, Ohio; and on August 1, 1897, Candidate August Biester was ordained and installed as Saint John's third resident pastor. In September, 1898, R. Wambsganss was "hired" as teacher with a monthly salary of twenty-five

*See Chapter 94, page 337.)

dollars. He served for about two years. A student, Mr. Dukow, then taught for one year, and O. Faster took his place in the school.

In 1901 Saint John's was "shaken to its roots" as a result of the "lodge question." Several of the charter members severed their connection with the congregation, and others their connection with the lodge. It was during this year also that the Geo. H. Hammond Packing Company's plant was completely destroyed by fire and that many of the employees followed the company to the Union Stock Yards in Chicago. The majority of Saint John's members remained in West Hammond (Calumet City) and found employment in other nearby industries.

In April, 1904, Saint John's gratefully accepted the offer of Mrs. Freitag to donate one of the three lots on Sibley (147th) and Harrison Streets on the condition that the congregation purchase the two adjoining lots for three hundred dollars. About fourteen years previously her husband, Frederick Freitag, who owned a large part of the real estate in the village, had offered these three lots as an outright donation to the young and struggling congregation; the offer was rejected because of the conviction on the part of many members that the village would expand toward the west, in which case the church "center" would soon be in a very disadvantageous location. The deal proposed in 1904 was soon consummated. During the summer of 1905 William M. E. Laufer succeeded Mr. Faster in the school. Construction work on a new church at the newly acquired site was begun in 1905. The church was dedicated on April 29, 1906—eleven days after the great earthquake in San Francisco, Calif. The first English service in Saint John's history was conducted in the evening of dedication Sunday. The sermon was preached by the Rev. Arthur H. C. Both, pastor of Trinity in Crown Point, Ind.*

*The Rev. A. H. C. Both in March, 1910, succeeded the Rev. Louis Lochner as pastor of First Trinity, Chicago.

In July, 1906, the Rev. Wendelin Linsenmann of Wanatah, Ind., succeeded Pastor Biester, who had accepted a call to North Judson, Ind. By this time the pastor's salary had risen to forty dollars a month. In 1907 Mr. Laufer was succeeded by a student, R. Bruesehoff, who remained for one year. Then came Theo. Breihan. In January, 1901, Saint John's decided to have one English service each month. A Sunday school was established in the same year. In 1910 Mr. Breihan was replaced in the day school by Fred Priehs. In the same year the congregation became a member of the Missouri Synod.

Pastor Linsenmann died on January 20, 1911. His successor, the Rev. Henry P. Prekel of North Plato, Ill., was installed on April 23, 1911. He held this pastorate until June, 1914, when he accepted a call to Waterloo, Iowa. Once again Saint John's looked toward the north and called the pastor of nearby Trinity in Hegewisch, the Rev. A. Wagner. His installation took place on September 6, 1914. At this time also the congregation entered into an agreement with Trinity in Hegewisch by which Pastor Wagner was to reside in West Hammond (Calumet City) but serve both congregations by preaching in Saint John's Church in the afternoon of the first Sunday of each month and in the forenoon on all other Sundays and, vice versa, in Trinity Church. On festival days, however, an assistant was to be provided, so that services could be held in both churches in the forenoon. Trinity of Hegewisch, in turn, agreed to contribute one third of the pastor's salary.

In April, 1919, Pastor Wagner submitted his resignation, because his health was failing. The congregation, however, was slow in accepting it, because it was hoped that his health would improve; but three months later, in July, the pastor's desire was fulfilled. On October 5, 1919, the Rev. Gotthold G. A. Elbert of Park City, Mont., succeeded to this pastorate. At this time the pastor's salary was advanced to one hundred dollars a month. Services in both German and English were begun in January, 1921. After serving Saint John's for about fourteen years, Pastor Elbert in 1933 accepted a call to Grace Congregation in Chicago (formerly known as the Crawford community, with its present "center" at West Twenty-eighth Street and Karlov Avenue). Saint John's next pastor was the Rev. Walter F. Krahn of Neudorf, Saskatchewan, Canada, who served from August 6, 1933, until August 13, 1941, and then resigned. His successor, the Rev. Edward H. H. Gade* of Cherokee, Okla., was installed at Saint John's on November 2, 1941. In August, 1945, Pastor Gade accepted a call to Emerald, Wis., and the Rev. Albert Krahenbil of Oliver, British Columbia, Canada, succeeded him in Calumet City on December 30, 1945.

In addition to those already mentioned, the following trained teachers have served in Calumet City: M. Krueger, Theo. Fruend, Mrs. Werth, Arthur Messerschmidt, H. E. Bundenthal, Erwin J. Buls, Robert Nieting, W. G. Schumann, Miss Faith Brenner, Erlo Warnke, and Richard G. A. Bendick.

After forty-one years of uninterrupted service as chairman of the congregation, Johann Rohloff in December, 1933, was made "honorary president"; he died, aged ninety-two, on February 10, 1935.

113. Chicago, Saint Stephen's

A brief reference to a community on Chicago's South Side, known as Englewood, was made in Chapter 86. Englewood, however, was not this community's original name. Its history goes back to the days when the territory was regarded as some of the most fertile farmland of the prairie. That was when Chicago itself was but a hamlet in the swamp. In the spring of 1852 the first railroad† was built through this territory. "In 1864 there was no Englewood, and even Chicago

*Son of the Rev. E. H. H. Gode, pastor of Immanuel Congregation in Dundee, Ill.
†Now part of the New York Central System.

Junction was a transfer house, or shed, and the depot was at Barney Street (now West Sixty-second). In the latter part of 1852 the Rock Island Railroad was built, coming from the west, and formed a junction and crossed the Michigan Southern at what is now Sixty-third and La Salle Streets. There was a large grove of trees in the vicinity, and the name applied to the district was Junction Grove." Prior to the coming of the railroads the "Grove" was a stopping station on the old stage road from the east. Sixty-third Street was then called Junction Avenue. The first building in this community was a frame school, located on State Street, near Sixty-fifth Street. Later a large brick school building was erected at Sixty-second and School Streets. The name of the latter street has since been changed to Princeton Avenue. The school building for some time served as a town hall and as a school as well as a "church" for all denominations. This entire area was part of what in previous chapters is referred to as the Town of Lake, which was bounded on the north by Thirty-ninth Street, on the east by State Street, on the south by Eighty-seventh Street, and on the west by the Township of Lyons. In 1865, the year in which the third Missouri Synod congregation in Chicago was organized,* the Town of Lake had a population of about seven hundred. In 1868, when First Trinity, Chicago, purchased property for its first school district, in "Bridgeport," from which Holy Cross developed in 1886, the name Chicago Junction was officially changed to Englewood. "At that time the locality—Englewood—was literally a forest of luxuriant oak trees. When the settlers came, the oaks were wantonly cut down, and the maples and elms which today shade the streets have been planted in recent years to take the place of those which were originally placed by the hand of nature."

About the time of Chicago's Great Fire, October, 1871,

*First Trinity—then at West Twenty-fifth and Canal Streets.

there was a rush for homes in Englewood, and the population increased very rapidly. The first church in Englewood was the Presbyterian, at Yale Avenue and Sixty-third Street. In 1882 Lewis I. Musser was the official cow puncher. He herded 110 cows belonging to the people of Englewood and pastured them between Sixty-third and Sixty-seventh Streets, from Wallace to Halsted Streets, and from Sixty-third to Seventy-fifth Streets, west of Morgan. In the summer of 1882 the first street railway was extended to Englewood, the State Street line, and the second, the Wentworth Avenue line, in 1884. On March 16 of the same year the Rev. Fred C. Leeb, since 1882 assistant pastor of First Trinity Congregation, was installed as pastor of that congregation's second "daughter," Saint Martini, then located at Forty-eighth and Ada Streets. In 1886 Saint Martini purchased two lots at Green and Fifty-ninth Streets, which cost $550, and upon them erected a school, which was dedicated on the First Sunday in Advent in 1886. On the same day H. Schulte was installed as teacher of this school. From then on Pastor Leeb came to this branch school every other Sunday to conduct worship services, while the schoolteacher conducted "Christenlehre" every Sunday.

On January 16, 1889, nine members* of the "mother" congregation, Saint Martini, together with seven other Lutheran men, organized "Sankt Stephanus" (Saint Stephen's) Congregation and at once called their own pastor, the Rev. Adolf J. Buenger of Steeleville, Ill. The "mother" congregation sold its property at Green and Fifty-ninth Street for five hundred dollars and permitted Pastor Leeb to serve until the pastor-elect could be installed, which occurred on the first Sunday after Easter, April 28, 1889. In June, 1889, Saint Stephen's purchased five lots on Englewood Avenue (now

*Theo. Budach
R. C. Lange
E. Koch
A. Wettstaedt
C. Orth
F. Boehm
J. Guderjahn
William Dohl
D. C. Cohrs

Sixty-second Place), near Halsted Street, for $3,500 and shortly afterward moved the school from Fifty-ninth and Green Streets to the new site. Before the end of the year also a new church, 45x70 feet, had been built and dedicated (December 15). Three special services were conducted; two in German and one in English, the latter conducted by Professor William Mueller of Concordia College,* Milwaukee, Wis. In 1890, South Englewood was annexed to Chicago, together with a number of other communities, including Washington Heights and Roseland.†

The first day school teacher of Saint Stephen's was teacher-candidate H. C. Wehrs, who was installed on August 10, 1890, but died, after having served only about eight months, on April 22, 1891. He was succeeded by O. F. Rusch of Ottawa, Ontario, Canada, on August 16, 1891. In November of the same year a second class was started in the "vestry" by Miss M. Merbitz. In the summer of 1892 the school building was enlarged; and in 1895 a branch school was opened in a rented building at Sixty-seventh Street and Loomis Avenue, to which Richard Erdmann of Lone Elm, Mo., was assigned. An assembly hall was built in 1897 and a new school in 1902. In 1906 Saint Stephen's purchased property at Sixty-fifth and Peoria (formerly, Spencer Avenue) and in 1907 erected a new school on this site. The old property was sold for six thousand dollars. On January 7, 1909, the church was totally destroyed by fire.

On March 6, 1910, Pastor Buenger conducted a service in a vacant store building at 2041 West Sixty-third Street for a group of Lutherans who one month previously had organized Golgotha Congregation. (See Chapter 171, page 509.)

Saint Stephen's dedicated its new church on September 18, 1910. At that time two English services a month were introduced, and a Sunday school was established.

*Founded in 1881.

†As a result of these annexations, Chicago became the second American city, with a population of 1,100,000.

After serving this congregation for thirty-three years, Pastor Buenger died on September 17, 1924.* His successor at Saint Stephen's, the Rev. Oscar Fedder of Seattle, Wash., was installed on February 8, 1925.

In addition to those already mentioned, the following have taught in Saint Stephen's School:

Robert List	Orville Richter	Miss Ardis Thurow
Miss Helen Pfotenhauer	A. V. Maurer	Edwin L. Kirchhoff
Mrs. Sophie Wassmann	Walter Bleke	Berwyn F. Lemke
Miss Mary Wittrock	E. H. Eggersmann	Fred Hamman
Mrs. Roy Wempen	C. H. Deffner	Candidate Arthur Teschke
Theo. Breihan	Ed. W. Klammer	E. Denys
Bernard Mieger	Miss Bernice Jaster	Miss Milda Naumann
		Mrs. H. Bishton

On February 24, 1946, the Rev. John F. Bauermeister of Fresno, Calif., was installed as assistant pastor. "It is a coincidence that both Pastor Fedder and his assistant are natives of Hammond, Ind., and that both have been called to Saint Stephen's from the Pacific Coast. Both families live in the same house, the congregation having converted the second floor of the parsonage into an apartment."

Mr. Erdmann, who resigned in 1936 after fifty years in the teaching profession, forty of them at Saint Stephen's, continued serving the congregation as financial secretary. He died on July 3, 1944, at the age of seventy-six. A daughter was married to the Rev. Paul G. Prokopy, successor of the Rev. Walter A. Maier as executive secretary of the Walther League, whose headquarters for some years were at 6438 Eggleston Avenue (formerly Dickey Street).†

114. Chicago, Gethsemane

Reverting briefly to the days when the area south of Thirty-ninth Street was still known as the Town of Lake (prior to July 15, 1889), it will be recalled that out there "in the woods and in the prairie" Saint Peter's Congregation was organized on September 5, 1871—a little more than one month before Chicago's Great Fire—by Lutherans who for the most part had

*Lies buried in Bethania Cemetery, on Archer Avenue, near Summit, Ill.
†Formerly the William Tatge residence.

been "guests" of First Trinity at Twenty-fifth and Canal Streets. In the early 1880's that congregation established a branch school at Forty-sixth Street, between School Street (now Princeton Avenue) and Atlantic Street, to which P. Bonneront was assigned. The school opened with twenty-five pupils.

Forty members of Saint Peter's were released to organize a congregation of their own. This was done on June 10, 1889, and the name Gethsemane was adopted. Gethsemane's first pastor, the Rev. John G. Nuetzel of Oshkosh, Wis., was installed on December 22, 1889. Shortly afterward two teachers were called, G. Garbisch for the upper classes and C. F. Martini for the lower. In April, 1893, Mr. Garbisch was succeeded by Carl H. M. Wagner, and Mr. Martini, who had resigned, by Oscar Damkoehler of Colehour (South Chicago) in September, 1895.

The growth of the congregation was rapid, which fact prompted the purchase of a new building site on Dearborn, near Forty-ninth Street, for $4,500. A church was erected here at a cost of $9,185.* Dedication took place the Sunday before Christmas, in 1891.

Pastor Nuetzel served until September, 1916, when ill health compelled him to resign.† His successor, the Rev. Frederick G. Miessler of Hanson Park (Chicago), was installed on December 3, 1916. A Sunday school was organized in 1920. In 1922 the old church was sold, and during the same year a new one was erected at the southeast corner of West Forty-fifth Place and Princeton Avenue (formerly School Street) at a cost of $55,000. It was dedicated on February 4, 1923.

Pastor Miessler retired from the active ministry on July 15, 1942, and moved to Beverly Heights, on Chicago's far South Side. His successor at Gethsemane, the Rev. Paul J. Eickstaedt of Saint Paul's Congregation, two miles northwest of Beecher, Ill., was installed on January 17, 1943.

*The pipe organ cost an additional $2,100.

†Pastor Nuetzel died on Dec. 15, 1918.

The following trained teachers have served in Gethsemane School: B. E. Petrowsky, R. Kassner, B. Zimdahl, C. Boehm, George Duensing, Edward Stelter, W. L. Meyer, and Mrs. W. L. Meyer.

The school was discontinued in June, 1946.

The charter members of Gethsemane were forty in number.*

115. Waukegan, Immanuel

Having visited a large number of cities, villages, hamlets, and crossroads in Lake County, the Trail has not yet stopped at the county seat, Waukegan, Ill.† Until about 1760 there was a French outpost where Waukegan now stands. For a long time after this region had become a part of the United States (1783), the Potawotami Indians continued to live here; in accordance with a treaty, white men were not permitted to settle here until after August, 1836. The first white settler came here in 1835, and the place was known as Little Fort. In 1849 the village was incorporated under the name "Waukegan"—meaning precisely the same thing, "Little Fort." A city since 1859, Waukegan is situated on a bluff about eighty feet above the lake level. Many ravines in the city are bridged for highways. From its elevated site it can be seen for miles, and its proximity to both Chicago and Milwaukee have made the beautiful city a favorite place of resort or summer residence for citizens of both municipalities. "Little Fort Trail,

*Gottlieb Heitner
Robert Haberichter
Ludwig Wehrmeister
Carl Berndt
Herman Voss
August Voss
W. Neumann
August Post
William Freier
Carl Beyer
Frederick Voss
August Bonow
Gustav Wegner
August Hupe
F. Zemke
John Schlaack
Carl Schneider
J. D. Heitner
F. Priebe
Martin Ziemer
R. Riewoldt
F. Thrun
Fred. Paris
Wm. Muschler
Ernst Bruesch
Fred. Jahnke
Fred. Raasch
Henry Drews
Frank Kittler
Jacob Kaross
Ferdinand Roepke
Herman Koehler
Fred. Heger
Fred. Pagel
Theo. Fraedrich
Fred. Klemz
Herman Wachholz
Albert Linde
Julius Voss
William Bonow

†1940 census: 34,241.

a little to the west of the main Green Bay Trail, led from Chicago to Waukegan."

At the corner of South Chapel Street and Glen Rock Avenue, in Waukegan, is Immanuel Church, the oldest and first Lutheran church. Immanuel Congregation was founded by pastors of the Wisconsin Synod in 1890 and organized in 1891,* when the congregation was composed of only nine Lutheran families. A Sunday school was established at that time. From 1889 until 1892 Immanuel was served once a month by Pastors August Bendler and E. Dornfeld of Milwaukee, Wis., and A. Jackel of Racine, Wis. Since 1892 the following served as resident pastors: the Rev. J. W. Koch, 1892-1893, who then accepted a call to a suburb of Milwaukee; the Rev. John Plocher, 1893, who within the same year accepted a call as missionary to the Apache Indians in the State of Arizona; the Rev. Julius Gamm, 1893-1895, who thence went to La Crosse, Wis.; the Rev. Martin Sauer, from 1895 to 1900, when he accepted a call to Brillion, Wis.; the Rev. Theodore Volkert, 1900-1908, then going to Racine, Wis.; the Rev. Richard O. Buerger, 1908-1923, when he accepted a call to Milwaukee, Wis. The Rev. A. C. Bartz has held this pastorate since 1923.

116. Rugby

The Trail now goes on a long stretch—a distance of about 110 miles—from Waukegan, county seat of Lake County, to Pontiac, county seat of Livingston County, in the heart of Illinois' corn belt, this time, however, merely to get acquainted (with more things than the State Reformatory). As yet the Missouri Synod is not represented by a church in this beautiful village on the Vermilion River. It is the year 1890. The Trail is scheduled to return to Pontiac about forty-two years hence, in 1932. About seven miles east by northeast from Pontiac is a very small community known as Rugby, for which

*Charter members: Gustav Geither, H. Zoehler, J. Braasch, Otto Mueller, Nicholas Hette, August Soldan.

no census figure is given, but here is a Lutheran church, organized in 1890 and named Saint Mark's. In recent years this congregation was served as an affiliate of Trinity in Pontiac, by the Rev. Otto C. Simonsen.* In 1947 the Rugby parish was merged with Trinity in Pontiac. Saint John's Congregation in Union Township is also served by him. Unfortunately there are no other historical facts available for inclusion in the Trail's narrative.

117. Pingree Grove

Northward from Rugby through the counties of Grundy and Kendall, and into the northeastern part of Kane—a total of about eighty miles—to another "Grove." Several years have elapsed since the Trail contacted a "grove"—away down south in Iroquois County, Ash Grove—and now it has arrived at one called Pingree, a name of perplexing origin. What is or are "Pingree"? Pending search for the etymology of this word, inquiry will proceed about the development of Lutheranism at Pingree Grove, Ill.† The hamlet is located about eight miles northwest of Elgin, but an additional perplexity is that the past history of Pingree Grove is "hazy, because the records were lost in a fire."

It is assumed that the Rev. Herman F. Fruechtenicht, pastor of Saint John's Congregation in Elgin, at intervals conducted services here in the middle 1880's. During the latter part of 1889 the Rev. Otto Gruner, pastor of Saint Peter's at North Plato, began to conduct services here. In the following year, 1890, Saint Peter's Congregation at Pingree Grove was organized.‡ In 1895 Pastor Gruner followed a call to Saint

*The names of only two former pastors were available up to the time of "going to press": Otto Pannkoke and Henry F. Meyer; the latter has been pastor of Saint John's Congregation at Coopers Grove since 1929. In 1947 Saint Mark's Congregation jointly with Trinity in Pontiac built a new church in the latter village.

†1940 census: 130.

‡Charter members:

Albert Bahr
William Braun
Albert Kremp
Herman Mick
Ferdinand Nimtz
Ferdinand Radde
Albert Thrun
Herman Thrun

Paul's in Rockford, Ill., and his successor at North Plato was the Rev. Ernst August Sieving, who continued the precedent set by Pastors Fruechtenicht and Gruner. In September, 1896, a school building, which had been purchased and converted into a church, was dedicated. In 1900 Pastor Sieving accepted a call to Lincoln, Nebr. At this time, then, Saint Peter's at Pingree Grove called its own pastor, the Rev. William Otto Joseph Kistemann, who served from 1900 until 1907, when he accepted a call to Emmanuel Congregation in Dwight, Ill. Then came the Rev. Henry P. Prekel from Hubbell, Mich., who served from September 15, 1907, until April, 1911, and then accepted a call to Saint John's Congregation in Calumet City (formerly, West Hammond), Ill. For about one year then Saint Peter's of Pingree Grove was without a resident pastor, but the Rev. Mr. Hamann of Elgin conducted services until the next pastor, the Rev. Otto Hitzeroth of North Prairie, Wis., was installed on April 21, 1912. Pastor Hitzeroth's pastorate here extended over a period of about twenty-five years.*

In June, 1935, Saint Peter's at Pingree Grove purchased the church building belonging to the Congregationalists, remodeled it for Lutheran worship, and dedicated it on June 21, 1936.

Other facts concerning this congregation are included in the history of Saint Peter's at North Plato. (See Chapter 82, page 319.)

118. Lena

From Pingree Grove the Trail proceeds to Rockford, and from there another forty miles west by northwest to Lena, Ill.,† where the Rev. Henry G. Schmidt, pastor of Immanuel Congregation in Freeport, came to gather in the Lutherans

*The Rev. Otto Hitzeroth died May 22, 1937.

†1940 census: 1,169. Named from the Plain of Lena in the poem "Fingal," by Ossian.

of this region and in 1890 organized Saint John's Congregation. But they did not build a church. Instead, they bought the old Methodist church; and for a while their existence was exiguous. From 1890 until 1920 the expense of maintaining the pastor was shared with Salem Congregation of Richland, about eight miles northeast of Lena, likewise organized under the leadership of Pastor Schmidt, in 1890. From February 1, 1891, until July, 1903, these two parishes were served by the Rev. Emil Meyer, called from Cordova, Nebr. He then accepted a call to Saint John's in Pecatonica, Ill. On January 17, 1904, the Rev. Frederick August Scharfenberg, heretofore pastor of Saint Paul's at Elizabeth, Ill., was installed as pastor of the dual parish. He served for almost five years, until November, 1908.* His successor, the Rev. Frank C. Ahrens of Bertha, Minn., was installed in December, 1909; he served until April, 1911, and then accepted a call to Sabin, Minn.† Then came the Rev. O. Johannes Buenger of Iuka, Ill. Installed in May, 1911, he served until September, 1919, when he accepted a call to Mount Carroll, Ill. The Rev. Louis H. Beto of New Rockford, N. Dak., was installed on December 21, 1919. In 1923 the Rev. Frederick Kroeger of Hinckley (Squaw Grove), Ill., was placed in charge of Salem Congregation at Richland and of Faith Congregation,‡ whose center is located about three miles west of Winslow, sometimes called "Christian Hollow," about a mile from the Illinois-Wisconsin State line. After fifty-one years of service in the active ministry Pastor Kroeger retired on January 1, 1940.§ Since that time Pastor Beto of Saint John's in Lena has also been serving Salem Congregation.

Two "sons" of Saint John's entered the ministry within recent years: George J. Beto, since January 16, 1949, president

*It was he with whom the Mission Board publicly sympathized. See "Elizabeth"—Chapter 91.

†Pastor Ahrens died on Jan. 3, 1945.

‡Formerly a member of the Ohio Synod (American Lutheran Church), Faith Congregation in August, 1923, joined the Missouri Synod.

§Pastor Kroeger died on Jan. 20, 1943, aged eighty-one.

of Concordia College, Austin, Tex.,* and Lee W. Steffen, pastor of Immanuel Congregation in Clearwater, Nebr.

119. Highland Park

In the history of Glencoe (Gross Point), Ill., reference was made to a near-by community known as Highland Park,† where in the middle 1840's a number of German immigrants had settled who shortly afterward requested the Rev. C. August T. Selle, pastor of the first Missouri Synod congregation in Chicago—First Saint Paul's—to minister to their spiritual needs. Beginning in 1850, Pastor Selle came up here by oxcart and once a month conducted worship services in private homes. A congregation was organized in 1853. Pastor Selle's successor, the Rev. Henry Wunder, or one of his assistants, continued this activity until August, 1874, when Trinity Congregation at Glencoe called its own pastor, the Rev. Edward Doering. The Lutherans of Highland Park were served as an affiliate of Trinity. Beginning in May, 1888, they had their worship services in McDonald's Hall and later in Evans Hall. In May, 1890, the Rev. John Adam Detzer became the first resident pastor of the Lutherans in Highland Park. In the same year the congregation purchased property on Central Avenue, at the foot of McGovern Street. Here a church was erected during the following fall and winter. Formal organization of the congregation took place on January 1, 1891.‡ The new church was dedicated on April 26, 1891. The church architect, Andrew A. Beck, constructed an altar and donated it to the congregation; Charles Unbehauen, in 1895, donated the church bell. In 1897 a school was opened, and taught by the pastor until 1906, when it was closed.

*Founded in 1926.

†1940 census: 14,476. So named from its high elevation above the lake, and because it was located in a natural park.

‡Charter members:

Fred Arnswald	Julius Johnson	Fred Rudolph
Gottfried Arnswald	Henry Lawrentz	Henry Ohlwein
William Arnswald	George Leffert	George Schumann
Fred Garling	William Markgraf	Christoph Staebling
George Huber		Charles Wetzel

Pastor Detzer resigned on April 25, 1897. His successor, the Rev. August F. A. Sallmann, temporarily without a charge, previously at Ashland, Ky., was installed as Redeemer Congregation's second resident pastor. In 1898 Redeemer Congregation joined the Missouri Synod.

From a report submitted to the Illinois District convention in 1900 comes this quotation: "Die dortige Gemeinde kann nicht von grossem Zuwachs reden. Es ist eine aristokratische Vorstadt, ein theures Pflaster." ("The congregation there"—in Highland Park—"cannot speak of much accession. It is an aristocratic suburb, an expensive place to live in.")

Pastor Sallmann died on October 8, 1900, aged about thirty-five. On November 25, 1900, his successor, the Rev. Albert Baumann of Kouts, Ind., was installed as the flock's third resident shepherd. He served until October, 1905, when he accepted a call to Immanuel Congregation in Elmhurst, Ill.

The Rev. Alvin W. C. Starck of Clay Center, Kans., succeeded Pastor Baumann at Redeemer on January 28, 1906, and served until December, 1910, when he accepted a call to Bergholz, N.Y.* His successor in Highland Park was the Rev. William F. Suhr, "Reiseprediger" in Oregon and Washington. His installation took place on May 21, 1911. In the same year a graded Sunday school was established. One of its teachers, Mrs. W. E. Hundley, served for thirty years. After Pastor Suhr's resignation in 1941 the Rev. H. K. Platzer of Cleveland, Ohio, became Redeemer's sixth resident pastor on January 11, 1942. The following Redeemer members continued their membership unbroken for fifty years: Mrs. Edward Eichler, Mrs. Charles Geminer, Otto Lawrentz, Miss Anna Ohlwein, and Mrs. Minna Quadt.

120. Chicago, Bethany

En route to Chicago this time the Trail picks up a printed reproduction of a recent India-born visitor's impressions of

*Pastor Starck died on Aug. 20, 1936, in Detroit, Mich.

"America's second city." "I have struck a city—a real city, and they call it Chicago. I urgently desire never to see it again. It is inhabited by savages. Its water is the water of the sewers, and its air is dirt. I spent two hours in the huge wilderness, sauntering through miles of those terrible streets, and jostling some few 100,000 of these terrible people who talked through their noses." One wonders how far Rudyard Kipling got beyond the Loop during his two-hour visit. Perhaps it was at about the time of this English novelist's visit that First Saint John's Congregation (1890) established a school district in the Humboldt community, purchased two lots for $1,150, and moved its old original school* to the new site, corner of Cortez Street, near Rockwell Street. Here worship services were conducted by the Rev. Edward Pardieck, assistant pastor of First Saint John's since the previous summer (1890)—at first, every two weeks and, a little later, every Sunday. On May 28, 1891, eighteen men gathered in this school for the purpose of organizing their own congregation.† The name Bethany was adopted. Its first pastor was the Rev. Edward Pardieck, who also continued teaching school until January, 1892, when L. H. Gilster assumed this responsibility. First Saint John's donated the entire property to Bethany. The building, "the old cradle" of First Saint John's, was still standing at 2612 Cortez Street a few years ago.

In August, 1892, Bethany purchased five lots at the corner of Humboldt Avenue and North Rockwell Street for thirty-five hundred dollars, and a twenty-thousand-dollar church building was erected on this site. The church, of brick con-

*This school originally stood at the corner of Cornell and Superior Streets. It contained one classroom and a "home" for the teacher.

†Charter members:

John Kuenn
William Rennhack
Carl Gierke
Fred Hoeft
Carl V. Marozick
Carl Drewitz
Fred Bresemann
Fred Dettmann
Carl Moench
Julius Kusch
C. Nimtz
Robert Schmidtke
John Marozick
Fred Holz
August Marozick
August Kassulke
Ernest Mueller
William Burchat

struction, was equipped with a 125-foot steeple and two bells in the tower. A second classroom was opened in June, 1893, and Carl Winter succeeded Mr. Gilster as teacher. On September 10, 1893, while the World's Columbian Exposition on Chicago's South Side was in full swing, Bethany Church was dedicated. In the same autumn the Misses Marie Strieter and Ida Drews were added to the teaching staff. In 1896 it became necessary to build a larger school, costing about eight thousand dollars; it was dedicated on August 9, 1896. The old property was sold. Others who served in Bethany School during this period were C. Strieter, J. Kalbfleisch, J. Zitzmann, E. Harks, Chr. Voss, and Carl H. M. Wagner.*

In the fall of 1902 Pastor Pardieck accepted a professorship at Saint Paul's College in Concordia, Mo. His successor, the Rev. August Burgdorf of Lincoln, Ill., was installed as Bethany's second pastor on October 26, 1902. At this time the congregation's communicant membership was 931; the enrollment in the day school was 215. The first English service, combined with the rite of confirmation, was conducted on December 27, 1908. The peak of Bethany's "prosperity" was reached in 1910: 1,103 communicants and a school enrollment of 230.

Because of adverse living conditions in this community early in the 1920's, many members moved away and joined "sister" congregations. Threatened with gradual disintegration, the congregation resolved to sell the property at Cortez and Rockwell and to move farther west.

During the preceding period, beginning 1911, the following were added to the teaching staff: Emil G. Garske, R. J. Schulz, Theo. Wunderlich, Walter Berndt, Miss Hagg, and Miss Th. Ferber.

In 1924 Bethany purchased several lots at the corner of Harvey and Greenfield Avenues in "the world's largest vil-

*His father, the Rev. Anton Wagner, was pastor of First Zion, Chicago, 1868-1909.

lage," Oak Park, with the intention of erecting temporary buildings. The price was $14,658. Local sentiment against the erection of a public building in a strictly residential zone, however, prevailed against carrying out this plan; those lots, therefore, were sold, and instead, the northeast corner of Wabansia and Narragansett Avenues in the Galewood community, was purchased for $12,350. A combination church and school was erected at the far eastern end of the site, facing Wabansia Avenue. Dedication took place on April 11, 1926. The old property was used for several more years, and Pastor Burgdorf conducted worship services in the new building twice a month. A Sunday school was begun with only four pupils, and the day school with eleven. The first teacher in the latter was H. Boester. He was succeeded by E. Nickel, and he, in turn, by John Kosche.

The old property on Cortez Street, which had previously been sold, was completely vacated on November 1, 1930. On the previous evening a stone was hurled through a window, almost striking the chairman of the voters' assembly. A costly Hallowe'en prank!

In 1933 Elmer F. Fiebig joined the teaching staff. Five years later, on July 15, 1938, Pastor Burgdorf died.* His successor, the Rev. Paul J. Roeder, heretofore pastor of Messiah Congregation in the Clearing industrial area in the southwestern part of Chicago, was installed on November 13, 1938. Mr. Kosche resigned in July, 1944, and Walter Mueller succeeded him in October, 1944. In May, 1945, Mr. Fiebig accepted a call to Fort Wayne, Ind. In November, 1945, Mr. Mueller accepted a call to Frohna, Mo., and Arthur Scheiwe came to Bethany. On the teaching staff, more recently, have been Miss Gertrude Pennekamp, Mrs. Augusta Mensing, and Arnold Bathje, Jr.

On May 4, 1947, ground was broken for the erection of a

*In 1922 Pastor Burgdorf visited the mission fields in South America for the Missouri Synod.—He is buried in Saint Lucas Cemetery, Chicago.

new church of Gothic design, with a seating capacity of 340 in the nave and 325 additional in the annex. The dedication followed on June 20, 1948. The cost of the new church, completely furnished, is $116,000.

121. Chicago, Concordia

When visiting First Bethlehem's "daughter," Christ Congregation in the Logan Square community, it was reported that this "daughter" opened a branch school in the Avondale area, where many of its members were residents. In 1888 Mrs. Sophie Bauermeister provided the building for the new venture, and shortly afterward the school was opened with an enrollment of seven children, in charge of Student Siegert of Concordia Seminary, Springfield, Ill. On alternate Sundays the Rev. Ernst Werfelmann, pastor of Christ Congregation, conducted worship services here. On June 29, 1891, six members* of this congregation organized Concordia and immediately called its first pastor, the Rev. Paul Brauns, then assistant pastor of Saint Matthew's Congregation in Chicago (2100 West —2100 South). His installation took place on July 19, 1891. At a special meeting held on July 22, 1891, the offer of Mrs. Sophie Bauermeister to donate two lots on California and Center Avenues as well as the school building was gratefully accepted. The membership grew very rapidly as this community was being populated by Chicagoans from the older settlements and by immigrants from Europe. In the autumn of 1891 the building which had been used since 1888 had become too small to accommodate the worshipers. In December the congregation received as a gift a good portion of the southeast corner of Belmont and Washtenaw Avenues. Here, then, a large church was erected within the next year. It was dedicated in April, 1893. The first day school teacher,

*Charter members:

F. Bauermeister	C. Brietzke
H. Kummer	A. Rehbein
C. Schuenke	J. Bauermeister

Paul Appelt, was installed in the following September. A second classroom was opened in 1894.

In May, 1895, Pastor Brauns unexpectedly resigned his pastorate at Concordia and with a majority of the members organized an "opposition congregation," with which he then joined the Evangelical Church. Reminding Lutherans of a statement made by the first President of the Missouri Synod, the Rev. C. F. W. Walther: "Sollte jemals der unter uns gegenwaertig noch helleuchtende Leuchter von seiner Staette gestossen werden, so geschaehe dies allein aus unserer eigenen, grossen, schweren, erschrecklichen Schuld." ("Should the now bright-shining lamp in our midst ever be thrust from its position, it would be by our own great, grievous, and terrible fault.")

The small "remnant" of Concordia was in a difficult and precarious situation. However, its spiritual needs were soon supplied when another pastor, the Rev. Carl F. Dietz of Cummings Corner (Oak Glen), Ill., was installed as its pastor; the financial needs were supplied largely by "sister" congregations, not only in Chicago, but in various parts of Illinois.* Within one year after the unfortunate disruption Concordia's membership had doubled, and the second class in the day school, which had been temporarily discontinued because of the defection, was again established, with the pastor serving as teacher until 1900, when Ernest J. Kemnitz assumed this responsibility.†

In the summer of 1901 Concordia Congregation established a mission in the Irving Park community—about a mile and a half northwest of Belmont and Washtenaw. The Rev. Ferdinand Doederlein of Jackson, Mo., was called as assistant pas-

*The distressed condition of his congregation was presented by Pastor Dietz to the delegates at the Illinois District convention in Chicago, 1897, who resolved to recommend that the congregations of this District contribute toward the support of this needy congregation, Concordia.

†Deafness compelled Teacher Kemnitz to resign in 1930. He died on June 29, 1942. A son, the Rev. Walter J. Kemnitz, has been pastor of Saint Paul's, Dolton-Riverdale, Ill., since 1924.

tor, with the special assignment of conducting worship services and carrying on mission work in the Irving Park community. In November, 1906, Pastor Dietz accepted a call to Milwaukee, Wis. At the same time the Irving Park mission was organized as an autonomous congregation and named Tabor. Its first pastor was the Rev. Ferdinand Doederlein, the "mother's" assistant pastor. O. H. Ziemann was the first day school teacher. (See Chapter 156, page 482.) Succeeding Pastor Doederlein to the Concordia pastorate was the Rev. Alfred E. Reinke, since 1900 pastor of Zion Congregation in Roseland (far South Side of Chicago). He was installed on December 16, 1906. At the same time F. Meyer was added to the teaching staff.

In 1931 a ninth grade was added to form a junior high school; this was discontinued when the Board of Education of Chicago abolished the plan.

After serving Concordia Congregation for about thirty-six years, Pastor Reinke died very suddenly during the second worship service on Sunday, January 24, 1943. As he stepped into the vestry after completing his second sermon, he collapsed and died instantly. He lies buried in Saint Lucas Cemetery. Concordia's fourth pastor, the Rev. Frederick John Pfotenhauer* of Trinity Congregation at Bachelors Grove (two miles north of Tinley Park), Ill., was installed on April 4, 1943. In September, 1948, he accepted a call to New Germany, Minn., and on January 23, 1949, the Rev. August C. Waechter of Bunker Hill, Ill., was installed as his successor at Concordia.

In addition to those already mentioned, the following teachers have served Concordia's day school: Miss Clara Doederlein, 1897-1905; Miss Emma Doederlein, 1902-1905; John H. F. Vornsand, 1917-1924; William Gutowski, 1920; Theodore Zwick, 1924-1939; Theodore Gassner, 1926-1930; Miss A. Nolte, 1930; Hugo Gehrke, 1932-1939; George Albers, 1940-1948;

*Youngest son of the Rev. Frederick Pfotenhauer, D.D., President of the Missouri Synod, 1911-1935.

Herman Ernst, 1940-1948; Miss Holst, 1900-1930; Armin Gutekunst, Victor Kalbfleisch, Mrs. J. Rieck, Miss Esther Seegert, Student C. Sieving, C. A. H. Eickemeyer, Elmer L. Bellhorn, Werner von Behren, and Mrs. Howard Kraegel.

122. Chicago, Christ (English)

Tarrying a little longer in Chicago, because its schedule does not call for another visit until 1893, the Trail at this time seeks to ascertain what truth there is in the reported organization of a Lutheran congregation "which was not involved in the German-language problem." This particular congregation originally was not an English-speaking one. It evolved from the first Norwegian Lutheran congregation in Chicago, whose place of worship was located at Erie and Franklin Streets, a comparatively short distance from the site of the little church in which the Missouri Synod was organized (Superior and La Salle Streets). The first pastor of this Norwegian congregation was the Rev. A. Mikkelsen.

About eight months after the Missouri Synod had been organized, the Rev. Paul Anderson came to Chicago for the purpose of organizing a mission started by a certain Mr. Thompson, into a congregation. On February 14, 1848, about thirty members of this mission were organized as the First Norwegian Lutheran Congregation. According to another source, the Rev. John G. Schmidt, delegated to Chicago by the Evangelical Lutheran Synod of New York . . . succeeded in the winter of 1847-1848 in inaugurating a Norwegian Evangelical Lutheran church and in erecting a place of worship on the north side of the river "capable of accommodating all the Norwegian population in this city." "Migrations of Norwegians to the United States on a large scale began in 1825, when the small sloop *Restaurationen,* which sailed from Stavanger, Norway, on the ninth of October, landed in New York with fifty-three immigrants . . . the majority of whom settled on farms in Morris and Kendall Townships, Orleans County, New York." Later, immigrants from Norway were directed to Illinois, more specifically to the fertile valley of the Fox River; a few of them settled at Beaver Creek, about ten miles south of Lake Michigan on the Illinois-Indiana State line. An estimated half million Norwegians had settled in the United States by the turn of the century. According to W. W. Sweet, "from 1870 to 1910 one and three-quarter million Northmen came to American shores, one half of whom were Swedes, while Norway furnished one third, and Denmark a sixth of the total."

In a comparatively short time, Pastor Mikkelsen's field of activity in Chicago became an industrial area, which resulted in the congregation's decision to sell its property at Erie and Franklin Streets and to disband. In 1891 the proceeds of the sale were divided between two groups which had already drawn up plans to organize two separate congregations. One of these was then organized as Lake View Lutheran Church, the other as Christ English Evangelical Lutheran Church. The latter received $5,556.90 as its share of the property's sale. Meanwhile two other Scandinavian congregations had been organized, Saint Paul's Norwegian at 2219 West North Avenue and Saint Peter's. The pastor of the former, the Rev. I. B. Torrison, and the Sunday school superintendent of the latter, Dr. J. K. Bartholomew,* deeply interested in the English movement, called upon the Rev. Louis Hoelter, pastor of First Immanuel Congregation (Ashland Boulevard near Twelfth Street) and with him discussed the feasibility of organizing an English Lutheran congregation to be fostered by the Missouri Synod. Pastor Torrison guided the movement until the Rev. A. Sloan Bartholomew of Springdale, Ark., and member of the Norwegian Synod, arrived in May, 1891, to take charge of the new venture, which was partially subsidized by the "German Pastoral Conference."

*Not a clergyman; presumably, a physician.

The new congregation, Christ English, was organized on September 14, 1891, by eight men.* Pastor Bartholomew's pastorate was very brief. He died at the age of thirty-three years, about three months after the congregation had been organized. Thereupon the Rev. Frederick W. Herzberger, pastor of Saint Paul's Congregation in Hammond, Ind., assumed the pastoral duties at Christ English until the Rev. H. J. G. Bartholomew† of Franklin, Pa., a brother of the deceased pastor, was installed on June 19, 1892. Shortly afterward the congregation purchased property on North Hoyne Avenue and Augusta Street, within one block of First Saint John's Church, and there built a "basement church." It was used for services for the first time in September, 1893; the superstructure was built within the next two years, and on November 10, 1895 (the 412th anniversary of Dr. Martin Luther's birthday), the church was dedicated.

A grievous difficulty resulted from the resignation of Pastor Bartholomew on October 3, 1898. Calls were issued to various pastors, but all were declined. Then a call was sent to the Rev. Ernest F. Haertel in Baltimore, Md., and it, too, was declined. The latter call was repeated, but forwarded to the Rev. William Dallmann, also stationed in Baltimore, with the request that he present it in person with cogent reasons for accepting it. He did this; and the pastor-elect came to Chicago to be installed on October 15, 1899. During the previous year, 1898, Christ English Congregation's very close neighbor, the German First Saint John's, became "particularly interested in English missions, primarily in the struggling English Lutheran Christ Church on Hoyne and Augusta. There was

*Charter members:

Rev. A. S. Bartholomew	Louis W. Peterson
Dr. J. K. Bartholomew	Charles A. Peterson
George Markhus	Herman Arneson
Niles Peterson	Louis O. Hauge

†A "colloquium committee," composed of the Rev. W. H. T. Dau and the Rev. William Dallmann, examined him and declared him qualified as a Lutheran pastor. Christ Congregation's second pastor became a member of the English Missouri Synod in May, 1893.

a heavy debt of $6,000 at 6 percent interest on the property, too heavy a load even to raise the interest. In our July meeting, Pastor Succop made a strong Pentecostal appeal, urging support of this our only English Lutheran congregation in Chicago, as well as organizing more English congregations, in order that Lutheranism may be preserved in Chicago. The voters heartily concurred, took the matter up in the August meeting, and a committee of five was elected to make recommendations.... In November the committee recommended that the Chicago sister congregations should be asked to raise the entire interest for five years. It was voted annually to lift an offering for Christ Church and to try to find a few members to pay the interest on $1,000. In a later meeting it was reported that this had been accomplished, a few members paying the necessary $60. When Pastor Haertel came to Christ Church, he was repeatedly invited to preach English in our church, and Christ Church was given the offering. —This is the place to answer the question why St. John's did not itself much sooner take up the work in English. The answer is: There was no demand to preach English until much later. The very few whom the pastors of St. John's found on their visits who preferred English they gladly turned over to Christ Church, especially since we located within one block of Christ Church on Hoyne Avenue."* About two years after Pastor Haertel's arrival, Christ English became self-sustaining. After worshiping at North Hoyne Avenue and Augusta Street for about thirty years, the congregation "avoided the fate of the 'mother' church" by selling its property to the Armenian Apostolic Church and moving westward about five miles, to the northeast corner of North Long Avenue and Le Moyne Street, in the Austin area. The property was purchased at a very reasonable price from Saint Mark's Norwegian Congregation. (See Chapter 140, page 450.) The first

*First Saint John's sold its property on Superior Street and moved to Hoyne Avenue and Walton Street in 1905.

service at the new location was conducted on April 8, 1923.

On September 6, 1925, the old property on Hoyne Avenue was sold, with the right to use it every Sunday and three days a week until May, 1926. Meanwhile a new church was being erected at the new location. Dedication took place on December 12, 1926.

Pastor Haertel, who had participated in the establishing of not a few other congregations in Chicago and vicinity, died on January 24, 1938.* His successor, the Rev. Warner H. Grothman of Berwyn, Ill., was installed as Christ English Congregation's fourth pastor on May 15, 1938. He served for nearly nine years, when he died on January 6, 1947, at the age of forty-eight years.† On July 6, 1947, the Rev. Richard C. Stuckmeyer of South Bend, Ind., was installed as Christ Congregation's next pastor.

123. Chicago Heights

The Trail proceeds to the "Heights," found by following Halsted Street in Chicago to its extreme south limit, in Chicago Heights, Ill.,‡ "at the crossroads of the nation"—Lincoln and Dixie Highways. The original name was Bloom, the name given to the district by a shoemaker of Chicago, Karl Sauter, in honor of Robert Blum, son of the cooper of Cologne, in whose person the liberty of Germany was saved by the declaration of martial law in Vienna.

The first Lutheran service in the Bloom community was a funeral service for the little daughter of Mr. and Mrs. Theodore Griese, in 1882. It was conducted by the Rev. Barthold Burfeind, pastor of Immanuel Congregation at Skunks Grove, (Sauk Trail and Cicero Avenue), in the Griese home on McEldowney Place. For some time services were continued there

*Pastor Haertel is buried in Saint Lucas Cemetery, Chicago.

†Pastor Grothman preached for the last time on Sunday, Dec. 29, 1946, on the words: "Lord, now lettest Thou Thy servant depart in peace." Luke 2:29.

‡1940 census: 22,461. Named from Chicago by a real estate company. It is located upon higher ground than Chicago.

until the Rev. Carl Keller of Thornton assumed charge of the little flock as an affiliate of his congregation. Then services were conducted in the old Presbyterian church, which was provided free of charge. Organization of the congregation took place on January 10, 1892, and it was called Saint Paul's. On September 28 of the same year the young congregation purchased a lot on the northeast corner of Chicago Road and Fourteenth Street for $350 and upon it erected its first church building, 26x40x12, including a steeple. Dedication followed on January 22, 1893. On August 18, 1895, Candidate Karl Henry Schroeder, graduate of Concordia Seminary, Springfield, Ill.,* was ordained and installed as Saint Paul's first pastor. On September 4 a day school was established and, presumably, taught by the young pastor. During the school year 1894-1895 Student Carl Gutekunst was in charge, and from 1895 to 1899 the pastor also served as schoolteacher.

On November 26, 1899, Saint Paul's second church was dedicated. About two months previously L. Homeier, graduate of the Teachers' Seminary at Addison, had been installed as teacher. After serving for only about one and a half years, he died; his successor, L. Fuhrmann, was installed on August 18, 1901. In 1902 another instructor was added, Miss Christine Schweer, who served for almost twenty-five years. In August, 1924, L. Brackmann replaced Mr. Fuhrmann. He remained until 1907, when he accepted a call to Danville, Ill. His successor at Saint Paul's was teacher-candidate F. C. Wilker. In October of the same year Pastor Schroeder accepted a call to Tobias, Nebr., and on October 13 the Rev. Henry G. Sandvoss, assistant pastor at First Zion Church in Chicago,† became Saint Paul's second resident pastor. In June

*His brother, the Rev. Gottlieb Schroeder, was pastor of Immanuel Congregation at Squaw Grove (near Hinckley), Ill., 1888-1905.

†West 19th and Peoria Streets. (Pastor Anton Wagner was Pastor Sandvoss' stepfather.)

Mr. Wilker resigned, and Arthur H. Eggers took his place. In May, 1911, Mr. Eggers followed a call to First Saint Paul's School in Chicago, and Frank Himmler of Immanuel Congregation, Elmhurst, Ill., succeeded him.

In February, 1913, Pastor Sandvoss accepted a call to Saint Peter's Congregation in Joliet, Ill., and on July 20 the Rev. Henry G. W. Kowert of Cordelia, Calif., succeeded him as Saint Paul's third pastor. A serious throat ailment compelled him to resign temporarily from the active ministry in December, 1914.* The next pastor was the Rev. Gottlieb Bauer of Decatur, Ind. During his pastorate in Chicago Heights the day school enrollment grew to more than 150 pupils. Christian Seidel replaced Mr. Himmler in 1917, but resigned about two years later, in July, 1919. Then came Walter Gotsch; Martin Hesemann of Zion Congregation in Summit, Ill., was also added to the teaching staff.

Because of failing health Pastor Bauer resigned on April 14, 1926; and in the fall of the same year Miss Christine Schweer died. Pastor Bauer's successor was the Rev. Arthur August Brauer† of Webster City, Iowa, who was installed as Saint Paul's fifth pastor on June 27, 1926. During the same year P. W. Wassmann took charge of Miss Schweer's former classes, and Louis Heidemann of Port Huron, Mich., replaced Mr. Gotsch, who had resigned because of impaired health in June, 1928. Other teachers at Saint Paul's, in recent years, were Mrs. A. A. (Dorothy) Brauer, Mrs. Raymond Stelter, Clifford Braun, Mrs. Otto Stogentin, Miss Frieda Strasen.

Plans for the erection of a new church are now being formulated by Saint Paul's Congregation in Chicago Heights.

*Pastor Kowert was installed as First Saint Paul's (Chicago) pastor on Sept. 16, 1917; he held this pastorate until Aug. 18, 1944, when he died (at Wheat Ridge, Colo.)

†Son of the Rev. Albert H. Brauer, pastor of Saint Paul's Congregation, two miles northwest of Beecher, Ill., 1880-1915. Arthur August Brauer was born there about twenty days before the official opening of the World's Columbian Exposition in Chicago, May 1, 1893, on April 11, 1893.

124. Elmhurst, Immanuel

Some of the early settlers a few miles southeast of Duncklees Grove were either natives of the South Midland area in England or people who had a liking for Middle English words, of the style used by the "father of English poetry," Goeffrey Chaucer.* "Hurst" means "grove." The settlement there was named Elmhurst† instead of Elm Grove, or Elmgrove, Ill., formerly known as Cottage Hill.

It is not surprising that Lutheranism spread to this area; surprising it were if its influence had not been felt also in Elmhurst, in view of the fact that for quite a number of years the community was virtually surrounded by German Lutherans, with centers at Duncklees Grove, Schaumburg (Sarah's Grove), "Franzosenbusch" (Proviso), York Center, and others. But almost fifty years elapsed before a Lutheran congregation was organized in Elmhurst, formerly known as Cottage Hill. It is true that one of the professors at the Teachers' Seminary at near-by Addison, the Rev. T. Johannes Grosse, did mission work here, or at least supervised it, beginning on March 9, 1879. It was then that seven members of Zion Congregation‡ established a school district in Elmhurst. It was at once decided to purchase four lots for $265 and to erect thereon a school building, 34x22x12, adorned with a small steeple ("mit einem kleinen Thuermchen geziert"). By the following August the building was complete. The total cost, including all appurtenances,§ amounted to $821.31. The "mother" congregation agreed to call a teacher for this southern district school. The teacher's salary—if single—was to be two hundred dollars plus free board

*Died 1400 A.D.

†1940 census: 14,458.

‡Charter members:

Louis Balgemann	Wilhelm Gaedke
Friedrich Rohmeyer	Heinrich Plagge
August Graue	Wilhelm Hanebut
Ernst Balgemann	

§The price included a well.

and laundry. The choice was left to the faculty of the Teachers' Seminary. August Baeder was chosen. His installation was combined with the dedication of the school building on August 3, 1879. A few years later Mr. Baeder took to himself a wife, and Zion Congregation placed an $825 home at the disposal of the young couple and doubled the teacher's salary. Free board and laundry, of course, ended.

On March 14, 1892, the group at Elmhurst organized its own congregation, which it named Immanuel, and coincidently joined the Missouri Synod. Until the completion of Immanuel's first church, at the corner of Michigan and Third Streets, Mrs. J. B. Bryan's chapel (mortuary?)* on Saint Charles Road was used for worship services without cost to the congregation. Immanuel's first pastor, the Rev. John George Hild of Altamont, Ill., was installed on August 7, 1892, in the local public school auditorium. The new church was dedicated on October 23, 1892.

In 1894 small bells were attached to the contribution baskets, or bags, so that the worshipers might hear when the receptacles were coming for their "gifts" ("damit die Leute hoeren, wenn der Klingelbeutel kommt"). "Some of these Klingelbeutel were masterpieces in their field. Handles were beautifully carved, and the bags, generally of velvet, were hand-embroidered and weighted by a golden tassel." Whether or not in any of the churches of the northern Illinois area devices were used to awaken sleepers during church services has not been determined. John Rudge, in the year 1725, bequeathed to the parish in Trysall, Shropshire, twenty shillings a year that a poor man might be employed to go about the church during the summer and keep the people awake. At Acton Church in Cheshire one of the church wardens used to go around in the church during service with a huge wand in his hand, and if any of the congregation were asleep, they were instantly awakened by a tap on the head. At Dun-

*Cottage Hill was renamed Elmhurst by Thomas H. Bryan.

church in Warwickshire a similar custom existed. A person bearing a stout wand, shaped like a hayfork at the end, stepped stealthily up and down the nave and aisles, and wherever he saw an individual asleep, he touched him so effectually that the spell was broken—this being sometimes done by fitting the fork to the nape of the neck. A more playful method is said to have been used in another church, where the church officer went around the edifice during service carrying a long staff, at one end of which was a fox's brush, and at the other a knob. With the former he gently tickled the faces of the female sleepers, while on the heads of the male offenders he bestowed with the knob a sharp rap. Thus far such or similar customs have not come under the Trail's observation.*

In 1894 Mr. Baeder followed a call to Christ Congregation in Cleveland, Ohio,† and shortly afterward G. H. Abel took his place in Elmhurst. A second school building was erected in 1901 for the accommodation of the ever-increasing day school enrollment. In 1904 Miss Anna Hild was placed in charge of the lower grades.

After a pastorate of a little more than thirteen years, Pastor Hild died of a heart ailment on December 16, 1905, at the age of about sixty-two years. In the same month—at Christmas time—the Missouri Synod's new Catechism‡ was introduced as a "gift to the school children." Pastor Hild's successor at Immanuel, the Rev. Albert Baumann of Highland Park, Ill., was installed on November 5, 1905. About two years later Otto Stahmer was called to relieve the pastor of the duties in the school. In 1910 Mr. Abel resigned, and Frank

*Neither has it come across problems arising from a certain weed, which in certain places warrants the "friendly" advice of a certain lecturer, who said: "Take your quid of tobacco out of your mouth on entering the house of God, and gently lay it on the outer edge of the sidewalk or on the fence. It will positively be there when you come out, for a rat won't take it, a cat won't take it, a dog won't take it, neither will any other animal. You are certain of your quid when you go after it." *Lutheran Witness*, VIII, No. 16, p. 102.

†The third Missouri Synod congregation in that city—organized two years before Immanuel in Elmhurst, 1890. The first Missouri Synod congregation in Cleveland, Trinity, was organized in 1857.

‡Dr. H. C. Schwan's *Exposition*.

Himmler took his place, serving from September, 1910, to July, 1911. On March 5, 1911, Pastor Baumann reported that because of a nervous affliction ("Nervenleiden") he was compelled to resign. His successor, the Rev. Carl Abel of Mount Olive, Ill., was installed on May 11, 1911; during the same summer Ed. Matthes of Portage, Wis., was installed as teacher in the upper class. In 1912 the first English services were conducted in Immanuel Church, and an English mission was begun on the south side of the village. Sixteen years later a congregation was organized in that area and named Redeemer.

In 1914 the two old school buildings, having become inadequate, were sold and a new four-classroom brick school was erected on Third and Illinois Streets at a cost of about fifteen thousand dollars. The dedication took place on December 27, 1914. At the same time English services were begun on Sunday mornings. In 1920 another teacher was added to the staff, Ed. Piepenbrink; in October, 1922, F. A. Meitz was installed. In 1926, for the first time in Immanuel's history, the rite of confirmation was performed in the English language. Paul G. Kolander served in the day school from 1925 to 1926; Miss Ada Gresens, 1926-1928; and Mrs. Elenor Rathjen, 1928. William F. Bertram came in January, 1930. In addition to the latter, the following have served in more recent years: Miss Lorraine Pflug, M. F. Wessler, Miss Lenore Kluender, Miss Erica Runge, and Carl Burger. Mr. Stahmer died in 1944. Candidate John A. Mau was ordained and installed as assistant pastor on February 7, 1937. He served until August, 1943, when he accepted a similar position at Zoar Congregation in Elmwood Park, Ill. Pastor Abel retired on July 12, 1943, but upon the congregation's request remained as honorary pastor. The Rev. E. T. Lange of St. Louis, Mo., was installed as Immanuel's fourth pastor on January 30, 1944. Pastor Abel died suddenly on March 13, 1947.

125. Melrose Park

Hursts and groves, glens and dales, prairies and fields, gardens and forests, springs and lakes, brooks and ports, points and heights, hills and ridges, moors and parks, burgs and shires, villas and villages, towns and townships, cities and skyscrapers—what an array of words to designate localities and communities! Elm, Oak, Ash, Willow, Walnut, Sycamore, Cherry, Deer, Wolf, Skunk. All picturesque except the last (that one, too, if at a safe distance)! But who ever heard of a melrose? Referring to the Italian language "de celesta" the word "mela" means "apple"—also the word for "rose" is "rosa." Putting these two words together produces "Melarosa" —hence the English "Melrose," as confirmed by the dictionary: "Melarosa is a fragrant fruit of the genus 'Citrus' as 'Citrus Bergamia,' the bergamot orange or 'Citrus Limetta,' a kind of lime."

Melrose Park* is twelve miles west of the Loop—on the old Indian trail, now Lake Street—or less than ten miles southeast of Duncklees Grove. An early record states that "many years before the turn of the century" Saint John's Congregation at Harlem (Forest Park) had debated the advisability of conducting preaching services somewhere in Maywood† in order to serve the numerous German Lutherans who were moving into this new territory. The records of this congregation indicate that such services were held.

Beginning in April, 1889, worship services were conducted on alternate Sunday afternoons in the town hall of Maywood, at Fifth Avenue and Saint Charles Road. Meanwhile a school building was being erected at Eleventh Avenue and Lake Street. After its dedication on July 28, 1889, the services were conducted in this building. On June 8, 1892, twenty-four

*1940 census: 10,933. Named from Melrose Abbey in Scotland.
†Maywood is located about one mile east by southeast of Melrose Park.

voting members* of Saint John's Congregation in Harlem (Forest Park), under the direction of the Rev. F. Martin Grosse, organized Saint Paul's Congregation. Shortly afterward a church was erected on the Eleventh Avenue-Lake Street site, and the dedication took place on November 26, 1893. Saint Paul's first day school teacher was William Leeseberg, who served until 1899, being succeeded at that time by Herman Voigt. In 1903 the old school building was replaced by a new four-room brick building. Saint Paul's first resident pastor, the Rev. Emil Zapf, assistant pastor at First Saint John's in Chicago, was installed on December 11, 1892, in the town hall of Maywood. In 1894 the congregation became a member of the Missouri Synod. Pastor Zapf taught school for about eight years, 1894-1902. In 1901 Mr. Leeseberg was replaced by Theo. J. Wichmann; in the same year Karl Markworth was added to the teaching staff. Meanwhile L. Dethen had served from 1890 till 1899. O. Sippel relieved Pastor Zapf of classroom work in 1902 and served until 1904. M. Heinicke was added to the staff in 1903. F. Meitz came in 1906 and served until 1912. In 1909 Mr. Markworth's place in school was taken by L. Rehwinkel, who served until 1911. Herman G. E. Maudanz served during the years 1913 and 1914; C. Wild in 1921; Armin Zapf, 1921-1922; E. Trusheim, 1922-1934; John Schroeder,† 1922-1941; E. Lewerenz, 1925-1932; H. Nichol, 1929-1930; R. Rosenthal, 1940; Paul Bussert, 1940-1942; and Mrs. E. Danker, 1940-1942. Other teachers in recent years were

*Charter members:

Carl Schnake	Wilhelm Radke	Ernst Amling
C. A. Amling	Albert Kuhlmann	Wilhelm Andermann
Christoph Warnecke	Heinrich Warnecke	William Leeseberg
Albert Amling	Friedrich Koehn	John Mueller, Jr.
William Haase	Christoph Wichtendahl	Hermann Bloedel
Johann Link	Fritz Epske	Peter Wuemede
Christian Amling	Friedrich Kurdt	John Mueller, Sr.
Fritz Koch	G. Ellberg	Gustav Schmidt

†Teacher Schroeder died on June 12, 1942—about two and one-half hours before a congregational meeting at which he was to be officially informed of having been elected as honorary elder of St. Paul's. He was a native of Woodworth, Ill.

A. H. Kramer,* A. E. Doering, Louis H. Phillips, P. F. Stohlmann, M. J. Weiss, R. A. Wetzstein, Miss Rose Backhaus.† Miss Myrtle Krause, Herman Krafft, Mrs. Carl Halter, Paul B. Bouman, Miss Phyllis Wisniewski (now Mrs. George Yursky), M. W. Eggerding, Miss W. Schroeder, R. E. Rickels, Miss Beatrice Kimblin, Edward V. Nolte, Emil H. Deffner, Miss Veleda Kelm, Miss Frieda Daenzer, Arnold C. Erxleben, Elmer Arnst, Miss Ethel Novak, Mrs. Marvis Middendorf, Miss Hertha Gotsch, Miss Anne Eissfeld, Mrs. Mildred Seboldt, and Gerhardt F. Klammer.

The Rev. Paul Kolb served as assistant pastor at Saint Paul's from 1906 until 1942, when he died.

In 1924 a third building was erected on Saint Paul's property; this building comprised additional classrooms, meeting rooms, bowling alleys, and another auditorium. The high point of enrollment in the day school was 641, in 1926. In 1927 failing eyesight prompted Pastor Zapf to relinquish his pastorate. Soon after, he accepted a position as missionary for the Lutheran City Mission Society of Chicago and environs.‡ His successor at Saint Paul's was the Rev. Paul L. Kluender, formerly of Ellendale, N. Dak., who had been previously installed as assistant pastor, on April 8, 1923. His son, Marcus Richmann Kluender, was installed as assistant pastor on September 8, 1935.

Saint Paul's has two "daughter" congregations: Bethlehem in River Grove (organized in 1896) and Bethlehem in Broadview, about two miles south of Melrose Park (organized in 1925). In other cases Saint Paul's encouraged—specifically by the release of members—the founding of congregations in Maywood and Bellwood—the latter, about one mile southwest. Saint Paul's School has maintained a perfect dental

*Commissioned April 20, 1947, as Assistant Director of Christian Education, Northern Illinois District.

†In September, 1944, she had completed 40 years as teacher of the first grade at St. Paul's School, Melrose Park, Ill.

‡Pastor Zapf died on July 22, 1937.

NOTE: On Sept. 21, 1947, members of St. Paul's Congregation joined with Mr. Ferdinand Jeschke—a member since March, 1893—in celebrating his 100th birthday.

record for sixteen consecutive years.* On January 19, 1947, the children's chorus appeared in a concert in Rockefeller Memorial Chapel on the campus of the University of Chicago.

Other clergymen who have served as assistant pastors at Saint Paul's, Melrose Park, in recent years were the Rev. Edward A. Koehler, D.D., professor at Concordia Teachers College, River Forest, and the Rev. Carl S. Meyer, principal of Luther Institute, Chicago.

Mr. H. G. Amling and his wife, prior to celebrating their golden wedding on August 27, had requested relatives and friends not to remember them with personal gifts. When such, nevertheless, arrived, the jubilarians remitted the $2,075 which they received to various treasuries of our Church. Mr. Amling is a prominent Chicago layman who has served the Northern Illinois District for many years and is still a member of its Home Mission Board. The Lutheran Laymen's League and the Valparaiso University Association have also been the beneficiaries of his talents and gifts.†

126. Chicago, Saint Philip's

The year 1892 had ushered in the World's Fair era for Chicago, "giving beauty to the world as well as commercial and industrial skill."

In 1893 the World's Columbian Exposition occasioned much excitement, particularly on Chicago's South Side, with its Ferris Wheel and White City. There was excitement, too, on the city's North Side, more subdued and unnoticed by the general public—in the Ravenswood community. It was here that the Rev. John E. A. Mueller, pastor of Saint Luke's Congregation, in what until 1890 was known as Lake View, on December 11, 1892, conducted the first service for a small group of Lutherans in a little Swedish church located

*This record was held by the graduating classes. The school's health and dental programs have received State and national recognition in the publications of the medical profession.

†*Lutheran Witness*, LXVIII, 19, p. 302.

at the corner of Robey (now Damen Avenue) and Ainslie Streets. On August 6, 1893, Saint Luke's placed William H. Ganske* in charge of its branch school in this community and gave him the additional assignment of carrying on missionary activities. Within about forty days this school district developed into an autonomous congregation. On September 16, 1893, organization of "Die evangelisch-lutherische Sankt Philippus-Gemeinde zu Ravenswood, Ill." was effected by thirty-three men.† While a church was under construction at Lawrence and Oakley Avenues, Pastor Ganske conducted worship services in a vacant store building at Seeley and Lawrence Avenues. On September 25, 1896, the new church was dedicated. The building which up to this time had served as a place of worship was moved to the new site and converted into a school. In 1905 the congregation became self-sustaining. In the same year a trained teacher, E. Karnatz, relieved Pastor Ganske of the schoolteaching responsibilities. Mr. Karnatz served for about five years, and F. Ziegele‡ took his place in Saint Philip's School. In 1926 a breakdown in health necessitated granting leave of absence for Pastor Ganske. His resignation followed before the close of the same year.§ On November 7, 1926, Candidate Edward C. Kuehnert was ordained and installed as assistant pastor, with the more specific assignment of taking charge of all pastoral activities in the English language. Great losses of membership had resulted from the continuance of the day school in the German

*A son of William H. Ganske, first day school teacher at Saint Matthew's in Chicago, born on Aug. 14, 1870.

†Charter members:

Otto Ristow	Carl Godglick	Carl Fielehr
Ferdinand Rehfeldt	Carl Hoppe	Ludwig Ristow
Carl Mueller	August Duwe	Henry Dierks
Matthew Jenne	George Kroeck	August Lohrke
Fritz Pagels	Carl Kunow	Ernest Ristow
Julius Vorkastner	Albert Kerbs	Wm. Amtsfeld
Andrew Martins	Ernst Bucholz	Carl Bernhard
William Lange	William Schultz	Carl Engel
Carl Koth	Albert Kunow	C. W. Behm
Henry Schwartz	Ferdinand Rehfeldt, Jr.	Fred Kasch
Carl Kasehull	August Fehlberg	Adam Trendel

‡Mr. Ziegele died in March, 1926.

§Pastor Ganske resigned in October, 1926. He died on Oct. 15, 1943.

language exclusively—the principal factor in the decision to close the school in 1929. A Mrs. Arnswald was placed in charge of the school in March, 1926, to complete the school year. In September, 1927, Mrs. Scheel* succeeded her in school and served until the congregation closed the school.

For some time Saint Philip's had given serious thought to disposing of its property and moving to a more quiet neighborhood; the site finally selected was at the northeast corner of Bryn Mawr and Campbell Avenues. From 2300 West and 4800 North the congregation's "center" was changed to 2500 West and 5600 North in 1928—from a commercial center to a rapidly growing residential community. In 1929 the old site was sold to the Northern Athletic Club. The final services in the old church were held on May 26, 1929. The new church was dedicated on July 15, 1929. Soon afterward occurred the economic depression, which "left its mark of calamity also upon Saint Philip's Congregation."

In September, 1937, the day school was reopened and partially supported by the Mission Board of the Northern Illinois District. Milton E. Marten, graduate of Concordia Teachers College, River Forest, Ill., took charge of the school at that time. In 1939 a kindergarten was started, with Mrs. Estelle Wolter, a member of the "mother" congregation, Saint Luke's, in charge. In 1940 a second classroom was opened, and Miss Marie Meyer was assigned to the lower grades. Miss Edna Messerschmidt replaced Miss Meyer in September, 1942; and Lawrence Rush was added to the staff in September, 1944. Others who have recently served were Miss Pauline Beyer, Miss Norma Mueller, W. M. Borchers, Miss Ann Pigors, Mrs. W. M. Borchers, and Rudolph W. Dobberfuhl.

In June, 1941, Pastor Kuehnert accepted a call as chaplain in the United States Army, and Candidate Victor C. Rickman was engaged to serve during the leave of absence. When

*The former Miss Flora Kuehnert, sister of the Rev. Edward C. Kuehnert. Their father, the Rev. F. G. Kuehnert, former executive secretary of the Missouri Synod's Board of Support and Pensions.

Chaplain Kuehnert, however, informed the congregation of his intention to continue in the military service longer than the period of time agreed upon, Saint Philip's retained the substitute as its pastor. Pastor Kuehnert's resignation became effective in February, 1942,* and Candidate Rickman was ordained and installed as Saint Philip's third pastor on April 12, 1942.

127. Chicago, Holy Trinity (Slovak)

In connection with the review of First Saint John's history, attention was directed to a group of Lutheran Slovakians, which had its services in the large hall of the three-story school building at Superior and Bickerdike (now Bishop) Streets under the leadership of the Rev. Ladislav Boor. This was in the year 1890. "In 1888 there were at the most fifty or sixty Slovaks in Chicago, but by 1892 there were between five and six hundred." Many of them were Lutherans. After years of oppression in their homeland they took advantage of every opportunity which the United States offered. On October 8, 1893, these Slovak Lutherans organized Trinity Congregation—the first Lutheran congregation in Chicago to be organized by Americans of Slovak descent.† Many at first refused to affiliate because it was not their intention to remain in this country, but to recoup their family fortune and then return to Slovakia. Meanwhile they lived in crowded boarding houses.

The scarcity of Slovak Lutheran pastors in the United States induced the "fathers" to look across the sea to Slovakia for a pastor. They selected and called the Rev. Ladislav Boor. A church was erected in 1901.

*In October, 1945, the Rev. E. C. Kuehnert, discharged from the chaplaincy, was installed as institutional missionary at Saginaw, Mich.

†A partial list of charter members:

Joseph Dianis	Paul Surak	John Bliska
John Svatik	Samuel Papanek	John Rechtoris
Paul Kvorka	Martin Papanek	Paul Cermak
John Vrablik	Stephen Mosny	Joseph Domko
Joseph Miskoci	Daniel Bella	Samuel Seplak
John Slahor	John Bozik	John Sopocy

In the era 1894-1914 many immigrants came from Nitra and Turiec in Slovakia. "In keeping with their clannish custom, they invariably settled in one certain section of the city; they saw certain advantages in living and being together." The areas around Milwaukee and Elston Avenues, and those adjacent to Halsted and Eighteenth Streets on the near South Side were almost entirely Slovak. Slovakian was the medium of conversation in the streets and in the stores.

In 1901 Trinity opened a branch congregation on the West Side, which was named after Saints Peter and Paul; and in 1902 they jointly became members of the Slovak Evangelical Lutheran Synod, but this affiliation was terminated in 1909.

In October, 1904, Pastor Boor accepted a call to Braddock, Pa. His successor was the Rev. John Somora of Slovakia, who was installed as Trinity's pastor in April, 1905, and shortly afterward opened a day school. He was "a stern disciplinarian . . . and caused great dissatisfaction among the members." In 1909 he resigned, and the same year Samuel Durkovic was placed in charge of the school. Pastor Somora's successor, the Rev. Samuel Lichner, was installed in July, 1910. On June 8, 1911, Trinity purchased Saint Peter's Lutheran church building at Chicago Avenue and Noble Street for twenty-three thousand dollars; it was rededicated as Trinity Church on Trinity's eighteenth birthday, October 8, 1911. In more recent years many members of Trinity have been moving to other parts of the city, particularly into the Mayfair and Jefferson Park districts. Therefore, in 1923 Trinity made provision for the northwestward trend and changing conditions. A corner lot at Kilbourn and Wilson Avenues was purchased and a chapel with a seating capacity of 175 erected, the basement being equipped as a schoolroom.

After serving for twenty-seven years, Pastor Lichner was compelled by failing health to resign in 1937.* His successor

*Trinity Congregation retained Pastor Lichner as "pastor emeritus."

was the Rev. Jaroslav J. Pelikan. Then regular services in the English language were begun at both churches. In the same year Mr. Durkovic, who resigned because of illness, was replaced by John Bezek; in 1942 Mr. Bezek, in turn, was replaced by Andrew Socha.

Several years ago Trinity purchased a new building site on the west side of Lacrosse Avenue, between Elston and Foster Avenues, an "irregular quadrangle," comprising almost two acres. A new church costing approximately $500,000, was erected on this site during 1949.

The Slovak Lutheran Church "has emerged from the state of seclusion into which we were placed by our language. We were spoken of, often in somewhat of a condescending tone, as 'the Slovak Church,'" according to the Rev. Stephan G. Mazak, editor of *The Lutheran Beacon*. "Not so long ago your Editor was called by a pastor of one of the synods affiliated with us 'a missionary among the Slovaks,' and amazement was expressed by this pastor that we could speak English so fluently. Of course, we are proud of that title 'Slovak.' But conditions have changed. Our youth has become Americanized and in many instances is marrying those of other nationalities. These changing conditions brought about the result that in all of our churches English services are being conducted."

Pastor Pelikan's son, Jaroslav Jan Pelikan, Jr., graduate of Concordia Seminary, St. Louis, Mo., was installed as assistant pastor of Trinity in June, 1946.*

128. Chicago, Bethel

The year 1894 vividly recalls Coxey's Army and the Pullman strike. The latter caused great suffering among the Lutherans of Zion Congregation in Roseland on Chicago's

*The young assistant pastor received the degree of Doctor of Philosophy from the University of Chicago on Dec. 20, 1946. (At age 24.) In the fall of 1946 he accepted a professorship at Valparaiso University, Valparaiso, Ind. In the fall of 1949 he became instructor at Concordia Seminary, St. Louis, Mo.

far South Side. The World's Fair "Dream City" was gone; so was Mayor Carter H. Harrison—the victim of an assassin's bullet, on October 28, 1893. Chicago suddenly became a "black city." The Trail, therefore, leaves the city briefly to explore the then so-called "outskirts of Chicago."

Early in 1891 a certain man came to the Rev. Martin Fuelling, pastor of Emmaus Congregation, the center of which was at California and Walnut, with the information that a number of Lutherans had located in a district a few miles to the northwest. A personal canvass helped this pastor to verify the report, which was soon brought to the attention of the Illinois District's Mission Board, and permission was granted to open a school in that community. Pastor Fuelling's congregation, Emmaus, was requested by the Mission Board to furnish several school desks, which request was readily granted; and soon afterward Pastor Fuelling began teaching in the new school housed in a frame store building at the northwest corner of Lawndale and Chicago Avenues. After about four months he was assisted by a seminary student. After some time the combination church and school was transferred to a home on Fortieth Avenue, now Monticello Avenue; thence to a home on Avers Avenue; from there to Star Hall at Grand and Crawford Avenues (now Pulaski Road—in the city). It was here that five members of Emmaus Congregation together with several other Lutheran men on June 22, 1894, organized Bethel Congregation.* Its first pastor, Candidate Eugen Pfund, was ordained and installed on September 2, 1894. For some time afterward church and school were at Kamerling and Crawford Avenues. At this juncture, mention should be made of the 300th birthday anniversary of King Gustav Adolf by the Missouri Synod congregations

*Carl Palenski
Johann Hinz
Johann Hauht
Christoph Gellersen
Heinrich Leverenz
Otto Mews
Friedrich Urban
Johann Henning
Johann Ruettenborges
Albert Zobel

in Chicago, held in Central Music Hall* on December 9, 1894.

On July 10, 1895, Bethel Congregation purchased two lots at the northwest corner of Springfield Avenue and Frederick (now Hirsch) Street and upon it erected a school and a parsonage. Pastor Pfund taught school for about six years, assisted at first by his wife and later by students. In 1901 J. Stellwagen was installed as teacher. He served for about three years, until 1904, when he was succeeded by George W. Nolting. Miss Paula Duever assisted in the lower grades for about three years, when she accepted a similar position at Christ School of Logan Square, Chicago. Her successor in Bethel School was Miss Emily Buszin. Mr. Nolting died on September 30, 1910, and P. F. W. Otto took his place in Bethel School. During 1910-1911 a new church was erected for $37,645.35 and dedicated on May 14, 1911.

Ill health prompted Pastor Pfund to resign in June, 1914.† His successor, the Rev. Leo Schmidtke, professor at Concordia Collegiate Institute,‡ Bronxville, N.Y., was installed on August 9 of the same year. In the following month Herman Schroeder was added to the teaching staff. He served until 1918, when he accepted a call to Saint Andrew's School in Chicago. Fred J. Uttech taught in Bethel School until the spring of 1926, when he accepted a call to Saint Andrew's School in Park Ridge (Brickton), Ill. Herold H. Pollex became his successor on July 20, 1926. Mr. Otto died on March 30, 1927, and his place was taken by E. Born on June 12, 1927.

A new school costing $77,557 was erected in 1929, and dedication took place on September 16 of the same year. Walter C. Berndt was then added to the teaching staff, and

*Opened on December 5, 1879, by the Apollo Musical Club concert, this hall was razed in 1901 to make room for enlargement of Marshall Field & Co. store The hall was located at the southeast corner of Randolph and State Streets.

†Assisted in schools of Immanuel in Des Plaines and Saint Peters, Schaumburg, 1914-1926; also assisted in the Orphan Home, Addison, 1926-1933. From there he went to Mondovi, Wis., where he made his home with a brother.

‡Founded in 1881.

NOTE: A son, Werner Schmidtke, was pastor of Trinity Congregation, Hampshire Ill., 1929-1947.

in the following year Mrs. Danker was engaged as assistant teacher.

Pastor Schmidtke died on November 8, 1934. His successor, Candidate William Boehm, a "son" of Bethel Congregation, was ordained and installed on January 27, 1935. In June, 1937, Miss Buszin was relieved of her work in the school and awarded a pension; she died at the age of 81 years on May 5, 1947. On August 29 Karl Helmkamp, Jr., was installed as teacher. Candidate Victor Kamprath was installed on September 29, 1940. Other teachers in Bethel School were Miss Minnie Kohn, Mrs. A. Barman, Mrs. T. Gose, Miss Esther Abel, Miss T. Leitz, Miss Norma Kretzmann, Miss Marg. Preuss, and Miss Anna Jean Petersen.

129. Chicago, Trinity, Hanson Park

Reference to Hanson Park was made in Niles (Dutchman's Point) by the Rev. J. Adam Detzer, Sr. He mentioned something about starting Lutheran mission work in that community 'way back in the year 1894—the year of so many disturbances here and elsewhere; the year also when the inhabitants of Cuba revolted against their Spanish overlords.

The first Lutheran worship service in what was then regarded as the northwest corner of Chicago was conducted in a public hall on October 25, 1894. This was continued on alternate Sundays for about a year, and on January 13, 1895, eight men organized Trinity Congregation. Shortly afterward a building site was acquired on Major Avenue, near Belden Avenue, and a frame church erected, dedication taking place on August 18, 1895. Candidate Henry Moldenhauer was installed as Trinity's first pastor on August 18, 1895. The church was partitioned off to provide room for school purposes, and the pastor taught four and a half days a week. Pastor Moldenhauer served until September, 1900, when he accepted a call to Saint John's Congregation in

Algonquin, Ill. He was succeeded at Trinity on November 25, 1900, by the Rev. Fred W. Mahnke of Joplin, Mo., who remained only until January, 1902, when he accepted a call to West Chicago (formerly Turner Junction), Ill. After a vacancy of a few months the Rev. Herman L. Pflug became Trinity's third pastor on March 9, 1902. He served until November, 1909, and accepted a call to Bethlehem Congregation in South Chicago (formerly Colehour); his successor at Trinity, Hanson Park, the Rev. Frederick G. Miessler of Batavia, Ill., was installed on January 16, 1910. Trinity's first day school teacher, Daniel L. Toenies, was installed on September 1, 1907. In 1912 the old school was set upon a concrete foundation and remodeled. Then, in 1915, Mr. Toenies followed a call to Grace Congregation's day school in Chicago (the former Crawford community), and J. Kastner of First Saint John's, Chicago, took his place at Trinity.

In November, 1916, Pastor Miessler accepted a call to Gethsemane Congregation in Chicago, and his successor, the Rev. F. C. Israel of Glencoe, Ill., was installed in Hanson Park on January 7, 1917. In the following summer Mr. Kastner was forced by illness to resign, and Carl Busse of Yorktown, Iowa, replaced him in September. When Mr. Busse left in 1919, August C. Bernahl of Fergus Falls, Minn., took charge of Trinity School. For several years students from Concordia Teachers College, River Forest, assisted in the school: O. Schuettel, 1918-1919; Arthur Messerschmidt, 1919-1920; and Walter Lauing, 1920-1921. The last mentioned, upon graduating, was formally added to Trinity's teaching staff.

In August, 1921, Pastor Israel accepted a call to Clarinda, Iowa, and was succeeded on October 30, 1921, by the Rev. J. C. G. Horsch of Yellowhead (about six miles northeast of Grant Park), Ill. In March, 1922, Mr. Lauing followed a call to Immanuel Congregation in Des Plaines, Ill., and G. Derer served as substitute until June. Mr. Bernahl followed a call to Saint Paul's Congregation at Dolton-Riverdale, and William J. Eggers of Uniontown, Mo., succeeded him in Hanson Park in August, 1922. In the same year Miss L. Engel was engaged to teach, and in September, 1924, Miss J. Wegmann came. The last to serve in the second classroom was Mrs. H. Luecke, from September, 1929, to December, 1930. Abrupt changes occurred during the ensuing economic depression, and many of Trinity's members moved to other sections of the city, which resulted in closing the second classroom on January 1, 1931. Pastor Horsch died suddenly on October 6, 1934, and Candidate Stuart William Nothnagel was engaged to serve as "interim pastor," but on December 9, 1934, he was installed as the congregation's seventh pastor. In September, 1937, Sunday school was started in a store at 6005 Diversey Avenue, and the first worship service was conducted on November 25, 1937. This place served as church and school for almost a year. In the fall of 1939 the old property at Major and Belden was sold with the proviso for use until July, 1940. On March 23, 1941, the new church at the corner of Wrightwood and Meade Avenues was dedicated. In 1942 Pastor Nothnagel was granted leave of absence to serve as "service pastor" for the Missouri Synod's Army and Navy Commission for one year. Candidate Richard J. Krueger, graduate of Concordia Seminary, Springfield, Ill., was appointed to serve during his absence, but when Pastor Nothnagel decided to remain in the service of the Army and Navy Commission, Candidate Krueger was ordained and installed as Trinity's eighth pastor on June 20, 1943.

Besides those already mentioned, the following have served in Trinity School: Mrs. Herbert Loose, W. J. Eggers, Miss Betty Humphrey, Student Robert Mueller, Miss Alyce Birr, Lewis J. Kuehm, and Miss Margaret Alt.

130. Momence

Momence, Ill.,* is a village located about ten miles east of Kankakee on the Kankakee River. It was named for a half-breed Potawatomi chief, Momenza, and is near the point where Colonel Gurdon S. Hubbard and his troops crossed on their way from Danville to Fort Dearborn (Chicago) at the beginning of the second quarter of the nineteenth century, during the Black Hawk campaign.

As early as 1885 Danish Lutherans began to settle in this section of Illinois. For some time worship services were conducted in private homes, usually on Sunday afternoons, by neighboring clergymen belonging to the Norwegian Synod. The first church building was erected in 1897 on the south side of the village, and south of the river.

In 1930 the members of this congregation applied to the Rev. Daniel C. Hennig, pastor of Calvary Congregation in Watseka, about twenty-seven miles south of Momence, for services, and in 1931 the congregation's desire to be served by pastors of the Missouri Synod was fulfilled. Pastor Hennig served the congregation, known as Our Savior, for about one year.† On July 26, 1931, the Rev. Frederick A. Graef of Rochester, N.Y., became Our Savior Congregation's first resident pastor. He likewise served for about one year and then accepted a call to Delray Beach, Fla. During a prolonged vacancy the Rev. Karl A. Guenther of Yellowhead served, and in the fall of 1934 the Rev. Chr. Adam of Emblem, Wyo., became the congregation's second resident pastor. A short time later, in December, 1934, the old church was destroyed by fire,‡ whereupon the congregation worshiped in a vacant store building on Washington Street, near the heart of the village. In the fall of 1938 Pastor Adam

*1940 census: 2,452.

†Pastor Hennig served the congregation in Momence as an affiliate of Calvary Congregation in Watseka, Ill.

‡All the church records were destroyed at that time.

accepted a call as institutional missionary for the Northern Illinois District in the State Hospital at Manteno, Ill., about eight miles northeast of Kankakee. His successor in Momence, the Rev.Louis Otto Walper of Waverly and Denver, Iowa, was installed as the third resident pastor of Our Savior Congregation on November 5, 1939. On July 12, 1941, Pastor Walper and his wife met with a serious accident; the automobile in which they were riding was struck by another automobile traveling at terrific speed through the village on the Dixie Highway. Mrs. Walper was fatally injured.

On April 4, 1943, a new church of brick construction, 32x65 feet, at Second and Pine Streets, was dedicated. By the end of the same year Our Savior Congregation in Momence was out of debt.

131. Chebanse

About eighteen miles southwest of Momence is another village which does honor to a former Indian chief of the Potawotami tribe, Chebanse, which means "Little Duck.*

It is the year 1895. The Trail finds a group of Lutherans in Forester Hall, Chebanse, intent upon organizing a congregation. The effort failed at this first meeting, principally for the reason that there was no Lutheran pastor to guide them. It was therefore decided to meet again for the same purpose on August 3 and to invite the Rev. Frederick Schroeder, pastor of Saint Paul's Congregation in Kankakee, to assist them. A constitution was adopted† at this meeting, and Zion Congregation came into being. Plans for a new church were presented and adopted at a meeting held on August 11, 1895. Within less than four months the church was completed, and

*1940 census: 603.

†Among the signers were:

Henry Lesch
Edward Irps
William Wilkin
William Friese
William Behm
George Ritter
C. Ruebensam
William Schultz
John Konow, Sr.

it was dedicated on December 22, 1895.* Zion's first pastor, the Rev. Ferdinand W. Seehausen of Clay Center, Kans., was installed on February 16, 1896. He served Zion Congregation for about twenty-eight years, resigning on account of failing health on July 6, 1924.† He preached his farewell sermon on Sunday, August 10, on the lawn of the Otto Nordmeyer home. In the same year the church was enlarged and a basement constructed at a cost of about twelve thousand dollars. In November, 1924, Zion extended a call to the Rev. Walter W. Winter at Cushing, Okla. His installation as Zion's second pastor took place on February 8, 1925, which was also the occasion for the rededication of the remodeled and enlarged church building. In 1927 the congregation became a member of the Missouri Synod.

In the July, 1925, voters' meeting the matter of establishing a day school was submitted but postponed for two weeks. By a "ballot vote" it was then resolved to proceed with definite plans, which included the calling of a trained teacher. A piece of property comprising two and 65/100 acres, including a building, was purchased in January, 1926. The building was remodeled and arranged for school purposes, and in September, 1926, the school began to function. The following have served as day school teachers: Waldemar Graf, A. Boehme, M. Wunderlich, C. Brauer, L. Winter, R. Finke, W. Haak, E. Schuricht, W. Rittmueller, H. H. Lipske, and A. H. Peters.

In January, 1946, the congregation resolved to erect a new school building of fireproof materials. On February 15, 1948, the new L-shaped brick building, costing $26,000, was dedicated.

*The first services were held in the local Methodist church.

†Pastor Seehausen was born at Crete, Ill., in 1869. After his resignation at Chebanse he moved to Indianapolis, Ind.

132. Des Plaines, Saint Matthew's

1896 is the year in which William B. McKinley, Republican, defeated William Jennings Bryan, Democrat, for the Presidency, and became the twenty-fifth President of the United States. In this year, so far as it has been possible to determine, only one Synodical Conference congregation was organized in the Northern Illinois area. That was Saint Matthew's, whose center is located about four miles east of the "City of Roses," Des Plaines, and which is affiliated with the Wisconsin Synod. Saint Matthew's was organized on January 29, 1896, and the first church was dedicated on Pentecost Sunday of the same year. Its first pastor was the Rev. Carl H. Buenger, who served until 1902, when he followed a call to Friedens (Peace) Congregation in Kenosha (formerly Southport), Wis.* His successor at Saint Matthew's, the Rev. J. Toepel, was installed in March, 1903. A school was erected in 1932. The following have served as day school teachers: Kurt Rode and Miss A. Timm.

133. Chicago, Our Savior (Deaf-Mute)

In 1893 a certain deaf man in Michigan City, Ind., wrote to the director of the Lutheran School for the Deaf in Detroit, Mich. which he had attended for a number of years, requesting that, if possible, arrangements be made to have services conducted for the deaf. This letter was forwarded to the Rev. Augustus Reinke, pastor of First Bethlehem Congregation in Chicago, with the urgent plea that he take this matter under advisement, particularly for the reason that twelve graduates of the institution in Detroit were members of First Bethlehem in Chicago. Assisted by the deaf-mute in Michigan City, Pastor Reinke began studying the sign

*"In the spring of 1854 the German Catholic priest here, Rev. D. Huber, who a short time before with liberal sentiments had emigrated from Switzerland, turned to Protestantism, and particularly to the Lutheran Church, and organized at Kenosha the first German Lutheran congregation." (*Cf. Ninety Years*, 1856-1946, Friedens Ev. Lutheran Congregation, Kenosha, Wis., Sept. 1, 1946.)

language, and a month later he was able to conduct the first Lutheran service in the sign language in the United States with an attendance of sixteen deaf persons. Calls for similar services came from Lutheran deaf-mutes in other cities, and soon Pastor Reinke was conducting services in Milwaukee, Wis., Fort Wayne, Ind., Louisville, Ky., St. Louis, Mo., Peoria and Galesburg, Ill., and other places. At Concordia Seminary, St. Louis, Mo., he also instructed four members of the graduating class in the sign language. In 1896 he requested the Missouri Synod's delegates assembled for convention in Fort Wayne, Ind., to take over the missions in Milwaukee, Wis., and Louisville, Ky. The request was heeded. Pastor Reinke, however, still had charge of the work in Chicago and, under the leadership of Ed. J. Pohl, organized Our Savior Congregation on October 2, 1896. For some time this congregation came together for worship services on the fourth Sunday of each month in the afternoon in First Bethlehem Church, Paulina and McReynolds Streets (now Le Moyne Avenue). The Rev. Arthur L. Reinke, assistant pastor of First Bethlehem and son of the founder, served as pastor to the deaf-mutes from 1897 until 1912, when the Rev. Nathanael Paul Uhlig succeeded him and then served until 1918. For the following nineteen years this work was performed by the Rev. Arthur C. Dahms. Upon his acceptance of a call to First Saint James Congregation in Chicago the Rev. Ernest J. Scheibert assumed charge of the deaf-mute missions in this region.

In 1904 a church was erected on Crystal Street, near Hoyne Avenue, in Chicago. This building was sold in 1920. Two years later a new building, containing a chapel, meeting rooms, and a parsonage, was built at 1400 North Ridgeway Avenue, where for several years services have been held every Sunday at 10:30 A.M. "No sound is heard during the service, unless the pastor speaks with his signs for the benefit of hearing visitors . . . . The congregation 'sings' hymns in the sign language; sometimes a soloist or a quartet in the conventional choir robes renders a hymn before the congregation."

The Chicago missionary travels to Michigan for services in Grand Rapids, Muskegon, and Ludington. South Bend, Ind., has been served monthly or oftener for about forty years. Fort Wayne, Ind., has been served out of Chicago and out of Detroit, Mich. Other places served out of Chicago were St. Joseph, Mich., Bremen, Ind., Crystal Lake, Elgin, and Kankakee, Ill. Former deaf-mute missionary Dahms tells about a certain man who attended his services in South Bend. The man walked home after the evening services, following the railroad track to his home town—a four-hour walk. (No train service was available at that time of the night.)

The Missouri Synod's mission to the deaf has spread over the entire country. Today more than twenty men are serving the deaf in nearly three hundred cities. In eleven cities the deaf have their own churches.

134. Libertyville

About eight miles southwest of Waukegan ("Little Fort") is a village known as Libertyville, Ill.* The first Lutheran service here was a funeral service for Rudolph Sitz in the old Union church (where the Episcopal church now stands), with the Rev. Martin Sauer of Waukegan officiating. The Lutherans of this region continued to worship in this church for about nine years. "Some claim that the first service was held in a private home on February 28, 1897." At first Pastor Sauer came once a month; later, twice a month. "Members would get him with horse and buggy or by handcar." Saint John's Congregation was organized on October 10, 1897.

In 1900 Pastor Sauer accepted a call to Brillion, Wis., and

*1940 census: 3,930.

was succeeded at Saint John's by the Rev. Theodore Volkert, who likewise served the congregations in Waukegan, Lake Forest, and Libertyville. In 1904 Saint John's Congregation purchased property, which was "more or less of a swamp or slough," for $540.65. Soon afterward a church was erected at a cost of $2,725.49 and dedicated on October 29, 1905. In 1908 Pastor Volkert accepted a call to Racine, Wis., and his successor in the triple parish was the Rev. Richard Buerger. On March 8, 1914, it was resolved to have English services once a month. In February, 1918, Saint Paul's Congregation in Lake Forest was disbanded, but the members promised to join near-by "sister" congregations. In September, 1923, the Waukegan and Libertyville parishes separated, so that each could call its own pastor. The Rev. Elmer C. Kiessling became Saint John's pastor. (See Chapter 115, page 396.) Less than four years later, in April, 1927, Pastor Kiessling accepted a professorship at Northwestern College, Watertown, Wis., but agreed to serve until the latter part of August. He was succeeded at Saint John's, Libertyville, on September 11, 1927, by the Rev. W. H. Lehmann of Darfur, Minn.

Saint John's Congregation is a member of the Wisconsin Synod.

135. Ontarioville

Approximately six miles from the western end of the Du Page-Cook county line is a hamlet called Ontarioville.* "Ontario" is a word of Iroquoian origin, signifying "The Great Lake." But this hamlet is not located at any kind of lake, great or small. Island Lake,† very small, is about two and a half miles west of Ontarioville. In the hamlet the Trail easily discovers a little church which for some years prior to 1899 belonged to the Evangelical denomination. On July 26, 1899, the members of the congregation here re-

*1940 census: 149.

†Not to be confused with a lake of the same name on the boundary of Lake and McHenry Counties. See Chapter 241.

solved to join the Missouri Synod and to request the Rev. Charles J. Fricke of West Chicago (Turner Junction)—about eight miles south—to be their pastor. A Lutheran constitution was adopted and signed by sixteen men on August 10, 1899.* At this time Pastor Fricke reported that it would be impossible for him to accept the pastorate, not even to serve Ontarioville as an affiliate of Trinity in West Chicago. Thereupon the congregation, organized under the name Immanuel, called the Rev. Frederick G. Miessler of Staplehurst, Nebr., who served until December, 1902, when he accepted a call to Immanuel Congregation in Batavia, Ill. Immanuel of Ontarioville had no pastor from that time until the summer of 1904, when the Rev. M. Guebert came; he served until 1908. His successor, the Rev. William H. Kowert, Sr., of St. Charles (Orchard Farm), Mo., held this pastorate until June, 1916. The next pastor, Candidate Eugene Schmid, recent graduate of Concordia Seminary, St. Louis, Mo., served until December, 1918, and was succeeded in Ontarioville by the Rev. H. J. F. Meier of Laurel, Mont. In September, 1920, Pastor Meier accepted a call to Hampshire, Ill. Immanuel's sixth and present pastor, the Rev. William F. Jiede of Kearney, Nebr., was installed on January 23, 1921. On November 21, 1948, he assumed charge of Saint John's Congregation at Roselle (Rodenberg) as an affiliate of Immanuel in Ontarioville.

136. River Grove

While paging through the records of Saint Paul's Congregation in Melrose Park, reference was made to the establishment of a congregation in River Grove, Ill.† This village's "center" is at Grand and First Avenues, about two and a half

*Charter members:

A. Kauke	C. L. Feuerhaken	L. W. Kauke
H. R. Troyke	W. Leiseberg	H. W. Schnadt
H. W. Hitzemann	E. Scholer	F. Koch
L. L. Leiseberg	L. Leiseberg	S. H. Harmening
H. Feuerhaken	F. Hitzemann	H. Hanke
	L. Knief	

†1940 census: 3,301.

miles northeast of Melrose Park and about a half mile east of the Des Plaines River, near the Che-Che-Pinqua Forest Preserve. "Che-Che-Pinqua"—the name of a Potawatomi Indian chief—means "Blinking Eyes." The chief's "civilized name" was Alexander Robinson. His mother was a part-French woman of the Ottawa tribe. It was on August 5, 1812, that Che-Che-Pinqua "beached his canoe on the Chicago shore to aid the fleeing survivors of the Fort Dearborn Massacre, which he had witnessed." When the peace treaty was signed at Prairie du Chien, Wis., this Indian chief received a grant of two sections of land on the Des Plaines River. He was a witness in the "Sand Bar Case," handled by Abraham Lincoln in 1858. In August, 1946, "the carved and inscribed stones which marked the last resting places of the chief, his wife, and several children were overthrown and shattered . . . by unknown creatures, no doubt of the white race, known under such circumstances as vandals."

In 1896 the Rev. Emil Zapf, pastor of Saint Paul's Congregation in Melrose Park, began conducting worship services in a public school house on Thatcher Avenue, River Grove. About two years later, on October 15, 1898, Bethlehem Congregation was organized. A building site at 2636 Oak Street was donated for religious purposes by a Mrs. Carey, a member of the River Grove community. Bethlehem's first resident pastor was the Rev. John Fred Starke, who was ordained and installed on August 12, 1900. In 1901 a school building was erected. In August, 1904, Pastor Starke accepted a call to Des Moines, Iowa. His successor, the Rev. John Schert of Sharon, Wis., was installed as Bethlehem's second pastor on September 18, 1904. He served until March, 1908, when he accepted a call to Lyons, Ill. Bethlehem's next pastor was the Rev. Otto Gurschke of Elma, Iowa. He held this pastorate from May, 1908, until March, 1911, and then assumed a pastorate at Falls City, Nebr. During the following nine years the pastorate was held by the Rev. Carl F. Eissfeldt, formerly superintendent of the "Kinderfreund-Gesellschaft" of Wisconsin (The Lutheran Children's Friend Society of Wisconsin), Wauwatosa, Wis. It was in this period that the Young People's Hall was built by Bethlehem in River Grove. In August, 1919, Pastor Eissfeldt accepted a call to Fair Haven, Mich.* His successor as Bethlehem's fifth pastor was the Rev. William H. Lippmann of Bovina, Colo. He was installed on September 13, 1919. During the first six years of his ministry in River Grove, Pastor Lippmann also taught school. In the fall of 1925 the congregation's first trained day school teacher, H. G. Ahrens, was installed. In 1935 another classroom was opened and taught by Paul H. Groenke; in 1940 he was replaced by William H. Franck. About four years later Mr. Franck followed a call to Hilbert, Wis., and Miss Luella Spitzack succeeded him in River Grove.

Plans for a larger church as well as a larger school are being formulated.

137. Chicago, Holy Cross, North Side

A little more than four miles directly east from River Grove is a community which at the turn of the century was largely settled by Americans of Polish descent. On September 4, 1898, twenty-one men adopted and signed a constitution and under the direction of the Rev. Ferdinand Sattelmeier of Bible Grove, Ill., organized a congregation which was named Holy Cross. According to a report which was read at the convention of the Illinois District, Missouri Synod, in 1900, this "Polish Mission" was begun upon the recommendation or advice of the Chicago Lutheran Pastoral Conference.

In May, 1899, Pastor Sattelmeier accepted a call to a Polish-German congregation in Scranton, Pa., which he had won for the Missouri Synod. On August 12, 1900, he was succeeded to the Holy Cross pastorate by the Rev. Stanislaus

*He died in Mount Prospect, Ill., March 14, 1935.

Mlotkowski of Palmer, S. Dak. In 1905 Holy Cross purchased the property of Saint Paul's Congregation on Campbell Avenue, near Fullerton Avenue. Up to this time the congregation had been worshiping in First Immanuel Church, Ashland Boulevard, near Twelfth Street. In 1916 the property on Campbell Avenue was sold, and a combination church-school building was erected on Lamon Avenue, just south of Wrightwood Avenue. Dedication took place on June 24, 1917. A day school was established at this time and taught by the pastor. The congregation's first trained teacher, John Steiner, was installed on April 2, 1922. In March, 1928, Pastor Mlotkowski accepted a call to Glendora, Mich. His successor at Holy Cross, the Rev. Paul Sich of Inglis, Manitoba, Canada, was installed on August 26, 1928. In the same year Mr. Steiner followed a call to Saint Andrew's Congregation in Chicago. Others who served in the day school of Holy Cross were A. C. Abel, Theodore E. Lange, Paul E. Raatz, Miss Irmalyn Klamt, L. Brands, and Victor Kalbfleisch.

The Northern Illinois District in 1930 adopted the recommendation submitted by the Committee on Memorials to "grant the request of Holy Cross Church at Wrightwood and Lamon to the effect that the Secretary of Synod be instructed to omit any reference to the Polish origin of this congregation in printing the name of said church in the roll of Synod, since such reference may be misunderstood, easily conveying the impression that work in this church is done preponderantly in the Polish language, while the fact is that the use of Polish is negligible, German and English being used mostly. Confusion with the name of Holy Cross on the South Side could be eliminated by designating north or south." In the course of an essay delivered at the convention of the Missouri Synod in 1934, the Rev. Martin Graebner, D.D., president of Concordia College, St. Paul, Minn.* said: "Let us not battle for a language, but let us contend for the Gospel."

*Founded in 1893.

138. Columbia Heights

Once more the Trail goes to the southern end of Cook County, stopping on the Cook-Will County line at a place known for some time as Columbia Heights, but now called Steger, Ill.* This village is located about one-half mile south of Brown's Corners, the intersection of the once highly important Sauk and Vincennes Trails, each of which fed the traffic of the other for many years prior to the advent of the railroad and the automobile. The village was called Steger for the founder and owner of the Steger Piano Company.

In 1896 the Rev. Friedrich E. Brauer, pastor of Trinity Congregation at Crete–about two miles south of Steger–and the Rev. Karl Schroeder, pastor of Saint Paul's Congregation in Chicago Heights (formerly known as Bloom)–about two miles north of Steger–began conducting services in the firehouse on Thirty-first Street. Later in the same year a storeroom in the Old Berchem Building, at the northwest corner of Chicago Road and Thirty-fourth Street, was rented for worship purposes. The other section of the building was used as a saloon. Members recalling those days say that the noises emanating from this drinking establishment were often so great that, although Pastor Brauer shouted, it was difficult for the congregation to understand him. After two years of worshiping under these unfavorable conditions the work was placed upon a more permanent basis. In the summer of 1898 Helmuth F. C. Schulz, student at Concordia Seminary, Springfield, Ill., was called to serve as student-pastor and as teacher in the day school. On November 15, 1898, the school was opened by Vicar Schulz with fourteen pupils, which number was increased by five before the end of the first week.

*1940 census: 3,369.

On January 1, 1899, seven men* adopted and signed the constitution. The name Immanuel, suggested by Vicar Schulz, was adopted by the new congregation. On the following day, work was started on a lot donated by a member of Trinity at Crete; a combination church and school building was erected on this site, at 3419 Chicago Road. This building, a frame structure, was dedicated in May, 1899. On August 21, 1899, Vicar Schulz was succeeded by another student, E. H. Felten, who came to Steger in time to open the new school year. In June, 1900, enrollment was forty-three.

Immanuel's first resident pastor, Candidate Helmuth F. C. Schulz, was ordained and installed on July 29, 1900.†

A short time afterward the congregation purchased property at the corner of Emerald Avenue and Thirty-fourth Street, the "avenue" paralleling the right of way of the interurban electric line which connected Kankakee with Chicago.

In November, 1910, Pastor Schulz accepted a call to Ashland, Wis. His successor at Immanuel in Columbia Heights (Steger) was the Rev. H. William Meyer of "Yellowhead"—Saint Paul's Congregation—six miles northeast of Grant Park, Ill. He was installed as Immanuel's second pastor on the first Sunday in January, 1911. During the same year a new parsonage was built, and work on a new church was begun at the same time, the dedication of the church taking place in May, 1912. Meanwhile the old church building was moved from Chicago Road to the new site and remodeled to serve as a school. The first trained teacher, W. Wilker, came to Steger in the fall of 1910, but resigned a year later. Walter Brown served in Immanuel School until Carl Homeier was installed as Mr. Wilker's successor.

*Charter members:

Friedrich Fedtke	Eduard Goers	Carl Kritsch
Fritz Teifke	Johann Gast	Karl Rekau
	Edward Gluth	

†As a student, Mr. Schulz had a room in the home of Fritz Fedtke and ate his meals in the homes of various members. As pastor he roomed at the Johann Gast home and ate his meals at Personke's. On July 16, 1902, he married Miss Ida Henning of Crete, Ill.

In 1915 Pastor Meyer accepted a call to Hampton, Nebr., and shortly afterward was succeeded in Steger by the Rev. G. J. C. Koch of Preble, Ind. On October 28, 1923, Pastor Koch suffered a heart attack while conducting the opening devotions of the Sunday school and died shortly thereafter. Succeeding him in the Immanuel pastorate on January 6, 1924, was the Rev. Peter Clausen of Vincennes, Ind. Pastor Clausen "ministered to the congregation during exceedingly difficult times." During his ministry the Steger piano factory closed, throwing many members of Immanuel out of employment. The local bank failed, and Immanuel and its pastor as well as most of the individual members lost all their funds. The closing years of his active ministry in Steger were those including the Second World War. In April, 1946, Pastor Clausen suffered a heart attack, which forced him to resign. The congregation accepted the resignation on September 1, 1946, but retained him as "honorary pastor."* On September 18, 1946, the pastorate was assumed by the Rev. William G. Mehringer, who had served as chaplain in the U.S. Army for almost three years. Recently he re-entered the chaplaincy. His successor, the Rev. Henry W. Niermann of Alamosa, Colo., was installed on June 26, 1949.

With the death of Mr. Homeier on April 8, 1942, there began a series of disheartening events which ultimately led to the closing of the congregation's day school in 1944. The original church building was then sold and razed.

"Waldemar J. Koch, owner of a hardware store and also village clerk of Steger for many years, has regularly taught a Sunday school class in Immanuel Church for the past 27 years." (*Lutheraner*, Northern Illinois District Edition, Vol. 103, No. 8.)

From Sycamore to Columbia Heights! A total of sixty-four places have been visited since the Trail left Sycamore toward

*He died May 9, 1949.

the close of the year 1876, the anniversary year (centennial) of the adoption of the Declaration of Independence. The nineteenth century closed about one year after the 136th congregation affiliated with the Evangelical Lutheran Synodical Conference of North America was organized. Inexorable is the flight of time; and the Trail will continue to observe the recording of events by "Father Time"—particularly in this part of the world.

Part Five

From Columbia Heights to Homewood

139. Rochelle

The twentieth century has arrived. The Spanish-American War was officially ended with the United States Senate's ratification of the peace treaty in 1899. The United States battleship *Maine,* which was sunk from an explosion in Havana Harbor, Cuba (February 15, 1898), led to the coining of the slogan "Remember the Maine!" In "Far Cathay"—China—another pot was boiling just before the turn of the century. The "I Ho Ch'uan" ("Righteous Harmony Fists"—"Boxers") were coining slogans like these: "Protect the country, destroy the foreigners!" "Protect the Ch'ing (dynasty), destroy the foreigner!" The Empress Dowager, Tz'u Hsi, or "Old Buddha," had virtually declared war upon the whole world. Throughout the Chinese Empire aliens were in danger of being killed, especially missionaries, for by the nature of their profession the latter were more frequently beyond the shelter of the treaty ports than were merchants. In 1900 Christians in Chihli (Hopei) Province were being massacred in large numbers.

Back to peaceful America, and to "good old" Illinois!

When the Lutheran Trail was in the northern district of this great Prairie State, the last stop of the nineteenth century was made at a village near the intersection of two great trails, Sauk and Vincennes, at Columbia Heights (Steger), Ill. Now, in this first year of the twentieth century, the Trail is resumed at a village some twenty miles directly south of Rockford, Rochelle,* formerly called Lane, for Dr. Robert P. Lane of Rockford, one of the founders. It was on February 24, 1897, that the first German Lutheran service here was held in the home of William Woodrick on Tenth Street by the Rev. Adolph C. Staats, pastor of Immanuel Congregation in Lynville (now Lindenwood). On January 14, 1900, Saint Paul's Congregation was organized. Its first pastor was Pastor Staats. On March 8, 1900, the congregation purchased property from the Norwegian Lutherans for twelve hundred dollars. On January 8, 1905, Pastor Staats accepted a call to Marengo, Ill., and on the following April 30 was succeeded by the Rev. Herman H. C. Schoenbeck of Natoma, Kans. He served Saint Paul's for a little more than five years, until November 20, 1910, when he accepted a call to Immanuel Congregation in Lynville (Lindenwood). The Rev. William John Voeltz, formerly missionary at Cupar, Saskatchewan, Canada, was installed as Saint Paul's third pastor on May 28, 1911. After serving here for a little more than four years, Pastor Voeltz in October, 1915, accepted a call to Sterling, Ill. Then came Candidate Gottlieb John Starck. He was ordained and installed on November 15, 1915. During his pastorate a new church was erected and dedicated. In February, 1919, he accepted a call to Clay Center, Kans., and on August 3 of the same year his successor, the Rev. Herman E. Brauer, was installed. During his pastorate an annex was built on the church to serve as a schoolroom, and a day school was founded. In August, 1924, Pastor Brauer accepted

*1940 census: 4,200. Named from the city in France.

a call to Marengo, Ill., and was succeeded by the Rev. Emil A. Bartusch of Sycamore, Ill., on October 12, 1924. He served Saint Paul's at Rochelle until his sudden death, which occurred on June 2, 1928. The next pastor, the Rev. Otto H. Linnemeier of Union, Ill., was installed on August 5, 1928. About three years later Pastor Linnemeier reported to the Mission Board of the Northern Illinois District that "previous to the beginning of this year (1931) it seemed as though we would be able to become self-supporting, but then in February the bank, which ninety per cent of my people patronized, closed its doors. Thus my people lost what they had, in addition to the general depression." Because of the steady decrease in enrollment the day school was discontinued in 1933. The two canneries located in Rochelle "are constantly moving their men around and are occupying more and more ground near Rochelle." This fact accounts for the moving of Saint Paul's members to places eight to sixteen miles from their church.

All preaching in the German language was discontinued on December 7, 1941.

140. Chicago, Saint Mark's (Norwegian)

During the sojourn amidst Emmaus Congregation in Chicago there was related the interesting experience of the Rev. Martin Fuelling in the founding of a mission at Fortieth Avenue (now Pulaski Road), near Grand Avenue. However, no mention was made of the presence in that community of Norwegian Lutherans. They were there, however, and very active in church work as early as 1900. It was then that a Sunday school was organized, which later was moved to the "German" Bethel Church, Springfield Avenue and Frederick (now Hirsch) Street. That school was for some time conducted by the Rev. Olaf E. Brandt and continued by his successor, the Rev. S. T. Reque, until the autumn of 1897. In that year the school was made part of a mission in charge of the Rev. John R. Birkelund, who had returned from the mission field in Japan in the same year. Worship services were also conducted in a public hall at Hancock Street and Bloomingdale Road. As the work progressed, the field became too expansive for Pastor Birkelund; therefore the congregation called an assistant pastor, the Rev. O. K. Ramberg, and divided the territory into two parishes, the one becoming Saint Matthew's of Logan Square and the other Saint Mark's.

The first congregational (voters') meeting of Saint Mark's was held on March 2, 1900, in Bethel Church. Four men* then adopted and signed a constitution. A vacant store building on North Avenue, between Harding and Springfield Avenues, which was rented almost at once, remained Saint Mark's meeting place for more than four years. In September, 1901, the same month in which President William B. McKinley was assassinated,† Pastor Ramberg was succeeded by the Rev. Theodore Ringoen, who remained here until July, 1904. During that summer Saint Mark's was served by the Rev. M. K. Bleken, pastor of Saint John's, and John A. Moldstad, student at Concordia Seminary, St. Louis, Mo. In August, 1904, a "basement" church was constructed on previously purchased property at North Tripp and Wabansia Avenues. On the eleventh of September Saint Mark's new pastor, the Rev. Lauritz S. Guttebo, was installed, and on the following November 20 the "basement" church was dedicated and occupied. About a year and a half later, April 15, 1906, Pastor Guttebo was forced by illness to resign. Thereupon a call was extended to Mr. J. A. Moldstad at the

*Charter members:

O. K. Ramberg, pastor	Hans E. Herwig
Theodore Olsen	Bernhard Anderson

†President McKinley was shot by an anarchist named Leon Czolgosz on Sept. 6, 1901, while attending the Pan-American Exposition at Buffalo, N.Y. Theodore Roosevelt succeeded him as President of the United States.

seminary in St. Louis, who soon after his graduation was ordained and installed as Saint Mark's fourth pastor, on July 15.* In the fall of 1945 Pastor Moldstad was stricken with an illness which gradually sapped his vitality. He died on June 4, 1946, at the age of seventy-two years. He was buried in Norway Grove Cemetery near Madison, Wis. On October 13, 1946, his successor at Saint Mark's, the Rev. Ahlert H. Strand of Saint Luke's Norwegian Congregation (5916 Rice Street), Chicago, was installed. Shortly afterward, Saint Luke's sold its property to Saint Paul's Congregation (Austin) and joined Saint Mark's. (See Chapter 94, page 347.)

Saint Mark's established a day school in the fall of 1947.

141. Chicago, Our Redeemer

Chicago Junction is the next stop. The name of this community was changed to Englewood in 1868, and in 1889 Englewood, together with a number of other formerly independent villages, was annexed to Chicago. One reads that "while at times there was considerable need of a police force in the Stock Yards district, Englewood pursued the even tenor of its way with very little necessity for their appearance other than to ornament the landscape and to see that the cows were not disturbed in their peaceful pastures."

A few facts were learned about Englewood while observing the origin and growth of Sankt Stephanus (Saint Stephen's) Congregation, which for some time worshiped in a small frame church on Englewood Avenue (now Sixty-second Place). It was here that the first Lutheran mission of the Missouri Synod in Chicago in which the English language was used exclusively was begun on February 17, 1901. The primary cause for the establishment of such a mission in this community was the request made by Paul Appelt, son of a

*Pastor Moldstad was one of the founders of the Norwegian Synod of the American Ev. Lutheran Church, which joined the Synodical Conference in 1920 and of which St. Mark's is a member.

parochial school teacher, Louis Appelt.* The former's wife, a Scandinavian, did not profit much from attendance at German worship services; so the considerate husband appealed to the Rev. William C. Kohn, president of the Northern Illinois District, for English services. Such services were soon started in Saint Stephen's Church on Sunday evenings, where they were continued until the mission was transferred to a public hall on West Sixty-third Street (formerly Junction Avenue), near Yale Avenue. The congregation was organized on April 19, 1901, and the first name chosen was Grace English.† A short time afterward the name "Grace" was changed to "Our Redeemer," because the former was constantly being confused with a church of the same name on the northwest side of Chicago. By 1902 the membership had increased to such an extent that it was decided to erect a church of yellow brick at West Sixtieth Place and Princeton Avenue. The membership grew rapidly. The building was enlarged; a balcony was installed, and yet within a brief space of time the congregation could not be adequately accommodated.

Our Redeemer's first pastor was the Rev. Guido Rohe Schuessler,‡ who for about five years prior to his coming to Chicago (Englewood) had served as pastor and teacher in mission churches at Coal City and Morris, Ill. He was installed on February 17, 1901.

In the years 1922 and 1923 a large stone church of Gothic style was erected on the west side of Harvard Avenue, between West Sixty-fourth and Sixty-fifth Streets. In 1932, late

*Louis Appelt was the first teacher at First Saint John's branch school in the Holstein community; when this school became the center of a new congregation (First Bethlehem) in 1871, he was retained as the first teacher. He taught there from 1868 to 1913.

†Charter members:

F. W. Fromm	W. A. Wettstaedt	Fred Funk
H. M. Bates	J. L. Sengstock	Otto Knitter
August F. Narten	E. W. Smalley	

‡The Rev. Guido R. Schuessler served as president of the English District of the Missouri Synod, 1927-1936; for three years prior to this period he was vice-president of this District and for about nine years a member of its Mission Board. He was a "fundamental and conservative theologian," and an "outstanding, silver-tongued orator."

summer, his son, Luther, since 1926 pastor of Good Shepherd Congregation in Maywood, Ill., was called as assistant pastor. Upon his father's retirement from the active ministry, in 1943, he became Our Redeemer's "first" pastor, while his father was made "pastor emeritus" and granted a pension for the rest of his life. Pastor Guido R. Schuessler died on July 6, 1946.

On April 27, 1947, the first seven of a total of forty-one hand-carved reliefs depicting the "Sermon on the Mount" were dedicated, three of them to the memory of Pastor Schuessler; one to the memory of Warren Winterhelt, who died during World War II while serving in the Merchant Marine; one to the memory of Dr. Charles E. Clapper; one to the memory of Mr. and Mrs. Ernest Schau, "former octogenarian members of the church"; one in memory of Carl Gross, longtime sponsor of youth work in the church; in addition, a bronze missal stand was dedicated to the memory of Mr. and Mrs. Herman C. Freadrich.* Scripture passages lettered in gold leaf on the frieze of the church and chancel were dedicated to the memory of Herman and Mary Poehler and Paul and Martha Brooks. The forty-one reliefs were executed by John O. Torell, Swedish-American sculptor of Chicago.

"Daughter" congregations of Our Redeemer are Faith, whose church is located at West Eighty-third Street and Sangamon Avenue, Hope, at West Sixty-fourth Street and Washtenaw Avenue, and Windsor Park, at East 76th Street and Saginaw Avenue.

142. Chicago, Ebenezer

Chicago's street-numbering system is an admirable one; the dividing line between the North and the South Sides is Madison Street, and between east and west, State Street, the continuation of the old Vincennes Trail and Hubbard's

*Herman C. Freadrich was chief usher at Our Redeemer for more than thirty years. He died in 1946.

Trace. Where the two lines cross, in the heart of the Loop, it is never "night"—the intersection which is appropriately called "the world's busiest corner." From this point the Trail now proceeds to South Harding Avenue and West Thirteenth Street, where pause is made to read from a report which was submitted to the Illinois District, Missouri Synod, in the year 1900. Translated, it reads in part: "At the western limits of Chicago there is a vast territory without a Lutheran church or school, although as yet sparsely settled by Lutherans. In a rented building the first worship service was held in November, 1899, and since that time regularly on Sunday evenings, by Pastors Theodore Kohn, Martin Fuelling, Louis Hoelter, and Edward Hoelter. The teachers A. B. Johnson and Abraham have been conducting Sunday school; the latter has now also established a day school. The attendance is fairly good. The Mission Board is of the opinion that the beginning of just such missions must be cheerfully greeted, not only because the sects encourage many pastors who are equipped ('ausgeruestet'), according to their manner, to establish mission stations everywhere, particularly in the larger cities, wherever they can firmly establish themselves for the sake of supporting themselves ('schon um der Brotfrage willen'), and experience teaches how difficult the work is when we everywhere arrive late—but also because it is expected ('voraussichtlich') that an increasing number of Lutherans will build their homes at the city limits, and such missions undoubtedly are the beginning of populous congregations." That seems to indicate that the first Lutheran service in this section was held in a store building, referred to in an anniversary booklet published twenty-five years later, at Twelfth Street, near Kostner Avenue. However, in the latter record it is stated that a candidate, H. Kettler, taught school and that the enrollment was twenty-eight, which was regarded as "fairly good."

On May 9, 1901, Ebenezer Congregation was organized by thirteen men.* A chapel near South Keeler Avenue, near West Thirteenth Street, was purchased for one thousand dollars and dedicated on July 7. The congregation's first pastor, Candidate William Gahl, graduate of Concordia Seminary, St. Louis, Mo., was ordained and installed on July 28, 1901. In 1905 Maurice L. Gotsch of Soest, Ind., was installed as teacher of Ebenezer School. In 1906 the congregation joined the Missouri Synod. Evening services in English were inaugurated in 1909. In 1910 a second classroom was opened and taught by Miss R. Feiertag; in 1911 the German in religious instruction in the day school was replaced by English. On February 23, 1913, Ebenezer's new church at South Harding Avenue and West Thirteenth Street was dedicated and a Sunday school established. In 1914 two English evening services a month were introduced. Two years later, in 1916, Miss Feiertag was succeeded by Miss Huettermann in the second classroom. In 1917 one English service a month was included in the Sunday morning schedule. In 1920 Mr. Gotsch followed a call to Peace Congregation, Chicago. His successor was Herman Maudanz, who served for about one year, to be succeeded by Ed. M. Streufert; in the same year Miss Julia Wegmann succeeded Miss Huettermann as teacher in the lower grades. In 1925 Mr. Streufert followed a call to Saint John's Congregation in Lansing, Ill., whereupon the Rev. Adolph C. Staats, a retired pastor,† took charge of the school. Since June, 1945, Herold H. Lipske of Chebanse, Ill., has been serving in Ebenezer School, assisted by Student J. Roberts and, later, by Miss Lois Sagehorn.

*Charter members:

August Rahn
Frederick Bruhnke
K. Boldt
Emil Bartz
Rud. Herhold
C. Bartel
Albert Moritz
Frederick Rahn
August Fett
Herman Bartel
Gottfried Bartel
August Baumann
Herman Wickboldt

†Had held pastorates at Lynville (Lindenwood), Rochelle, and Marengo; at the latter place he served from 1905 until 1924, and then resigned. See footnote, p. 307.

At the 50th anniversary celebration of the school's founding, November 20, 1949, it was announced that A. Bruhnke, Sr., and Anna Herhold (Mrs. W. Siegler), two of the first pupils, "are still members of Ebenezer."

Services in German and English every Sunday morning have been conducted since 1921.

143. Aurora, Emmanuel

It is certain that the English poet Alexander Pope did not have in mind a village or city in Illinois when he translated Homer's *Iliad* or the *Odyssey*. Pope died more than two hundred years ago, in 1744. His reference to "Aurora" reads thus: "Soon as Aurora, daughter of the dawn, Sprinkled with roseate light the dewy lawn." In the *Iliad* he speaks of "Aurora" in this wise:

"The morning planet told th' approach of light,
And, fast behind, Aurora's warmer ray
O'er the broad ocean pour'd the golden day."

Has not the Trail crossed Aurora before? Yes; in 1856. And that growing village justifies a second call, there to visit another Missouri Synod congregation. Aurora claims the distinction of being the first city in the world to use electricity for street lighting and for this reason has come to be known as the "City of Lights."

On June 5, 1901, twenty-one voting members of Saint Paul's Congregation, Aurora, under the leadership of two officials of the Illinois District, Missouri Synod, the Rev. T. Johannes Grosse of Zion Congregation at what is now called Churchville (originally Duncklees Grove), and the Rev. Louis Lochner, pastor of First Trinity Congregation in Chicago, organized Emmanuel Congregation in Aurora, near the "center" of the "mother" congregation. Emmanuel's* first place of worship was Saint Olaf's Norwegian Lutheran Church at

*"Emmanuel" is a variant of "Immanuel," the Hebrew name of Christ, meaning "God with us."

Clark Street and Bevier Place. The Rev. John W. Rabe of Yorkville, ten miles southwest of Aurora, had charge of the young congregation until December 8, 1901, when the Rev. Charles J. Fricke of West Chicago (formerly called Turner and Turner Junction), Ill., was installed. Emmanuel School was started in the front hall of the above-mentioned Norwegian church with an enrollment of eleven pupils. During the following year a church was erected at the northeast corner of Jackson Street and Fourth Avenue. Dedication took place on January 18, 1903. Emmanuel's first day school teacher, E. C. Hoffmann, since 1891 on the teaching staff at near-by Saint Paul's School, was installed on August 31, 1902. A new school was adjoined to the rear of the new church and completed before the latter; it was occupied and dedicated on November 30, 1902. In July, 1906, Emmanuel became a member of the Missouri Synod. In the same year Pastor Fricke started a second class of the day school in the study of the parsonage. Less than three years later this class was discontinued when Pastor Fricke on February 21, 1909, accepted a call to Knoxville, Tenn. His successor in Aurora, the Rev. J. F. Karl Schmidt of Mobile, Ala., was installed as Emmanuel's second pastor on May 9, 1909. He remained for about three years and then accepted a call to Bethany College, Mankato, Minn.* The congregation then turned its thoughts to the South again—to Tennessee this time—and recalled its former pastor. For the second time Pastor Fricke was installed on April 14, 1912. Shortly afterward a building at the southwest corner of Jackson Street and Fourth Avenue was purchased by the congregation; this building was used temporarily for the second classroom, on the first floor, while the upper floor was arranged as a home for the congregation's second day school teacher, A. H. Brinkmann of Seymour, Ind., who was installed on April 19, 1914. In the

*An institution belonging to the Norwegian Synod of the American Ev. Lutheran Church, organized in 1918.

fall of 1916 a new and larger building, comprising classrooms, recreation rooms, and an auditorium, was erected, dedication following on June 10, 1917. In the fall of the same year a third class was begun, with Miss Esther Schwermann in charge of the primary grades. Erwin Burgdorf, a student at Concordia Seminary, St. Louis, Mo., replaced her in 1924.* Upon his return to the Seminary in 1925, Miss Minna Fricke was placed in charge of this department. About two years later she was succeeded by Miss Norma Voigt of Danville, Ill. Mr. Hoffmann, the first teacher, died on July 17, 1930. Pastor Fricke then took over some of the duties of the upper grades until Walter Gotsch of Chicago Heights, Ill., was installed on April 26, 1931. On September 27 in the same year Paul G. Witte, graduate of Concordia Teachers College, River Forest, was installed, succeeding Miss Voigt in the primary department. Mr. Gotsch resigned from the teaching profession on October 14, 1934. His successor, Norman Himmler of Maywood, Ill., was installed on January 13, 1935.

Pastor Fricke served Emmanuel Congregation, Aurora, until his untimely death, which resulted from an automobile accident at Gettysburg, Pa., on August 19, 1939. He and his wife were on their way to Europe to spend their vacation. Mrs. Fricke was killed instantly, but Pastor Fricke lingered until September 10, 1939. A retired pastor and member of Emmanuel, the Rev. Herman Hagist,† served the congregation until the Rev. Theodore F. A. Nickel of Eau Claire, Wis., was installed on February 25, 1940. About four years later Pastor Nickel accepted a call to Jehovah Congregation, Chicago, and on April 16, 1944, his successor in Aurora, the Rev. Albert E. Richert of Detroit, Mich., more recently associated with the Missouri Synod's Army and Navy Commission with the special assignment to establish "service centers," became Emmanuel's fourth pastor.

*Pastor of St. Mark's Congregation, St. Charles, Ill., since July 24, 1938.

†Formerly pastor at Elberfeld, Ind. He died on July 23, 1948.

In addition to those already mentioned, the following have served on Emmanuel's teaching staff: Mrs. Theo. F. A. Nickel, R. O. Krause, Student R. Krueger, A. L. Amt, Miss Irma Gade, Paul F. Stohlmann, Mrs. Viola Vomhof, Mrs. Harry Ilsemann, and Alvin Hitzemann.

144. Chicago, Grace

The twentieth congregation of the Missouri Synod in Chicago, Saint Mark's, founded on November 16, 1887, established a branch school in a rented store building on Forty-second Avenue (now Keeler), between Twenty-seventh and Twenty-eighth Streets, in what then was known as the Crawford community. The Rev. Theodore Kohn opened this school with five pupils. In 1898 the same congregation purchased two lots at the northwest corner of Twenty-eighth Street and Forty-first Avenue (now Karlov). A frame building erected there was dedicated a few days before Christmas, 1898. On October 31, 1901, Grace Congregation was organized by a group of men heretofore in membership with Saint Mark's. The school property was donated to the "daughter" congregation, whose first pastor was the Rev. T. Edmund Brueggemann of Castello, Mo. He was installed on November 3, 1901. In the afternoon of that day the cornerstone of the new church and school was laid. The combination building, costing $3,450, was dedicated on December 22, 1901. In the same year Grace Congregation joined the Missouri Synod. On July 19, 1904, contracts for the erection of a new church at the northeast corner of Twenty-eighth Street and Karlov Avenue were let. A building, of brick, and costing $32,762.51, was dedicated on May 7, 1905. Three years later, in the summer of 1908, Pastor Brueggemann retired. His successor, the Rev. Henry H. F. Boester of Mishawaka, Ind., was installed on October 25, 1908. On February 13, 1910, one English evening service per month was introduced; and on

February 9, 1919, two English services a month on Sunday mornings were started. For some years services in both German and English have been held every Sunday morning.

In the early 1920's a new school building was erected on the northwest corner of the same intersection at a cost of $69,930.65. A Sunday school was organized on March 1, 1925. Two years later, in August, 1927, the German language was replaced by the English in the religious instruction in the day school. In 1933 Pastor Boester resigned. He was succeeded at Grace Church by the Rev. Gotthold Gerhard August Elbert of Calumet City (formerly known as West Hammond), Ill.

The following have served on the teaching staff of Grace School:

Gustave Eberhardt, 1897-1909
Paul Juengel, 1902-1912
Charles Ruff, 1907-1941
Amandus L. Wendt, 1909-1919
Adam M. Reinhardt, 1911-1914
Paul Wendler, 1912-1918
Daniel L. Toenies, 1914-
Henry J. Lange, 1918-
Theophil A. Wunderlich, 1919-1925
L. B. Abraham, 1925-
Theodore Preuss,
Adam Scheffler
Elmer H. Huedepohl
Arnold Bathje
Herbert Gade

and the Misses Lydia Meyer, Jessie Jamann, Minnie Kohn, Marie Gremel, Lora Beenders, Ruth Helmkamp, Gertrude Dahms, Alberta Koss, Faith Brenner and Mrs. C. Werner.

145. River Forest

History now looks back over the line marking the end of the nineteenth and the beginning of the twentieth century, this time to the year 1896. It was in the spring of that year that Saint John's Congregation in Harlem (Forest Park) purchased a lot at Augusta Street and Belleforte Avenue, Oak Park, and thereon erected a small school building to accommodate the children of its members residing in that community. A retired pastor, the Rev. Leopold C. A. Wahl, formerly at Tavistock, Ontario, Canada, opened the day school in the fall of 1896. Several months later, H. F. Renken took charge of the day school and served until 1898. On August 12, 1898, P. J. Schroeder assumed these responsibilities.

On March 17, 1902, a number of Lutherans* residing in this part of Oak Park—"the world's largest village"—met to organize a congregation, calling it "Gnaden-Gemeinde" (Grace Congregation). Worship services were conducted in the schoolroom for almost two years. The desks were fastened on boards so they might easily be moved to provide room for the Sunday audiences. Boxes were placed along the walls, and planks were placed upon them to serve as seats. The congregation's first pastor, the Rev. George William Wolter of Sturgis, Mich., was installed on January 1, 1903. In the same year a frame church was built on the northwest corner of Augusta Street and Belleforte Avenue. In 1905 Miss Sophie Schultz was engaged to assist Mr. Schroeder in the school. She was succeeded on June 2, 1907, by Walter F. Hann. In 1909 Mr. Hann followed a call to Saint Paul's, Austin (now part of Chicago's West Side), and shortly afterward Miss Paula Duever was placed in charge of the lower grades. Within five years the congregation's membership had increased by three hundred per cent.

Failing health forced the resignation of Pastor Wolter on February 5, 1911. His successor, the Rev. William Martin Roecker of Champaign, Ill., was installed on May 21, 1911.

The removal of the Teachers' Seminary from Addison to River Forest in 1912† helped to increase the membership and also ushered in a new era for the day school. In order to give the graduating students an opportunity to do practical

*Charter members:

Albert Schneider, Sr.	William Langreder	Charles Uteritz
Albert Schneider, Jr.	Henry W. Schultz	William Kuthe
E. C. Amling	E. J. Gotsch	Paul F. Grupe
Herman Mueller	Charles Lussow	Charles Tesnow
Henry Lussow	William Reich	Fred Tesnow
Carl Pries	Fred Schmidt	Fred Wehrmann
Henry C. Schultz	Henry Schroeder	Albert Miessler
John Lussow	Fred Mueller	H. J. Renken
	Henry Schneider	

†Since its removal to River Forest the institution's official name is Concordia Teachers College.

classroom work and to enable the professors to teach their students by practical demonstration of applied methods, the congregation complied with the faculty's request and placed the four lower grades of its day school into the college training school.

A nervous breakdown forced the resignation of Pastor Roecker on February 13, 1918. He was succeeded by the Rev. Herman C. Engelbrecht, a student at the University of Chicago and assistant pastor at First Saint James Church, Chicago.

Already during Pastor Wolter's pastorate attempts at introducing English services were made; and during Pastor Engelbrecht's pastorate services in both German and English became the accepted arrangement.

Mr. Schroeder resigned on August 4, 1918, and William Wegner succeeded him on the day before the Armistice of World War I, on November 10, 1918.

In the summer of 1922 Pastor Engelbrecht accepted a professorship at Concordia Collegiate Institute, Bronxville, N. Y., and on September 24, 1922, the Rev. Otto A. Geiseman of Pekin, Ill., succeeded him to the pastorate of Grace Congregation.

In 1929 a new church was erected at the northeast corner of the Concordia Teachers College campus, West Disivion Street and Bonnie Brae, River Forest.

The teaching staff of Grace School in recent years consisted of the following: H. J. Speckhard (1929-1943), Prof. Albert V. Maurer, Ernest E. Yunghans, Carl Halter, and the Misses Elfrieda Miller, Morella Mensing, Norma Cimaglio, Marie Henriksen, and Mrs. Clara Christopher, Miss Gertrude Drews, Victor Waldschmidt, Miss Evelyn Peck, and Edward F. Krueger.

On January 6, 1946, the Rev. James G. Manz of New Lenox, Ill. was installed as assistant pastor at Grace, River Forest. In October, 1949, he accepted a call to First St. Paul's Congregation in Chicago.

"An Ash Wednesday sermon by Dr. O. A. Geiseman . . . has been chosen as the 'Sermon of the Year' by Dr. Andrew W. Blackwood, professor of homiletics at Princeton Theological Seminary. The sermon appeared in the February issue of the *Pulpit Digest* . . . . " (*Cf. The Lutheran Witness,* LXVII, 21, p. 330.)

146. Chicago, Peace

Still in the preceding century. Enquiry must now be made as to how the Lutherans in the "Hamburger" district are faring in 1897. Some of the members of Saint Andrew's Congregation in that community have established homes a few blocks southwest, a mile or so from their church and school. These people desired to have these institutions for themselves. After several attempts to realize their desire, the "mother" congregation finally yielded to the extent of establishing a school for their children. On August 15, 1897, a school was dedicated at 2711-13 West Forty-third Street. Later, during the seasons of Advent and Lent, the Rev. William C. Kohn, pastor of Saint Andrew's Congregation, conducted "some services" in this school building. Five years after the school had been established, twenty-two men on May 14, 1902, organized Peace Congregation. At its second meeting, on June 12, 1902, Peace Congregation called its first pastor, the Rev. Frank C. Streufert, "Reiseprediger" in Nevada and California, with headquarters at Lodi, Calif. He was installed on August 31, 1902. Within another year seven lots at the corner of Mozart and West Forty-third Streets were purchased, upon which a combination church and school was erected, with the dedication taking place on August 16, 1903. In 1909 five more lots on the southwest corner of South California Avenue and West Forty-third Street (one block east of the original property) were purchased. Fourteen years after the dedication of the first school, and eight after the dedication of the dual-purpose building, the cornerstone of the new church was laid, on August 13, 1911, with dedication following in June, 1912.

In August, 1932, Pastor Streufert accepted the position as executive secretary of the Missouri Synod's Board of Home Missions in North and South America, with headquarters in St. Louis, Mo. The Rev. Luther Streufert served Peace Congregation from August until November 27, 1932, when the congregation's second pastor, the Rev. Franz Julius Theodore Frese of St. Libory, Nebr., was installed. He served here until his death, which occurred on February 29, 1948. The Rev. Herman M. Bauer of Belvidere, Ill., succeeded him to the Peace pastorate on July 11, 1948.

The following have served as teachers in the day school: Maurice L. Gotsch, G. H. Abel, K. Schmid, William Helmkamp, Alfred D. Abraham,* Richard C. Engelbrecht, Mrs. Hugo Bloedel, Erich Haase, Emil Becker, Miss Carolyn Bauer, Mrs. Erich Haase, Richard E. Keb, Miss Luella Mickley, Miss Betty Junkhan, and Mrs. May Hennig.

147. Brookfield

The Trail now proceeds directly westward a distance of seven miles to Brookfield†—about a mile beyond the Des Plaines River—a village formerly known as Grossdale, named for one of its founders, E. A. Gross. In 1890 the Rev. Johannes Strieter, pastor of Immanuel Congregation at Proviso ("Franzosenbusch"), about three and a half miles northwest of Grossdale (Brookfield), made the first attempt at establishing a mission in this place. Services were conducted in Gross Hall, opposite the depot of the "Q" (Chicago, Burlington and Quincy Railroad), on Prairie and Brookfield Avenues. Many of the German families, "being rather unsettled," soon moved to other localities. Most of those who remained attended serv-

*Died March 30, 1947 (65)

†1940 census: 10,817.

ices at Saint John's Church in La Grange—a little more than a mile to the southwest. Another effort to promote Lutheran mission work here was made in 1894 by the Rev. Alex Ullrich, pastor of the La Grange congregation. He conducted services on Sunday afternoons in the anteroom of Gross Hall, which also served as the village's public school, and, later, in Rossler's Hall, at Burlington and Vernon Avenues. In 1896 the Rev. F. A. Luedeke of Crawford (now part of Chicago) conducted services and a day school in a building at 3513 Grand Boulevard and founded Saint Paul's Congregation according to the principles of the Evangelical Church. However, in the spring of 1902, after the unexpected resignation of Saint Paul's pastor, the Rev. R. Fischer, three men* on behalf of the congregation requested Pastor Ullrich to take charge of Saint Paul's in Grossdale. At a meeting on June 3, 1902, at which also two Lutheran pastors, the Rev. Alex Ullrich and the Rev. Louis Hoelter, pastor of First Immanuel, Chicago, and member of the Illinois District's Mission Board, were present, it was decided to sever connections with the afore-mentioned synod, to reorganize as the German Evangelical Lutheran St. Paul's Congregation of Grossdale, Ill., and to ask the Missouri Synod for support.† Thereafter services were conducted regularly every Sunday afternoon by Pastor Ullrich. A day school was opened in January, 1903, and taught, consecutively, by the following: Student W. L. Peterson (January-June, 1903); Student Neumann (until June, 1904); George Seitz, a retired teacher, who served until June, 1908, when he resigned because of his advanced age; and Miss Erna Homann of Addison, Ill., who served until Sep-

*August Gieseke
Emil Albany
Fred Simoneit

†Charter members:

Ernest Weiss
Emil Albany
August Gieseke
Adolph Schmuckal
Edward Schmuckal
Henry Berg
Philip Jacob
Gustav Brozio
Fred Werner
Fred Simoneit
Adolph Klabuhn
Christian Jacob
Louis Bricko
August Holes

tember 16, 1910, when Pastor Ullrich assumed this responsibility for about six weeks. In 1908 Saint Paul's Congregation decided to call its own pastor, but its quest was futile for nearly two years. Then, on November 6, 1910, the Rev. Frederick William Falkenroth of Holden, Alberta, Canada, was installed as the first resident pastor. He also taught school, which until this time and for about two more years was located in a rear room of the church. On May 9, 1912, the congregation resolved to purchase two lots east of the church for $615. Upon this site a dual-purpose building—school and parsonage—was erected at a cost of $4,697.16. Dedication took place on October 6, 1912. In 1913 the congregation joined the Missouri Synod. In August, 1915, the congregation voted to grant Pastor Falkenroth leave of absence for one year for the sake of his health. During this year the congregation was served by students of theology: Martin Buenger, H. Schleef, and H. Meyer. In 1918 the school was forced to close "because of local conditions, chiefly caused by World War I." Pastor Falkenroth resigned in September, 1919, and moved to Clements, Minn. Candidate Oscar A. Rockhoff, graduate of the Lutheran Theological Seminary, Wauwatosa, Wis.,* succeeded to Saint Paul's pastorate on October 26, 1919.

In the spring of 1921 the congregation became self-supporting. In the same year efforts were made to reopen the day school, and in the fall the pastor took charge of this responsibility, beginning with an enrollment of twelve. A year later the enrollment was only four, and therefore it was decided to close the school "for the coming year." Mrs. William Verdon sometime during that winter aroused the interest of "numerous other members" in the day school by means of a letter which she addressed to the congregation. On May 17, 1923, at a meeting of the voters, at which Paul T. Buszin, superintendent of Lutheran Schools in the Northern Illinois District, was the principal speaker, it was resolved to reopen

*Institution belonging to the Wisconsin Synod.

the day school and to call a trained teacher. This teacher, William F. Wittmer, graduate of Concordia Teachers College, River Forest, was installed on September 2, 1923. Two years later a second classroom was opened; a new parsonage was erected; the second floor of the school building was remodeled to serve as a schoolroom; and Pastor Rockhoff again taught school, taking charge of the three lower grades until the fall of 1926, when Miss Olga Knust,* daughter of the Rev. Henry C. Knust of Hamler, Ohio, assumed the work. She served until March, 1930, and was succeeded by Mrs. Louise Stennes; she, in turn, was succeeded by Miss Hilda Anderson† in September, 1931, who served for about six years. In June, 1936, Mr. Wittmer accepted a call to Nazareth Congregation, Chicago. His successor in Saint Paul's School was Herbert Nickel. In the same year Albert Guemmer, Jr., was given charge of the lower grades. In April, 1942, Mr. Guemmer's place was taken by Edgar Abraham. In October, 1942, Mr. Nickel accepted a position offered by the Civil Service Commission; whereupon Mr. Abraham was transferred to the upper grades, and in February, 1943, Edward Lange took charge of the lower grades.

In January, 1938, several lots at the southeast corner of Grant and Park Avenues were purchased for $2,500, and contracts were signed for the erection of a new church to cost $55,000. Application for priorities was made, but when the materials were not forthcoming, building operations were postponed until after the war. A new contract was let in September, 1945, for an additional ten thousand dollars. The new church was dedicated on November 17, 1946.

The Rev. August Oltroge, now pastor of First Immanuel in Chicago, is a "son" of Saint Paul's in Brookfield (Grossdale), Ill.

The teaching staff in recent years consisted of Edgar A.

*Now Mrs. Reinhold Gurgel. Her father, retired, now resides at Plain City, Ohio.

†Now Mrs. Walter Knabusch.

Abraham, and the Misses Ruth Wilkins, Flora Kaiser, Caroline Mueller, Marie Sutton, Elsie Zimmermann, Ruth Warnke, Nanett Neidhold, and Mrs. Elsie Ostien.

148. Morton Grove

About two miles north of Niles (formerly known as Dutchman's Point) is a village called Morton Grove, Ill.* In an old folks' home there the Rev. Frederick W. Detzer of Niles Center (now Skokie) occasionally conducted worship services. Later, as the attendance increased, the services were conducted in the local public school house. As the mission expanded, Pastor Detzer found a willing helper in the Rev. Carl H. Buenger of Maine Township, alternating with him in preaching in Morton Grove; and before long the latter had complete charge of the work, because the former could no longer spare sufficient time to serve here. On July 5, 1902, nine men† met in the village hall and organized Jerusalem Congregation. For the next two years the young congregation was served as an affiliate of Saint Matthew's Congregation in Maine Township by its pastor, the Rev. Carl H. Buenger. Meanwhile the congregation had purchased a plot of ground, 96x125 feet, at the corner of Fernald and Capulina Avenues. In 1902 Pastor Buenger accepted a call to Kenosha, Wis. In March, 1903, the Rev. Julius Toepel succeeded Pastor Buenger at Saint Matthew's and also served Jerusalem Congregation as an affiliate. In the same year the latter congregation erected its first church building and dedicated it on September 27, 1903. Less than a year later, August 14, 1904, the Rev. Theodore Thurow became Jerusalem's first resident pastor. Already in the following year, however, he

*1940 census: 2,010.

†Charter members:

Adolph Poehlmann	Julius Geweke
August Poehlmann	Ludwig Freier
Fred Dilg	John Hillmann
Henry Budde	Charles Peschke
	Charles Blischke

NOTE: For a brief history of St. Matthew's Congregation see Chapter 132, page 436. The church is located four miles east of Des Plaines.

accepted a call to Litchfield, Wis., and during the ensuing vacancy the congregation was served by John Moussa, student at The University of Chicago. The Rev. O. P. Heidtke was installed as Jerusalem's second pastor in April, 1906. In the fall of that year, Pastor Heidtke started a seven-grade school, which he taught for fifteen years. In 1921 Otis Stelljes took charge of the day school; in 1925 he resigned, and C. Kraemer replaced him. In 1929 the church was destroyed by fire, and the services and day school were held in the public school building. In 1930 a new building, serving as church and school, was erected. Financial difficulties resulted in the closing of the day school in 1935. In 1946, however, a new school project was launched—a consolidation of the schools maintained by Saint Paul's, Skokie, Saint John's, Niles, and Jerusalem, in the new building erected by the latter in Morton Grove. This school was opened with an enrollment of 107, in charge of three teachers: Edward M. Lindemann, Walter L. Papenberg, Mrs. Mable Windhorn, Mrs. Elinor Behrens, and Mrs. Elizabeth Bolin were added more recently.

The house next to the parsonage in 1944 was bequeathed to the congregation by William Geweke and now serves as a teacher's residence.

149. Harvey

The year 1903 was noted for many interesting events, not the least significant of which was the first successful heavier-than-air flying-machine flight at Kitty Hawk, N. C., by the two brothers Wilbur and Orville Wright of Dayton, Ohio. During the last week of this year, in the afternoon of December 30, a tragedy occurred in Chicago. 596 persons lost their lives in a fire which destroyed the new and "completely fireproof" Iroquois Theater.

The place next scheduled on the itinerary of the Lutheran Trail is one visited in the 1890's in company with the Rev.

Carl Moritz Noack, who at the time was serving Saint Paul's Congregation at Dolton-Riverdale. It is Harvey, Ill.,* named for its founder, Turlington W. Harvey. In other words, the Trail is now in the 14700-15700 blocks, 17 to 18 miles south of Chicago's Loop, where Halsted Street jogs somewhat to the southeast through the adjacent village of Phoenix, then continuing south for another seven miles into Chicago Heights.

When Pastor Noack in 1897 accepted a call to Sioux City, Iowa, the Rev. Matthew H. Feddersen, pastor of Saint John's Congregation at Coopers Grove, took under his wing the few Lutherans in Harvey. Early in 1898 he and Henry Tegal canvassed the village with a view to organizing a congregation. A small public school house was used as a place of worship. The first service held there on June 4, 1899, was attended by fifteen persons, five of whom were children. For nearly three years worship services were conducted in the German language on alternate Sunday afternoons. In the summer of 1902 the mission in Harvey was taken over by the Rev. Henry F. Wind, Pastor Noack's successor at Saint Paul's, Dolton-Riverdale, chiefly because it was comparatively easy for Pastor Wind to reach Harvey by train, while from Coopers Grove the trip was somewhat difficult, Pastor Feddersen's home being located about three miles west of the Illinois Central Railroad's depot, at Homewood (formerly known as Thornton Station).

On February 8, 1903, a congregation was organized by ten men† and named Trinity. In June of the same year Trinity purchased a 37x60-foot lot at 129 East 153d Street for $115. On this site a frame chapel costing twelve hundred dollars

*1940 census: 17,878.

†Charter members:

Henry Tegal	George Greiner, Sr.	Edward Schroeder
Emil Rohrdanz	Adolph Lehmann	Chas. Seams
Christian Hieber	George Greiner, Jr.	John Rusch
	Carl Staack	

was erected, and dedicated on September 13, 1903. In the spring of 1918 the faculty of Concordia Seminary, St. Louis, Mo., assigned Candidate Rudolf L. Geffert to Trinity Congregation in Harvey. He was installed as its first resident pastor on August 28, 1918. From then on German and English services were conducted on alternate Sundays. On August 5, 1920, Trinity purchased the Presbyterian church at 15316 Center Avenue for $18,000. After the interior had been remodeled, this church was dedicated on October 24, 1920. The old chapel on East 153d Street was sold to the Seventh Day Adventists for fifteen hundred dollars. On June 28, 1922, Trinity became a member of the Missouri Synod. In January, 1924, the congregation became self-supporting; and in the same year services in both languages, German and English, were instituted for every Sunday morning. In the same year Pastor Geffert received permission from his congregation to start mission work in the village of Hazel Crest, about two miles south of Harvey. Two years later a "basement" church was constructed on Wood Street, at West 169th, and services were held there on Sunday evenings or afternoons. This small parish is now being served jointly with Concordia (Midlothian) by the Rev. Walter C. Johannes, who was installed on June 5, 1949.

150. Chicago, Saint Paul's

Back to Chicago. At 5600 North and 7900 West, which is the intersection of Higgins and Canfield Roads, the Trail makes a brief pause in the summer of 1903—at the "Big City's" northwestern limits, where the folks living on the east side of Canfield Road can converse with their Park Ridge neighbors on the other side of the road.

In the early days, quite a number of members of Saint John's Congregation in the village of Mayfair, Jefferson Township, were residents in this community, about one and a half miles northwest of Saint John's Church. In a meeting held on July 7, 1903, these members were granted permission to organize their own congregation. This was accomplished two weeks later, on July 26, when thirteen men adopted and signed a constitution and chose the name Saint Paul. Almost immediately steps were taken to build a church. By the end of February, 1904, the building, 36x60 feet, was completed. Dedication took place on March 6, 1904. Saint Paul's first pastor was the Rev. August Lange, who was called from Brownton, Minn. His pastorate here extended over a period of about twelve years, from 1903 to 1915. He was succeeded by the Rev. Herman C. Schoenbeck of Lynville (now Lindenwood), Ill., who served from 1915 to 1920. Then came the Rev. Paul W. Roehrs from Altamont, Ill., who remained here until 1927 and then accepted a call to Wausau, Wis. Shortly afterward the present pastor came from Okawville, Ill., the Rev. Albert H. Zimmer. He was installed October 23, 1927.

A day school has been maintained since the year of organization. From a one-room school in the rear of the church, taught by the pastors, the school has grown steadily. The following trained teachers have been in charge of the school in more recent years: H. E. Meyer, Miss Dorothy Kurth, Mrs. Lydia Werth, Albert F. Sachtleben, Miss Sophia von Bergen, Miss Lois Schwanenberg, Mrs. Ilene Koehler, and William H. Tetting.

151. Wilmette

Fourteen miles north of Chicago's Loop, or about three miles north of Evanston on the Lake, is a large village whose name honors the memory of an Indian half-breed, "Billy" Ouilmette, who helped prevent a massacre of white settlers at Lake Geneva, Wis., during the latter part of the 1820's.

On August 27, 1893, the Rev. John D. Matthius, pastor of Bethlehem in Evanston and of Trinity in Glencoe, preached to an audience of about fifteen people in Wilmette, which was considerably smaller then than it is now; by 1940 it had gained about 16,226 inhabitants over the estimated 1,000 in 1893. For about three years Pastor Matthius conducted services in Wilmette on alternate Sunday afternoons. In 1896 the Rev. Fred Knief, assistant pastor of First Zion Congregation in Chicago,* began preaching here every Sunday afternoon. In the following year, the year of the memorable gold rush to the Klondike region in Alaska, Saint John's Congregation was organized in Wilmette. In 1898 the Rev. Barthold Burfeind, who because of ill health had resigned from the active ministry in Lemont, Ill., in the summer of 1895, came from his home in Chicago to conduct services and also sought to organize a congregation in near-by Winnetka. In 1902 ill health again forced him to resign. Then a somewhat disheartening chapter in the history of the two parishes followed: the people who were to constitute the nucleus for a new congregation rejoined the congregations to which they had previously belonged, principally Bethlehem in Evanston and Trinity in Glencoe.

In 1903 the Chicago Lutheran Pastoral Conference requested and encouraged Pastor Matthius to make another attempt at gathering the Lutherans of Wilmette into a congregation. The attempt was fruitful. On November 8, 1903, twelve men adopted a constitution and organized Saint John's Congregation. A student of theology, F. H. Kretzschmar, was engaged to serve temporarily. A Sunday school was established, and worship services were conducted in various homes, public halls, and church buildings of other denominations.

Saint John's first resident pastor, the Rev. Victor F. Richter of Centerville, Mich., was installed on March 19, 1905. In the following year two lots on the corner of Prairie and Linden Avenues were purchased for twelve hundred dollars, and soon afterward a frame church building, 50x26 feet, was

*Located at West Nineteenth and Peoria Streets.

erected, dedication following on November 11, 1906. On the very next day a day school was opened with ten pupils; nine more came during the first term. In September, 1909, Pastor Richter accepted a call to Billings, near Springfield, Mo. After a long vacancy the Rev. Fred W. G. Mueller, assistant pastor of Saint Luke's Congregation, Chicago, was installed on March 4, 1910. Ill health interrupted his pastorate, and he resigned in February, 1913.* His successor in Wilmette, the Rev. Herman W. Meyer of Millstadt, Ill., was installed as the third pastor of Saint John's on April 13, 1913. A short time prior to his arrival the congregation had become self-supporting.

In March, 1922, a lot at Wilmette and Park Avenues was purchased, and upon it a new church was erected in the following year, dedication taking place on December 16, 1923. About ten years later, on November 6, 1933, Pastor Meyer died. His successor, the Rev. Julius Herman Gockel, since 1929 hospice secretary at the Walther League office, 6438 Eggleston Avenue, Chicago, was installed as Saint John's fourth pastor on January 28, 1934. In 1944 a fifty-foot lot, adjoining the east line of the church property, was purchased for the purpose of erecting upon it a parish hall.

152. Beecher

It seems like ages ago since the Trail was in the vicinity of Beecher, Ill.† Two miles northwest of this village is Saint Paul's Church. Now, in the village itself acquaintance is made with some of the Lutherans residing there. They are members of Saint Paul's‡ out there in the country, but they are

*Later he re-entered the active ministry; was pastor of St. Peter's Congregation, residing in Florida, Ohio; now retired and living in Napoleon, Ohio.

†1940 census: 742.

‡Charter members:

Henry Stade	Fred Kegebein	William Ahrens
C. B. Boicken	J. W. Knuth	Henry Hartman
Martin Arfmann	William Rump	H. Behrens
Ed. Langreder	H. F. Wilke	Ernest Fette
Fred Schuette	(:)William J. Hinze	Louis Stade
	H. Seitz	L. Oldenburg

(:)Treasurer of the Northern Illinois District, Missouri Synod, 1907-1945.

discussing the advisability of organizing their own congregation in Beecher. This took place on November 29, 1903; and on the following December 18 they met in the home of H. F. Wilke, where they adopted a constitution which had been drawn up for them by the Rev. Albert H. Brauer, pastor of Saint Paul's. They organized as Zion Congregation, calling their own pastor, the Rev. Louis J. F. Going of Elmore, Ohio. At that time also the congregation voted to join the Missouri Synod. Pastor Going was installed on June 12, 1904.

For the first ten months worship services were held in the village hall of Beecher. During this time, however, a church was being built on the corner of Elliott and Indiana Streets.* This building was dedicated on October 16, 1904. A day school was established in the same year and taught by the pastor until 1914, when a trained teacher, V. J. Schultz, was placed in charge of this work. Six years later a second classroom was opened, and Miss Ruth Rump was engaged to teach the lower grades. During the summer of 1923 Pastor Going resigned.† His successor in Beecher, the Rev. William Henry Louis Schuetz of Monticello, Iowa, was installed on September 16, 1923. About three years later Mr. Schultz followed a call to Grand Rapids, Mich., and was succeeded in Zion School on October 17, 1926, by Paul E. Leimer‡ of Falls City, Nebr. In 1927 the congregation expended $14,600 for the erection of a parsonage and a teacher's residence. In 1931 Miss Rump's place in school was taken by Miss Clara Maschhoff, who served for one year. In 1932 a Sunday school was organized. At that time, in September, Miss Esther Thoen began teaching the lower grades. Three years later she was replaced by a former teacher, Miss Rump, who served for the next three years. Then came Miss Lucille Wassmann and

*This site, comprising three lots, was purchased for $400.

†Pastor Going died in 1925 in Des Plaines, Ill., and was buried in the Lutheran cemetery near Beecher, Ill.

‡A brother of the Rev. John A. Leimer, pastor of Hope Congregation in Chicago since Jan. 7, 1917.

taught for four years; after her, Miss Fern Lange and Miss Pauline Beyer; and more recently, Darrel H. Naber, Mrs. William Deutsch, and Miss Esther Adam.

Pastor Schuetz resigned in the spring of 1943.* Zion's third pastor, the Rev. Harold J. Wunderlich of Fredericksburg, Iowa, was installed on June 6, 1943.

153. Harvard

1904—the year in which the United States occupied the Panama Canal Zone and began digging the canal under the direction of Colonel George W. Goethals. However, there is no indication of any new Missouri Synod congregation being organized in northern Illinois during this year. Hence the Trail returns in the direction of Duncklees Grove to get a glimpse of something that has been going on for a good many years. Harvard† is the "milk center of the world," and back in the 1870's and 1880's the scattered Lutherans in and round about this village were served by the Rev. Henry G. Schmidt of Crystal Lake and later by the Rev. Walter von Schenk of Algonquin. Under the leadership of the latter the building of the Congregationalists on Hart Boulevard was rented for worship purposes. On July 7, 1889, the Rev. Frederick Caemmerer of Sturgis, Mich., became the first resident pastor. During his pastorate a new church and parsonage were built on the northeastern edge of the village. The church was dedicated on October 31, 1892. In 1897 Pastor Caemmerer severed connections with the Missouri Synod. Disunity in the congregation, then known as Trinity, came to an unfortunate climax when the Mission Board of the Illinois District (Missouri Synod) suggested that the Lutherans residing at Big Foot‡ on the Illinois-Wisconsin State line, five miles north

*For several years during World War II, Pastor Schuetz served Trinity Congregation at Paw Paw, Mich., during the Rev. H. J. Maleske's leave of absence as chaplain in the U.S. Army; more recently he has been serving as assistant pastor at First Saint James Church, Chicago.

†1940 census: 3,121. Named by Judge Ayer, an early settler, for Harvard University.

‡A very small community.

of Harvard, request the pastor of Zion Congregation at Sharon, Wis., to serve them as an affiliate. Pastor Caemmerer violently disagreed with the suggestion; after a number of unsuccessful meetings with the synodical officials in Illinois and Wisconsin, Trinity in Harvard, on the insistence of its pastor, in October, 1897, severed its connection with the Missouri Synod and became a member of the General Synod.* However, a short time afterward eighteen families severed their connection with the new congregation and returned to worship in the church on Hart Boulevard. Then the Rev. F. Gerhard Kuehnert, who on June 28, 1896, had assumed the Zion pastorate at Sharon, Wis., was requested to serve the now nameless group in Harvard. He received an "informal call" and on February 27, 1898, conducted his first service in the church where Lutheranism in Harvard was born during the seventh decade. Upon Pastor Kuehnert's acceptance of a call in June, 1900, to Omaha, Nebr.,† the Rev. John Schert, his successor at Zion in Sharon, continued to serve the Harvard group as an affiliate. In 1905, however, the Illinois District's Mission Board (Missouri Synod) assigned the Rev. Raymond R. Reinke to take charge of the nameless and shepherdless flock in Harvard. On June 11, 1905, this group was organized as Saint Paul's Congregation. Pastor Reinke began mission work in near-by Alden shortly after his arrival in Harvard. In December, 1909, he accepted a call to the newly organized Salem Congregation in Blue Island, Ill., and was succeeded in Harvard by an elderly pastor, the Rev. F. Kleist, who lived in Alden, about ten miles northeast of Harvard. At the 1910 convention of the Illinois District (Missouri Synod) it was reported that "not only is there strong opposition on the part of a congregation which formerly belonged to us, but also the lodges have gained control of everything ("haben

*The General Synod was one of the many which in 1918 entered the merger which since then has been known as the United Lutheran Church in America.

†The Rev. F. G. Kuehnert served Immanuel Congregation in Crystal Lake, Ill., 1904-1934.

hier alles eingenommen"). In 1913 the Rev. F. G. Kuehnert, who had served the "orphaned" congregation as an affiliate of his congregation in Sharon, Wis., 1898-1900, and since 1904 pastor of Immanuel Congregation in Crystal Lake, Ill.,* was requested to take charge of the congregation, now known as Saint Paul's, on a temporary basis. In 1919 the congregation purchased the property it had been renting for many years; the following year extensive improvements were made, the greater part being done by Saint Paul's members.

When in 1925 Pastor Kuehnert reported that he found it impossible to continue serving this flock any longer, the Mission Board requested the Rev. Herman E. Brauer of Marengo, about twelve miles south of Harvard, to serve Saint Paul's as an affiliate. He did this until 1929. His successor at Marengo, the Rev. Edward A. Nauss, served in a similar manner until August, 1931, when he died. According to a report submitted by the Mission Board at the 1931 convention, a candidate was designated to serve in Harvard. This was W. Martin Rupprecht, graduate of Concordia Seminary, St. Louis, Mo. He served as Saint Paul's pastor until 1937, when he accepted a call as assistant pastor at Jehovah Church in Chicago. Pastor Rupprecht's successor in Harvard was Candidate William J. Danker, who was installed on July 4, 1937. In the summer of 1942 he accepted a call to West Chicago (formerly known as Turner Junction), Ill., and the Rev. Paul F. Huxhold of Bridgeview, Ill., was installed as Saint Paul's pastor on August 9, 1942.

154. Chicago, Bethany, Uptown

Near the water's edge, about eight miles north of the Loop in Chicago, the Trail enters into the "uptown" community known as Edgewater. It was in the afternoon of Sunday, June 11, 1905, when a small group of people gathered in a public hall at the corner of North Clark Street and "the

*Crystal Lake is located about 20 miles southeast of Harvard.

Ridge" for a worship service conducted by the Rev. Ernest F. Haertel, pastor of Christ English Congregation, whose center at that time was at North Hoyne Avenue and Augusta Street, Chicago.* For seven months the small flock worshiped in that public hall, during which time Pastor Haertel was in charge. An urgent request for a special meeting of "all interested in the organization of an English congregation" in the Edgewater community was heeded by comparatively few people. Nevertheless, the meeting was held in the evening of November 15, 1905, and Bethany Congregation came into being. Assisted by the Mission Board of the Illinois District (Missouri Synod), the small congregation called the Rev. Karl G. Schlerf of Hillside, Mich. At the time of his installation, on January 7, 1906, it was found that Bethany's membership was composed of seventeen adults and eight children, the latter constituting the first Sunday school enrollment. In February, 1906, Bethany rented a vacant store at 2561 Evanston Avenue (now 5540 Broadway), where the services were conducted from March 4, 1906, until January 10, 1909. On April 3, 1906, eleven Lutheran men signed Bethany's constitution.† Meanwhile two lots at the corner of Thorndale and Magnolia Avenues had been purchased for $3,800, and upon this site a so-called Bible Chapel was erected at a cost of approximately $14,500, inclusive of furnishings and appurtenances. This building was dedicated on January 17, 1909. Less than seven years after its founding, Bethany resolved to erect a new church directly east of the Bible Chapel and adjoining it. A hundred-foot frontage was acquired by three members and presented to the congregation as the site of a parish house and a parsonage. At its tenth anniversary in 1915 Bethany had increased to 288 communicants (400 baptized members), and the Sunday school to 283.

*New location, since 1926, North Long and Le Moyne Avenues.

†Henry C. Bartling—August Heuer, Jr.—A. P. Handke—Henry C. Knoll—Robert C. Cook—William H. Eggebrecht—William H. Heuer—A. H. Lachmann—George J. Kroeck—William F. Detering—Karl G. Schlerf, pastor.

On July 22, 1945, Candidate Ralph Justin Pomeroy, graduate of Concordia Seminary, St. Louis, Mo., was installed as assistant pastor. Bethany had its first pastor until June 26, 1949, which marks the date of his retirement from the ministry.

155. Addison

Time is short, so back directly to the Duncklees Grove neighborhood—to Addison,* a small village, whose name unwittingly reminds one of Addison's disease, a disease traced to its source by Dr. Thomas Addison of London, England. Presumably, however, the village's name is derived from an eminent English essayist, Joseph Addison, the cause of whose death (June 17, 1719) was dropsy and asthma.

The historical background of the Lutheran congregation in Addison is identical with that of Zion Congregation, two and a half miles to the east. (See Chapter One, page 15.) Beginning in 1893, worship services were held in the chapel of the Teachers' Seminary, directly northwest of the village. In the course of time the inadequacy of this arrangement was keenly felt, and the "mother" congregation at Duncklees Grove (now known as Churchville) was requested to devise ways and means toward solving the problem. Favorably inclined toward rendering special assistance, Zion Congregation on July 10, 1906, released forty-five of its voting members for the purpose of organizing a congregation in the village. Five days later the congregation, Saint Paul's, called its first resident pastor, the Rev. Adolph Pfotenhauer of Lemont, Ill. He was installed on September 16, 1906. In the same year a large brick church was erected at a cost of $30,716, and because the church was designed to serve both the faculty and the students of the Teachers' Seminary, Saint Paul's was granted permission to solicit funds from member congregations throughout the Missouri Synod. The records reveal that such financial assistance was given and received.

*1940 census: 819.

During Pastor Pfotenhauer's pastorate, Saint Paul's developed into a congregation of more than eight hundred baptized members, and on July 5, 1936, gave its pastor an assistant, Candidate Daniel E. Poellot,* graduate of Concordia Seminary, St. Louis, Mo. Less than three years later, on April 29, 1939, Pastor Pfotenhauer died, and the assistant pastor was formally placed in charge of the pastorate on September 24, 1939.

Two day schools—the one adjoining the church and founded in 1848, the other in Bloomingdale Township and founded in 1880—were taken over from the "mother" congregation in 1906. In 1942 the latter property was sold at public auction. In 1925 a new school building was erected directly west of the new church at a cost of forty-three thousand dollars, one half of which was contributed by the Lutheran Orphan Home Association, for the reason that the orphans attended this school.

The following have served as teachers in this day school:

H. Bartling, 1849-1891
G. Seitz, 1861
Miss Regina Rotermund, 1861-1865
A. Albers, 1856-1867
J. Brackmann, 1867-1868
Adolph Gruhl, 1866-1871
Karl Koebel, 1871-1874
Wm. Kammann, 1872-1874
Christian Greve, 1874-1887
Edmund Brust, 1887-1902
Miss Lisette Leeseberg, 1880-1882
Miss Bertha Heidemann, 1882-1885
Miss Amalia Brauer, 1885-1887
G. Ritzmann, 1888-1902
Miss Johanna Bartling, 1891
A. Weise, 1891-1898
G. F. Wagner, 1902
William Helmkamp, 1902-1908
Paul Buuck, 1908
Arnold Felten, 1908
H. William Koch, 1903-1946
Miss Louise Pfotenhauer, 1907-1913
Hugo Oldsen, 1908-1923
O. H. Buerger, 1913-1941
Mrs. Paula Pfotenhauer, 1922
Chr. Seidel, 1923
E. Ritzmann, 1923-1924
Rev. Adolph C. Staats, 1924
William C. Marten, 1924-1943
Miss Ada Gresens, 1925-1926
Miss Anita Spaltholz, 1926-1929
Miss Emma Heidemann, 1929-1940; 1942-
Daniel E. Poellot, 1935
R. C. Engebrecht, 1943-
Mrs. D. E. Poellot, 1944-1945; 1946-1947
Milton W. Schmidt, 1946-1948
M. J. Kaste, 1948-

156. Chicago, Tabor

During sojourn in the Avondale community on the northwest side of Chicago acquaintance was made with First Bethlehem's "granddaughter," Concordia Congregation, and "her"

*His father, the Rev. Siegfried Daniel Poellot, was pastor of Immanuel Congregation, Palatine, Ill., 1910-1940; he died at Addison Jan. 12, 1942.

pastors. The records show that the latter's second pastor, the Rev. Carl F. Dietz, in 1901 established a mission in the Irving Park community on Kimball Avenue, north of Irving Park Boulevard, where a vacant store served as a place of worship for Concordia's members living in that community. Soon afterward the "mother" congregation's newly installed assistant pastor, the Rev. Ferdinand Doederlein, was placed in charge of this new mission, then generally referred to as "Konkordia Mission." A centrally located lot with a frame building at Montrose and Central Park Avenues was purchased by the Mission Board of the Illinois District (Missouri Synod). The building was remodeled to serve as a combination church and school. On November 26, 1906, the "Konkordia Mission" was organized as Tabor Congregation.* "An ancient tradition, traceable back as far as Jerome and Origen, associates Tabor with the scene of the Transfiguration, but in Christ's time the top of the mountain was probably covered with houses, ruins of which and of an old fortress, as well as of churches and monasteries with pools and cisterns, are still to be found on it." On the day of organization Tabor Congregation called the "mother" congregation's assistant pastor. The first day school teacher was Otto Ziemann, graduate of the Teachers' Seminary at Addison. In the summer of 1907 Pastor Doederlein suffered a stroke, which weakened him to such an extent that he felt constrained to resign "only for the welfare of Tabor." His successor, the Rev. Albert D. Wangerin of Hampshire, Ill., was installed on February 23, 1908, and Pastor Doederlein was made "honorary pastor," with the understanding that he would assist the new pastor "as much as his strength would permit." Mr. Ziemann at this time followed a call to Cincinnati, Ohio, and Pastor Wangerin took charge of the day school. By October, 1908, the enrollment had increased to sixty, and the congregation called Henry Lotz of

*Charter members: Chas. F. Brack—Emil Weber, Sr.—Theodore Glienke—Fred Lemke—Paul R. Stark—August Spiekermann.

Whiting, Ind., to relieve the pastor from school teaching.

In January, 1909, Tabor purchased property on the northwest corner of Sunnyside and Drake Avenues. It joined the Missouri Synod in the same year. On April 25, 1909, a second classroom was opened and taught by Pastor Wangerin until November, when Edward H. Karnatz took charge. On December 5, 1909, the combination church and school was dedicated. "After a short farewell service in the chapel on Montrose Avenue, the congregation, under a downpour of rain, marched to Sunnyside and Drake Avenues and entered the new building." The entire cost of the building and lots was $18,705.88. In 1911 a church bell was purchased from Bethel Congregation, Springfield Avenue and Hirsch Street, and English services were introduced. In February, 1911, Mr. Lotz followed a call to Saint Matthew's Congregation at Russells Grove (Fairfield), Ill., and in May Miss Marie Lietzow took his place in the day school. In January, 1915, Tabor became self-supporting. On July 3 of the same year Pastor Doederlein died at the age of eighty-three.

In November, 1916, Mr. Karnatz followed a call to the "Kinderheim" at Addison, Ill., and on April 22, 1917, E. L. Marquardt of Christ Congregation of Logan Square was installed as teacher. In 1920 two additional classrooms were opened, and on August 20, 1920, E. H. Brunn was installed. Miss Martha Burger of Sheboygan, Wis., took over Miss Lietzow's classes. Soon afterward, owing to scarcity of day school teachers, Mrs. William Arnswald (the former Miss Marie Lietzow) was again placed in charge of two classes until J. H. Maschhoff's induction on September 4, 1921. After one year's service the latter resigned, and Albert O. Heldt, graduate of Concordia Teachers College, River Forest, succeeded him on September 3, 1922. On November 19 M. E. Klausmeier of Beemer, Nebr., succeeded Mr. Brunn, who resigned in order to devote himself entirely to music. In 1924 Mr. Klausmeier followed a call to Milwaukee, Wis., and on November 30 John G. Rieck* of Edwardsville, Ill., was installed.

During 1926 and 1927 a new church was erected at a cost of $125,000. Dedication took place on September 25, 1927. On May 17, 1940, Pastor Wangerin died at the age of fifty-nine. The Rev. Carl R. Matthies of Blackwell, Okla., became Tabor's third pastor by installation on October 6, 1940. Mr. Heldt died on November 6, 1942.

In addition to the teachers already mentioned, the following have served in Tabor School: H. J. Eschbach, Miss Irmalyn Klamt, Elroy L. Venzke, Miss Anita Scher, Mrs. Dorothy Neumann, Miss Esther Kretzmann, and Armond Schoof.

A motion-picture film in technicolor, titled "Tabor Church, 1944" and produced by Edgar Neitzel and Fred Krefft, with the assistance of other members, several years ago drew an overflow crowd to Tabor's assembly hall. "Every phase of congregation work and activity at Tabor is shown."

Mr. and Mrs. Walter Rodgers and their family, evicted from their apartment near Tabor Church, found shelter in the kindergarten room of Tabor School during the night of March 5, 1947. The mother, smoothing the blankets around the baby, Harold, who was laughing unconcernedly, said: "I didn't know anything like this could happen." (No doubt, referring to the eviction.)[95]

157. Oak Park, Trinity

1907—the year in which the Illinois District of the Missouri Synod was divided into three Districts: Northern, Central, and Southern. Organization of the Northern Illinois District was effected on May 23, 1907, in First Bethlehem Church, North Paulina and McReynolds (now Le Moyne) Streets. The Illinois District was a part of the Western District, established by the Missouri Synod in 1854, until 1875, when Illinois be-

*Mr. Rieck directed the children's chorus at the Centennial celebration in Chicago, on July 23, 1947, in the Medinah Temple.

came a separate District. The first president of the Northern Illinois District was the Rev. William C. Kohn, at the time pastor of Saint Andrew's Congregation in Chicago. He was elected at the District's first convention in Chicago in 1909 and served in this capacity until 1913, when he accepted the directorship of Concordia Teachers College in River Forest, Ill.

The Trail moves on, this time to Kettlestring's Grove, first settled in 1835, but not incorporated as a village until 1901. This place has the distinction of having been renamed several times: first, Kettlestring's Grove; then Oak Ridge; for some time it shared honors with a close neighbor and was known as Harlem; then it was called Noyesville, but now this village, the world's largest, 'tis said, is known as Oak Park, Ill.* Oak Park "is an attractive residential center and has a thriving retail trade, several private as well as public schools, a public library, Scoville Institute, various literary, art, music, and other cultural organizations. . . ."

One of those private schools is the day school maintained by Christ Congregation at Harvard and South East Avenues, which will be considered in a subsequent chapter. Immediate concern is how Lutheranism found its way into the northern part of this village.

It was on Sunday, October 28, 1906, that the Rev. Ernest F. Haertel, pastor of Christ English Congregation, began preaching services in a public hall located at the corner of Lake Street and Lombard Avenue in Oak Park. On April 4, 1907, six Lutheran men organized Trinity Congregation and joined the English Missouri Synod. On June 23, 1907, Candidate Jean M. Bailey, graduate of Concordia Seminary, St. Louis, Mo., was installed as Trinity's first pastor. A year later a large lot at Sixty-fourth Avenue (now Ridgeland) and Erie Street was purchased, upon which a chapel was erected, and

*1940 census: 66,015.

dedicated on August 15, 1909. In 1910 the congregation became self-supporting.

The increase in membership necessitated the erection of a new place of worship in 1915. The dedication took place on November 26, 1916. In 1920 Pastor Bailey accepted a call to Baltimore, Md., and his successor, the Rev. Herman W. Prange of Minneapolis, Minn., was installed on March 13, 1921. Pastor Prange served Trinity for eighteen years and on October 17, 1939, died suddenly while conducting a vestry meeting at church. He was succeeded on April 7, 1940, by the Rev. Harold W. Romoser of Pittsburgh, Pa. In 1946 Trinity joined the Northern Illinois District.

158. Itasca

About five miles northwest of Zion Church in the well-known community of Duncklees Grove (now Churchville) is a village located on the Chicago, Milwaukee, St. Paul, and Pacific Railroad, Itasca, Ill.,* named for a lake in the State of Minnesota. "The word itself was coined by Mr. Schoolcraft from the Ojibway 'totosh,' meaning 'a woman's breast.' " The members of Zion residing in this community in the 1870's already agitated for the establishment of a school district, but because the number of children who were of school age was very small, the congregation at Duncklees Grove postponed the matter until more Lutherans settled there. In 1885 the Itascans felt that the opportune time had come to repeat the former request. At first, however, they agreed to making an attempt at establishing a school in the local public school during the summer vacation, for a period of about three months. They were granted the free use of the classrooms for this purpose. A Mr. Richter, student at Concordia Seminary, Springfield, Ill., was placed in charge of this branch school, which was attended by more than twenty pupils. During July the Itascans had additional courage to come before

*1940 census: 787.

Zion Congregation. The latter, in a special meeting on July 27, 1885, granted the petition and provided for a special collection in the entire congregation for this cause. Two days later, on July 29, the Itasca school district was organized by six men in the home of Louis Magers.* Two acres of land with a dwelling were purchased for nine hundred dollars. Upon this site a school was erected (24x30x12) at a cost of $512.70. This building was dedicated on September 13, 1885. Student Richter consented to remain here and teach during the following school year. In April, 1886, Zion Congregation extended a call to a student at the Teachers' Seminary, Addison, Theodore Hinz. He graduated in June, and on the following August 22 he was installed as teacher in Itasca. His annual salary was fixed at $250. By summer, 1888, the enrollment in the day school was twenty-seven. For almost twenty more years Zion Congregation maintained this school district. Then, on July 14, 1907, seventeen voting members residing in the Itasca territory were peacefully released to organize their own congregation, which was named Saint Luke. Its first pastor, the Rev. Frederick Zersen of Hankinson, N. Dak., was installed on August 25, 1907. He took charge of the school and taught for about two years, when a trained teacher, Gerhard Elbert, assumed these duties. During the year 1907 a church costing ten thousand dollars was erected on South Walnut Avenue and dedicated in December. In 1908 Saint Luke's joined the Missouri Synod.

In 1921 an addition was built to the school, and a second teacher, Miss Gertrude Doederlein, was given charge of the lower grades.

The language question "solved itself."

Pastor Zersen's son, the Rev. William Louis Zersen, for about ten years pastor of a congregation at Kelowna, British Columbia, Canada, died on March 27, 1938.

*Eduard Fiene—Heinrich Droegemueller—August Kaehler—Louis Magers—August Buchholz—August Wede.

Pastor Zersen retired from the active ministry on August 31, 1945.* His successor, the Rev. Kurt Victor Grotheer† of Foley, Ala., was installed as Saint Luke's second pastor on October 28, 1945.

In addition to the teachers already mentioned, the following have served in Saint Luke's day school: Student P. Droegemueller, Mrs. William J. Danker, and Miss Edna Bonitz. Since 1945 this school has been maintained jointly by Saint Luke's and its "mother"—Zion of Churchville (formerly Duncklees Grove.)[96]

159. Oak Park, Christ

Back again to the world's largest village—Oak Park, Ill.—formerly and consecutively known as Kettlestring's Grove, Oak Ridge, Harlem, and Noyesville. It was upon the suggestion and with the willing assistance of Leo Goetz, a resident of Oak Park, that the Rev. George William Wolter, pastor of Grace Congregation, whose center at the time was at the northwest corner of Augusta Street and Belleforte Avenue, canvassed the southern section of the village during the summer of 1907. In the following November a congregation, Christ Church, was organized there under Pastor Wolter's direction. Worship services and Sunday school sessions were conducted every Sunday afternoon in a rented hall on Clarence Avenue in South Oak Park (Berwyn) by Pastor Wolter, assisted by the Rev. William Gahl, pastor of Ebenezer Congregation, Chicago. Christ Congregation's first resident pastor, the Rev. Ernest T. Lams, graduate of Concordia Seminary, St. Louis, Mo., 1903, was installed on August 16, 1908. Several weeks later the new pastor organized a day school, which

*Frederick Zersen was born on a farm near Lake Zurich in 1869; attended St. Matthew's School at Russells Grove (Fairfield), Ill. Died April 25, 1949.

†Son of the Rev. Louis A. Grotheer, pastor of St. John's, Niles (Dutchman's Point), Ill., 1914-1942.

NOTE: The Rev. Ernest T. Lams was president of the Northern Illinois District from 1936 until 1945. He received the honorary degree of Doctor of Divinity from Concordia Seminary, Springfield, Ill., in 1944.

he taught for two years. In December, 1908, the congregation's first church building, constructed of wood and located on Harvard Street, was dedicated. This building served as church and school for about five years. During this period it had to be enlarged to provide more room for the steady increase in church membership and in school enrollment.* In 1913 a new church of brick was erected at the southwest corner of South East Avenue and Harvard Street. A new and larger school was built and dedicated in 1924. On December 6, 1936, Candidate Edgar Ernest Lams, one of the pastor's sons, graduate of Concordia Seminary, Springfield, Ill., was ordained and installed as associate pastor of Christ Congregation.

The teaching staff comprises the following: C. H. Meier (principal); A. C. Wissmueller, H. E. Boester, Miss Elsa M. Pigorsz, and Miss Bertha Tjernagel. Others who have served as teachers in the day school were Ottomar Kolb, Jr., H. Borchers, Miss Rosena Porth, Miss Elfrieda Miller, Miss Esther Luebke, Miss Phyllis Wisniewski, Miss Dorothy Gurske, Mrs. Boger, Wm. Wegener, and Mrs. M. C. Duensing.

160. Bellwood

Four miles west of Oak Park is a village called Bellwood.† The Rev. Henry Roehrs, pastor of Immanuel Congregation at Proviso ("Franzosenbusch"), in 1907 canvassed this village and found many Russians from the Volga district. He evidently conversed with them in the German language and also began conducting worship services for them. On December 15, 1907, Saint John's Congregation was organized in Bellwood; in the following year a chapel was built. It seems that Pastor Roehrs continued to serve this new congregation for the next five or six years as an affiliate of Im-

*This building still stands on the present church property. It is utilized as a meeting place for various auxiliary organizations and for classrooms.

†1940 census: 5,220.

manuel at Proviso. Christian Scheiderer of Quincy, Ill., was called to take charge of the day school, which opened with seventeen pupils in September, 1908. After about six years the enrollment had increased to 106. Saint John's first resident pastor, the Rev. Herman Meyer, for the past ten years pastor of Trinity Congregation at Willow Springs, Ill., was installed in Bellwood on August 24, 1913. Mr. Scheiderer died unexpectedly on March 26, 1916.* E. W. Grothe of Belvidere, Ill., took his place in Saint John's School. At the same time Miss Stehr of Chicago was engaged to teach the lower grades. In 1917 ill health caused Mr. Grothe's resignation; thereupon two men were called, Paul M. Schroeter and William Krueger. Two years later, in 1919, both teachers followed calls elsewhere; then M. G. Seitz of Kendallville, Ind., was given charge of the upper grades, and the pastor taught the lower grades.

On March 1, 1925, Pastor Meyer resigned for reasons of health. His successor, the Rev. John H. Mueller of Zion in Summit, Ill., was installed on June 7, 1925. In December, 1926, Pastor Mueller accepted the superintendency of the Kinderheim at Addison, and the Rev. William L. Kupsky of Lace, Ill., succeeded him in Saint John's pastorate on January 23, 1927.

Other teachers who have served in Saint John's School were Milton Eggerding, Ralph T. Appelt, William H. Tetting and Miss Carol Sauer.

At the 1918 convention of the Northern Illinois District (Missouri Synod) it was reported that "in Bellwood the first portable school in Synod was erected at a cost of $75".

In September, 1948, a mission was begun in South Bellwood. The first service was conducted on September 12 by Dr. Arthur W. Klinck, president of Concordia Teachers College,

*Mr. Scheiderer was born in Neuendettelsau (a German settlement) south of Marysville, Ohio; was baptized and confirmed in St. John's Church—one of the original congregations of the Missouri Synod. His wife, the eldest daughter of Mr. and Mrs. Ottomar Kolb, Amanda, died suddenly a short time before her young husband.

River Forest, who remained in charge of the mission until April 30, 1949, when the Rev. H. W. Hitzeman of Honey Creek, Iowa, was installed as missionary-pastor. A. H. Kramer, assistant director of education, Northern Illinois District, was in charge of the Sunday school. In 1949, a portable chapel was erected at Linden and Monroe Avenues. Meanwhile, worship services and Sunday school sessions were conducted in a vacated public school on Wilcox Avenue, near Linden Ave. Organized on March 29, 1949, the name of this new congregation is Faith.

161. Chicago, Jehovah

Chapter 91 related that Christ Congregation of Logan Square, on Chicago's northwest side, on March 29, 1903, established a branch school at 2420 North Lawndale Avenue and placed A. M. Reinhardt in charge. The Rev. Ernst Werfelmann, pastor of Christ (Christus) Congregation, also conducted worship services in that building twice a month in the German language. On January 14, 1908, twenty-six voting members of Christ Congregation gathered in the same building in the so-called Pennock district to organize their own congregation, which they named Jehovah. On May 10 Jehovah's first pastor, the Rev. Theodore Graebner was installed. Less than a month later the cornerstone of the church was laid, and on October 18 the church was dedicated. The cost, including equipment, was $14,513.86. The old school on North Lawndale Avenue was then sold for $1,650. School had been opened with fourteen* pupils, and at the time of church dedication the enrollment had increased to fifty-nine, which fact necessitated assistance in the school, meaning, in this case, that the pastor also served as schoolteacher. In November, 1909, the Rev. Stanislaus Mlotkowski, pastor of Holy Cross (See Chapter 137, p. 442), was engaged to teach the lower grades. In 1910 one English service a month was in-

*When opened as a branch school on April 1, 1903, the enrollment was sixteen pupils.

troduced. In 1911 Mr. Reinhardt followed a call to Grace Congregation (Crawford), Chicago, and on April 23 he was succeeded by John Zitzmann. In order to provide a playground for the school children, an additional frontage of fifty feet was purchased for one thousand dollars, thus giving the congregation a 206-foot frontage on Belden Avenue. On November 19 of the same year Andrew B. Johnson was installed as Jehovah's third member of the teaching staff, and the eighth grade was added.

Pastor Graebner terminated his pastorate at Jehovah on August 10, 1913, and accepted a professorship at Concordia Seminary, St. Louis, Mo. His successor at Jehovah, the Rev. Arthur W. Lussky of Hopkins Township, Sterling, Ill.,* was installed on September 21, 1913. In December of that year it was resolved to erect a new church with a seating capacity of nine hundred, the cost not to exceed fifty-five thousand dollars. Two days before the outbreak of World War I, on July 26, 1914, the cornerstone was laid. The new building, on the northwest corner of Belden and Ridgeway Avenues, was completed at a cost of $66,623.94 and dedicated on July 25, 1915. By this time the congregation's membership had increased to 1,650 baptized members, 985 of whom were communicants and 195 voters. A fourth teacher, Walter Wendt, was added to the staff, and a Sunday school was established. Mr. Johnson died on March 16, 1920, and E. A. Mueller was installed on September 3, 1920. The following month, Pastor Mlotkowski terminated his school teaching at Jehovah in order to give full time to his own congregation. Miss Elfrieda Steinkraus was engaged to take his place, and another teacher was called, A. G. Ortlip. In July, 1924, Mr. Mueller was forced by illness to resign; his place was taken by C. A. Luhmann, on December 28, 1924.

*"The First German Ev. Lutheran Church of Hopkins Township"—organized under the direction of the Rev. John Carl Frederick Lussky in 1875, father of Jehovah's second pastor. The Rev. Arthur W. Lussky served the "Hopkins Township" parish, now known as Our Savior's Ev. Lutheran Congregation, from 1908 to 1913. (See Chapter 69, page 282.)

In 1928 the school was enlarged to include four additional classrooms, a gymnasium, and six bowling alleys. The old section of this building was the congregation's first church. The enlarged building was dedicated on November 4, 1928. In September, 1931, a kindergarten department was established and Miss Gertrude Doederlein placed in charge.

In 1937 the Rev. W. Martin Rupprecht of Harvard, Ill., was installed as associate pastor. He served until 1941, when he was succeeded by the Rev. Robert G. Lange of Pine Bluff, Ark.* About two years later the latter accepted a call to Zion Congregation, St. Louis, Mo. On March 19, 1944, the Rev. Theodore F. A. Nickel of Aurora (Immanuel Congregation), Ill., became Jehovah's pastor, and Pastor Lussky voluntarily occupied the position of associate pastor. During the year 1945 the sanctuary was completely remodeled. The altar is constructed of Italian Powanaza marble. The steps and floor are of pink Tennessee marble; the borders and central runner are of dark-green Vermont marble. The inlaid medallion at the center of the chancel floor is of variegated marble and other stones from the far corners of the earth. The dedication took place on December 2, 1945.

Other teachers more recently in Jehovah School were Fred Eggerding, Mrs. Charles Nestel, Mrs. Helmuth A. Stahlecker, Floyd H. Rogner, Werner P. Grams, Miss Dorothy Asch, Miss Emma Burmeister, and Miss Arlette Eisenberg.

162. Crete, Zion

In connection with the history of Trinity Congregation at Crete† attention was directed to an unfortunate incident—a lawsuit resulting from the unwillingness of a group of seventy-six members to abide by the resolution, unanimously adopted, to have the old church transferred to the village

*A "son" of St. Stephen's Congregation, Chicago, Ill.

†Prior to 1858, this congregation's name was Zion.

of Crete. (See Chapter 7, page 591.) "Forced by circumstances to seek a new church home," these former members of Trinity met for a discussion of the entire problem in their school building, which had been quickly erected and used temporarily also as a place of worship. It was at first decided to build on the old site. However, the opposition to this proposal was overwhelming. Thereupon Philip Engelking offered to sell them the present church property at the southern end of the village for two hundred dollars. His offer was accepted, and shortly afterward construction work on a church was begun under the direction of their pastor, the Rev. H. Wente, and the trustees, C. Behrens, Henry Kracke, Otto Piepenbrink, and Henry Sporleder. The church was dedicated on September 10, 1911. The total cost of the building was thirteen thousand dollars. To the original price was added the price of the bell, which weighed two thousand pounds and cost fifteen cents a pound. This bell was hauled from the local freight depot (Chicago and Eastern Illinois Railroad) on a hayrack by Louis Plagge. Mr. Piepenbrink, who resided about three miles from the church, wanted to be sure that he and his family could hear the bell. Mrs. J. Meyer was requested to telephone them when the bell would be tolled. The first time she did so, Mr. Piepenbrink answered the call by loudly saying: "We hear it!" Pastor Wente served Zion from 1909 until 1939. His successor was the Rev. Gerhard Redlin of Allenton, Wis. Dr. Wente was made "pastor emeritus." In 1949 Pastor Redlin followed a call to Watertown, Wis.

Zion Congregation is a member of the Wisconsin Synod.

Trinity and Zion are again united in spirit, having celebrated their first joint Reformation festival in 1946.

163. Downers Grove

Chatty reminiscenses of church folk in Hinsdale (formerly known as Fullersburg) indicate that about 1890 the Rev. Herman C. Guebert, pastor of Zion Congregation in that village, started mission work in several near-by places, including the village of Downers Grove,* about four miles west of Hinsdale, where on February 8, 1909, he assisted in the organization of Immanuel Congregation. During the following twelve years Immanuel was served by the pastors of Saint John's Congregation at Lace, first by the Rev. Martin Nickel and then (1913-1921) by the Rev. Walter Burmeister. In the fall of 1921 Candidate Otto F. Arndt, graduate of Concordia Seminary, St. Louis, Mo., was installed as Immanuel's first resident pastor. Soon afterward the congregation joined the Missouri Synod and erected a bungalow chapel at the intersection of Grove and Carpenter Streets, dedicating it in October, 1924. In the course of a few years Immanuel became self-supporting. Because of the steady increase in membership, plans for the expansion of the facilities for worship were formulated. In 1913 the Mission Board reported to the delegates assembled for convention of the Northern Illinois District that Immanuel Congregation "prefers to remain small rather than to receive such as do not adhere to the Lutheran Confessions." The economic depression temporarily halted execution of the plans for expansion. In 1942 a new church was erected on the original property. In November, 1931, Pastor Arndt accepted a call to Niles Center (now Skokie), Ill., and the Rev. Milton Augustus Reinke succeeded him in Downers Grove on December 18, 1931.

164. Glen Ellyn

The ill-fated lover's motif is back of the name Glen Ellyn, which according to Bernadine Skeels, comes from the legendary "King Groynllin, who courted the Lady Grolodys." According to another source, this village in Du Page County, Glen Ellyn (Glenellyn),† Ill., is named from reference to a

*Mission work was carried on several decades before this, in Downers Grove as well as in Naperville. (See Chapter 21, page 129.) Named for Pierce Downer, who located there in 1830.

†1940 census: 8,055.

near-by glen, the last syllable being added for euphony." In the latter part of the first decade of the twentieth century definite action was taken to provide the Lutherans of this village with spiritual care. In this instance the initial steps in that direction were taken, not by neighboring ministers, but by a pastor in Chicago, the Rev. Ernest F. Haertel, pastor of Christ English Congregation, whose "center" at the time was within one block of First Saint John's Congregation—North Hoyne Avenue and Augusta Street. He conducted the first worship service on February 28, 1909, in Kindle Hall, Glen Ellyn. In the same year the group of Lutherans here organized as Grace Congregation. Its first pastor, the Rev. C. H. Kenreich of Scranton, Miss., was installed on January 10, 1910. He served until July 16, 1916, when he accepted a call to South Sodus, N.Y. He was succeeded on August 12, 1917, by the Rev. Karl Schleede, recent graduate of Concordia Seminary, St. Louis, Mo., who had been ordained on the previous July 15 in Kingston, N.Y. However, already in the following November he resigned to become chaplain in the United States Army. His successor, the Rev. Ben. A. Maurer, "Reiseprediger" in western Ontario, Canada, was installed as the third pastor of Grace on February 3, 1918. The ceremony was conducted in the hall of the public library. In 1920 the congregation purchased a church building formerly occupied by the Congregationalists, at the corner of Forest and Pennsylvania Avenues. On May 22, 1923, Pastor Maurer accepted a call to Milwaukee, Wis., and on the following June 10 his successor, the Rev. Henry Mackensen of Trinity Congregation, Hammond, Ind., was installed. He served Grace for a period of almost nineteen years. Early in the morning of May 13, 1942, he was fatally injured in an automobile accident at West Twenty-second Street and State Highway 83, about six miles southeast of Glen Ellyn, on his way to visit his wife, who was a patient in a La Fayette (Ind.)

hospital.* On October 4, 1942, the Rev. Carl H. Harman of Milwaukee, Wis., was installed as the congregation's fifth pastor.

165. Park Ridge, Saint Andrew's

About sixteen miles northeast of Glen Ellyn, or fourteen miles northwest of downtown Chicago, is the village of Park Ridge, formerly known as Brickton, Ill.† On June 27, 1909, twelve Lutheran men, hitherto members of Saint John's Congregation at Niles (Dutchman's Point), organized Saint Andrew's Congregation. Its first pastor, the Rev. Paul Hans Reinhold Guelzow of Muskogee, Okla., was installed on February 6, 1910. In 1911 a church was erected at the southeast corner of Northwest Highway and Elm Street. Meanwhile a day school had been established, which was taught by the pastor. On July 6, 1913, Pastor Guelzow accepted a call to East Peoria, Ill., and was succeeded in Park Ridge by Candidate Henry Carl August Richter, who likewise served as schoolteacher, until May, 1921, when Walter Gerth was called to fill that position. He, however, remained only one year, and in November, 1922, F. J. Priehs took his place. A new school was built in 1923; in 1925 another classroom was opened, with Fred J. Uttech serving as teacher of the lower grades. In 1929 Alfred F. Fricke succeeded Mr. Uttech, and Mr. Priehs resigned. Then came Miss Flora Kuehnert, Orville Richter, and Miss Gertrude Richter, each serving for one year.

With a nucleus of members of Pilgrim Congregation in Chicago the English District in 1931 organized Redeemer Congregation on the south side of Park Ridge, and "because of disturbing conditions in Saint Andrew's Congregation many members left to join" the new congregation. (See Chapter 215, page 578.)

*A son, Gordon, was pastor of Grace Congregation in Wilmington, Ill., July 1, 1944-May, 1948. Now pastor at El Centro, Calif.

†1940 census: 12,063.

In the summer of 1934 Mr. Fricke followed a call to Zoar Congregation in Elmwood Park, Ill., and M. D. Schultz of North East, Pa., succeeded him in Saint Andrew's School. The following December Pastor Richter resigned from the active ministry, and the Rev. Arnold H. Semmann of Waterloo, Iowa, succeeded him in the Park Ridge pastorate on January 27, 1935. In 1936 Mr. Schultz resigned, and teacher-candidate L. W. Beer replaced him, also in the capacity as principal. In addition to those mentioned, the following have served as teachers in Saint Andrew's School in more recent years: Mrs. Myra Roberts, Miss Rose Sachtleben, Miss Elda Halfpap, Miss Norma Mueller, Walter G. Nau, John Bolz, Miss Irma Gade, Paul G. Witte, L. W. Beer, Miss Helen Meyer, Mrs. Dorothy K. Witte, Miss Marion Maurer, Herman T. Staiger, and Mrs. Herman T. Staiger.

In 1946 the Mission Board of the Northern Illinois District extended a call to Pastor Semmann to serve as senior chaplain and mission counselor. "It was not an easy matter for him to accept the call, and it was with much reluctancy that Saint Andrew's Congregation released him." His successor in the Saint Andrew's pastorate, the Rev. Paul Mehl, executive secretary of the Missouri Synod's Armed Services Commission* and prior to his acceptance of this position (during the Second World War) pastor at Hutchinson, Kans., was installed on April 20, 1947.[97]

166. De Kalb

In 1721, in Huettendorf, Germany, there was born a peasant boy who was destined to become an officer in the French army. In 1777 he came to the United States with Marquis de Lafayette and later, having received from the Congress of the United States the appointment as major general, served in General George Washington's army. In 1780 he was second

*Headquarters at 221 N. La Salle Street, Chicago, until April, 1948; thence moved to Washington, D.C.

in command under General Gates in the South and was killed in the Battle of Camden. That soldier, of German extraction, was John De Kalb, for whom the next village to be visited by the Lutheran Trail was named, De Kalb, Ill.,* about fifty-eight miles west of Chicago. In 1898 the Rev. Gottlieb Schroeder, pastor of Immanuel Congregation at Squaw Grove (Hinckley), began mission work in this community. For about seven years he came once a month and conducted worship services in the old Swedish Lutheran church at De Kalb. Later this pastor stated that "because of the floating and transient character of the population"—between 1898 and 1905—"no real footing was gained during that time." In 1905 the Rev. Frederick Kroeger, Pastor Schroeder's successor at Squaw Grove, continued serving the De Kalb group in the same place and in a manner similar to that of his predecessor. Within a short time some of Immanuel's members moved to De Kalb. One of them, Henry Ilsemann, made the rounds and invited the people to come to church and in other ways manifested a keen personal interest in the cause. By spring of 1909 the flock had become too large for Pastor Kroeger to give it adequate pastoral care and attention. It was then that the group in De Kalb and Saint John's Congregation in Sycamore—five miles northeast of De Kalb—jointly called the Rev. August Fred Parge of Bemidji, Minn. His installation took place on April 25, 1909. In the following October six members organized Immanuel Congregation in De Kalb. The worship services were continued in the Swedish church.† Pastor Parge preached in both churches, alternately in German and English, every Sunday, until autumn, 1917, when ill health forced him to resign from the active ministry. His successor, the Rev. Emil A. Bartusch of Havelock, Nebr., was installed on August 4, 1918. He resided in Sycamore and served the dual parish until the fall of 1924, when he accepted a call

*1940 census: 9,146.

†A new church had meanwhile been erected by the Swedish Lutherans.

to Rochelle, Ill.* In 1925 the two congregations again jointly extended a call; this time to the Rev. Erdmann W. Frenk, also of Bemidji, Minn. He was installed on January 18, 1925. He also conducted services in German and English, not, however, in the Swedish church, but in the Welfare Hall of the American Steel and Wire Works, De Kalb. The service schedule was changed to the forenoon in both parishes.

On the fourth of October, 1925, the cornerstone of Immanuel Church was laid, on the northwest corner of North Fifth Street and Fisk Avenue. The building itself was dedicated on October 17, 1926. On May 13, 1928, Pastor Frenk became the full-time pastor of Immanuel in De Kalb, which he then served for another two and a half years.† In October, 1932, he accepted a call to Saint Peter's Congregation in Joliet, Ill. On January 5, 1933, his successor, the Rev. Paul E. Schauer of Joliet, was installed as Immanuel's pastor.‡ Then came the economic depression, and Immanuel found itself heavily burdened with debt. However, by 1942 the debt was liquidated, and a year later the congregation became self-supporting. Immanuel, the youngest of three Lutheran congregations in De Kalb, joined the Missouri Synod in 1943.[98]

167. Chicago, Zion (Slovak)

The organization of one congregation composed of Slovakian Lutherans (Holy Trinity) has already been told. Now a second one, also in Chicago, enters into history, having its origin in the first one. (See Chapter 127, page 425.) It was in the year 1909 that the Rev. John Somora and about one hundred members of Holy Trinity, amid misunderstandings and dissensions, withdrew and on November 30 established Zion Congregation. "As a matter of record, this severance came

*Pastor Bartusch died suddenly on June 5, 1928.

†Presumably Pastor Frenk served Saint John's in Sycamore as an affiliate of Saint John's in De Kalb; the Rev. H. H. Tessmann, then at Genoa, Ill., was called upon to serve the former as an affiliate after Pastor Frenk's departure from De Kalb.

‡Temporarily without charge; formerly in Mokena, Ill. (1930-1932.)

not as a direct result of difference on the fundamental points of doctrine, but rather as a result of misunderstanding, which strained the bond of fellowship to the breaking point. It is gratifying to note that the past is being forgotten and that, instead, there is a growing spirit of mutual understanding."

The first church of Zion Congregation was located at the corner of West Huron and Bickerdike (now Bishop) Streets and was purchased for twelve thousand dollars.

"The years under Pastor Somora were spent delving into the treasury of faith, discussing and studying article after article. A thorough process of indoctrination allows for no middle ground, not a spirit of indifference and lukewarmness. As a result there was a sifting of membership, and a sizable number of members severed their relations with Zion. Some left because of finances; others, owing to misunderstandings; others yet, because of the legalistic attitude of the pastor. It is difficult for an outsider properly to diagnose the conditions of that time. There is always a spirit of the time, known only to those who have had the personal experience. Even today opinion is prevalent that the spirit of that time was more legalistic than evangelical. However, these very people will admit that, though the pastor was intensely strict, he was unsurpassed as a preacher." Pastor Somora's long and difficult pastorate at Zion came to an end in March, 1924, when he accepted a call to a Slovak Lutheran mission in Czechoslovakia, at Velka pod Tatrou and at Illiasovce. Following his departure, Zion called the Rev. George Gona of Massillon, Ohio. Increased church attendance and amalgamation of Bethlehem Congregation with Zion caused the membership to proceed with plans for the erection of a new church. Instead a new brick church and a new two-story house were purchased about three years later from the Norwegian Lutheran congregation for fifty thousand dollars. Zion's new property since 1928 is located at the corner of

Iowa Street and Springfield Avenue. On November 21, 1942, Pastor Gona met a tragic death when he fell from a window in a Loop building.* His successor in the Zion pastorate, the Rev. John Bajus of Granite City, Ill., was installed on March 28, 1943.

168. Blue Island

From May 1, 1839, until February 24, 1843, the official name of the post office at what now is known as Blue Island was Portland. From February 24, 1843, until April 20, 1850, it was "Blue Island." In 1850 the United States Post Office Department in Washington, D.C., enacted legislation naming the village Worth—same as the township—until January 10, 1860. Then the Postmaster General changed the name of the post office from Worth to Blue Island.† Originally the latter name applied to the entire ridge, about six miles in length, about four miles west of Lake Calumet. The village was called Blue Island "because when viewed from a distance by the early settlers it appeared like an island covered with blue flowers."

It may appear rather strange that in the review of "Missouri" Lutheranism Blue Island is mentioned thus late in the history of the Northern Illinois District. It will be recalled that First Bethlehem Congregation in Chicago (Holstein community) called its first pastor, the Rev. Augustus Reinke, from Blue Island and installed him on October 1, 1871, nine days before the Great Fire in Chicago; and that a decade before that, 1860-1861, there were found from time to time small groups of German settlers gathered in various private homes in Blue Island for religious observances; also, that in 1862 the Rev. Wolfgang S. Stubnatzy of Saint John's Con-

*"Nasa draha cirkev navstivena bola bol'nou a t'azkou ranou, ked' nas drahomilovany duspastier za vyse 17 rokov, dvjct. pan farar Juraj Gona, po tri mesacnej nemoci, skoncili cestu svojho zivota v dolnej casti nasho mesta, v sobotu, 21. novembra roku Pana 1942." (Zapisnica.) (Cf. "Pamaetnik"—Zion Ev. Lutheran Church, Chicago, Ill.—p. 21.)

†1940 census: 16,638.

gregation at Coopers Grove (or Yankee Settlement, as it was known in the 1830's) assumed charge of those meetings and "gathered about him quite a following among the German-speaking residents of the village." At first these meetings were held in the home of Peter Engelland at the southern limits of Blue Island (the original Portland), and later, as the attendance increased, in the Bauer Brick Building at the foot of Western Avenue. On January 23, 1863, an organization of the German Evangelical Lutheran Society was effected with a membership of sixty-six. On May 26, 1863, the cornerstone of the church on Grove and Ann Streets was laid. "During the building of the church a man named Israel had been appointed to the pastorate, but he served the congregation only nine months, when he was dismissed for non-Lutheran teachings." Shortly before the dedication of the new church the Rev. Augustus Reinke was called, and he served the congregation for seven years. During his ministry the congregation was put upon a doctrinally solid foundation. A parsonage and school building were erected during this time.

Pastor Reinke's successor was the Rev. H. Ernst, who served for about eight years, 1871-1879;* then came the Rev. H. P. Duborg, hitherto pastor of the two parishes in what is now South Chicago (Bethlehem and Immanuel) and of Saint John's, Whiting, Ind., who now served Zion in Washington Heights as an affiliate of his Blue Island parish until 1881. In that year occurred the Predestination and Election Controversy in the Synodical Conference. Virtually the entire congregation in Blue Island then, together with Pastor Duborg, joined the Ohio Synod,† which withdrew from the Synodical Conference. The comparatively few remaining "Missourians" joined the remnant in Washington Heights in building up Zion Congregation, at first under the leadership

*Pastor Ernst accepted a call to Michigan City, Ind.

†Now a member of the American Lutheran Church, organized on Aug. 10, 1930, in Toledo, Ohio.

of the Rev. Henry Theo. L. Felten. (See Chapter 48, page 227.)

On May 16, 1896, the greater portion of three blocks in the central business section of Blue Island was devastated by a fire. Almost fourteen years later, on September 29, 1909, another Missouri Synod congregation was organized* in Blue Island under the direction of the Rev. Ferdinand Sievers of Immanuel Congregation, South Chicago. For a year worship services were conducted by Pastor Sievers in the Congregationalist church on York Street. Meanwhile a church was being built by the new congregation, known as Salem ("Peace"), at the southeast corner of Maple Avenue and High Street. This building was dedicated on December 11, 1910. The Rev. Raymond R. Reinke of Harvard, Ill., fourth son of the first pastor of the first Lutheran church in Blue Island, was installed as Salem's first resident pastor.

Among the teachers in Salem School were the following: Miss L. Zebell, W. Kluth, H. F. W. Hoppe, Mrs. H. Hoppe, Mrs. C. Leiger, Mrs. B. Reichow, Student R. Trusheim, and Mrs. L. E. Burmeister.

One of the ten-dollar bills in the fifty-thousand-dollar ransom given to the kidnapers of Charles S. Ross, Chicago manufacturer, was found in the Blue Island district on October 21, 1938.

Pastor Reinke's father was a "son" of Zion Congregation at Duncklees Grove. From Duncklees Grove the parents of Pastor Augustus Reinke, probably during the early 1870's, moved to Fort Wayne, Ind., where they were placed in charge of the commissary department of Concordia College. The Rev. Ludwig Ernest Fuerbringer, D.D.,† who began his studies in

*Charter members:

Louis Storz	John Schwartz
William Siemsen	John Wolz

†Professor at Concordia Seminary, St. Louis, Mo., from 1893 until 1947. He died on May 6, 1947, at the age of 83.

that institution in 1877, relates that "the attachment between them [Mr. and Mrs. Reinke] and the students was so close that once when they attended a college festivity—I think it was the fiftieth anniversary of the founding of the college—I remember seeing Mrs. Reinke caressing in a motherly way Pastor Charles Frincke, at that time a prominent minister on Staten Island, N.Y." The Rev. Augustus Reinke in 1896 founded the Deaf-Mute Mission of the Missouri Synod and led in the organization of Our Savior's Congregation of the Deaf in Chicago; he was also one of the founders of the Lutheran Old Folks' Home in Arlington Heights (Dunton), in 1892. His eldest son, Edwin, served as assistant pastor at First Bethlehem, Chicago, until December, 1899,* when he succeeded to the full pastorate of this large parish. On June 17, 1900, his brother Arthur L. was installed as assistant pastor. Upon the death of Pastor Edwin Reinke the assistant pastor assumed the full pastorate. Pastor Arthur L. Reinke died in 1934. Another brother, Alfred E., served as pastor of Zion Congregation in Roseland, Chicago, from 1900 to 1906, and of Concordia Congregation in the Avondale community, Chicago, from 1906 until his sudden death during a worship service in his church on January 24, 1943. Pastor Raymond R. Reinke was born in First Bethlehem's first "parsonage"— in the church basement. The Rev. Leonard A. Reinke, pastor of Trinity Congregation at New Lenox, Ill., since 1946, is a son of Pastor Edwin Reinke; the Rev. Milton A. Reinke of Immanuel Congregation in Downers Grove is a son of Pastor Arthur Reinke; and the Rev. Manfred E. Reinke of Saint John's Congregation in La Porte, Ind., is a son of Pastor Edwin Reinke. Pastor Raymond R. Reinke died suddenly on January 30, 1947. His successor in the Blue Island pastorate is the Rev. Carl F. Selle of St. John's, Eagle Lake, Ill., he was installed on June 8, 1947.[99]

*The Rev. Augustus Reinke died on Nov. 18, 1899.(See Chapter 15.)

169. Herscher

Almost fifty miles southwest of Blue Island, or, more specifically, about thirteen miles southwest of Kankakee in Kankakee County, is a quiet little village named Herscher.* If the "r" were double, the name would signify "ruler" or "commander." But such a name is hardly applicable to any clergyman who might have had anything to do with the beginning of church activities in this community, because all planning and execution prior to organization were accomplished without the advice or aid of clergymen.

In 1909 a number of consecrated men, who had reached the conclusion that a church was a necessity in Herscher, met and discussed the advisability of separating from the "mother" congregation, Zion, at "Townline" (Bonfield) and organizing their own congregation in the village. On April 9, 1909, thirty-four† men gathered in the home of Henry Appel and organized Trinity Congregation.

A building site comprising several lots was donated by Mrs. Caroline Diecke. Here a church costing $9,082.81 was erected soon after organization had been effected. The dedication took place on February 13, 1910. The Rev. Paul C. Engelbert of Leland, Mich., became Trinity's first pastor on July 24 of the same year. The congregation was self-supporting from the beginning and flourished under Pastor Engelbert's leadership. On August 29, 1920, this first pastor accepted a call to Saint Matthew's Congregation in Buffalo, N.Y.‡ His successor in Herscher, the Rev. Rudolf John Sauer of Tracy, Ind., was installed on October 31, 1920 (Reformation Day). During the next several years the congregation grew to such an extent that more room in the church became necessary; hence

*1940 census: 416.

†Charter members (partial list):

Henry Appel	R. Schmidt
Henry Siedentop	J. Reinhart
D. L. Frieling	William Dickmann

‡The Rev. Paul C. Engelbert died on Aug. 8, 1946, in Buffalo, N.Y.

a balcony was added to accommodate about one hundred people.

The transition period from German to English was passed without any difficulty.

170. Dundee, Bethlehem

The Lutheran Trail turns north again, to arrive at Dundee, first visited in the 1860's, to observe the development of Lutheranism in that community, which is divided by the Fox River into East and West Dundee.

In the fall of 1909 a number of "west siders" asked the "mother" congregation, Immanuel, to release them for the purpose of organizing their own congregation and their own day school. The request was granted, and forty-two members organized Bethlehem Congregation on December 5, 1909. While awaiting the arrival of its own pastor, Bethlehem was served by neighboring pastors, notably by the Rev. Herman F. Fruechtenicht, pastor of Saint John's Congregation in Elgin. On September 18, 1910, the Rev. Edward Sylvester of Milwaukee, Wis., was installed as Bethlehem's first pastor. The first church was a small frame structure, which had served as a meetinghouse for the German Methodists. A building site "at the top of the hill" was chosen as the site of a new church—West Main and Fourth Streets—which was erected in 1911 and dedicated on January 28, 1912. In 1928 the day school was discontinued, and arrangements were made with the "mother" congregation on the east side of the river for Bethlehem's children to attend school there.

After thirty-three years of service, Pastor Sylvester was compelled by ill health to retire, in 1943. His successor, the Rev. Herbert Mueller of York Center (about one mile southeast of Lombard), was installed as Bethlehem's second pastor on September 5, 1943.

171. Chicago, Golgotha

The Trail now leads back to Chicago, which has grown by leaps and bounds since the last Missouri Lutheran congregation was organized there—Jehovah, in the Pennock community. Chicago Junction (Englewood) had long since been absorbed by the Big City, as also many other formerly independent communities, such as Lake View, Hyde Park, Colehour, Roseland, and Jefferson. Meanwhile two "Missouri" congregations had been established in Englewood, Sankt Stephanus (Saint Stephen's) and Our Redeemer (at first known as Grace). Over a period of some fifteen years, members of Saint Stephen's, Saint Martini, Saint Andrew's, Holy Cross, and others, were settling in the vicinity of Ashland Avenue and West Sixty-third Street; and on February 7, 1910, a meeting was called of all Lutherans in this new development, and the nearest Lutheran clergyman, the Rev. Adolf J. Buenger, pastor of Saint Stephen's, was invited to attend. It was then that Golgotha Congregation was organized by ten men.* One month later, on March 6, the first worship service was conducted by Pastor Buenger in a vacant store at 2041 West Sixty-third Street. A day school was founded at the same time. The ministerial acts were temporarily performed by the Rev. R. C. Kissling, and the day school was in charge of John List until August 7, 1910, when Candidate William L. Mueller, graduate of Concordia Seminary, St. Louis, Mo., was ordained and installed as Golgotha's first resident pastor.

On September 11, 1910, Golgotha purchased property on Lincoln Street (now Wolcott Avenue), near West Sixty-fifth Street, upon which a two-story chapel was erected, and dedi-

*Charter members:

A. Petersen	J. Sievert
A. Kluck	W. Oestermeyer
E. Bruhl	H. Klopp
C. Stoehr	G. Hornbostel
H. Wehmhoefer	E. Hornbostel
L. Landeck	

cated on March 26, 1911. In 1912 property on the northeast corner of Lincoln Street and Marquette Road (also regarded as Sixty-seventh Street) was purchased. Two years later, on February 8, 1914, the first trained teacher, Theodore J. Wichmann, was installed. On October 31, 1915, a new four-room school was dedicated at 1848 West Marquette Road. Two years later a second teacher was added to the staff, William C. Marten; and in August, 1919, a third teacher, Edward C. Recknagel. In addition to the teachers mentioned, the following have served in Golgotha's day school: Miss Frieda Joss, Robert Metzger, A. Alwes, Robert W. Ahlbrandt, Theobald Breihan, Walter H. E. Schlueter, Miss Esther Engel, Mrs. Rita Bruhl, Miss Cordelia Ferber, Miss Dorothy Wilcer, Mrs. Louise Rutz.

Golgotha's present church, at the northeast corner of Marquette Road and Wolcott Avenue, was dedicated on August 2, 1925.

172. Roselle

About six miles beyond Duncklees Grove (Addison) is the little village of Roselle, Ill.* For eleven years this community was served as a school district by Saint Peter's Congregation of Schaumburg. When B. F. Dehn, the teacher, in 1910 followed a call elsewhere, the Lutherans of Roselle—some of them members of Saint Peter's and some of Saint John's, two miles west of the village—felt that this was the opportune time to organize their own congregation in Roselle. The Rev. Gottlob Theiss, pastor of Saint Peter's Congregation, served as their spiritual adviser, and on September 12, 1910, Trinity Congregation was organized by nine men.† Property

*1940 census: 694.

†Charter members:

Conrad Biesterfeld
Carl Trost
Henry Hattendorf
Adolph Troyke
August Scharlau
Fred Haak
William Bokelmann
Henry Botterman
Henry Steinbeck

at Park and Elm Streets was purchased, and upon it a frame church was erected, the dedication taking place on January 29, 1911. Trinity's first pastor, the Rev. Paul W. Luecke* of Mena, Ark., was installed on June 11, 1911. After serving for about five and a half years, Pastor Luecke accepted a call to Bethlehem Congregation in Evanston, Ill. His successor, the Rev. Ernest A. Brauer,† was installed on April 15, 1917.

In 1920 a new and larger school was erected. In October, 1922, Pastor Brauer accepted a call to Immanuel Congregation in Dundee, Ill. On December 17, 1922, his successor, the Rev. Edward A. Nauss of Milaca, Minn., was installed. He remained in Roselle for about seven years, until January, 1930, when he accepted a call to Marengo, slightly less than thirty miles northwest of Roselle. On the following May 11 the Rev. Walter H. Mehlberg of Iron Mountain, Mich., was installed as Trinity's fourth pastor. A Sunday school was established in September, 1937.

Prior to the organization of Trinity, the day school was in charge of the following teachers: F. C. Biermann, 1899-1903; W. Kath, 1903-1905; B. F. Dehn, 1906-1910. Since 1913: A. Stellhorn, 1913-1920; A. J. Binneboese (since 1920), and Mrs. Martin Kruse.

173. Cary

Almost twelve miles due north of Elgin, near the southeast corner of McHenry County, is a village called Cary, Ill.‡ In 1911 a Lutheran congregation was organized by five Lutheran men under the guidance of the Rev. F. Gerhard Kuehnert, pastor of Immanuel Congregation in Crystal Lake—five miles to the northwest—and named Holy Cross.

In 1931 Holy Cross Congregation acquired its own church

*Son of the Rev. Paul Luecke, pastor St. John's, Mayfair, Chicago, 1886-1937.

†Brother of the Rev. Arthur A. Brauer, pastor of St. Paul's, Chicago Heights, Ill., since June 27, 1926. Their father, the Rev. Albert H. Brauer, was pastor of St. Paul's, northwest of Beecher, Ill., 1880-1915.

‡1940 census: 707. Named for W. D. Cary, owner of the site.

home by purchasing the former Free Methodist church for $1,550. A considerably larger amount has since been expended for repairs and improvements.

Pastor Kuehnert served Holy Cross until 1941, when, because of his additional duties as chairman and later as executive secretary of the Missouri Synod's pension system, he withdrew as regular pastor but consented to serve as assistant pastor.* On September 27, 1942, the Rev. Theodore Bornemann was installed as pastor of Holy Cross, which, however, he is serving as an affiliate of his parish, Saint John's, at Algonquin, about four miles to the southwest.

174. Hodgkins

Returning from Cary, southeastward, by way of the Northwest Highway, the Trail passes through Barrington, Palatine, Arlington Heights (Dunton), and Mount Prospect, and goes as far as Des Plaines; there it turns south on Lee Street, which crosses Higgins Road at the northeast corner of the Douglas Airport and then bears the name Mannheim Road; continuing straight south, the name of the highway has been changed to La Grange Road, then suddenly it becomes Fifth Avenue. About three miles south of the village of La Grange and a half mile east of the multinamed highway is the little village of Hodgkins.† (See Chapter 50.)

Thoughts of organizing a Lutheran congregation here were entertained as far back as 1865—the end of the Civil War. At that time several Lutheran families here were members of Saint John's in La Grange and others of Trinity near Willow Springs. The inconvenience of attending services and the hardships encountered by the children in trudging to and from school created a desire for a church and school of

*On July 16, 1947, the Rev. Edwin A. Sommer became associate secretary of the Missouri Synod's Board of Support and Pensions and, upon Pastor Kuehnert's resignation, Nov. 1, 1948, full-time executive secretary; he first resided in Park Ridge, Ill., and is now living in St. Louis, Mo.

†1940 census: 331.

their own. Perhaps a certain "religiously inclined" merchant of La Grange, John Witsan, who peddled his wares in Hodgkins, lent some inspiration to the organization of a congregation in this village. Through Witsan's efforts a Sunday school was organized—"though of a sectarian nature." As a result of this experience, Reinhart Leu, a member of Trinity at Willow Springs, and Henry Bloedorn, whose residence was in Hodgkins and who was a member of Saint John's in La Grange, soon afterward approached the Rev. Alex Ullrich, pastor of the latter congregation, with the plea that he assist in establishing a congregation in Hodgkins. The pastors of both congregations concurred in the idea, and on February 5, 1911, the Rev. Herman Meyer of Willow Springs conducted the first Lutheran service in the old village hall in Hodgkins.

On April 23, 1911, twenty-six men gathered in that hall and with the help of Pastors Meyer and Ullrich organized Immanuel Congregation in Hodgkins. The former was called as "first" pastor, and the latter as assistant pastor.

Shortly afterward, Saint John's Congregation offered its old school building for sale, and Immanuel purchased it for nineteen hundred dollars. Men, women, and children of the congregation soon were busily engaged in dismantling the old building, transferring the material some three miles south, and reconstructing it in Hodgkins. The work was completed during the same winter, and on March 10, 1912, the building, 26x38 feet, with a schoolroom annex, was dedicated.

In August, 1913, Pastor Meyer accepted a call to Saint John's Congregation in Bellwood. Thereupon Pastor Ullrich assumed charge of the congregation, serving it as an affiliate of Saint John's, La Grange, until 1930, when he became president of the Northern Illinois District. He was succeeded by the Rev. Herman C. Seitz, who served Immanuel as an affiliate of Grace Congregation in Western Springs, about a mile and a half west of LaGrange, or about four miles northwest of Hodgkins.

After the sudden death of Pastor Seitz on December 18, 1945, the Rev. Harry Fricke,* pastor of Faith Congregation in the community known as Clyde in South Cicero, took charge of this congregation, serving it as an affiliate of Faith.

"A large influx of people, attracted by a vast building program in South Clyde, has increased the work of Pastor Fricke and compelled him to relinquish the reins at Hodgkins. Immanuel Congregation is also experiencing a healthy growth," according to a report published on April 15, 1947. The Rev. Gerhardt W. Leverenz, a former chaplain in the United States Army and a student at the University of Chicago, served Immanuel at Hodgkins until 1948, when he accepted a call to the Lutheran mission in the Panama Canal Zone.

From the summer of 1948 until the summer of 1949 this parish was served by Student D. W. Olson; during the "coming months" Candidate Henry Schroeter is serving Immanual Congregation.

175. Cicero

Had he been living in the third decade of the twentieth century, the Roman namesake of this Chicago suburb would have been aghast at its social and political corruption—appropriately he might have delivered another oration, likewise beginning: "Quousque tandem," Etiamne ad Catilinam? Non vero; autem "de mortuis . . . !" However, long before Cicero had acquired a reputation notorious as any "city of the plain," Missouri Synod Lutheranism had planted its standard, and Cicero today, purged from its Prohibition Era dross, is mightily civic-minded. Early in 1912 three Missouri Synod clergymen, the Rev. Herman H. Engelbrecht, pastor of Saint Matthew's Congregation, and his assistant, the Rev. Theo. F.

*The Rev. Harry C. Fricke held the Saint Peter's pastorate in Arlington Heights (Dunton), Ill., from 1927 until 1943; in the latter year he entered military service as a chaplain in the U.S. Army.

Siemon, and the Rev. Henry Boester, pastor of Grace Congregation in the former Crawford community (Chicago's near southwest side), made efforts toward gathering all the Lutherans who held membership in various Lutheran churches in Chicago for the purpose of organizing a congregation in Cicero.* Services at first were held in Albert Kurscher's vacant store at 5113 West Twenty-second Street (also known as Cermak Road). Business meetings were held in Fred Jochens' kitchen at Forty-eighth Avenue and West Twenty-second Place. On September 22, 1912, a congregation was organized under Pastor Engelbrecht's direction and named "Erloeser" (Redeemer). A constitution was signed by nine Lutheran men.†

At first Redeemer Congregation was served by a student, Charles Voelz. On December 8, 1912, the Rev. Louis J. C. Millies of Elk Grove, Ill., was installed as the congregation's first resident pastor. Shortly afterward two lots at Fiftieth Avenue and West Twenty-third Street were purchased, and a combination church and school was erected. Dedication took place on September 13, 1913. Pastor Millies taught school until April, 1914, when Ernest Jahn was installed as teacher. In August, 1919, he was succeeded by Edward G. Warmann;‡ in 1920 Miss Elizabeth Miller was engaged for the lower grades. Others who have served as teachers in Redeemer's day school were Miss Olga Knust, Miss E. Hohmann, Miss Florence Kuehnert, Miss Loretta Jagusch, Miss Marie Neitsch, Oscar Wilde, R. J. Schulz, Miss Viola Pauvola, Ralph A. Pingel, and Miss Evelyn Halamka.

During 1924-1925 a new church was erected at the corner of Fifty-third Avenue and West Twenty-third Street, the dedication following on April 28, 1925.

*1940 census: 64,712.

†Charter members:

Herman Christen	William Selig
Fred Schultz	Adolph Koenemann
Charles Troike	Louis Kramp
William Arndt	Fred Witt
Fred Jochens	

‡Ed. G. Warmann died on Jan. 13, 1949, in Melrose Park, Ill.

In the fall of 1945 Pastor Millies suffered a nervous breakdown. The Rev. John Klotz, instructor at Concordia Teachers College, River Forest—about five miles northwest of Cicero—served as substitute for the stricken pastor. In December, 1945, Mr. Wilde followed a call to Kankakee, Ill., and Armin Grams took his place in Cicero, remaining here until September, 1946. In 1946 Redeemer resolved to call an associate pastor. The Rev. Martin C. Lopahs of Odem, Tex., chosen for this position, was installed on March 31, 1946. During the same year Mr. Grams was replaced by Ralph J. Schulz of Lansing, Mich.

Pastor Millies died on November 13, 1946, at the age of sixty-nine, after having served Redeemer Congregation for thirty-four years, less one month. He was laid to rest in Concordia Cemetery, Forest Park. His successor as Redeemer's second pastor is the Rev. Martin C. Lopahs.

176. Chicago, Saint Luke's (Norwegian)

Back in Chicago, in that part which formerly was an independent village known as Austin, is another Norwegian Lutheran congregation. The Mission Board of that church body* in the summer of 1911 called the Rev. J. C. Tweten of Norge, Va., to begin mission work in Austin and Oak Park. The invitation came partially from the Chicago Lutheran Pastoral Conference and partially from a number of families which had moved into those communities and thus were far removed from their Norwegian "sister" congregations. Worship services and Sunday school sessions were held in the school building of Saint Paul's Congregation, Menard Avenue and Iowa Street. The first one, on August 24, 1911. The first three Sunday school pupils were Rudolph Onsrud, Borghild Klovjan, and Trennor Jacobsen. The first organizational meeting of the small group was held on January 3, 1912, and the congregation was named Saint Luke. Organization

*The Norwegian Synod, founded in 1853.

was completed on January 17. On the following February 20 the property of the First Baptist Church* was purchased for $3,250, and the first worship service was held there on March 3. An early issue of the program leaflets bore this statement: "Remember that St. Luke's Church is an English Lutheran church. When we represent St. Luke's Congregation as an English Lutheran church, the purpose is not to slight the Norwegian work. Just as a 'Norwegian' congregation does not carry on its work exclusively in the Norwegian language, so it is not necessary for an English congregation to pursue its work exclusively in the English language. The Norwegian services will be continued just as long as it is apparent that they are necessary and desired."

On March 21, 1915, Pastor Tweten accepted a call to Lee, Ill. His successor, the Rev. H. A. Preuss of Spokane, Wash., was installed on July 18 of the same year. When in the fall of 1917 Pastor Preuss was called by the Army and Navy Board of the Missouri Synod to serve as camp pastor, Saint Luke's Congregation was drawn into the union of Norwegian churches. The Mission Board of the Norwegian merger promised aid in securing a "permanent" pastor in the near future. Temporary pastors came and soon left again. The "officials" made it plain that they did not intend to supply funds for a permanent pastor, and it was their advice that the congregation be dissolved. External pressure soon resulted in internal dissatisfaction, and a flourishing congregation soon wilted to a mere handful of members—unable to carry on alone. On June 19, 1918, the decision was reached to dissolve, lock the doors of the church, and offer the property for sale. The ladies' aid society, however, had not disbanded; and through this organization Saint Luke's was kept alive. The meetings of this society had been attended by the Rev. John A. Moldstad, pastor of Saint Mark's Norwegian

*Locted at 5916 West Rice Street.

Congregation,* and the Rev. George Gullixson, pastor of Saint Paul's Norwegian Congregation†—both of whom with their congregations had not joined the union of Norwegian churches in 1917. When the society sought advice as to what to do in the circumstances, these two pastors urged a meeting of those interested in maintaining a congregation. The meeting was held in the home of the Saxon family, with both clergymen present; the latter pointed out that the congregation alone and no other body had the power to decide whether they should disband or continue. "Weary but valiant hearts were refilled with hope." At a voters' meeting, at which Pastor Gullixson presided, resolutions concerning the dissolution of the congregation and sale of the property at 5916 Rice Street (passed at the June 19 meeting) were rescinded, and action was decided upon *de novo* to join the reorganized Norwegian Synod, which had continued in affiliation with the Evangelical Lutheran Synodical Conference of North America, and immediately to resume worship services and Sunday school sessions.

On December 22, 1918, the Rev. H. A. Preuss for the second time was installed as Saint Luke's pastor. About four years later there was serious discussion about the advisability of changing the location of Saint Luke's and uniting with the mission established by the Rev. John A. Moldstad at Long Avenue and Le Moyne Street.‡ In 1924, however, the congregation outlined an extensive building program. The basement and the foundation were rebuilt of brick and concrete, and both the interior and the exterior were redecorated at a cost of seven thousand dollars.

On May 3, 1925, Pastor Preuss accepted a call to Calmar, Iowa, and was succeeded in Saint Luke's pastorate on the following Sunday by the Rev. J. J. Strand of St. Peter, Minn.

*Located at North Tripp and Wabansia Avenues, Chicago.

†Located at 2215 West North Avenue. Its present pastor, the Rev. Eivind G. Unseth.

‡This property was purchased by Christ English Congregation in 1922.

Five years later he was stricken with apoplexy and granted a year's leave of absence. During the interim Saint Luke's was served for some time by the Rev. J. M. Bailey, then director of religious education, and later by the Rev. Hugo Goetz.* By the end of 1930 it became evident that Pastor Strand could not resume active charge of the parish, and he, therefore, submitted his resignation.† His successor, the Rev. H. A. Theiste of Forsyth, Mont., was installed on August 30, 1931. Six years later, in August, 1937, Pastor Theiste accepted a call to Minneapolis, Minn., and on September 6 the Rev. Ahlert H. Strand of Duluth, Minn., son of the former Pastor Strand, was installed. After the death of the Rev. John A. Moldstad, on June 4, 1946, Pastor Ahlert H. Strand accepted a call to Saint Mark's Congregation, whose center is at North Tripp and Wabansia Avenues, Chicago. In the fall of 1946 Saint Luke's united with Saint Mark's and sold its property at 5916 Rice Street to Saint Paul's Congregation, whose church had been destroyed by fire on October 11, 1946.

177. Chicago, Pilgrim

During the night of April 14, 1912, one of the greatest disasters recorded in the history of ocean travel occurred some distance southeast of Newfoundland, when the S.S. *Titanic* sank with a loss of 1,635 lives.‡ 1912 also was the year in which the twenty-eighth President of the United States, Woodrow Wilson, was elected.

On June 2, 1912, the Rev. Fred W. G. Mueller, pastor of Saint John's Congregation, Wilmette,§ organized a congregation in a public hall on Lincoln Avenue and called it Saint

*Pastor of Griffith Lutheran Congregation, Griffith, Ind., since 1941.

†The Rev. J. J. Strand died on Sept. 3, 1933.

‡Various figures of the death toll have appeared.

§Son of the Rev. J. E. A. Mueller, first pastor of Saint Luke's, Chicago, and first child to be baptized in Saint Luke's Church (1884).

Paul's.* The young congregation's first resident pastor, the Rev. Henry C. Steinhoff of Milwaukee, Wis., was installed on September 1, 1912, in Saint Paul's newly acquired frame church at Cuyler and Lincoln (now Wolcott) Avenues. The building, which cost $5,500, was dedicated on November 10, 1912 (Martin Luther's 429th birthday). In May, 1913, the congregation became self-supporting. In 1917 the old church was enlarged, and the congregation's name was changed to Pilgrim.

Among the missions begun by Pilgrim Congregation were Mount Olive (1917), whose "center" now is at West Byron Street and North Tripp Avenue; Redeemer in Park Ridge (1931); Redeemer in Hinsdale (1922); Concordia in Berwyn (1923); Jefferson Park (1923); and Mount Calvary, located at North Mozart Street and Ardmore Avenue (1926).

On January 31, 1921, a day school was opened, with A. A. Rumsfeld in charge. In the same year a school was erected on West Cullom Avenue, near Winchester Avenue, and dedicated in 1922. In 1927 a second teacher, Edgar Steinbach, was called; two years later Walter L. Sassmannshausen of Christ (Christus) Congregation of Logan Square was installed.† Others who have served as teachers in Pilgrim School: M. Gehrs, the Misses Olinda Roettger, Beatrice Strahl, Clara Firnhaber, L. Predoehl, D. Ehler, Helen Geiseman, Pauline Beyer, Carola Novak, Mrs. Estelle Wolter, Mrs. Norman Luecke, William F. Wittmer, and Miss Jeanne Ladewig. The goal of a current church building campaign is set at $100,000 cash before building construction begins.

*Charter members:

Martin Brockmann	William H. Ehlenfeld	W. A. Sass
John F. Semmlow	R. W. Doederlein	H. A. Zorn
Otto F. Skibbe	George H. Hemler	A. J. Koehneke
Otto T. Lachmann	William H. Jacobs	C. H. Mundstock
Gustav C. Sass	Martin Kemnitz	R. Frank
Edwin H. Bohnsack	Arthur L. Kemnitz	L. G. Moeller
James Wilkens	Chas. E. Kemnitz	C. H. Bernhard
Charles Kemnitz	John Streit	August Bernhard
Charles H. Piske	William Streit	E. H. Stoebig
	A. P. Wollermann	

†Mr. Sassmannshausen died on Aug. 29, 1945.

178. Mount Prospect

About two and a half miles southeast of Arlington Heights (formerly Dunton), on the Northwest Highway, is a village known as Mount Prospect.* It can be readily understood why there was no Missouri Synod congregation in this community until the beginning of the second decade of the twentieth century: the Lutherans residing here and in the vicinity found it comparatively easy to attend services in the neighboring Lutheran churches, at Elk Grove, Des Plaines, and Arlington Heights. However, in July, 1912, twenty-five of these people† met to organize their own congregation, naming it Saint Paul. The Rev. Carl Moritz Noack, pastor of Saint Peter's Congregation in Arlington Heights, directed them in this venture.

Saint Paul's at the beginning was served by the Rev. Walter F. Pieper, pastor of Immanuel in Des Plaines, who conducted worship services on Sunday afternoons in the public school of Mount Prospect. The first resident pastor to be installed was the Rev. John E. A. Mueller, "Reiseprediger" in North Dakota, with headquarters at Napoleon, N. Dak. The installation took place on January 12, 1913.‡ About a week later Pastor Mueller opened a day school with seven pupils in a small cottage on Main Street. Meanwhile the church building was in course of construction on a section of a two-acre piece of property, donated by William and Edward

*1940 census: 1,720.

†Charter members:

Henry Haberkamp	Edward Busse	Henry Reese
Henry J. Ehard	Albert Sporleder	Albert Wille
§William Busse	Herman Oelerking	Fred Biermann
Henry Beigel	Herman Beigel	Christ. Wille
William Busse, Jr.	Louis Katz	William Bargmann
William Wille	Joseph Ehard	Albert Busse
Ernst Busse	Louis Haberkamp	Henry Glade
Henry Hammer	John W. Pohlmann	

§Now (1949) in his 48th year as county commissioner of Cook County.

‡Son of the Rev. J. E. A. Mueller, first pastor of St. Luke's, Chicago. The father died on Aug. 25, 1917.

Busse. During a blizzard which raged on March 2, 1913, the church, located at the corner of Busse and Elm Streets, was dedicated. In the summer of the same year a one-room school building was erected near the church. The congregation's first trained teacher, Martin H. Hasz, was installed in September, 1917. In 1921 Miss Edna Taege of Arlington Heights was engaged for the lower grades. In 1925 several small school buildings were added, and Elmer Jackisch was added to the teaching staff. In 1928 all the wooden buildings were sold and moved off the property. Shortly afterward a fifty-thousand-dollar school building was erected, and dedicated in January, 1929. Serving as teachers also, more recently, were Mrs. Edward Busse and Mrs. Robert Bayne.

179. Chicago, Zion (Lithuanian)

The Evangelical Lutheran Synodical Conference of North America consists of German Lutherans, English Lutherans, Norwegian, Danish, Swedish, Slovak, Polish, and Lithuanian Lutherans—all of these nationalities, in addition to others, being represented in the Northern Illinois District area. The last-mentioned group has a congregation in the neighborhood which has been designated as "2100 South and 2100 West"—in the old "Lime Kiln" territory. On December 4, 1912, these Lithuanian Lutherans organized Zion Congregation and called as their first pastor a young graduate of Concordia Seminary, Springfield, Ill.—Candidate John J. D. Razokas. He served the congregation until his death in January, 1921, and was succeeded in May of the same year by the Rev. John Rozak of Fairland, Okla. In November, 1934, he* was succeeded in this pastorate by the Rev. Ewald Kories, who served for about twelve years, resigning in the latter part of 1946. His successor, the Rev. Elmer H. Nauyok, was installed as Zion's fourth pastor on January 10, 1947. Early

*Without a charge for a number of years, the Rev. John Rozak was installed as pastor of St. John's, Rodenberg, on Jan. 31, 1943.

in the fall of 1949, Pastor Nauyok resigned the pastorate, and the Rev. John Paupera* was installed as his successor.

Two "sons" of this congregation have entered the Lutheran ministry: George Jurkshaitis, who graduated from Concordia Seminary, Springfield, Ill., in 1917; and Elmer H. Nauyok, who graduated from Concordia Seminary, St. Louis, Mo., in 1945.

180. Chicago, Doctor Martin Luther

The fourth Slovak Lutheran congregation to be organized in the Chicago area now has its center at West Fiftieth and South Honore Streets. Organization of Dr. Martin Luther Congregation was effected by fifty-two Lutheran men† on April 6, 1913. The Rev. John S. Bradac, who in 1913 was serving Bethlehem Slovak Congregation, was instrumental in bringing this to pass. During the first five years of its existence, Doctor Martin Luther Congregation held its worship services in the school of Saint Martini Congregation, at West Fifty-first Street and Marshfield Avenue. Its own church was

*The Rev. John Paupera of 4826 South Lawndale Ave., Chicago 32, Ill., compelled to flee to Germany because of the "Red tide," has made his way to America. Since coming to Chicago, he has rendered "great physical and spiritual help to his Lithuanian brethren who in recent months have come to Chicago." He has now successfully passed his colloquy, held at Chicago on Nov. 5. The examination was conducted by Pastors Arthur A. Brauer, Herbert H. A. Harthun, and Theodore F. Nickel. Pastor A. H. Werfelmann, President of the Northern Illinois District, served as moderator. The Examining Committee of The Lutheran Church—Missouri Synod hereby declares *Pastor John Paupera* eligible for a call. Signed G. Chr. Barth, D.D.; Louis J. Sieck, D.D.; F. A. Hertwig, *Chairman*. *The Lutheran Witness*, LXVIII, No 26 (Dec. 27, 1949.)

†Charter members:

John Kristof	Michael Rigan	John Vojtek
Matt. Baranovic	Paul Basnar	Charles Zak
Michael Somovic	Martin Drzik	Michael P. Stancik
Martin Drobena	Martin Nebes	Michael Sadkib
Michael T. Stancik	Stephen Batka	Paul Jesko
John Hucko	George Stancik	Matt. Stancik
John Tenjak	John Pilat	George Ruman
Samuel Trlak	Martin Mihalik	Martin Vaclavek
Charles Shvets	John Vitek	Michael Barancin
Samuel Arvet	Paul Shvets	Martin Kostial
Peter Valach	Stephen Klc	Martin Stancik
John Simovic	Paul Matejak	Michael Marchalik
Matt. Tenjak	John Miklas	Michael Cermak
George Hlatky	Michael Hucko	Martin Gregor
Stephen Pijacek	John Valek	John Sefara
Stephen Cibula	Matt. Hulata	Michael Vojtek
Martin Rohacek	George Valach	Stephen Gergel
	Samuel Galandak	

erected during the fall and winter of 1917-1918, dedication taking place on April 28, 1918. This church is located at 4953 South Honore Street. The congregation has been served by the following pastors: Robert Schnirch, John Pribula, George Roh, Jaroslav J. Pelikan, and John Mihok (since 1933).

181. Chicago, Windsor Park

Windsor Park is located about ten miles south of the Loop. "The Church of Our Redeemer, Chicago (Englewood), offered $50 monthly for six months in addition to her regular mission collections, on condition that a mission be begun in Windsor Park." On June 8, 1913, the Rev. Arthur Henry Kaub* of Dallas, Tex., was installed in Immanuel Church, East Ninety-first Street and Houston Avenue, South Chicago, as missionary for the territory of Windsor Park and vicinity. "A most welcome surprise was sprung when the Rev. Ferdinand Sievers in a short address following the act of installation committed the spiritual welfare of seventy-one souls of his congregation to the care of the newly installed pastor. Of this number, thirty-five were communicants and formed the nucleus for the new mission." Two English services were conducted by Pastor Kaub in Immanuel Church. On June 29, 1913, the first in a series of services was conducted in a vacant store in the Windsor Park community, at 2625 East Seventy-fifth Street. It was here that Windsor Park Congregation was organized on July 20, 1913, with fifty-seven communicants, nine of whom were voting members. Beginning on November 1, 1913, services were conducted in Jones Hall, at East Seventy-fifth Street and Coles Avenue. Meanwhile property measuring 72x167 feet at the southwest corner of East Seventy-sixth Street and Saginaw Avenue was purchased for four thousand dollars, and plans were formulated to

*Pastor Kaub was born on Oct. 12, 1880, at Thirty-seventh and State (extension of the old Vincennes Trail) Streets, Chicago—several blocks from St. Peter's Church, erected in 1874, at Dearborn and West 39th Streets. St. Peter's center now is at East 74th and Michigan.

build a church. The foundation was laid early in April, 1914. Labor troubles in the brickyards delayed construction work for about two months. A little more than a month after President Woodrow Wilson had announced the neutrality of the United States, the church was dedicated, September 13, 1914. Two months later, on December 13, the news came that the American Marines had seized Haiti (San Domingo).

Rapid growth during the next ten years necessitated the erection of a larger church. On the occasion of its tenth anniversary the congregation witnessed the laying of the cornerstone of its new church at the corner of the previously mentioned site. Dedication took place on March 30, 1924.

On February 21, 1939, mission work was begun in Chatham Fields, a community about two miles southwest of Windsor Park. (See Chapter 227, page 594.) The Hyde Park mission, organized in March, 1940, although originally sponsored by the Northern Illinois District, was heartily supported, morally, by Windsor Park Congregation and its pastor. On June 2, 1940, a second mission was started by Windsor Park; this one in Markham, a comparatively new subdivision approximately two miles west of Harvey. (See Chapter 231, page 600.)

In November, 1945, the Rev. Ervin H. Hartman, until recently chaplain in the United States Army and prior to that pastor of Saint Paul's Congregation in Utica, Nebr., was installed as assistant pastor in Windsor Park. Upon Pastor Kaub's resignation at the end of June, 1948, the assistant pastor was formally installed as Windsor Park's pastor on Sunday, September 12, 1948. On September 11, 1949, John F. Buelow, graduate of Concordia Teachers College, River Forest, and of the American Conservatory of Music, was installed as director of music and education. In Jánuary, 1949, Pastor Kaub organized a congregation for the English District in Tuscon, Ariz.

182. Chicago, Lord Jesus

Prior to 1913 the Polish Lutherans were scattered through the city of Chicago. Holy Cross, on the city's northwest side—at Lamon and Wrightwood Avenues—was the only congregation affiliated with the Synodical Conference which conducted work among the Polish-speaking Lutherans in their mother tongue. In order to promote this activity more systematically and to maintain unity in the congregation's far-flung mission projects, special men were selected for the various congregational districts in Chicago. Fifteen members of Holy Cross were residing on the South Side; one of these, Paul Wilcopolski, was the official "collector." He and a student, J. Olszar of the Wisconsin Synod's theological seminary at Wauwatosa, Wis., with whom some of these South Side Poles became acquainted when he preached in Holy Cross Church during his vacation, called a meeting for the purpose of organizing a congregation on the South Side. Needing help and support for the new venture, the group consulted with the Rev. Frank C. Streufert, pastor of Peace Congregation at West Forty-third Street and California Avenue. They were advised by him to dissolve, to return to their "mother" congregation, and to petition their own pastor, the Rev. Stanislaus Mlotkowski, to assist them in organizing a congregation. This advice was heeded, and on August 10, 1913, a Polish congregation was organized in Peace Congregation's school, at West Forty-third and Mozart Streets, and named Lord Jesus.* Pastor Mlotkowski, who presided at this meeting, was asked to serve as the first pastor. Shortly afterward property at 3042 West Thirty-eighth Street was purchased by the new

*Charter members:

Adam Riczko	Adam Dora	Adolf Mikilon
John Bransteyder	Paul Pulkos	Paul Wilcopolski
Julius Henzel	Michal Mikolon	Jacob Mikolon
Adolf Kucewski	Andrew Pulkos	Julius Sadowski
Karol Marcowka	Frank Kucewski	Adam Kucewski
Michal Wroblewski	Ludwig Brodowski	

congregation and a church erected. While the building was under construction, Lord Jesus Congregation held its worship services in Peace School. The new church was dedicated on November 29, 1914. After Pastor Mlotkowski's resignation from this part of his large mission field, Pastor Streufert and Student Olszar took over the ministerial work. Upon graduating from the seminary, Candidate Olszar became the first resident pastor of Lord Jesus Congregation and served here until November, 1919. His successor, the Rev. Theodore Engel, "Reiseprediger" in Wisconsin, Minnesota, and Iowa, was installed about ten months later, on September 26, 1920. Up to this time all congregational work had been done through the medium of the Polish language. With the coming of Pastor Engel, the children of the parish received their religious instruction in the English language. Beginning in 1929, English worship services were conducted on alternate Sundays, and in 1934, every Sunday.

Not strong enough, financially, to support a day school of its own, Lord Jesus Congregation urges its children to attend school either at Peace or Saint Andrew's School.

183. Villa Park

If some people would have had their way about it, the area between Elmhurst and Lombard—the hearts of which two cities are only about four miles apart—would have been set apart as a cemetery. However, in 1909 a realty firm, recognizing the possibilities of a subdivision for the living rather than for the dead, established not only one community, but two communities between the two already mentioned. The two new settlements were called Villa Park and Ardmore; but the latter was later swallowed up by Villa Park, by incorporation.* A very important factor in the development also of this community, about eighteen miles due west from Chicago's Loop, was the Chicago, Aurora, and Elgin Rail-

*1940 census: 7,072.

road, whose fast electric trains enter Chicago above traffic congestion, over the tracks of the Chicago Rapid Transit ("L" or "El") Company (now part of CTA, Chicago Transit Authority).

In the fall of 1913 the Rev. C. H. Kenreich, pastor of Grace Congregation in Glen Ellyn, about two and a half miles west of Lombard, saw in this yet small but flourishing dual settlement possibilities for the establishment of a Lutheran mission. Through the efforts of Charles Biermann, a Lutheran of York Center and member of the local public school board, the use of the public schoolhouse was secured for the first worship service, on November 16, 1913. This continued for two years, and in 1915 a building site was donated by Ballard & Pottinger, real estate operators. In the summer of the same year a church was built, the dedication following on November 15. The name Trinity already had been adopted. The congregation received as a gift the church bell which had served its purpose in Saint John's Church, Forest Park (Harlem), Ill., since 1867.

Pastor Kenreich served Trinity as an affiliate of Grace in Glen Ellyn until the summer of 1916, when he accepted a call to South Sodus, N.Y. During the ensuing vacancy, Student Edgar F. Witte of Concordia Seminary, St. Louis, Mo.,* assumed the responsibility and served for about one year. Trinity's first resident pastor, Candidate Arno Schlechte, was ordained and installed on August 5, 1917. On October 16, 1949, the Rev. Harry N. Huxhold, assistant executive secretary of the Lutheran Child Welfare Association at Addison, Ill., was installed as Trinity Congregation's assistant pastor. Trinity is a member of the English District.

Miss Alma Fendt, who began teaching in the Sunday school of Trinity Congregation in 1922, continued this work with-

*Since June 1, 1944, executive director of the Lutheran Charities of Chicago; formerly pastor of Pilgrim Congregation, St. Paul, Minn.

out a break for 25 years, and on the occasion of the anniversary in the fall of 1947 the congregation presented her with a certificate of appreciation.[101]

184. Chicago, Faith

About four miles southwest of Windsor Park is Auburn Park, likewise a part of the Big City. Near the end of 1913 Our Redeemer Congregation in Englewood offered the Mission Board of the English District fifty dollars a month for a period of six months for the purpose of starting a mission in the rapidly developing Auburn Park community. The offer was accepted, and shortly afterward a call was extended to the Rev. Elmer V. Haserodt of Freeport, Ill., to serve as missionary in the districts known as Auburn Park and Gresham. He was installed on February 8, 1914; and the first service was conducted on the following Sunday, February 15, in Cosmopolitan Hall, 7938 South Halsted Street. Twenty-three people were in attendance. The mission was formally organized by nine men as a congregation and named Faith, on April 8, 1914. World War I began on July 28.

Two years later, in May, 1916, Faith Congregation purchased five lots at the southwest corner of West Eighty-third and Sangamon Streets, and upon this site the Mission Board of the English District erected a portable chapel in August of the same year. On April 6, 1917, the United States formally entered the European War. As a result of this unfortunate development, building operations in Auburn Park, like in thousands of other places, were postponed. On March 1, 1919, Faith Congregation became self-supporting. A little more than three years later, in May, 1922, ground was broken for a new church building on the original site. Then, for several years, the "basement" served as a place of worship. In 1925 the superstructure was completed, and on September 27, 1925, the new brick church was dedicated.

A collation of Bible portions, which harmonize with the 660 hymns of the *Lutheran Hymnal* was recently completed as the private study of Pastor Haserodt. He has added the portions of the Bible that harmonize with the thoughts in the hymn. (Cf. *Lutheran Witness*, English District edition, LXVII, No. 22.) The Rev. A. Fred Grothe, ex-chaplain and graduate student at The University of Chicago, has been assisting Pastor Haserodt for more than a year.

185. Chicago, Nazareth

In 1915 the Northern Illinois District (Missouri Synod) instituted a "Hausmission" (house mission)* in Chicago and placed the Rev. William F. Burhenn in charge of it. Pastor Burhenn started this work on December 1, 1915, visiting people in their homes, distributing German and English religious tracts, and urging the Lutherans to join near-by congregations. Among the first sections of the city to come under his observation was the new development in the Central Park-South Kedzie Avenue area, north and northwest of Marquette Park. With a group of Lutheran men† Pastor Burhenn organized Nazareth Congregation in 1917. He had charge of this mission until June, about the time when the first American soldiers arrived in France, when he was succeeded by the Rev. Eugene Theodore Lochner of Storm Lake, Iowa. After having served for a little more than a year, Pastor Lochner accepted a call to Vincennes, Ind., and the Rev. C. F. Worthmann of Alliance, Nebr., succeeded him on November 10, 1918—the day before the Armistice was signed in

*In 1918 it was reported at the District convention that there was very little apparent success ("wenig augenscheinlicher Erfolg"). The mission was discontinued in the same year. According to the report, Pastor Burhenn organized Nazareth and Golgotha Congregations. (See *Proceedings* of the Northern Illinois District, 1916 and 1918.)

†Charter members:

W. Kissmann	E. Raschke	H. Czichilski
John Rohde	C. Bohl	J. Kujatt
G. Kissrow	Leo Weiss	William H. Nagel
J. Kruger	H. Haebel	William C. Zemke
G. Tucholke	A. Ahrendt	Fred Mader
	G. Preuss	

Europe. Pastor Worthmann opened a day school with seventeen pupils, and in 1919 William H. Nagel became its first teacher. In the same year Nazareth, assisted by the District's mission treasury, purchased property at the corner of West Sixtieth Street and Hamlin Avenue, on which it erected a portable chapel. A thorough canvass of the neighborhood revealed that the selected location was by no means the most desirable in the community and that the new mission's center was about five blocks farther east. While the matter of relocation was under advisement in 1920, Pastor Worthmann accepted a call to Corder, Mo. During the ensuing vacancy the Nazareth mission almost lost its identity, although the day school continued to function. In September, 1920, those interested in the school retained the idea of proceeding with the original plans and with the aid of the Rev. Frank C. Streufert, pastor of Peace Congregation (West Forty-third Street and California Avenue), purchased several lots at the northeast corner of West Sixtieth Street and South Spaulding Avenue. In August, 1921, a resolution to erect a chapel on this site instilled new enthusiasm into the small group of Lutherans. Loans were secured from the general Church Extension Fund of the Missouri Synod and from the mission treasury of the Northern Illinois District. In January, 1922, the chapel was dedicated. Then came a real estate boom which lured many more Lutherans into this section of Chicago. On May 13, 1923, when the Rev. Herbert Kohn* of Ferguson, Mo., was installed as Nazareth's pastor, the communicant membership was sixty-nine. In June, 1925, Mr. Nagel followed a call to Fort Wayne, Ind., and Armin G. Zapf succeeded him here.† During these years of development Pastor Kohn taught the lower grades, and student vicars had

*Son of the Rev. William C. Kohn, D.D., pastor of St. Andrew's, Chicago, 1889-1912, and first president of the Northern Illinois District, 1909-1913.

†Son of the Rev. Emil Zapf, pastor of St. Paul's, Melrose Park, Ill., 1892-1927, and Chicago city missionary, 1927-1937.

charge of the intermediate grades until September, 1927, when Arthur L. Miller was added to the teaching staff. One year later, Arthur Petrowsky assumed charge of the primary grades.

In May, 1928, a new church, costing approximately eighty-eight thousand dollars, was dedicated, and the chapel was converted into a school building. In 1935 Mr. Zapf followed a call to Detroit, Mich., and William F. Wittmer of Brookfield (formerly called Grossdale), Ill., replaced him in Nazareth School. In 1946 Mr. Miller followed a call to St. Louis, Mo., to serve as executive secretary on the Missouri Synod's Board for Parish Education. In 1947 Mr. Petrowsky followed a call to Detroit, Mich. Mr. Wittmer followed a call to Pilgrim School on West Cullom Avenue, near Winchester Avenue. Succeeding these two teachers on Nazareth's teaching staff were Walter G. Nau* and Paul E. Doerrer.† Other members of the teaching staff in recent years were Miss Marie Wilharm, Miss May Henning, Miss Charlotte Schupmann, James S. Strayer,[102] Carlos Messerli, and Miss Carola Novak.

186. Chicago, Hope

From 6000 South and 3300 West the Trail now proceeds a short distance toward the southeast, to 6400 South and 2700 West. The southwest corner of this intersection, West Sixty-fourth Street and Washtenaw Avenue, constitutes the center of interest for well-nigh five thousand Missouri Lutherans. Hope Congregation was organized in February, 1917, in a vacant store at 2552 West Sixty-third Street. During the previous year the area had been canvassed, and large numbers of Lutherans, affiliated with one or another near-by congregation, expressed their willingness to affiliate with the new mission in their midst.

The first worship service was conducted in October, 1916,

*Mr. Nau resigned in 1948.

†Mr. Doerrer accepted a call to the Western District in January, 1949.

by the Rev. J. C. Anderson, principal of Luther Institute, and he took charge until January 7, 1917, when the Rev. John A. Leimer of Goodfarm, Ill., was installed as Hope's first pastor.

In 1918 a "basement" church was built. The growth in membership was rapid, so that the superstructure had to be erected in 1921. Seven years later an annex was built, and dedicated on July 7, 1929. The enlarged church represents a right angle in the form of the letter L, with the pulpit standing in the apex and the pews in two separate wings.

When by fall of 1933 the attendance overtaxed the enlarged church building, the congregation decided upon having two identical services on Sunday mornings. Hope's church council consists of twenty-four deacons and three trustees, the pastor serving as chairman. These deacons are the spiritual leaders of the church and assist the pastor.

For fifteen years, Immanuel Carl Strieter, a former day school teacher, served as organist and choirmaster. In June, 1939, the Rev. Oscar Rauschelbach was called as assistant pastor, to serve especially as organist and choirmaster. He served in this capacity until a few months before his death, which occurred on July 9, 1944.

"Through all the years of our ministry at Hope Church, the members of our council have set our congregation a beautiful example in church attendance and in loyal service. Ever have they been eager to co-operate with the pastor in working out the plans and problems for the extension of the work, and, next to God's grace, we owe much of the success attained by Hope Church to these faithful leaders."

Hope Congregation conducts a Saturday Bible school as well as a Sunday school. According to the Missouri Synod's *Statistical Yearbook*, Hope Congregation's Sunday school is the largest in this Synod, having 1,058 pupils. The original constitution was signed by fourteen men.* The baptized membership now is 4,366.

Hope Congregation is a member of the English District. "There are within a radius of one mile of Hope Church nine Reformed churches, six other Lutheran churches (three of the Missouri Synod), and nine Catholic churches." (Cf. *Lutheran Witness*, LXI, 18, p. 308.)[103]

187. Chicago, Mount Olive

Approximately thirteen miles due north of the community discussed in the preceding chapter there was similar mission activity during the same year, 1917. Urged by Pilgrim Congregation, whose "center" is located at Cuyler and Wolcott (formerly Lincoln Street) Avenues, the Mission Board of the English District established a congregation in the Albany Park community. Pilgrim agreed to subsidize this mission project to the extent of twenty-five dollars monthly for one year.

Candidate Bernard H. Hemmeter,† graduate of Concordia Seminary, St. Louis, Mo., was assigned to this mission. Upon arriving in Chicago, the young clergyman was "taken for a ride" by the Rev. Ernest F. Haertel, pastor of Christ English Congregation, on a Kedzie Avenue streetcar. Espying a vacant store at the southeast corner of West Cullom and Kedzie Avenues, they alighted and within a brief space of time completed arrangements to rent the store for worship purposes. The young candidate soon afterward washed the win-

*Charter members:

Aaron Meyers	William H. Ziervogel
John W. Utesch	Ferdinand C. Moench
John Thornmahlen	Edward W. Schwer
E. R. Wickstrom	William F. Moench
Harry Graefen	William Gehrke
Arthur C. Utesch	Charles Lausen

†Candidate Hemmeter was ordained at Conover, N.C., where his father, the Rev. Henry Bernard Hemmeter, was president of Concordia College, 1914-1918; the latter was president of Concordia Seminary, Springfield, Ill., 1937-1945, and died July 22, 1948, in Baltimore, Md., at age of 79.

NOTE: The Rev. M. Leimer of Beemer, Nebr., father of Hope Congregation's pastor, while visiting in Chicago, to assist at the Holy Week services, suffered a stroke on Easter Monday and died on May 2, 1943.

dows, mopped the floor, borrowed chairs and other essential furnishings from the "mother" congregation, and prepared for his installation, scheduled for September 23, 1917. On the following Sunday morning he organized a Sunday school with fifteen pupils and conducted the first service with an attendance of thirty-four persons. On November 8, 1917, the congregation was organized by nine members and named Mount Olive.* In the fall of 1918 Mount Olive began to conduct its services in a building "across the street," formerly places of business—the larger portion of it having been a saloon.

Mount Olive became self-supporting on March 1, 1919.

The members being drawn chiefly from the western parts of the community, the problem of a permanent location, with due consideration to near-by "sister" congregations, was solved by purchasing a building site in the Irving Park community, at the southwest corner of Tripp Avenue and Byron Street. In 1919 services were begun in another rented "center" near the proposed "permanent center" in the Myrtle Temple, corner of Tripp Avenue and Irving Park Road. On January 29, 1922, a chapel was dedicated and used for worship services and Sunday school sessions for a little less than six years. The church proper was dedicated on December 11, 1927. Although located in a community whose residents were predominantly "Protestant," of other than Lutheran antecedents, Mount Olive's growth in membership has been a healthy one, principally by "missionary accessions." Pastor Hemmeter writes: "We often think back to a Saturday afternoon when the members were felling trees in order to clear the ground for the parsonage, when the streets were filled with autos. Upon inquiry, we learned that it was the

*Charter members:
A. A. Faehse
William C. Faehse
G. H. Knitter
A. H. Sporleder
John A. Wagner
D. C. Hucksoll
M. J. Stuebe
M. F. Schmidt
Bernard H. Hemmeter, pastor

Ku Klux Klan gathering for a 'Konklave.' So, from the very beginning the congregation was compelled to emphasize the distinctive characteristics of confessional Lutheranism, witness against 'strange altars' and conduct an evangelizing program in the community."

Of the first fifteen persons in attendance at the first Sunday school session, on September 30, 1917, one continues as a member of the Sunday school: Mrs. Eugene F. Tegtmeier (the former Miss Ruth Faehse). During these thirty years the Sunday school has had two superintendents: William C. Faehse and John A. Wagner. Albert Hemler, grandson of a member of Pilgrim Congregation who "did much to encourage and help the mission" in its early stages of development, G. E. Hemler, is Mount Olive's present secretary. Of the thirty-four who attended the first service, the following still are members of Mount Olive: A. A. Faehse, Mr. and Mrs. William C. Faehse, Mr. and Mrs. John A. Wagner, A. H. Sporleder, and Mrs. G. H. Knitter.

In January, 1948, the Rev. Richard Luecke, son of the Rev. and Mrs. George L. Luecke of Norwood Park (Chicago), was installed as assistant pastor of Mount Olive Church.

188. Homewood

The Trail has not been outside Chicago since 1913. It now goes from the Irving Park community (Mount Olive Church) in Chicago to a place once known as Hartford, about six miles from the Cook-Will county line, on the Illinois Central Railroad. During the early years of the Missouri Synod's existence—especially during the 1850's and 1860's—this place was invariably referred to as Thornton Station. Officially it has been known for a good many years as Homewood, Ill.*

On December 25, 1905 (Christmas Day), a small group of

*1940 census: 4,078. The name "Homewood" was suggested by Mrs. J. C. Howe after a village near Pittsburgh, Pa.

"German" Lutherans gathered in the Homewood home of John Diekmann for a worship service conducted by the Rev. Matthew H. Feddersen, pastor of Saint John's Congregation at Coopers Grove—about three miles west of Homewood. For a time, then, the services were held once a month in the home of John Kaehler on North Morris (now Harwood) Avenue, next door and adjoining the building in which Mr. Kaehler operated a blacksmith shop. As more people became interested in the venture, the group in 1909 rented the old Presbyterian church, which stood directly east of the present Illinois Central Railroad "underpass" (Dixie Highway). On April 11, 1915, the last service was held there, and shortly afterward the building was razed. During the following four years the services were held in the village hall on Clark Street (now Chestnut Road).

On August 10, 1919, eight men* organized their own congregation in Homewood and named it Salem ("Peace"). The congregation thereupon purchased two lots on South Morris Street for four hundred dollars, and a carpenter shop, 16x25 feet, which stood on this property, for an additional five hundred dollars. Remodeled during the summer and fall, this building was dedicated as a church on November 9, 1919. The Rev. Rudolph L. Geffert, pastor of Trinity Congregation in Harvey—about three and a half miles north by northeast of Homewood—assisted Pastor Feddersen in serving Salem with an English worship service once a month. On March 8, 1925, the congregation extended a call to the Rev. Louis J. Schwartzkopf, at the time on a lecture tour for the Board of Foreign Missions in the eastern part of the country. Pastor Schwartzkopf, on a two-year sick leave, accepted this call while in Cleveland, Ohio. He was installed as Salem's first resident pastor on March 29, 1925. Within a few weeks

*Charter members:

William Adam
Henry Butze
Walter Gomoll
Herman Stogentin
William Kaehler
Christ. Retschlag
John Kaehler
Albert W. Tatge

the congregation resolved to erect a larger church.* Another lot, adjacent to the original property on the north side, was purchased for nine hundred dollars. While the church was being constructed, plans were formulated for a day school. On September 6, 1925, the church with a full basement was dedicated. On the folowing day the pastor opened the day school with an enrollment of eighteen; within two weeks three more children were added. A total of six had been "promised." The "old" church served as the schoolhouse, but not for long. In 1926 plans for a new and modern school building were formulated, and on August 28, 1927, the congregation witnessed the ceremony attendant on laying of the cornerstone for a new face-brick school building of modern design and facilities. In its report to the Northern Illinois District in 1926, the Mission Board stated: "The congregation in Homewood has doubled all its figures since the previous synodical convention . . . . The parish school, in which the pastor is active five days each week, has an enrollment of 26 children, and more have been promised for the next school year."

Prior to November, 1929, German and English services were held on alternate Sundays. Since that time English services have been conducted every Sunday, and German services twice a month. In September, 1929, the enrollment had risen to forty-seven. With the consent and co-operation of the Mission Board the congregation then gave its pastor an assistant, Miss Christine Eickemeyer,† who taught the lower grades. In the fall of 1934 Pastor Schwartzkopf resigned He was succeeded in Homewood by Candidate Armin H. Breihan, who was installed on January 27, 1935. Five years later Pastor Breihan accepted a call to Redeemer Congregation in Park Ridge, Ill. His successor as Salem's third resident pas-

*The subsidy of the congregation began in 1925; in 1930 the Northern Illinois District began to subsidize the school.

†Daughter of Teacher Christian Eickemeyer, then at St. John's School, Eagle Lake, Ill.

tor was the Rev. Walter William Paul Wilk of Amherst, Colo., who was installed on July 21, 1940.

In addition to those already mentioned, the following have served in the day school: Miss Ruth Adams, Miss Frieda Strasen, Theo. F. Ries, and Walter J. Schmaedeke.

Since the turn of the century the Lutheran Trail has visited fifty congregations, and a total of 188 at the end of the second decade of the twentieth century.

During this same period a multitude of discoveries have been made in the fields of science; and numerous inventions have brought hitherto unheard-of conveniences to most Americans, particularly to those living in the larger cities and environs. Since about 1914 the Trail has been finding its way in dark places by means of flashlights—pocket size! In most directions from now on the Trail will not follow mud roads or gravel roads, but wide roads constructed of macadam or concrete; if necessary, it will take to the sky by means of an airplane or helicopter![104]

Part Six

From Homewood to Arlington Heights

189. Chicago, Bethesda

The last year of the twentieth century's second decade, 1920, is known, at least in America, principally for the addition of the Nineteenth Amendment to the National Constitution, giving equal suffrage to American women, which went into effect in that year, when Warren Gamaliel Harding was elected President of the United States.

The Trail's first stopping place listed on this itinerary is a community in the northern section of Chicago known as Rogers Park. "Missouri" Lutheran mission work was started here in March, 1905, in an abandoned church belonging to another denomination. The place, which included a schoolroom, was rented for ten dollars a month, and worship services were conducted by the Rev. Victor F. Richter, pastor of Saint John's Congregation in Wilmette,* for about five years. In 1910 the Mission Board of the Northern Illinois District reported to the delegates at the second convention of this body that half of the eleven members had moved away

*Pastor Richter was installed in Wilmette on March 19, 1905.

and that the congregation dissolved before the board could deal with it. "That this mission ended so abruptly is attributable to the dishonesty of the congregation's treasurer."

Ten years later, in October, 1920, six Lutheran men* organized another congregation in this community, presumably much farther to the west, and named it Bethesda. Its first resident pastor was the Rev. Herbert W. Luecke of Wadena, Minn. He was installed on October 24, 1920. For several years Bethesda's services were held in a vacant store at 8107 North Western Avenue. In December, 1925, a brick bungalow chapel was dedicated about a mile and a half south of that store, at North Campbell Avenue and West Farwell Street, on property purchased in 1923. Ill health compelled Pastor Luecke to resign at the beginning of the following year, 1926. His successor, the Rev. Frank P. A. Wittmer of Marseilles, Ill., was installed on February 6, 1926. A new church of brick and Lannon stone, with a seating capacity of three hundred and fifty, was erected near the southeast corner of the same intersection and dedicated on January 20, 1935. The former chapel, facing Farwell Street, was converted into a parsonage. Recently nine additional lots directly south of the church were purchased as the site for a four-room day school and recreation hall. One family contributed five thousand dollars toward this project.[105]

190. Chicago, Grace

Grace Church is located at 2700 North and 5200 West, near the "center" of Holy Cross, which was founded in 1899 as a Polish Lutheran congregation. On May 11, 1919, Holy Cross called Candidate August Jarus, graduate of Concordia Seminary, St. Louis, Mo., to take charge of the English work and to teach in its day school. A canvass of the community

*Charter members:

Carl Schoen	William Gedons	August Diesterheft
Herman Kuk, Sr.	Adolf Litwitz	Gustav Sasse

revealed that many Lutherans had no inclination to affiliate with the "Polish" congregation,* but that there was a definite sentiment toward the founding of a new congregation. This led to the organization of Grace Congregation in November, 1920† Because no other place of worship was available, the congregation's English services were held at 9:30 on Sunday mornings. Beginning July 3, 1921, these services were held in the Lloyd Branch Public School at North Cicero and Fullerton Avenues. Meanwhile a brick church was being erected by Grace Congregation at the southeast corner of Parker and Laramie Avenues. On September 6, 1921, a day school was opened in the unfinished building with an enrollment of twelve pupils. The church was dedicated September 18. In the same month the congregation's first trained teacher, John Maschoff, was installed; he left the same fall and was succeeded by Ernest A. Harks on January 3, 1923.

In 1926 a new church was erected, the dedication following on October 24. In January, 1928, A. L. Wendt was installed as day school teacher.‡ In September of the same year, Edgar G. Krenzke was added to the staff; he served until 1933, when he followed a call to the staff of Saint Luke's School, Chicago. He was succeeded in 1934 by E. E. Yunghans. Others who have served in Grace School in more recent years were W. C. Loek, Delmar R. Lorenz, Miss Thea Schwich, Mrs. Elizabeth Birr, Mrs. Ruth Lorenz, C. F. Berndt, D. Zimmermann, Miss Ruth Kluender, H. W. Grueber, Mrs. D. Butcher, Mrs. M. Covington, Miss Inez Cizek, Mrs. D. N. Gross, and Mrs. A. Nottke.

*At that time, Holy Cross conducted services in three languages: German, Polish, and English.

†Charter members:

F. Faulhaber	A. Arlt	M. Struzt
O. Krack	G. Fritz	H. Mickow
J. Breitzke	G. Fick	M. Hoy
E. Kline	C. Boness	C. Stapelmann
H. Kline	H. Nemitz	J. Rode
J. Thrun	A. Hofstetter	F. Kline
Ernest Graves	R. Geschke	A. Buelow
	A. Stroemer	

‡Mr. Wendt died suddenly on Nov. 6, 1939.

191. Chicago, Our Saviour

The Trail now winds to the extreme northwestern limits of Chicago, 6200 North and 6000 West—Norwood Park.

During World War I, at the instigation of members of St. John's Congregation at near-by Niles (Dutchman's Point) and other Lutherans residing in the Norwood Park area, worship services and a Sunday school were established in a Methodist church on Nickerson Avenue, at Hood Avenue, with the stipulation that all the work be carried on in the German language. The *Fibel* (Primer) was used for instruction of English-speaking children of largely English-speaking parents. The Rev. Louis A. Grotheer, pastor of Saint John's, Niles, was in charge. During the war, however, this arrangement became impossible, and the project was discontinued. Thereupon several people addressed an appeal to the Mission Board of the English District for action which would lead to the establishment of a mission in Norwood Park. After considerable delay, caused partly by objections raised by neighboring Lutheran congregations and partly by the difficulty in securing a pastor to start this work, the Rev. John C. Anderson, principal of Luther Institute in Chicago, was empowered to serve the small flock.

The first service was conducted on Sunday morning, October 31, 1920, in the Masonic Hall, East Circle and Nina Avenues. During the following week the interior of the little Episcopal Church of Saint Alban, on West Circle, near Nickerson Avenue, was made ready for succeeding services, and the twenty-six children of the Sunday school began to prepare for a Christmas program under the direction of O. P. Behnke and Edward Stoebig, members of Mount Olive Congregation in the Irving Park community. By January 1, 1921, the increased membership indicated that the young mission was ready to be organized as a congregation. On January

16 nine men gathered for this purpose. Professor Anderson presided at the meeting, which was also attended by the Rev. Ernest F. Haertel, pastor of Christ English Congregation, Chicago, and member of the English District's Mission Board. The name chosen was Our Saviour.

In February, 1921, a call was extended to Candidate George L. Luecke, graduate of Concordia Seminary, St. Louis, Mo., and at this time student at The University of Chicago. He was ordained and installed as Our Saviour's first resident pastor on March 13, 1921. In February, 1922, an inside lot, 50x200 feet, on Northcott Avenue, at West Circle, was purchased for $1,250. "No sooner did we get the sweet taste of debt than we wanted more; and ere the year was up, we had arranged for the loan of $8,500 toward the erection of our first chapel." This chapel, Our Saviour's first church, was dedicated on March 18, 1923. "For more than two years we had dwelt in 'tents.'" Shortly after this event in the congregation's history, the Sunday school enrollment had risen to 140. In the following year, 1924, a day school was established, and the first trained teacher, Paul W. Moll of Altamont, Ill., was installed on August 24. The school was opened with six grades, comprising forty-two pupils, divided into two classes. Pastor Luecke taught the lower grades for one year; after this the lower grades were taught successively by Miss Stella Wuerffel, Miss Velma Schroeder, Mrs. Eugene Ford, Miss Virginia Moll, and Erich W. Christian. In 1928 a school building was erected near the rear of the church.

The growth of Our Saviour's was never rapid. There are "sister" congregations one and a half to two miles away in all directions, and Lutherans of other synods in Norwood Park as well as in Edison Park. However, in 1933 "double" services on Sunday mornings were instituted, and within the next five years even these were overcrowded.

In 1941 an effort was launched with an insurance plan

to raise forty thousand dollars to liquidate the debt of twenty thousand dollars and to erect the first unit of a new church with the remainder. On a corner piece of property, 156x270 x200 feet (corner of Nickerson and Northcott), one block northwest of its present property, a new church was erected in 1949, which cost $10,000;[106] the dedication took place on Sunday, December 4, 1949.

192. Maywood, Good Shepherd

From Norwood Park the Trail goes about seven miles south to Maywood,* first visited in 1892. (See Chapter 125, page 419.)

Late in the summer of 1919 three Lutheran clergymen, Emil Zapf, pastor of Saint Paul's Congregation in Melrose Park—about a mile west of Maywood—Ernest F. Haertel, pastor of Christ English Congregation, Chicago, and Jean M. Bailey, director of religious education, were cruising about in the community then known as South Maywood and discussing the possibilities of starting a congregation in the latter community. The most directly concerned with the project was Pastor Zapf. The other two men, therefore, conferred with him about the proposed new congregation, and by the time the cruising for the day was over, it had been unanimously agreed a new mission be started "anywhere south of Madison Street, or else very close to Madison Street."

In the spring of 1921 the Rev. Guido R. Schuessler, secretary of the English District's Mission Board, requested the Rev. Martin F. Buenger, temporarily without a charge and residing in Chicago,† to canvass Maywood with the view to organizing a mission. With the name and address of a former member of Pastor Schuessler's parish,‡ Richard Esemann, Pastor Buenger soon afterward began working in this community. The names of former members of Pastor Bailey's

*Named by Col. W. T. Nichols, one of the owners of the site, for his daughter, May.

†Pastor Buenger resigned his pastorate at Strasburg, Ill., June 20, 1920.

‡Our Redeemer Congregation in the Englewood community, Chicago.

congregation, Trinity in Oak Park, (since March, 1921, served by Pastor H. W. Prange) were added to this list, which then constituted the nucleus for the new congregation, thenceforth designated Good Shepherd, and formally organized on May 2, 1921.* The first service was held on March 27, 1921, in the Yale Theater, Fifth Avenue and Madison Street, and later the services were conducted on the second floor of a building on the northwest corner of Washington Boulevard and Fifth Avenue. In the early part of 1926 Pastor Buenger accepted a call to Warren, Minn. On April 17, 1926, a young clergyman in Birmingham, Mich., while studying his sermon for the following day, "Good Shepherd Sunday" ("Misericordias Domini"), received a call from Good Shepherd Congregation in South Maywood, Ill. This young man, the Rev. Luther Schuessler, was installed as Good Shepherd's second pastor in May, 1926. In the following year a church of varicolored Lannon stone was erected at Sixth and Warren Avenues, and dedicated on January 15, 1928. A contribution of one thousand dollars was received from Samuel Insull† and twenty-five hundred dollars from Mr. John P. Schaefer of Pittsburgh, Pa., through the good offices of the Mission Board's secretary, Pastor Guido R. Schuessler.

In the latter part of the summer of 1932 Pastor Luther Schuessler accepted a call to Our Redeemer Congregation in Englewood, Chicago, as assistant pastor. His successor at Good Shepherd in South Maywood, the Rev. J. M. Bailey,‡ since January, 1931, serving as the Walther League's director of religious education in Chicago, was installed on November 27, 1932.

*Charter members:

Richard Esemann	John Kautz
Gustav A. Lueck	Lester Gurke
Paul Weiss	Clarence Engel
Herbert Diesner	

†Public Utilities magnate in Northern Illinois since about 1907; died suddenly in 1938, in Paris, France.

‡Served as pastor of Trinity, Oak Park, from 1907 until 1920, and then accepted a call to Baltimore, Md.

193. Hinsdale, Redeemer

The Trail passed through Hinsdale (formerly known as Fullersburg) in 1888. In 1922 the situation in this village was similar to that prevailing in Norwood Park after World War I. A group of six families belonging to Zion Congregation, whose "center" is at Grant and Second Streets, realizing the need for exclusively English services in Hinsdale, principally in order to prevent the younger generation from drifting away from the Church, met in April, 1922, for the purpose of organizing such a congregation.* This group organized under the name Redeemer. The young congregation was served at the beginning by the Rev. John C. Anderson, principal of Luther Institute, Chicago. A Sunday school was organized on April 16, and the first worship service was held in the afternoon of May 7, in the Butte Building. Beginning June 11, Professor Anderson conducted the services on Sunday mornings. On September 3 Redeemer's first resident pastor, the Rev. Carl F. Dankworth† of Port Huron, Mich., was installed. A year later a building site at First and Blaine Streets was purchased for $4,500. On March 1, 1925, in subzero weather, the cornerstone of the chapel was laid. The dedication took place on August 30, 1925. The cost was approximately $23,500.

One son of the congregation, H. F. Dorn, has entered the Lutheran ministry.

On March 13, 1949, Miss Marie Homann's services as a Sunday school teacher for 20 years were recognized by Redeemer Congregation.

*Charter members of Redeemer, Hinsdale:
Mr. and Mrs. J. H. Steben
Mr. and Mrs. E. H. Maier
Mr. and Mrs. W. F. H. Graue
Mr. and Mrs. C. J. Schwendener
Mr. and Mrs. W. H. Papp
Mr. and Mrs. J. A. Schmidt
Mrs. B. Maier
Mr. and Mrs. F. M. Schmidt
Mr. and Mrs. William Waisanen
Mr. and Mrs. George Karnatz
The Misses Augusta and Henrietta Biermann, Ruth Graue, Gertrude Lochman, and Ruth and Evelyn Papp

†Since 1945 secretary of the English District.

NOTE: In 1921 the word "German" was deleted from the constitution of the Northern Illinois District.

194. Berwyn, Concordia

In the spring of 1923, the city of Berwyn,* so named by P. S. Eustis, passenger traffic manager for the "Q" Line (C. B. & Q. R.R.) in memory of the suburb of Philadelphia, Pa., in which he was reared, was canvassed, and occasional services were conducted. Berwyn is located less than two miles southwest of Cicero, or about ten miles west–southwest of Chicago's Loop and crossed by Ogden Avenue (the old Southwest Plank Road). In June, 1923, Candidate Warner H. Grothman, graduate of Concordia Seminary, Springfield, Ill., was called to assume charge of this prospective mission field. On August 19—about two weeks after the death of President Warren G. Harding in San Francisco, Calif. (August 2)—Candidate Grothman was ordained as a Lutheran minister. On October 14, 1923, services were held in the Odd Fellows Hall, at Oak Park Avenue and Windsor Street. The increasing attendance at the services encouraged the members of this mission to take steps toward organizing a congregation. A preliminary meeting was called for January 15, 1924, in the home of R. C. Bischof. Eleven men attended this meeting.† The organization meeting was held on February 6, at which time a constitution was signed by eight men.‡ On the following June 4, Concordia joined the English District of the Missouri Synod. On November 30 the congregation purchased an old Presbyterian church at Thirty-second Street and Home Avenue for nine thousand dollars and dedicated it on December 21. On January 1, 1928, the congregation became self-supporting. In 1932 a canvass of the Stickney community, directly south of Berwyn,

*1940 census: 48,451.

†Attending the preliminary meeting: Pastor Grothman, Fred Schroeder, W. O. Bendler, Otto Albert, H. Nuecke, A. Janowsky, M. Hillmer, H. Schwartz, H. Wollenberg, and F. W. Brockmann, and the Rev. H. W. Prange of Oak Park.

‡Charter members:

Wm. Steinhauser	Fred Schroeder
Otto Albert	H. Nuecke
W. O. Bendler	H. Schwartz
R. C. Bischof	F. W. Brockmann

was conducted by a number of Concordia Sunday school teachers. This resulted in the establishment of a branch Sunday school on May 22, 1932, in the home of a Mrs. Cobb. On June 4, 1933, another branch Sunday school was organized in the home of Mrs. E. Brandner in North Riverside, about one mile west of Berwyn. Preaching services were begun here in March, 1934.

On May 15, 1938, Pastor Grothman accepted a call to Christ English Congregation in Chicago as successor of the Rev. Ernest F. Haertel, whose death occurred on the previous January 24.* His successor as Concordia's second pastor, the Rev. Edmund G. Kleidon of Wolf Point, Mont., was installed on September 25, 1938. He served this parish until October, 1944, when he accepted a call to Mishawaka, Ind. Concordia's third pastor, the Rev. Daniel R. Ludwig of Boonville, Mo., was installed on February 4, 1945.

Plans for a new church and educational building have been completed. The estimated cost of the project is $110,000. The cornerstone of the new building was laid on Sunday, October 9, 1949. "The old church was moved to the back of the old property, set on a new foundation, and faced with brick, to serve as a parish hall."

195. Jefferson Park

About one hundred and eighty years after the birth of our country's third President, Thomas Jefferson (1743), the Trail leads to a town named in his honor, formerly known as Plank Road. Reference to a township called Jefferson was made in several previous chapters. (See Chapter 66, page 281.) Now, in 1923, the name graces a section of northwest Chicago, originally an independent village, where are seen two Lutheran clergymen, the Rev. B. H. Hemmeter, pastor of Mount Olive Congregation, Chicago, and the Rev. George

*The Rev. Warner H. Grothman died on Jan. 6, 1947, at the age of forty-eight.

L. Luecke, pastor of Our Saviour Congregation in Norwood Park (Chicago), and two laymen, enthusiastically discussing the prospects of a mission in the Jefferson Park community, recently surveyed by a general canvass. The Mission Board of the English District regarded favorably the project and promptly gave material support. In June, 1924, the congregation was organized by eight men* and named Jefferson Park Lutheran Church. The Mission Board extended a call to the Rev. August F. Lindenmyr of Oakmont, Pa. His installation took place on May 9, 1924, in Mount Olive Church, North Tripp Avenue and Byron Street. The first services were conducted in the "hall" of the Democratic Party (Forty-first Ward) on the second floor of the present Wolke and Kotler Department Store, at the intersection of Milwaukee and Lawrence Avenues.

Because this was one of the first Protestant churches in Jefferson Park and the first English Lutheran church, the mission grew rapidly and became self-supporting within one year after its organization. "Possibly none of the mission congregations of our District has enjoyed a more steady and remarkable growth than this church," was the English District Mission Board's printed comment in June, 1927.

In 1925 the congregation purchased property at Long Avenue and Northwest Highway, and in the following May the brick church, 40x90 feet, was dedicated. "The church became a vital factor in the expanding community. Building an aggressive Sunday school organization, the church attracted hundreds of children." The economic depression, however, nullified plans for the construction of completely adequate facilities.

In May, 1944, Pastor Lindenmyr, after twenty-one years

*Charter members:

Martin Gerse	Ed. Kowalke
Henry Nemitz	C. Rauschenberg
Charles Belzer	William Jehs
M. Thompson	Henry Wessel

in the Jefferson Park pastorate, accepted a call to Los Angeles, Calif. In September, 1944, his successor, the Rev. William F. Eifrig,* former service pastor for the Missouri Synod's Army and Navy Commission, was installed as the congregation's second pastor.

In 1946 the congregation called a full-time director of Christian education Armin Grams, and now is contemplating a building program, which will include a day school and an enlarged church building.

196. Chicago, Messiah

In the fall of 1924 the rapidly developing community known as Clearing, in one of Chicago's southwest corners, was canvassed by the Rev. John H. Mueller, pastor of Zion Congregation in Summit, a few miles west of Clearing, and the Rev. Herbert Kohn, pastor of Nazareth Congregation, West Sixtieth Street and Spaulding Avenue. The first business meeting of a group of men, including the two clergymen mentioned, was held in the home of Mr. Kraai. Five of these men volunteered to "follow up" on the canvass that had been made, and on November 16, 1924, services were held in a Methodist church. Shortly afterward the Clearing Town Hall was secured, free of charge, for this purpose. Two men served each Sunday, sweeping, building the fire, and arranging the chairs. In February of the following year a congregation was organized and named Messiah. In the same month also a lot on the northeast corner of West Sixty-second Street and Mansfield (now Monitor) Avenue was purchased. A small brick church was erected, and dedicated on October 11, 1925. Pastor Kohn conducted the worship services from November, 1924, till December, 1926; then, under his direction, the mission was served by the Rev. Louis H.

*Prior to becoming service pastor, the Rev. W. F. Eifrig, son of Prof. Charles W. G. Eifrig, professor at Concordia Teachers' College, River Forst, Ill. (1909-1943), served a pastorate at Carlinville, Ill. Professor Eifrig died Nov. 1, 1949, at Orlando, Fla.

J. Steinbach from January until May, 1926. The Rev. Frank C. Streufert, pastor of Peace Congregation, West Forty-third Street and California Avenue, Chicago, supervised the mission from June, 1926, until June, 1927. On June 5, 1927, the Rev. Paul Julius Roeder, missionary of "the Western Slope" in Colorado, was installed as Messiah's first resident pastor. He also taught school for some time. Assisting in this work for several seasons were Students E. Burgdorf and Paul Schmanke. In November, 1938, Pastor Roeder accepted a call to Bethany Congregation* as successor of the Rev. August Burgdorf, who died on July 15, 1938. In the same year Messiah Congregation became self-supporting. Its second resident pastor, the Rev. Walter H. Vatthauer of Clinton, Ill., was installed on December 4, 1938. Messiah's day school was discontinued during the depression in the 1930's

In 1949 the church building was completely remodeled; it now is "an outstanding structure of modified English Gothic design." The cost was $49,500, which includes the chancel "Trinity" window.

197. Chicago, Messiah

It is becoming increasingly apparent that the Mission Board of the Northern Illinois District (Missouri Synod) was ever on the alert to establish new missions in Chicagoland at every opportunity. On Chicago's northwest side a canvass was conducted under the board's direction in the vicinity of Patterson Street and Melvina Avenue (6200 West and 3600 North), which resulted in the establishment of a mission in the fall of 1924. On October 24 invitations were sent out to a number of prospects, and two days later the first worship service was conducted in a community hall on West Addison Street by the Rev. Theodore L. Blanken. Nine adults and four children attended. On February 8, 1925, a constitution

*Located at Cortez and Rockwell Streets, 1891-1926; since then, at Narragansett and Wabansia Avenues.

was adopted and Messiah Congregation (the second by the same name within the same month in Chicago) was organized. Two weeks later, on February 22, the Rev. Theodore L. Blanken, formerly in Champaign County, Ill., was installed as Messiah's first pastor. There were fifteen charter members. Four months later the congregation was faced with the need for larger quarters. A building committee, therefore, was appointed, and construction of a combination church and school building was begun at 3640 North Melvina Avenue. Dedication took place on August 29, 1926. Ten years later the membership had so greatly increased that three services had to be arranged for Sunday forenoons. In December of the same year, Pastor Blanken contracted a severe throat ailment, and his physician advised him to spend a half year in the "Sunny South." The congregation granted its pastor an indefinite leave of absence. During this time he received a call from the Central Illinois District (Missouri Synod) to serve as institutional missionary at Bartonville, near Peoria, Ill. After receiving the call for a second time and admitting that his physical condition would not permit his return to Messiah Congregation, he asked to be released so that he might accept the call. At a special meeting on July 7, 1937, he bade farewell to Messiah, at which time he received a "testimonial for his faithful services." During Pastor Blanken's illness the congregation had called Candidate Franklin C. Giese, graduate of Concordia Seminary, St. Louis, Mo., to serve during the vacancy. On August 1, 1937, he succeeded to the pastorate relinquished by Pastor Blanken.

The following trained teachers have served in Messiah School: Herold P. Wukasch, E. K. Eckert, Arthur L. Amt, J. M. Roth, Rudolph T. Stahlecker, Mrs. G. Hedges, Miss Helen Rotermund, Mrs. R. Michaelson, J. Bolz, and Norman C. Niles. Miss Lois Schauer, winner in the Chicagoland Music Festival (1943) vocal contests, is a Messiah graduate.

*Sonsored by the *Chicago Tribune*.

Plans for expansion of church and school facilities are now under way.

198. Midlothian

About three miles southwest of Blue Island is a village known as Midlothian, Ill.,* a far cry from Edinburghshire in Scotland! The Rev. Walter J. Kemnitz, while serving Immanuel Congregation in Mokena (1918-1924), some ten miles to the southwest, canvassed this village and found a "sufficient number" of interested Lutherans to warrant organization of a congregation. After considerable delay on the part of those who might have supported the venture, the Mission Board of the Northern Illinois District instructed its missionary at large, the Rev. Daniel C. Hennig, to conduct another canvass. He reported as follows: "I was told to find a place for worship and to get the ball rolling. That wasn't easy. Nothing at all was available. Still I had written to all the prospects that the first service would be conducted on a certain day and had advised them to look at the bulletin board in the railroad station (Rock Island R.R.), where full information would be posted. In desperation, the Friday before the appointed Sunday, I persuaded a gentleman by the name of Schroeder to permit me to use his half-finished garage on the back of his lot (only walls—no roof) for the first service. I posted the information on the bulletin board, and the first service was attended by twenty-eight people. In the course of the next week I persuaded the Mission Board to buy a circus tent and induced a realtor to permit us to use one of his lots for location of the tent. All went according to schedule, and on the following Sunday evening the second service was conducted in that tent..... When summer began to draw toward its close, I spoke of Christian education to the members and succeeded in getting thirty-three children for a school. The Mission Board engaged Student Herbert

*1940 census: 2,430.

R. Neitzel* of Concordia Seminary, Springfield, Ill., and a day school was begun in that tent, which was heated with several small kerosene stoves." Meanwhile the Mission Board had purchased a lot at 148th Place and Hamlin Avenue, Midlothian, and soon afterward, aided by a loan of $3,600 from the Church Extension Fund, a chapel was erected on this site. Toward the end of November the congregation and the school moved into this chapel. Formal organization of the congregation, which was named Concordia, took place in the spring of 1925. A Pastor Klaus served the congregation and taught school for a short time; his successor, the Rev. Louis H. J. Steinbach, also remained here for a very brief period. During the intervening vacancies the congregation was served by the Rev. Paul Roesener, who was living in retirement at Mokena. On January 22, 1928, the Rev. Ernest Theodore Blau of Tampa, Kans., was installed. Shortly afterward the school was discontinued. In its report to the delegates assembled in convention in June of the same year, the Mission Board stated: "Although there are a few faithful souls here who wish to be served by the Missouri Synod, the majority of the people here who have been invited and admonished to attend services were indifferent." The convention delegates thereupon resolved that this congregation "be served henceforth, as soon as possible, by any of the neighboring pastors, and that the school children attend the school of a neighboring congregation, if feasible."

In the summer of 1943 Pastor Blau accepted a call to Gage Park Congregation in Chicago. Thereupon Concordia became an affiliate of Salem Congregation in Homewood, about five miles southeast of Midlothian, and was served by the Rev. Walter W. P. Wilk from October 1, 1943, until September 1, 1946. At that time the Midlothian parish became an affiliate of Mount Greenwood Congregation, West 109th

*Assistant executive secretary of the Lutheran Child Welfare Association (Kinderheim), Addison, Ill., 1946-1949.

Street and Trumbull Avenue, and was served by its pastor, the Rev. William J. Rohlwing. More recently, the spiritual requirements of Concordia and of Trinity, Hazel Crest, were combined to constitute a dual parish under the guidance of the Rev. Walter C. Johannes of McHenry, Ill.; he was installed on June 5, 1949.[107]

199. Saint Charles

From Midlothian the Trail leads in a northwesterly direction, a distance of about thirty-seven miles, to St. Charles, Ill.,* on the Fox River—about ten miles south of Elgin.

Information on the inception of "Missouri" Lutheranism in St. Charles indicates that since about 1912 preaching services had been conducted in the village by the following clergymen: Charles J. Fricke, pastor of Emmanuel Congregation, Aurora; J. Martin Grosse of Batavia; Herman Harms of Batavia; Frederick G. Miessler of Batavia; John F. C. Molthan of Batavia; and Henry W. Rabe of Elgin.† In 1913 the Mission Board in its printed report, submitted to the delegates assembled in convention, included the statement that Pastor Harms succeeded in "giving new life to the dying plant" ("das sterbende Pflaenzlein neu zu beleben"). Pastor Rabe, in 1924 or 1925, preached here every Sunday, German and English, in a lodge hall. Organized in 1925, the congregation was named Saint Mark's. Its first resident pastor was the Rev. Wilbert Frederick Theiss,‡ who served until 1935 and then resigned. His successor, the Rev. Edwin H. Pflug of Oswego, Kans., was installed a short time later. In July, 1938, Pastor Pflug accepted a call to Saint Paul's Congregation in Grand Crossing on Chicago's South Side. His successor, the Rev.

*1940 census: 5,870. First named Charleston by Ira Minard, an early settler, from the town of that name in New Hampshire.

†Retired pastor.

‡Later he resumed pastoral work in Sharon, Wis. From 1943 to 1945 he was pastor of Immanuel Congregation, Belvidere, Ill.; thence he went to Port Washington, Wis. His father, the Rev. Gottlob Theiss, was pastor of Saint Peter's, Schaumburg, Ill., 1906-1935.

Erwin L. Burgdorf of Wessington Springs, S. Dak., was installed on July 24, 1938. Pastor Burgdorf also served the near-by State Training School for Boys. In September, 1947, Pastor Burgdorf accepted a call to Marseilles, Ill., and his successor in St. Charles, the Rev. Alex F. C. Pfotenhauer of Monroe, Mich., was installed on November 30, 1947. He is a son of the Rev. Martin A. Pfotenhauer, pastor of Holy Cross Congregation, Chicago, until his death, May 16, 1949.[108]

200. Western Springs

From St. Charles the Trail once more goes directly eastward, following St. Charles Road, which eventually becomes North Avenue, and at the intersection of the "Avenue" and Wolf Road—about a mile northeast of Elmhurst (Cottage Hill)—it turns south, passing "Franzosenbusch" (Proviso), and about two miles south of this place enters a village situated almost halfway between Hinsdale (Fullersburg) and La Grange. Its name is Western Springs.*

It was on June 26, 1925, that the Rev. T. W. Strieter, pastor of Zion Congregation in Hinsdale, conducted the first worship service in the public school building in Western Springs. Services were held in the same place for the remainder of the summer, and in the fall a Sunday school was organized in the home of Mr. and Mrs. L. H. Winkelmann on Central Avenue. Mr. Winkelmann served as superintendent. On November 15, 1925, Grace Congregation was organized. Soon afterward a building site at the corner of Wolf Road and Forty-first Street was purchased. Although the building was not completely finished, the first service was conducted here on Christmas Eve, December 24, 1925. The church was dedicated on January 17, 1926. Groups of men assisted in the construction work, and both members and friends gave and loaned liberally in a financial way. Seminary students assisted Pastor Strieter in the mission activities,

*1940 census: 4,856.

among whom was Walter R. Roehrs, student at the University of Chicago. He became Grace Congregation's first resident pastor on June 27, 1926, being installed by his father, the Rev. Henry F. Roehrs, pastor of Immanuel Congregation at Proviso. Arrangements were made with Saint John's School in La Grange—about two miles to the east—to have the children attend there. Pastor Roehrs also served Bethel Congregation at Westmont—about four miles west of Western Springs—for two years. On January 12, 1930, Pastor Roehrs accepted a professorship at Saint Paul's College, Concordia, Mo.* His successor, the Rev. Herman Christian Seitz of Ponchatoula, La., was installed on February 9, 1930. For ten years, beginning 1934, he also taught school—all grades—until the latter part of 1944, when a member of the congregation, Mrs. Renetta Griese, assisted in this work. On March 1, 1945, Arthur Schaefer was installed as teacher. On the following December 18 Pastor Seitz died suddenly "while performing some customary household duties." His successor in the Western Springs pastorate, the Rev. Randolph E. Muller of Columbus, Ind., was installed on May 19, 1946. In June, 1949, Pastor Mueller accepted a call to Spencer, Wis. Grace Congregation's fourth resident pastor, the Rev. Arthur E. Bohlmann of West Point, Nebr., was installed on November 13, 1949.

201. Broadwiew

Less than five miles northeast of Western Springs, or two miles directly south of Melrose Park, is a village known as Broadview.†

Here again are evidences of alertness on the part of the Northern Illinois District's Mission Board, for it is recorded that in November, 1925, that agency of the Missouri Synod

*For several years in the early 1940's he was a member of the Concordia Teachers College faculty, River Forest, Ill.; more recently, at Concordia Seminary, St. Louis, Mo.

†1940 census: 1,457.

purchased from the United Lutheran Church a "basement" church and a small three-room cottage at the rear of the lot located at South Fifteenth Avenue and Harvard Street. Five families, totaling thirteen communicants, constituted the original membership of this mission, which was named Bethlehem. Its first resident pastor, the Rev. Arthur Charles Hallmann of Brimfield, Ill., was installed on April 4, 1926. By the end of the year the communicant membership had increased to thirty-seven. The growth continued at the rate of from fifty to ninety per cent each year, until the economic depression caused many members to lose their homes and seek residence elsewhere. When the depression was nearly over, only about ten of the original members remained, but with the advent of 1945 Bethlehem declared itself self-supporting.* The day school was established in September, 1926, with an enrollment of twenty-six pupils, with the pastor in charge. In 1927 a student was placed in charge of this work, and in 1928 E. H. Dieckhoff was installed. Two years later Alfred Richter was added to the staff. Others who have served as teachers in Bethlehem School were: Edgar A. Meyer, Paul F. Steffens, Edward Stelter, Miss Hulda Jung, Miss Betty Humphrey, and Miss Betty Albrecht.

202. Chicago, Mount Calvary

Mission work in the neighborhood of Arcadia Terrace and Peterson Woods, a few miles west of the Edgewater territory in "uptown" Chicago, was begun in 1926 by the Rev. Carl H. Eberhard from Roanoke, Va., whom the Mission Board of the English District had called in the spring of that year. The first service was held in his home at 2610 Ardmore Avenue on Easter Day, April 11, 1926. Subsequently the services were held in the De Witt Clinton Public School

*The Mission Board of the Northern Illinois District had paid somewhat more than $20,000 for this property, which included the super-structure. Prior to Pastor Hallmann's arrival the mission was served by the Rev. John H. Mueller and the Rev. Emil Zapf.

at Fairfield and Glenlake Avenues. In August, 1926, the congregation was organized and named Mount Calvary. Its first pastor was the Rev. Carl H. Eberhard. Because the rental of the school auditorium was "too high," the small group resolved to seek its own place of worship. A 20x40-foot chapel, formerly the property of Christ English Congregation, was purchased with the assistance of the Lutheran Church Extension Association (English District), and the C. & R. Rauchert & Co. granted free use of a lot on Lincoln Avenue, near the intersection of Peterson Avenue, where the chapel was dedicated and Pastor Eberhard installed on October 17, 1926.

In October, 1927, Pastor Eberhard accepted a call to Louisville, Ky., and the Rev. Carl Louis Rutz of West Frankfort, Ill., was installed as Mount Calvary's second pastor on January 8, 1928. In 1929 the chapel, previously moved and set up on the congregation's new building site at Ardmore Avenue and Mozart Street, was enlarged. In 1935 an "English brick basement" was built to serve as a more desirable place of worship. The superstructure was completed early in the year 1941 and dedicated on February 16.

203. Elmwood Park

A few miles south of Chechepinqua Forest Preserve, or about ten miles northwest of Chicago's Loop, the Trail enters Elmwood Park,* where for the first time the name Zoar is found for a Missouri Synod congregation in this territory. Zoar Congregation was organized on January 19, 1927, in Belmont Heights—a half mile north of its present location, by the Rev. Theodore L. Blanken, pastor of Messiah Congregation, whose "center" is at Melvina Avenue and Patterson Street, Chicago. It was in May of the same year that Col. Charles A. Lindbergh made his epochal solo flight from New York to Paris. On September 18, 1927, the Northern Illinois District's Church Extension Board dedicated a chapel

*1940 census: 13,689.

at Seventy-fifth Court and Roscoe Street. Candidate Herman P. Meyer was called to assume charge of both church and school work. He served in this capacity until January, 1929, when he accepted a call to Woodstock, Ill. When the subdivision known as Westwood was developed, the Mission Board caused this territory to be canvassed by its missionary at large, the Rev. Horace Henry Hartman. Members of "sister" congregations moved here in large numbers, and before long a mission was established in the Westwood community. Because the two missions were so close together, the Mission Board requested the members of the two congregations to merge. A union was effected on February 6, 1929, and at a joint meeting on February 9, 1930, Zoar Congregation in Elmwood Park was organized. A plot of ground was purchased at Seventy-fifth Court and Wellington Avenue by the Church Extension Board, and a two-story building, 35x60 feet, designed to serve as a church and school, was erected.

On April 14, 1930, the Rev. Horace H. Hartman was called as Zoar's first pastor, and shortly afterward Norman Himmler was called as teacher. The following year a second teacher, H. T. Ellermann, was added to the staff. Students Enno Gahl and John A. Mau* served as teachers from 1932 to 1935. In 1934 Alfred F. Fricke of Park Ridge, Ill., replaced Mr. Himmler. The years 1933-1935 were "very trying for Zoar." Many members lost their homes and many more their employment, but the few who kept their employment carried Zoar's financial burden. Beginning in 1936, the congregation gradually was re-established, and by the end of 1939 seventy-five per cent owned their homes. In 1940 Zoar became self-supporting.

During 1941 a tower was erected on the southeast corner of the chapel, which provided more room in the chapel,

*Enno Gahl, son of the Rev. William Gahl, Chicago, has been pastor of Saint Paul's (Austin—Chicago) since 1938. John A. Mau served as assistant pastor at Immanuel, Elmhurst, 1937-1943; now at Havertown, Pa.

added fifty to the seating capacity, and afforded a third classroom.

Miss Minnie Kohn was engaged in 1936 to teach the primary grades, and in 1941 Edward Eckhardt taught the intermediate grades. And when in August, 1943. Mr. Fricke followed a call to Cleveland, Ohio, Werner E. Diercks succeeded to the principalship. In September, 1946, he followed a call to Fort Wayne, Ind. In 1946 Warren F. Schmidt, hitherto on the staff of Immanuel School in South Chicago, was installed in Elmwood Park. Others who have served as day school teachers were: Mrs. D. P. Kautz and Miss Bernita Voltz. In June, 1948, Pastor Hartman resigned the Zoar pastorate, and on September 12, 1948, the Rev. Walter Schmidt of Salina, Kans., succeeded him.[109]

204. Chicago, Good Shepherd

The Trail now goes to the West Lawn community on Chicago's southwest side. On September 18, 1927, the first "Missouri" Lutheran service was conducted in a portable school building at West Sixty-second Street and Kostner Avenue by the Rev. Paul William Czamanske of Sheboygan, Wis., where on the previous August 28 he had been ordained by his father; his installation in Chicago took place on September 11. About three months later three lots were purchased, and a portable chapel was erected at the northwest corner of West Sixty-second Street and Keeler Avenue.

Pastor Czamanske served in this mission until July, 1930, when he accepted a call to Hazel Park (in Detroit), Mich. His successor, the Rev. Walter Louis Fred Baumgartner of Milk River, Alberta, Canada, was installed on September 7, 1930.

Seven years later there appeared in the official organ of the Chicago Lutheran Church Extension Association, *The Ambassador,* the following description of conditions here: "The Church of the Good Shepherd can truthfully be called a favorite child of the Association, inasmuch as it has been signally blessed with assistance in a financial way on several occasions. At its beginning Good Shepherd received a loan of three thousand dollars for the erection of a small portable building and the purchase of several lots. This amount was reduced by only six hundred dollars when the depression struck. (Just six days before the congregation was to make payment on its loan, the local bank closed its doors, and all the congregation could boast of at the time was the offering received on a certain Sunday morning in June of that year.) In 1930 . . . a large sum of money was urgently needed to meet financial obligations to the city of Chicago for five special street assessments amounting to $473.73 each..... The mistake was apparent, namely, that Good Shepherd had more real estate than funds to make payment for street paving."

On December 21, 1944, the church which had been erected in 1927 was burnt out, and the interior appointments which escaped the flames were water-soaked. Plans for a new church were soon made; meanwhile, services and meetings were held in the portable parish hall.

Exclusive of "much donated labor," the new brick church, with a seating capacity of 450, was erected at a cost of $85,000. The dedication took place on January 23, 1949.[110]

Several months later the contractor, William Zimmermann, was fatally injured in an automobile accident near his summer home at Benton Harbor, Mich.

205. Waukegan, Redeemer

For the second time the Trail proceeds from Chicago northward along the lake shore to a place once known as "Little Fort" but since 1849 as Waukegan,* an Indian name having the same meaning.

It is the year 1927, in which year, on August 2, Calvin

*1940 census: 34,241.

Coolidge, thirtieth President of the United States since August 3, 1923, handed out a written statement to newspaper correspondents at Rapid City, S. Dak., bearing the now historic phrase: "I do not choose to run for President in 1928."

In Waukegan acquaintance is made with the second Synodical Conference congregation,* this one a member of the Missouri Synod. In October, 1927, twenty-three voting members, together with their families, were released from the former congregation (Immanuel), to organize their own congregation. For a time this group was served by Pastors Adolph C. and Carl H. Buenger of Kenosha, Wis., about fifteen miles north of Waukegan, services being held in the German Congregational church opposite the Lake County courthouse. At a meeting of the temporary board, or council, in the home of E. Burandt at Wilson Station, in the presence of the Rev. Alex Ullrich, president of the Northern Illinois District (Missouri Synod), the Rev. T. W. Strieter of Hinsdale, Ill., and the Rev. D. C. Henry Heise, circuit visitor, the last-named was requested to serve as supply pastor until the embryo congregation could be formally organized with its own pastor.

The circuit visitor then called a meeting for December 15, 1927, in the home of C. Bockeloh, 814 Franklin Street, in the basement of which many subsequent meetings were held. At the first meeting a Lutheran constitution was discussed, and at the next meeting, December 21, the document was signed by twenty-four members, who then also applied for membership in the Missouri Synod. At the same time a call was extended to the circuit visitor, the Rev. Daniel Christoph Henry Heise, then pastor of Saint Matthew's Congregation at Fairfield (Russells Grove), Ill.—about sixteen miles southwest of Waukegan. He was installed as the first resident pastor of this new congregation, named Redeemer, on February 5, 1928. Soon afterward a lot at 626 Grove Avenue

*Immanuel Congregation, a member of the Wisconsin Synod, was organized in 1891.

was purchased for about ten thousand dollars, and the Mission Board approved plans for a church building to cost $25,000. The new church was dedicated on July 7, 1929. Redeemer Congregation for some time was subsidized by the Northern Illinois District to the extent of a hundred dollars a month. The congregation grew and prospered in its new surroundings until the economic depression came. Then there were many removals and transfers. In 1929 the congregation's indebtedness amounted to fifty-eight thousand dollars; by the beginning of 1945 it had been reduced by almost forty per cent.[111]

206. Westmont

Following the old Green Bay Trail, the Lutheran Trail now goes back to Chicago, and near the southwestern side of Lincoln Park connects with Ogden Avenue, which it pursues through Douglas Park, Cicero, Berwyn, Lyons, Brookfield, La Grange, Western Springs, Hinsdale, until it comes to a cross-road named Cass Avenue—about two and a half miles west of Hinsdale—and then turns south to Westmont.*

When the village of Westmont was in the first stages of development, the Rev. T. W. Strieter, pastor of Zion Congregation in Hinsdale, observed not only the transformation of fruitful farmland into a lively village, but also the influx of a considerable population. He canvassed the territory, and soon afterward services were held there by the Rev. Otto F. Arndt, pastor of Immanuel Congregation in Downers Grove. Interest which had been aroused gradually waned, until at length the field was abandoned so far as public services were concerned. Pastor Strieter, however, repeated his attempt to establish a mission and for some time conducted services and Sunday school sessions in a vacant store. Again a failure! In the fall of 1924 a plot of ground was purchased by the Mission Board of the Northern Illinois District, and upon it

*1940 census: 3,044.

a portable chapel was erected. During this somewhat more hopeful attempt the Rev. William L. Kupsky, pastor of Saint John's Congregation, whose "center" is located about three miles south of Westmont—on Cass Avenue—had charge of the services and the Sunday school. In the hope that a day school might serve as a more tangible means of starting a mission, such an institution was established in 1925. The Mission Board engaged Ewald F. Lorenz,* student at Concordia Seminary, Springfield, Ill., for two years, and the mission was served as an affiliate of Grace Congregation in Western Springs by its pastor, the Rev. Walter R. Roehrs.

In the fall of 1927 Bethel Congregation was organized by twenty men, who then called the Rev. Ernest F. Kavasch of Danbury, Conn., to serve as pastor and teacher. He was installed on December 4, 1927. In 1929 the cornerstone of a church was laid at Grant and Irving Streets, Westmont, and, when it was completed, the portable chapel was converted into a school. The first primary teacher was Miss C. M. Reinke; she served from 1931 until 1940. In 1932 L. Lessel took charge of the upper grades. Others who have served as teachers in Bethel School were C. J. Gehrs and the Misses M. Gieschen, F. Seitz, G. Beldenow, Marie Gorr, and Mrs. A. Anderson.

During the economic depression many of Bethel's members lost their homes and moved away. Since then practically a new congregation has developed and a new school is being planned. On November 21, 1948, the cornerstone was laid.

207. Chicago, Saint Philip's

The Evangelical Lutheran Synodical Conference of North America has varied interests, including mission work among the Negroes; one such is the affiliated congregation in the extensive area sometimes referred to as Bronzeville on Chicago's South Side.

In the fall of 1921 the Rev. Marmaduke N. Carter was

*Pastor of Saint Matthew's, Chicago, since Sept. 22, 1946.

requested by the Synodical Conference authorities to relinquish his activities as missionary in the State of Alabama and, instead, to devote his time to lecturing and preaching in churches of the "Conference" for the purpose of acquainting its members with the Negro Mission. In January, 1922, the lecturer-preacher was stationed in Chicago, with the understanding that at the conclusion of his tours he would start working as missionary among his own people in this city. Such work was begun by him in March, 1924. Services were conducted in the auditorium of the Young Men's Christian Association (Building for Negroes) on Wabash Avenue for about two and one half years. Rental for two hours on Sunday mornings was $4.50. In 1927 the Northern Illinois District convention was held in Peace Church, West Forty-third Street and California Avenue; at one of the sessions the resolution was passed to devote fifteen thousand dollars to local Negro mission work. Also, a committee, consisting of Pastors August Burgdorf, Leo Schmidtke,* and Ernest G. Jehn, was chosen to advise and assist Missionary Carter in the selection of a building site and the erection of a church.

This congregation is appropriately named in honor of a zealous missionary of Hellenic origin, Philip, the evangelist who met an Ethiopian eunuch on the way from Jerusalem to Gaza and explained to him the Prophet Isaiah's declaration concerning the suffering and death of the Messiah. After being baptized by Philip, the Ethiopian (Negro) "went his way rejoicing." (Acts 8:26-40.)

A lot at the southwest corner of East Sixty-fourth Street and St. Lawrence Avenue was purchased, and toward the end of May, 1926, building operations were commenced. Saint Philip's Church was dedicated on October 17, 1926. "In the spring of 1928, as far as human vision could reach, it was a question as to whether Saint Philip's would stand or be wrecked. By God's grace, the storm was weathered, and Saint

*Later, Pastor Schmidtke was replaced by the Rev. Oscar Fedder.

Philip's stood." By the year 1933 the first church (chapel) had outlived its usefulness, and serious consideration was given to the idea of enlarging it, but the economic depression disrupted the plan. In the same year Saint Philip's started a mission among the Negroes in Evanston. Candidate L. L. Charles was ordained in November, 1933, and placed in charge of this mission, which for some time was conducted in the building of the Young Men's Christian Association. In 1937 a chapel was opened for this purpose; the building, which had living quarters for Pastor Charles, cost about seven thousand dollars, provided by the Mission Board. This mission was discontinued "because of lack of membership." The building was sold in 1941. In September, 1941, Saint Philip's purchased Trinity Congregational Church at 6232 Eberhart Avenue for twenty thousand dollars, assisted by a seven thousand dollar loan from the Northern Illinois District's church extension fund. The entire indebtedness was liquidated in December, 1946.

"There are in Chicago today over 375,000 Negroes, a tenth of the population, and the second largest urban concentration of Negroes in the United States."—"Bronzeville* is a community of grim contrasts, the facets of its life as varied as the colors of its people's skins."[112]

Since October, 1947, the Rev. Andrew Schulze, formerly of St. Louis, Mo., has been carrying on mission work among the Negroes of Chicago.

On June 9, 1949, Pastor M. N. Carter was made Doctor of Divinity by Concordia Seminary, Springfield, Ill.

208. Naperville

In Chapter 34, page 179, attention was directed to a village in the southwestern corner of Du Page County called Naperville.† This village, the oldest in Du Page County, is

*Chicago Negroes prefer this appellation to "Black Belt."
†1940 census: 5,272.

located about nine miles east of Aurora. It was founded in 1831 by Captain Joseph Naper and his brother John of Ashtabula County, Ohio. Abraham Lincoln lodged at the Pre-Emption House in Naperville during the night of February 13, 1858. It seems that Lutheranism could not find a lodging place in this village, possibly because the early settlers and their descendants were determined to make Naperville "Evangelical."

However, in the year 1927 the Missouri Synod finally extended its activities into this community. The first worship service was held on October 16 in a small store on West Chicago Avenue, and on the following January 15 a congregation was organized and named Bethany. On March 3, 1928, the Rev. Adolph E. Ullrich,* missionary in the State of Nevada, was installed as Bethany's first resident pastor. Then for some time the worship services were conducted in the Women's Club rooms of the old stone church at 14 North Washington Street. In 1928 and 1929 a stone church was erected at 632 North Washington Street and dedicated on June 16, 1929. In September, 1930, a day school was opened and taught by the pastor. In November, 1932, Bethany organized a Sunday school in Warrenville, a village about three miles northwest of Naperville. (See Chapter 239, page 613.) In March, 1933, the congregation established a mission in the village of Lisle, about four miles northeast of Naperville.

209. Elmhurst, Redeemer

From Naperville the Trail goes across the prairie in a northeasterly direction, a distance of about fifteen miles to Elmhurst (formerly Cottage Hill)—the city whose early citizens, presumably, preferred the Middle English word "hurst" to the more common word "grove."

It is Easter Day, 1928, and a Lutheran service is being

*Nephew of the Rev. Alex Ullrich, pastor of Saint John's, La Grange, Ill., 1893-1942, and president of the Northern Illinois District, 1927-1936.

conducted in the Hawthorne Public School on the city's south side by the Rev. Horace H. Hartman, missionary at large for the Northern Illinois District. Immanuel Congregation on the north side is in full and hearty accord with the founding of a new congregation in the fast-growing suburb. It will be recalled that Immanuel had begun an English mission on the south side in 1912.

Pastor Hartman and other pastors conducted services regularly until the Rev. Worth A. Setzer of Hickory, N.C., was installed as this congregation's first pastor on October 7, 1928. In the same month the congregation was formally organized and named Redeemer. Shortly afterward a lot at a prominent corner of the city, at the intersection of St. Charles Road and Kenilworth Avenue, was purchased for $15,250. Here a church was erected at a cost of $86,750 and dedicated on May 15, 1930. The final payment on the mortgage, which included a gift in the amount of ten thousand dollars, was made in May, 1946.

In 1931 Pastor Setzer was appointed chaplain in the United States Chaplains Reserve Corps. In August, 1942, he was called to active duty in World War II. A leave of absence "for the duration" was granted him by Redeemer Congregation. During the interim the congregation was served by the Rev. E. M. Biegener of St. Louis, Mo. In December, 1945, Pastor Setzer resumed the pastorate of Redeemer in Elmhurst.

Redeemer Congregation is a member of the English District, Missouri Synod.

210. Chicago, Irvingwood

Another mission project was begun in 1928 by the Northern Illinois District in the Irvingwood community, a section which constitutes Chicago's westernmost limits on the North Side. Four blocks east of these limits (Cumberland Avenue), west of which is the Che-che-pin-qua Forest Preserve, is Pioneer Avenue. A short distance south of Addison Avenue, and on the west side of Pioneer Avenue, a chapel was built in 1928 and dedicated on October 4. The mission's first pastor was the Rev. Herman P. Meyer, who served it as an affiliate of his mission in Belmont Heights. The first day school teacher was H. C. Meier. On March 30, 1930, the Rev. Henry F. Buettner of Hampton, Iowa, succeeded Pastor Meyer to the Irvingwood pastorate. In the same year a building was moved from 74th Court and Roscoe Street (See Chapter 203, page 560) and placed directly in the rear of the chapel on Pioneer Avenue, to serve as a school. During the following ten years the Irvingwood congregation struggled valiantly for its existence. In 1941 Pastor Buettner resigned from the ministry. He was succeeded on February 16, 1941, by the Rev. Ray E. Miller* of Wallula, Kans. In 1948 the congregation adopted a new name: "The Church of St. Michael."

211. Berwyn, Good Shepherd

About eight miles south of Irvingwood is a village through which the Trail has passed a number of times—Berwyn. Knowing that it has a population of nearly fifty thousand, it is not surprising to find Lutheran activities in every section of Berwyn. Five years after Concordia's founding, the Rev. Horace H. Hartman, missionary at large for the Northern Illinois District, made a thorough canvass of the northern section and, at the behest of the Mission Board, secured a place for worship services in the basement of a private home at 2327 South East Avenue, where the first service was held on May 15, 1928. After about two months a tent was pitched at the southeast corner of Oak Park Avenue and West Twenty-second Street. The rental of the premises for three months was one hundred dollars. When the lease expired and the weather was growing cold, the worshipers agreed to rent a

*Pastor Miller was born at Long Grove, Ill., on July 6, 1908.

vacant store at 6710 West Twenty-second Street. On July 25, 1928, eleven men met in the home of Elmer F. Jacobs at 1920 South Oak Park Avenue and organized a congregation. Plans for a church building were discussed, and a building site was selected. On August 23 an architect was engaged to draw up plans for the building, and the name Good Shepherd was adopted.

Among the outstanding events that served to make history in the United States during 1928 were the Presidential election and the tremendous financial transactions that developed into a frenzied orgy of speculations with subsequent heavy profits and losses; the unprecedented prosperity that smiled upon "Big Business" and the enormous commercial mergers or combinations effected during the year. Herbert Hoover became the thirtieth President, and the country enjoyed what was called "Hoover Prosperity." Then came October, 1929; with little warning the stock market crashed; unemployment followed; then "relief" and "emergency relief," W.P.A., and all the other adjuncts of a planned economy.

On January 27, 1929, Good Shepherd Congregation in Berwyn for the first time worshiped in the basement of the new church building, located at Thirty-second Street and Home Avenue, the superstructure of which was not completed until April, with dedication on April 14. The cost of the building was $18,430.

Good Shepherd's first pastor, the Rev. Karl F. Lohrmann of Lemont, Ill., was installed on June 2, 1929. At the close of 1930 the congregation became self-supporting; the entire indebtedness was liquidated on December 10, 1944. According to the pastor, there was never a spurious money-making scheme set in motion at any time. Bunco, bazaars, sales, suppers, for the purpose of making money for the church are unknown here. In the course of an essay read by the Rev. Edward H. Gade, pastor of Immanuel Congregation, Dundee, the following question was posed by him: "My brethren, shall we engage in raffles and lotteries and games of chance and then sanctimoniously approach the holy Son of God and offer Him His rake-off?"*

Good Shepherd maintains a Sunday school as well as a Saturday school for the education of the young, and the confirmed youth is required to attend a Junior Bible class on Sunday morning for four years after confirmation.

Until December 7, 1941 ("Pearl Harbor"), services in Good Shepherd Church, Berwyn, had been conducted in both German and English. Since then the former has been discontinued, and two English services are held every Sunday morning. The one member who could not understand English was transferred to a "sister" congregation, which still had German services.

212. Chicago, Pilgrim, South Side

About four miles southeast of Berwyn is a community long since incorporated within the limits of Chicago and known as Archer Heights. In the fall of 1928 the first Lutheran services were held in a vacant store on West Fifty-first Street, between Kolin and Kostner Avenues, and conducted by the Rev. Horace H. Hartman, missionary at large for the Northern Illinois District. Manifesting confidence in the future of this field, this District's Mission Board financed the erection of a chapel at the northeast corner of Kildare and Archer Avenues. This building, which cost $3,613.83, was dedicated on November 11, 1928. A day school was opened on November 13 with an enrollment of three pupils. By the end of the first school year the enrollment was thirty-three. The Rev. Hugo S. Bloedel of Hubbell, Mich., was placed in charge of this mission, which for some time was known as the Archer Heights mission, and all the canvassing of this territory was

*Convention, Northern Illinois District, Missouri Synod, River Forest, Ill., June, 1936. *Proceedings*, page 53.

done by him. At first he also served as teacher in the day school. For some time, then, his wife relieved him of these responsibilities, until William J. Danker* was engaged for this work; he was succeeded by Ernest A. Boseck.† During the economic depression the school was closed.

For a brief time this mission, organized in January, 1929, was known as Resurrection; later it was renamed Pilgrim. More recently the qualifying word "South Side" was added to distinguish this congregation from that of the same name at Cuyler and Wolcott Avenues on Chicago's North Side. Pastor Bloedel, installed as Pilgrim's pastor on August 11, 1929, ten years later canvassed the newly developed settlement adjoining his parish on the west side and on November 12, 1939, conducted the first service there in a vacant bungalow, on the northeast corner of West Fifty-second Street and Parkside Avenue. Shortly afterward he was called as pastor of this new mission. His successor at Pilgrim South Side was the Rev. Wilbert M. Weber of Chicago, who served in Archer Heights until October, 1945, when he accepted a call to Trinity Congregation, La Porte, Ind. On Wednesday, February 27, 1946, the Rev. Henry G. W. Wolter of Martinsburg, Nebr. was installed as Pilgrim's third pastor.

Since Armistice Day, 1928, this little congregation has been worshiping in its small and very unpretentious "chapel."‡ Long ago someone wrote: "As long as a congregation is poor, they can well do with an humble, unostentatious church building. For the efficacy of the Word is the same if preached in a log hut or in a magnificent cathedral. But when members of a congregation can afford to live in spacious, commodious dwellings and to surround themselves with the comforts of

*Pastor of Trinity Congregation, West Chicago, 1942-1948; on June 27, 1948, he was commissioned as the Missouri Synod's first missionary to Japan.

†Retired teacher, formerly in Michigan and Iowa.

‡In 1934 the Northern Illinois District's Mission Board reported to the delegates assembled in convention at River Forest that "its growth has been quite slow, and it has been obliged to wrestle with many problems; there are sister congregations at no great distance." *Proceedings*, 1934, p. 62.

life, it does not look well for them to serve their God in a scant and dismal-looking hut." On March 3, 1947, the voters of Pilgrim South Side resolved "that ground be broken for construction of the proposed church and parsonage at the earliest possible date; that means, as soon as various minor financial and business details have been concluded." . . . "The plan is to build as much of the church and parsonage as funds on hand will permit. At present we do not have enough on hand, including possible loans, to build more than a 'basement' church and a one-story parsonage . . . . Construction costs would be anywhere from twenty thousand to twenty-five thousand dollars."

213. Chicago, Saint John the Divine

The name of the next place included in the Trail's itinerary may suggest places on the East and West Coasts of the United States. Eighteen miles northeast of Boston, Mass., there is a seaport with a splendid harbor, good fisheries, and a summer resort named Beverly; a suburb of yet more famous Los Angeles, Calif., is known as Beverly Hills. However, the Beverly Hills presently concerned is an important section of Chicago's great South Side.

On October 31, 1928, the Rev. Elmer V. Haserodt, pastor of Faith Congregation in the Auburn Park community, conducted a worship service in a vacant store at 10241 South Western Avenue. Less than a year later, in September, 1929, the Rev. Roger L. Sommer* of St. Louis, Mo., was placed in charge of the new mission project. On the following November 10 eleven Lutheran men and twenty-eight communicants met with the young pastor for the purpose of organizing a congregation. It was named Saint John the Divine. In June, 1930, the congregation joined the Missouri Synod and became self-supporting in October of the same year. In 1932 property

*Son of the Rev. Martin S. Sommer, D.D., professor at Concordia Seminary, St. Louis, Mo., 1920-1947. The father died Dec. 16, 1949.

at West 105th Street and Oakley Avenue (150x124 feet) was purchased for $11,500, and a church building with a seating capacity of three hundred was erected at a cost of $12,500.

In 1937, thirty members of Saint John the Divine residing in Evergreen Park—about two miles west of their "center"—* were released to organize Bethel Congregation in that suburb, which was served as an affiliate by Pastor Sommer until January 22, 1939, when the Rev. A. Fred Grothe was installed as its first pastor.

In 1942 the church building at West 105th Street and Oakley Avenue was enlarged toward the north side, to provide additional space for the Sunday school and overflow church attendance. In the following year the "Emergency Trailer Unit," conducted by the Missouri Synod, came to Mount Greenwood, a community approximately one and a half miles southwest of Saint John the Divine Church, and with the assistance of Pastor Sommer founded a new mission there. Again, thirty communicants and twenty-five Sunday school pupils were released to organize Mount Greenwood Congregation.

On the occasion of its fifteenth anniversary, in 1944, Saint John the Divine Congregation declared itself debt free of a $7,500 obligation through a person-to-person campaign of debt liquidation. An anniversary offering of $3,360 in cash was received.

Assisting in the ministerial work in recent years were the Rev. Edgar F. Witte, executive director of Chicago Lutheran Charities, and the Rev. Frederick G. Miessler, retired pastor.†

214. Watseka

Approximately seventy-five miles straight south from the Loop, or about eight miles northeast of the community known

*Evergreen Park is a community, beyond Chicago's limits, at West Ninety-fifth Street and Kedzie Avenue. (See Chapter 225, page 592.)

†Pastor Miessler resigned as pastor of Gethsemane Congregation, Chicago, on July 15, 1942, and moved to Beverly Heights.

as Woodworth,* is a pleasant country town called Watseka,† named for a mythical Indian girl, who saved her tribe from disaster.

While pastor of Trinity Congregation near Crete, the Rev. Gottlieb Traub carried on mission work in Woodworth, Watseka, and other places in Will and Iroquois Counties, from 1866 to 1878.

More than half a century has elapsed since then. It is now the year 1929, and it seems that the Northern Illinois District's missionary at large, the Rev. Horace H. Hartman, put in some of his last "licks" in this part of the prairie before he settled down as pastor of Zoar Congregation in Elmwood Park, Ill., on April 14, 1930.

In the summer of 1929 Missionary Hartman explored the possibilities of establishing a Lutheran congregation in this quiet and airy town, the county seat of Iroquois County. He procured, free of charge, an old vacant frame church building in September and, assisted by neighboring pastors, conducted worship services and a Sunday school.

In January, 1930, Missionary Hartman's successor as missionary at large, the Rev. Daniel C. Hennig, was placed in charge of the small flock by the District's Mission Board. Pastor Hennig with his family moved to Watseka, and seven months later, on August 25, Calvary Congregation was organized with a communicant membership of fifty-six. The first resident pastor was the Rev. Herbert A. Dick, who came to Watseka as a ministerial candidate and was installed on August 23, 1931. He also served a group of Lutherans in Milford, a village about ten miles south of Watseka. In 1932 the Milford group organized Our Savior Congregation, which for approximately ten years was served as an affiliate of Calvary at Watseka. In January, 1935, Pastor Dick accepted a call to Bridgeton, N.J., and his successor, the Rev. Bruno F. Prange

†First visited in 1872.
†1940 census: 3,744.

of Joliet, Ill. (Redeemer Congregation), was installed as Calvary's third pastor on April 6, 1935.

In the summer of 1940 Calvary Congregation purchased property at Fourth and North Streets, which included the old frame church it had been using free of charge since its inception; the large house on the same property has served as parsonage and parish house.

From September, 1941, until July, 1942, Pastor Prange was assisted by Candidate William Timm. In the latter year both congregations petitioned the Northern Illinois District, assembled in convention at River Forest, to approve the division of the dual parish, so that each congregation might have its own pastor. This was done for the reason that the parish was receiving subsidy from the District's mission funds. Approved, the division was effected, and Pastor Prange was called to serve Calvary Congregation only, as of September 1, 1942. This congregation became self-supporting in February, 1944. The congregation is debt free and has been gathering funds and making plans for an extensive building program.

215. Park Ridge, Redeemer

Park Ridge is another place which the Trail crossed in 1909. In the twenty-two years elapsed since then there has been an increase in its population, as in all the suburbs just outside the northwest limits of Chicago.

On February 15, 1931, the Rev. Henry C. Steinhoff, pastor of Pilgrim Congregation in Chicago, conducted the first worship service primarily for the benefit of Pilgrim's members who had established their homes in that suburb. (See Chapter 165, p. 498.) On March 22 a Sunday school was founded with an enrollment of nine pupils; and a month later, April 20, Redeemer Congregation was organized by six Lutheran men.*

*Charter members:

Walter Schramm	George Hemler
Walter Keuer	A. C. Sommer
Edward Keuer	Herbert Stoffels

The growth in membership was such that the congregation, with the approval of the English District's Mission Board, called its own pastor, the Rev. Raymond C. Hohenstein of Chicago. He was installed on August 30, 1931. By the end of the first year, Redeemer Congregation had a baptized membership of more than one hundred. From its inception the congregation worshiped in various places: in a vacant theater, in a small empty store in the business district, and in an automobile showroom. In 1933 a piece of property, 142x177 feet, at the northwest corner of Gillick and Clifton Streets—on the south side of Park Ridge—was purchased. A chapel was erected here in the following year and dedicated on September 16, 1934. Redeemer Congregation became self-supporting on October 1, 1935.

In the spring of 1940 Pastor Hohenstein entered the chaplaincy of the United States Navy. Redeemer's second pastor, the Rev. Armin H. Breihan of Homewood, Ill., was installed on May 19, 1940. In the spring of 1942 he likewise entered the chaplaincy, in the Army. On November 15, 1942, the Rev. Waldemar Ralph Kissling, missionary in the State of Montana—with headquarters at Anaconda—became Redeemer's third pastor.

216. Rockford, Our Redeemer

At Rockford on the Rock River, eighty-five miles northwest of Chicago, Saint Paul's Congregation was organized early in 1888 and located on Horsman Street, on the west side of the city. About forty-three years later, on Thursday, May 21, 1931, the first meeting of Lutherans on the city's east side was held. Members of the Northern Illinois District's Mission Board and about twenty local men were present. On May 24 (Pentecost Sunday) the first worship service was held in the International Order of Good Templars Hall on Third Avenue. This hall remained the group's place of worship for about seven and a half years, until September 4, 1938.

On August 9, 1931, nineteen men signed the constitution of the congregation, which was named Our Redeemer. Candidate Elmer C. Kieninger of Forest Park, Ill., was placed in charge of the flock. During the same year a Sunday school, an adult Bible class, a men's club, a ladies' aid society, and a young people's society were organized. The Northern Illinois District's missionary at large, the Rev. William H. Medler, successor in this position of the Rev. Daniel C. Hennig,* served as Our Redeemer Congregation's adviser until July 30, 1933, when the Rev. Elmer C. Kieninger was installed as first resident pastor. The first church building, erected at the corner of Sixteenth Street and Fifth Avenue, was dedicated on September 11, 1938. Three years later, in January, 1941, the congregation became self-supporting. In June, 1943, Pastor Kieninger accepted a call to St. Louis, Mo. His successor in Rockford, the Rev. Edwin C. Beversdorf of Iron Mountain, Mich., was installed on October 3, 1943. On April 30, 1944, the congregation became free of debt and on June 1, 1945, was transferred from the English to the Northern Illinois District.

217. Milford

A short time ago the Trail led through Watseka in Iroquois County. About ten miles south of Watseka is the village of Milford,† to which this history alluded in Chapter 214, page 576. In June, 1931, the Rev. Daniel C. Hennig, in charge of Calvary Congregation at Watseka, conducted the first Lutheran worship service here in Foremen's Hall. In the course of a canvass he found twenty-four Lutheran families, eighty-seven unchurched families, and ninety-three children who

*Missionary Hennig was installed as pastor of Our Savior Congregation in Addison Heights (northwest side of Chicago) on June 17, 1934.

†1940 census: 1,628.

were not attending Sunday school. Accordingly, on August 23 administration of the mission was taken over by the Rev. Herbert A. Dick, who was also in charge of the parish at Watseka. On February 6, 1932, the group in Milford organized with eight voting members and sixty communicants and named the congregation Our Savior. In 1935 Pastor Dick accepted a call to Bridgeton, N.J., and his successor, the Rev. Bruno F. Prange of Joliet, Ill. (Redeemer Congregation), was installed as pastor of the dual parish on April 6, 1935. During the latter's pastorate the services were conducted in the Herald-News Building, and later in the Williamson Funeral Home. During the winter of 1938-1939 a church was erected at West Jones Street and dedicated on March 5, 1939.

On April 12, 1942, the congregations, Calvary in Watseka and Our Savior in Milford, resolved to become separate parishes. On August 2, Candidate William Timm, who had served as Pastor Prange's assistant since September, 1941, was installed as pastor of Our Savior's in Milford. In January, 1945, Pastor Timm accepted a call to Faith Church, Flora, Ill. During the vacancy, from February through June, the congregation was served by the Rev. Norman H. Heimsoth of Woodworth, about eight miles west of Milford, and by Pastor Prange of Watseka. On July 1, 1945, the Rev. Paul E. Meyer,* hitherto missionary at the "Ida B. Wells Housing Projects for Negroes" as well as in Chicago's "Chinatown," was installed as the congregation's second resident pastor.

218. Barrington

The Trail now leads back to Chicago and thence northwest to a village about forty miles from Chicago's Loop on the Cook-Lake county line, Barrington,† named for Great Barrington, Mass., the home of several of the first settlers.

*The Rev. Paul E. Meyer was pastor of Immanuel Congregation at Glenview, Ill., 1932-1943.

†1940 census: 3,560.

The beginning of "Missouri" Lutheran activity in this village dates back to the year 1930, when the first services were held here in private homes and conducted by the Rev. Paul G. Gerth, pastor of Saint Matthew's Congregation near Fairfield (Russells Grove), about six miles northeast of Barrington. At various times prior to that year sections of this village had been canvassed, with the result that the parties interested felt that there was little promise of success. For some time services were held in the old Catlow Theater Building on West Station Street; then in Groff's Hall in the business district. The Mission Board of the Northern Illinois District, under whose direction the work had been begun, now realized that prospects for the establishment of a church in Barrington were good and therefore in September, 1931, requested its missionary, the Rev. Daniel C. Hennig, to conduct worship services regularly on Sundays. After the first class of six adults had been confirmed in the spring of 1932, organization of Saint Matthew's Congregation was effected by nine Lutheran men on April 27, 1932. In September of the same year the Rev. Alfred Theodore Kretzmann* of Forest Park, Ill., was sent to Barrington to continue the work. On October 8, 1933, he was installed as Saint Matthew's first resident pastor. In the fall of 1933 a lot at the corner of Coolidge Avenue and Lill Street was purchased. Early in 1934 a former Free Methodist church building in Algonquin—eight miles west of Barrington—was purchased for $150 and moved to Barrington. After untoward delay, caused by an injunction against the moving of the building to the proposed site, the structure was placed upon the previously constructed basement walls and then completely remodeled. On February 1, 1943, the congregation became self-supporting.

In January, 1945, Pastor Kretzmann accepted a call to Trinity Congregation in Crete, Ill. His successor in Barrington,

*Son of the Rev. M. F. Kretzmann, D.D., Kendallville, Ind., Secretary of the Missouri Synod since 1920.

the Rev. Herbert H. Heinemann of North Plato and Pingree Grove, Ill., was installed on April 29, 1945.

The children of Saint Matthew's Congregation attend the day school of Immanuel Congregation in Palatine—about six miles southeast of Barrington, on the Northwest Highway.

219. Pontiac

In 1890 the Trail passed through "the heart of the corn belt" and paused in the county seat of Livingston County, Pontiac*—about ninety-five miles southwest of Chicago.

"Missouri" Lutheran mission work in Pontiac was begun by the Rev. D. C. Hennig, missionary at large for the Northern Illinois District; it was continued for some time by the Rev. Ernest A. Brauer, institutional missionary for the same District, and by the latter's son-in-law, the Rev. Martin Frick.

Services were conducted in a funeral home, a parlor of which was rented for twenty dollars a month, later for fifteen dollars. Pastor Frick made his home with his in-laws and thus saved considerable rent for the mission. In February, 1935, he accepted a call to Trinity Congregation at Bachelors Grove—two miles north of Tinley Park, Ill. In 1935 the Rev. Otto C. Simonsen of Junction City, Wis., came to Pontiac.

On February 1, 1931, a Lutheran congregation was organized in this city and named Trinity. The congregation's new church building, dedicated on January 9, 1949, is located at Prairie and Oak Streets. (See Chapter 116.)

220. Chicago, Our Savior

It was during the "dark days" of the depression in 1932 that the Northern Illinois District's missionary at large, the Rev. Daniel C. Hennig, canvassed the territory centering at about 3500 North and 7200 West and known as Addison Heights. On March 1, 1932, newspaper headlines carried the

*1940 census: 9,585. Pontiac was named for the famous Indian chief, leader of the revolt against the British in 1763.

news of the Lindbergh kidnaping.* Mission work in the Addison Heights community seemed to be an utterly futile undertaking, particularly because there were already two established congregations, one affiliated with the Evangelical denomination and the other with the United Lutheran Church; in addition, three congregations affiliated with the Missouri Synod, not far from this territory, objected to the possibility of unpleasant overlapping activities. Nevertheless, an attempt to start a mission was made in the sombre basement of a private home at 3537 Nottingham Avenue. This soon proved to be a failure. After another canvass, which indicated that a sizable number of people would lend support to the project, the Mission Board of the District resolved to make another attempt under Missionary Hennig's direction. However, the neighborhood being "painfully residential," there was no place available for worship services. A basement in another bungalow was rented in November, 1932, and arranged in such a manner that at least a hundred persons could be comfortably accommodated. The missionary moved into this bungalow on November 8. On October 25, 1932, seventeen Lutheran men organized Our Savior Congregation and voted to pay forty dollars monthly toward the pastor's salary.

On February 15, 1933, Mayor Anton J. Cermak of Chicago was fatally wounded at Miami, Fla., by a gunman attempting to kill the President-elect, Franklin Delano Roosevelt, during a celebration in honor of the latter, who had recently returned from a fishing trip. Other outstanding events of that year were the moratorium on banking, beginning on February 14, which paralyzed the nation's banking system; the inauguration of the "New Deal"; repeal of prohibition following fourteen years of "dryness"; the setting up of Federal projects like WPA and PWA to relieve bread lines and hunger marches; and the *Akron* dirigible disaster—the worst in aeronautical

*The twenty-month-old son of Col. and Mrs. Chas. A. Lindbergh was kidnaped from his parental home near Hopewell, N.J., on March 1, 1932; on May 12 the lifeless body of the child was found in the woods five miles away.

history—which on April 4 fell into the Atlantic Ocean about sixty miles south of New York Harbor, with a loss of seventy men.

In November, 1933, the parsonage and church were moved to 3500 Nottingham Avenue. Here the services and Sunday school sessions were held until August, 1935. At the same time tentative arrangements were made with Messiah Congregation* to provide room for its school children. The Mission Board agreed to subsidize another teacher in Messiah's day school if a sufficient number of children could be gained from the new territory. When thirty children from Our Savior parish were enrolled at the beginning of September, 1934, the Mission Board placed J. M. Roth there. In September, 1935, the number of children from the new territory had increased to forty-eight; therefore the Mission Board subsidized a second teacher, Ernest A. Boseck.

On April 25, 1934, a call was extended to Missionary Hennig. The decision of relinquishing the office of missionary at large in the Northern Illinois District to resume pastoral work was a difficult one for the Rev. Daniel C. Hennig to make. Nevertheless, on May 23, after a month's consideration, he decided to take charge of the young and struggling congregation. He was installed as Our Savior's first pastor on June 17.

The combination parsonage-church served manifold purposes. Early in the winter of 1935 one of the pastor's children contracted scarlet fever. Overnight the "church" was moved to a basement at 3624 Neva Avenue, where the services were continued until the quarantine was lifted. In the fall of 1936 the congregation was informed that the bungalow would not be available after the following spring. A committee chosen by the congregation approached the Mission Board for a loan for the erection of a church; the need was recognized. With its own funds, however, the congregation forthwith purchased a lot at Neva and Cornelia Avenues.

*Located at Melvina Avenue and Patterson Street. (Organized in 1925.)

When the enrollment of Our Savior's children in Messiah School reached the sixty mark, the latter congregation resolved not to accept any more children from the former. Then befell an unexpected contretemps: the bids submitted indicated that a total of sixteen thousand dollars would be needed for the proposed building, and, secondly, the request for a loan of that amount was denied by the Mission Board. However, within the space of a few weeks the plan for the construction of a smaller building, to cost three thousand dollars less, was adopted. The Mission Board granted the loan, and soon afterward the building was erected, dedication taking place on June 5, 1937.

In August, 1937, the congregation was notified by Messiah Congregation that its sixty-one children could no longer be accommodated.* The day for the opening of the new school year was only two weeks away. What to do? The auditorium of the new building was too large for such a purpose; there were no desks, no maps, no equipment, no teacher, and very little money with which to purchase essential equipment. Nothing daunted, the voting members unanimously resolved to open a school in the new church, determined that by the opening day all difficulties would be overcome. A sliding partition was constructed by the men themselves at a cost of only $205, the price of the materials; sufficient second-hand equipment was secured; and on September 7 two well-equipped rooms were ready for occupancy. The enrollment was seventy. The Mission Board then transferred Mr. Boseck to this school. Pastor Hennig taught the upper grades until October 24, when Arthur L. Amt of Messiah School was called and installed as principal of Our Savior School. In June, 1938, Mr. Boseck, who had been temporarily engaged, was dismissed. Because the Mission Board considered the large amount required for

*NOTE: A teacher in Chicago carried on a canvass of a certain well-populated community "through the entire year" (presumably 1933), and then he was able to say; "I have nine very sure prospects for the coming year." (*Proceedings*, Northern Illinois District, 1934, p. 67.)

the salaries of two teachers unjustifiable, especially in view of the fact that a single man could take over at least one of the teaching positions, M. F. Luebke, recent graduate of Concordia Teachers College, River Forest, began work here in September; on June 4, 1939, he was installed. In March, 1942, Mr. Amt followed a call to Emmanuel School, Aurora, Ill., and Mr. Luebke succeeded to the principalship, while teacher-candidate Theodore Leitz took charge of the lower grades. In March, 1944, the latter joined the staff of First Saint John's School in Chicago, and his successor at Our Savior School was Elmer Hausermann.

On September 1, 1944, the congregation became self-supporting.

In 1945 Mr. Luebke went to First Bethlehem School, Chicago, and on November 25, 1945, A. E. Christian of Northbrook, Ill., came to Addison Heights. On December 4, 1944, a resolution was passed to launch a campaign for the building of a new church.

221. Joliet, Redeemer

The Trail has traversed Joliet several times. Ninety years ago, in 1857, it "witnessed" the founding of Saint Peter's Congregation on Broadway. In 1931 this veteran congregation established a mission in a community known as Ingalls Park in the eastern section of the city, and the Mission Board of the Northern Illinois District assisted by subsidizing it. The first missionary stationed here was the Rev. Bruno F. Prange. He served until the spring of 1935, when he accepted a call to the dual parish at Watseka and Milford in Iroquois County, Ill. Then the Rev. Ernest A. Brauer, institutional missionary, assumed charge of the mission on a temporary basis, followed soon afterward by the Rev. Henry C. Richter* on the same basis. The Rev. William H. Medler served for about two

*Pastor of Saint Andrew's, Park Ridge, Ill., 1913-1934.

years; his successor, the Rev. Luther G. Schliesser,* who came to Joliet as a ministerial candidate, likewise served for about two years. At the beginning of 1942 the difficulties and "future hopes" of this mission were carefully studied by representatives of the Northern Illinois District and the English District, the result being that the mission was transferred to the latter, which recently established a mission about two miles west of Ingalls Park. On January 25, 1942, the two missions were combined, and the Rev. H. William Lieske became the congregation's first pastor. In 1946 Pastor Lieske accepted a call to St. Louis, Mo., and was succeeded on November 24, 1947, by the Rev. Armin H. Breihan, recently discharged chaplain in the U.S. Army.† Redeemer Congregation's center is at 100 South Briggs Street, Joliet. A new "basement" church costing $12,000 was erected during the winter months of 1947-1948, and this portion of the new building was solemnly dedicated on March 14, 1948.

222. Chicago, Timothy

In its sixtieth year, First Trinity Congregation, which in May, 1865—about a month after the Civil War had ended—was organized as the third "Missouri" congregation in Chicago, acting upon the encouraging advice of the Mission Board of the Northern Illinois District, rented a vacant store at 1446 West Seventy-ninth Street to accommodate particularly those of its members emigrating to that territory.‡ The first worship services and Sunday school sessions were held in that store building on July 15, 1925, by the Rev. Arthur H. C.

*His father, the Rev. Ad. J. Schliesser, served as chaplain in the U.S. Army during World War I. He himself served as chaplain in the U.S. Army in World War II. The former, having retired from the ministry, Nov. 1, 1939, now resides in Joliet.

†Was pastor of Redeemer, Park Ridge, Ill., 1940-1942.

‡The Mission Board, at the 1925 convention, reported as follows: "Suedlich von der 79. Strasse und westlich von Ashland Ave., fanden wir ein aussichtsvolles Missionsfeld. Da jedoch eine Anzahl Glieder der Dreieingkeitsgemeinde in der Naehe dieses Feldes wohnen, so trafen wir ein Abkommen mit jener Gemeinde, nach welchem sie die Pflege dieses Gebietes uebernahm." (Trinity Congregation already had purchased property in this community and decided to begin church services and a day school in the fall of 1925.)

Both, pastor of First Trinity, a "mother" congregation of numerous "daughters." In September a day school was opened with twelve pupils, taught by Edwin F. Langrehr. About a month later a new two-story building at 8248 South Paulina Street was dedicated, the lower story serving as schoolrooms and the upper as a chapel. In 1928 a new combination church-school building was erected at the northeast corner of South Hermitage Avenue and West Eighty-third Street* and dedicated in September of the same year.

At first the mission prospered; however, in the 1930's the economic depression caused extremely serious difficulties with legal complications of a threatened foreclosure by the mortgagors. This was fortunately averted by a favorable court decision, and the congregation ultimately became solvent.

On January 1, 1934, the mission was organized by forty voting members as Trinity-Eighty-third Street. In April, 1934, the Rev. Edward Hoeferkamp was installed as pastor. In November of the same year he was compelled by ill health to resign.† During the ensuing vacancy the congregation was served by the Rev. Herman E. Brauer, pastor of Saint Martini Congregation, one of the "daughters" of First Trinity. On January 3, 1935, the congregation was reorganized and incorporated as Timothy. On October 6, 1935, Candidate Otto G. Thieme, graduate of Concordia Seminary, St. Louis, Mo.‡ was installed as pastor and Ed. F. Langrehr as teacher, the latter serving until 1946, when he resigned. Others who have served in this congregation's day school were E. R. Bode, H. Prischmann, L. Beer, Erwin Witzke, Arthur Teschke (student), Mrs. Rita Bruhl, Mrs. Mary Flicek, Walter F. Becker, Mrs. W. Becker, and Martin W. Klammer.

*Located within the same block—southwest of the two-story building at 8248 South Paulina Street, now serving as parsonage.

†Some time later he assumed a pastorate at Jonesville, Ind.

‡His father, the Rev. Traugott Thieme was pastor of Bethlehem Congregation in South Chicago (Colehour), Ill., 1913-1937, and since then institutional missionary in Chicago.

223. Aurora, Our Savior

Aurora, for the third time, now claims attention; but it is the first visit since 1901, at which time the Trail crossed only the city's east side. In 1902 Aurora, the "City of Lights," was linked to Chicago by the Chicago, Aurora and Elgin Electric Railroad, which since then has afforded this city all the "manifold advantages of urban life" and leaves it without the "disadvantages that accrue to those who must dwell in the heart of that sprawling giant"—Chicago. Arching trees shade its miles of paved streets, many of them improved a short time before its centennial celebration in September, 1937, by the removal of streetcar rails and substitution of a modern bus system.

In February, 1935, the English District's Mission Board placed into Aurora's east side a student of Concordia Seminary, St. Louis, Mo., George Weiss, to carry on mission work. The Chicago Lutheran Church Extension Association and several Lutheran pastors were keenly interested in this project. On June 4, 1935, eleven men* gathered in the home of Albert W. Thurow and signed the constitution of a new congregation, which was named Our Savior. At first the services were conducted in the chapel of the Healy Funeral Home. When Student Weiss returned to the seminary, the Mission Board extended a call to the Rev. Paul G. Krentz at Harrisburg, Pa. On December 1, 1935, he was installed as Our Savior's first resident pastor. Shortly afterward the congregation purchased the Kilbourne residence with additional vacant building space at 420 Downer Place. The ground floor of this large building served as a chapel and the upper floor as a

*Charter members:

David Kollmann	Martin Eygabroad
Frank C. Schaefer	Edward Koepke
Albert W. Thurow	Francis Morey
William J. Sass	Carl Wolff
Charles DesJarden	Herman Wollenweber
Marcus Albrecht	Louis Kollmann

parsonage. Within five years the congregation became self-supporting.

In 1942 a new church was erected on the same site at a cost of approximately sixty thousand dollars and dedicated on November 15, 1942.[113]

On September 28, 1947, Herbert F. Toensing of Wellston, Mo., was installed as director of music and education; however, in the fall of 1948 he returned to Wellston.

The congregation's new building program, which calls for an expenditure of approximately $150,000, is expected to be completed during 1950.

224. Riverside

Returning from Aurora by way of Ogden Avenue, the Trail goes as far as Lyons, and thence north on a winding road to Riverside.* It is the year in which Franklin Delano Roosevelt was re-elected for a second term as President of the United States and John L. Lewis set up the Committee for Industrial Organization (CIO). On May 27, 1933, a ray of light from Arcturus, which had taken 40 years to travel from the star to the earth, even at a rate of 186,000 miles a second, was trapped by delicate instruments, magnified, and by means of photo-electric cells turned on the lights and started the wheels of A Century of Progress Exposition on Chicago's front yard. Mission work in the Riverside territory was begun in June, 1933, under the guidance of the Rev. Warner H. Grothman, pastor of Concordia Congregation in Berwyn—less than two miles east of Riverside—who opened a branch Sunday school in the home of Mrs. E. Brandner. Beginning in March, 1934, regular forenoon worship services were conducted in the village hall. In 1936 the Mission Board of the English District "took the young congregation under its wings" and organized a congregation with fifty-four communicant members, naming it Ascension. On September 20 of the

*1940 census: 7,935.

same year, Candidate Lee G. Egloff was installed as the congregation's first resident pastor. In June, 1937, the congregation, with the aid of the Chicago Lutheran Church Extension Association and the English District, purchased a hundred-foot lot at the corner of Nuttall and Southcote Roads for $2,900. On September 10, 1939, the cornerstone of a church seating 150 and valued at thirty thousand dollars was laid. The dedication took place during Thanksgiving week, at the end of November. Having accepted a call into the chaplaincy of the United States Army, Pastor Egloff preached his farewell sermon on June 7, 1942. His successor, the Rev. Arthur A. Yoss of Camden, N.J., was installed on September 20, 1942.

Instead of starting a branch Sunday school in near-by North Riverside, Ascension Congregation by means of a bus brings children of that community to its own church; several rooms in the public school building opposite the church had to be rented to accommodate the increase in enrollment.

Plans for the construction of a new church have been formulated; work on the "first stage" is to begin in 1950.

225. Evergreen Park

Continuing from Riverside one mile south to Ogden Avenue, the Trail turns east and soon connects with Harlem Avenue (now State Route 4-A); seven miles south of this intersection it again turns eastward and continues a distance of five miles, into a village called Evergreen Park.* In the latter part of 1937 thirty members of Saint John the Divine Congregation, whose "center" is at West 105th Street and Oakley Avenue—about two miles southeast of Evergreen Park—requested their pastor, the Rev. Roger L. Sommer, to prepare for the organization of a congregation in their community. On September 26 the first worship was held in the public

*1940 census: 3,313.

school of Evergreen Park. In the following summer, Candidate A. Fred Grothe, graduate of Concordia Seminary, St. Louis, Mo., was placed in charge of the mission; and after his ordination in Milwaukee, Wis., he was installed as first resident pastor of the flock, organized as Bethel Congregation. On January 22, 1941, he accepted a chaplaincy in the United States Army, whereupon Candidate Melvin Blume, also a graduate of the above-named seminary, was engaged to serve during Pastor Grothe's leave of absence. When, however, Pastor Grothe resigned the pastorate and continued in the military service, Candidate Blume was ordained in Hope Church at West Sixty-fourth Street and Washtenaw Avenue, his "home" church, and installed as Bethel's second pastor on March 15, 1942.

In the same year, 1942, a church was erected, and dedicated on January 24, 1943. In September, 1946, a day school was opened in the basement of this church, with Carl Rogahn, graduate of Concordia Teachers College, River Forest, in charge. A school building has since been erected at the corner of West Ninety-eighth Street and Kedzie Avenue.

Recently, Pastor Blume gathered a nucleus of Lutherans residing in the vicinity of West 94th Street and 53d Avenue, in Oak Lawn, for a new congregation. Worship services now are being held in the Legion Hall. "A large church site has been donated as an incentive toward a new church."

226. Evanston, Grace

In November, 1938, twenty-six voting members of Bethlehem Congregation, whose "center" is at Greenwood Street and Wesley Avenue in Evanston—first visited in 1872—received releases for the purpose of organizing their own congregation. At the request of Circuit Visitor Frank Wittmer, the first service was conducted by the Reverend Louis J. Schwartzkopf of Chicago on December 3, 1938, in the Nichols

Public School. The congregation organized under the name of Grace. The Mission Board of the English District agreed to sponsor this new project. From January, 1939, until June, 1942, Grace Congregation was served by the Rev. Rudolph F. Zimmermann, for some time prior to that time without a charge, who then accepted a call to Mount Vernon, Ill. His successor, the Rev. Henry C. Duwe of Oberlin, Ohio, was installed on February 7, 1943. Plans for the erection of a church are now being formulated.

Somewhere along the route the Trail has picked up several very unusual news items. "All Chicago marriage license records were broken as prospective brides and bridegrooms rushed to get marriage licenses before an Illinois bill requiring them to show doctor's certificates went into effect June 30, 1938. 1,407 applied today." "The historic battle of President Roosevelt to enlarge the membership of the United States Supreme Court was ended July 22, 1938."[114]

227. Chicago, Chatham Fields

The genesis of Chatham Fields coincides with the sounding of drums of war along the Rhine, the Seine, and the Thames. Be it peace or war, however, in 1939 nothing arrests the work of the Church; her destiny, unmindful of the finite, is ever expansion and construction!

In February of that year the voting membership of Windsor Park Congregation, whose "center" is at East Seventy-sixth Street and Saginaw Avenue near the shore of Lake Michigan, resolved to petition the Mission Board of the English District to begin work in the Chatham Fields community—about two miles southwest of Windsor Park—on Chicago's South Side, and to call Candidate Laurance A. Boseck to serve as missionary in that area. His ordination and installation took place on April 30, and the first worship service was conducted in a vacant store at 8112 Cottage Grove Avenue on May 7, 1939.

On June 13 forty-six members of Windsor Park Congregation, together with three other Lutherans and Pastor Boseck, organized a congregation, naming it Chatham Fields. At the same meeting it was resolved to purchase property at the northwest corner of St. Lawrence Avenue and East Eighty-first Street and to build a church. Ten days later, June 23, the congregation became a member of the Missouri Synod. From October 1 to December 23, 1939, worship services were conducted in a vacant store at 7909 Maryland Avenue, about three blocks from the former place. On the day before Christmas, 1939, the first service was held in the basement of the unfinished church. On April 28, 1940, one year after Pastor Boseck's installation, the completed church was dedicated. The congregation became self-supporting on July 1, 1944, and free of debt at Easter time, 1947.

228. Franklin Park, Church of the Apostles

The next place may be somewhat difficult to find; it is located a few miles north of Melrose Park, one-half mile south of Grand Avenue, in Leyden Township. During the month of December, 1938, this territory was canvassed for the first time by the Rev. Daniel C. Hennig, pastor of Our Savior Congregation in Chicago,* and the Rev. Alfred T. Kretzmann of Barrington, Ill. On July 16, 1939, the first worship service was held in a chapel which had been erected at the expense of the Northern Illinois District.† At this service the chapel was dedicated, and Candidate Robert A. Spletzer was ordained and commissioned as missionary of this territory. A congregation was organized on March 3, 1940, and named the Evangelical Lutheran Church of Leyden Township. Some time later the present name was adopted: Church of the Apostles.

*Addison Heights, on Chicago's northwest side (Cornelia and Neva Avenues).
†The District's Church Extension Fund Committee was the intermediary.
NOTE: A few years ago (1945?) a member of the Church of the Apostles donated the use of one acre of ground which other members of the same parish tilled in their spare moments. The onion crop which they harvested brought $300, which amount was turned over to the Lord's treasury. (*Lutheran Witness* LXV, No. 11, p. 170.)

The entire cost of the lot and the chapel, $3,943.39, was assumed by the young congregation. A little more than four years later, on May 25, 1944, Pastor Spletzer was instantly killed in an automobile accident near Bloomington, Ill. His father-in-law, Ernest H. Lessmann, parochial school teacher in Milwaukee, Wis., also was killed. They were en route to St. Louis, Mo., to attend the graduation of Paul G. Lessmann from Concordia Seminary.*

Pastor Spletzer's successor, the Rev. William L. Bartling of Willow Springs, Ill., was installed on August 6, 1944.

A day school was established with Herbert C. Laubenstein (in Fort Smith, Ark., since 1948) and Elmer Arnst (in Bellwood, Ill., since 1948) in charge. Others who have served as teachers were Norman Vonderheid, Raymond Ritt, Students R. Dornfeld, G. Janke, H. Bunge, and J. Nauss; F. J. Luebke, R. F. Nordbrock, Miss Donna Nordbrock, and John D. Bruns.

229. Chicago, Gage Park

The president of the World's Columbian Exposition, held on Chicago's South Side in 1893, was Lyman Judson Gage. From 1897 to 1902 he was Secretary of the United States Treasury during the administrations of William B. McKinley and Theodore Roosevelt. On Chicago's southwest side there is a community known as Gage Park, named for Mr. Gage.

In 1902 Saint Martini Congregation, whose "center" is at West Fifty-first Street and Marshfield Avenue, established a mission school on South Western Avenue in this neighborhood. In 1927 this mission school was discontinued. In 1931 a day school was reopened and taught by Herold H. Lipske. On October 13, 1939, seventeen Lutheran men† of the commu-

*Presently pastor of a congregation in Towson, Md.

†Charter members:

Marvin Pansegrau	Norman Schmidt	William Koppitt
John Schmidt	John Rossau	Theo. Buszin
Rud. Gleisner	Theodore Dehn	Chas. Pelton
Martin Buszin	Norman Pansegrau	Bernard Kloos
	Arthur Kloos	

‡1940 census: 3,007.

nity, mostly members of Saint Martini, met for the purpose of organizing their own congregation, which they named Gage Park. At the same meeting a call was extended to Candidate Luther W. Roehrs, whom the Mission Board of the Northern Illinois District had assigned to the school after Mr. Lipske had followed a call to Emmaus School in Chicago. Candidate Roehrs was installed as Gage Park Congregation's first pastor on November 5, 1939. An old frame church at 5230 South Artesian Avenue was purchased from the Methodists for $2,-100 and dedicated as a Lutheran church on December 3. In August, 1943, Pastor Roehrs accepted a call to Wausau, Wis., as assistant pastor in his father's congregation.* His successor, the Rev. Ernest T. Blau of Midlothian, Ill., was installed at Gage Park on September 19, 1943. One year later the congregation became self-supporting.

230. Chicago, Hyde Park

On a certain afternoon in the spring of 1938 Edward W. Jaeger, a diligent worker for the Lutheran Church, and this writer were standing before a window in one of the latter's offices in the Loop. The discussion centered chiefly around the fact that between this place and Grand Crossing—7600 South—where Mr. Jaeger is a member of Saint Paul's Congregation, there was no church belonging to the Synodical Conference. At that time the writer was living in the Woodlawn community and conducting a letter mimeographing and duplicating business in the Loop. Shortly afterward the situation was explained to the Rev. Arnold H. Semmann of Park Ridge, chairman of the Northern Illinois District's Mission Board. During the following summer preparations for the beginning of missionary activities in the communities of Hyde Park, Woodlawn, Kenwood, and Oakland were made by way of a partial canvass of the approximately three hundred thou-

*Pastor Luther Roehrs' father, the Rev. Paul W. Roehrs, was pastor of Saint Paul's Congregation (Higgins and Canfield Roads), Chicago, 1920-1927. (Chapter 150.)

sand inhabitants. A vacant church building at 5487 Dorchester Avenue was rented, and here the first worship service was conducted on Sunday afternoon, September 10, 1939, and the Rev. William H. Medler of Maywood, Ill.,* was installed as missionary-pastor. On January 15, 1940, nine men met to consider a Lutheran constitution. Subsequently five† of these men declared their readiness to join the new congregation. Organization of the congregation was effected on March 10, 1940, and the name Hyde Park adopted. In October, 1930, the Mission Board of the English District, into whose membership the newly organized congregation had been admitted by being transferred from the Northern Illinois District on the previous June 19, purchased from the Methodist Church the property at 5487 Dorchester Avenue, including the flats at the rear of the lot, for five thousand dollars.

On October 3, 1943, Pastor Medler resigned the pastorate.‡ For a while the little group was threatened with disintegration. But the determined efforts of several devoted lay people led to a revival. Pastor Medler's successor, the Rev. Louis J. Schwartzkopf, hitherto assistant pastor at Christ Church of Logan Square, Chicago, was installed on January 2, 1944.

In December, 1943, the Mission Board disposed of the church building;§ shortly afterward, however, upon invitation from the University of Chicago, principally through the good offices of Dr. Carl F. Huth,¶ Hyde Park Congregation on February 6, 1944, transferred its services to the Joseph Bond Chapel on the campus.

In June, 1946, the Rev. Martin L. Graebner, ex-chaplain in the United States Army and student at the University,

*Recently in charge of Redeemer Congregation in Joliet, Ill.

†Charter members:

Ernest Polzin	Alvin Wiedenheft
Andrew Ruwald	Thorvald Kargard
William Etscheid	

‡Re-entered the active ministry in the fall of 1946—near Jefferson City (Honey Creek), Mo.; now in the service of the Lutheran Hour.

§It is now used as a place of worship by the Chicago Buddhists (Japanese)!

¶Son of the Rev. Carl Frederick Emil Huth, D.D., professor at Concordia College, Milwaukee, Wis., 1881-1926 (died 1926)—member of the University's faculty.

was appointed chaplain to the Lutheran students on the campus.* Dr. John G. Kunstmann and Pastor Schwartzkopf in September, 1946, appeared before the Mission Board of the English District in Detroit, Mich., with the plea that the spiritual care of students be provided through co-operative effort and subsidized by the District. Subsequently the latter was invited to attend a joint meeting of the District's officers and the Mission Board, again in Detroit. At this meeting "Executive Secretary Jesse outlined the situation, and the secretary read a summary of the proposed program prepared by the Lutheran Student Council at Chicago University. After an extended discussion of the principles, responsibilities, possibilities, opportunities, and consequences involved, it was decided to consider this request a challenge to our courage, ambition, vision, and willingness to do the same work that other Districts are doing in their areas. However, in order not to establish a precedent, the staff resolved that the work at Chicago University should be taken over in connection with the Hyde Park Mission until the next convention, 1948, with the understanding that as soon as it is practical in the opinion of the Mission Board the entire work be done by one man. Thereby the cost of the project is to be kept as low as possible. The Mission Board concurred in this decision. An appropriation of $125 per month was made from the District treasury in support of this endeavor, and any special contributions made to this cause are to be applied to this cause." To this report the president of the English District, the Rev. Herman W. Bartels of Cleveland Heights, Ohio, attached the question: "Would you personally send in a contribution earmarked 'Hyde Park'?" Pastor Martin L. Graebner† was formally installed as student pastor by Pastor

*NOTE: Called by the Mission Board of the Northern Illinois District, the Rev. Louis Steinbach was installed as student pastor at the U. of C. on March 8, 1925; at the convention of the same District in June, 1927, the Mission Board reported that the "work at the U. of C. has been discontinued."

†Son of the Rev. Martin Graebner, D.D., president of Concordia College, St. Paul, Minn., 1927-1946.

Schwartzkopf on January 26, 1947. (See *Proceedings* of English District, 25th Conv., p. 38f.) In September, 1949, Student Pastor Graebner began to conduct services on Sunday mornings in the Thorndike Hilton Memorial Chapel, 1150 East Fifty-eighth Street.

Hyde Park Congregation became self-supporting on July 1, 1949.

Two "sons" of Hyde Park Congregation, Elmer J. (born in Hankow, China) and Luther E. Schwartzkopf (born in Ichang, China), are Missouri Synod pastors.

Before proceeding to the next scheduled stop, the Trail presents a seventy-year-old "news item" concerning Hyde Park, which up to 1889 was an independent community: "In 1869 there was agitation for a gravel road to Hyde Park, a suburb six miles south of Chicago."[119]

231. Markham

The Trail now leaves Hyde Park and, following the Illinois Central Railroad a distance of about fourteen miles, goes in a south–by–southwesterly direction to Harvey, where in 1903 it witnessed the organization of Trinity Congregation. It is the year 1940–a "red-letter year" in the annals of history principally by reason of the fact that for the first time a United States President was re-elected for a third term.

Frank Gabriel, feeling the need of a Lutheran congregation in this community, found his way into several homes, which resulted in a gathering of seven people on May 9, 1940, all of whom expressed a desire to found a congregation. B. C. Goers, acting as representative of this group, presented its need to and enlisted the aid of the Rev. Arthur H. Kaub, pastor of Windsor Park Congregation. The latter proposed a meeting of all residents of Markham* interested in forming a Lutheran church for Sunday, May 26. An enthusiastic group

*Originally, the Markham "subdivision" was located south of Harvey—adjoining the Illinois Central R.R.

met in the home of Mr. and Mrs. B. C. Goers, at which time they voted to establish a congregation immediately and to build a chapel as soon as circumstances permitted. Among those present were Mr. and Mrs. Frank Gabriel, Mrs. Frank Baumgarten, Mr. and Mrs. R. N. Germany, Mrs. Fred Peters, Mrs. W. A. Valentine, Mrs. William Fischer, and Carl Widule.

The real beginning of a "Missouri" congregation in this comparatively new suburb, about three miles southwest of Harvey, was made on June 2, 1940, when a Sunday school session was held in the McLaughry Public School at the corner of West 157th Street and Homan Avenue. On the following Sunday the first worship service was held in the same place, under the leadership of the Rev. Arthur H. Kaub, pastor of Windsor Park Congregation in Chicago. On July 8 sixty-five Lutherans in Markham organized a congregation and named it after the village. Shortly afterward a plot of ground, 97x142, at West 160th Street and St. Louis Avenue was purchased. Meanwhile worship services were conducted by Pastor Kaub, then circuit visitor, in the McLaughry School. Markham's first resident pastor, the Rev. Charles W. Tedrahn, temporarily without a charge,* was installed in Trinity Church, Harvey. A church was erected in 1940, and the first service was held in the basement of the unfinished church on Christmas Eve. The completed building was dedicated on March 16, 1941. In November, 1946, Pastor Tedrahn accepted a call to El Cajon, Calif. His successor, the Rev. Marvin Nicolaus of La Valle, Wis., was installed as Markham's second pastor on January 26, 1947.

232. Chicago, Gloria Dei

A short distance beyond Archer Heights on Chicago's southwest side a building boom was in progress in 1939. The Rev. Hugo S. Bloedel, pastor of the near-by Pilgrim South Side

*He had served as pastor of Saint Peter's Congregation, Chicago, 1923-1936.

Congregation, canvassed the territory and, convinced that the time for missionary action had come, secured a vacant bungalow at the northeast corner of West Fifty-second Street and Parkside Avenue as a temporary place of worship. The first service was held here on November 12, 1939. In order to accommodate the sixty-two worshipers, shelves were taken from the pantry and placed in various parts of the house. The pastor occupied a position about halfway between either end of the bungalow, which was partitioned down the middle; thus he had to speak into two rooms. Forty-seven children were enrolled in the Sunday school. "A modest slowing down of business tempo occurred at this time. Economists called it a normal readjustment after the sharp rise in the last quarter of 1939."* Early in the year 1940 the congregation was organized and named Parkside. On January 24 Pastor Bloedel was called to serve this parish; a week later it was decided that he should serve both Pilgrim and Parkside. He was installed in the latter place on March 31. During the latter month, lots at the northeast corner of West Fifty-third Street and Major Avenue were purchased, and a church was erected on this site.

In December, 1940, Pastor Bloedel assumed full charge of Parkside Congregation. In the following year the congregation's name was changed to Gloria Dei. The church was dedicated on September 28, 1941.

It will be observed that the dedication took place less than two years after the first efforts of Pastor Bloedel had been put forth in this community. The church has a seating capacity of two hundred and is "remarkable for its pleasing exterior brickwork and stone trim, the churchly dimensions, and the rich symbolism of the interior . . . . The structure, without furnishings or ground, cost nineteen thousand dollars. . . . The handsome church should be, under God, a tool in carrying on the work so auspiciously begun." The Rev. Prof.

**Commerce, Business Voice of the Middle West*, February, 1940, p. 7.

Theodore Graebner, D.D., who officiated at the installation of Pastor Bloedel, March 31, 1940, wrote: "If you would know why the Chicago area looks to us like a mission field of unapproached possibilities (except by Greater New York), read the story of Gloria Dei Church, the Rev. H. Bloedel, pastor. Founded 1940, independent 1944, property now worth $26,500."

On February 12, 1946, Pastor Bloedel received a peaceful dismissal from Gloria Dei Congregation and shortly afterward became a member of the Missouri Synod's Emergency Planning Council in St. Louis, Mo. His successor, the Rev. Henry J. Behrens, ex-chaplain in the United States Army and, prior to his chaplaincy, pastor at Junction City, Wis., was installed on March 10, 1946.[120]

233. Oak Lawn

A short distance beyond the village of Oak Lawn, Ill.,* about thirteen miles southwest of Chicago's Loop, is a subdivision known as Columbus Manor. One of the early settlers in this community, Mrs. E. J. Desmond, member of Hope Congregation, West Sixty-fourth Street and Washtenaw Avenue, in the late 1930's took it upon herself to write to the Missouri Synod's headquarters,† suggesting the possibilities of opening a mission station at Columbus Manor and offering to assist in a canvass of the rapidly developing subdivision. The matter was referred to the Mission Board of the Northern Illinois District, and on October 12, 1939—Columbus Day—Columbus Manor and its environs were canvassed. Ten days later, October 22, the first worship service and Sunday school session were conducted in the home of one of the Lutheran families, with twenty-one adults attending the service and nineteen children the Sunday school. The Rev. Ernest T. Blau of Midlothian—about seven miles southeast of Oak Lawn—

*1940 census: 3,483.
†St. Louis, Mo.

served this mission for the first few months of its existence. On April 12, 1940, the congregation was organized and named Faith. Two months later the congregation joined the Missouri Synod. With the aid of a loan from the Northern Illinois District's Church Extension Fund, Faith Congregation erected a church at West Ninety-seventh Street and Melvina Avenue in Oak Lawn. On the day of dedication, October 6, 1940, Candidate Albert G. Hoffmann was ordained and installed as Faith's first pastor. In September, 1941, a day school was opened in the church basement and taught by the pastor. In 1942 Pastor Hoffmann accepted a call to Cissna Park, Ill., and his successor, the Rev. Raymond W. Fechner, then assistant pastor at First Saint John's Church in Chicago, was installed on November 15. The congregation became self-supporting on September 1, 1944. In 1945 Pastor Fechner accepted a call to Conroy, Iowa. He was succeeded in Oak Lawn on November 4, 1945, by the Rev. Reinhart R. Steinly,* without a charge at the time and residing in Chicago.

234. Elgin, Good Shepherd

The difference between a beeline from Oaklawn to Elgin and the State routes connecting the two communities is only about five miles. The Trail, quite properly, follows the "terra firma" route and, as the jovial Negro said in reply to an invitation to ride in an airplane, "I'se stickin' to terra firma, and da firma da betta!"—U.S. 12 and 20 to Ninety-sixth Avenue (5.7 miles), which, now combined with U.S. 45, leads directly northward across Archer Avenue, the Illinois-Michigan Canal and the Des Plaines River, through the village of Hodgkins, then La Grange, and, by-passing Bellwood and continuing about two miles beyond, the Trail connects with the old Indian Trail, Lake Street (U.S. 20)—U.S. 12 and 45 continues northward. Add 12.1 to 5.7 miles. Six miles

*His former charge was near Merrill, Wis.

northwest of this important junction is "old Addison"; 5.3 miles beyond is the small village of Bloomingdale, where "old Zion of Duncklees Grove" maintained a school district from 1880 to 1907; at the western end of the village the Trail now passes a Baptist church. Remaining on the "through route," the Trail, after another 4.4 miles, allows little more than a glimpse of Immanuel Church in Ontarioville. The remaining 7.2 miles are replete with scenic beauty—whether covered during the pristine freshness of springtime or during the approaching or receding splendor of a northern Illinois autumn. The meter registers 40.4 miles as the Trail once more enters the city of Elgin. Many changes have taken place also here since the Trail crossed the Fox River here in 1859. Confidently the Trail now follows Chicago Street through the somewhat hectic business section to the West Side, where additional evidences of Saint John's mission consciousness "must" appear, for near the end of Chapter 20 reference is made to that congregation's "West Side" mission. It is the summer of 1938. From Paris, France, comes the report that Samuel Insull—former Public Utilities magnate in Chicago—has died of a heart attack. On February 21, 1938, the Rev. Andreas Christian Landeck,* pastor emeritus, died at the age of 84 years here in Elgin. In that summer, then, Candidate Louis W. Schuth, who for about two years previously had been serving the congregations belonging to the Missouri Synod in this territory as a "circuit rider," was requested to canvass the West Side of Elgin with a view to developing the new mission. On November 20 he conducted the first Sunday school session and the first worship service in the city's fire station No. 4, at Van and DuBois Streets. Reminiscing upon experiences there, Pastor Schuth writes: "We remember with a twinge of sorrow . . . the fact that Pastor Kowert was never able to attend one of the services. One morning

*Formerly pastor at Hamburg and Glencoe, Minn., professor at Concordia College, St. Paul, Minn., pastor at St. Paul, Freeport, Pecatonica, Ill.

he had time to peek through the front windows at the three rings of children gathered for Sunday school. Just a month later, year's end 1938, his earthly work was done." A short time later it became necessary for the mission congregation to look for another meeting place, because the fire station was to be renovated and restored to its original purposes. Authorized by Saint John's Congregation, the trustees in April, 1939, purchased six lots at the southeast corner of Van and South Aldine Streets for $3,500. In June ground was broken, and the erection of a church building begun. Meanwhile, beginning May 20, 1939, worship services and Sunday school sessions were held in the gymnasium and library of the Abbott Junior High School. Formal organization of the congregation, adoption of a Lutheran constitution,* and selection of the name Good Shepherd took place on July 24, 1939.

In the evening of August 13, 1939, the new house of worship, erected at a cost of $6,500, was dedicated, and Candidate Schuth was ordained and installed as pastor of Good Shepherd Congregation. Generously supported by the "mother" congregation, the "West Side" mission was declared "debt free" on July 11, 1941. In May, 1948, a $40,000 drive toward a new church fund was inaugurated, and on the occasion of its tenth anniversary, August, 1949, it was reported that a little more than $37,000 had been contributed toward this fund. Plans for a new church indicate a corner of Alfred and Van Streets as the building site.

*Charter members:

Frank W. Hopp
B. C. Lessing
William C. Wolff
Herman Matthies
Harry Witt
Henry Krueger
Elmer Werrbach
Frederick Hopkins
John Rambow
Charles Smith
Walter Witt
David Spicer
Otto Niethammer
Edward Lohse
Lester Braun
George Nickel
Charles Fevrier
Hans Schudel
Henry Bartelt
Alvin Bramer
Harold Laseman
Charles Paulin
Ralph Kluender
Russell Krahn
Gustav Scherer
Fred Handrock
Charles Seelhoff
Lyman Mittlestaedt

235. Round Lake

Twenty-five miles northeast of Elgin, or, more specifically, thirteen miles due west from Waukegan ("Little Fort"), is a small village which goes by the name of Round Lake.* Near by there is a more or less round lake of the same name. In the vicinity there are two communities, Renehan and Round Lake Beach. Toward the close of the third decade, William Bendien, a member of Saint Peter's Congregation in Arlington Heights (formerly Dunton)—about eighteen miles southeast—while driving about in this part of the country in his automobile, was deeply impressed with the large number of community developments. Everywhere he saw new houses, schools, store buildings—but no churches. He discussed the situation with his pastor and fellow church elders, with the result that an agreement was made with the congregations at Mount Prospect, Northfield, Barrington, Fairfield (formerly Russells Grove), and Arlington Heights to raise sufficient funds to engage a ministerial candidate to conduct a religious survey of the entire territory from Rand Road to the Wisconsin-Illinois State line. A meeting of representatives of these congregations was held in March, 1939. The Mission Board of the Northern Illinois District, informed of the proposed survey, declared its wholehearted approval of the venture.

In June, 1939, Candidate Raymond T. Eissfeldt entered into this field; and during that summer he made approximately five thousand missionary calls. On October 1 a mission station with a Sunday school was opened in the Renehan community—two miles east of the village of Round Lake. A month later, on November 5, another mission was opened at Round Lake Beach. When, however, on July 7, 1940, a church building was dedicated in Renehan, the Round Lake mission was merged with it. The congregation was organized in Au-

*1940 census: 359.

gust, 1940, and named Saint Paul, while the merging of the Sunday schools followed in March, 1941.

Although the community is principally a summer resort, people who originally came to live here only during the summer months have settled permanently, so that the population has gone far beyond the Government's census figure for 1940; it is approximately two thousand. Soon after the congregation had been organized, a day school was founded. The first trained teacher was Raymond H. Sprehe, and as the enrollment increased, Norman Utech was added to the staff. In March, 1944, Pastor Eissfeldt accepted a call to the Kinderheim in Addison, Ill., to serve as assistant executive secretary of the Lutheran Child Welfare Association. His successor at Round Lake was the Rev. Herman C. Noll, formerly on the Isle of Pines, Cuba. In 1946 E. H. Klemp succeeded Mr. Utech in the day school, and a third teacher, Miss Marie Bauer, was appointed.

236. New Lenox

About six miles east of Joliet, on the Lincoln Highway, is a little village called New Lenox.* Originally a fur-trading center, this place was known for some time as Hickory Creek Settlement. Its present name, adopted in 1832, was suggested by one of the settlers who had moved here from Lenox, Mass. In May, 1850, the Rev. Anton August Philip Weyel, for a short time pastor of Zion (in 1858 changed to Trinity) Congregation at Crete, Ill., came to this territory, which is drained by Hickory Creek, and founded a Lutheran congregation a few miles east of New Lenox, between Mokena and Frankfort. In 1915 this congregation moved its church into the village of Mokena, about three miles to the northwest. In 1852 Pastor Weyel accepted a call to Darmstadt, Ind. (See Chapter 8, page 69.)

According to Le Baron and Co., *History of Will County*, page 503, the village New Lenox was named by J. Van Dusen, the first supervisor for the Town of Lenox, N.Y.

In the fall of 1931 the Rev. Paul E. Schauer,* pastor of Immanuel Congregation in Mokena, began to conduct worship services in Grace Episcopal Church, New Lenox, and carried on mission activities in this community until 1933. His successor in Mokena, the Rev. Walter J. Geffert, resumed mission work here in 1940, conducting his first service on March 10 in the gymnasium of the public school. On the twentieth of the same month he established a Sunday school with an enrollment of fifteen pupils. In the following September a congregation was organized by nine men† and named Trinity. In February, 1942, plans for the erection of a "basement" church were completed, and on June 28 the cornerstone was laid. The first service in the basement was held on Christmas Eve, 1942, and the dedication followed on January 31, 1943. Stone blocks, measuring twelve to sixteen inches and eight feet in length, were cut to desired shapes and sizes by Ernest C. Rydberg, who devoted the evening hours of several months to this task. The excavation, as well as much of the grading, carpentry work, painting, etc., was done by the members themselves, often assisted by Pastor Geffert. Neighbors, although not members of the congregation, gave ready assistance whenever it became necessary to "keep certain work ahead of the contractor." Lester E. Brown and Mr. Rydberg made an altar of plywood donated by the New Lenox Lumber Company. The lectern was made as a WPA project under the direction of local officials.

In 1947 the congregation purchased another tract of land, 147 by 110 feet, north of the present church.

In May, 1943, Pastor Geffert accepted a call to Kingfisher, Okla. On July 18 Candidate James G. Manz, graduate of Con-

*Pastor Schauer resigned in 1932, but on Jan. 5, 1933, assumed the pastorate of Immanual Congregation, De Kalb, Ill.

†Charter members:

Lucius J. Boynton	Lester E. Brown
Ernest Gernenz	Edward Kersten
G. Fred Krog	Ernest C. Rydberg
Harold F. Triebe	George G. Webster
Leo C. J. White	

cordia Seminary, St. Louis, Mo., was ordained and installed as Trinity's first resident pastor. He served until December, 1946, when he accepted a call as assistant pastor at Grace Church in River Forest, Ill. His successor, the Rev. Leonard M. Reinke of Shawnee, Okla.,* was installed on May 5, 1946.

The enlarged and improved church building was dedicated on April 24, 1949.

237. Bridgeview

The Trail now follows Lincoln Highway eastward in the direction of Chicago Heights, but about eight and a half miles east of New Lenox connects with Harlem Avenue, on which it proceeds due north to a community called Bridgeview, two miles south of Summit. In 1939 the Rev. August H. Lange, pastor of Zion Congregation in Summit, at the request of the Northern Illinois District's Mission Board, canvassed this territory. The first "general" meeting was held in the home of Herman Krieger at Harlem Avenue and West Seventy-first Street, with seven persons attending, not including members of the Mission Board. The Kriegers then and there offered the use of their home for church and Sunday school purposes; it was used for the first time on September 17. The attendance at the service, conducted by Pastor Lange, was forty-three, which number included thirty-two children from the Sunday school. On March 31, 1940, the group moved to the basement of Belasco's store across the street. On the following October 27 the young congregation dedicated its own chapel at Harlem Avenue and West Seventy-third Street. On March 23, 1941, Candidate Paul F. Huxhold, graduate of Concordia Seminary, St. Louis, Mo., and native of Forest Park (Harlem), Ill., was installed as the first resident pastor of this congregation, named Holy Trinity. He served until July 31, 1942, when he accepted a call to Harvard, Ill. Can-

*Son of the Rev. Edwin Reinke, pastor of First Bethlehem, Chicago, 1893-1919 (died March 12, 1919).

didate William J. Rohlwing, graduate of the same seminary, succeeded to the Holy Trinity pastorate on August 30. In July, 1943, the chapel was converted into a two-story building, providing space for a day school on the second floor. The school was opened with an enrollment of forty-three on September 14, 1943. Ernest R. Ebert, graduate of Concordia Teachers College, River Forest, was the first teacher. In June, 1944, Pastor Rohlwing accepted a call to the newly organized congregation in the Mount Greenwood community, about seven miles southeast of Bridgeview, but continued serving Holy Trinity Congregation as an affiliate of the younger parish. In February, 1945, the chapel was destroyed by fire. While the building lay in ruins, worship services were conducted in Messiah Church, West Sixty-second Street and Monitor Avenue, in the Clearing Industrial District,* and the day school was housed in the Nottingham Fire Department's building and later in the Hartfield home. A new chapel was dedicated on July 22, 1945. Holy Trinity's third pastor, Candidate Milton W. Beer, was ordained and installed on September 2, 1945. He also took charge of the school. In 1947 he accepted a call to Roanoke, Ill.

At the time of Holy Trinity's inception at Bridgeview, mission work was begun in a small community located at Eighty-seventh Street and Roberts Road, concerning which Pastor Huxhold had the following to say at the time: ". . . . plans were made to erect a tavern. A fine building was completed. Of course, it had to have one large room so that ample space might be provided for the patrons after the equipment peculiar to a tavern had been installed. Everything was in readiness. Night life and its inseparable companions of lust were to have an early beginning in the young community." . . . But "the people of the community objected strenuously to the tavern and were successful in preventing

*About a mile west of the Chicago Municipal Airport—within the city limits.

its doors from opening. Pastor A. H. Lange heard of this while ministering to one of the Lutheran families living there. He immediately contacted the Mission Board. The large room offered splendid facilities for a place of worship. The building was rented. On September 1 the opening service was held. The Holy Trinity supplants the 'Unholy Trinity'!" Holy Trinity was served by Vicar D. W. Olson from the summer of 1948 until the summer of 1949; Candidate ~~Henry~~ Schroeter, a recent graduate of Concordia Seminary, St. Louis, Mo., is now serving in a similar capacity.

238. Wooddale

Toward the beginning of the fourth decade of this century a building boom was in progress also in the village of Wooddale, about ten miles west of the northwestern limits of Chicago—on Irving Road. Its population soon made the official 1940 census figure (738) appear very obsolete. Vital statistics derived from a canvass conducted by the Rev. Daniel C. Hennig and the Rev. Raymond T. Eissfeldt prompted the Mission Board of the Northern Illinois District to begin mission work here at the earliest possible time. More than seventy families "had begged for a sound, fundamental church." In 1940 Calvary Congregation was organized. However, there was no vacant store or public hall in the village where services could be held. So Zion Congregation of Churchville (Duncklees Grove) offered to move its school, together with the teacher, to Wooddale, to assist in organizing a central school and to permit the use of this building also for church purposes. A down payment was made on a building site. And by the time everything was in readiness to complete the arrangements, the village board declared its objection to the placing of a frame structure within the village limits for school purposes. That was that! Then the Mission Board sought other ways and means. Behind a filling station a former cow barn was found;

this was rented and reconstructed for use as a religious institution. Shortly afterward, on November 16, 1941, Candidate Norman Streufert was ordained and installed as pastor of Calvary Congregation. He also took charge of the school. In August, 1943, Pastor Streufert accepted a call to Thornton, Ill. Thereupon the Rev. Fred E. Bartling, pastor of Christ Congregation at North Lake Village (about seven miles to the southeast), began to serve the Wooddale flock as an affiliate.

239. Warrenville

The Trail now makes a beeline of fourteen miles in a southwesterly direction from Wooddale to Warrenville.* According to recent reports concerning the development of this village (about eight miles northeast of Aurora) a zero ought, perhaps, to be added to the figure printed at the bottom of this page. In 1942 the Rev. Adolph E. Ullrich, pastor of Bethany Congregation in Naperville, founded Good Shepherd Congregation and served it until the Rev. Frank Frese took it over as an affiliate of his congregation, Saint John's, in Wheaton, about four miles northeast of Warrenville. When in 1944 Pastor Frese accepted the position as service pastor for the Missouri Synod's Army and Navy Commission, his successor in the Wheaton parish, the Rev. Harold H. Tessmann of Raleigh, N.C., on February 27, 1944, also assumed charge of Good Shepherd Congregation in Warrenville. The congregation's first place of worship was a concrete-block factory building, which was used until a chapel located on Aurora Road and Rockwell Street was dedicated. Good Shepherd's first resident pastor, the Rev. Frederick Dankert† of Horicon, Wis., was installed on September 29, 1946. On December 11, 1947, he accepted a call to Trinity Congregation, six miles southeast of Bay City, Mich. Recently application was made for a

*1940 census: 150.

†A brother of the Rev. Wm. J. Danker, pastor of Trinity Congregation, West Chicago (Turner Junction), Ill., 1942-1948.

vicar, who is to serve Good Shepherd Congregation, Warrenville, the mission station at Moecherville, and the area northeast of Aurora.

240. Mount Greenwood

Early in 1939 the Mount Greenwood territory, in the vicinity of West 111th Street and Trumbull Avenue, had been canvassed, and divine services were conducted in the public school building of Alsip, a small village three miles west of Blue Island. During the same summer, however, this venture was discontinued. In 1942 the same territory and vicinity was again canvassed, but no further action was taken. Then, in July, 1943, the "Emergency Trailor Unit,"* conducted by the Missouri Synod, was set up at the corner of West 111th Street and Trumbull Avenue, and open-air tent services were held each evening. The attendance increased. Three months later the trailer unit moved away from this territory, and the Rev. William J. Rohlwing, pastor of Holy Trinity Congregation at Bridgeview, was called to serve in this community, besides attending to his own little parish. Services were conducted in a small building which had served as a warehouse for a hardware merchant. In June, 1944, seventy-six Lutherans, including thirty communicant members of Saint John the Divine Congregation, whose center is located at West 105th Street and Oakley Avenue, Chicago (Beverly Heights)—about one and a half miles northeast of Mount Greenwood—organized Mount Greenwood Congregation. Pastor Rohlwing was installed as this congregation's first pastor on August 20, 1944. He served here until April, 1949, when he accepted a call to Madison, Wis. His successor, the Rev. Arthur C. Hellert of Ironwood, Mich., was installed on September 4, 1949.

*The equipment of the E.T.U. included a tent, folding chairs, sound amplifiers, movie projector, sound films, stripfilm projector, mimeograph, camp stove, house trailer, an automobile, and a crew of at least two men. (*Concordia Theological Monthly*, St. Louis, Mo., Vol. XVII, No. 2, p. 110.)

241. North Lake Village

This community, located a short distance west of River Grove and southwest of the Che-che-pinqua Forest Preserve, was canvassed in the fall of 1940 by students of Concordia Teachers College and members of the "Mission Activities Group" of that institution in River Forest. The first service, attended by seven people, was conducted in the back room of a drugstore on December 15, 1940. When the final service was held there on February 2, 1941, the attendance was thirty-eight. In the afternoon of the same day a chapel erected at a cost of $6,500 at Hyde Park and Fullerton Avenues was dedicated. On the following day a day school was opened with an enrollment of twelve pupils. The first teacher was Frank H. Colba, student of Concordia Teachers College and organizer of the "Mission Activities Group." On October 19, 1941, the congregation was organized and named Christ. On December 7 the Rev. Fred E. Bartling, formerly pastor of Saint Mark's Congregation in Chicago,* was installed as this congregation's first pastor. In June, 1944, Candidate Norman W. Vonderheid took charge of the day school. About one year later the school was discontinued.

242. Island Lake

On the boundary between Lake and McHenry Counties is a small lake, known as Island Lake.† On its shore is a recently developed community of the same name. After a canvass in the fall of 1941 by members of the Mission Activities Group of Concordia Teachers College, River Forest, the first worship service was held on November 9 in Beu's tea room by the Rev. Alfred T. Kretzmann, pastor of Saint Matthew's Congregation in Barrington, about eight miles south–southwest of the lake. A Sunday school was organized on the same

*Pastor of St. Mark's, Chicago, 1937-1941.

†Not to be confused with the lake of the same name directly west of Ontarioville.

day. For an entire month Pastor Kretzmann and his family lived in Island Lake "to give more adequate attention to the enormous amount of work involved in getting this large group of men and women with more than a dozen different denominational backgrounds ready to be received into church membership on October 4, 1942." It was at this time that thirty-three members organized Saint John's Congregation at Island Lake. An abandoned school was purchased at an auction and moved to "the best lots in the community."

In May, 1943, a group of members, dissatisfied because the church had not turned out to be a "community church in doctrine and practice," separated from Saint John's Congregation to establish that kind of congregation. Several years prior to this unfortunate event, the Rev. Ernest T. Lams, president of the Northern Illinois District,* in the course of his opening address at the 1937 District convention, said: "There must be oneness in teaching all the articles of our holy Christian faith. Dissensions and compromises definitely must be ruled out. There must be perfect oneness in the conviction of our hearts in prosecuting the identical purposes and aims of our beloved Evangelical Lutheran Church." Since May, 1943, the worship services, Sunday school sessions, and meetings have been held in a reconstructed garage adjoining the W. E. Dorn residence. When Pastor Kretzmann in April, 1945, accepted a call to Trinity Congregation in Crete, Ill., his successor in Barrington, the Rev. Herbert H. Heinemann of Hampshire, Ill., continued to serve Saint John's in Island Lake. On May 22, 1949, a new church valued at $15,000 was erected in Island Lake.

President Franklin Delano Roosevelt died unexpectedly at 3:35 P.M., Chicago time, of a cerebral hemorrhage at Warm Springs, Ga., and two hours and 34 minutes later, Harry S. Truman, "one-time Missouri farm boy, was sworn in as the 33d individual to become President of the United

*The fourth president of this District; 1936-1945.

States in a simple ceremony in the cabinet room of the executive offices of the White House." (*Chicago Tribune*, April 13, 1945.)

243. Wilmington

In 1857 the Trail en route from Aurora to Bonfield crossed the Kankakee River at Wilmington,* a village located about fifteen miles south of Joliet and named from the city in Ohio (40 miles northeast of Cincinnati). About eighty-five years have elapsed since then. On August 8, 1942, this community was canvassed in the interest of the Missouri Synod. A public garage on State Highway 66 was rented at the rate of $65 dollars a month, and the first worship service was held here on December 6, 1942.

The Rev. H. William Lieske, pastor of Redeemer Congregation in Joliet, served this mission until December, 1943, when the Rev. Adolph J. Schliesser, a retired pastor† residing in Joliet, took charge of the mission, serving it until July 1, 1944, when the Rev. Gordon Mackensen‡ came to Wilmington. In the fall of 1945 a congregation was organized and named Grace. With the aid of the Chicago Lutheran Church Extension Association, Grace Congregation was able to purchase a large house at 214 South Main Street, which was converted into a combination church and parsonage. Plans for the erection of a church on the property adjacent to this building are under way. In May, 1948, Pastor Mackensen accepted a call to El Centro, Calif., and Gerald Thies,¶ a 1948 graduate of Concordia Seminary, St. Louis, Mo., became second resident pastor of Grace on August 1, 1948.

*1940 census: 1,921.

†Formerly held a pastorate at Lincoln, Ill. Served as chaplain in the U.S. Army during World War I. His son, Luther, for about two years served Redeemer Congregation in Joliet, Ill.

‡Son of the Rev. Henry Mackensen, pastor of Grace Congregation, Glen Ellyn, Ill., 1923-1942. (Killed in auto accident May 13, 1942.)

¶Pastor Thies is a son of the Rev. Clemens Thies, a former pastor of First Bethlehem, Chicago, and presently a faculty member of Luther Institute in Chicago.

244. Clyde

A canvass in this new housing project revealed to the Mission Board of the Northern Illinois District that a mission should be begun at this place at the very earliest possible time. Clyde is a community located near the famous Hawthorne Race Track, directly south of Cicero. A vacant building, somewhat on one side (east) of the mission field but easily accessible from all parts of the community, was secured. The Rev. Ernest Wenz of Marseilles, Ill., was placed in charge of this mission field on January 21, 1945. One month later, on February 25, a congregation was organized with forty charter members and named Faith. A Sunday school, which had been nursed along by Mrs. Albert Stoike, soon had an enrollment of more than one hundred pupils; during the following summer the Bible class was attended by sixty-one children. Pastor Wenz resigned on March 1, 1946. His successor in the Faith pastorate is the Rev. Harry C. Fricke, formerly pastor of Saint Peter's Congregation, Arlington Heights (Dunton), and more recently chaplain in the United States Army. He was installed on June 23, 1946, at Faith Chapel, 3627 South Sixty-first Avenue, Clyde, Ill.

245. Des Plaines, Good Shepherd

During the economic depression of 1873 the Trail led to Des Plaines, where at that time a group of Lutherans was busy organizing Immanuel Congregation. That was seventy-two years ago. In July, 1945, a preliminary canvass was made of a comparatively new section of the community within the corporate limits of "the City of Roses." The Rev. Arthur A. Yoss, pastor of Ascension Congregation, Riverside, the Rev. Arno Schlechte, pastor of Trinity Congregation, Villa Park, and the Rev. Roger L. Sommer, pastor of Saint John the Divine Congregation, Chicago, all of whom served as members of the English District's Survey Committee, together with members of Lutheran congregations—"volunteers from near and far"—participated in the canvass. Shortly afterward the Mission Board of the English District extended a call to the Rev. Herbert Henry Nagel of San Diego, Calif. He accepted and in the middle of September began surveying the territory. Property of suitable character was not available, but at the first meeting of a group of interested people, on October 9, in the home of Mr. and Mrs. Arthur Neumann, 1973 Illinois Street, it was decided to erect a building to serve as church. On November 7 the organization of a congregation was effected by eleven Lutheran men* in the home of Edward Beyer in Glen Acres. The name Good Shepherd was adopted on the 13th, and the incorporation was completed on the 20th. Shortly afterward property at the corner of Prospect Avenue and Illinois Street was purchased. Building operations were begun on January 19, 1946. Meanwhile the congregation worshiped in "the upper room" of Mr. and Mrs. Arvid Jacobson's home on Pratt Avenue, near Mannheim Road. That was from December 2, 1945, until April 19, 1946, when Good Shepherd Congregation entered the new chapel located at Prospect Avenue and Illinois Street. Formal dedication took place ten days later, on April 29. In October the young congregation purchased a building for use as a parsonage. On November 9, 1947, a new addition to the chapel was dedicated, providing—in its entirety—seating space for 150 persons.

246. Chicago, Jeffery Manor

During World War II an entirely new home-building proj-

*Charter members:
Mr. and Mrs. Warner Nagel
Mrs. Carl Salamann
Fred Meinshausen
Mrs. Gertrude Johnson
Mrs. Martha Weichbrodt
Edward J. Beyer
Miss Hattie Beyer
Mr. and Mrs. Albert Dallmann
Elmer Dallmann
Miss Evelyn Dallmann
Mr. and Mrs. Walter Dallmann
Mr. and Mrs. Arvid Jacobson
Mr. and Mrs. Alvin Nagel
Mrs. Jane Reiter
Mr. and Mrs. Richard Stratton
Mr. and Mrs. Rudolph Strahs
Miss June Strahs
Mrs. Gudereit
Mrs. Herbert Nagel
Mr. and Mrs. Frank Roll

ect was begun under Government direction in the territory bounded by Jeffery and Torrence Avenues and East Ninety-fifth and One Hundred and Second Streets, on Chicago's far southeast side. Single and duplex houses of brick were hurriedly erected in Jeffery Manor and Calumet Gardens, including a public school building. Initially these buildings were intended for war plant workers. By January, 1945, some 1,100 homes housed more than five thousand people.

Mr. and Mrs. M. H. Burton, members of Saint Paul's Congregation, whose "center" is at East Seventy-sixth Street and Dorchester Avenue (Grand Crossing), aware of the mission opportunities, offered their home at 2100 East Ninety-eighth Place as locale for the opening of a Sunday school. In fact, they made the beginning on March 18, 1945. Before long every room in their home, including the basement, was filled with Sunday school pupils on Sunday mornings. The Rev. Edwin H. Pflug of Grand Crossing and the Rev. Edgar R. Pflug, pastor of Bethlehem Congregation in South Chicago (Colehour), took an active interest in the undertaking. Through them the Burtons approached the Mission Board of the Northern Illinois District with the request for more space. Arrangements were made to use the Luella Public School building, Luella Avenue and East One Hundredth Street. On the first Sunday in October, 1945, worship services were begun there. The first three were conducted by Dr. Arthur W. Klinck, president of Concordia Teachers College, River Forest; the following seven, by Candidate Robert Stade, who was awaiting orders from the Board of Foreign Missions to proceed to the mission field in Nigeria, Africa. Thereafter various pastors and students were asked to serve on Sunday mornings until January, 1946, when the Mission Board requested the Rev. T. W. Strieter, who in the previous year had left his congregation in Evansville (Saint Paul's), Ind., to serve as director of the Lutheran Commission for Prisoners of War with offices in Chicago. On June 16, 1946, he was installed as the first resident pastor of Jeffery Manor Congregation. Formal organization had been effected on April 7 by eight men, and the name chosen was Our Savior. In June the congregation joined the Missouri Synod.

(The Trail during recent days devoted much attention to the report regarding cessation of hostilities in Europe—VE Day, May 8, 1945; soon after this came VJ Day, August 14, 1945.)

By the end of 1946 Our Savior Congregation comprised eighty communicant members, and the Sunday school enrollment was 151.

On January 30, 1949, Our Savior Congregation dedicated its new "basement" chapel.

In an editorial captioned "Chicago, the City with Elbow Room," we are told that "Chicago still has many square miles of vacant territory suitable for residential construction. Its zoning has always been fantastically optimistic. Someone once figured out that if all of the lots in the city zoned for commercial use were developed, the stores and business establishments placed on them would serve the entire population of the United States, and that if all of the land zoned for tall apartment buildings were so developed, most of the American population could live in them." (*Chicago Tribune*, September 25, 1946.)

247. Chicago, Ashburn

The Ashburn mission is located at West Eighty-third Street and Hamlin Avenue, a short distance northwest of Evergreen Park, Ill. Upon the suggestion of the Rev. Adolph Lach, pastor of Christ Congregation in Orland Park, Ill., who had members residing in the Ashburn community, the Rev. Roger L. Sommer detailed a student, Paul Shippert of Concordia Seminary, St. Louis, Mo., and member of Saint John the Divine Congregation, Chicago, to make a canvass of the entire area extending from Western Avenue to Southwest Highway and from West Seventy-ninth to West Eighty-third Streets. The first worship service was conducted by Pastor Sommer on February 17, 1946, in the basement of a restaurant at Western Avenue and West Seventy-ninth Street, with an attendance of eleven persons. On March 10, 1946, services and Sunday school sessions were started in the Ashburn Public School, West Eighty-third Street and Hamlin Avenue, at a rental of fifteen dollars per Sunday. On August 2, 1946, the Rev. H. Fred Goetze, formerly with the American Lutheran Church,* was placed in charge of this mission project. Organization of a congregation was effected on December 11, 1946. Mr. and Mrs. William Raney, members of the young congregation, have presented six lots at West Eighty-third Street and Homan Avenue for church and parsonage sites. On October 31, 1948, the cornerstone of a combination chapel-parsonage was laid. This building was dedicated on June 26, 1949, on which occasion this writer was privileged to preach the dedicatory sermon.

248. Arlington Heights, Faith

Approximately eighty-seven years ago the Lutheran Trail witnessed the organization of Saint Peter's Congregation in Dunton (now Arlington Heights), on March 30, 1860. (See Chapter 25, p. 139.) On March 10, 1947, a "daughter" congregation of Saint Peter's was organized with 190 of its communicant members in a new community at the southwestern limits of the village known as Scarsdale, "where no other church as yet is located," and named Faith. The first service was conducted on February 23 by the Rev. Arthur A. Yoss, pastor of Ascension Congregation, Riverside, and survey director for the English District of the Missouri Synod. The attendance was 210. The Rev. Gerhardt Leverenz, ex-chaplain in the U. S. Army and student at the University of Chicago, was in charge as temporary pastor until September 14, 1947,

*Was received into membership with the Missouri Synod in June, 1946.

when the Rev. Edgar H. Behrens of Philadelphia, Pa., was installed as the congregation's first resident pastor. Several months previously the following news item appeared in the Northern Illinois District edition of the *Lutheraner* (Vol. 103, No. 7): "143 communicant members have been given a release from St. Peter's, Arlington Heights (Pastor L. V. Stephan), so that under the sponsorship of the English District they might form a new congregation in the town's expanding residential district. Pastor Arthur A. Yoss of Riverside, survey director of the English District, is the group's adviser . . . . St. Peter's School will serve both congregations. Present building operations in the town as well as the number of prospects and transfers moving in from the metropolitan areas indicate strongly that the field of opportunity for both congregations to flourish is ripe unto the harvest."

Construction of a church building on South State Road, four blocks south of Northwest Highway, was begun in the spring of 1948. On Sunday, September 25, 1949, the new church, constructed of Wisconsin limestone, was dedicated.

249. Bellwood, Faith (See chapter 160, p. 490)

250. Chicago, Christ the King (See p. 668)

Havoc Wrought By Fire, Storm, etc.

Date	*Place*	*Church (Parsonage or School)*	*Cause*
1859	Elk Grove	St. John's, parsonage	Fire
?	Goodfarm	Trinity, parsonage	Fire
Oct. 9, 1871	Chicago	First St. Paul's Church *(2d)*	Fire *(total loss)*
May 3, 1876	Chicago	First Trinity Church, *(steeple)*	Tornado
Jan. 24, 1880	Yellowhead *(Grant Park)*	St. Paul's Church and parsonage	Fire
July 5, 1881	Crete	Trinity School	Fire
Dec. 25, 1883	Bachelors Grove	Trinity Church	Fire
Nov., 1886	Evanston	Bethlehem Church *(under construction)*	Tornado
May 1, 1887	Kankakee	St. Paul's Church	Fire
July 23, 1887	Chicago	St. Matthew's Church	Fire *(total loss)*
1889	Algonquin	St. John's, parsonage	Fire
May 29, 1896	Chicago *(Logan Square)*	Christ Church	Fire
1896	Belvidere	Immanuel Church, steeple	Lightning
1898 (?)	Woodstock	St. John's Church	Fire
Jan. 29, 1899	Chicago	St. Luke's Church	Fire
July 11, 1904	Schaumberg	St. Peter's Church, steeple and organ	Electric storm
Aug. 11, 1905	Marengo	Zion Church and School	Lightning *(fire)*
Jan. 7, 1909	Chicago	St. Stephen's Church	Fire
Aug. 23, 1910	Rodenberg	St. John's Church	Fire *(lightning)*
Feb. 28, 1914	River Forest, Ill.	Concordia Teachers College, Adm. Bldg.	Fire *(lightning)*
May 6, 1914	Aurora	St. Paul's Church	Lightning
June 24, 1914	La Grange	St. John's Church steeple	Lightning *(fire)*
May 15, 1915	Northbrook *(6 S. W.)*	St. John's Church	Fire
June 9, 1915	Willow Springs	Trinity Church	Lightning *(fire)*
Apr. 26, 1916	Forest Park	St. John's *(old)* Church	Fire
May 26, 1917	Eagle Lake	St. John's Church, steeple	Tornado

Date	*Place*	*Church (Parsonage or School)*	*Cause*
1917	Sieden Prairie	St. Paul's, parsonage	Fire
1917	Yellowhead *(Grant Park)*	St. Paul's Church *(organ)*	Fire
Jan. 18, 1918	South Chicago	Bethlehem Church	Fire
Jan., 1918	Lemont	St. Matthew's Church	Fire
Spring, 1919	Riverdale *(Chicago)*	St. Paul's Church	Lightning *(fire)*
Spring, 1922	Glenview	Immanuel Church *(partially)*	Storm
Aug., 1922	Elk Grove	St. John's Church *(partially)*	Storm
1926	Union	St. John's Church	Lightning *(fire)*
1927	Churchville *(Duncklees Gr.)*	Zion Church *(windows)*	Hailstorm
1929	Morton Grove	Jerusalem Church	Fire
Feb. 22, 1929	Hinckley *(Squaw Grove)*	Immanuel, parsonage	Fire
July 2, 1933	Proviso	Immanuel Church, steeple	Tornado
Dec., 1934	Momence	Our Savior Church	Fire
Aug. 10, 1935	Chicago	First St. John's, steeple	Lightning *(fire)*
Aug. 19, 1937	Churchville *(Duncklees Gr.)*	Zion Church	Fire
Dec. 25, 1937	South Chicago	Immanuel Church *(partially)*	Fire
1943	Union	St. John's Church *(interior)*	Fire
Dec. 21, 1944	Chicago	Good Shepherd Church	Fire
Feb., 1945	Bridgeview *(Chicago)*	Holy Trinity Chapel	Fire
Feb. 19, 1945	Roseland *(Chicago)*	Zion Church	Fire
June, 1946	Chicago *(Austin)*	St. Paul's Church, steeple	Lightning
Oct. 11, 1946	Chicago *(Austin)*	St. Paul's Church	Fire *(blowtorch)*
July 13, 1948	Ash Grove	St. John's Church	Lightning *(fire; total loss)*

Part Seven

Organization of the Missouri Synod

Leisurely returning from Arlington Heights, the last place in its itinerary, the Lutheran Trail passes through a veritable shower of printed matter, directing attention to the "Centennial, Celebration" to take place on Sunday, July 27 1947, in Soldier Field on Chicago's attractive lake front. "Special trains, busses, and chartered planes will bring Lutherans from distant points for this great Centennial celebration!"—"Over 120,000 Lutherans are expected to attend."—"All seats free!"—"The Convention sessions will be held in the Palmer House." One hundred years, 1847-1947!—"The congregations of the English District are contributing an equal assessment toward the expenses involved and therefore received recognition in the appointments of the committee personnel."(!) (*Northern Illinois District Messenger*, 1945, p. 40.)

The Centennial Convention sessions, attended by a total of 876 delegates, were held from July 20 through 29, 1947, in a hotel in downtown Chicago, the Palmer House! The proceedings are recorded in a 798-page book published in 1947 by Concordia Publishing House, Saint Louis, Mo. On Wednesday, July 23, a "Lutheran Centennial Concert" was presented in the Medinah Temple, 600 North Wabash Avenue,* by the Lutheran Centennial Choir,† directed by Gerhard Schroth, and the Lutheran Centennial Children's Choir, directed by John G. Rieck.‡ The concert manager was George E. Merker, Jr., John L. Astley-Cock, writing in the *Chicago Tribune* on the following day, referred to the concert as "the cultural highlight of the centennial anniversary." In the last portion of the program the two choirs combined and, accompanied by members of the Chicago Symphony Orchestra, gave a splendid rendition of Johann Sebastian Bach's Reformation Cantata. A full-page display advertisement in the *Chicago Tribune*¶ on the day of the concert contained the names of some 240 "Chicagoland Churches" and its pastors, a large reproduction of the official Centennial emblem, a few historical data, and, across the bottom, in bold letters, an invitation to the "gigantic religious demonstration" (*Chicago Daily News*, July 26) in Soldier Field on Sunday afternoon, July 27. The festival sermon was preached by the Rev. John W. Behnken, D.D., re-elected at the Centennial Convention for a fifth consecutive triennium as President of the Missouri Synod. His text was: "For unto whomsoever much is given, of him shall be much required" (Luke 12:48b). Brilliant decorations adorned Soldier Field; on a huge platform stood a 25-foot cross, and around it were grouped the flags of the sixty-four countries in which the Lutheran Church carries on its religious and educational activities. On the following day the religion editor of the *Chicago Herald-American* (the Rev. St. John Tucker) made this comment: "Sixty-five thousand Lutherans lifted

*Originally scheduled to be held in the Chicago Civic Opera House, 20 North Wacker Drive.

†This choir has been continued under the name "The Lutheran Choir of Chicago" and remains under Mr. Schroth's direction.

‡This choir has been continued under the name "The Chicagoland Lutheran Children's Choir"—under Mr. Rieck's direction.

¶"The Only Chicago Newspaper Ever to Reach 100" on Tuesday, June 10, 1947, published a fifty-four page Centennial Edition as a feature of the celebration of its founding. In the evening of the same day, a mile-long stretch of the lake, between Roosevelt and Cermak Roads, was "a battlefront." "Seated in comfort and safety on the broad and grassy expanses of Burnham Park, fronting the lagoon, which separates the mainland from Northerly Island, a great crowd" witnessed "a fire-works display on a scale never attempted before." (Same source.)

their voices at Soldier Field yesterday, in the brilliant sunlight of a perfect day, in praise of God for the first 100 years of life of the Missouri Synod. The deep thunder of their voices in the Nicene Creed alternated with great chorales of the Lutheran movement. A massed choir of 5,000 trained voices from 80 churches rendered a cantata of praise, partly in song, partly in choral verse." Anthony Czarnecki used the figure 50,000 in reporting on the festivities; and the Rev. John Evans simply referred to it as "a throng numbering in the thousands." (The *Chicago Daily Tribune,* July 28, 1947.)

At this Centennial Convention also the constituent congregations of Synod were called upon to approve the change of its official name to THE LUTHERAN CHURCH–MISSOURI SYNOD. On the editorial page of the *Lutheran Witness,* LXVII, 9 (May 4, 1948), appeared this formal announcement:

Re: Changing Name of Synod

Synod in 1947 resolved to adopt a new name: "The Lutheran Church — Missouri Synod." (Cf. *Synodical Proceedings* 1947, page 447.) This constituted an amendment of the Constitution, Article I. Therefore this amendment, according to Article XIV, had to "be submitted to the congregations of Synod by means of three announcements in the official synodical organs within three months after the close of the convention." A one-third vote of the congregations would have been necessary to defeat the amendment. The required time for such votes was allowed. The six months after the last publication were up on April 7, 1948. By that time only 302 votes had been received by the Secretary. The amendment therefore becomes effective at this time. The official name of the former Evangelical Lutheran Synod of Missouri, Ohio, and Other States now is: The Lutheran Church — Missouri Synod.

M. F. Kretzmann, Secretary of Synod

Kendallville, Ind., April 8, 1948

Let us set the clock back a century. Let us talk about the beginnings of the Missouri Synod. Here in Chicago stood its cradle. At that, the Missouri Synod, from the start, was not a "local" affair. A hundred years ago, even as today, Chicago was a hub and a magnet. Here was brought to fruition what had been started in Cleveland, Ohio. There a number of Lutheran ministers in September, 1845, had a meeting for the purpose of discussing and formulating a set of rules and regulations intended as a guide or basis for the formation of a union of Lutheran congregations "built upon" the Bible and the confessional standards of the Evangelical Lutheran Church. Representatives of this group in the spring of the following year journeyed to St. Louis, Mo., where, during an eight-day conference, May 13-20, 1846, they discussed their plans with the spiritual leaders of the Saxon immigrants. In July of the same year a similar meeting was held by a group of Lutheran clergymen in Fort Wayne, Ind., and vicinity. Here the proposed constitution was thoroughly discussed, and a "final draft" was worked out, with the understanding that definitive action be taken by members of the three groups who were in agreement with the proposed "union" at a meeting scheduled to be held in Chicago in April, 1847. Arrangements were also made to have the plan published as widely as possible. This was done principally by means of a German church paper, *Der Lutheraner*, edited by the Rev. C. F. W. Walther and published by Trinity Congregation in St. Louis, Mo., since 1844 and adopted by the Missouri Synod, in 1847, as its official organ.*

The opening service of the Chicago Convention was held at 9 A.M. on Sunday, April 25, 1847, in the little church of Saint Paul's Congregation, located in the swamp at the southwest corner of Ohio and La Salle Streets. On the following day the first in a series of eighteen public sessions was held.

*Still being published; now in its 106th year, it has approximately 37,000 subscribers.

After the pastor of the host congregation, the Rev. C. August T. Selle, had explained the purpose of the convention, the preliminary signing of the constitution took place. It was signed by those pastors and laymen who in the preceding year at Fort Wayne had taken part in its drafting. These, then, constituted the synodical body, which thereupon received other qualified applicants into membership. The first officers, elected pro tempore, were: the Rev. C. F. W. Walther, president; the Rev. Frederick William Hussmann, secretary; the Rev. William Sihler, Ph.D., treasurer.

Once more the constitution was discussed, and, together with a new paragraph pertaining to the relation of the individual congregation to the new synod or union, it was formally adopted at the first session, April 26, 1847. Only two Lutheran pastors of the northern Illinois area attended this convention, viz., the Rev. C. A. T. Selle, pastor of Saint Paul's, Chicago, and the Rev. Francis Arnold Hoffmann, pastor of Zion Congregation at Duncklees Grove. (See Part Two, Chapters one and two, pages 15 and 24.)

Permanently elected near the end of the convention sessions, May 6, 1847, were the following: the Rev. C. F. W. Walther, president; the Rev. William Sihler, Ph.D., vice-president; the Rev. Frederick William Hussmann,* secretary; and F. W. Barthel, a layman from St. Louis, Mo., treasurer.†

Conventions of the new Synod were held annually in the following cities: St. Louis, Mo. (1848, 1850, and 1854); Fort Wayne, Ind. (1849 and 1852); Milwaukee, Wis. (1851); and Cleveland, Ohio (1853). At the eighth annual convention, June 21-July 1, 1854, in St. Louis, Mo., Synod put into effect a resolution passed at the two previous conventions to divide Synod into Districts. Thus came into being the first four syn-

*A son of Synod's first secretary, the Rev. F. W. Hussmann, died on Sept. 10, 1948, in San Bernardino, Calif., at the age of 90 years.

†For details concerning the manifold transactions of this first convention, see *Erster Synodal-Bericht der deutschen evangelisch-lutherischen Synode von Missouri, Ohio und andern Staaten vom Jahre* 1847," second edition, printed by that Synod's publishing house in St. Louis, Mo. (1876). An English translation of the main parts appears in the *Concordia Historical Institute Quarterly*, Vol. XIX, No. 3, pp. 97-129.

odical Districts: *Western*, comprising the States of Missouri and Illinois; *Central*, Indiana and Ohio; *Northern*, Michigan and Wisconsin; and *Eastern*, New York, Maryland, Pennsylvania, and the District of Columbia. This subdividing was continued from time to time as the territory occupied by Synod grew wider and the number of pastors, teachers, and congregations increased year by year. Since 1854 the entire Synod met in joint session only every third year, each District meeting separately once a year during the two intervening years. The first officers of the Western District were the Rev. G. A. Schieferdecker, president; the Rev. J. F. Buenger, vice-president; the Rev. C. A. T. Selle, secretary; and Mr. E. Roschke, treasurer.

In 1874 there were in the State of Illinois alone 139 pastors and 114 day school teachers belonging to the Western District. In view of this fact, Synod advised organization of a separate District. The advice was heeded. The first president of the Illinois District (founded in 1874) was the Rev. Henry Wunder, pastor of First Saint Paul's, Chicago. In 1880 the Illinois Synod, formerly a part of the General Synod,* joined the Illinois District of the Missouri Synod, a sudden increase of ten congregations and twenty-two pastors.

In 1907 the Missouri Synod decided to divide the Illinois District into three parts, to be known as the Northern, the Central, and the Southern Illinois Districts. The first president of the Northern Illinois District was the Rev. Wm. C. Kohn, pastor of Saint Andrew's Congregation, Chicago. The first convention of the Northern Illinois District was held in Saint Mark's Church, West Twenty-third Street and California Avenue, Chicago, June 2-8, 1909. Pastor Kohn held the presidency until 1913, when he accepted the directorship of the Teachers' Seminary, which in that year was trans-

*The first federation of Lutheran synods in the U.S.A., organized on Oct. 22, 1820, at Hagerstown, Md., by pastors and congregations of the New York Ministerium, the Pennsylvania Ministerium, the North Carolina Synod, and the Maryland-Virginia Synod.

ferred from Addison to River Forest and since then known as Concordia Teachers College. (See page 636.) The following have served as presidents of the Northern Illinois District since 1913: the Rev. Frederick Brunn of Oak Glen-Lansing, 1913-1927; the Rev. Alex Ullrich of La Grange, 1927-1936; the Rev. Ernest T. Lams of Oak Park, 1936-1945; and the Rev. Arthur H. Werfelmann of Elgin, since 1945. William H. Hinze, layman, of Beecher, Ill., served as the District's treasurer from 1907 until 1945. His successor is Fred C. Schmitt of River Forest.

Meantime, inquiry must be made into the source whence the Missouri Synod, which at this time (1949) comprises thirty-four Districts, obtains the majority of its pastors and teachers. In 1839 the Saxon immigrants came up the Mississippi River from New Orleans, La., the port of entry, and debarked at St. Louis, Mo. The majority of them, after a brief sojourn there, preferring to establish their homes far away from the "big city," moved some one hundred miles south, to Perry County, to occupy a tract of land, comprising 4,440 acres, which had previously been purchased out of a common fund raised by the immigrants themselves in Europe. At a place which they called Altenburg the settlers constructed dwelling places and a one-room log cabin which was to serve as a high school. The official announcement, which appeared in the *Anzeiger des Westens* (St. Louis) in August, 1839, and signed by C. F. W. Walther, Ottomar Fuerbringer, Th. Jul. Brohm, and John F. Buenger, clearly indicates that this school originally was not intended to be a theological institution. At its first convention (1847) the Missouri Synod received this institution, together with the seminary in Fort Wayne, Ind., as the first nucleus for its educational program. Two years later the school was transferred to St. Louis, and the Synod's first President, the Rev. C. F. W. Walther, was chosen as the institution's head. In the course of a few years the theological purpose of the school began to stand out ever more clearly; it developed into a theological seminary. The institution, known as Concordia Seminary, was located on St. Louis' south side ("St. Louis Commons") from 1849 until 1926. In the latter year the present institution, consisting of eighteen buildings of Tudor-Gothic design, was dedicated. Located a few blocks west of Forest Park in the suburb of Clayton in St. Louis County, the new seminary, including fifteen professors' residences, cost approximately three million dollars. On the seminary campus is the Missouri Synod's radio station, KFUO—"The Gospel Voice"—founded on Sunday, December 14, 1924, "when a 500-watt transmitter with other necessary equipment, also a control room and a studio, were dedicated to the glory of God in the attic of the old Seminary on South Jefferson Avenue at the cost of $14,000...." (Dedication Program, May 31, 1942.)

In 1846 a seminary was established in Fort Wayne, Ind., with a department added shortly afterward for the training of day school teachers. This institution was likewise transferred to the Missouri Synod in 1847. Because of its rapid growth a pro-seminary (preparatory department) was added. In 1861 the seminary proper was moved to St. Louis, Mo., and combined with Concordia Seminary, while the undergraduate department was in the same year moved to the former city. In 1874 the Missouri Synod purchased the property of the former Illinois State University in Springfield, Ill., and set it apart as a short-course, "practical" seminary.

In 1855 three pastors, Philip Fleischmann, L. Dulitz, and F. J. C. Lochner of Milwaukee, Wis., together with Christian Diez, a day school teacher, had established as a private venture a school for the training of day school teachers. From this humble beginning in Milwaukee grew in the course of time one of Synod's largest educational institutions, Concordia Teachers College, now located in the northern Illinois area, in River Forest. Before the new school had been able to establish itself firmly, a meeting was held in 1857 in Duncklees Grove (Zion Congregation), a few months after the Rev. A. G. G. Francke had assumed the pastorate there, for the purpose of discussing the matter of finding a more suitable location for the new "normal school." A member of Zion, Friedrich Meyer, declared: "Kerls, dat lat uesch hierher bring, wi hebt Platz!" ("Fellows, let us bring it here; we have room!") Soon afterward Zion Congregation offered a tract of land and, in conjunction with neighboring congregations, promised to gather most of the funds required for the erection of needed buildings. The congregation instructed its pastor and its lay delegate, F. Fiene, to make a strong appeal at the synodical convention in Fort Wayne, Ind. (October 14-24, 1857), for the removal of the Milwaukee normal school to Addison, Ill. However, Dr. Sihler, who had been asked to recommend to the synodical convention a plan for teacher training, succeeded in persuading the delegates that the removal of the Milwaukee normal school to Fort Wayne and the combination with the Fort Wayne institution would be, for the time being, the easiest and most practical solution, even though the Chicago Teachers' Conference had called attention to certain disadvantages which might result from such a combination.* Consequently, the Missouri Synod in 1857 took over the struggling Milwaukee institution, transferred it to Fort Wayne, Ind., and combined it with the seminary in that city. The first instructor of the normal department was the Rev. Philip Fleischmann. As the number of students increased, a second instructor, the Rev. C. August T. Selle of Rock Island, Ill.,† was called in 1861.

In the early part of this year (1861), a student of the Fort Wayne institution, Seitz by name, was assigned to Zion's west-

*See *Synodalbericht*, 1857 (2. Auflage, 1876), p. 357.

†Pastor Selle in 1846 came from New Lisbon, Ohio, to Saint Paul's Congregation, Chicago; in 1851 he accepted a call to Zion (in 1858 named Trinity) at Crete, Ill.; in 1858 he assumed a pastorate in Rock Island, Ill.

ern district day school (Duncklees Grove) on a temporary basis. One day, while a school board meeting was in progress in the home of Teacher Henry Bartling, the postman brought a letter from Professors Fleischmann and Selle, intimating that it would be better if the Teachers' Seminary were located at Addison. After considerable discussion, interspersed with laughter and much headshaking ("Kopfschuetteln"), one of the members finally said: "I know why the seminary has not been established at Addison—lack of funds!" He continued: "Folks, I have sold several heads of cattle, and the proceeds have been donated to our building fund. Now, I still have a young horse ("ein Fuchs"—chestnut or light bay horse), which I shall sell, and the proceeds will go for the new seminary at Addison. This remark aroused more laughter, and another member interjected: "Oh, if that's the case, then I can also convert a pair of pigs into cash!" Youthful George Bartling then was asked to produce a sheet of paper, pen, and ink. A letter in German was dictated to him: "If the seminary is transferred to Addison, I will pledge . . . . " Amounts ranging from $100 to $200 were promised by every man present. Mr. Bartling was speechless. Deeply moved, he finally declared: "Do you know what you have done today? I believe you have brought the teachers' seminary here!" On November 14, 1863, Zion's western school district resolved to sell six acres of land, heretofore used by Teacher Bartling as a pasture, to the Missouri Synod for the nominal sum of ten dollars. Another site was offered to Synod: an "inexpensive farm on the lake front at Diversey Avenue," in Lake View (annexed to Chicago in 1899). Evidently northern Illinois was determined to have the Teachers' Seminary located in its territory! In fact, Synod decided to locate the institution at Addison—"behind the bush," in the words of William Meyne. Many of the "Duncklees Grovers" worked daily for two weeks in the interest of the institution, hauling building material to the site. The first building at Addison was dedicated on December 28, 1864. The first director of the new Teachers' Seminary was the Rev. J. C. W. Lindemann.* According to a resolution passed by Synod in 1908, a $100,000 building was to be erected at Addison. Of this amount, $30,000 was pledged by the Northern Illinois District. But then, during the latter part of 1910, an "Away from Addison Movement to River Forest" was started in First Saint John's Congregation, Chicago (Dr. Henry Succop, pastor). When on February 2, 1911, the total contributions in this area amounted to $15,000, a violent opposition toward retaining the Teachers' Seminary at Addison arose in Chicago.† In June, 1911, the Chicago Pastoral Conference adopted resolutions in this matter, paragraph 3 of which read: "We recommend that all congregations adopt and carry out the plan according to which the work is done in Pastor Succop's congregation." The Lutheran Education Society of Chicago offered to Synod a tract of land comprising about forty acres in the residential district of River Forest. Thus it happened that during the sessions of the Missouri Synod's convention in May, 1911 (St. Louis, Mo.), it was resolved to transfer the institution to River Forest, Ill. During the years 1912 and 1913 the first units of the new institution were erected. On October 12, 1913, the normal school, now known as Concordia Teachers College, was dedicated. Six addresses, three in German and three in English, were delivered simultaneously in various parts of the campus. The college's first president was the Rev. William C. Kohn.‡

A fire in the new administration on February 28, 1914, did damage to the extent of about $75,000.

From 1908 to 1933 a two-year normal school training was offered in addition to four years of high school. In 1933 Synod extended the teacher-training program proper to three

*Director Lindemann died in 1879.

†See Diamond Jubilee Booklet, 1867-1942.

‡Director Kohn died on March 13, 1943. Made honorary president of the college in 1939, Dr. Kohn was succeeded by the Rev. Dr. Arthur W. Klinck.

years. Since the fall of 1939 the four-year teachers' college has been in operation.

At its convention in 1938 the Missouri Synod authorized the college and its high school department to enroll a limited number of girls and women for teacher training.

In 1894 Synod established a second teachers' seminary, at Seward, Neb.*

Included in the aims and purposes of the Missouri Synod is "the publication and distribution of Bibles, church books, schoolbooks, religious periodicals, and other books and papers." Prior to 1869, the printing was done in a Roman Catholic printing establishment in St. Louis, Mo., and some in New York and in Reading, Pa. In 1869 three† wealthy members of Old Trinity Congregation in St. Louis each gave a thousand dollars toward the founding of a "synodical press" ("Synodaldruckerei") in the same city. This printing establishment was located in a building on the campus of Concordia Seminary and was "rather under the personal supervision of Dr. Walther." In 1874 a new structure was erected on the northwest corner of Indiana Avenue and Miami Street, about two blocks northeast of the "old" seminary.‡ In 1878 the name "Concordia-Verlag" (Concordia Publishing House) was adopted. The original building (1874) was enlarged in 1882 and again in 1887. In 1893 an office building was erected on the corner of south Jefferson Avenue and Miami Street. In 1911 a unit on Jefferson Avenue was added to the corner structure. In 1925 a complete factory was erected north of and adjoining this structure at a cost of $260,000. Further additions and renovations were completed in 1941

*This institution remained a three-year school until 1905. Upon completion of the course, the students of Seward were expected to complete their training for the teaching profession in the Addison institution. Subsequently, this arrangement was discontinued, and the Seward institution became a full teachers' seminary, which meant that its graduates were prepared to accept teaching positions. (Herman O. A. Keinath, Ph.D.)

†"In 1867 five members of Old Trinity put equipment valued at three thousand dollars into a room of the seminary, as the nucleus of a synodical printery." *The Work of Our Hands*, C. P. H. 1869-1944.

‡The new plant was completed at a cost of $20,964.

and 1942. "The institution is, while operated under a separate charter of its own, entirely the property of the Missouri Synod, and all its profits or surplus have always been turned over to Synod for use in missions and other synodical activities." The first "general agent," in charge of production and sales, was M. C. Barthel, who served in this capacity from 1874 till 1891; his successor was Martin Tirmenstein, who served until 1907. On March 18 of that year Edmund Seuel* took over the managerial responsibilities and "piloted the firm through the era of its most signal expansion." In 1941 Otto A. Dorn† entered the firm as assistant general manager. In March, 1944, he succeeded Mr. Seuel as general manager, the latter being retained as "manager emeritus."

In September, 1940, thirty-two young men and women of the college department of Concordia Teachers College, River Forest, organized the *Concordia Mission Activities Group.* "Only two desires prompted this organization: to learn how to do mission work; to do mission work."

The *Concordia Teachers College Men's Club,* composed of pastors, teachers, and laymen, was organized in 1936. Its aim is "to arouse a deeper interest in the River Forest Concordia, to give moral and financial aid to the school's physical education program, and to foster the spirit of Christian fellowship." A project recently completed by this organization was the purchase and installation of a public address system in the gymnasium.

"We Lutherans should have the best schools in the country. At no place and at no time should we content ourselves with having achieved only the most essential purposes; to the glory of our heavenly Father and for the welfare of our

*Mr. Seuel was graduated from Concordia Seminary, St. Louis, Mo. (1886); served as pastor at Ogallala, Nebr. (1886-1888); then as professor and president of Walther College, St. Louis, Mo. (1888-1907).

†Son of the Rev. Prof. Louis W. Dorn, pastor of Saint Paul's Congregation in Rockford, Ill., 1888-1895; Belleville, Ill., 1895-1900; and professor at Concordia College, Fort Wayne, Ind., 1900-1918. Mr. Dorn's previous position was that of assistant executive secretary of the Walther League, Chicago.

own children, yea, for the welfare of the whole country, we should be diligent, and shun no sacrifice, in the establishment of the best possible (' moeglichst vollkommene') schools and to have the most competent teachers."* The foreword to the twelfth volume of the *Schulblatt* opens with this sentence: "Eine herrliche Zierde unserer Synode, eine schoene Krone, welche Gottes unaussprechlich grosse Gnade derselben auf das Haupt gesetzt hat, ist ohne Zweifel unser Schulwesen." (A glorious ornament of our Synod—a beautiful crown—which God's unspeakably great grace has placed upon its head, doubtless is our school system.)

The *Chicago Teachers' Choir* was organized on March 16, 1896. Its first director, W. Kuntze, served until June, 1900. A Mr. von Oppen served in this capacity during the following five years. Prof. Hans Biedermann succeeded in 1905; he served until 1926, when he died. Then came George L. Tenney ("Uncle George"), who directed the choir until the beginning of World War II, when it disbanded.

On May 27, 1918, the Northern Illinois District resolved to call a "Schulinspektor" (school superintendent). The call was extended by the Board of Christian Education to Paul Theodore Buszin, at the time on the teaching staff of the First Bethlehem School, Chicago. He served in this capacity from October 1, 1918, until June 25, 1942, which date marked the fiftieth anniversary of his graduation from the Teachers' Seminary, Addison. On that occasion the delegates attending the convention of the District in River Forest (June 22-26, 1942) passed congratulatory resolutions in recognition of Superintendent Buszin's services. Responding, Mr. Buszin "felt constrained to address a few words to the convention—from a full heart." "This new, until 1918 unexplored, service within our Synod . . . has been one replete with labors, functions, solicitude, and study which proved trying and testing to me indeed, but, moreover, a service of joy, animation,

**Schulblatt*, II, 1875, p. 2.

and satisfaction as well . . . . " In the official "proceedings" of that convention reference is made to Mr. Buszin's twenty-four-year service as superintendent of schools. "This service is unique in that he is not only the *first* and *only* superintendent to serve this District, but also the pioneer superintendent in the entire Synod."*

Grouping the purposes of the Lutheran day school, the Northern Illinois District's school catalog lists these essential endeavors: "To assist in preserving the child in the discipleship of Christ begun in his Baptism; to be of service so that the education in behalf of the child at his Baptism, by the Church, the parents, and the sponsors, be as thorough as possible; to educate the child evenly, consistently alike, in the Christian home, the Christian church, and the Christian school; to teach and learn God's Word regularly, diligently, and faithfully; to teach and learn all other common school subjects in agreement with the truths of the Bible; to train children in godly living; to help in every way to rear true Christians, reliable Lutherans, and dependable, intelligent citizens of the nation."† Presently the director of Christian education, Northern Illinois District, is the Rev. Albert G. Merkens, M.A., Ph.D.‡ His installation took place on May 20, 1945.

There are at the present time thirty-three pastors and congregations in the Northern Illinois District area (Note) who are affiliated with the English District of the Missouri Synod. The "English District" has an interesting history. "On hearing that name today, the outsider, not knowing the history of our organization," recently wrote Dr. W. G. Polack, "is apt to set 'American' in contrast to 'English' and draw the conclusion that our English District is that section of our

*Northern Illinois District *Proceedings*, 1942, p. 71.

†Also quoted in the *Northern Illinois Messenger*, XIV, 8, p. 2.
(NOTE: Includes those in northwestern Indiana.)

‡Pastor Merkens received the Ph.D. degree in 1947 from the University of Pittsburgh.

PLATE VII

CENTENNIAL CELEBRATION

THE EVANGELICAL LUTHERAN SYNOD OF MISSOURI, OHIO AND OTHER STATES

founded at St. Paul's Church, Chicago, Illinois, April 26, 1847. Memorial Plaque to be found at southwest corner of LaSalle and Ohio Streets.

✠

THE EIGHTH SUNDAY AFTER TRINITY
July Twenty-seventh, Anno ✠ Domini 1947

✠

SOLDIER FIELD
ON THE LAKE
CHICAGO, ILLINOIS
three-thirty in the afternoon

1847 ✠ 1947

PLATE VIII

LUTHERAN · SYNOD · OF · MISSOURI ·
OHIO · AND · OTHER · STATES ·
· THE · EVANGELICAL ·
A ✠ D
MDCCC
XLVII
A ✠ D
MCM
XLVII
Spiritus
Gladius
DOMINUS
ILLUMINATIO
MEA ET SALUS
MEA QUEM TIMEBO
CENTENNIAL CONVENTION · CHICAGO · 1947 ·

Synod which has its antecedents in England."* Inasmuch as "English District" pastors, teachers, and congregations are playing an important role in Northern Illinois Lutheranism, a few remarks on the history of the English District are in place.

At the convention of the *Evangelical Lutheran Synodical Conference of North America*, July 15-21, 1874, in Pittsburgh, Pa.; the following excerpt from a report submitted by the Rev. Jonathan R. Moser in Missouri reads: "At the last meeting of our conference (composed of Lutheran pastors who used the English language in their pastoral work) in Webster County, Missouri, some action was had as to the propriety of uniting with the Synodical Conference with a view to finally becoming a part of that body." This *English Lutheran Conference* was organized by the three pastors Polycarp Henkel, Jonathan R. Moser, and Andrew Rader and the lay delegates of their congregations, at a convention held from August 16 to 20, 1872, at Gravelton, Wayne County, Mo. Shortly afterward Prof. C. F. W. Walther editorially expressed his interest in that conference. He concluded his comments with these words: "May it please God to lay His further gracious blessing on this small but blessed beginning of organized care for the scattered children of our Church in the West who speak the English language! May everyone who loves our Zion assist in requesting this from the Father of mercy in Jesus' name. Amen."†

The fifteenth convention of the English Lutheran Conference was held in 1888 in St. Louis, Mo. Upon the recommendation of the "German Missouri Synod" (1887), to the effect that an independent English synod be organized, the Conference adopted the name "The General Evangelical Lutheran Conference of Missouri and Other States." In the *Lutheran Witness*, shortly afterward, there appeared a "Draft

**The Lutheran Witness*, LXIII-3, p. 35.

†*Der Lutheraner*, XXIX, p. 180 (1872).

of a Constitution for a General Body of All English Lutherans Within the Synodical Conference." The preamble concludes with the sentence: "We, the Evangelical Lutherans of the English tongue, connected with the Synodical Conference, do hereby adopt the following constitution." The document, which contained seven "Articles," was signed by A. W. Weber and W. Dallmann.* At the 1891 convention the name of the "Conference" was changed to "Synod." At the third convention of the "English Synod," May 3-10, 1893, in Chicago,† the Rev. F. Kuegele, its president, submitted for discussion seven "Theses on Parish Rights." He introduced the theses with the following remarks: "Since the organization of our Synod in 1888, God has awakened among our German brethren an interest for the English work which is steadily growing. It cannot be otherwise but that those observing the drift of the times with an unprejudiced eye, must see the urgent necessity of establishing an English Lutheran Church having the same platform and practice as the strictly confessional German and Norwegian churches. Many are losing the language of their fathers, and finding no opportunity to worship in a Lutheran church, they either become utter strangers to the house of God or wander into sectarian folds."‡

At the English Synod's sixth convention, July 5-11, 1899, in Detroit, Mich., the vote on the "advisability of inquiring of the German Missouri Synod whether they could find ways and means to remove the barriers that ten years ago prevented us from becoming an English District of the German§ Missouri Synod" was taken and resulted in sixteen affirmative and eight negative votes.¶

A union of the two synods was consummated on Monday, May 15, 1911, while both were conducting their conventions

*_The Lutheran Witness_, VII, No. 5, p. 33.
†In First St. John's Church (Pastor Henry Succop).
‡English Synod _Proceedings_, 1893 (Harry Lang, Printer—Baltimore, Md.), p. 37, This record also contains the Constitution of the new synod.
§The term "German" was officially expunged from the Missouri Synod's name in 1917.
¶English Synod _Proceedings_, 1899, p. 53.

in St. Louis, Mo. The English Synod joined the "German" Synod as one of its Districts, with no territorial limitations.* What may be regarded as a dramatic scene is depicted thus: "Our Synod marched in a body to Holy Cross Church, where the German Delegate Synod was in session, and was received at the door by a special committee, which escorted us to seats of honor in the front of the church. The words spoken on that occasion will never be forgotten by those who were fortunate to be present on that memorable afternoon. The Spirit of God moved us deeply. We all felt the importance of what was transpiring. We preserve the words of the speakers. Pastor Biewend welcomed us as follows: 'We thank God, our heavenly Father, that He has fulfilled our hopes. You, dear brethren, have come back to your mother; you have come back to your brethren. You, indeed, ever were our brethren, but you did not dwell in the same house with us. Now you come to live under our roof. This has not come to pass by our wisdom and power, but by the hand of God. We also know that this is pleasing and acceptable to God, our heavenly Father. Yea, the angels of heaven rejoice. We have no doubt but that our dear Savior will say 'Well done!' President Eckhardt then responded as follows: 'Mr. President and Brethren of the Venerable German Synod of Missouri, Ohio, and Other States: The honor has been conferred on me to represent the English Synod of Missouri, acting as its first spokesman on this momentous and significant occasion. It is an honor of which I am not worthy. In the name of our body I heartily thank the preceding speaker for his kind words and hearty welcome extended to us in behalf of

*H. P. Eckhardt writes: "The plain facts are that in 1887 the small English group in Missouri petitioned the German Synod to be received as a separate English District and that the German Synod not only declined the petition, but also advised the organization to form a separate and independent English Synod. The German Synod was still altogether German and at that time both wanted and expected to remain German." (*The English District, a Historical Sketch*—printed and distributed by resolution of the English District convention, June, 1945, page 17.) Pastor Eckhardt, president of the English Synod, 1905-11, and a vice-president of the Missouri Synod, 1917-26, died on May 11, 1949, in Pittsburgh, Pa., at the age of 82.

your venerable body. We feel certain that we are finding a cordial reception and welcome among you. Our final vote on this union proposition was not unanimous. A few votes were recorded in the negative. But these were cast by delegates who felt that they must refer the matter back to their congregations. And such were their final declarations that we have every reason to hope and trust that not one of our congregations will be lost to us. Mr. President, I have the honor and pleasure to formally announce the final decision of our Synod as being favorable to district union. And we have come here in a body to ratify in this general meeting the common resolutions of both bodies. Such has been the spirit that has manifested itself in our deliberations, and yours, that we are convinced it was none other than the Holy Spirit of God, who ruled and led both bodies. Therefore we see in this result the hand of God pointing out to us the way in which we should go. And this fact is also our hope for the future. It is significant that this union is being consummated in this city of St. Louis, Mo. For it was in this place that our fathers wrote the early chapters of your venerable German Synod's history. It was in this city, twenty-three years ago, that our English Synod was organized and its opening chapter written. It is in this same place that this new chapter is now being written, telling of the union of the two Missouri bodies. May our God in heaven close this chapter with an approving Amen. And we add to it the old motto of Missouri: Soli Deo Gloria!' . . . Pastor Kuegele then gave expression to his joy in the following words in German: 'It is thirty-two years ago that our heavenly Father led me out of the Synod of Missouri. This took place when I accepted a call to an English congregation of the Ohio Synod. Heavy conflicts have passed over our American Lutheran Zion in these thirty-two years. This is well known to our older pastors, especially to all those that took a stand in the midst of the struggle. Our Great Shepherd, the Lord

Jesus Christ, frustrated the purpose of the evil Foe, and the true Lutheran Church came forth out of the Election Controversy strengthened and rejuvenated....' In conclusion, the venerable President of the German Synod, the Rev. F. Pfotenhauer, spoke the following words in German: 'This day is a day of great joy for the English and German Missouri Synods, not in this respect that we today for the first time greet one another and sit together as brethren. We have always been brethren, children of one Church. But in this respect is this day a day of great joy, because from today on we shall walk together hand in hand the same way which we regard as most advantageous for the work of our dear Church in this glorious land, which is our and our children's earthly fatherland. Now let us give all glory to Him to whom alone it is due, and unite in the singing of the Te Deum.' Dr. Luther's version of the Te Deum was then sung responsively between the teachers' choir and the delegates and guests. The exercises concluded with the Lord's Prayer and benediction."* "The answer to the question of amalgamation in the last analysis rests entirely with the English District."†

During the triennial convention of the Missouri Synod in June, 1917, its President, the Rev. Frederick Pfotenhauer, D.D., was instructed to appoint a committee to "look after the spiritual needs of our men called to the colors." The *Lutheran Church Board for Army and Navy* was composed of the following: the Rev. Carl Eissfeldt of River Grove, Ill., chairman; the Rev. F. C. Streufert, pastor of Peace Congregation, Chicago, secretary; Fred H. Wolff, layman of Chicago, treasurer; and the Rev. Karl G. Schlerf, pastor of Bethany (Eng-

*English Synod *Proceedings*, 12th Convention (Concordia Publishing House, St. Louis, Mo., 1911), pp. 73-76.

†"Amalgamation?"—a treatise by R. Jesse, mimeographed by request of the English District Pastoral Conference, East and West Detroit Circuits—page 2. NOTE: It is interesting, perhaps surprising, to learn that in Perry County, Missouri, efforts in English missions emanated even from the thoroughly German Saxons. Candidate Theo. Julius Brohm, who had taught English at the Hellweg Institute in Dresden, Germany (later pastor in New York City) in a letter dated in the year 1841 writes that "at the request of neighboring Americans he had a number of times preached in English in Perry County." The Rev. Andrew Baepler, in the early 1880's, did mission work among them.

lish) Congregation, Chicago, editor of the *Lutheran Soldiers' and Sailors' Bulletin.* The first of these bulletins was issued in December, 1917. "We had thirteen chaplains in the Army and Navy, five of whom were overseas, three in the Navy and five in different camps. We salaried seventy military pastors who gave full-time, and 124 camp pastors who gave part-time service."

During the triennial convention of the Missouri Synod in Cleveland, Ohio (June 19-28, 1935), several overtures appertaining to the appointment of "qualified pastors" to chaplaincy in the Army and Navy of the United States of America, "both in times of peace and war," were presented for discussion. A resolution was adopted, "that a committee be appointed to investigate the chaplaincy in order to ascertain whether or not a Lutheran pastor could serve in the chaplaincy in the Army and Navy without compromising the tenets of the Lutheran Church and violating conscience." A favorable report having been prepared and submitted to the Board of Directors of the Missouri Synod, a committee of five pastors* was chosen to represent Synod in this new field of church activity. The first meeting of this group, thenceforth officially called the *Army and Navy Commission of the Evangelical Lutheran Synod of Missouri, Ohio, and Other States,* to Serve Chaplains, Soldiers, and Sailors, was held on June 3, 1936, in Bronxville, N.Y. "Quietly the Commission went to work to fill the Church's quota of regular Army and Navy chaplains and to build a Chaplains' Reserve Corps," and when in the fall of 1940 the National Defense Program was put into effect, the Commission had on its roster the names of three regular Army and two regular Navy chaplains and of forty in the Reserve Corps. In November of the same year the offices of the Commission were established at 82 West Washington Street in Chicago,

*Pastors Geo. A. Romoser, D.D.; Paul L. Dannenfeldt, H. D. Mensing, F. C. Proehl, and Karl Schleede. Pastor Dannenfeldt was appointed chairman after Pastor Mensing's death (Dec. 16, 1940).

with the Rev. Edmund Weber in charge as executive secretary. In the following year, 1941, larger quarters were found in the La Salle-Wacker Building, 221 North La Salle Street. Being a Reserve Corps chaplain, Pastor Weber was called to active duty in the spring of 1942. His successor, the Rev. Paul Mehl, entered upon his duties here in the following October. Serving as director of public relations and as editor of publications and tracts for servicemen was the Rev. Lambert Brose, formerly pastor in Los Angeles, Calif. Other local men associated with the Commission were Theodore H. Schlake, treasurer; Otto C. Rentner, and the Rev. Louis J. Schwartzkopf, contact key pastor. One of the Commission's "Servicemen's Centers"*—supported, like many others, also by the National Lutheran Council—was maintained at 65 East Randoph Street, opposite the Chicago Public Library. This "Home Away from Home" was closed during the summer of 1946. In the spring of 1947 the Commission began to wind up its "war service" activities. Writing about the Commission's postwar activities, Pastor Brose in November, 1946, reported to this writer: "One of our biggest jobs at the present time, of course, is ministering to the sick and disabled veterans. More than 100 hospital pastors and chaplains are working in co-operation with the Commission in Veterans Hospitals, and a considerable amount of literature is now being prepared for their use." A profusely illustrated brochure depicting the Commission's postwar work was published for general distribution in the late spring of 1947 under the caption "Remember Me?" On the cover are a photographic reproduction of a smiling ex-serviceman on crutches and the following legend: "For Ninety Thousand Americans the War Is Not Over. They are still fighting—fighting to get well, fighting to learn to live with their disabilities, fighting to return to their homes. These men we dare never forget."

*The Church's slogan was: "They Shall Not March Alone."

On April 20, 1947, the Rev. Paul Mehl was installed as pastor of Saint Andrew's Congregation in Park Ridge, Ill., and on May 25, 1947, the Rev. Lambert Brose was installed as assistant pastor of Layton Park Congregation (the Rev. F. C. Proehl, pastor) in Milwaukee, Wis.* In April, 1948, the offices were moved to 736 Jackson Place, N.W., Washington, D.C.

In the fall of 1940 Henry Worthmann, an aged architect, and his grandson, Henry Wolter, then a student at Concordia Seminary, St. Louis, Mo., came to this writer's downtown office to discuss with him the advisability of conducting *Sunday worship services in Chicago's Loop.* On November 10,† the spacious anteroom of the writer's offices at 82 West Washington Street was converted into a chapel, and Student Wolter assumed charge. In the course of time, a more suitable place in the Kimball Building, at the northwest corner of Wabash Avenue and Jackson Boulevard, was rented for the purpose. Various pastors of the Synodical Conference, choirs, and soloists volunteered their services. Originally intended as an accommodation for downtown hotel guests, the services in 1941 were combined with a "social hour" for service men and women. Two special groups of singers, the Lutheran Vespers Ensemble, composed of seven girls,‡ and the Lutheran Vespers Treblettes, composed of five girls,§ participated, jointly on special occasions. Among the consistent promoters of this project, in addition to those already named, were William Bargmann, Arthur C. Schreibeı, Otto Reiner, and Mrs. Louis J. Schwartzkopf. A list of names of

*In 1946 the Rev. Lambert Brose married Miss Christine Biedermann, member of St. John's Congregation, Elgin, Ill.

†Dr. Martin Luther's birthday (Nov. 10, 1483).

‡The Misses Ethel Hoger, Irene Stringham, Edna Sommer, Dorothy Henle, Dorothy Carnitz, Alma Weisenstein, and Lucille Carnitz. This group appeared in white blouses and blue skirts.

§The Misses Ethel, Lorraine, and Carola Novak (sisters), Grace Buszin, and June Bunde. Others who for some time sang with the Treblettes were the Misses Carol Strehlow and Lois Dreyer. This group appeared in red jackets and white skirts. (In June, 1948, Miss Dreyer became the wife of the Rev. Frederick W. Danker; in June, 1949, Miss Ethel Novak, the wife of the Rev. Carvel V. Plitt.

those who in various ways supported the project, especially during the years 1942-1944, woud fill several pages of this book. The vespers were discontinued in June, 1944, when this writer, in charge of a pastorate on Chicago's South Side, was called upon to serve as missionary in a near-by public institution. A portable altar and a lectern which had been designed, manufactured, and donated to the cause by Henry Danker, a member of Jehovah Congregation, together with candleholders, crucifix, etc., were transferred to the auditorium of the Parkway Lodge, East Fifty-first Street and Vincennes Avenue (on the "Old Trail"). The Lutheran Vespers Treblettes won first-place honors on two Chicago radio "amateur hours" and during the year 1946 made ten one-half hour recordings for the Missouri Synod's radio station KFUO on the campus of Concordia Seminary, St. Louis, Mo. In recent years they have caroled during the Christmas holidays at various Chicago hospitals and convalescent homes.

The *Lutheran Publicity Association of Greater Chicago*, organized in 1926, emanated from what during the previous eight years had been functioning as the Lutheran Noonday Lenten Service Committee* of the Chicago Lutheran Pastoral Conference. From the latter committee the new organization "inherited" an operating fund of a thousand dollars. Representing the congregations affiliated with the Synodical Conference in the Chicago area, the Association extended its activities to other phases of dignified church publicity. From the beginning the administrative work was carried on by a board of directors consisting of five pastors elected by the Chicago Pastoral Conference, five laymen elected at the annual meeting of the Association, and one day school teacher elected by the Chicago Teachers' Conference. The Associa-

*The first specific reference to organized publicity efforts is found in the minutes of the English District Lutheran Pastoral Conference, Chicago, Feb. 6, 1917. "The Publicity Committee reported on advertising in the newspapers. The committee recommends: 30 times in the *News*, $14.50; 12 times in the *Examiner*, $3.30; 12 times in the *Staatszeitung*, $3.30."

tion distributed religious tracts, copies of the *Lutheran Witness*, and Luther's Small Catechism; conducted radio programs* on various Chicago stations, principally WAAF, and prepared news articles for the metropolitan and community newspapers. In 1929 it sponsored the four hundredth anniversary of the publication of Luther's Small Catechism in Soldier Field; the attendance was somewhere above the sixty-thousand mark. In 1930 the four hundredth anniversary of the Augsburg Confession was observed, with the presentation of a drama depicting the historical event, in the Civic Opera House. At the hundredth anniversary of Chicago's "birthday" (Century of Progress) in 1933 two exhibits were placed in the Hall of Religion. Nearly 100,000 persons† signed the guest register. On October 18, 1936, a drama portraying the life and work of Dr. Martin Luther, under the title "Luther, the Liberator," was staged in the Civic Opera House. The cast comprised five hundred people, augmented by a chorus of 420 voices. This drama was repeated on October 31, 1937, under the auspices of the Northern Illinois District Walther League, in the same auditorium.‡

In the spring of 1937 an office was established in the quarters occupied by the Schwartzkopf Mimeo Service at 82 West Washington Street. The telephone of this firm—Franklin 9733—was shared by the Association, and the proprietor of the "Service" (and his wife) received all calls for the Association and gave information concerning the Lutheran Church to inquirers who called by 'phone or in person. Re-

*Sermons by various local pastors; music by soloists and choirs.

†Men and women from every State in the Union and many foreign countries.

‡On Feb. 18, 1937, there appeared in the *Chicago Daily News* an editorial entitled "Luther, the Emancipator." " . . . . What other lessons may Americans draw from the life of the good and great man who, all unknowing, worked so marvelously for the freedom we enjoy? Particularly in this year when dictatorships in Europe are trampling down the rights of man, when certain elements in our own country seek to sap our constitutional guaranties, Americans of every creed may find Luther's qualities a wellspring of encouragement to persevere. He showed a lion's courage against entrenched authority. He hated cunning and intrigue. He argued—as in the Peasants' Revolt—for conference and conciliation rather than for tyranny or the mob's rule. Today, for many millions, this rugged peasant, this humble monk, this genial and charitable and dauntless champion of man, stands forever as the symbol of the free soul."

ferring to "professional church publicity representation," the Rev. John Evans, religion editor of the *Chicago Tribune*, on February 3, 1943, stated that the Association "maintains 24-hour-a-day newspaper service under the Rev. Louis J. Schwartzkopf." Between office hours the residential 'phone was used for such purposes. In June, 1938, this writer was appointed as the Association's "publicity director," and the congregations in Chicago and vicinity were informed by letter that the Publicity Office would be prepared to handle their news items. Thenceforth, at least once a week a set of brief stories concerning various "Lutheran Activities" was forwarded to the daily newspapers in Chicago. Beginning in January, 1944, the newspaper work and the information service were continued in this writer's residence. On January 20, 1947, the Association turned its various projects over to the newly established public relations department of the Northern Illinois District.* For several years a list of available student pastors, retired pastors, and theological professors was maintained. "All of this activity was carried on without any salary or other tangible compensation," wrote Edward W. Jaeger in a circular letter addressed to all pastors and delegates in the Chicago area shortly after the name of the Association was changed to "The Lutheran Bureau, Incorporated" (1942). From January 1, 1944, until January, 1949, the information service was carried on jointly with the central office of the Northern Illinois District, 77 West Washington Street, and this writer's household on the Midway Plaisance (site of the world's Columbian Exposition in 1893), the service at the latter place being rendered principally over the week ends.

In November, 1948, the Rev. A. H. Werfelmann, president of the Northern Illinois District, appointed a Public Rela-

*Resolutions concerning the creation of such a department were made during the 25th convention of the Northern Illinois District, June 25-27, 1945 (assembled at First St. Paul's Church, Chicago).

tions Committee, consisting of five members, to serve during the following three years; the Chicago Pastoral Conference of the English District added two men to this committee.

In Aurora the three Missouri Synod congregations* in December, 1946, issued the first edition of *The Aurora Lutheran*. The first major project of the Aurora Lutheran Publicity Bureau, this monthly publication "grew out of the *Emmanuel Messenger*," which (had) just completed its second year of publication . . . . Upon investigation it was decided to publish this enlarged paper in newspaper form rather than in that of a magazine. The managing editor is the Rev. A. E. Richert; the pastors of the two other congregations serve as associate editors. Its first advertising committee was composed of Benjamin F. Lewis, Ernest Rowoldt, and Arthur Ninke.

Efforts along the same lines had been repeatedly made in Chicago, but they ended in failure.

A periodical devoted to evaluating the past history of the Chicago area was published in May, 1942.† The feature article, titled "Grooming for the Reception," dealt with the problem of finding ways and means of gathering historical data for publication during the Missouri Synod's Centennial year (1947). The response was insignificant. However, on January 28, 1944, a Chicago Area Chapter of the Concordia Historical Institute‡ was organized in a meeting room at the Central Y.M.C.A., 19 South La Salle Street. "Two aged veterans in the ministry, Pastor Adolph Bartling and Dr. Wm. Dallmann, refused to miss the opportunity to attend. . . . Actually the meeting—after a buffet supper—lasted but two hours; however, during this period a constitution was adopted, twelve officers were chosen, addresses were made by the

*Emmanuel (A. E. Richert, pastor), St. Paul's (Walter G. Stallmann, pastor), and Our Savior (Paul G. Krentz, pastor).

†Edited by Victor W. Richter and this writer.

‡The Concordia Historical Institute, organized on March 31, 1927, has its headquarters at Concordia Seminary, St. Louis, Mo.

two veterans referred to and also by Pastors (Henry) Kowert and (John) Bajus, the latter representing the parent society, whose headquarters are in St. Louis, Mo. There was still room for two musical numbers, these being furnished by the Treblettes, prize singers of the downtown Lutheran Vespers . . . . The following officers were elected by ballot: Mr. E. G. Reimer, president; the Rev. Thomas Coates, vice-president; the the Rev. A. T. Kretzmann, recording secretary; Mr. V. W. Richter, corresponding secretary; Mr. A. W. Nimmer, treasurer; the Rev. L. J. Schwartzkopf, librarian and research director. The Board of Directors, also serving as trustees, was composed of the following: Prof. Carl S. Meyer of Luther Institute (Chicago), and Mr. F. W. Heuer for a three-year term, Mr. Otto Wachholz and Teacher C. H. Meier for a two-year term, and Pastors A. R. Kretzmann and Paul Roeder for a one-year term."* A spirit of lethargy has all but annihilated this "chapter."

The Lutheran Trail, the reader will have noticed, passes by and through cemeteries, too!

Prior to the year 1859 the city of Chicago maintained a common cemetery where Lincoln Park now is located.† At a meeting held on October 16, 1859, the only two Missouri Synod congregations within the city limits (First Saint Paul's and First Immanuel) decided to found a Lutheran cemetery in "faraway" Lake View. Fourteen and a half acres of land, partly on the east and partly on the west side of Green Bay Road (now North Clark Street) were purchased for $1,685, and the cemetery was dedicated on Pentecost Monday, 1860. In 1865 ten acres on the west side of the road were exchanged for the same number on the east side (adjoining the formerly purchased land), plus several acres which were swampland. Later this swamp was filled in with sand from Lake Michigan. The remains of many Lutherans were dis-

*_Concordia Historical Institute Quarterly_, XVII, 1, p. 3.

†The cemetery was transformed into a park a few years before the great Chicago Fire (Oct. 9, 1871).

interred from the old "city cemetery" and reinterred in the Lutheran cemetery, which according to its charter is known as the "German Evangelical Lutheran Cemetery," more popularly, however, as "*Wunder's Cemetery*," in memory of its original and principal promoter, the Rev. Henry Wunder, D.D., second pastor of First Saint Paul's Congregation. Because the Lake View* City council refused to grant permission to extend the cemetery area farther, the other Lutheran congregations in Chicago had to look elsewhere for burial plots. Thus came about the *Concordia Cemetery Association.* This association was organized on June 10, 1872, by the following congregations: First Saint John's, First Saint James, First Bethlehem, First Trinity, and First Saint Paul's. First Immanuel and Saint Matthew's joined within the next two years. The cemetery of the association, called "Concordia," is located at 8000 West Madison Street, near the Des Plaines River, in Forest Park (Harlem). The first sixty acres were purchased from a Mr. Haase at $800 the acre. On June 30, 1872, the cemetery was dedicated. The first burial here was on July 7, 1872. On February 25, 1884, the association was incorporated with a capital stock of $70,000, which amount was divided into seven hundred shares, each of the seven member congregations assuming 100 shares. In the same year the cemetery was enlarged by the purchase of ten adjoining acres, which cost $450 the acre. Two years later, in 1886, the Chicago Great Western Railroad Company laid tracks through the cemetery, for which $8,860 indemnity was awarded the association by the court. In 1889 the Entrance and Office Building and the Vault were erected at a cost of $14,573. In 1904 the obligation assumed by the seven congregations (ten thousand dollars each) was considered paid in full. In 1907 the association began to manufacture the "Concordia Burial Vaults." In 1913 the association (as a stock company) was dissolved, and a new corporation char-

*Lake View was annexed to Chicago in 1889.

ter was applied for (dated December 4, 1913) for the organization of the Concordia Association, the membership of which was limited to forty-two members, these being six members of each of the seven member congregations. In 1926 the Chicago, Aurora & Elgin Electric Railroad proposed constructing a railroad through the cemetery, but the plan was frustrated by the economic depression.

In April, 1894, the *Bethania Cemetery Association* ("Bethania Gottesacker Gesellschaft") was organized by seven congregations on Chicago's South Side: Holy Cross, Saint Andrew's, Saint Martini, Saint Stephen's, Bethlehem (Colehour—South Chicago), Saint Mark's, and Saint Paul's (Grand Crossing). The association purchased 114 acres of land at $200 the acre, on Archer Road (Avenue) and West 79th Street, near Summit, Ill. Dedication took place on July 15, 1894. The first burial was made here on July 22, 1894. The remains of the Missouri Synod's fifth President were laid to rest in Bethania Cemetery. (See plate after page 656.)

The principal reason why Zion Congregation, Nineteenth and Peoria Streets, did not join the association was that its pastor, the Rev. Anton Wagner, opposed the project on the grounds that it was not the business of congregations as such to engage in such enterprises. Later, however, when success was apparent, Zion Congregation was eager to join the association. Dr. Wunder's answer to Pastor Wagner was concise and decisive: "Anton, erst wolltet ihr nicht; jetzt sollt ihr nicht!" (Anton, at first you did not want to; now you shall not!)

On September 16, 1900, a meeting of the pastors and delegates of Missouri Synod congregations on Chicago's northwest side was held in the church of Saint Luke, Belmont and Greenview Avenues, for the purpose of obtaining another cemetery for the benefit of that territory. The following congregations were represented: Saint Luke, Christ (Logan

Square), Saint Philip's, Concordia, and Saint John's (Mayfair). However, only two of the five congregations, Christ and Saint Luke, took part in the founding, on October 19, 1900. A seventy-one acre tract of land on North Crawford Avenue (now Pulaski Road), near Foster Avenue, was purchased. The cemetery, named *St. Lucas*, was dedicated on October 21, 1900. About a week later, on October 29, the first burial took place here. At the time of the purchase there was a saloon on a piece of property near the entrance to St. Lucas Cemetery. The proprietor refused to sell to the association. However, he finally yielded, and this property was added to the area in 1919.*

The Missouri Synod Lutheran churches were the first Protestants to begin mission work in the public institutions of Chicago and Cook County. The beginning was made in 1895, when several Christian men and women began visiting a number of aged and forsaken Lutherans in the Cook County Poor House, then located in the community known as Dunning, in the northwestern part of Chicago. The Chicago Lutheran Pastoral Conference in 1896 officially recognized the missionary opportunities among the thousands of unfortunate and spiritually neglected inmates of the public institutions and placed the Rev. Paul Luecke† in charge of this venture. He was assisted by several other pastors, including pastors Ernst Werfelmann, Carl F. Dietz, and Martin Fuelling. On May 19, 1901, the Rev. August Schlechte of Mishawaka, Ind., was installed as the first regular city missionary, supported by the *Chicago Lutheran City Mission Society*, which was organized on June 10, 1900. On May 4,

*NOTE: At the 65th general assembly of the State Legislature in Springfield, Ill. (1946), certain cemetery bills were presented which were designed to govern the cemeteries within the State of Illinois. A commission was appointed by Governor Dwight Green to study the laws of other States, with the view to preparing a cemetery code for Illinois. Ernest H. Kieper, business manager of St. Lucas Cemetery and member of Christ Congregation (Logan Square), was appointed to serve on this Commission. The official report was published in June, 1947.

†Pastor of Saint John's Congregation, Mayfair, Chicago, 1886-1944.

PLATE IX

Programm

— für die —

Einweihungsfeier

— des —

Evang.-Luth. Concordia-Colleges

— zu —

River Forest, (Chicago), Ill.

Sonntag, den 12. Oktober 1913.

---

1. **Posaunenchor.**
   Dirigent: E. G. Hoffmann.

2. **Eröffnung der Feier** durch Pastor Fr. Brunn, Präses des Nord Illinois-Distrikts.

3. **Gemeindegesang:** Nr. 10, 1—5. „Nun jauchzet dem HErrn alle Welt."

4. **Männerchor.** „Jauchzet Gott, alle Lande." Dirigent P. D. Frieser.

5. **Die deutschen Redner:** Dr. F. Pieper vom Concordia-Seminar in St. Louis, Mo., Direktor E. Albrecht vom Concordia-College in Milwaukee, Wis. und Direktor M. Luecke vom Concordia-College in Ft. Wayne, Ind.

6. **Kinderchor.** „Dir, HErr, sei Preis." J. J. Wachsmann. Dirigent: T. T. Buszin.

7. **Gemeindegesang.** Nr. 158. „Ein feste Burg ist unser Gott."

8. **Die englischen Redner:** Prof. F. Bente vom Concordia-Seminar in St. Louis, Mo.; Pastor W. Koepchen aus New York City und Direktor G. Weller vom Lehrer-Seminar in Seward, Nebr.

9. **Gemischter Chor.** "The heavens resound." Dirigent: O. F. Rusch.

10. Hymn:

Praise God, from whom all blessings flow;
Praise Him all creatures here below;
Praise Him above, ye heavenly host;
Praise Father, Son, and Holy Ghost.

11. **Posaunenchor.**

II.

1. **Weiheakt.** Ueberreichung der Schlüssel durch Herrn Paul Schulze, dem Vorsitzer des Baukomitees, an den Vertreter der Allgemeinen Synode. Dieser schließt die Tür auf, und übergiebt dann im Namen der Synode dem Direktor der Anstalt, Herrn W. C. Kohn, die Schlüssel zur Verwahrung.

2. **Weihgebet,** gesprochen von Pastor Theo. Kohn, dem Sekretär der Aufsichtsbehörde.

3. **Segen und Vater Unser,** gesprochen vom Direktor der Anstalt, W. C. Kohn.

4. **Posaunenchor.**

5. **Besichtigung der Anstalt.** Die Besichtigung der Anstalt geschieht nach dem Gottesdienst. Eingang nur vorn bei den großen Säulen. In den Hallen sind Führer postiert, welche den Zug leiten. Alle Räume stehen offen, sollten aber nicht betreten werden, weil sonst alles in's Stocken gerät. Von der Halle aus kann man bequem die Zimmer überschauen.

Festkollekte.

Die Festkollekte wird vor und nach dem Gottesdienste von Kollektoren erhoben, welche am Ärmel ihres Rockes ein Abzeichen tragen mit der Aufschrift "C. T. C." (Concordia Teacher's College). Jedem, der eine Gabe gibt, wird ein "Souvenir" überreicht, welches er anstecken kann. Auf diese Weise wird es ermöglicht, jeden Festgenossen um eine Gabe anzusprechen, und wird auch vermieden, daß viele mehrere Male um eine Gabe angegangen werden. Die Kollekte wird zur Herrichtung des Anstalt-Grundstückes verwandt werden.

Erfrischungen.

Kaffee und Brödchen sind in Zelt 1 und 2, **Getränke** in Zelt 3 und **Ice Cream** in Zelt 4 zu haben. Diese Zelte werden hinter den Gebäuden aufgerichtet sein.

Redner.

Die deutschen Redner, die zu gleicher Zeit reden werden, sind folgende: Dr. F. Pieper vor dem Lehrgebäude; Direktor E. Albrecht neben dem östlichen Wohngebäude; Direktor M. Luecke, neben dem westlichen Wohngebäude. — Die englischen Redner, die auch zu gleicher Zeit reden werden, sind: Prof. F. Bente vor dem Lehrgebäude; Pastor W. Koepchen neben dem östlichen Wohngebäude; Direktor G. Weller neben dem westlichen Wohngebäude.

PLATE X

1919, a second missionary, the Rev. J. H. Witte* of Cleveland, Ohio, was installed. In October, 1920, Pastor Schlechte was succeeded by the Rev. Henry G. Sandvoss of Joliet, Ill. In 1927 the Rev. Emil Zapf of Melrose Park, Ill., was added to the missionary staff. Others who have served in this field of activity were (are) the Rev. Traugott Thieme, the Rev. Gerhard Roehrs, the Rev. William Greve, the Rev. Alex Ullrich, and the Rev. Marcus Wagner, D.D. Deaconesses assisting the missionaries were the Misses Louise Wegner and Frieda Bremermann. The *Lutheran Welfare Society*, organized in 1901, placed its resources at the disposal of the city missionaries and specialized in the distribution of alms and edibles among the Lutheran communicants at the Cook County Infirmary and Tuberculosis Hospital (Oak Forest), at the State Hospital for the Insane (Dunning), at the Lutheran Old Folks' Home (Arlington Heights), and other institutions. At the delegate meeting of the Chicago Lutheran City Mission Society, January 30, 1944, the chairman of the Lutheran Welfare Society (F. Zirzow) reported that "over 6,000 Christmas packages were distributed at Christmas time (1943) alone at the following institutions: Old Folks' Home, 75; County Jail, 675; Juvenile Home, 275; State Hospital, 1,058; County Hospital, 1,780; Municipal Tuberculosis Sanatorium, 1,202; County Infirmary, 902; two Orphan Homes, 200, and Home for the Blind, 6. In addition, the Society gave food to 500 at the annual outing; 2,400 were served at Dunning with tobacco, candy, or fruit; over 6,000 were served with coffee cake; the Society donated $100 for chairs at the Municipal Tuberculosis Sanatorium, etc."

On July 1, 1944, the Chicago Lutheran City Mission Society was merged with the Northern Illinois District. In the same year a committee representing both the Northern Illi-

*A son, the Rev. Edgar F. Witte, has served as executive director of the Chicago Lutheran Charities since June, 1944. Pastor J. H. Witte died on Sept. 18, 1947, in Ann Arbor, Mich., at age 76.

nois and the English District congregations in the Chicago area was appointed to develop a plan "to co-ordinate the efforts of the several congregations . . . in the support and maintenance of charitable and educational institutions." This resulted in the founding of *The Lutheran Church, Missouri Synod, Charities Fund.* Provision was made for an equitable distribution of funds received from the congregations and individuals in accordance with the needs of specified institutions of charity.

The *Lutheran Charities of Chicago,* organized on November 24, 1936, is a federation of twenty-three Lutheran charitable agencies and institutions in northern Illinois, comprising institutions operated by the Missouri Synod, the American Lutheran Church, the Danish Ev. Lutheran Church, the Augustana Synod, the Illinois Synod of the United Lutheran Church, and the Norwegian Lutheran Church of America. This federation's office budget is met by subsidy from the Community Fund, by appropriations from synodical boards and fund-raising bodies, and by contributions from interested individuals. It acts as fiscal agent for its member agencies in applying for and distributing funds from the Community Fund. It co-ordinates the services and programs of all Lutheran agencies in this area and thus prevents overlapping of effort and duplication of services. It provides common services for the mentioned agencies, representation in the Juvenile Court and in social planning bodies, and conducts a central referral service, to which other welfare and social agencies may refer Lutherans for welfare service. Its headquarters are now located at 343 South Dearborn Street, Chicago, with the Rev. Edgar F. Witte, formerly pastor of Pilgrim Congregation (Missouri Synod) in St. Paul, Minn., serving as this organization's executive director since June 1, 1944.

The story of the origin and development of the *Lutheran*

*Old Folks' Home** in Arlington Heights is graphically told in the "service booklet" distributed on the occasion of this institution's fiftieth anniversary, July 12, 1942. "'Great oaks from tiny acorns grow.' The acorn from which this institution grew was planted quite casually by a nameless, obscure Lutheran, evidently in poor circumstances. But fortunately it fell on good ground, on the warm and fertile heart of a great leader of Chicago's early Lutheranism, the Rev. August Reinke, then the pastor of (First) Bethlehem Church (Chicago). It happened thus. Always alert to the challenge of new fields of service, Pastor Reinke in an address to his congregation had referred to the necessity of providing a place of refuge for old homeless, neglected Lutherans. Two days later he received an unsigned letter, urging him to proceed with the establishment of an 'Altenheim' (home for the aged) and enclosing a gift of twenty-six cents for a building fund." Pastor Reinke "forwarded it to the District Treasurer, and this methodical person listed it in his annual reports as 'for the building of an Altenheim, 26 cents . . . . In 1892 life began to stir in the little mustard seed. [Acorn!] Disturbed by the annual appearance of those twenty-six cents in the financial report, Pastor Reinke . . . resolved to arouse wider interest in an institution for old brethren of the faith. In the post-Easter conference of Chicago's (Lutheran) pastors he pleaded for the cause . . . . The pastors approved the project wholeheartedly and backed their interest by appropriate action. A general meeting of all Missouri Synod churches of the metropolitan area was called for the following month to discuss the forming of an 'Altenheim-Gesellschaft' (Old Folks' Home Association) and the building of an institution . . . . Before the close of the year the association was organized." Four acres of land were purchased in Arlington Heights (formerly called Dunton) for $500, and a building was erected at a cost of $25,000. Dedication took

*Recently renamed "Lutheran Home and Service for the Aged."

place on August 20, 1893. The first chaplain was the Rev. John Edmund Roeder, pastor of the near-by Saint Peter's Congregation. A west wing was added at a cost of $7,000 in 1902 and 1903, with dedication on August 8, 1903. A south wing was erected in 1921 and 1922 at a cost of $30,000 and dedicated on July 9, 1922. This section provided a small chapel and living rooms for forty more persons. Plans for the erection of a new and larger building have been made. Pastor Roeder's successor as chaplain was the Rev. Carl M. Noack (1899-1944). In charge of the "Home" from 1893 to 1897 were Mr. and Mrs. Frederick Bornhoeft; from 1897 to 1907, Mr. and Mrs. Henry Studtmann, Sr.; from 1907 to 1928, Mr. and Mrs. Carl Stier; from 1928 to 1938, Mr. and Mrs. Julius Stahmer. Following the death of her husband on July 4, 1938, Mrs. Stahmer carried on alone as superintendent until 1941. On December 10, 1941, the Rev. John Kempf* assumed the superintendency of the Home, being formally inducted into his office on January 18, 1942, in Saint Peter's Church, Arlington Heights.

The *Evangelical Lutheran Orphan Home* at Addison was brought into being as the result of a somewhat casual remark made at the convention of the Missouri Synod in St. Louis, Mo., in May, 1872. Someone suggested the desirability of having an orphan home in the vicinity of the Teachers' Seminary in that village, "damit aus den Waisenkindern eine Uebungsschule fuer die Seminaristen gegruendet werden koennte" ("so that a practice school for the students could be developed from the orphanage"). No official action was taken at that time. However, a report was circulated by the public press to the effect that the Missouri Synod had resolved to erect such an institution. A month after the synodical convention a certain congregation sent a contribution to Addison "fuer das Waisenhaus" ("for the orphan home").

*Pastor Kempf came from Detroit, Mich., where he had been serving as field secretary for the Lutheran Institute for the Deaf.

This contribution was followed by many others, a fact which induced a number of Lutherans in northern Illinois to do something about the matter. An *Orphan Home Association* was organized on June 27, 1873, in the Teachers' Seminary at Addison by fourteen congregations.* The first building was erected on a thirty-acre piece of land, directly west of the village and near the Teachers' Seminary.† Dedication took place on October 12, 1873. In the following year a larger building was erected with provision for about fifty children. The first "Orphan Home Festival" took place on September 27, 1877. The attendance at these festivals increased year by year, particularly after the Illinois Central in 1890 had constructed a branch line to Addison. Another building, providing for fifty additional children, was erected in 1878; a small two-story addition, primarily for sick children, was built in 1889. Then, in 1896, an 80x50 foot annex was erected at a cost of approximately $11,000. In charge of the home temporarily were Mr. and Mrs. F. G. Albers of Town Rich (Skunks Grove). Others, subsequently, were: Mr. and Mrs. John Harmening (1874-1891); Mr. and Mrs. Ernst Leubner (1891-1902); the Rev. and Mrs. H. Merz (1902-1917); the Rev. and Mrs. A. Klaus; the Rev. and Mrs. M. K. C. Vetter.

In 1934 the Addison Orphan Home Association absorbed the Lutheran Children's Friend Society of Peoria, Ill.

The Rev. August Schlechte, first city missionary of the Missouri Synod in Chicago, frequently had occasion to seek suitable homes for children who, according to ordinary rules, could not be placed into an orphan home. A special home for such children ("Kinderheim") was established in 1909 by the Chicago Lutheran City Mission Society at 2929 Warren

*First St. Paul's, First Trinity, First St. John's, First St. James, and First Zion of Chicago; St. Peter's, Schaumburg; Zion, Addison (Duncklees Grove); Immanuel (Proviso); St. John's (Forest Park—Harlem); St. John's, Rodenburg; Immanuel, Dundee; Trinity, Crete; Cross, Yorkville; and St. Paul's, Kankakee.

†The original purchase included 54 acres; 15 were sold to the Missouri Synod in the interest of the Teachers' Seminary.

Avenue, Chicago. Within a few months this place had become too small. A larger building was erected at Rockwell and Hirsch Streets and dedicated in June, 1910. In 1914 the Chicago Lutheran City Mission Society purchased the building formerly occupied by the Teachers' Seminary at Addison. After the work of remodeling the building had been completed, the "Kinderheim" (children's home) was moved to Addison in December, 1916. In 1924 the "Kinderheim Association" made arrangements with the City Mission Society for the erection of a large building, which cost about $225,000. This new "Kinderheim" was dedicated on December 27, 1925. "Pastor Schlechte recognized the valuable contribution which ministering women could offer his new activity, and together with his wife he began to organize women into groups who would gather in his home to sew and work for the children . . . . In 1916 these women organized the *Kinderheim Auxiliary,* one of the earliest auxiliaries within our Synod and the first in Chicagoland." On May 15, 1934, another society was organized for the purpose of giving special assistance to the children in the Orphan Home. This organization was known as "*Adoha,*" a name composed of the first letters of these words: "**A**ddison **O**rphan **H**ome **A**id." The society's slogan was "**A**rdent **D**oers **O**f **H**is **A**ssignments."

In 1940 plans for the reorganization and amalgamation of the Orphan Home and the "Kinderheim" were formulated. At a meeting of the delegates of seventy member congregations on July 21, 1940, the two organizations were merged, and the new organization was named the *Lutheran Child Welfare Association.* The first executive secretary of this new association was the Rev. T. H. Thormahlen, Jr., who came to Addison from Mattoon, Wis., in October, 1937; his assistant was the Rev. John H. Mueller, who had served as superintendent of the "Kinderheim" from 1927 till 1940;*

*Miss Lulu Kropp, assistant superintendent and matron of the "Kinderheim," 1922-1940, died in December, 1940.

soon afterward Pastor Mueller was succeeded by the Rev. Reinhold Albert Marquardt. In March, 1944, Pastor Marquardt accepted a call as executive secretary of the Lutheran Child Welfare Association at Indianapolis, Ind. He was succeeded in Addison by the Rev. Herbert R. Neitzel. In August, 1946, Pastor Thormahlen accepted a call to the Bethlehem Lutheran Children's Home, Staten Island, N.Y., and Pastor Marquardt succeeded him to the superintendency at Addison. Early in 1949 Pastor Neitzel also accepted a call to Staten Island, N.Y. In a special evening service on Sunday, October 23, 1949, the Rev. Harry N. Huxhold of Darien, Wis., was installed as Pastor Neitzel's successor at the "Kinderheim."

The *Lutheran Hospital,* located at 1116 North Kedzie Avenue, Chicago, in 1923 was "dedicated to the service of God and humanity and to the memory of Lutheran soldiers and sailors who died for their country in the World War." In 1939, the year which marked the centennial of the Saxon immigration to the State of Missouri, the hospital's name was changed to Walther Memorial Hospital, in memory of the Rev. C. F. W. Walther, D.D., first President of the Missouri Synod. This hospital "can never be operated for profit, nor can any profit accrue to anyone as a result of its activities. All surplus over and above operating charges and debt liquidation must be devoted to improvement or expansion of the service it renders. Fees received from those able to pay have enabled the hospital to extend approximately $12,000 in charity service annually to the deserving and worthy poor."

In the *Chicago "Medical Center,"* which now covers about a square mile on Chicago's near West Side and includes four large hospitals, four medical schools, two schools of nursing, and the schools of dentistry, pharmacy, and embalming, mission work has been carried on since about the turn of the century. Regular services have for some time been conducted in the chapel of the Cook County Hospital. On May 18, 1947, the Rev. William R. Miessler of Herington, Kans., was commissioned missionary of this "Center."

At its convention in June, 1939, the Northern Illinois District established the *Office of Stewardship Secretary,* and elected the Rev. Martin Piehler* to assume this responsibility. The formal installation of the secretary took place during the last session of the convention, on Friday afternoon, June 28, 1940, with the Rev. Ernest T. Lams, D.D., president of the District, officiating and the Rev. Oscar Fedder giving the formal address.

At this time, 1940, it was found necessary to centralize the ever-expanding activities of the District's boards, commissions, and committees. To effect this, a small office was rented in the Chicago Temple (Methodist) Building, 77 West Washington Street, Chicago, and on September 15, 1942, Pastor Piehler and his secretary, Miss Johanna Runge, began occupying this office. Three months later the District's Board of Directors rented additional space to satisfy the demands for more meeting rooms. The office at this time, 1949, occupies approximately two thousand square feet and employs five full-time secretaries. All District officials, boards and committees, many of the Missouri Synod's committees, boards and officials, and all non-budget charitable and educational agencies are using its facilities. Adjacent to the District's office the Missouri Synod has leased offices for its Student Service Commission and the Board for Higher Education. Dr. Piehler serves also as Transportation Secretary for the Missouri Synod.

The *Lutheran Laymen's League* had its inception during the convention of the Missouri Synod in June, 1917, in Milwaukee, Wis. "The social and economic upheaval caused by

*Pastor of Zion, 113th Street and Edbrooke Avenue, Chicago (Roseland), 1928-1940. He received his honorary degree, D.D., from Concordia Seminary, Springfield, Ill., in June, 1946.

the war had affected the work of the Church .... A hitherto unheard-of deficit of about $100,000 was burdening the Synod's treasury." A group of lay delegates, wealthy businessmen, at that time met in the home of Fred C. Pritzlaff to discuss the problem of liquidating all or part of that debt. Before the meeting was over, $26,000 had been pledged. After the meeting, about midnight, a terrific thunderstorm raged in Milwaukee. "The next morning, while talking about the storm, Mr. Bosse (of Evansville, Ind.) remarked that it had been such a wonderful exhibition of God's power that the Lord thundered another thousand out of him; and he made good by raising his subscription from one to two thousand." Each man present expressed the willingness to "cover a certain prescribed territory of Synod, and thus the money was collected." The second meeting was held on October 1, 1917, in Chicago (in the Sherman Hotel). At this time a resolution to make the Lutheran Laymen's League (L.L.L.) a permanent organization was passed. On December 3, 1917, the League set as its next purpose the gathering of a fund of $250,000 or more to be presented to Synod in 1920 as a "Permanent Endowment Fund for the better support of superannuated professors, pastors, and teachers or their widows or orphans." The first president of the Northern Illinois L.L.L. was Martin L. Daib of Chicago. For a number of years the latter group sponsored a "Christian Free Employment Bureau" and an agency for the collection of used household furnishings for the needy. The League's most comprehensive project is the support of the Lutheran broadcast known as the Lutheran Hour,* the first of which took place on October 2, 1930, over Station WHK, Ceveland, Ohio. The speaker was Dr. Walter A. Maier, and the musical portion of the half-hour program was presented by the Cleveland Bach Chorus.

*Lutheran Hour rallies have been held annually, with few exceptions, in the Amphitheater (Stockyards), the Chicago Stadium, and Medinah Temple.

In 1939 several "mission-minded laymen" of the northwest suburbs of Chicago surveyed the northern area of the District and found a decided need for churches. They interested neighboring congregations, and soon afterward another society came into being, this one known as the *Lutheran Mission Crusaders.* Their object was to find mission opportunities and with the aid of the Mission Board of the Northern Illinois District to establish new congregations. The first spiritual adviser was the Rev. J. E. A. Mueller of Mount Prospect. Meetings are held once a month, and dues are one dollar per year.

Mission work in *Chicago's "Chinatown,"* which occupies several blocks centering at Wentworth Avenue and West Cermak Road (22d Street), was begun in October, 1936, by Mrs Verna Schulz, a lay worker.* For about eighteen months she worked in this community, paying her own expenses and supplying the necessary material, such as Sunday school leaflets, etc. Encouraged by several pastors, she requested the Mission Board of the Northern Illinois District either to take over this work or to give her some assistance. Agreeing to lend financial aid, the board also requested the Rev. Arnold H. Semmann, a member of the board, to supervise this mission endeavor. On May 9, 1937, a Sunday school was established in the Chinese Y.M.C.A. building, on Cermak Road, near the western end of "Chinatown." On the following Sunday the first preaching service was conducted here.† Soon afterward another place was rented, at the northeast corner of West Twenty-second Place and Shields Avenue. On December 12, 1937, fourteen children, which included Chinese, Mexican, and Italian pupils of the "Chinatown" Sunday school, were baptized in a special afternoon service held

*She and her husband are members of St. Paul's, Austin (Chicago); Mr. Schulz is a son of the Rev. John H. H. Schulz, pastor of St. John's, Ash Grove, Ill., 1921-1923; died Aug. 27, 1923.

†Sermons by the Rev. Arnold H. Gebhardt and this writer, both for some years missionaries in China. (Language: English.)

in Saint Andrew's Church, Park Ridge, by Pastor Semmann. In 1940 the following report was submitted at the Northern Illinois District's convention in River Forest: "After many efforts have failed, after many disappointments and discouraging experiences, after many ups and downs in the mission in Chinatown, your Reviewing Committee believes your Mission Board is planning wisely by trying to find a consecrated servant of the Lord of mature age and experience in the ministry who would also be willing to organize a Christian day school." On December 23, 1943, all preparations had been made for the Christmas services; on the following day a fire broke out in the "chapel," destroying, among other things, all the newly acquired choir robes. Other pastors who have served in "Chinatown" were the Rev. Robert W. Rippe, now missionary in Argentina, South America; the Rev. L. A. Buuck, former missionary in China, now at Arcadia, Ind.; the Rev. R. J. Mueller, former missionary in China, now at Chaska, Minn.; the Rev. Daniel Wenz;* the Rev. Paul E. Meyer, now at Milford, Ill.; and the Rev. Edmund Puseman, now U.S. Army Chaplain, Washington, D.C.

In recent years, the work in "Chinatown" was connected with the mission among the Negroes occupying the "Ida B. Wells" Government Housing Project located at 3700 Cottage Grove Avenue. Co-operating in the latter for some time was the Mission Activities Group of Concordia Teachers College, River Forest.

Because of the rise in rental "to exorbitant heights" the building on Cottage Grove Avenue was abandoned in 1948. The only available place in the area for services and Sunday school was Mr. Sims' undertaking establishment, which he made available for these purposes. The school with its teacher and children was moved into "Chinatown." Recently, however,

*Pastor of St. John's, Niles (Dutchman's Point), Ill., 1942-46.

because of transportation hazards, this school was closed, pending the erection of a chapel at the corner of East thirty-seventh Street and Lake Park Avenue, where a building site was acquired for about $4,000. The Senior Chaplain and Mission Counselor of the Northern Illinois District reports that "frequently one or several corpses are present during the Sunday school sessions and worship services." Concerning the mission in "Chinatown," he recently said to this writer: "Many of the Chinese have moved away; but the work among these people was not in vain. Missions in other parts of the country have been started among the Chinese with a nucleus of people who had joined our church in Chicago's 'Chinatown.' The few remaining members of the flock, mostly Negroes, are now meeting with the group in the afore-mentioned undertaking parlors." On Sunday, November 13, 1949, the new chapel, 30x57 and constructed of brick, was formally dedicated as the Lutheran Church of Christ, the King.

Mission work among the Jews was begun by the Missouri Synod in 1881 in New York City, N.Y. In the 1930's the Rev. Isadore Schwartz began mission work among the Jews of Chicago. At the 1933 convention of the Northern Illinois District it was reported that this mission "will no longer be financed by the General Synod,"* and the question "What is to be done?" was answered with a formal resolution to the effect that the matter be placed "into the hands of the Mission Board of the Northern Illinois District, with the plea to continue in this work, if possible." Soon afterward this work was discontinued, and Missionary Schwartz severed his connections with the Missouri Synod.†

In 1923 the Missouri Synod referred the matter of preparing literature for the blind to the Board of Missions for the Deaf. In 1926 Synod resolved to print literature for the blind,

*Meaning the Missouri Synod as a body.

†His son, the Rev. Arthur N. Schwartz, graduate of Concordia Seminary, St. Louis, Mo., served as institutional missionary in Norfolk, Nebr. (1945-47). Since November, 1947, he has held a pastorate in Pasadena, Tex.

and in the fall of that year Dr. Luther's Small Catechism, with brief explanations by Dr. William Dallmann, was published in Braille. The first issue of the *Lutheran Messenger* in Braille appeared in January, 1927. The first Moon Type magazine appeared in February, 1928. The *Lutheran Library for the Blind* is located at 11251 South Homewood Avenue, Chicago.* The Rev. Otto C. Schroeder has served as librarian and manager since 1941, when Synod took over this project. In December, 1943, the Rev. Clarence Bremer, missionary to the deaf and blind in the State of Wisconsin, became assistant librarian, a position which he held until 1945, when he accepted a call to a congregation in Minneapolis, Minn. Lutheran periodicals now serve approximately five thousand blind persons and groups of blind in nearly all the States of the Union and in the Provinces of Canada, as well as in foreign countries: England, Scotland, Ireland, Australia, New Zealand, the West Indies, the Philippines, the Fiji Islands, South Africa, China, Egypt, Palestine, Holland, Sweden, Denmark, Romania, Latvia, Switzerland, Poland, Hungary, Estonia, Iceland, Syria, India, Greece, Italy, and, in normal times, also Germany. Mr. and Mrs. E. D. Diener and their son, Jimmy, who is blind, are members of the Congregation of St. Luke, Chicago. Mrs. Diener several years ago "took up Braille . . . primarily to help Jimmy with his learning of Braille. When she heard of our Lutheran Library for the Blind, she offered her services as a transcriber direct from ink print into Braille, so that our Lutheran literature can be the more quickly put into the code of the blind."

Shortly before the turn of the century the *Evangelical Lutheran Associated Young Men's Societies* was organized in Chicago, principally for the purpose of "keeping our young people in our midst and in proper surroundings on Christian social and athletic matters." Its first president was Frank C.

*Acquired by Synod in April, 1943, the building was dedicated on Nov. 28, 1943. The building, of brick construction, has six rooms for living quarters on the first floor and a second-floor room, 22 x 46, for shelves and tables.

Haeger. In 1907 this association became the source of still another organization, known as the *Concordia League*, which included in its chief objectives the promotion of higher education. An office was established and maintained at 77 South Clark Street, with William Gakemeier serving as the first business manager. Its official organ was *The Concordia League Messenger*. The first officers were: Robert A. Schoenfeld, president; Martin C. Koebel, secretary; and Frank C. Haeger, treasurer. Successors in the presidency were Albert W. Beilfuss, Paul Schulze, William Busse, and Frank C. Haeger. On March 11, 1907, a committee was appointed to devise ways and means for the establishment of a Lutheran high school in Chicago. A special meeting, to which also pastors and teachers were invited, was held on May 27, 1907, in the downtown office of Gustav J. Tatge. At this meeting a board of directors, comprising Pastors Ferdinand Sievers, A. J. Buenger, and J. H. Haake, Teachers William Burhop, M. Gotsch, and O. F. Rusch, and League members Julius Geweke, William Schulz, C. F. Claussen, Chas. H. Zuttermeister, F. Buszin, William Seehausen, C. F. Ziegler, Chas. F. Thoms, and H. Utpatel, was elected. On August 6, 1908, the charter for a *Lutheran high school in Chicago* was granted by the Secretary of State (Illinois). Formal opening of the institution, known as *Luther Institute*, took place on April 19, 1909, in the school building of the First Immanuel Congregation, Marshfield Avenue and Twelfth Street (Roosevelt

*Among the organizers:
William G. Bock
William E. Brockschmidt
Claus S. Claussen
P. J. Claussen
F. Dabelstein
Theo. H. Doering
William C. Faehse
Andrew Fuhrmann
O. C. Holtz
John A. Keil
John C. Krietenstein
Theo. H. Lambrecht
William L. Laib
William R. Lense
J. J. Luening
Chas. H. Marquardt
William A. Narten
H. A. Raddy
Emil Ramming
F. W. Roepstorf
E. P. Richter
F. A. Schroeder
Albert Segler
Gustav J. Tatge
Edward W. Tatge
Chas. F. Thoms
Paul G. Ullrich
C. D. Ziegler
Chas. H. Zuttermeister
F. W. Volkert
Paul L. Haertel
Edward Thiele
Henry Gruetzmacher
Pastors Active in League:
August Schlechte
A. J. Buenger
Ernest T. Lams
Guido Schuessler
Karl G. Schlerf
Ernst Werfelmann
Carl F. Dietz
Theo. Graebner
Teachers Active in League:
Oscar F. Rusch
R. F. Nimmer
Henry Burmeister
E. J. Kemnitz
H. T. Ellermann

Road). The school's first president, the Rev. W. C. Hermann, B.A., was installed at a special evening service in First Immanuel Church on the previous evening by the Rev. Louis Hoelter. Others serving on the original faculty were David Gamble Chase, M.A., Luther T. Smith, and the Rev. Edward Hoelter. At that time the enrollment was sixty-six students. On November 11, 1909, Luther Institute was given wide publicity in a Luther Day celebration at Orchestra Hall on South Michigan Avenue. The principal speakers were Dr. A. Hoermann of Northwestern College, Watertown, Wis., and Dr. William H. T. Dau of Concordia Seminary, St. Louis, Mo. The first graduation exercises were held in the evening of October 14, 1910, at Schiller Hall.* In 1912 the enrollment increased to 154, which meant that the school board was face to face with a difficult problem: either curtail the enrollment or provide more classrooms. The cost of building another story on Immanuel's school building was estimated at ten thousand dollars, while an entirely new building was expected to cost approximately eighty thousand dollars. On June 4, 1913, a meeting was held in which the Concordia League was induced to relinquish its rights and surrender the school's charter to the Lutheran congregations of Chicago. The direct result was the organization of the *Luther Institute Association of Chicago.* In July, 1915, a contract for a new building at 120 North Wood Street was signed, and on September 19 the cornerstone was laid. The Rev. J. H. Haake preached the German and the Rev. Arthur H. Kaub the English dedicatory sermons. Dedication of the completed building took place on August 27, 1916, with the Rev. J. W. Miller, pastor of Saint Paul's Congregation, Fort Wayne, Ind., preaching the sermon. In 1923 the enrollment had increased to such an extent that the question of expansion again had to be discussed, with the result that

*First graduates: Walter Schroeder, Walter Brand, Alice Eifert, Emil Wittman, Meta Thiele, Alma Carstens, Ada Palenske, Louise Gramath, Adelheid Duever, Magdalene Foerster.

a branch school was established at 6309 Yale Avenue, in the Englewood community, on Chicago's South Side. The formal opening took place on September 4, 1923; John C. Anderson served as director here for about two years. In August, 1926, President Hermann accepted a professorship at Northwestern College, Watertown, Wis., and Professor Anderson of the branch school was placed in charge of the main school. Prof. Carl Scaer succeeded to the directorship of the branch school. In 1931 the branch school was discontinued. "The deterioration of the neighborhood in which Luther Institute is located makes it almost imperative that this school be relocated in a better environment," according to the Rev. Carl S. Meyer, M.A., president of Luther Institute since October, 1943. In 1945 the *Lutheran High School Association* was organized for the purpose of raising two million dollars for the erection of three high schools in Chicago.

In 1947, arrangements were made to provide for the greatly increased enrollment at Luther Institute by establishing branch schools in various parts of the city, including the school building of First Trinity Congregation, at West Thirty-first Street and Lowe Avenue. Eighty-one years ago the first President of the Missouri Synod, Dr. C. F. W. Walther, declared: "If we German Lutherans in America are not forever to play the part of woodcutters and water boys like the Gibeonites in Canaan (Joshua 9:21), and if we wish to do our part in promoting the general welfare of our new fatherland, we must also establish higher educational agencies, schools that go beyond our parochial schools, no matter how high we may raise the standards of the latter." In the course of an address, on April 28, 1946, in Chicago, E. F. Eggold, president of the Lutheran high school at Racine, Wis., said: "Your program of secondary education is just what Chicago Lutheranism needs to keep it a healthy, growing, dynamic organism."

Building sites for two Lutheran high schools have been

PLATE XI

Extent of the United States of America
at the Time the Missouri Synod was Founded

PLATE XII

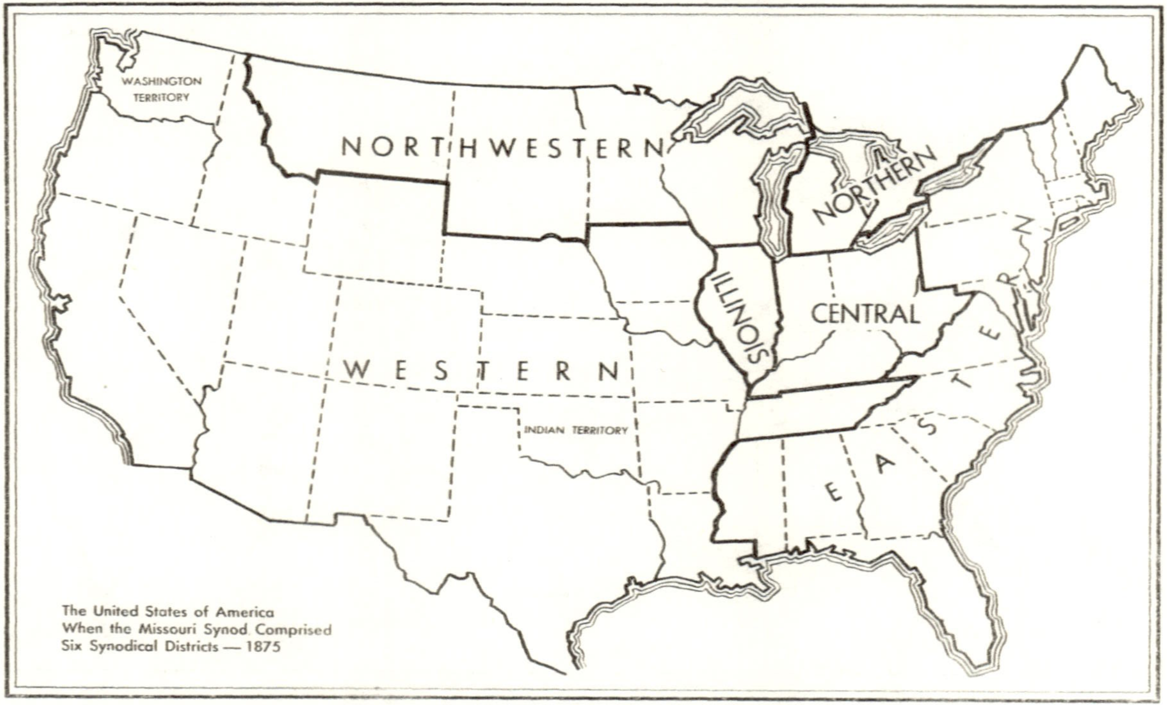

The United States of America
When the Missouri Synod Comprised
Six Synodical Districts — 1875

PLATE XIII

The United States of America
When the Missouri Synod was Divided into
Thirteen Territorial Districts — 1900

PLATE XIV

The United States of America when the Missouri Synod was Divided into Thirty-Three Districts. The English District Alone is Non-Territorial

acquired: one on the South Side, at West 87th Street and Kedzie Avenue (1948), and another on the North Side, at West Cullom and North Menard Avenues (1949). Early in 1949 Leo Buehring, a former business manager in the Lutheran Youth Building (Walther League), was secured by the association to serve as executive secretary and director of public relations, succeeding Carl F. Wolff, who had served in this capacity for several years previously.

At a meeting of delegates representing the Luther Institute Association and the Lutheran High School Association of Greater Chicago, held on April 27, 1949, in First St. Paul's Church, Chicago, the question concerning amalgamation of the two groups was discussed. Effective as of July 1, 1949, Luther Institute, maintaining its identity, continues under the board of directors of the High School Association.

The Trail now turns our eyes from Luther Institute in Chicago to a "wooded hill one mile from the center of the straggling little village of Valparaiso, Ind."* where in September, 1859, a college† was opened with six instructors and seventy-five students. Quite destitute of resources, attributable to the storm and stress of the Civil War, the school was forced to cease functioning in 1869. About four years later (September, 1873) the institution was re-opened as the Northern Indiana Normal School and Business Institute under the leadership of Henry Baker Brown. In 1900 its name was changed to Valparaiso College, and in 1907 to *Valparaiso University.* In the summer of 1925 this institution was purchased by the Lutheran University Association, an Indiana corporation composed of Lutheran men and women affiliated with the Evangelical Lutheran Synodical Confer-

*Formerly known as Portersville. "In 1836 a party of sailors stopped overnight at Hill's Tavern, and after entertaining the natives with stories, one suggested that since the county was named for Commodore David Porter, who was in command of the *Essex* during a battle near Valparaiso, Chile (South America), it would be appropriate to name the county seat after that town. The suggestion was accepted." (Meyer, quoting from *Works Progress Administration Bulletin*, p. 119. *Toponomy*, p. 157).

†Valparaiso Male and Female College.

ence of North America. Its first president was Dr. William H. T. Dau (1926-1930), formerly professor at Concordia Seminary, St. Louis, Mo. His successor was Dr. Oscar C. Kreinheder (1930-1939). On October 5 and 6, 1940, the fifteenth anniversary of its reorganization and its annual homecoming for alumni, the University celebrated the inauguration of its new president, the Rev. Otto Paul Kretzmann. At the beginning of World War II, Valparaiso University "offered integrated programs of study in fields necessary for national defense, such as chemistry, physics, pre-medicine, pre-dentistry, pre-nursing, business management, civil engineering, mechanical engineering, electrical engineering, and chemical engineering. Courses less directly essential for national defense were offered in the biological sciences, the social sciences, the modern languages and literatures, and law." The "total strength" of the institution was pledged to the President of the United States in that national crisis. On the occasion of the twentieth anniversary of the reorganization it was stated that "Valparaiso University is today ready to be obedient to the vision of its founders. The first twenty years under Lutheran administration were years of testing and trial. The University had to find its way and set its course . . . . The second twenty years will, I am sure, under the compelling pressure of the hand of God in history, be years of relentless building on the foundations which were laid with such care and devotion. They may well be decisive."*

On October 27, 1946, a memorial service took place in Graceland Cemetery, Valparaiso, in honor of Ensign Eric Andres,† first Valparaiso University alumnus to fall in World War II. The inscription on the memorial marker reads: "Pro Patria Mortuus, Vivit in Christo." ("He died for his native country, but lives in Christ.")

According to Robert Allett, Valparaiso University "is more

*Valparaiso Bulletin XVI, 9.

†Son of Rev. and Mrs. Theo. Andres, Madison, Wis.

than an institution of higher learning. It is the expression of an educational ideal . . . . A truly Christian education, Valparaiso contends, is possible only when Christian conviction underlies not a part but all of its curriculum. It is in accord with the great Reformer Martin Luther, who said: 'Where God's Word does not reign supreme, there I advise no one to send his child'."*

Valparaiso University's motto is: "In luce tua videmus lucem." ("In Thy light shall we see light.")

A large and comprehensive expansion program is presently being executed. Students of the University's engineering school in 1948 erected and financed a building "which the University could not at the time afford to build."†

The *Lutheran Women's Mission Endeavor,* an association of women's societies of local congregations, was organized on May 5, 1938, for the purpose of aiding the Church in its mission program at home and abroad. At the second meeting, October 26, 1938, fifty-four societies were added to the original nucleus of twelve societies. The first officers were Mrs. Hugh A. Bresemann of Oak Park, president; Mrs. Henry Kehe of Des Plaines, Mrs. Edward Kasch of Chicago, and Mrs. Edward M. Streufert of Lansing, regional vice-presidents; Mrs. Otto Koch, of Arlington Heights, corresponding secretary; Mrs. Luther Kohn of Chicago, recording secretary; and Mrs. Walter M. Samuels of Berwyn, treasurer.‡

In November, 1945, the name of this association was changed to Lutheran Women's Missionary League, a national organization within the Evangelical Lutheran Synodical Conference of North America, which had been organized in July, 1942. "Every participating society is given a sufficient number of 'mite boxes' for the personal use of members and interested women. Those who accept these mite boxes may deposit a small coin each day or each week as their love and

**American Lutheran,* XX, 5, p. 17.

†*Valparaiso Bulletin,* September, 1948. p. 4.

‡*Lutheran Witness,* LXI, 16, p. 278ff.

ability may dictate." No resort is had to money-making schemes, such as sales, bazaars, dinners, card parties, etc.

The *Chicago Lutheran Church Extension Association* was organized on January 28, 1924, by the congregations* of the English District in Chicago and vicinity. Among the purposes stated in its constitution are: to help found new missions where they are needed, to assist newly formed congregations in acquiring property and places of worship, and in every possible way to further and promulgate the cause of missions. Its first president was Henry C. Bartling, who served in this capacity until his death in 1934. Its official organ, *The Ambassador,* was discontinued with the advent of the English District edition of the *Lutheran Witness.* In recent years this association has sponsored "caravan trips" to various mission stations in the northern Illinois area.

The *Walther League* is an international association of young people's, young men's, and young ladies' societies within the Evangelical Lutheran Synodical Conference of North America. Its origin is traced to a mass meeting held by the young men's societies of three congregations in Buffalo, N.Y., on February 21, 1893. At that meeting it was resolved to issue a call for a general young people's convention to be held in the same city, from May 20 to 23, in the same year. Twelve societies responded to the call by sending delegates to Buffalo. Herman C. Gahwe† of Buffalo was elected first president of the new organization, which for a little more than one year was known as the General Alliance of Young People's and Young Men's Societies of the Synodical Conference. During the next convention, in June, 1894, at Fort Wayne, Ind., the organization adopted the name Walther League,‡ in honor of Dr. C. F. W. Walther, whose death had occurred seven years before.§ "It was a small beginning, and there were many

*Then eighteen in number.
†Died on Feb. 18, 1941, at age 75.
‡At this convention also the now popular ten-pointed star enclosed in a circle as the League's emblem was adopted.
§Dr. Walther died on May 7, 1887.

who viewed with alarm this projected union of young people's societies in our Missouri Synod. Their fear was that such an organization might encroach upon the rightful domain of the local congregation and interfere with the organized work of Synod." The principal object of the League was then, as it is now, "to assist in keeping our young people within the Church." But over a period of quite a number of years the opinion prevailed in various sections of the country that this youth organization was virtually only a sort of "matrimonial agency,"* and such criticism doubtless constituted the one principal factor in the slow progress during the first tweny-five or thirty years of the League's existence. At the turn of the century it was composed of only fifty societies. In 1910 there were only sixty-nine. "After that, however, when the work of the League was better understood, it grew rapidly . . . ."†

In 1914 the League was organized in the State of Illinois. Miss Lydia Jorn,‡ a member of First Trinity Congregation, Chicago, served as the first delegate from Illinois to the League's general convention in Detroit, Mich., in 1913. The second Illinois society to join was that of Emmaus Congregation, under the leadership of Miss Elfrieda Blank and Miss Ruth Fuelling. At the same time, Victor Walther, a descendant of Dr. Walther, organized societies in Aurora and Joliet. Soon afterward St. Paul's of Rockford also joined. Five societies constituted the League's original Illinois District. Its first president was the Rev. Karl J. Fricke of Aurora. Mr. Walther's successor as "field secretary" was Albert H. Miller of La Grange. In 1924 there were 175 societies in the State of Illinois.§ In the same year the Northern Illinois District of the Walther League was organized. The following have served as presidents of this district: Albert H. Miller,

*Miss Emma Gerlach was one of the delegates attending a Walther League convention in Lima, Ohio, in 1915; among the visitors was this writer. In June, 1919, Miss G. became Mrs. L.J.S.

†Walther League, *Fifty Years*.

‡Now the wife of Edward W. Jaeger of Chicago.

§In 1920 the societies in the southern part of Illinois formed the Southern Illinois District of the Walther League.

the Rev. Karl Kurth, the Rev. Adalbert R. Kretzmann, Otto A. Koeneke, Paul G. Vetter, George Cramer, Edwin A. Kuecker, Hugo F. Malte, William Zeiter (now president of the International Walther League), Erwin Greifendorf, Milton Eggerding, Leo Kraft, and Arthur W. Streit.

In January, 1922, the League's offices were moved from Milwaukee, Wis., to 6438 Eggleston Avenue (formerly Dickey Street), in the Englewood community, Chicago. Through the raising of a $115,000 "Golden Anniversary Fund" the erection of a new building, known as the Lutheran Youth Building, at 875 North Dearborn Street, was made possible. Dedication took place on September 20, 1942. The building "stands as a memorial to the faith and courage of those who planned and labored under the blessing of God in days past, and as a sure sign to the Leaguers of tomorrow that the faith in the Savior which built the League and the building is still the only hope of the children of men."* The purpose of the League itself, in the words of Hugo F. Malte, a former president of the Northern Illinois District Walther League, is "not just social, but fundamentally and primarily spiritual."

In the spring of the year 1923 the Rev. Paul Sauer, pastor of First Saint John's Congregation in Chicago, began a campaign for the founding of a choir which would specialize in singing compositions of Johann Sebastian Bach. Although buffeted by various winds of opposition, he hopefully looked forward to the formal organization of a *Bach Association* in June, 1925. Then, however, "Mother Nature" interfered by making the whole Midwest swelter and causing cancellation of the proposed meeting. Hardly had the heat wave subsided, when two of "the foremost Lutherans interested in the choir, the Messrs. Theodore Fathauer and William Schlake," set out on a voyage across the ocean waves to Europe. Shortly before their departure, Mr. Schlake assured Pastor Sauer by telephone: "I am with you with my heart and pocketbook." The

*Dedication program, Lutheran Youth Building, Sept. 20, 1942.

first layman to advocate the enterprise was William Schulze. Gustav A. Fleischer, editor of the *Concordia* magazine, rendered invaluable services by placing the columns of this periodical at the disposal of the association, which was formally organized on September 15, 1925. The first director was William Boeppler. The *Chicago Bach Chorus* made its debut on May 12, 1926. On the following day, Herman DeVries, music critic of the *Chicago Evening American* (now *Herald-American*), commented as follows (quoting in part): "My ears are still warm with the glories of the Bach Society and their magnificent singing under the masterly and inspiring baton of William Boeppler, that concert of unforgettable joys." Prof. Karl Haase of Concordia Teachers College, Seward, Nebr., addressed the following words to the founder and first president of the *Bach Association,* Pastor Sauer. "You are to be complimented on the success of this grand undertaking. Really, you are, in a way, a second Mendelssohn, bringing Bach to Chicago Lutherans."

Pointing to the general lack of interest in, or appreciation of, Bach's compositions, a writer in the *Lutheran Witness* recently stated that "on this side of the water we have merely scratched the surface of Bach research and in the presentation of his masterpieces to the public . . . . The other day they packed the pews in the chapel of the University of Chicago,* brought extra chairs, and then had people line the walls until more than 3,000 were gathered to hear a concert made up of Bach's organ music . . . . The artist was Marcel Dupre, organist of the Church of St. Sulpice of Paris . . . . A reviewer in the *Chicago Tribune* said: 'Bach, two centuries dead, seems at last to have come into his rightful kingdom.' "

The *Lutheran Bar Association,* comprising lawyers affiliated with Missouri Synod congregations in the Chicago area, was incorporated under the laws of the State of Illinois in 1943. Its offices are located in Room 1805, 77 West Washing-

*Rockefeller Memorial Chapel.

ton Street, Chicago. The association came into being as a result of a certain desire that a group of Lutheran lawyers cherished to provide an opportunity for becoming acquainted with one another and exchanging ideas concerning legal matters.

A Chicago chapter of the *Lutheran Collegiate Association* was organized in November, 1945. "Consisting of college-trained members of the Synodical Conference, its purpose is to encourage higher education and a greater measure of service to the Church as well as participation in public affairs in the spirit of Lutheran polity; to develop a bolder confessionalism in our laity in their contacts with non-Lutherans, and to promote lay leadership by an interest in student welfare work and by assisting worthy men and women financially and informationally in research and scholarship."*

On April 4, 1948, the Chicago chapter conducted a forum on the question: Should we, as Christians, take an aggressive part in breaking down racial barriers?" The forum was held in Our Redeemer Church, 6430 Harvard Avenue, Chicago.

Originally scheduled to be held in St. Louis, Mo., the Third Lutheran Race Relations Convention and Institute was held on April 23-25, 1948, in First Saint Paul's Lutheran Church, LaSalle and Goethe Streets, Chicago.

The *Doctor Martin Luther Guild of Chicago* was organized in October, 1948, for the purpose of holding Lutheran church services in the German language and to work among German-speaking immigrants in order to win them for The Lutheran Church—Missouri Synod. Such services have since been conducted once a month in the Woodlawn Boys Club Building and in the Thorndike Hilton Memorial Chapel on the campus of the University of Chicago.

"History means inquiry into facts that the deeds done . . . . should not be forgotten."

Herodotus, "The Father of History"

*(*Northern Illinois Messenger*, LXVII, 2), *Lutheran Witness*.

Bibliography

1

Jacobs, Chas. M., *The Story of the Church* (Philadelphia, Pa., 1925), p. 314 f.

Latourette, K.S., *The Great Century in Europe and the United States of America,* A.D. 1800-A.D. 1914, IV, p. 381 f.

Qualben, Lars P., *A History of the Christian Church* (Thomas Nelson & Sons, New York, 1940), p. 421 f.

Finck, Rev. Wm. J., D.D., *Lutheran Landmarks and Pioneers in America* (The United Lutheran Publishing House, Philadelphia, Pa., 1913), Third Edition, pp. 65, 94.

Loeher, *Geschichte und Zustaende der Deutschen in Amerika* (Cincinnati, Verlag von Eggers und Wulkop, 1847; Leipzig, bei K. F. Koehler), p. 210.

Carlyle, Thomas, *Hero Worship, and the Heroic in Society* (Scribner & Sons, Chicago, Ill.).

Concordia Historical Institute Quarterly (St. Louis, Mo.), I, 2, p. 34; II, 1, p. 8.

Fairbanks, *The Spaniards in Florida,* p. 17 (quoted in *Concordia Historical Institute Quarterly,* I, 2, p. 34).

Sweet, William Warren, *The Story of Religion in America* (Harper Bros., The University of Chicago, 1939), pp. 34, 35.

Americanized Encyclopedia Britannica (Riverside Publishing Co., Chicago, 1898), Latest Edition.

Wolf, Edmund, D.D., *The Lutherans in America* (J. A. Hill & Company, New York, 1890), p. 206.

Graebner, A. L., *Geschichte der Lutherischen Kirche in Amerika* (Concordia Publishing House, St. Louis, Mo., 1892), pp. 50-54, 60.

Krauss, E. A. Wilh., *Lebensbilder aus der Geschichte der Christlichen Kirche* (Concordia Publishing House, St. Louis, Mo., 1913), pp. 684 ff.

2

Graebner, A. L., *op. cit.*, p. 88 f.

Wentz, Abdel Ross, Ph., D.D., *The Lutheran Church in America* (United Lutheran Publishing House, Philadelphia, Pa., 1923), Chapter 5, p. 172 f.

Neve-Allbeck, *History of the Lutheran Church in America* (The Lutheran Literary Board, Burlington, Iowa, 1934), Third Edition, p. 30.

3

Sweet, William Warren, *op. cit.*, p. 171f.

Polack, W. G., *The Building of a Great Church* (Concordia Publishing House, St. Louis, Mo., 1941), Second Edition, pp. 14-22.

Spaude, Paul W., M.A., S.T.D., *The Lutheran Church Under American Influence* (The Lutheran Literary Board, Burlington, Iowa, 1943).

Mann, W. J., *Heinrich Melchior Muehlenberg, Leben und Wirken* (Pastor A. Hellwege, Publ., Roxborough, Philadelphia, Pa., 1891).

Graebner, A. L., *op. cit.*

The Cresset (International Walther League, Publ., Minneapolis, Minn.), V, 9, p. 6.

4

Phillips, Geo., *Chicago and Her Churches*, 1868, p. 12.

5

Hageman, G. E., *Sketches from the History of the Church* (Concordia Publishing House, St. Louis, Mo.), p. 211.

6

Neve-Allbeck, *op. cit.*, Third Edition, p. 65.

7

Neve-Allbeck, *op. cit.*, p. 67.

8

Edward J. Barrett, Secretary of State, *Guide to Illinois State Buildings* (pamphlet), Revised Edition, 1946. (No printer mentioned.)

9

Richardson, James D., *Messages and Papers of the Presidents* (Bureau of National Literature and Art), I, p. 615.

The History of Nations (P. F. Collier & Son Corp., New York, 25 vols. XXIII, pp. 434-458.

10

Benton, Thomas H., *Thirty Years in the United States Senate* (D. Appleton & Co., New York, 1903), I, p. 104.

11

Forman, S. E., *Our Republic* (D. Appleton & Co., New York, 1937), p. 222.

12

Wagner, Martin L., *The Chicago Synod and Its Antecedents* (Wartburg Publishing House, Waverly, Iowa, no year, Preface 1909), p. 7.

13

Polack, W. G., *op. cit.*, p. 22.

14

Wagner, Martin L., *op. cit.*, p. 26.

15

Wagner, Martin L., *op. cit.*, p. 26.

16

For general information regarding Chicago and Illinois see following sources:

Chicago Sunday Tribune, issue of February 9, 1947, "Makers of the Middle West," Graphic Section, p. 2.

Phillips, Geo., *op. cit.*, p. 121f.

McClure, J. B., *Stories and Sketches of Chicago*, pp. 27, 58, 69, 81.

Encyclopedia Americana. VI, p. 438f.

Chicago und sein Deutschtum (German-American Biographical Publishing Co., Cleveland, Ohio, 1901-1903), p. 23 ff.

Lloyd Lewis-Henry Justin Smith, *Chicago* (Harcourt, Brace & Co., New York, 1929), pp. 37, 39.

Forman, S. E., *op. cit.*, p. 348.

Winslow, Chas. S., *Indians of the Chicago Region* (Soderlund Printing Service, 216 Institute Place, Chicago 10, Ill., 1946), Second Edition.

Early Chicago Reminiscenses, Fergus Historical Series, No. 19 (Fergus Printing Co., Chicago, 1882, p. 24).

17

Chicago Herald-American, January 25, 1947, p. 5, "Church Begins Jubilee Week."

18

Forman, S. E., *op. cit.*, p. 348.

19

Kohl, J. G., *Reisen im Nordwesten der Vereinigten Staaten* (D. Appleton & Co., New York, 1857), Chapter 35, p. 459 ff.

Grosse, T. J., *Geschichte der Deutschen Evang. Luth. Gemeinden zu Addison, Ill.*, p. 14.

Lutheran Witness, VII, 6, p. 46.

20

Lutheraner, IV, 23, p. 184.

Chicago Tribune, February 9, 1947, Part 1, Sec. 2, p. 4.

Feiertag, Johannes, *Geschichte der Ev. Lutherischen Gemeinden U.A.C. zu Chicago*, 1846-1896, pp. 17, 18, 24.

Kinsley Philip, *The Chicago Tribune—Its First Hundred Years* (Alfred A. Knopf, New York, 1943), I, p. 14.

Pierce, Bessie Louise, *A History of Chicago* (Alfred A. Knopf, New York and London, 1937), I, pp. 202, 207, 326, 352; II, p. 3f.

Proceedings, The Missouri Synod, 1849, p. 81.

Umbeck, Sharvey G., *The Social Adaptations of a Selected Group of German Background Protestant Churches in Chicago* (The Chicago University Press, December, 1940), pp. 4-7.

Buck, Solon Justus, *Illinois in* 1818 (Illinois Centennial Com., Springfield, 1917), p. 173.

Chicago und sein Deutschtum, op. cit., pp. 31, 66 ff.

Phillips, Geo., *op. cit.* (re Huffert).

Concordia Historical Institute Quarterly, III, 4, p. 118.

Chicago Tribune, October 6, 1946, Voice of the People, by Pat Maloney.

McClure, J. B., *Stories and Sketches of Chicago* (Rhodes & Mc Clure, Chicago, 1880), p. 130 (*re* fire).

Reed, Thomas B., *Modern Eloquence* (John B. Morris & Co., Philadelphia, Pa., 1900), IV, p. 268 ff. (*re* fire); V, p. 425 (one year after fire).

News Service (St. Louis, Mo.), XXV, 2, p. 10.

21

Diamantenes Jubilaeum der Evang. Lutherischen St. Petri Gemeinde U.A.C. zu Schaumburg, Ill., 1922.

Vorbericht in *Proceedings*, Missouri Synod, 1847-1860 (St. Louis, Mo.), Second Edition, 1876, p. 3.

Concordia Historical Institute Quarterly (St. Louis, Mo.), XIX, 3, p. 97.
Ludwig Catechism was published in New York.
Memorial Addresses for Abraham Lincoln (Government Printing Office, Washington, D.C., 1903), p. 38. (The quotation is from an address prepared by Chas. Rowley Cushman and delivered by George Bancroft.)
Pierce, Bessie L., *op. cit.*, II, p. 256.
Kinsley, Philip, *The Chicago Tribune* (Alfred A. Knopf, New York, 1943), I, p. 193.

22

Anniversary Booklet.
Selle, C. A. T., Autobiography, *Der Lutheraner,* LIV (1898), p. 92ff.
Hesler, Geo., *The Glencoe News,* April 6, 1944.

23

Anniversary Booklet and Church History.
Lutheraner, Aug. 12, 1856; also XII, 26, pp. 206, 207.
Concordia Historical Institute Quarterly, XVIII, 2, p. 45.
Proceedings, Eighth Convention of Missouri Synod, Pittsburgh, Pa. (American Lutheran Publication Board, Pittsburgh, Pa.), June 24, 1903, p. 25 (re *Christenlehre*)
Spaude, Paul W., M.A., S.T.D., *op. cit.,* p. 95 (re *Christenlehre*).

24

Grosse, T. J., *op. cit.,* p. 46.
Lutheraner, V, 26, p. 201.
Kinsley Philip, *op. cit.,* I, p. 63.
Volp, John H., *The First Hundred Years,* 1835-1935, of Blue Island, Ill., p. 50.
The Lutheran Witness, Northern Illinois District Edition, LXVII, 12.

25

Meyer, Alfred H., *Toponomy in Sequent Occupance* (Valparaiso University), p. 151.
Concordia Historical Institute Quarterly, XI, 1, p. 14 ff.

26

Concordia Historical Institute Quarterly, XI, 1, p. 17.

27

Anniversary Booklet of St. Peter's Lutheran Church of Schaumburg.

28

Lewis & Smith, *op. cit.*, p. 29.
Sechster Synodal-Bericht der deutschen Ev. Lutherischen Synode vom Jahre, 1852 (St. Louis, Mo., 1876), Second Edition, p. 61.
Kinsley, Philip, *op. cit.*, I, p. 20.

29

Lutheraner, II, 4, p. 32.
Concordia Cyclopedia (Concordia Publishing House, St. Louis, Mo., 1927), p. 684.
Kinsley, Philip, *op. cit.*, I, pp. 28, 30, 39, 285, 292, 316.
Pierce, Bessie L., *op. cit.*, II, pp. 6, 17, 59.
Umbeck, Sharvey G., *op. cit.*, p. 202.
Chicago Tribune, January 1, 1869 (re Washington Street Tunnel); February 9, 1947, Part 1, Sec. 2, p. 4 (re plank road); November 10, 1929, p. 1 (re steeple, by Oney Sweet).
Chicago Daily News, April 17, 1947, p. 17 (re neighborhood).
Chicago-Herald-American, March 4, 1947 (re Addie Hibbard Gregory).

30

Kinsley, Philip, *op. cit.*, I, p. 47.
Roosevelt, F. D., Greetings to Albert M. Hirsch, President and Publisher of *Aurora Beacon News,* Aurora, Ill. (Letter of August 5, 1937. The White House.)

31

Kinsley, Philip, *op. cit.*, I, pp. 26, 63, 64.
Aurora Beacon News Centennial Edition. Section 2.

32

Volp, John H., *Blue Island Historical Review* (Blue Island, Ill., 1935).
Kinsley, Philip, *op. cit.*, I, pp. 233, 250; II, pp. 48, 64.

33

Loeher, *op. cit.*, p. 540.

34

Pierce, Bessie L., *op. cit.*, II, p. 313.
Proceedings, Missouri Synod, 1851, Second Edition, 1876, p. 160.

35

Synodalbericht, Wisconsin-Distrikt, 1910 (Concordia Publishing House, St. Louis Mo.), p. 32.

36

A Guide Book for Greenfield Village of the Edison Institute, Dearborn, Mich., 1941, p. 25.

37

Kinsley, Philip, *op. cit.*, I, pp. 83, 128, 133.
Volp, John H., *op. cit.*, p. 14.
Chicago Tribune, May 17-19, 1860.

38

Proceedings, Northern Illinois District, June 30, 1933, p. 47.

39

Sechster Synodal-Bericht, Missouri Synod, 1852, Second Edition, p. 10.

40

Birkigt, Brunhilde, *They Rehearsed All That God had Done with Them* (Acts 14:27). Booklet about St. John's of Forest Park.

41

Immanuel Church History, Dundee, Ill., 1937.

42

Clipping from Ottawa newspaper (date missing).

43

Kinsley, Philip, *op. cit.*, I, p. 286.
Richardson, James D., *Messages and Papers of the Presidents,* 11 volumes (Bureau of National Literature and Art, 1910), *op. cit.*, V. p. 3477.

44

Kinsley, Philip, *op. cit.*, I, p. 350, 351; II, p. 10.
Ida M. Tarbell, *The Life of Abraham Lincoln* (Lincoln Historical Society, New York, 4 vols.), IV, p. 35f. pp. 50ff.
"Abraham Lincoln" (National Park Service; Source Book Series, No. 2), pp. 48-53.

45

Kinsley, Philip, *op. cit.*, II, p. 35.

46

Aurora Beacon News Centennial Edition, September 5, 1937.

47

Feiertag, Johannes, *op. cit.*, p. 48.

48

Kinsley, Philip, *op. cit.*, II, pp. 26, 86.
Forman, S. E., *op. cit.*, p. 22.
Sauer, Paul, *op. cit.*, Diamond Jubilee Booklet (1867-1942), First St. John's Evangelical Lutheran Church, Chicago, Ill., p. 4.

49

Grosse, T. J., *op. cit.*

50

Kinsley, Philip, *op. cit.*, II, pp. 99, 117, 126.

51

McClure, J. B., *op. cit.*, p. 57.

52

Volp, John H., *op. cit.*, p. 75.

53

Northern Illinois District *Lutheran Witness* Supplement, March 25, 1947. No. 6.

54

Proceedings, Northern Illinois District, 1918, p. 56.

55

Church History of Summit.

56

The Lutheran Missionary Editorial. (One week after fire in 1871.)
Concordia Theological Monthly, I, 7 (July, 1930), p. 481.

57

Fritschel, *Quellen und Dokumente*, p. 27.

58

Church History of St. Matthew's.

59

Evanston, Ill., *Index Newspaper*, November 27, 1886.
Kinsley, Philip, *op. cit.*, I, p. 163; II, pp. 145, 154, 174.

60

Der Lutheraner, XIII, 26, p. 203.
Proceedings, Western District, Missouri Synod (St. Louis, Mo., 1876), p. 12.

61

Kinsley, Philip, *op. cit.*, II, p. 289.

62
Meyer, Alfred H., *Toponomy*, p. 150.
63
Skeels, Bernadine, *Public Service Bulletin.* (Chicago, Ill.)
64
Flower and Leaf, p. 54.
Skeels, Bernadine, *op. cit.*
65
Skeels, Bernadine, *Western United Service Bulletin.* (Chicago.)
66
Kinsley, Philip, *op. cit.*, III, p. 8.
67
Meyer, Alfred H., *op. cit.*, p. 152.
68
Proceedings, Northern Illinois District, 1931, p. 61.
69
Kinsley, Philip, *op. cit.*, III, pp. 54, 58.
70
Proceedings, Northern Illinois District, 1913 and 1915; also 1942, p. 57.
71
Feiertag, Johannes, *op. cit.*, p. 111.
72
Lewis & Smith, *op. cit.*, pp. 160-166.
Larned, J. N., *History for Ready Reference* (The C. A. Nichols Co., Springfield, Mass., 1895), V, pp. 4-10.
73
Chicago Tribune, "Line o' Type or Two," August 8, 1946.
74
Feiertag, Johannes, *op. cit.*, pp. 121, 122.
75
Strieter, Johannes, Lebenslauf. (By J. M. F. Leutner of Cleveland, Ohio, Zion Lutheran Church, 1905.)
76
Feiertag, Johannes, *op. cit.*, p. 130.
Lewis & Smith, *op. cit.*, p. 59 ff.

77

Proceedings, Illinois District, 1900, p. 69.

78

Volp, John H., *op. cit.*, p. 44.

79

Englewood Businessmen's Association, *The Story of Englewood, 1835-1923.* (Copyright 1924, by Foster & McDonnell, Chicago, Ill.)

80

Winslow, C. S., *op. cit.* (See Footnote 16.)
Winston Encyclopedia.
Encyclopedia Americana.

81

Kinsley, Philip, *op. cit.*, III, p. 166.

82

Walther, C. F. W., *Brosamen*, p. 507.

83

Sweet, Wm. Warren, *op. cit.*, p. 488.
Northern Illinois District *Lutheran Witness* Supplement, January 29, 1946.
Grace for Grace (Lutheran Synod Book Co., Mankato, Minn., 1943), pp. 9-11.
Weekly Chicago Democrat, November 9 and December 7, 1847.
Pierce, Bessie L., *op. cit.*, I, p. 231.

84

Chicago und sein Deutschtum, *op. cit.*, p. 46 f.
Brauer, Albert, *Lebensbild, Pastor Ernst August Brauer.*

85

Lutheran Witness, VI, 18, p. 142.
Northern Illinois District Stewardship Bulletin, April, 1947, p. 3.

86

The Lutheran Beacon (Slovak Ev. Lutheran Church; Editor, Stephen G. Mazak; Publ., Concordia Publishing House, St. Louis, Mo.), III, 1, p. 3.

87

Concordia Cyclopedia (Concordia Publishing House, St. Louis, Mo., 1927), p. 503.

88

Chicago Tribune, "Line o' Type or Two," December 10, 1946.
Winslow, C. S., *op. cit.,* pp. 13, 114, 115.

89

Proceedings, Illinois District, 1900, p. 74; *Proceedings,* Northern Illinois District, 1930, p. 89; 1934, p. 49.

90

Latourette, Kenneth S., *The Chinese, Their History and Culture* (The MacMillan Co. New York, N.Y., 1946), Third Edition. p. 390 ff.
Williams, Edward Thomas, *China, Yesterday and Today* (Thomas Y. Crowell Co., New York, N.Y., 1923), pp. 413 ff.
Proceedings, Northern Illinois District, 1931, p. 56.

91

Englewood Businessmen's Association, *op. cit.,* p. 49.
Chicago Tribune, April 27, 1947.

92

Proceedings, Illinois District, 1899, p. 70.

93

Homer's *Odyssey,* Book 19: 61; *Iliad,* Book 23: 281-283.
Aurora Beacon News Centennial Edition, Sec. 5, Part I; Sec. 3, p. 3.

94

Proceedings, Northern Illinois District, 1910, p. 56; 1931, p. 61.

95

New Standard Bible Dictionary, p. 884.
Chicago Daily News, March 6, 1947.

96

Grosse, T. J., *op. cit.*

97

Northern Illinois District *Lutheran Witness* Supplement, December 31, 1946.

98

Winston Encyclopedia
Encyclopedia Britannica.

99

Journal, Illinois State Historical Society, October 2, 1936, p. 201.
Feiertag, J. H., *op. cit.,* p. 66.
Volp, John H., *op. cit.,* pp. 32-34.
Chicago American National Almanac and Yearbook, 1938, p. 99.

Fuerbringer, Ludwig Ernest, 80 *Eventful Years* (Concordia Publishing House, St. Louis, Mo., 1944), p. 31.

100

Lutheraner, CIII, 8.

101

Battle, Chas. S., *Centennial Biographical and Historical Record of Aurora* for 100 Years. 1834-1937. (*Aurora Beacon News*, Aurora.)

102

Proceedings, Northern Illinois District, 1916 and 1918.

103

Lutheran Witness, LXI, 18, p. 308.

104

Northern Illinois District Mission Board Report of 1925, p. 50; 1927; 1931, p. 57; 1933, p. 58.

105

Proceedings, Northern Illinois District, 1910, p. 57.

106

Proceedings, English District, 1927, p. 4.

107

Proceedings, Northern Illinois District, p. 104.

108

Proceedings, Northern Illinois District, 1925.

109

Northern Illinois Messenger, XVI, 16, 5.

110

Chicago Lutheran Church Extension Association.—*The Ambassador*, XI (October, 1937), p. 1.

111

H. F. McGee and I. Schulman, *World Progress* Supplement, 1929 (Cincinnati, Ohio).

Proceedings, Northern Illinois District, 1928.

112

Lutheran Witness, LXI, 8.

Holiday Magazine (Curtis Publishing Co., Independence Square, Philadelphia 5, Pa.), II, 5, p. 675.

113

Aurora Beacon News Centennial Edition, Sections 6 and 7.

Encyclopedia, John H. Winston Co. (Chicago-Philadelphia-Toronto, in 12 volumes). Cumulative Revision, 1933.

"Abraham Lincoln" (National Park Service Source Book Series, No. 2.) p. 16.

Proceedings, Northern Illinois District, 1913, p. 62; 1928; 1930, p. 62; 1933, p. 33; 1936, p. 53; 1937, p. 40.

114

Proceedings, Northern Illinois District, 1913, p. 62; 1928; 1930, p. 62; 1933, p. 33; 1936, p. 53; 1937, p. 40.

World Progress Standard, V, 2.

115

Lutheran Witness, VI, 23, p. 183.

116

Proceedings, English District, 1942, June 16-19.

117

Aurora Beacon News Centennial Edition, Part 1, pp. 3, 6.

118

Chicago-American National Almanac and Year Book, 1938 (Curtis D. MacDougall, Editor. National Survey and Sales), p. 90.

119

Kinsley, Philip, *op. cit.*, II, p. 99.

120

Lutheran Witness, LX, 23, p. 388.

Commerce, Business Voice of the Middle West, February, 1940.

Northern Illinois District *Lutheran Witness* Supplement, LXV, 7.

Index of Congregations

Inside Front Cover

The Lutheran Trail

By

LOUIS J. SCHWARTZKOPF

Martyrdom marks the beginning of THE LUTHERAN TRAIL, and glorious spiritual victory crowns all its subsequent history.

This is the triumphant historical account of the development of Lutheranism in the Northern Illinois District.

Interest for the general reader is heightened as the histories of the congregations in this region are thrown against the background of the contemporary political, social, and economic history of the United States.

The first section sets down a brief narrative of Lutheran activity in various sections of the eastern part of the United States. The major portion of the book presents short accounts of the 250 congregations affiliated with the Evangelical Lutheran Synodical Conference of North America in Northern Illinois. The arrangement is in chronological sequence according to the date of origin of each congregation.

The last section supplies vital information concerning the organization and development of the Missouri Synod as well as information on the development of the various Lutheran educational institutions and charitable organizations in the Northern Illinois area.

Out of the maze of manifold obstacles inherent in the gathering of the necessary data for this volume has finally emerged this belated Centennial offering. May this factual account be a blazing forerunner of the Kingdom advances to be won in the second century of Lutheranism in Northern Illinois.

CONCORDIA PUBLISHING HOUSE
SAINT LOUIS 18, MISSOURI

Inside Back Cover

WRITING OF THE BOOK

THE LUTHERAN TRAIL was begun in 1944 at the instigation of the Centennial Historical Committee of Synod. The original title of the book was "TRUE LUTHERANISM, ITS PART IN THE DEVELOPMENT OF GREATER CHICAGO."

Naturally a work of this magnitude entails most careful research and investigation. Most of the actual work was done by the author and his wife. Personal visits were made by them to many sources of pertinent information: to the homes of pastors, teachers, laymen; to libraries and historical deposits, resulting in a tremendous amount of copying. Most of this copying was competently done by Mrs. Schwartzkopf.

From more than 6,000 standard-size, double-spaced type sheets, progress toward adequate conciseness was understandably slow. With the unstinted aid of John J. Astley-Cock, associate editor of Religion and Education of the *Chicago Tribune* and Dr. John G. Kunstmann, associate professor in the Department of Germanic Languages and Literatures, the University of Chicago, the basic objective was reached during the winter months of 1946—1947.

Difficulties which arose in the printing trade, however, delayed the publication of this historical volume. The title of the book was altered to THE LUTHERAN TRAIL during the Missouri Synod Centennial year, which came to a grand climax with a mass celebration in Chicago's Soldier Field in the spring of 1947.

CONCORDIA PUBLISHING HOUSE
SAINT LOUIS 18, MISSOURI

www.ingramcontent.com/pod-product-compliance
Lightning Source LLC
Chambersburg PA
CBHW021412300426
44114CB00010B/462
* 9 7 8 0 7 5 8 6 7 6 1 0 8 *